WORD TO KINDLE FORMATTING MAGIC

Chris McMullen

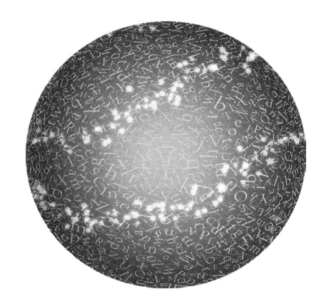

Zishka Publishing
ISBN: 978-1-941691-22-9
Version 3.19.18A

Books > Reference > Writing, Research & Publishing Guides > Authorship
Books > Arts & Photography > Graphic Design > Desktop Publishing

—Contents—

—Introduction—

FORMATTING AN EBOOK for Kindle can seem mysterious: A book may appear perfect on a computer monitor at home, yet show unexpected problems on one or more Kindle devices or apps. New authors often come across inconsistent indentations, alignment issues, unsupported characters, missing images, unwanted sections of italicized text, unexpected paragraph spacing, and other formatting problems—even when no such issues were observed in the original Word file.

Although there really is no *magic* involved in formatting a Kindle eBook, this guide will help take the mystery out of Kindle formatting. A successful transition from Word to Kindle begins with learning how to properly prepare your Word file. We will tackle this challenge one step at a time.

The chief problem lies in the way that Kindle interprets the eBook file that you prepare. Many Kindle formatting issues relate to 'hidden' formatting instructions (hidden so much that even Word's Show/Hide button can't reveal them). Chapters 2-4 describe how to format your Word file in order to better control Kindle's interpretation of your eBook file. In Chapter 5, we'll actually learn how to go one quick step beyond Word to reveal the otherwise 'hidden' formatting instructions.

Chapter 7 shows you how to preview the results before you publish, including how to side-load your book onto actual devices. This important step will help you catch potential problems *before* you publish your Kindle eBook.

In this book, you'll learn how to optimize your eBook in Microsoft Word. If you upload your Word document following the instructions set forth in this guide, the result will be pretty good. Chapter 5 shows you how to go a step beyond Word to tweak your eBook. This extra step offers many subtle improvements, like gaining control of how pictures display on a variety of screen sizes, or improving indents so that they look good across all devices (instead of being a fixed value in inches or points). Don't worry: There is a cookbook recipe for how to do this.

Some authors are satisfied with the results they achieve exclusively from Word. Others will make subtle improvements by going a step beyond Word. You don't need to decide until your Word file is complete. Then, if you're undecided, upload your Word file to KDP and view the result on the Kindle previewer. This will show you how your Kindle eBook looks before going a step beyond Word. You may be satisfied with that.

This book is focused on creating an eBook in a reflowable format, which is the standard format recommended for most eBooks. Almost all eBooks use the reflowable format, meaning that the text adapts to the dimensions of the screen and the customer's display settings. A novel definitely requires a reflowable format, as does any other book that primarily consists of text to read. (The alternative, called fixed format, applies mainly to eBooks that have a picture on nearly every page. If you have a children's fully-illustrated picture book, a comic book, or a richly formatted textbook, consider using—or at least trying—Amazon's free Kindle Kids' Book Creator, Kindle Comic Creator, or Kindle Textbook Creator. Much of the information in this guide *doesn't* apply to fixed format eBooks.)

The instructions in Chapters 2-4 that relate to Microsoft Word are specifically given for version 2013 for Windows, which is very similar to Microsoft Word 2016, 2010, and 2007. (The main ideas also apply to most features of Word 2003 for Windows and to most versions of Mac, but some features are implemented in another way.)

Formatting is an art. There are many different ways to do it, and there are different levels at which it can be applied. Some of it can be subtle. Learning how to optimize Word for Kindle formatting is a good place to start, and when you're finished you retain the flexibility to later go a step beyond Word to make subtle improvements (Chapter 5 shows you how to make those improvements).

When it comes to Kindle formatting, simple and efficient designs tend to work best. You want the formatting to work across *all* devices so that *every* customer enjoys the reading experience.

Note that this guide is focused on Kindle formatting. If you also decide to publish your eBook with Nook, Kobo, or other retailers,[1] note that the formatting is slightly different for other platforms. You may wish to do a little research into possible differences between Kindle, Nook, and Kobo formatting, for example. (If your eBook has many images, note also that other retailers don't have such general file size limits as Amazon does: You'll want to make sure that your eBook file size isn't too large to publish elsewhere.) In Sec. 6.12, we will consider the pros and cons of enrolling your eBook with KDP Select, which is Amazon's incentive for authors to publish the eBook version exclusively with Kindle (authors who do this don't need to learn how to reformat their eBooks for other platforms).

I sincerely hope that you learn much from this guide, that you have an enjoyable experience formatting your Kindle eBook, and that you have a successful book launch.

Good luck with your book,

Chris McMullen

---

[1] The simplest way to publish with other retailers is to use an aggregator—like Smashwords, Draft2Digital, or BookBaby—as described in Sec. 6.16.

—Chapter 1—

Considerations

1.1 Reflowable Format

W HAT YOU SEE on the screen in Word isn't the same as what you get on the screen of a Kindle device or app. That's partly because Word shows definite pages, while Kindle adopts a reflowable format. It's also partly because Kindle interprets the file differently from the way Word displays it on your monitor.

A printed book has a fixed format. It consists of definite pages. When designing a print book, you can control which text and images appear on which pages. You can even refer to pages by number.

None of this is true for a typical (reflowable) eBook. An eBook can be read on a small screen like a cell phone, or a large screen like an iPad. For a typical eBook, the customer can change the font style, font size, line spacing, and internal margins. There is no way to predict which information will appear on the screen at any given time. A typical eBook doesn't consist of definite 'pages.'

It's necessary to format an eBook with a reflowable layout in mind. For example, pagination, navigation, horizontal spacing, and vertical spacing work much differently from print books. Don't worry: We'll learn how to do this one step at a time. The important point for now is to realize that your eBook design must accommodate the reflowable nature of a typical eBook. (If you've never read an eBook before, I strongly encourage you to at least download some free samples of Kindle eBooks and browse through them with one of the free reading apps, such as Kindle for PC, Kindle for Mac, Kindle for Android, Kindle for iPad, Kindle for iPhone, etc. You can do this for *free*—you don't even need to own a Kindle device—and it will give you some valuable insight into the customer reading experience.)

There is an alternative eBook format called fixed format. The reflowable layout is generally better,[2] as it provides the optimal reading experience across all devices. Fixed format is designed for picture books, where each page includes a picture (perhaps with some text). This applies to many illustrated children's books, comic books, and manga, for example.

If you have a fully illustrated children's book (with pictures on virtually every page), a richly formatted textbook, or a comic book, the convenience of preparing it for fixed format with Amazon's free tools may appeal to you. Amazon's free Kindle Kids' Book Creator tool works well for fully illustrated children's books, even allowing for pop-up text. You can find a free tutorial on my blog:

http://chrismcmullen.com/2014/09/04/how-to-use-the-new-kindle-kids-book-creator-tutorial

---

[2] However, there are a few exceptions. Most comic books and fully illustrated children's books, for example, are inherently designed to function with a fixed layout.

Amazon has a free Kindle Textbook Creator for richly formatted textbooks. The Kindle Textbook Creator allows the inclusion of audio and video files, though they are presently available only for third-generation (and newer) Kindle Fire devices and may not function in the Look Inside. There are also free tutorials for the Kindle Textbook Creator on my blog:

https://chrismcmullen.com/2015/01/23/how-to-use-amazons-new-kindle-textbook-creator-tutorial
https://chrismcmullen.com/2015/07/30/optimizing-amazons-free-kindle-textbook-creator-publishing-tool

Amazon also has a free Kindle Comic Creator for comic eBooks:

http://www.amazon.com/gp/feature.html?docId=1001103761

Here are some reasons that a reflowable layout is generally better (except for picture books where virtually every page is a picture):

- Fixed-format books aren't available for all devices. For example, eBooks created with the Kindle Kids' Book Creator only work with Kindle Fire devices and the Kindle apps for iPad, iPhone, and Android. This excludes the popular Paperwhite and older Kindle devices, for example.[3]

- A reflowable eBook can offer easier reading by placing text in body paragraphs between images. This allows the customer to resize the text and line spacing, for example. In fixed format, features like pop-up text or pinch-and-zoom can help the customer read the text, but this becomes a very tedious way to read several pages of text.

- A well-designed reflowable eBook can format better across all devices, from a small cell phone screen to a large HD tablet.[4] Since every page appears as a picture in a fixed-format book, the fact that Kindle Fires, cell phones, iPads, and other screens have different aspect ratios serves as a limitation.[5]

- Reflowable books with text in body paragraphs are more customer-friendly. Fixed-format books embed the text in the image. Customers can't adjust the font size or line spacing to suit their vision needs and preferences like they can in reflowable books.

- Reflowable format offers the book designer greater flexibility with the design of the eBook.

---

[3] The Kindle Kids' Book Creator lets you create pop-up text, which is designed to work on the listed devices.

[4] The key term here is "well-designed." Don't just judge the design by how it looks on your screen in Microsoft Word. Create a preview (see Chapter 7) and judge how it looks on a variety of devices. You don't have to wait until the book is complete to upload a file and preview it at Kindle Direct Publishing (just sign up for a new account and visit your KDP Bookshelf).

http://kdp.amazon.com

[5] In Chapter 4, we'll see that aspect ratio is important for images even in reflowable layout, but unlike fixed format, the *entire book* isn't composed of pictures. In reflowable format, large images simply need to fill the width of the screen on any device (and the text before and after may help to fill up any remaining space).

For fully illustrated picture books, Sec. 4.12 discusses a few other differences between reflowable and fixed formats.

This guide focuses exclusively on how to format a Kindle eBook with a reflowable layout. Much of the formatting discussed in Chapters 2-3 specifically relates to the fact that most eBooks are reflowable in nature.

1.2 Word DOC or DOCX?

Microsoft Word 2007 and beyond allow you to save your work with DOC or DOCX file extensions. When you click Save As from the File menu, you can choose Word Document (for DOCX) or Word 97-2003 Document (for DOC). In Microsoft Word 2003 and earlier, DOCX isn't an option.

For those using Word 2007 and later, the question arises: Which file format is better—DOC or DOCX?

In the early days of Word 2007, the best format was DOC, but times have changed. Kindle software has improved, Microsoft Word has been updated, and even Windows has evolved. The original problems associated with DOCX have been resolved, and DOCX now actually appears to be friendlier for converting a properly formatted Word file to Kindle. Specifically, the hidden formatting alluded to in the Introduction may now translate better with DOCX.

Currently, I prefer **DOCX** for Kindle formatting. There may be a rare book that formats better as DOC instead of DOCX. You can try it both ways: Once your Word file is complete, it's easy to use the Save As feature and try it both ways.

Actually, what I recommend is **neither** uploading DOC nor DOCX, as I'll outline in Chapter 5. I begin with a Word file in DOCX format, implement all the suggestions in Chapters 2-4, and then follow the prescription in Chapter 5 to perfect the file in another format.

When you reach Chapter 5, you can save your file with both DOC and DOCX extensions, and you can try converting to yet another (which can be better in a few ways) file format specified in Chapter 5 from both DOC and DOCX formats to see which one turns out best. So you really don't have to choose now. (There are a few features that DOCX supports—which DOC doesn't support or which come out differently in DOC format—but if you design your Kindle eBook well, you shouldn't be using most of those features anyway.)

1.3 Print Edition, too?

If you may make a print edition of your book—now or in the future—you really need two separate files for your book. The reason is that print formatting and eBook formatting are considerably different. Rich formatting (fancy fonts, textboxes, bullet sublevels, etc.) and page information (headers, footers, page references, etc.) are either redesigned in a simpler way or are stripped out in eBook design, but you want those features in your print book.

This book was first written as a manuscript without *any* formatting. Obviously, neither the eBook nor the print editions look anything like that now. My current strategy is to perfect the text first, with a simple plain format, and then add formatting later.

The simplest way to create both eBook and print editions of the same book is to begin with a plain text manuscript. Don't worry about *any* formatting. (If you prefer to do a little formatting as you go—for some authors, making the book appear professional is a helpful motivator—at least try to avoid doing any formatting that is different between your eBook and print editions, as it will just take more work later to change it.)

Revise, edit, and proofread your plain-text manuscript until you have it perfected. Get the manuscript as well-written as possible before you begin formatting. Why? Because you'll eventually make both eBook and print editions, which have different formatting. Once you have two separate files, any changes that you make must be done twice. Proofreading and editing are simpler when you only need to work with one file. (Invariably, though, you'll catch more typos when you proofread your formatted eBook and print book. It's wise to create a proof of your print book and read that carefully before publishing your eBook because it's very common to find typos in print that are missed on the screen. Another tip is to use text-to-speech and listen for mistakes: Do that in addition to reading the text, **not** as a substitute for proofreading.)

At some point, you'll need to save your Word document with two different filenames, like SciFiKindle.docx and SciFiPrint.docx. From then on, the two files need to have the same text, but different formatting. Any time you make revisions to the text in one file, remember to also revise the text in the other file.

Tip: Save two copies of your book file—one for the eBook and one for the print book.

When is the best time to start working with two files instead of one? As soon as you apply any formatting that is specific to just one format or the other. Before you reach that point, it's simpler to work with a single file.

Note that Microsoft Word's paragraph styles make it easy for you to change your formatting. We'll learn how to use Word's paragraph styles efficiently in Chapter 3. Paragraph styles aren't just convenient: They are *necessary* to achieve reliable Kindle formatting from Microsoft Word—efficiency isn't the main reason for learning how to use Word's styles.

Paragraph styles automatically update throughout your book when you modify them (provided that you don't apply formatting directly to the paragraph—e.g. by highlighting the paragraph and selecting formatting options for it; the correct way is to create a paragraph style for every kind of paragraph formatting you need, and simply associate each paragraph with a paragraph style) when you follow the directions given in Chapter 3. This way, all you need to do to change your paragraph formatting is modify each of the paragraph styles. (This makes it easy to adjust the font style and font size for your print book, along with other paragraph features, such as leading. There will still be page features—like headers and page numbers—and other formatting features that need to be implemented manually.)

So here's what I would do: First use Word's styles to properly style the eBook (as described in Chapter 3). Next save your file separately for print and eBook formats. Then make changes that are specific to one format or the other (like special characters, headers, footers, textboxes, etc.).

Note that this guide is organized logically by topic (i.e. understanding the various aspects of eBook design), and wasn't organized in the order that you should implement the changes if you'll be formatting both an eBook and print book. However, for your convenience, the following list suggests the order in which to make the changes:

1. First, carry out the changes outlined in Sec.'s 2.1 thru 2.3. There is no reason to have tabs, extra spaces, or extra Enters in either edition of your book. (We will learn more reliable and efficient methods for controlling horizontal and vertical space in Chapter 3.)

2. Find the features from Sec.'s 2.4 thru 2.9 that are the same for both your eBook and your print book. Implement these features now, but save the others for later.

3. Style your book as outlined in Chapter 3 (but save Sec. 3.8 and Sec.'s 3.10-3.12 for later).

4. Save your Word document with two filenames—one for your eBook and one for your print book. If you later revise any text, remember to change both files.

5. Carry out the features of Sec.'s 2.4 thru 2.9 that are specific to each format. For example, a print book supports a wide range of special characters and fancy formatting, whereas Kindle has a limited set of supported characters (Appendix A) and formatting features.

6. Follow the instructions in Sec.'s 3.8 and 3.10 for your eBook. For your print book, you want your table of contents to include page numbers instead of hyperlinks.

7. If you have tables or equations, you may need to format these differently for your eBook and print book. See Sec.'s 3.11-3.12.

8. Proceed to Chapter 4 and onward for your eBook. If you have pictures, you may need to size and format them differently for your print book (Sec. 8.11).

9. Read Sec. 8.11 for a list of other features that you will need to add for your print book.

1.4 Back-up

Save your Word document regularly. Back your file up by saving it in (at least) two different locations (e.g. hard drive, jump drive, email). After making significant progress, add a version number to the filename, like Mystery3.docx instead of Mystery2.docx. You want to avoid the worst-case scenario where your file becomes corrupt and you must start over.

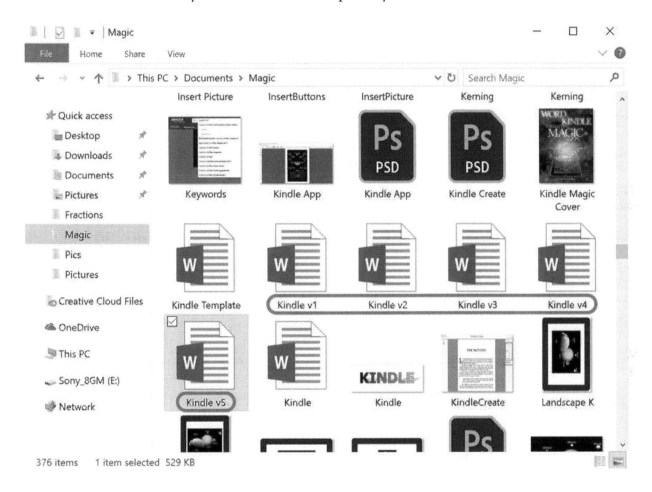

1.5 Alternative Formatting

Word is just one of the many ways to produce an eBook. Kindle is fairly Word-friendly, especially when all paragraph formatting is achieved through Word's styles (as described in Chapter 3). However, there are other ways to produce a quality Kindle eBook. Note that *every* method has its own pitfalls; no single method is foolproof.

- Write the book in HTML. This option appeals to many web designers. You have to be careful though, as designing a Kindle eBook is significantly different from designing a webpage. Many HTML features don't work on Kindle devices, and some features work on newer devices, but produce poor formatting on older devices. You must also be careful about which HTML editor you use, since some produce less Kindle-friendly results than others. I recommend instead starting with Word, and then switching to HTML after it has been properly styled. Chapter 5 of my book will help you with the transition.

- First type a rich text file. Then format the eBook in Sigil and create an ePub file. Many eBook formatting experts prefer to work with a program like Sigil (presently free). However, if you follow this guide—especially, styling your document according to Chapter 3—it will produce relatively clean HTML that you could then tweak in Sigil or Notepad. (On the other hand, a Word document that *isn't* styled cleanly as described in Chapter 3 can produce rather convoluted HTML.) Especially, if you may be creating a print book in addition to an eBook, it may be handy to have a properly styled Word document (see the note in Sec. 1.3) before perfecting your eBook with Sigil or Notepad. In Chapter 5, we'll learn how to use Word to produce HTML, which you can then edit in Notepad or Sigil, for example. So this option is very much in line with the formatting guide that you're reading now. (Plus, here is a secret: Many formatting experts who advocate Sigil or other programs actually begin with a Word document before using those other programs. There are a few exceptions, but the use of Word, at least in the beginning, is highly common.)

- A relatively new option is to use Amazon's new Kindle Create software. Actually, you can use this tool and still follow my book. What Kindle Create really does is provide a simplified alternative to using Word's paragraph styles. In that case, when you read Chapter 3, you would style your paragraphs using Kindle Create instead of using Word. The only chapter of this guide that doesn't apply when you use the Kindle Create software is Chapter 5 (you won't be able to go a step beyond Word and still use Kindle Create).

- Some authors prefer to use an alternative word processing software, such as Open Office (free), Atlantis, Jutoh, or Scrivener. It's not that these other programs are better, as a properly styled Word document can produce a very good Kindle eBook (especially, if you follow Chapters 3 and 5 of this guide). If you're already familiar with Word, it's much more convenient to learn how to modify your Word file for Kindle than it would be to learn new software.

- Yet another option is to submit your manuscript to Kindle Scout—Amazon's eBook publishing company. Authors submit their complete manuscripts to Kindle Scout, and prospective readers vote on them. If you price your book $2.99 or higher, you can earn higher royalties by self-publishing via KDP, but Kindle Scout offers an advance if they accept your book. It may help if you've already built an active following through marketing (Sec. 8.7) to help recruit votes. A possible downside is that if your book isn't accepted, Amazon will email the people who voted on your book to let them know (unless this feature has changed)—although if your book is accepted, the same feature becomes an upside.

https://kindlescout.amazon.com

- Some authors publish their eBooks through an aggregator, and then the aggregator distributes the eBook to a variety of eStores. A few popular aggregators include Smashwords, Draft2Digital, and BookBaby. The way that you go about the formatting varies with the aggregator. For example, with Smashwords, following the *Smashwords Style Guide* isn't too different than following the information in my book. Aggregators offer convenience if you wish to publish your eBook with multiple outlets, but they also introduce new formatting challenges. For example, a few of the formatting solutions that we implement for Kindle may cause problems with other eReaders (such as Nook), which means you must research the differences (note that my guide is focused on Kindle). Another issue is that you can't enroll your eBook in KDP Select (however, BookBaby is unique in that it currently offers this option—though it still requires exclusivity, no different than if you publish with KDP), which is beneficial to many authors. I recommend that you read Sec.'s 6.12 and 6.16 first if you're considering whether or not to use an aggregator. If your book has pictures, note that other distributors don't offer the generous file size limit that Amazon does, so you may wish to explore their file size limits before you commit. For most aggregators, I still recommend that you follow this guide to prepare your Kindle edition, and then consider revising your file for the aggregator (but you should first research the formatting requirements of the aggregator you wish to use before you do the formatting work, just to make sure it will work for you).

www.smashwords.com
www.draft2digital.com
www.bookbaby.com

- Note that it is possible to find a Word template for Kindle formatting, yet no template is foolproof. One problem with a Word template is that formatting can change when you copy and paste text into it, and copying and pasting can even be inconsistent in Word. Another problem is when you advance onto a new paragraph, you can sometimes begin a different paragraph style than you expected. A template also doesn't understand your unique book: It's common for a relatively simple and common thing not to have been anticipated by the designer. You are more likely to understand formatting that you do yourself than you are to understand somebody else's template, which means you're more likely to get your own Word file to format properly than you are to get a template to work properly. In my opinion (shared by many other eBook formatters), learning how to use Word's styles, understanding eBook formatting options, and learning basic eBook design is better than using a template. Plus, it's relatively easy to do, as this guide will show you.

- If you have a fully illustrated children's book, a comic book, or a richly formatted textbook, an alternative is to create a fixed format eBook using one of Amazon's free publishing tools.

Kindle Kids' Book Creator

https://kdp.amazon.com/en_US/kids

http://chrismcmullen.com/2014/09/04/how-to-use-the-new-kindle-kids-book-creator-tutorial

https://chrismcmullen.wordpress.com/2017/06/13/how-to-add-url-hyperlinks-with-the-kindle-kids-book-creator-kkbc

Kindle Textbook Creator

https://www.amazon.com/gp/education-publishing

https://chrismcmullen.com/2015/01/23/how-to-use-amazons-new-kindle-textbook-creator-tutorial

https://chrismcmullen.com/2015/07/30/optimizing-amazons-free-kindle-textbook-creator-publishing-tool

Kindle Comic Creator

https://www.amazon.com/gp/feature.html?ie=UTF8&docId=1001103761

- The other option is paid formatting. Amazon has a short list of paid formatting services on the KDP website (if the link below no longer works—which may happen, as Amazon updates the KDP website periodically—try typing "conversion resources" without the quotation marks in the search field at the KDP help pages). On Amazon's list, I'm familiar with Booknook.biz: I haven't used this company, but I have interacted with the person who runs the company, who has appeared quite knowledgeable. If you visit the Smashwords website (find the link a couple of bullet points back), they have a list of inexpensive eBook formatters (and also a list of inexpensive cover designers). BookBaby (for which the link was also provided a couple of bullet points back) offers paid conversion (and other) services, which is convenient if you are looking for an eBook distributor and are also looking for paid services. If do decide to pay for formatting, you want to inquire about making changes to your file in the future before you commit. **I recommend investing the time to learn how to format your own eBook if you may publish additional books in the future.** If you wind up publishing several books and pay to have all of them professionally formatted, *you could have saved yourself a great deal of money by learning how to do it yourself in the beginning.* **Another advantage of doing your own formatting is that it's easy to make changes**: You won't have to contact the formatter, pay more money, and wait for the changes to be implemented (and what if the formatter has gone out of business?). (CreateSpace, which is an Amazon company, used to offer paid conversion services, but CreateSpace is discontinuing its paid service options. Note that if you publish a paperback with CreateSpace, *don't* accept CreateSpace's free offer to transfer your PDF files to Kindle: That free file transfer almost always results in formatting problems.)

https://kdp.amazon.com/en_US/help/topic/G200634410

You really don't need to look for an alternative. Microsoft Word is a great place to start (even if you're willing to go a step beyond Word):

- Microsoft Word is fairly Kindle friendly (and even friendlier if you follow the instructions in this guide). Amazon knows that most self-published authors use Word. You do need to learn how to modify your Word file to produce good Kindle formatting, like learning how to use paragraph styles and which features don't convert well to Kindle, but if you do this (as described in this book), then Word is very Kindle friendly.
- Word is convenient. Most authors have access to Word. It's fairly affordable and accessible. Most authors already have experience using Word, whereas starting with new software involves a large learning curve.

- You retain the flexibility to go one step beyond Word (for example, if you're willing to use a little HTML). If you style your Word file properly, this makes the transition relatively straightforward. In fact, many formatters who use other software like Sigil actually first prepare their manuscript in Word first. Chapter 5 discusses how to go one step beyond Word to make subtle formatting improvements (though if you submit your polished Word file, that should be pretty good, too).

- For authors who will publish a print book in addition to an eBook, Word can be used to do both (though, as noted in Sec. 1.3, at some point you will need to create two separate Word files for this). This makes Word even more convenient.

1.6 Other Formats, too?

This book is focused on how to format a Kindle eBook. If you also plan to publish your eBook with Nook, Kobo, etc., many of the formatting procedures are the same, but there are a few subtle differences. You'll want to research these differences when preparing your eBook file for other eBook retailers or distributors.

Also, note that Amazon has the most generous file size limits. Pictures take the most memory: If your book includes several images, you should explore the file size limits for other platforms before you commit to publishing elsewhere.

Amazon actually provides authors with an incentive to publish their eBook exclusively with Kindle. If you wish to take advantage of the benefits that KDP Select has to offer, you're **not** permitted to publish your eBook anywhere other than Kindle (via Amazon KDP). *Authors who enroll in KDP Select also don't have to learn how to format their eBooks for other platforms*, which simplifies the publishing process.

Sec. 6.12 discusses the pros and cons of enrolling your Kindle eBook in KDP Select. I recommend that you read Sec. 6.12 and consider this important decision before you commit to publishing your eBook elsewhere. If you're interested in publishing with Nook, Kobo, and other eBook retailers, Sec. 6.16 will help point you in the right direction.

—Chapter 2—

The Basics

2.1 Remove all Tabs

UNFORTUNATELY, USE OF the tab key to create indents isn't compatible with eBooks. The tab key can create indents nicely on the screen when you're using Word, and this can translate fairly well to print books, but it doesn't work well with eBooks. The big problem with the tab key is that it results in inconsistent indents throughout the book—sometimes smaller, sometimes larger. This really detracts from the reading experience. This particular formatting issue may vary from one device to another: Thus, it might seem okay when you preview it on one device, but it will have a problem on another device. Tabs are likely to look worst on the all-important Look Inside at Amazon (for which there is no preview, so the author doesn't realize it until the book is already published).

Pitfall: Use of the tab key results in inconsistent indentations throughout the eBook.
Solution: Don't use the tab key.

Good news: You can create perfectly formatted indents without using the tab key. We'll learn how to do this in Chapter 3.

Pitfall: Using the spacebar to create indents is also **not** recommended. It may also result in inconsistent paragraph indentations.
Solution: Don't use the spacebar (or the tab key) to create indents. In Chapter 3, we'll learn that the reliable way to indent paragraphs is to adjust the First Line Indent in a paragraph style.

In the meantime, if you've already used the tab key, you need to undo this mistake. Even if you believe that you *didn't* use the tab key, it's worth performing the following search just to be sure. (If you used the spacebar to create indents, Sec. 2.2 will show you how to remove those spaces.)

Tip: Remove all tabs from your Word file.

Follow these steps to remove all of the tabs from your Word document:
1. Go to the Home ribbon.[6]
2. Press the Replace button at the far right of the Home ribbon.
3. Click the More button.
4. Place your cursor in the Find What field.

---

[6] If you don't see the Home ribbon, hover your cursor over the icons at the top right corner of the screen until you find the Ribbon Display Options. Click the button for Ribbon Display Options and select Show Tabs and Commands.

5. Click Special and select Tab Character. It should display ^t.

6. Leave the Replace With field blank.

7. Press the Replace All button.

8. If asked to continue the search from the beginning of the document, press OK.

Don't worry: You'll learn the proper way to restore indents in Chapter 3. The first step is to remove the tabs.

Do you know about First Line Indent? Beware that you might not know *enough* about it. (If you don't know about First Line Indent, don't worry: We'll learn about it in Chapter 3.) If you highlighted paragraphs and applied First Line Indent to specific paragraphs (or if you used the paragraph options on the Home ribbon with your cursor placed in the paragraph), unfortunately this may result in formatting issues. There is a *better* way to do this. (Want to know *why*? Read Sec. 3.1.) You want to apply First Line Indent to the Normal style and associate the Normal style with indented paragraphs (as described in Chapter 3). Don't apply First Line Indents to high-lighted paragraphs, or apply the paragraph options on the Home ribbon with your cursor in a paragraph. (Too late? You can still clear the paragraph formatting and restyle the paragraphs properly, but wait until you read Chapter 3 and learn how to do this properly.)

Also, beware that multi-level indents often result in formatting problems. We'll discuss indents in Chapter 3, including the proper way to indent paragraphs via Word's paragraph styles.

Tip: Don't highlight paragraphs and set First Line Indent to highlighted paragraphs. Don't adjust the font or paragraph options on the Home ribbon and then proceed to type one or more paragraphs.[7] Instead, learn how to use the Normal style (Chapter 3) to do this without applying direct formatting.

2.2 Remove Extra Spaces

Did you press the spacebar twice after each period (and before the first letter of the next sentence) while typing your book? It's a common habit among writers, and many people learned that this was 'correct' in school (even in colleges). However, traditionally published books are **not** printed this way.

If you visit a bookstore and open a variety of books, you should notice that the space after a period matches the size of the space between words. That's because traditional publishers only use a single space after a period: two spaces after a period will seem *incorrect* by comparison.

---

[7] You can use either of these methods for *part* of a paragraph (for example, to italicize one sentence). However, if you need to apply font or paragraph changes to an *entire* paragraph (or more), Chapter 3 will show you how to use the paragraph styles feature instead.

Inconsistent Indents

light when you want one? I once drove 70 miles, getting every one of several lights red in two different cities. Oh, but that day I had been in a hurry.

I did manage to reach my destination and jot down some notes on a napkin. Then I went into the restaurant, only to think of yet another idea, with my napkin and pen back in the car.

Very funny, muse. We all know that muses have a great sense of humor. They really put the muse in amusement.

Of course, this isn't the only evidence. We have storage rooms full of it.

Your muse and Murphy's law: They're definitely in on it together.

What has your muse done to you lately?

One Problem with Tabs

in two different cities. Oh, but that day I had been in a hurry.

I did manage to reach my destination and jot down some notes on a napkin. Then I went into the restaurant, only to think of yet another idea, with my napkin and pen back in the car.

Very funny, muse. We all know that muses have a great sense of humor. They really put the muse in amusement.

Of course, this isn't the only evidence. We have storage rooms full of it.

Your muse and Murphy's law: They're definitely in on it together.

What has your muse done to you lately?

Consistency

getting every one of several lights red in two different cities. Oh, but that day I had been in a hurry.

I did manage to reach my destination and jot down some notes on a napkin. Then I went into the restaurant, only to think of yet another idea, with my napkin and pen back in the car.

Very funny, muse. We all know that muses have a great sense of humor. They really put the muse in amusement.

Of course, this isn't the only evidence. We have storage rooms full of it.

Your muse and Murphy's law: They're definitely in on it together.

What has your muse done to you lately?

One space after a period

If the book passes your examination, you take it out on a date. You begin reading the first chapter. The whole time the book is anticipating that first kiss, wondering if you will take it home with you. Meanwhile, you are analyzing the book's every move. Going steady with a book is a big commitment. You don't want to be disappointed.

How do you know if the relationship will work out? Curling up by the fireplace, snuggling in warm covers in bed with a book light, sneaking a quick page or two in the bathroom. You will share these intimate times with your book. You want to know that the book is Mr. or Mrs. Right for you.

When you look at the cover, you see the book's handsome or pretty face

Two spaces after a period

If the book passes your examination, you take it out on a date. You begin reading the first chapter. The whole time the book is anticipating that first kiss, wondering if you will take it home with you. Meanwhile, you are analyzing the book's every move. Going steady with a book is a big commitment. You don't want to be disappointed.

How do you know if the relationship will work out? Curling up by the fireplace, snuggling in warm covers in bed with a book light, sneaking a quick page or two in the bathroom. You will share these intimate times with your book. You want to know that the book is Mr. or Mrs. Right for you.

When you look at the cover, you see the book's handsome or pretty face

Are you still unconvinced? There is a fantastic *Slate* article entitled "Space Invaders" by Farhad Manjoo, which every writer should read: Visit the URL below to read that article.

http://www.slate.com/articles/technology/technology/2011/01/space_invaders.html

There are a variety of extra spaces that may result in formatting issues in a Kindle eBook:

- Two spaces after a period (instead of one).
- Pressing the spacebar key repeatedly to create indents.
- An extra spacebar accidentally typed at the end of a paragraph.

Again, these extra spaces may not seem to cause any problems when you're viewing your work in Word, but they may cause formatting problems when customers read the book on Kindle devices (or apps). Even if you don't believe you have extra spaces in your file, it's worth doing the following search just in case.

Tip: Remove all extra spaces from your Word file.

Follow these steps to remove strings of multiple spaces from your Word document:

1. Go to the Home ribbon.
2. Press the Replace button at the far right.
3. Place your cursor in the Find What field.
4. Press the spacebar twice.
5. Place your cursor in the Replace With field.
6. Press the spacebar once.
7. Press the Replace All button.
8. If asked to continue the search from the beginning of the document, press OK.
9. Press Replace All again and repeat until you don't get any matches.

In addition, you want to find any stray spaces that might lie at the end of a paragraph:

- Go to the Home ribbon.
- Press the Replace button at the far right.
- Click the More button.
- Place your cursor in the Find What field.
- Click Special and select Paragraph Character. It should display ^p.
- Place your cursor to the **left** of the ^p that appears and press the spacebar once. This will give you spacebar^p (but with an actual space instead of the word spacebar).
- Place your cursor in the Replace With field.
- Click Special and Select Paragraph Character. It should display ^p.

- Press the Replace All button.
- If asked to continue the search from the beginning of the document, press OK.
- Press Replace All again and repeat until you don't get any matches.
- Repeat the steps above using Manual Line Break (^l) instead of Paragraph Character (^p).

The reason for doing the last step is that there are two different kinds of line breaks. One line break is created by pressing the Enter key, while another can be created, for example, by pressing Shift + Enter. Pressing the Enter key creates a hard return, whereas pressing Shift + Enter creates a soft return. Visually, you can tell the difference in Word, but soft returns don't achieve the same effect with Kindle as you see in Word.

A stray space at the beginning of a paragraph isn't quite as common, but it does happen. To find and replace these, repeat the steps above, but in Step 6 put the spacebar to the right of the ^p instead of the left of it: You should now have ^pspacebar (but press the spacebar once to create a blank space—don't type the word spacebar as I have done here) in the Find What field.

2.3 Remove Extra Line Breaks

So far, we've looked at common *horizontal* spacing issues with the tab key and spacebar. Now we'll examine common *vertical* spacing issues associated with the Enter key.

One problem arises when using the Enter key to create blank lines. That is, you press Enter once to end a paragraph and a second time to create a blank line between paragraphs—or, more commonly, to create a blank line between a heading and a paragraph, or between a heading and a subheading. (Note that this is a problem regardless of whether you use hard or soft returns.)

Unfortunately, a single line space between paragraphs may not format as desired across all devices. Even worse, a blank line is likely to be stripped out of the important Look Inside feature at Amazon.

Another problem with using the Enter key to create a blank line is when the blank line happens to come at the top or bottom of a 'page' (or call it a 'screen' instead). You wouldn't want a blank line to appear at the top or bottom of a page in a printed book: You'd either omit the blank line in this case, or, if it is a section break, you might use asterisks (* * *) instead. However, you can't predict when a blank line would appear at the top or bottom of a screen in an eBook.

Pitfall: Don't press the Enter consecutively to produce blank lines.
Solution: Add space before or after the paragraph through the paragraph menu (but do it with Word's styles, as described in Chapter 3).

Blank lines (especially, two or more consecutive blank lines) may result in poor Kindle formatting. Blank lines may also be stripped out in some cases (such as in the Look Inside feature).

Fortunately, there is an alternative to using blank lines that works much better. In the paragraph options, you can add space before or after a paragraph to create this effect instead of using the Enter key. But don't highlight paragraphs and manually add space to them. Instead, learn how to add space before or after paragraphs through Word's styles, as explained in Chapter 3.

Another problem arises when the Enter key (or any other method for creating a return or forced line break) is used before reaching the end of a paragraph. You should press Enter once at the end of a paragraph to automatically begin a new paragraph (with **no** blank line between), but you should **not** press the Enter key in an attempt to control line breaks within a paragraph—since this results in poor Kindle formatting. There are two ways that this sometimes happens. One way is when someone who is knowledgeable regarding print formatting uses Shift + Enter to force a line break (to deal with a print formatting issue, such as a widow, orphan, or justification problem): While that may help *print* formatting, it can be disastrous for *Kindle* formatting. A more severe problem occurs when an author presses Enter at the end of each line in the paragraph, instead of only pressing Enter once at the very end of the paragraph. If your book has any Enters of this form, you need to search for them and remove them for your Kindle eBook. You can search for Shift + Enter line breaks with the Find or Replace tools (click the arrow to the right of the Find button, choose Advanced Find, click the More button, click Special, and select Manual Line Break), but if you pressed Enter at the end of a line before reaching the end of a paragraph, you will need to find and correct this manually.

The biggest vertical spacing problem arises from using the Enter key to advance to the next page. When viewing the screen in Word, this seems to work, but it doesn't work once the eBook is viewed on a Kindle device or app. The reason is that you can't predict how many Enter keys would be needed to advance to the next page, as you have no control over the screen size of the customer's device, font style or font size that the customer will select, or the margins setting that the customer will choose.

So if you use the Enter key to advance to the next page, the next chapter won't start where you'd like: On a large screen with a small font, it may not even reach the next page, while on a small screen with a large font, the next chapter may begin at the bottom of the next page—or worse, it might create one or more blank pages in between chapters. It's also possible that the extra line breaks will simply get stripped out of your converted eBook. (Of course, with eBooks, what I'm calling a 'page' isn't a page in the traditional sense. It would be better to call it a 'screen.') This will definitely create a poor reading experience.

Pitfall: Don't use the Enter key to start a new chapter.

Solution: Use a page break instead (but do it with Word's styles, as described in Chapter 3).

Any extra Enters create formatting issues:

- Pressing the Enter key repeatedly to create blank lines.
- Using the Enter key to begin a new chapter.
- Pressing the Enter key (or any alternative method for creating a return or forced line break) before reaching the end of a paragraph. (However, for bullet points and numbered lists, it is okay to press Enter at the end of each list item.)
- Two (or more) consecutive Enters for *any* reason.

Tip: Remove all extra Enters from your Word file.

Before you remove the extra Enters from your Word file, I recommend that you replace all manual line breaks (soft returns) with Enters (hard returns). Manual line breaks don't have the same effect on an eBook as they do on a print book, and if you used manual line breaks to control the appearance of paragraphs as you see them in Word, they may cause major formatting issues in your eBook (unless you remove them). After turning soft returns into hard returns, if there are any formatting issues with the hard returns, there is a better chance that you will catch the problem and correct it while you're formatting your Word file. Follow these steps to replace any manual line breaks (soft returns) with Enters (hard returns):

1. Go to the Home ribbon.
2. Press the Replace button at the far right.
3. Click the More button.
4. Place your cursor in the Find What field.
5. Click Special and select Manual Line Break. It should display ^l.
6. Place your cursor in the Replace With field.
7. Click Special and Select Paragraph Character. It should display ^p.
8. Press the Replace All button.
9. If asked to continue the search from the beginning of the document, press OK.

Don't worry: You'll learn the proper way to add space between paragraphs in Chapter 3. The first step is to remove the extra line breaks. Follow these steps to remove extra line breaks from your Word document:

1. Go to the Home ribbon.
2. Press the Replace button at the far right.
3. Click the More button.
4. Place your cursor in the Find What field.
5. Click Special and select Paragraph Character. It should display ^p.
6. Click Special and select Paragraph Character again. It should now display ^p^p.

7. Place your cursor in the Replace With field.

8. Click Special and Select Paragraph Character. It should display ^p.

9. Press the Replace All button.

10. If asked to continue the search from the beginning of the document, press OK.

11. Press Replace All again and repeat until you don't get any matches.

As explained at the end of Sec. 2.2, the last step deals with the two possible ways of creating a line break in a Word document.

2.4 Navigation and Reflow

When you paginate your way through an eBook, advancing one 'page' (or 'screen') at a time, the reading experience very much seems to mimic that of a printed book. However, when designing an eBook, it's important to keep in mind that the reading experience is different from that of a printed book in two significant ways: reflow and navigation.

An eBook is *reflowable*, but not in the same sense that a website is reflowable. When you visit a webpage, you read it by scrolling downward. You don't scroll through an eBook. The sense in which an eBook is reflowable is that the text automatically adjusts to fill the screen regardless of the screen size of the display (from a cell phone to a large tablet), the orientation in which it is held (portrait or landscape), and the reader settings (font style, font size, internal margins, and line spacing—selected by the customer).

When we say that a standard eBook is reflowable, what we really mean to emphasize is that you can't predict which information will show up on the screen at any given location in the eBook—because you can't predict the screen size, orientation, and reader settings that the customer will select.

One example of how the reflowable nature of eBooks impacts Kindle design involves scene breaks: In a print book, a blank line is used to indicate a scene break. The blank line may very well vanish in an eBook: Depending on the screen size, orientation, and reader settings, the scene break might appear at the very top or bottom of the screen—where it will likely go unnoticed.

We already saw an issue relating to the fact that eBooks don't have well-defined pages in Sec. 2.3: You must refrain from using returns (line breaks) to control when each line of a paragraph ends (instead, just press Enter once when you reach the end of the paragraph), and must refrain from using returns to advance onto the next page (use a page break instead). Similarly, if you used manual hyphens to control the appearance of your paragraphs as shown in Word, or if you applied typographical tricks to control widows, orphans, runts, and rivers, you will need to undo all of this for your eBook (because you can't predict how the text will appear on any given 'screen' when a customer reads your eBook).

Another way that the reflowable nature of eBooks affects Kindle formatting is that you can't refer to specific page numbers. It would be completely meaningless to say something like, "See page 42," in an eBook. Since different customers have devices with different screen sizes, and since the customer can adjust the font size, font style, margins, and orientation (portrait or landscape), there is no way of predicting which information would show on the 42nd screen from the beginning. You *can* reference a chapter or section (for example, "See Sec. 3.6").

An eBook actually offers a better way of referencing specific material compared to a print book. In a print book, if you write, "See page 42," the customer must thumb through the pages until finding page 42. In an eBook, you can create a bookmark hyperlink: When the customer clicks on the bookmark hyperlink, the eBook immediately takes the customer to bookmarked location in the book. (This makes it much easier to get eBook customers to visit websites, too.)

With bookmark hyperlinks, we see an example of how a customer may *navigate* rather than paginate through an eBook. Another way that customers may navigate—rather than turn pages—through an eBook is via an active table of contents. Unlike a print book, an eBook's table of contents doesn't include page numbers: It includes bookmark hyperlinks. Customers don't even need to return to the beginning of the book to access it: Kindle devices and apps have built-in navigation. Readers simply access the menu from the device or app to quickly visit a particular chapter.

Footnotes and endnotes automatically turn into bookmark hyperlinks. If you include footnotes or endnotes in your Word file, Kindle customers can click on them in the eBook. When a customer clicks on a footnote or endnote, the device or app takes the customer directly to the footnote or endnote. How does the customer return? It's automatic: The customer simply clicks the footnote or endnote number and the device returns the customer to the previous reading position (except that the text may shift on the page—compared to how it looked to the customer before clicking on the note—to place the footnote or endnote number at the top of the screen).

You might expect an index to similarly include bookmark hyperlinks instead of page numbers, but it turns out that an index is completely **unnecessary** in an eBook: Kindle devices and apps include a search feature. Customers can type any word or phrase into the search field and the eReader will show all of the matches.

Navigation and reflow are important to eBook design in a few ways:

- Some features, like page numbers and page headers (Sec. 2.5), don't apply to eBooks.
- Other features, like bookmark hyperlinks, must be added to eBooks. (We'll learn how to add bookmark hyperlinks in Sec. 3.10.)
- Other features, like endnotes (Sec.'s 2.5 and 3.4), apply to both eBooks and print books, but work differently in each case.

At first, this section break seems to be fine.

it needed a cover. He wasn't an artist or a photography. This wasn't going to be easy. As a businessman though, he understood the need to make a good first impression. He wouldn't show up to an interview without a tie, a pressed suit, and a clean shave. So he would get a book cover that could make the right impression. Fortunately, he was able to hire an inexpensive designer to put together a nice cover.

Wait. *The writing wasn't complete.* The book needed a description. At first, it seemed to be such a small thing. After all, he'd already written 50,000 words. What's a few hundred more?

Yet the more he tried to write a description, the harder this task seemed to be. Why was it so easy to write a story, but so hard to describe it? He knew it shouldn't be a summary: If you already knew what

At a different customer setting, the section break "vanishes" at the top of a screen.

work didn't end there. It was followed with formatting. He learned a great deal about the layout of a novel in his effort to master formatting. He would never look at a book the same way again. It wasn't easy, but he finally made the novel look as beautiful as she reasonably could.

The book was complete, but now it needed a cover. He wasn't an artist or a photography. This wasn't going to be easy. As a businessman though, he understood the need to make a good first impression. He wouldn't show up to an interview without a tie, a pressed suit, and a clean shave. So he would get a book cover that could make the right impression. Fortunately, he was able to hire an inexpensive designer to put together a nice cover.

Wait. *The writing wasn't complete.* The book needed a description. At first, it seemed to be such a small thing. After all, he'd already written 50,000 words. What's a few hundred more?

Yet the more he tried to write a description, the harder this task seemed to be. Why was it so easy to write a story, but so hard to describe it? He knew it shouldn't be a summary: If you already knew what happened, you wouldn't want to read the story. It needed a few hints regarding what the story was about: enough to know what type of story to expect, but not enough information to spoil it. The description also needed something to entice and interest the reader: a little suspense.

Asterisks would be visible wherever the break occurs.

* * *

Wait. *The writing wasn't complete.* The book needed a description. At first, it seemed to be such a small thing. After all, he'd already written 50,000 words. What's a few hundred more?

Yet the more he tried to write a description, the harder this task seemed to be. Why was it so easy to write a story, but so hard to describe it? He knew it shouldn't be a summary: If you already knew what happened, you wouldn't want to read the story. It needed a few hints regarding what the story was about: enough to know what type of story to expect, but not enough information to spoil it. The description also needed something to entice and interest the reader: a little suspense.

In a reflowable eBook, you can't predict which text (or how much text) will show up on a screen at any given location.

Device 1 (Kindle):

dog.

Unfortunately, he was barking up the wrong tree.

Fortunately, he had an ace up his sleeve.

Until he lost his shirt.

So he followed his nose.

He arrived just in the nick of time.

Better late than never.

The damsel was over a barrel.

A tiger was playing mouse with her.

The knight took the tiger by the tail.

Since he had a bone to pick with that tiger.

It was like playing with fire.

He cleaned the tiger's clock.

Then he rubbed salt in the tiger's wounds.

The tiger went stiff as a board and then bit the dust.

kindle

Device 2 (phone):

Fortunately, he had an ace up his sleeve.

Until he lost his shirt.

So he followed his nose.

He arrived just in the nick of time.

Better late than never.

The damsel was over a barrel.

A tiger was playing mouse with her.

The knight took the tiger by the tail.

Since he had a bone to pick with that tiger.

It was like playing with fire.

He cleaned the tiger's clock.

Then he rubbed salt in the tiger's wounds.

The tiger went stiff as a board and then bit the dust.

Next he buried the hatchet.

And the tiger was up a creek without a paddle.

When the knight and damsel met, it was love at first sight.

It was so romantic.

Device 3 (tablet):

in the morning.

Then he felt snug as a bug in a rug.

He turned nutty as a fruitcake and barked like a dog.

Unfortunately, he was barking up the wrong tree.

Fortunately, he had an ace up his sleeve.

Until he lost his shirt.

So he followed his nose.

He arrived just in the nick of time.

Better late than never.

The damsel was over a barrel.

A tiger was playing mouse with her.

The knight took the tiger by the tail.

Since he had a bone to pick with that

Device 4 (tablet):

The damsel was over a barrel.

A tiger was playing mouse with her.

The knight took the tiger by the tail.

Since he had a bone to pick with that tiger.

It was like playing with fire.

He cleaned the tiger's clock.

Then he rubbed salt in the tiger's wounds.

The tiger went stiff as a board and then bit the dust.

Next he buried the hatchet.

And the tiger was up a creek without a paddle.

When the knight and damsel met, it was love at first sight.

It was so romantic.

Because it takes two to tango and there's a crowd.

They were like two peas in a pod.

He was dressed to the nines and she had money to burn.

So they tied the knot.

They even put the icing on the cake.

And they lived happily ever after.

They were on cloud nine.

Until they kicked the bucket.

- You are severely limited in your control of which content will show on any given 'page' (screen!) and how it will appear. You do have a few tools that you can use, such as page breaks and non-breaking spaces (see Chapters 3 and 5).

- A well-designed eBook considers the reflowable nature of eBooks, assorted sizes of eReaders, possible customer selections (font size, font style, and margins), different technology (from old Kindle devices to the latest high-definition tablets), and the fact that not all customers are familiar with how to operate their devices. This impacts Kindle design choices, as we will explore in Sec. 3.7, for example.

This section was *conceptual*: The purpose of this section is to try and get you thinking about the nature of eBooks and how they differ from print books. Such a mindset will help you with Kindle design decisions that you will encounter as you follow this guide to format your eBook.

2.5 Page-related Features

Since standard (reflowable) eBooks don't have well-defined 'pages,' there are a variety of page-related features that must be removed (or modified) from your Word file. As we'll see in Sec. 2.10, you don't need to strip *every* page-related feature from your book to format it as an eBook. For example, you can actually leave page numbers (assuming that they were inserted through page headers or footers and propagated automatically through your Word file) and page headers in your Word document. Word's headers and footers (including page numbers that are part of headers or footers) simply won't show up in your eBook. In this section, we'll focus on page-related features that you *do* need to modify or remove.

The following are specific changes that you want to make with regard to pagination:

- Delete your table of contents, but save the Table of Contents heading. If you format your book as prescribed in Chapter 3, you will be able to use Word's automatic table of contents feature to quickly create an active table of contents. This is shown in Sec. 3.8. You'll want to have an active table of contents to provide easy navigation for your readers (Kindle will also build this into the menu on the device or app so customers don't need to scroll back to the beginning).

- You can have page breaks, but there is a better way: We'll learn how to build page breaks into one of Word's styles in Chapter 3. Thus, I recommend removing all page breaks for now, and then implementing page breaks through a heading or paragraph style when we reach the next chapter. You also want to consider how page breaks might impact the reflowable nature of the eBook. Most eBooks only include page breaks at the beginning of each chapter (by incorporating a page break into the Heading 1 style, as we'll learn in Chapter 3). If a chapter heading doesn't come with a page break, the chapter heading may appear awkwardly at the bottom of a 'screen.' There may be a few other places where a page break is helpful: For example, if you have a tall picture and don't want just a few lines of text to display below the picture, you could use a page break to force that text onto the next 'screen.' You probably *don't* want to force page breaks with *every* image or table (as this can create large sections of white space on the pages before and between them). With each page break, ask yourself if it's necessary and how it might impact the reader's navigation through the eBook. You'll also be able to try it out in the preview (Chapter 7) before publishing. I recommend avoiding most page breaks except with chapter headings.

- If you used Word's **section break** features (such as Next Page, Continuous, or Odd Page breaks—available in Page Layout > Breaks), you can leave them in your Word file. Since Word's section break features affect page headers and footers (for example, in a print book Next Page section breaks are used to create different page headers for different chapters), and since page headers and footers won't show up in your eBook, these section break features don't really matter. However, if you have a Next Page or Odd Page break, and if you wish to incorporate the page break into the heading style as recommended in Chapter 3, then you should remove the Next Page or Odd Page break now. If you have **endnotes**, note that Word's section break features affect the (automatic) placement of your endnotes in your eBook (this concerns endnotes, not footnotes). The text for your endnotes will appear at the end of each chapter if your Word file includes section breaks, whereas the text for endnotes are generally 'hidden' at the back of the eBook. Ordinarily, you want that text out of the way: When a customer clicks on a link for the endnote in an eBook, the eBook will take the customer to the otherwise 'hidden' endnote text, and then return the customer to the previous reading position after. Therefore, if you used endnotes (remember, this doesn't concern footnotes) in your Word file, consider removing the section break features from your Word file.

- Search for references that you may have made in the text with regard to **specific pages**. You may have written phrases like, "see page 14," "refer to pages 112-5," "as shown on p. 35," or, "from pp. 289-95." Use the Find tool on the right side of the Home ribbon. Search for "page" and "p. " to catch most of these page references (but without the quotation marks, but do include the space after the period in "p. "). Change these to refer to sections or chapters instead. You may also want to turn these into bookmark hyperlinks for easy navigation (see Sec. 3.10).

- Leave **footnotes** and **endnotes** in your Word file. Customers can click on any of these, read the note, and return to reading. Sec. 3.4 will show you how to format these properly.

- If you have an index, remove it from the Word document for your eBook. An index isn't needed in an eBook because eReaders include a search option. Customers can simply enter words or phrases into the search tool to quickly find them in the eBook. You will also have the option to add X-ray to your Kindle eBook after you publish (Sec. 8.14), which functions sort of like a handy glossary.

- Typographers often adjust features like tracking, kerning, scaling, font size, spacing between paragraphs, margins, and inter-word spacing, for example, in print books in order to prevent unwanted features like widows, orphans, and runts. However, you don't want features like tracking, scaling, and abrupt font size changes in your eBook. Suppose that you highlight a paragraph of text to adjust font size slightly in order to avoid a widow in your print book: This can cause chaos in your eBook, where widows and orphans are unpredictable (and therefore largely uncontrollable). Ideally, you would create two versions of your manuscript from which to format separate eBook and paperback files (see Sec. 1.3). However, if you already have a professionally formatted print book where the typographer dealt with features like widows and orphans, you want to strip out all this extra formatting. It is possible to clear formatting by highlighting text and pressing the Clear All Formatting button on the Font section of the Home ribbon, but this may clear out some formatting that you'd like to retain (like boldface and italics). So if you do clear all formatting, you'll need to put the more basic formatting back in afterward. There are also some types of formatting that Clear All Formatting *doesn't* clear: Don't take that word "all" too literally. A more extreme method of stripping out unwanted formatting is to cut and paste text into Notepad and then cut and paste it back into Word (but you will need to put back any formatting that you wish to retain, like boldface and italics).

- Similarly, print book formatters often add hyphenation to help improve the justification of paragraphs. You certainly don't want any manual hyphens that may have been added for print formatting. However, you *can't* simply remove every hyphen with the Replace tool because there probably are hyphens that you want to keep. For example, many compound words, like "one-half" or "father-in-law," are hyphenated; you don't want to remove *those* hyphens. Use the Find tool at the right side of the Home ribbon and comb through your document for unwanted hyphens. Also, turn off Word's auto-hyphenation: Go to Page Layout, click Hyphenation in the Page Setup group, and click None. Many Kindle devices now hyphenate automatically—there is *nothing* that you need to do in Word to make that happen (but you do need to remove manual hyphens from your Word file so that you don't get hyphens in unwanted positions in your eBook).

Kindle Hyphenates Automatically

If the book passes your examination, you take it out on a date. You begin reading the first chapter. The whole time the book is anticipating that first kiss, wondering if you will take it home with you. Meanwhile, you are analyzing the book's every move. Going steady with a book is a big commitment. You don't want to be disappointed.

How do you know if the relationship will work out? Curling up by the fireplace, snuggling in warm covers in bed with a book light, sneaking a quick page or two in the bathroom. You will share these intimate times with your book. You want to know that the book is Mr. or Mrs. Right for you.

When you look at the cover, you see the book's handsome or pretty face

Manual Hyphens Are a Problem

If the book passes your examination, you take it out on a date. You begin reading the first chapter. The whole time the book is anticipating that first kiss, won-dering if you will take it home with you. Meanwhile, you are analyzing the book's every move. Going steady with a book is a big commit-ment. You don't want to be disappointed.

How do you know if the relationship will work out? Curling up by the fire-place, snuggling in warm covers in bed with a book light, sneaking a quick page or two in the bath-room. You will share these intimate times with your book. You want to know that the book is Mr. or Mrs. Right for you.

When you look at the cover, you see the book's handsome or pretty

2.6 Special Characters

Unfortunately, there are many characters that you can type (or insert) on your computer that **won't** display on all Kindle devices or apps. These are called unsupported characters.

Browse through the list of supported characters in Appendix A:

- Note that supported characters are only supported if they are inserted properly. We'll discuss the proper and improper ways to do this in this section.
- Unsupported characters must be reformatted another way. We'll discuss alternatives later in this section.

Note: A special character may work on some devices and apps, but not others. A few of the older devices are especially problematic (and it's difficult to obtain a reliable preview for them unless you happen to own a variety of older devices). If you use a special character that isn't listed in Appendix A, you run the risk that it won't work on one of the older devices—even if it appears to work fine in the available previews (Chapter 7).

Let's first address supported characters. Some of these can be found on a standard keyboard, while others can't. Actually, both supported and unsupported characters *can* be typed from a keyboard using the Alt button (as we'll learn, there are better ways to insert supported characters that can't be found on a standard keyboard—I suggest *not* using the Alt button). When a supported character can be found on a standard keyboard, simply type it.

The following symbols can be typed with a standard keyboard:

- Uppercase letters: A-Z.
- Lowercase letters: a-z.
- Digits: 0-9.
- Symbols above digits: !@#$%^&*().
- Other symbols: -_=+`~<>,.;:/?'"[]{}\|.

Except as described in Sec. 2.7 for quotes, apostrophes, dashes, superscripts, and fractions, any other supported characters are **best** inserted as follows:

- Click Symbol from the Insert ribbon (but first read the notes about font style in the last two bullet points).
- Choose More Symbols.
- Select the Symbols tab; don't use the Special Characters tab.
- Select "(normal text)" from the dropdown menu in the "font" field at the top.
- Select "ASCII (decimal)" from the dropdown menu in the "from" field at the bottom right.

- Be sure to look at the character code at the bottom right. Some characters look very similar, yet aren't the same (and sometimes a character with similar appearance isn't supported). Only use character codes listed in Appendix A, using "(normal text)" with "ASCII (decimal)" selected—**not** "ASCII (hex)" or "Unicode (hex)."

- Note that some fonts may be troublesome. In Word, use the default font (Times New Roman or Calibri). Ideally, the end result will allow the reader to choose a font (see 5.6), but while working in Microsoft Word, it's necessary to specify *some* font (some work better than others). The best way to do this is to **not** adjust the font style at all: Just leave the default font (Times New Roman or Calibri) as it is. If you change the paragraph font from its default (not recommended), you want to do this by modifying the paragraph styles (Chapter 3), and not by highlighting parts of your document. Sec. 3.4 recommends font settings for working within Microsoft Word.

- Note that there are two places where you can make a mistake with the font. One place is where you see "(normal text)" in the font dropdown menu in the Insert > Symbol pop-up window: Don't adjust that to a different font style. The other place is the font style in the paragraph where the cursor is located when you use Insert > Symbol: Don't adjust that font to another style prior to inserting a supported symbol. If you somehow manage to insert a symbol with a nonstandard font, an otherwise supported symbol may not be supported on one or more devices or apps. (Some font styles that are very common among word processors and computers can be problematic with Kindle eBooks, which is why sticking with the default—Times New Roman or Calibri—is recommended.)

Only the symbols listed in Appendix A are supported across *all* Kindle readers and apps. Characters other than these are likely to be unsupported on one or more Kindle devices or apps.

> **Caution**: Beware that a few unsupported characters work on some Kindle devices, but don't work on other Kindle devices (especially, older devices). Just because you see the symbol work on one device doesn't guarantee that it will work across all devices and apps. There are a few symbols that appear to work in the Kindle previewer, but which are not actually supported by one or more devices or apps (note that the previewer *doesn't* offer a preview of *every* possible device or app). Check Appendix A to ensure that the character you wish to use is supported.

Don't enter supported characters with other methods (except as noted in Sec. 2.7):

- Don't use Alt codes because in some cases this may result in a slightly different symbol. Use Insert > Symbol as described previously and check that both the character code and symbol match that of Appendix A.

- Don't use HTML codes for symbols that can be inserted in Word using the Insert > Symbol method. HTML codes should only be used for the few symbols mentioned in Sec. 5.6, using the method described in Chapter 5. KDP recommends that you don't use HTML codes for supported characters from Appendix A that can be inserted in Word with the Insert > Symbol method. Also, note that HTML codes for other symbols besides the few mentioned in Sec. 5.6 may work only on selected devices, and aren't likely to work across all Kindle devices and apps (especially, older devices). It's best to stick with Appendix A using the Insert > Symbol method and only use HTML codes for the few symbols mentioned in Sec. 5.6—and to carefully preview your eBook on every device before publishing, just to be sure. (Regarding HTML codes, of course you shouldn't insert those into your Word file. Of the few Kindle-friendly HTML codes, which are mentioned in Sec. 5.6, you must wait until you have gone a step beyond Word before you may use them.)

- Don't change the font style so that you can use the keyboard to type the symbol. One problem with this method (even when the symbol looks like a supported character) is that the symbol may not be the *exact* same symbol as a supported character that looks very similar. Using Insert > Symbol is safer. Use the default font (Times New Roman or Calibri), with "(normal text)" and "ASCII (decimal)" selected in the dropdown menus.

- Don't use Microsoft Word's AutoCorrect feature to type symbols. For example, if you type a space, two hyphens, and a space (--), Microsoft Word automatically converts this to an en dash (–), unless you turn this AutoCorrect feature off (see Sec.'s 2.7 and 2.11). Instead, using Insert Symbol and selecting character code 150 is the more reliable way to create an en dash that is supported by all devices. (One exception, as we will discuss in Sec. 2.7, is that you may use the AutoFormat feature to create curly quotes and apostrophes.)

What happens when a Kindle eBook uses an **unsupported** character? The reader will either see boxes, boxed question marks, or a string of strange characters in place of the unsupported character. The same thing may happen when a character that's ordinarily supported is improperly inserted into the document. The following examples show a few different ways of how unsupported characters may appear on a Kindle device or app.

There are a couple of ways to reformat unsupported characters. If your book includes a symbol that doesn't appear in Appendix A, choose one of these options:

- Create the symbol as a picture and insert the picture in place of the symbol. First read Chapter 4 to learn how to properly insert pictures into your Kindle eBook. Note that pictures format best when placed on their own line—not as part of a paragraph. (First try this with a single picture, create a test file, upload the test file to KDP, preview the result on each device, and adjust the customer settings. Repeat this test as needed to get your picture 'right' before inserting pictures for several symbols. Chapter 4 discusses pictures and Chapter 7 shows you how to preview your eBook. Sec. 4.13 specifically discusses how to make a quick test file in order to test your pictures.)

- Settle for one of the supported characters from Appendix A, if a suitable substitute can be found. If your first choice was something you were hoping for, but didn't really need to use, this might be viable. But when the only symbol that will work satisfactorily can't be found in Appendix A, a properly inserted picture is the way to go.

Unsupported Characters

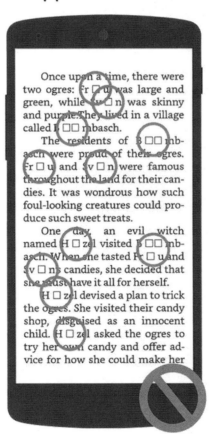

2.7 Punctuation Issues

In this section, we will discuss formatting options with some common punctuation marks—such as dashes, quotes, apostrophes, and ellipsis.

Microsoft Word's automatic curly quotes and curly apostrophes *do* result in supported characters (though you should always test everything carefully on all devices in the preview—as explained in Chapter 7), which is quite convenient. Therefore, it *isn't* necessary to use Insert > Symbol each time you wish to insert a curly quote or apostrophe, provided that you have this AutoFormat feature enabled (Sec. 2.11 describes how to enable AutoFormat for curly quotes, and also discusses which AutoFormat features you should disable for your eBook).

Note the distinction between **curly** quotes and **straight** quotes, and similarly with apostrophes:

- "curly double quotes"
- "straight double quotes"
- 'curly single quotes'
- 'straight single quotes'
- curly apostrophes: can't, won't, owner's
- straight apostrophes: can't, won't, owner's

It's generally viewed that the **curly** options appear more professional. However, you must watch Word's AutoFormat carefully: Occasionally, it gets the curly quote backwards, which would look unprofessional. There is a way to search for single and double quotes to help find instances that may be backwards, but it isn't foolproof—so it's best to get it right the first time.

How do you type curly quotation marks in the Find field of the Find tool? Don't use Shift + comma, since that results in straight quotation marks. Following is one method for inserting curly quotation marks into the Find field of Word's Find tool: First use Insert > Symbol with character code 147 (double open), 148 (double closed), 145 (single open), or 146 (single closed) to insert the character into your Word file (do this *before* you press the Find button to begin a search). Then cut and paste the curly quotation mark out of your Word file. Now press the Find button on the Home ribbon, and use Ctrl + v to paste the curly quotation mark into the Find field. (Alternatively, in the Find field, try holding down Alt while typing 0147, 0148, 0145, or 0146.)

Now we'll discuss how to use the Find tool to search for potentially problematic curly quotes. This is an important step, since Word's AutoFormat tool occasionally gets them backwards. Most quotations should have the form, "This sentence appears in quotes." Notice that the open curly quote (") has a spacebar before it, but not after it. Similarly, the closed curly quote (") has a spacebar after it, but not before it.

That's the way it *should* be, so to search for possible problems, in the Find field you want to enter it the way it *shouldn't* be: If there is a mistake, you want to find it and correct it. Therefore, use the Find tool on the Home ribbon to search for an open curly quote (search double and single separately—character codes 147 and 145) followed by a spacebar—since it should be preceded by a space, but not followed by one. Similarly, search for a spacebar followed by a closed curly quote (character codes 148 and 146). This will help you find possible matches where the curly quotes are backwards.

Another place to look is at the start or end of a paragraph. An open curly quote (" or ') may begin a paragraph, but should never end one. Similarly, a closed curly quote (" or ') may end a paragraph, but should never begin one. To catch possible mistakes, search for a paragraph mark followed by a closed curly quote (search double and single separately—character codes 148 and 146), since only an open curly quote should begin a paragraph. Type ^p" and ^p' (in two separate searches) in the Find field. Similarly, search for an open curly quote (character codes 147 and 145) followed by a paragraph mark, since only a closed curly quote should appear at the end of a paragraph. Type "^p and '^p (in two separate searches) in the Find field.

Remember: These are things you *don't* want to find. If these searches pull up any matches, they probably need to be corrected. This method won't catch *every* instance of a backwards curly quote, but it will help to catch many of them.

Any **apostrophes** that may be backwards are harder to catch. When you proofread your book, one thing to look for is possible curly quotes and apostrophes that appear backwards.

If your document already has straight apostrophes ('), straight single quotes ('), and straight double quotes ("), but you wish to change these to curly apostrophes and quotes, first enable Word's AutoFormat feature (not the same as AutoCorrect), as described in Sec. 2.11. If needed, next use the Replace tool. (As mentioned in Sec. 2.11, while you do want to use AutoFormat to make curly quotes and apostrophes, there are some AutoFormat and AutoCorrect features that you should disable.) Be careful though, it's not as simple as replacing straight quotes with curly quotes. You need to include a space along with the quotation mark. Use the Replace tool in the following order:

- Enter a space followed by a straight double quote (") in the Find What field, and a space followed by an open curly double quote (")—character code 147—in the Replace With field.
- Enter a straight double quote (") followed by a space in the Find What field, and a closed curly double quote (")—character code 148—followed by a space in the Replace With field.
- Enter a space followed by a straight single quote (') in the Find What field, and a space followed by an open curly single quote (')—character code 145—in the Replace With field.
- Enter a straight single quote (') followed by a space in the Find What field, and a closed curly single quote (')—character code 146—followed by a space in the Replace With field.

- Enter a straight apostrophe (') in the Find What field, and a curly apostrophe (')—character code 146—in the Replace With field. (Note that the curly apostrophe is identical to the closed curly single quote mark.)

Whether you use AutoCorrect, AutoFormat, or the Replace tool, beware that none of these options is foolproof. There is a good chance that a few will still come out backwards. A few of the punctuation marks may not change at all. Therefore, when you are finished, you should enter a straight apostrophe (') in the Find tool, then manually replace any straight apostrophes that Word finds. Do the same with the double straight quote (").

Note the distinction between a **hyphen** (-) and a **dash** (– or —). A hyphen joins two words together in some compound words, such as "one-fourth" and "mother-in-law." A dash is a separator—used to separate phrases, like this. There are two common dashes: the shorter en dash (–) and the longer em dash (—), both of which are longer than a hyphen (-). The en dash is surrounded by space – like this – whereas the em dash has no space around it—like this. Each dash is popular in different types of books, so it would be wise to see which is common in your genre or category. The em dash (—) used to have a subtle formatting issue with Kindle eBooks, but it appears to work better now, especially with Kindle's enhanced typesetting.

Hyphens (-), which are different from **dashes** (– or —), can simply be typed from a standard keyboard. The key for the hyphen can be found between the zero (0) and the equal sign (=).

The recommended method for creating dashes is to use Insert > Symbol and choose character codes 150 and 151, respectively, to create en (–) or em (—) **dashes**. This method is more reliable than using Word's AutoCorrect tool to format dashes as you type (e.g. you can type a space, two hyphens, and a space -- like this, and Word automatically converts this to an en dash if this AutoFormat feature is enabled—see Sec. 2.11). If you've already made en or em dashes with a method other than Insert > Symbol > 150 or 151, you can use the Replace tool on the Home ribbon to correct this. Cut and paste one of the dashes that you made otherwise into the Find What field, and make a dash with Insert > Symbol and cut and paste this symbol into the Replace With field.

It's important to check that your punctuation marks are not in an **unsupported font style**. A common way for this to happen is if you use Insert > Symbol and change the font from "normal text" to a specific font. Another way is if you adjust the font on the home ribbon (which you should never do for your eBook) and then proceed to insert a symbol. Another example of how this can happen is if you originally used WordPerfect and later imported your book into Word: In that case, your quotation marks may appear in an unsupported font.

If you have numerical superscripts besides the ^{2} and ^{3}, you might achieve more consistent formatting using superscripts instead of using character codes 178 and 179. Compare x^2, x^3, x^4 to

x^2, x^3, x^4. (Look closely.) The first set includes character codes for the ^{2} and ^{3}, while the second set was made using superscripts; in both cases, the ^{4} is a superscript (since there isn't a supported character code for that). There is a slight difference with the ^{2} and ^{3}, so if you're looking for consistency among superscripts, it's better to format the numbers as superscripts instead of using character codes 178 and 179. It's easier to see the difference like this: ^{22} and ^{33}.

There is a similar issue with fractions. If you use character codes 188-190 (¼, ½, and ¾) and also include other fractions like 2/3 or 5/8, you'll have to type the other fractions with the slash (/), in which case formatting will appear inconsistent. If you only need 1/4, 1/2, and 3/4, then you're better off using character codes 188-190. If you need other fractions too, using the slash for *all* of your fractions would result in consistency.

You can insert an ellipsis character (…) with Insert > Symbol > 133. The ellipsis is actually a single character, even though it may look like three separate periods. The ellipsis character (…) used to have a subtle formatting issue with Kindle eBooks, but it appears to work better now, especially with Kindle's enhanced typesetting. If you prefer to include spaces between the dots (. . .), type periods and use non-breaking spaces to join them together—though beware that non-breaking spaces aren't always as effective with all punctuation marks as they are with letters in Kindle eBooks (we'll discuss the non-breaking space later in this section, and again in Sec. 3.7).

Following are three ways to use the ellipsis:

- No space after the ellipsis… This option is compact.
- Space after the ellipsis … If you use an ordinary space, the ellipsis can wind up on a separate line. However, if you use a non-breaking space, it can increase justification issues.
- Space after the ellipsis with spaces between the dots . . . If you use ordinary spaces, the dots can get separated across different lines. Definitely, use non-breaking spaces between the dots in this case (but note that non-breaking spaces aren't always as effective with all punctuation marks as they are with letters in Kindle eBooks), though this option has the biggest impact on justification issues.[8]

Occasionally, it is helpful to create a non-breaking space between words. Unlike the ordinary space between words created by pressing the spacebar, a **non-breaking space** formed by Insert > Symbol > 160 keeps the words joined together. For example, one might use a non-breaking space in "3 cm" to prevent the possibility of the "3" and "cm" from appearing on different lines of a paragraph (with the "3" at the end of one line and the "cm" at the beginning of the next line).

---

[8] If you don't justify, but use ragged right, then the problem is that you may have a much shorter line in your paragraph. No matter what, there is a design issue. (Note that Kindle automatically justifies a book set in ragged right, unless you know how to prevent this, as discussed in Sec.'s 3.7 and 5.4.)

Never Join 3 Words Together with Non-breaking Spaces

Beware that the non-breaking space can introduce worse problems than you're trying to prevent. For example, suppose that you have a paragraph ending with the words "prevent it." You might be tempted to insert a non-breaking space between them in order to prevent a possible runt (one short word appearing on its own line at the end of a paragraph, sometimes also called an orphan). However, this strings 10 characters together, which could create large gaps in justified text. If you justify your body text (or if you leave the user the option to justify body text, as mentioned in Chapter 5—this isn't an option unless you go beyond Microsoft Word), avoid non-breaking spaces except between two very short elements (like "18 in."), and then only use it when the pros outweigh the possible cons. Stringing *three* or more elements together with non-breaking spaces becomes even more problematic: It's **not** recommended.

Note that non-breaking spaces *do* expand with justified text (that is, they are *not* fixed width). *Don't* string non-breaking spaces together in an attempt to create a long space.

You can also create non-breaking spaces with HTML characters (as described in Sec. 5.6). This option also lets you use the zero-width non-joiner. However, beware that many HTML characters don't work across all devices. Sec. 5.6 lists the few HTML characters which are safe to use. You should preview your book carefully on each device before publishing. (Don't insert HTML codes into your Word file. You must wait until you have gone a step beyond Word before you may use them. See Chapter 5.)

2.8 Font and Text Features

The following basic formatting should work without any hitches, provided that you are only highlighting a *portion* of a paragraph (like a phrase or sentence):

- **boldface**
- *italics*
- basic underline
- ~~strikethrough~~
- sub$_{scripts}$
- super^{scripts}
- CAPS

However, if you want to apply basic formatting to an *entire* paragraph (including a stand-alone line, like a *heading*), use Word's paragraph **styles** (see Chapter 3) to do it instead of highlighting the entire paragraph and applying formatting to what's highlighted (also *don't* adjust the font or paragraph settings and then proceed to type an entire paragraph).

If you just want to format *part* of a paragraph, *don't* use a style. In that case, highlight the selection and apply the formatting to the selection.

Changes in font **color** and size[9] are supported. However, you should **never** set any text color to black, white, sepia (a creamy color), or green because it would appear *invisible* under certain customer settings. For example, if you set the text color to black and the customer reads your eBook in night mode, the text won't be visible.

Your body text for normal paragraphs should have the font set to **automatic** (that way it will naturally appear black against a white background and white in night mode): Set the font color through Word's paragraph styles (Chapter 3). Most of your paragraph styles should have the font set to automatic. Color text should be used sparingly.

You can color selected text or headings, but beware of how it may look on black-and-white devices. For example, red stands out well on color devices, but has the opposite effect on the Kindle Paperwhite and other black-and-white devices, where red shows as gray. Similarly, colors that ordinarily contrast well may blend together or clash in grayscale. It's wise to test your color choices out on all devices, and against all possible backgrounds (white, black, sepia, and green). Chapter 7 will show you how to preview your eBook on different devices and apps, with different possible backgrounds.

---

[9] However, there are limitations on relative changes in font size. As we will see in Sec. 3.4, a font size of 12 points is recommended for body text (and this should be set through Word's paragraph styles—see Chapter 3). If you want the local font to appear a little smaller, try a font size of 10 points; if you want it to appear somewhat larger, try 16 points. You can find recommended font sizes in Sec. 3.4. Actually, the *best* method is to set the font size as a percentage rather than as a point value, which requires going a step beyond Word (Sec. 5.4).

If the entire paragraph (or stand-alone line, like a heading) needs a different font color or size, use one of Word's paragraph styles (see Chapter 3) to achieve this. However, if only a part of a paragraph requires a different font color or size, simply highlight the text and change its font color or size. Note that in Chapter 5 we'll learn a better way to set font size than by adjusting the font size in Word. Don't worry: You can change it in Word for now, and then update this later when you reach Chapter 5.

It's best **not** to apply a particular font style (like Garamond or Century) to *any* text. With eReaders, the user has the option to select the font style and size. If you try to force a particular font style (or if you try to embed a particular font), **it will likely result in formatting issues on one or more devices**. We'll discuss font style and size in Chapters 3 and 5. For now, the *best* thing is to just leave Word's *default* font style (Times New Roman or Calibri). Refrain from highlighting any text or paragraphs and applying *any* font style to it (if you do, the Clear All Formatting button can help you undo this mistake). Similarly, don't adjust the font style on the Home ribbon and then type with that style.

It's partly true that the font doesn't matter, but not entirely true. One way that it matters is when a character that would normally be a supported character in one of Word's default fonts becomes an unsupported character because some other font was used instead. It also matters when the file you upload embeds a font that a customer's device or app doesn't support. These are two reasons why you want to go with a default font style, and to refrain from setting any particular font.

I recommend that you **don't** use the font selection dropdown menu on the Font group of the Home tab for your eBook. (Similarly, don't open the font properties dialog box from the Font group of the Home tab to access the font selection dropdown menu.) If you feel that you must adjust the font style in Word (which goes against my recommendation: it's safer to leave the font style set to Word's default—Times New Roman or Calibri), do this through the paragraph styles (Chapter 3).

The fancier formatting options in the Font group on the Home ribbon should **not** be used for a Kindle eBook. If you already used them, these should be replaced with a simpler formatting option (or if you really need to preserve the original, consider doing so through an image instead, as described in Chapter 4):

- fancy underlining (like double underline)
- outline
- shadow
- reflection
- glow

KINDLE

Text that appears in **textboxes**, **WordArt**, and any **fancy text** should either be moved into a paragraph in the body of your text (with simple formatting), or it needs to be turned into an image as described in Chapter 4.

It's possible to format **drop caps**, provided that you keep them simple. Drop caps are discussed in Sec.'s 3.7 and 5.6.

Options for formatting **equations** are discussed in Sec.'s 3.11 and 4.9.

I recommend that you avoid using Word's highlighting tool (on the Font group of the Home ribbon) even if it seems to work for you when previewing your eBook on various devices. Kindle users can highlight text in their eBooks, so if the eBook already includes highlighting, that might be a problem.

Recall that special symbols were discussed in Sec. 2.6.

Don't use the font dropdown menu.

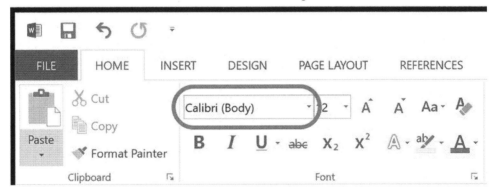

2.9 Special Formatting

Kindle supports some kinds of formatting, but not others, and what it does support is sometimes limited. When you're unsure, you can test it out by uploading a file to KDP and previewing it carefully on each device (Sec. 7.2 shows you how to upload a quick test file). Beware that there isn't a proper preview for older devices. If you still have doubts, try to find a simpler alternative.

There are some important subtleties involved in formatting **bullet points** (•) or **numbered lists** (1, 2, 3…):

- Word's default bulleted and numbered lists will work if you upload a DOC or DOCX file to KDP, provided that you don't try to adjust the settings and provided that you keep the list simple with single-level indents. However, the indent is somewhat large this way—

which makes Kindle justification issues more pronounced (although with Amazon's new enhanced typesetting, it's better than it used to be, except on older devices)—and the bullet symbol can appear relatively small. (Trying to shorten the large automatic indent for lists tends to cause more harm than good. If you want to use Word's list tools, leave them at their default settings.)

- Only use simple, plain, single-level bullet points and numbered lists in Word. Fancy bullets, multi-level lists, hanging indents, negative indents, and other fancy features will likely produce inconsistent or unexpected formatting on one or more devices (such as older Kindles).

- Some Kindle formatters use a block indent (setting a left indent in the paragraph settings: do this through the paragraph styles, as described in Chapter 3, not by highlighting paragraphs and adjusting the indent directly to what's highlighted) and simply create the bullet symbol by hand (in Word, this can be done using Insert > Symbol > 149). This avoids the problems associated with a hanging indent (or setting a negative indent), lets you set a narrower indent if you're uploading a Word file (compared to the relatively large indent that automatically results from Word's default list tools), and gives you more control in Word (for example, you can create a separate paragraph style for the last point on the list). If you choose this method, you want to do it via paragraph styles (find the recommendations for list paragraphs in Sec. 3.4).

- You can gain a little more control with bullet points and numbered lists by going a step beyond Word, as we'll learn in Chapter 5. Even then, you have to be careful not to get too fancy, and you have to consider the limitations of older Kindle devices. If you plan to go a step beyond Word, it's convenient to create a special paragraph style for lists (as mentioned in the previous paragraph), and then modify the paragraph style later after going a step beyond Word. (If you use Word's default bullet options, it creates convoluted instructions, which requires more work to clean up properly after going a step beyond Word.)

- **Keep it simple** and your lists are more likely to work as expected across all devices and apps. The more complicated you make your lists, the more likely it will backfire and result in a disaster on a specific device or app (such as older Kindle devices).

We will explore bullet points and numbered lists further in Sec.'s 3.4, 3.7, and 5.4.

The best way to control paragraph indentations is through Word's built-in styles (Chapter 3). It's best to avoid multi-level indentations (even if you go a step beyond Word). It's a challenge to get multiple levels of indentations to show consistently and as expected across all Kindle devices and apps (especially older devices), and the larger indent makes Kindle justification issues even more pronounced. **Note**: Even if multi-level indents appear to work okay in the Kindle pre-viewer, they might result in a serious issue on at least one device for which there isn't a proper preview. Simplicity of design tends to provide more reliable and predictable formatting.

There is support for basic **tables** with just a couple of columns. You really want to test your tables out on actual devices (especially, older ones) before publishing. We will explore tables further in Sec. 3.12. Another option for a complex table is to format the table as an image instead, although formatting a table as an image also introduces issues (Sec. 4.8). For some simple tables, the content of the table may format best as paragraph text (i.e. not in a table at all). You could use block indenting to help set off the text in this case.

You can have **images** that are wrapped in-line with text (instead of square, in front of text, or behind text). Pictures are discussed extensively in Chapter 4.

Horizontal lines (or borders) are best managed through the techniques described in Chapter 5 (and again may not work across all devices and apps).

Footnotes and endnotes work, so you should keep these features. However, you shouldn't get too fancy with them, like inserting unsupported characters using the Custom Mark option. Note that all of the standard Number Format options use supported characters; even the option with the *, †, ‡, and § symbols should be supported (but read the note at the end of Appendix A).

In a print book, footnotes show at the bottom of the page, while endnotes show at the end of the chapter or the end of the book. Kindle eBooks don't have pages, so the bottom of a page doesn't make sense. Instead, the footnote or endnote number turns into an active hyperlink. The reader clicks on the number to access the note, and clicks on the number again to return to the prior reading position. The note itself appears at the very end of the eBook, so as not to interfere with the reading experience. If you use endnotes, choose the option to place them at the end of the document (not the end of the section).

Recall that if you wish to remove formatting, you should use the Clear All Formatting button in the Font group on the Home ribbon: Highlight the text and press the Clear All Formatting button. If you wish to reformat text that is just *part* of a paragraph, first highlight the text and press the Clear All Formatting button, and then reformat the text as desired. (If you want to reformat an entire paragraph or multiple paragraphs, don't apply formatting directly to high-lighted paragraphs: Instead, apply paragraph styles as described in Chapter 3.) If you skip the Clear All Formatting step, this may create convoluted instructions in the hidden formatting in the background (which can impact how your Kindle eBook displays on one or more devices). Also recall that the Clear All Formatting button doesn't remove all types of formatting: In some cases, you need to copy and paste the text into Notepad, and then copy and paste it back into Word to completely remove the formatting (but if there was formatting like italics that you wished to retain, you will then need to add that back in).

Word's Default Bullet Tool

the cash register.

• Spellcheck, aisle three. If you can't get the spelling and grammar right in a hundred words or so... Look, it's not an option. You have to get it right.

• Vocabulary. It needs to match your target audience. Words they don't understand can scare them away (but if such words are common in the prose, you also don't want to create false expectations).

• Research. Do your homework. Check out blurbs of successful books similar to yours.

• Feedback. Ask for opinions on your blurb. Before you publish, this can help you generate buzz.

Here is a nonfiction blurb checklist:

• Be concise OR break up a long blurb into paragraphs with bullet points. Still, don't say anything that's unnecessary.

• Inform. Make it clear what information

kindle

Insert > Symbol > 149 + Block Indent

• Spellcheck, aisle three. If you can't get the spelling and grammar right in a hundred words or so... Look, it's not an option. You have to get it right.

• Vocabulary. It needs to match your target audience. Words they don't understand can scare them away (but if such words are common in the prose, you also don't want to create false expectations).

• Research. Do your homework. Check out blurbs of successful books similar to yours.

• Feedback. Ask for opinions on your blurb. Before you publish, this can help you generate buzz.

Here is a nonfiction blurb checklist:

• Be concise OR break up a long blurb into paragraphs with bullet points. Still, don't say anything that's unnecessary.

• Inform. Make it clear what information will be found in your book. If they aren't sure

kindle

Bear in mind that some formatting features may work on certain devices, but not all devices. In particular, older Kindle devices don't tend support as many formatting features (or don't support those features fully). This can be a problem when you're formatting your Kindle eBook. When in doubt, keep it simple (or, in some cases, you may be able to use an image to produce the effect instead). You can preview your book across several devices with the Kindle Previewer, and you can test your eBook out on any devices that you can get your hands on (see Chapter 7). Note that a few customers still have original Kindle devices with limited functionality (for which there isn't a proper preview unless you happen to have the same device).

Tip: Keep it simple. You can have a well-designed, well-formatted eBook that works across all devices without making it unnecessarily complicated. Those unnecessary complications can cause major problems on one or more devices; it often isn't worth the risk.

2.10 Irrelevant Features

Some features shouldn't impact your Kindle eBook at all, and will simply be ignored in the conversion process. (Always carefully preview your book on each possible device—including actual devices as well as Kindle apps—as described in Chapter 7, just in case.)

Page headers and footers, for example, which were added to your Word file via the Header or Footer buttons on the Insert ribbon do not show in the converted eBook. You can remove them if you wish, but they shouldn't show up. In the published Kindle eBook, whatever you enter for the title of your book (not in the book file, but during the publishing process) will automatically show at the top of the screen.

Don't confuse **headers** with *headings* or **footers** with *footnotes*. Headings and footnotes *do* matter; headers and footers do *not*. A chapter heading, like Chapter 1, appears in the text at the beginning of the chapter, whereas a page header is text (or a design, or both) that appears at the top of every page (or every other page). A page footer is like a page header, except that it appears at the bottom of the page, whereas a footnote is a numbered note that supplements the text.

Page numbers that were added to your Word file via the Page Number button on the Insert ribbon similarly do not show up in the converted eBook. However, if you managed to insert page numbers into your file without using the page header or page footer (for example, if you just typed the numbers on each page, instead of using the Insert > Page Number feature), then you will need to remove the page numbers from your Kindle eBook.

Unfortunately, Word's automatic widow and orphan control has no impact on the Kindle eBook. In the paragraph dialog box (accessed by right-clicking a paragraph and selecting Paragraph), on the Line and Page breaks tab, the top three boxes have no impact on Kindle formatting. The fourth box, Page Break Before, *does* work, and that's best incorporated into a paragraph style (Chapter 3).

Many traditionally published books don't begin a chapter at the top of a page of a printed book—or at the top of a screen for an eBook. Instead, it's common to drop the chapter heading down the equivalent of a few lines from the top of the page (or screen). The best way to do this in Word is to use the Spacing Before feature in the paragraph setting (using the Enter key to do this can lead to inconsistencies, even in print)—by modifying the Heading 1 style as described in Chapter 3 and associating the chapter heading with the Heading 1 style.[10]

The page size that you set in Word is irrelevant for your Kindle eBook; this information will be lost. The page margins that you set should also be lost in the conversion to Kindle. However, it only takes a moment to change all the margins to zero, being sure to select Whole Document in the Apply To field. (The Kindle device has its own *internal* margins, which you *can't* control, and the customer can actually adjust the margins on the screen to a degree.)

Note that **paragraph** margins are different from **page** margins. While Kindle will ignore *page* margins, if you set *paragraph* margins instead, those can cause mayhem, especially on devices with small screens. Paragraph margins should be set to zero (except for block indent, and then only using paragraph styles as described in Chapters 3 and 5—and even in that case, you should only use left margin, not right).

Word's Next Page, Odd Page, and Continuous section break features—which are needed to have different styles of page numbers or headers in the print edition—have no effect on the Kindle edition. An ordinary page break will do (in fact, an ordinary page break works *better* when it is applied through the paragraph styles, as shown in Chapter 3).

Word's spelling and grammar check feature, which adds little green and red marks to the document, can actually show up in the converted eBook (even though it's not supposed to, and usually doesn't). I have seen this (although rarely) in a Kindle eBook (even after turning this feature off in Microsoft Word), so you want to ensure that this doesn't happen to you. Sec. 2.11 will help you disable this feature before you save your finished file (leave the spelling and grammar checkers enabled until you finish working with your Word file, and then disable them before you save the final product), and Sec. 5.7 will show how to check if your finished eBook has this problem.

---

[10] Note that one or more Kindle devices or apps (especially older devices) may ignore the Spacing Before feature in Word when it is applied immediately after a page break. Using the Enter key to drop down a few lines from the beginning of a chapter may also be ignored—in fact, using blank lines is a less reliable and predictable way of adding vertical space. The most reliable way to add space to a heading (or paragraph) following a page break is to create an ePub file (Sec. 5.12). The ePub file format can divide your book up in such a way that Kindle devices and apps will respect the Spacing Before option at the beginning of a chapter. If instead you upload a DOC, DOCX, or HTML file (even a zipped file), it may not work across all devices and apps (especially older devices for which there isn't a proper preview).

Word's automatic hyphenation shouldn't impact your Kindle eBook in any way, but it's very easy to turn off (Page Layout > Hyphenation). However, if you manually hyphenated any words to improve the appearance of your print edition, those *manual* hyphens will carry over to your Kindle eBook, and they will look strange not appearing at the end of a line. (I'm not talking about hyphenated words, like merry-go-round. I'm talking about when traditional publishers add a hyphen to a long word so that the beginning of the word appears at the end of one line and the end of the word appears at the beginning of the next line.) Be sure to remove any manual hyphens (without removing hyphens from hyphenated words).

2.11 Spelling, Grammar, and AutoCorrect

You want to use Word's spelling and grammar checker just before you publish, as it will help you catch some obvious mistakes. However, you don't want those red and green marks to propagate through to your Kindle eBook. It *shouldn't*, but I have seen it show up (though rarely) in a Kindle eBook (even after turning this feature off), so you want to make sure it doesn't happen to your eBook.

Go to File > Options > Proofing, click the AutoCorrect Options button, and adjust the settings under the AutoCorrect, AutoFormat, and AutoFormat As You Type tabs:

- On the AutoFormat tab, check the box to replace "straight quotes" with "smart quotes," but uncheck the other boxes under the Replace section.
- On the AutoFormat tab, check the box to preserve styles.
- On the AutoFormat tab, the settings under the Apply section correspond to the paragraph styles discussed in Chapter 3. I recommend checking the boxes for "built-in heading styles" and for "other paragraph styles."
- On the AutoFormat tab, whether to check or uncheck the boxes for "automatic bulleted lists" and "list styles" depends on whether you will use Word's built-in list buttons (then check these two boxes) or whether you will define your own simple paragraph style for lists (then uncheck these boxes; you can find a recommendation for this type of paragraph style in Sec. 3.4). Recall that we discussed this choice in Sec. 2.9. We will discuss other settings relating to various styles in Sec. 3.3.

- On the AutoFormat As You Type tab, check the box to replace "straight quotes" with "smart quotes," but uncheck the other boxes under the Replace As You Type section. (Note that the AutoFormat tab is different from the AutoFormat As You Type tab. You must adjust the settings separately for each of these tabs.)
- On the AutoFormat As You Type tab, uncheck *every* box under the Apply As You Type section.
- On the AutoFormat As You Type tab, uncheck *every* box under the Automatically As You Type section.

When your book is ready to publish, first turn both the spelling and grammar checkers on. Go through your whole document, checking every issue that Word flags. Not every flag is necessarily a mistake, and some mistakes aren't flagged, but the spelling and grammar checkers can help you catch a few obvious mistakes before you publish.

After using the speller and grammar checkers and **before you upload your eBook to KDP** (or before you convert to another file format—see Chapter 5), turn the spelling and grammar checkers **off**. The bottom two checkboxes in File > Options > Proofing allow you to hide errors in the document. Even then, I recommend reading a note toward the end of Sec. 5.7 to ensure that spelling and grammar marks won't show up in your Kindle eBook.

Note that Word's spelling and grammar checkers won't catch *every* mistake. It isn't foolproof. For example, if you type, "Your welcome," instead of, "You're welcome," Word won't notice the difference.

Also, occasionally Word flags an issue that isn't actually a mistake. Not everything necessarily needs to be fixed.

Software called Grammarly can also help you catch some mistakes. Grammarly is a step up from Word's spelling and grammar checker, but again it isn't foolproof.

Spelling and grammar are your responsibility. A dictionary, thesaurus, and a guide to grammar and style serve as handy resources—every writer should use them. Even then, we always need proofreaders to help catch our mistakes, and it may be worthwhile to find a quality yet affordable editor.

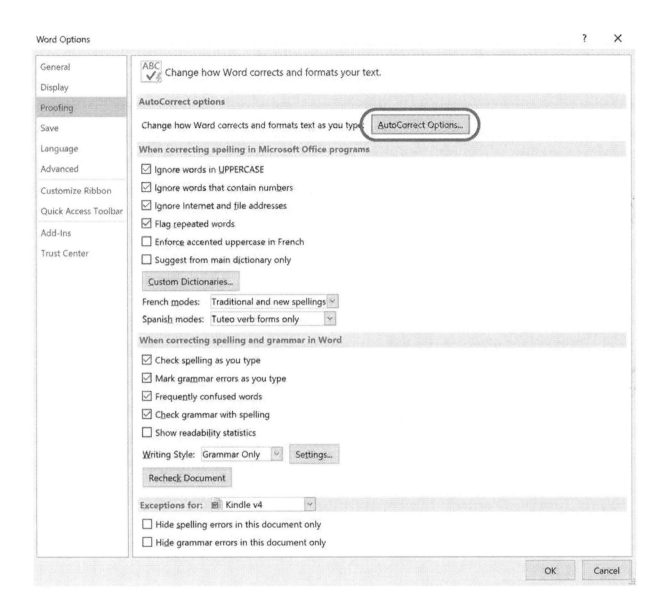

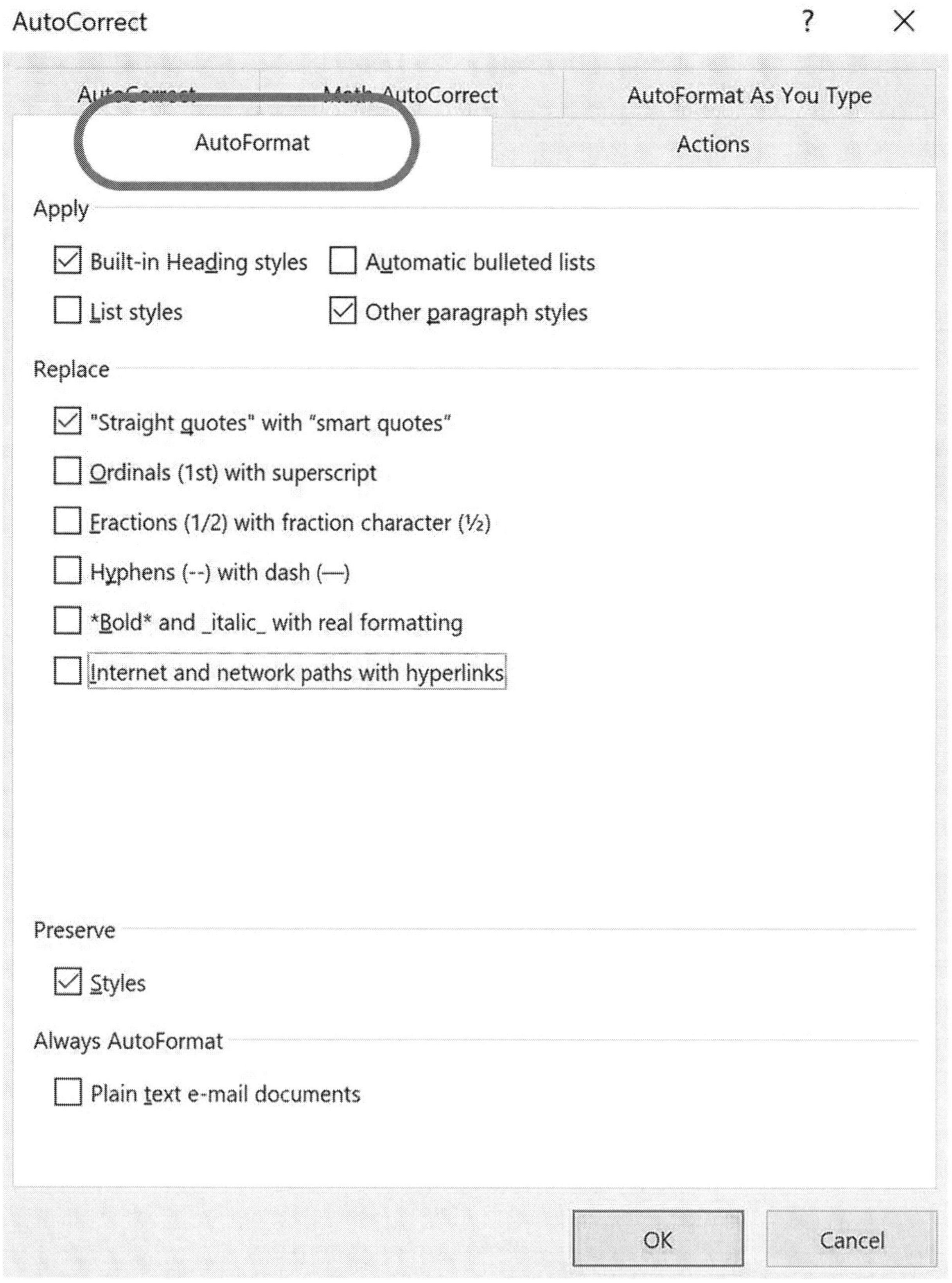

AutoCorrect   ?   ✕

AutoCorrect	Math AutoCorrect	AutoFormat As You Type
AutoFormat		Actions

Apply

☑ Built-in Heading styles   ☐ Automatic bulleted lists

☐ List styles   ☑ Other paragraph styles

Replace

☑ "Straight quotes" with "smart quotes"

☐ Ordinals (1st) with superscript

☐ Fractions (1/2) with fraction character (½)

☐ Hyphens (--) with dash (—)

☐ *Bold* and _italic_ with real formatting

☐ Internet and network paths with hyperlinks

Preserve

☑ Styles

Always AutoFormat

☐ Plain text e-mail documents

OK   Cancel

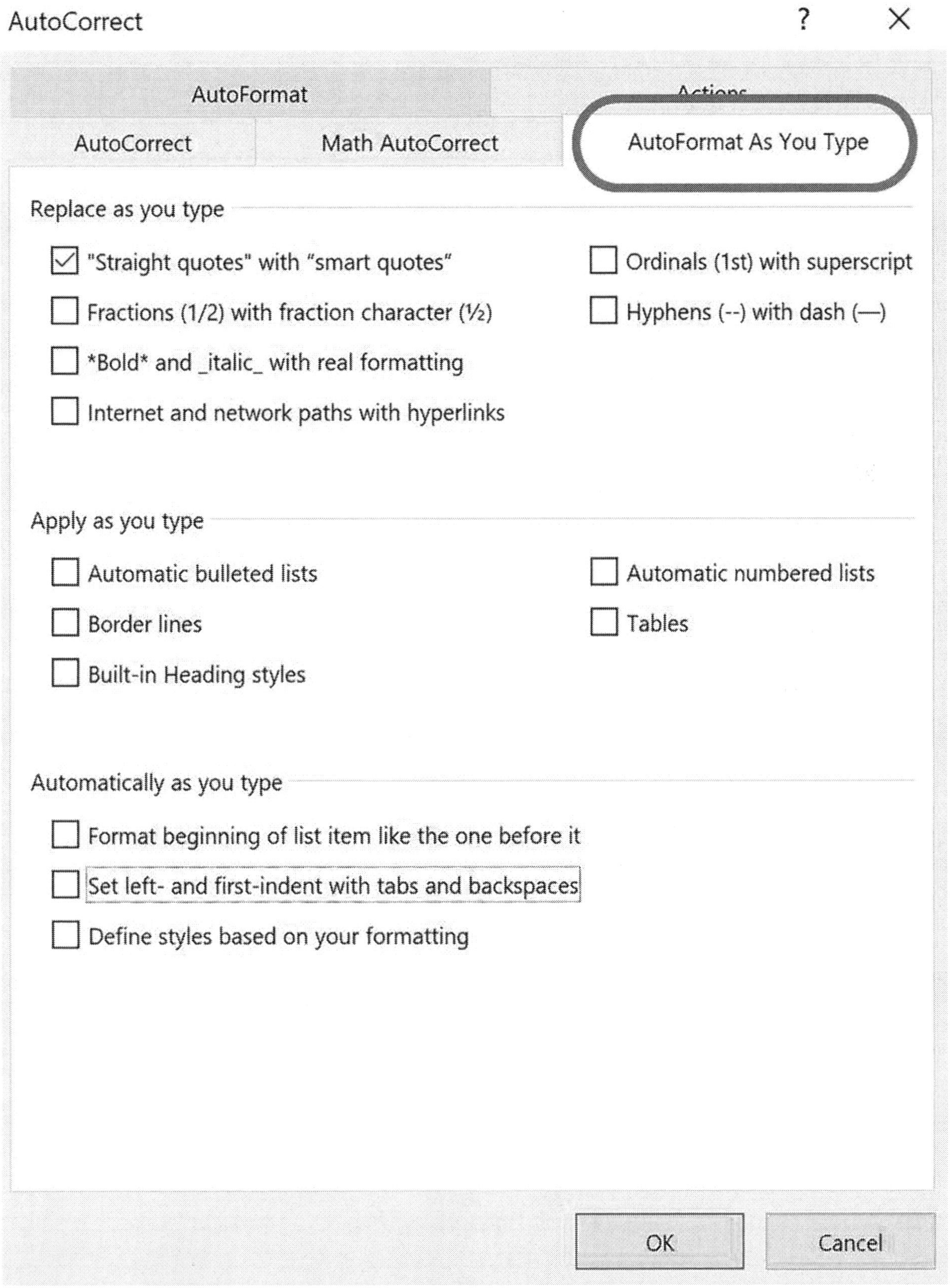

AutoCorrect   ?   ✕

| AutoFormat | Actions |

| AutoCorrect | Math AutoCorrect | **AutoFormat As You Type** |

Replace as you type

- ☑ "Straight quotes" with "smart quotes"
- ☐ Fractions (1/2) with fraction character (½)
- ☐ *Bold* and _italic_ with real formatting
- ☐ Internet and network paths with hyperlinks

- ☐ Ordinals (1st) with superscript
- ☐ Hyphens (--) with dash (—)

Apply as you type

- ☐ Automatic bulleted lists
- ☐ Border lines
- ☐ Built-in Heading styles

- ☐ Automatic numbered lists
- ☐ Tables

Automatically as you type

- ☐ Format beginning of list item like the one before it
- ☐ Set left- and first-indent with tabs and backspaces
- ☐ Define styles based on your formatting

OK   Cancel

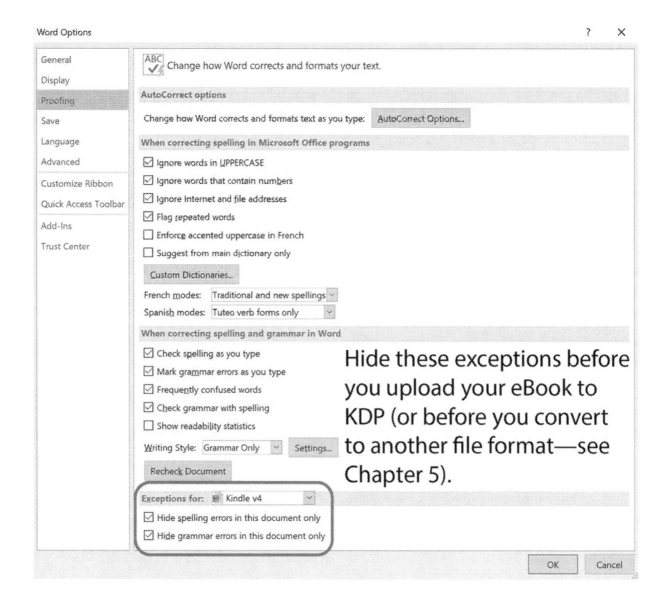

Hide these exceptions before you upload your eBook to KDP (or before you convert to another file format—see Chapter 5).

2.12 Pre-formatting Checklist

Following is a summary of changes you should have already made to the Word file for your eBook before proceeding to Chapter 3:

- Remove tabs (Sec. 2.1). Wait until Chapter 3 to replace them with indents (so that you can do this properly using paragraph styles).

- Remove two or more consecutive spaces made with the spacebar (Sec. 2.2).

- Remove any spaces made with the spacebar that (accidentally) appear at the end of a paragraph (Sec. 2.2).

- Remove blank lines and two or more consecutive Enters (Sec. 2.3). A better way to add vertical space will be introduced in Chapter 3.

- Remove the index, if you have one (Sec. 2.5).

- Remove the table of contents, except for the heading (Sec. 2.5). We'll replace it with a new table of contents in Chapter 3.

- Change page references (e.g. where you have text like "as shown on page 75"). These should refer to chapters or sections instead of specific page numbers (Sec. 2.5).

- Clear tracking, kerning, scaling, and other typographical features that may have been utilized to control issues like widows, orphans, and runts for a print book (Sec. 2.5).

- Turn off automatic hyphenation and then remove unnecessary manual hyphens that may have been inserted to adjust paragraph formatting for your print edition (Sec. 2.5). (However, don't use Replace All because you may have a few hyphens that you wish to keep. For example, if you typed the words "ice-cream" or "mother-in-law" in your book, you wouldn't want to inadvertently remove those hyphens.)

- Replace unsupported special characters with supported characters, or format each as a picture placed on its own line (Sec. 2.6).

- Replace straight quotes and apostrophes with curly ones (Sec. 2.7).

- Remove textboxes, WordArt, and unsupported fancy text formatting and replace them with ordinary text in body text paragraphs or replace them with pictures (Sec. 2.8).

- If you had highlighted entire paragraphs and applied formatting directly to those paragraphs,[11] highlight those paragraphs and press the Clear All Formatting button (Sec. 2.8). Use paragraph styles (Chapter 3) to apply formatting to *entire* paragraphs. (If instead you just need to format *part* of a paragraph—like putting a phrase in boldface or a sentence in italics—you should highlight and format for this. Don't apply a style to *part* of a paragraph.)

---

[11] Similarly, if you adjusted font or paragraph options on the Home ribbon and then typed one or more complete paragraphs, you want to redo this correctly.

- Review Sec. 2.9 regarding bullets, numbered lists, horizontal lines, borders, tables, and images. We will consider these topics again in Chapters 3-5.
- Try to keep your formatting simple (Sec. 2.9).
- Turn off the spelling and grammar checkers *after* you finish checking Word's suggestions for possible spelling and grammar mistakes (Sec. 2.11).

—Chapter 3—

Formatting

3.1 Styles: The Secret to Kindle Formatting

I F YOU UPLOAD a Word document to KDP, your Word document gets converted to a MOBI file. (No matter what kind of file you upload, it gets converted to MOBI format.) The MOBI file is basically a set of instructions for Kindle devices and apps to follow to display your book on the screen of the reading device.

These instructions don't interpret your Word document the same way as your computer does when displaying your original Word file on your monitor. Rather, Kindle devices and apps see your text along with formatting instructions. There are two kinds of formatting instructions in your MOBI file:

- One section of the MOBI file contains the style definitions, which describe the different kinds of paragraphs included in your Kindle eBook and how each type of paragraph should be formatted.
- In the body of the file, where the text appears, each paragraph calls one of the paragraph styles from the style definitions. The individual paragraphs can also include formatting instructions of their own.

If you highlight an entire paragraph in Word and apply formatting directly to what is highlighted, Word introduces formatting instructions for that specific paragraph which can contradict the style definition that it calls. You get similar contradictions when you adjust the font or paragraph options and proceed to type an entire paragraph (or more) with those settings. Such contradictions can lead to unexpected formatting on one or more devices.

Amazon's Look Inside feature is especially strict at interpreting the instructions in your MOBI file. Contradictions between the style definitions and specific paragraph instructions often result in formatting problems in the Look Inside. The Look Inside can serve as a great marketing tool for books, but instead waves a red flag when there are formatting issues.

There is no way to properly preview the Look Inside, yet the Look Inside interprets the MOBI file more strictly than Kindle devices and apps. As a result, sometimes the Kindle eBook looks great in the preview, but problems show up in the Look Inside (or on a specific device or app for which there isn't a proper preview). This is a common source of frustration for authors.

However, the problem is fairly avoidable. The first key to successful formatting across all devices, apps, and even the Look Inside is to use the **paragraph styles** religiously. **<u>Don't</u>** highlight an entire paragraph (or multiple paragraphs) and apply formatting directly to what is highlighted, as that will result in contradictions between the style definitions and the paragraph's formatting instructions. Similarly, **<u>don't</u>** adjust the font or paragraph options on the Home ribbon and proceed to type one or more paragraphs.[12] Instead, create a different paragraph style for each type of paragraph that you need, and simply associate the appropriate paragraph style with each paragraph (as described in this chapter). I realize that I've repeated this point several times in this book, but it's arguably the most important point relating to Kindle formatting: It can be stressed too little, but not too much.

> **Tip**: Avoid highlighting an *entire* paragraph or multiple paragraphs and applying any formatting directly to what you have highlighted. Also, avoid adjusting font or paragraph options on the Home ribbon and proceeding to type one or more paragraphs. Instead, use Word's paragraph styles to format paragraphs.

If you have already formatted one or more paragraphs by highlighting the paragraph and applying formatting directly to what is highlighted (or by adjusting font or paragraph options and typing one or more paragraphs), use the Clear All Formatting button in the Font group on the Home ribbon to undo it, and apply a paragraph style to that paragraph instead.

Parts of paragraphs are different. If you want just a part of a paragraph to have special formatting, you should highlight that phrase or sentence and apply formatting directly to it. This creates a span statement (mentioned in Chapter 5) in the formatting instructions, and that won't cause contradictions in paragraph instructions. If you only need to format *part* of a paragraph a certain way, *don't* use a style for that.

> **Tip**: Don't use styles to format only a *part* of a paragraph. First associate the entire paragraph with one paragraph style, and then highlight the *part* of the paragraph that you want to have different formatting (like italics or boldface) and apply formatting directly to that.

If you feel confused at this point, don't worry. The remainder of this chapter will show you exactly what to do. The goal of this first section was to stress the importance of using the paragraph styles and to help explain why it is necessary to use the paragraph styles.

It is possible to see hidden formatting by going a quick step beyond Word, as we will see in Chapter 5. The connection between the use of Word's styles and its impact on the hidden formatting is shown in Sec. 5.7.

---

[12] You can do either of these for *part* of a paragraph, like setting one sentence in italics (but *don't* adjust the font style). It's when you need to format an *entire* paragraph (or multiple paragraphs) a particular way that you must use the paragraph styles.

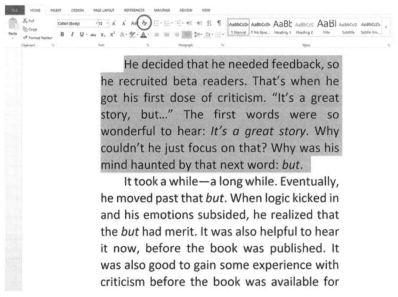

3.2 Proper Kindle Formatting

There are two main kinds of formatting:

- *Paragraph* formatting specifies the formatting of the paragraph. Paragraph formatting should be controlled through paragraph styles. Note that a paragraph can be as short as a single line, such as a heading or a picture placed on its own line. **Use Word's paragraph styles for all *paragraph* formatting.**

- *Character* formatting specifies the formatting of one or more characters (or words, phrases, or sentences), but *not* an entire paragraph. You should **not** use Word's styles to apply formatting to *part* of a paragraph. **Don't use Word's *character* styles.**[13]

Every *paragraph* in Word has a paragraph style associated with it. You will need a different paragraph style for every different type of paragraph in your Word document.

There are many different kinds of paragraphs:

- Most of the paragraphs in a book are usually body text. Word's Normal style is usually applied to the main body text.

---

[13] The one exception is a built-in character style called Hyperlink. When we create hyperlinks in Sec. 3.10, Word will automatically associate the Hyperlink character style with those hyperlinks. (If the hyperlink text serves as a complete paragraph of its own—like a website URL on its own line by itself, rather than being part of a paragraph of text—first associate the desired paragraph style with it, and then make the hyperlink as described in Sec. 3.10.)

- The first paragraph of each chapter is sometimes non-indented. If the main body text is indented, while the first paragraph is non-indented, a different style is needed for the first paragraph of each chapter.

- Special paragraphs, like quotations, may have a block indent where the whole left side is indented, not just the first line of the paragraph. Each kind of special paragraph needs its own formatting. (In print, the right side may also be indented, but in an eBook, it is best *not* to indent from the right side.)

- Chapter headings are paragraphs, too. The beginning of each chapter usually has a heading, like Chapter 3, placed on its own line. Even very short paragraphs like chapter headings need their own paragraph styles. Chapter headings should use the Heading 1 style (because Kindle automatically uses Heading 1 styles to build in-device navigation into the eBook).

- Some books have subheadings. Use Heading 2, Heading 3, etc. for different levels of subheadings.

- If your file has any pictures, each image should be placed on its own line with the Text Wrap set to In Line With Text. These are paragraphs, too. You need a centered style for image paragraphs. The same centered style can also be used to center text.

- The book title and subtitle usually appear in a larger font size. Use the title and subtitle styles for these 'paragraphs.'

- Any other type of paragraph with formatting different from these also needs its own paragraph style.

We will explore how to modify Word's styles and how to create a new paragraph style in Sec. 3.3, and we will consider several different common types of styles in Sec. 3.4.

You will need to associate the appropriate paragraph style for every paragraph in your book. Remember, don't highlight an entire paragraph to format it, don't right-click on a paragraph to adjust formatting, and don't adjust the paragraph options on the Home ribbon. Only adjust the font options for *part* of a paragraph (not for a complete paragraph or more). Instead, simply associate a paragraph style with the paragraph to set its default formatting. We'll discuss how to do this in Sec. 3.6, after we discuss how to modify Word's paragraph styles in Sec.'s 3.3-3.5.

However, if you only need to reformat *part* of a paragraph (anything less than 100%, from one character to several sentences), don't use a style for these. Although Word does have character styles in addition to paragraph styles, it's best **not** to use the character styles. Just highlight the part of the paragraph that you wish to reformat, and apply formatting directly to what is highlighted. This is common, for example, if you just need to render *part* (like a phrase or sentence) of a paragraph with bold or italics.

Following are several examples of the kinds of formatting that should be done using one of Word's paragraph styles (*not* by highlighting the paragraph, *not* by right-clicking the paragraph, and *not* by adjusting the font or paragraph options on the Home ribbon):

- Indent paragraphs applying a paragraph style (not using the tab key, not by highlighting a paragraph, not by right-clicking the paragraph, and not by using the paragraph options on the Home ribbon). Body paragraphs are indented by first modifying and then applying the Normal style.

- Non-indenting paragraphs must also be done using a paragraph style, e.g. if you want the first paragraph of a chapter to be non-indented (but—as we will learn—in Word the indent size must be set to 0.01", since "none" and zero won't work).

- Center a picture by placing the picture in its own (one-line) paragraph with the Text Wrap set to In Line With Text and applying a centered style to it. (First create the centered style as shown in Sec.'s 3.3-3.4.)

- Control paragraph alignment (left aligned, justified, centered, or right aligned) using suitable paragraph styles. Left alignment is a little tricky (see Sec. 3.4 and Sec. 5.4).

- You can even use a paragraph (or heading) style to achieve page breaks, such as Heading 1 to begin a new chapter on a new page. For an example of how to do this, see the recommended settings for the Heading 1 style in Sec. 3.4.

- Anywhere you would like to add space between paragraphs, such as between chapter headings and the first paragraph, use a paragraph style to add Spacing After (don't highlight a paragraph or use the paragraph dialog box to add Spacing After). It's more predictable and reliable to add Spacing After to the previous paragraph, rather than adding Spacing Before to the following paragraph. Note that adding Spacing Before to the first paragraph of a chapter following a page break may have *no* effect on certain[14] Kindle devices or apps (especially older devices—although Sec. 5.12 mentions a way to ensure that it works across all devices and apps).

- Any font properties that apply to an *entire* paragraph should be adjusted through paragraph styles, such as font size and color. Don't change the font style; just use the default font, Times New Roman or Calibri (and if you go a step beyond Word, as shown in Chapter 5, you can later remove these fonts, too). Sec. 3.4 recommends font sizes if you plan to upload a DOC or DOCX file, whereas if you will follow the prescription in Chapter 5, the font size that you set in Word won't matter. Chapter 5 shows you a better

---

[14] For years, attempts to add Spacing Before the first paragraph (or heading) following a page break didn't work on *any* Kindle devices or apps when uploading a Word or HTML file. Even if this changes, the best way to ensure that it works across all devices and apps is mentioned in Sec. 5.12 (the method mentioned there is reliable because it has *always* worked).

technique to control font size. If you plan to skip Chapter 5, you should still read the note in Sec. 5.6 about possible font issues, such as Times New Roman Italics (especially if you're a Mac user).

If you already did any of the above formatting by highlighting an *entire* paragraph (or more than one paragraph)—or by adjusting font or paragraph options on the Home ribbon and typing one or more paragraphs—instead of applying an appropriate paragraph style, see the next section to learn how to undo it and then reapply the formatting with a paragraph style.

Apply a Paragraph Style for an *entire* paragraph, but not for *part* of a paragraph.

An Entire Paragraph

have believed that he had an ounce of creativity. Yet on a train ride to work, in his imagination there emerged a story.

Characters came to life in his mind's eye, acting out scenes. A plot developed. Emotions stirred. The unthinkable happened.

The idea was too good to contain within his own mind. It was begging to be shared. But how could he, a common businessman, share this story? The answer, he reasoned, was to self-publish a book.

For months, in his spare time he sat at his computer, typing away. The words came to him easily, as if a muse were looking over his shoulder, reciting to him. It felt good to write the

Part of a Paragraph

out a way to answer it. Then he spent hours looking through pictures before he found the right look for his author photo.

The big moment had finally come. Press one button and the book would be published. Wait. Savor the moment for a while. Okay, do it. Now. Press that button.

A flood of emotions passed through him. It was incredible. Such relief. Finally, it was all over.

After a good night's sleep, he found his book on Amazon. *I'm a real author,* he thought.

That's when anxiety leaped out of the tall grass and tackled him. Will people like the story? Will customers post good reviews? Will anybody even buy the book?

3.3 Modify Word's Styles

Note: If you're reluctant to use Word's styles, see the note at the end of this section regarding Amazon's free app called Kindle Create. While I recommend learning how to use Word's styles, Kindle Create does offer a simplified alternative for those who need it.

In Microsoft Word 2007, 2010, 2013, and 2016 for Windows, the styles appear on the top right half of the Home ribbon.

You can find Word's styles on the Home ribbon.

Many of the style features that you need are located in the **styles menu**. To open the styles menu, click the funny little arrow-like icon at the bottom right corner of the Styles group on the Home ribbon (the following picture shows where this is).

Click the bottom-right corner to open the Styles menu.

This opens a styles menu in a small new window (which usually appears on the right-hand side of the screen). The **styles menu** should resemble the picture below.

The Styles Menu

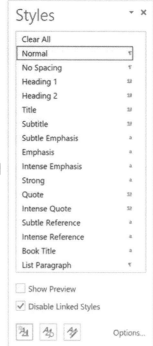

You will need to modify Word's existing paragraph styles, and you will probably need to create new paragraph styles. Don't worry: We will discuss how to do this in the remainder of this chapter. In addition, you will want to **avoid** *character* styles (for example, **don't** use the Strong or Emphasis styles).

How can you tell if a style is a character style or paragraph style? Right-click the paragraph style, click Modify, and look at the second line from the top, called Style Type. There are five different style types: paragraph, character, linked, table, and list.

Most of your book should use *paragraph* styles, like the Normal style (and variations of the Normal style that we will learn how to make). A few parts of your book will also use default *linked* styles, such as the Heading 1, Subtitle, Title, and Footnote Text styles. These linked styles also serve as paragraph styles (chapter headings and titles are really 'short paragraphs').

To **modify** an existing style, right-click on the style in the styles menu. When you click Modify, the **Format** button provides additional options, such as font and paragraph settings (but ignore the one called Tabs). Recommended settings for common styles are provided in Sec. 3.4.

To **create** a new paragraph style, open the **styles menu** (shown in the previous figure). Look for the three buttons at the bottom of the styles menu (these buttons have A's on them—look closely). Click the left button to create a new paragraph style.

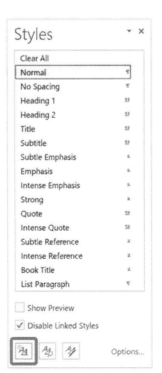

Create a new style

Now we will explore the style **options**. You can find the style options when you proceed to modify a style (by right-clicking on the style). It would be a good idea to open Microsoft Word, open the styles menu, right-click on the Normal style, select Modify, and explore the options that you see there. Click the **Format** button at the bottom left, choose **Paragraph**, and explore the settings that you see there. Next, right-click another style (like Heading 1), click Modify, and compare the options: Almost all of the same options will be available, but the settings will be a little different. Explore the Format > Paragraph settings again. This will offer you a little familiarity with the style options as we discuss them. It would also be wise to look for each option in Word as you read about it.

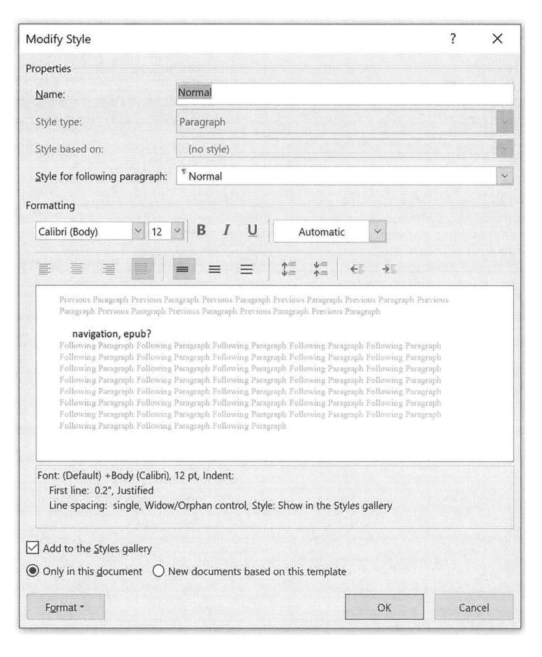

When you proceed to modify a style (by right-clicking on the style), note the options that appear at the *bottom* of the pop-up window: All of the styles *except* for the Normal style have a checkbox called Automatically Update. The Automatically Update checkbox has a somewhat misleading name. Most styles automatically update whether or not this box is checked. That is, if you modify the paragraph settings for a paragraph, it will automatically change every paragraph associated with that paragraph style (you can press Undo once to apply the change only to one paragraph, and Undo twice to completely undo it)—whether or not the Automatically Update checkbox is checked. However, this really isn't a problem because you *should* modify the paragraph *style* itself rather than apply changes to just one paragraph (except, as explained in Sec. 3.2, when you only want to modify *part* of a paragraph—in which case you shouldn't be using Word's style at all to apply the change).

What the Automatically Update feature does is automatically update *other* styles *associated* with a paragraph style that is modified. When you create a new paragraph style, styles can become linked through the Style Based On setting (one option is **No Style**). The Automatically Update checkbox is referring to linked styles. On the bottom of the styles menu (which usually appears at the far right of the screen, once opened—in order to open the styles menu, click the funny arrow-like icon on the bottom right corner of the Styles group on the Home ribbon), you can check a box to **Disable Linked Styles**.

The Options link at the bottom right corner of the styles menu lets you choose which styles to display on the menu. Uncheck font formatting since you should only use paragraph styles, and check the box for paragraph level formatting. The top dropdown menu can be adjusted to display just the styles in the document or just those in use, for example. This will filter out unnecessary styles from the styles menu.

Note that you may still see styles that you *don't* need at the top right half of the Home ribbon. You can remove styles that you don't need by right-clicking on the paragraph style on the Home ribbon and clicking the option to Remove from Quick Style Gallery. Sec.'s 3.4-3.5 will help you determine which styles you do need.

I remove all of the styles from the Quick Style Gallery and styles menu except for: Normal, Heading 1, Heading 2, Title, and Subtitle. (I also modify each of these, and add several others, as you will see in Sec. 3.4.)

I also prefer to use the styles menu that pops up in its own window—*not* the Quick Style Gallery that appears on the top right of the Home ribbon. The Show Preview option on the styles menu makes it easy to visually see which style is which.

There are two things to do with Word's paragraph styles:

- First, modify existing paragraph styles and add new paragraph styles until you have a paragraph style for every kind of paragraph (or heading) in your book. We'll discuss what styles you need and what parameters to set in Sec. 3.4.
- Next, assign the appropriate paragraph style to each paragraph (or heading) in your book.

There are a few different ways to assign styles to paragraphs. Here are a few examples:

- Place your cursor within the paragraph, and simply click on the appropriate paragraph style from the styles menu (click on the funny arrow-like icon on the bottom right corner of the Styles group on the Home ribbon to open the styles menu on the right side of the screen).

- Place your cursor within the paragraph, and simply click on the appropriate paragraph style from the list that appears on the top right half of the Home ribbon.

- Highlight multiple paragraphs and click on the appropriate style. Be careful not to accidentally select beyond the end of the last paragraph: If you select past the final period, sometimes the selection affects the paragraph after the selection. You don't actually have to select a *complete* paragraph in order to associate a paragraph style with it, so a safe practice is only to select *part* of the first and *part* of the final paragraphs when you highlight.

- In a paragraph with Normal style, simply press the Enter key to begin typing another paragraph of the Normal style.

- When you proceed to modify a paragraph style (right-click on it), the fourth option from the top is called "style for following paragraph." This allows you to set which style you want to serve as the default when you press Enter at the end of a paragraph of that paragraph style.

Before you proceed to modify a paragraph style, place your cursor in a paragraph of that same kind of paragraph style. Otherwise, you might accidentally apply the paragraph style that you modify to whatever paragraph happens to have your cursor in it.

Most paragraph styles automatically update every paragraph of that paragraph style when you modify the paragraph style. (For those styles, this also happens if you highlight a paragraph of that style and then reformat the highlighted paragraph, but you shouldn't do any formatting by highlighting paragraphs. Modify the paragraph style instead.)

Another way to update paragraphs associated with a particular style is to open the styles menu (click the funny-looking arrow-like icon on the bottom right corner of the Styles group on the Home ribbon). Hover your cursor over the desired paragraph style on the styles menu (not the paragraph style on the Home ribbon—the styles menu appears on the right, separate from the paragraph styles that appear on the Home ribbon), and click the dropdown arrow that appears at its right edge. Click Select All. Now when you modify the paragraph style, it will change every paragraph associated with that paragraph style.

If you will be going a step beyond Word, as described in Chapter 5, you could alternatively modify a paragraph style later. No matter how you choose to modify a paragraph style, it's easy provided that you didn't highlight any paragraphs and apply formatting directly to what was highlighted (and provided that you didn't adjust font or paragraph options on the Home ribbon and proceed to type one or more paragraphs).

Beware that some paragraph styles may be associated with one another. This can happen, for example, when you create a new paragraph style and base it on a preexisting paragraph style. **When two or more paragraph styles are associated with one another, modifying one paragraph style causes other paragraph styles to change, too.** (This also happens if you highlight a paragraph and format what is highlighted, but you shouldn't format by highlighting. Modify the paragraph style instead.) **Uncheck the Automatically Update box for associated paragraph styles** to disable this feature (recommended). You can find Automatically Update option by right-clicking a paragraph style from the Home ribbon or the styles menu and then selecting Modify. (When you apply a change to one paragraph style and it automatically updates an associated paragraph style, pressing Undo once undoes the update to the associated paragraph style, and it takes a second Undo to completely undo the action. Things are simpler when automatic updates for associated paragraph styles are disabled.)

> **Tip**: For each paragraph style, right-click the paragraph style, select Modify, and *uncheck* the box beside **Automatically Update**. With this box unchecked, modifying one paragraph style won't automatically update associated paragraph styles.

> **Tip**: Check the box next to **Disable Linked Styles** on the styles menu. (Read carefully: For Automatically Update, I recommend *unchecking* the box, whereas for Disabled Linked Styles, I recommend *checking* the box.)

You can also avoid associated paragraph styles by setting Style Based On to "no style."

> **Tip**: When you modify an existing paragraph style or when you create a new paragraph style, set Style Based On to "**no style**" in order to avoid associated paragraph styles.

If you wish to create a new paragraph style that is similar to an existing paragraph style, there is a simple way to do this without setting Style Based On to an existing paragraph style. First, create the new paragraph style. Set the Style Type to Paragraph, adjust Style Based On to "no style," choose a paragraph style for the following paragraph, *uncheck* the box for Automatically Update, and click OK. Find a paragraph that has a paragraph style similar to the paragraph style that you wish to create, and place your cursor within that paragraph. In the styles menu, hover over the newly created paragraph style, click the dropdown arrow that appears at the right of the style name, and select the option to update this newly created paragraph style to match the selection. Now modify the newly created paragraph style as desired.

All paragraph **indentations** should be controlled through paragraph styles. This includes non-centered (meaning justified or left-aligned) paragraphs that you *don't* want indented—as we will see, it turns out that non-indenting is tricky, too.

There are two common methods that writers often use to create indents, which are *problematic* for Kindle formatting:

- If you used the tab key at all, Sec. 2.1 shows you how to remove all of those tabs.
- If you used the paragraph dialog box to set the First Line Indent to selected paragraphs, that was also a mistake (there is a chance, for example, that it will impact the Look Inside). The instructions that follow show you how to correct this.

To undo manual First Line Indents and redo it properly via a paragraph style, follow these steps:

1. Place your cursor in a paragraph with a First Line Indent that needs to be undone (so that it can be redone).
2. Open the styles menu (click on the funny-looking arrow-like icon on the bottom right corner of the styles menu on the Home ribbon).
3. Hover your cursor over the paragraph style on the styles menu, and click the dropdown arrow that appears at the right edge of the paragraph style. Select all.
4. Right-click on the paragraph style to modify it, click **Format**, and choose **Paragraph**.
5. Change First Line Indent to none (don't worry: this is temporary).
6. Exit, then Select All for that paragraph style again, modify the paragraph style, click Format, choose Paragraph, and set First Line Indent to the desired value (see Sec. 3.4 for recommendations).

If you have a paragraph that you wish to be non-indented, and if the paragraph is non-centered, you must also apply the above steps, setting the value of First Line Indent to 0.01" (look closely: **don't** use 0.1", which is noticeably larger). The problem is that some Kindle devices or apps (or even the Look Inside) may automatically indent a paragraph where First Line Indent is set to "none" in Word (setting First Line Indent to exactly 0 suffers the same problem). Changing First Line Indent from "none" to 0.01" works around this problem. However, you should leave First Line Indent set to "none" for **centered** paragraphs and headings: It's only an issue for paragraphs or headings that are set to full (justified) or left alignment.

See Appendix B for a **quick hands-on tutorial** that will show you how to test out Word's styles before applying them to your book. Why not take a few minutes to master this tool before you get started?

Note that Amazon offers an alternative for authors who don't want to learn how to use Word's styles: Amazon's free app, **Kindle Create**, provides a simplified method of assigning paragraph (and heading) styles for your Kindle eBook. **My recommendation is to learn how to properly style your book using Microsoft Word.** However, if you're reluctant to use Word's paragraph styles, then using Kindle Create is better than not styling your paragraphs at all. (If the following URL is no longer working—which may happen as Amazon occasionally updates their help pages—try typing "Kindle Create" without the quotes in the search field in the KDP help pages.)

https://kdp.amazon.com/en_US/help/topic/GHU4YEWXQGNLU94T

If you use Kindle Create, I still recommend that you continue reading Chapter 3 of my guide, as it may help you learn more about Kindle design and the general process of styling paragraphs. The way you go about modifying and applying paragraph styles is different in Kindle Create (it's simpler) than it is in Word, but the design concepts are very similar. Beware that Kindle Create comes with a few **limitations**: Kindle Create doesn't permit all of the Kindle eBook features that are possible from Word, and it won't let you go a step beyond to make subtle improvements (so **you won't be able to follow any suggestions from Chapter 5**, for example).

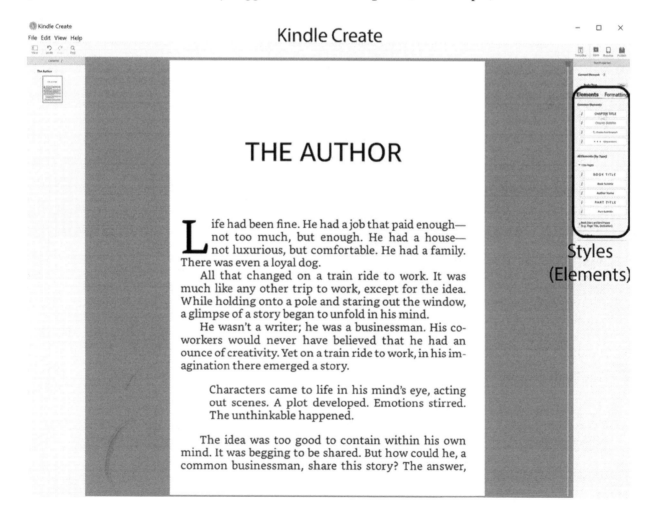

3.4 Recommended Settings

Before we begin, ensure that Word doesn't track changes, as that can lead to less predictable formatting in your eBook. Click File > Options > Advanced, look in the Editing Options, and make sure that the box next to "Keep track of formatting" is *unchecked*.

In each of these styles, be sure that Style Type is set to Paragraph (although Word's default styles with a Style Type called Linked are okay, too—this includes Heading 1, for example). Don't use any styles with other kinds of Style Types (besides Paragraph and Linked), such as Emphasis or Strong (which have Style Type set to Character).[13]

Where you find the dropdown menu for Style Based On, choose "(no style)." (Right-click a style on the styles menu and select Modify to get this option.)

Be sure to modify the paragraph style itself as described in Sec. 3.3, and **<u>not</u>** to apply these changes to highlighted text.

You may not need *every* paragraph style mentioned in this section. Find the paragraph styles that are relevant for your book. Depending on your design needs, you may also need a few styles that aren't listed in this section (a few examples are described at the end of this section).

Some books, such as novels, only need a few styles: Normal body text, non-indented body text, Heading 1, title, and subtitle may be sufficient. Other books, such as nonfiction books, require more styles: They may also need paragraph styles for bullet points, subheadings, footnotes, and other special paragraph formatting needs.

Note: When you right-click on a style and select Modify, you only see a few basic settings. Remember to click the **Format** button in the bottom left corner (after you click Modify) to find additional settings. Many of the most important settings (such as Special > First Line Indent, left indent, Spacing After, and line spacing) are found under Format > **Paragraph**.

You may wish to read the notes in Sec. 3.5 and the discussion on Kindle design in Sec. 3.7 before you implement the recommended settings in Sec. 3.4 for your Kindle eBook. It may also be helpful to work through the styles tutorial in Appendix B, and to study the sample eBook in Appendix C.

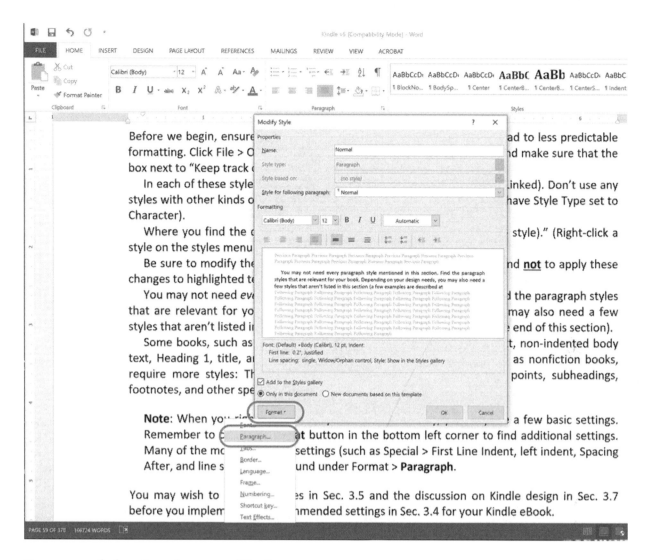

Recommended settings for **normal body text**:

- What it's for: Most of the paragraphs of your book should have normal body text.
- Font size: 12 pt.[15]
- Font style: Use the default font style (Calibri or Times New Roman).[16]

---

[15] We'll learn a better way to treat font size in Chapter 5.

[16] Times New Roman had long been the default font for Microsoft Word, and hence it is very Kindle friendly. The new default font is Calibri, and it is also Kindle friendly. A few Word-to-Kindle formatters recommend Georgia. **Don't** use Arial, even though it might seem like a common enough font to use—you can run into big problems. If you intend to submit a Word file to KDP, I recommend leaving everything in the default font (Times New Roman or Calibri). If you decide to use Georgia, you want to set this through the paragraph styles. The **best** option is to leave a default option for now, and then remove the font completely following the steps outlined in Sec. 5.6. The font that you set in Word is not what the user will get on the Kindle device or app anyway. Using a nonstandard font leads to formatting problems, while using a default Word font will let the Kindle user choose their own preferred font (provided that you only set the font through Word's styles, and not by highlighting text and applying the font

- Font color: Be sure this is set to Automatic. Do not set it to black, as that will cause your book to be unreadable when a customer chooses night mode.
- Alignment: Justified (i.e. full).[17]
- Indent: Format > Paragraph > Special > First Line > 0.2".[18] (Both Left and Right should be set to 0.)
- Line spacing: Single. Leave the At field empty.[19]
- Space before: 0 pt.
- Space after: 0 pt.
- Style for the following paragraph: Choose the same style (Normal, or whatever you choose to call the paragraph style for normal body text).
- Suggested name: Either modify the Normal style, leaving the name unchanged, or create a new paragraph style called BodyNormal and use it in place of the Normal style (in this case, change the Style Based On field to "no style"). I recommend modifying the Normal style and using Normal for main body text (unless you plan to force left-aligned body text, as outlined in Sec. 5.4—though I don't recommend that).

Recommended settings for **non-indented body text**:
- What it's for: The first paragraph of a chapter is often non-indented. There may also be other paragraphs that should have non-indented normal body text.
- Font size: 12 pt.
- Font style: Use the default font style (Calibri or Times New Roman).
- Font color: Automatic.
- Alignment: Justified (i.e. full).
- Indent: Format > Paragraph > Special > First Line > 0.01". Look closely to make sure it is 0.01", and not 0.1". Anything smaller than 0.01" can lead to big problems. (Both Left and Right should be set to 0.)
- Line spacing: Single. Leave the At field empty.

---

directly to highlighted text—and also not by adjusting the font on the Home ribbon and then typing text in that font).

[17] The choice between left alignment and justified (full) is discussed in Sec. 3.7. Note that left alignment set in Word may not carry over to the actual device or app. The most reliable way to create left alignment is described in Sec. 5.4.

[18] Almost all traditionally published books have indented paragraphs with no space between. This includes novels and most nonfiction. However, if you have one of the specialty books where block paragraphs are common, you would instead set the indent to 0.01" and put 12 pt in the Space After field (and then you wouldn't need a separate style for non-indented body text). Choose one or the other: Either have indented paragraphs with no space between paragraphs (recommended), or have non-indented paragraphs (meaning First Line Indent = 0.01") with 12 pt Space After.

[19] Be sure to select Single from the dropdown menu. Do not use Exactly or At Least for your Kindle eBook.

- Space before: 0 pt. (Although there is usually space between the chapter heading and the first paragraph of a chapter, it's better to achieve this by adding Spacing After to the previous heading or subheading than it is to use Spacing Before: Some older devices may respect Spacing After, but ignore Spacing Before.)
- Space after: 0 pt.
- Style for the following paragraph: Choose the paragraph style for normal body text.
- Suggested name: NoIndent.[20]

Recommended settings for body text where you want to **add space after the paragraph**:
- What it's for: Use this style when you want to add space following a paragraph of body text. For example, you might apply this style to a body text paragraph preceding an image, quote, block indent, or a section heading. This helps to create separation between the body text and whatever else follows it. Another place to apply this style is the last paragraph of a chapter: This helps to create space between the chapter ending and the chapter heading that follows (since the Look Inside strips out page breaks). See Sec. 3.7 for further discussion of this style.
- Font size: 12 pt.
- Font style: Use the default font style (Calibri or Times New Roman).
- Font color: Automatic.
- Alignment: Justified (i.e. full).
- Indent: Format > Paragraph > Special > First Line > 0.2".
- Line spacing: Single. Leave the At field empty.
- Space before: 0 pt.
- Space after: 12 pt.
- Style for the following paragraph: Choose a paragraph style that's likely to follow such a paragraph.
- Suggested name: BodySpaceAfter.

Recommended settings for **non-indented body text with space after the paragraph**:
- What it's for: Body text paragraphs where you don't want an indent, but where you do want to add space after the paragraph: For example, use this style if you want non-indented block paragraphs for your copyright page. (This style is not for centered paragraphs.) A book that uses block paragraphs would apply this style (whereas for most books, most of the paragraphs apply a Normal style with indented paragraphs).
- Font size: 12 pt.

---

[20] It's best to omit spaces from the names of any styles that you create. It's also wise to name the paragraph styles so that it will be easy for you to remember which style is which.

- Font style: Use the default font style (Calibri or Times New Roman).
- Font color: Automatic.
- Alignment: Justified (i.e. full).
- Indent: Format > Paragraph > Special > First Line > 0.01". Look closely to make sure it is 0.01", and not 0.1". Anything smaller than 0.01" can lead to big problems. (Both Left and Right should be set to 0.)
- Line spacing: Single. Leave the At field empty.
- Space before: 0 pt.
- Space after: 12 pt.
- Style for the following paragraph: Use the same paragraph style.
- Suggested name: NoIndentSpaceAfter.

Recommended settings for **block indents**:

- What it's for: Block indents set a paragraph apart by indenting the entire paragraph rather than just the first line. (Note the distinction between block indents and block paragraphs. The block indent style adds a left margin to indent the entire paragraph, whereas block paragraphs are non-indented: A book that uses block paragraphs would apply the style with the suggested name of NoIndentSpaceAfter.)
- Font size: 12 pt.
- Font style: Use the default font style (Calibri or Times New Roman).
- Font color: Automatic.
- Alignment: Justified (i.e. full).
- Indent: Format > Paragraph > Indentation > Left > 0.2" and Special > First Line > 0.01". This creates a block indent, i.e. it indents the entire paragraph instead of just the first line.[21]
- Line spacing: Single. Leave the At field empty.
- Space before: 0 pt.
- Space after: 12 pt. This will help create separation for the indented paragraph. The paragraph prior to the block indent should also add space after (if not, it may be hard to tell where the previous paragraph ends and the block indent begins—especially, when the last line of the previous paragraph happens to be about the full width of the screen).
- Style for the following paragraph: Choose the paragraph style for non-indented body text. (This is a design choice. The reason behind this suggestion is given in Sec. 3.7.)
- Suggested name: IndentBlock.

---

[21] It's recommended that you indent only from the left side. Indenting from the right side can cause formatting issues, e.g. on a cell phone there is limited space to begin with so indenting from both sides would amplify the usual problems with how text displays on devices with small screens.

Recommended settings for Heading 1:

- What it's for: Use Heading 1 for chapter headings. Heading 1 styles are automatically used for device navigation (see Sec. 3.8, where the distinction is made between navigation and the table of contents), so only use Heading 1 for headings that you want to appear in device navigation. For example, if you have an Acknowledgments section, but don't want this to show in device navigation, don't use a Heading style for the Acknowledgments heading.

- Font size: 20 pt.

- Font style. Use the default font style (Calibri or Times New Roman).

- Font color: Automatic.

- Font weight: bold.

- Alignment: Centered.

- Indent: Format > Paragraph > Special > First Line > "none."[22]

- Line spacing: Single. Leave the At field empty.

- Space before: 24 pt.[23]

- Space after: 12 pt.[24]

- Page break: Format > Paragraph > choose the Line and Page Breaks tab at the top of the pop-up window > Page Break Before. This is the best way to incorporate a page break with each new chapter. Apply the Heading 1 style to the text at the beginning of each chapter.[25]

- Style for the following paragraph: This depends. Choose the paragraph style for non-indented body text if body text will begin immediately after your chapter heading and you want to follow the convention of not indenting the first paragraph of a chapter. This way, after you press enter when typing a chapter heading, the next paragraph will automatically use the non-indented body text style. If, for example, you will have a sub-

---

[22] Choosing "none" only works for centered alignment. If you set the alignment to left or justified (full), you must set the first line indent to 0.01" (instead of "none") in order to avoid possible automatic indents on certain devices or apps. (I don't recommend justified full for headings, and I only recommend left alignment if you will be following Chapter 5.)

[23] Beware that certain Kindle devices or apps may not respect Spacing Before following a page break (even if you make a page break manually, and even if you use a section break instead)—unless you create an ePub (the problem occurs when you upload either a Word document or an HTML file) as mentioned in Sec. 5.12.

[24] We'll learn a way to improve upon this in Chapter 5.

[25] If you use an image at the beginning of each chapter *before* your chapter heading text, you will have to do things a little differently. Create a new paragraph style for the image at the beginning of each chapter (call it ImageHead, for example), incorporating the page break with the new paragraph style. Remove the page break from the Heading 1 style and apply the Heading 1 style to the chapter heading text that follows the image. (If you want to use an image that includes the chapter heading text—and don't want to include chapter heading text after the image—this creates another problem: Kindle devices and apps automatically use your Heading 1 text for device navigation, but you won't have *any* Heading 1 text for it to find. I **don't** recommend embedding your chapter heading text in a picture.)

heading following your chapter heading, you should set the paragraph style for the following paragraph to Heading 2 instead.

- Suggested name: Heading 1.[26]

Recommended settings for **Heading 2**:

- What it's for: Apply the Heading 2 style to any subheadings that you would like to include with device navigation. (Note that a heading or subheading, standing alone on a line all by itself, is its own paragraph.) Don't apply Heading 1 or Heading 2 styles to anything that you don't want to show up as a heading in device navigation.
- Font size: 16 pt.
- Font style: Use the default font style (Calibri or Times New Roman).
- Font color: Automatic.
- Font weight: bold. (This is optional, of course.)
- Alignment: Left.[27] (However, this may automatically become justified in a Kindle eBook or app, unless you follow the prescription in Chapter 5. See Sec. 5.4.)
- Indent: Format > Paragraph > Special > First Line > 0.01". (However, if you change the alignment to centered instead of left, use "none" instead, whereas "none" will backfire for non-centered paragraphs.)
- Line spacing: Single. Leave the At field empty.
- Space before: 0 pt.
- Space after: 12 pt.
- If you want your subheading style to incorporate a page break, achieve this through Format > Paragraph, choose the Line and Page Breaks tab at the top of the pop-up window, and check the box for Page Break Before. I'm not advocating this, just stating that it's an option. Since this book has lengthy subsections, I opted to include a page break with my subheadings.
- Style for the following paragraph: Choose the paragraph style for non-indented body text if you want the paragraph following Heading 2 to typically have non-indented body text.
- Suggested name: Heading 2.

---

[26] This is the default name. Kindle expects you to use standard Heading 1 and Heading 2 styles for chapter headings and subheadings that you would like to include with device navigation, so the best thing is to use the default names. (Ultimately, these will turn into h1 and h2, as we will see in Chapter 5—even if you skip Chapter 5 and upload a Word document, they will still function as h1 and h2.)

[27] Center would work, too; this is a design choice (though if you will be uploading a Word document instead of following Chapter 5, center alignment has the advantage: left alignment may automatically justify when uploading a Word file). Don't use justified (i.e. full) alignment for headings or subheadings, as that will lead to very large gaps between the words on small screens (or when a customer chooses a large font size). I only recommend left alignment if you will be following Chapter 5.

Recommended settings for **centered paragraphs**:

- What it's for: This style is for centered text or for section breaks (like * * *) where you don't wish to add space after the paragraph. (See the next style—called CenterSpaceAfter—for a centered style that adds space after the paragraph.)
- Font size: 12 pt.
- Font style: Use the default font style (Calibri or Times New Roman).
- Font color: Automatic.
- Alignment: Centered.
- Indent: Format > Paragraph > Special > First Line > "none."
- Line spacing: Single. Leave the At field empty.
- Space after: 0 pt.
- Style for the following paragraph: Choose the paragraph style for non-indented body text or for Normal text. (This is a design choice: It's not really necessary to indent a paragraph after a centered line, as we'll note in Sec. 3.7, but some books do indent such a paragraph anyway.)
- Suggested name: Center.

Recommended settings for **centered paragraphs that add space after**:

- What it's for: This style is for centered text or images where you wish to add space after the paragraph. (See the previous style—called Center—for a centered style that doesn't add space after the paragraph.) For a large image, you may prefer the paragraph style recommended in Sec. 4.7.
- Font size: 12 pt.
- Font style: Use the default font style (Calibri or Times New Roman).
- Font color: Automatic.
- Alignment: Centered.
- Indent: Format > Paragraph > Special > First Line > "none."
- Line spacing: Single. Leave the At field empty.
- Space before: 0 pt.
- Space after: 12 pt.
- Style for the following paragraph: Choose the paragraph style for non-indented body text or for Normal text. (This is a design choice: It's not really necessary to indent a paragraph after a centered line, as we'll note in Sec. 3.7, but some books do indent such a paragraph anyway.)

- Note: Since this style adds space after the paragraph, you want the previous paragraph style to also add space after, as this will help give some symmetry before and after the image (or centered text). For example, if body text precedes the centered image or text, apply the BodySpaceAfter style (described earlier) to the paragraph of body text immediately preceding the centered image or text.
- Suggested name: CenterSpaceAfter. The word 'After' may help remind you that this centered style adds space after the paragraph.

Recommended settings for **title**:

- What it's for: Use the title style for your book's title on the title page.
- **Note**: The default title style has an advanced font setting. When you click Modify, go to Format > Font, click on the Advanced tab, and change Spacing to Normal. Also, uncheck the box for kerning.
- **Note**: The default title style has a border setting. To remove it, click Modify and Format > Border and choose the icon for None at the top left.
- Font size: 24 pt.
- Font style: Use the default font style (Calibri or Times New Roman).
- Font color: Automatic.
- Font weight: bold.
- Alignment: Centered.
- Indent: Format > Paragraph > Special > First Line > "none."
- Line spacing: Single. Leave the At field empty.
- Space before: 24 pt.[28]
- Space after: 12 pt.
- Style for the following paragraph: Choose the subtitle style if the subtitle will follow your title.
- Suggested name: Title.

Recommended settings for **subtitle**:

- What it's for: Use the subtitle style for your book's subtitle on the title page.
- **Note**: The default subtitle style has an advanced font setting. When you click Modify, go to Format > Font, click on the Advanced tab, and change Spacing to Normal.
- Font size: 16 pt.

---

[28] This drops the title of the book down a couple of lines if it appears on the very first 'paragraph' of the book. If you try using this style after a page break, however, the Spacing Before field may be ignored on certain devices or apps (unless you format the file as an ePub—see Sec. 5.12).

- Font style: Use the default font style (Calibri or Times New Roman).
- Font color: Automatic.
- Alignment: Centered.
- Indent: Format > Paragraph > Special > First Line > "none."
- Line spacing: Single. Leave the At field empty.
- Space before: 0 pt.
- Space after: 12 pt.
- Style for the following paragraph: Choose the CenterSpaceAfter style (see the recommended style for centered images, even if you will have text following your subtitle) if you will have the author name follow the subtitle (or other centered text). This is just a

- Suggested name: Subtitle.

Recommended settings for **bullet points** or **numbered lists**: *Bullets*

- What it's for: To create a new paragraph style for ordered or unordered lists. Why do some authors create a new paragraph style for lists, instead of using Word's built-in list tools (available on the Paragraph group on the Home ribbon)? The built-in list tools result in somewhat quirky Kindle results (and may actually create several styles hidden in the background). The default settings for the built-in list tools include a negative indent (but not where you can see and adjust it within Word), which may cause problems on particular devices or apps. We will discuss Kindle design issues (which you won't see in Word) relating to ordered and unordered lists in Sec. 3.7.
- Font size: 12 pt.
- Font style: Use the default font style (Calibri or Times New Roman).
- Font color: Automatic.
- Alignment: Left. (However, this may automatically become justified in a Kindle eBook or app, unless you follow the prescription in Sec. 5.4.) Don't add a hanging indent or use a negative indent, as these features aren't supported across all devices.[29]
- Indent: Format > Paragraph > Indentation > Left > 0.2" and Special > First Line > 0.01". This creates a block indent, i.e. it indents the entire paragraph instead of just the first line.
- Line spacing: Single. Leave the At field empty.
- Space before: 0 pt. (If you wish to add space before the first point on your list, achieve that by applying a paragraph style to the preceding paragraph that adds space after.)

---

[29] Keep it simple, as that is more likely to work across all devices. Avoid multi-level lists and varied indent sizes, for example.

- Space after: 0 pt. (If you want to add space after the last point on your list, use the next style for the very last point on your list.)
- Symbols: Don't use Format > Numbering to insert symbols or numbers for your list, as this creates some design issues (see Sec. 3.7). Rather, insert the bullet (•) symbol for unordered lists or type the number (1, 2, 3… or Roman numerals or letters, for example) directly followed by a space. In Word, use Insert > Symbol, adjust Font at the top to "(normal text)" and adjust "from" at the bottom right to "ASCII (decimal)," then select symbol 149 to insert a bullet. We'll discuss lists again in Sec. 3.7.
- Style for the following paragraph: Choose the same list style.
- Suggested name: ListPoint.

Recommended settings for **the last element of a list**: *See List Paragraph*

- What it's for: Use this style for the very last element of an ordered or unordered list, if you wish to create vertical space between your list and the paragraph that follows. This is a design choice.
- Font size: 12 pt.
- Font style: Use the default font style (Calibri or Times New Roman).
- Font color: Automatic.
- Alignment: Left. (However, this may automatically become justified in a Kindle eBook or app, unless you follow the prescription in Sec. 5.4.)
- Indent: Format > Paragraph > Indentation > Left > 0.2" and Special > First Line > 0.01". This creates a block indent, i.e. it indents the entire paragraph instead of just the first line.
- Line spacing: Single. Leave the At field empty.
- Space before: 0 pt. (If you wish to add space before the first point on your list, achieve that by applying a paragraph style to the preceding paragraph that adds space after.)
- Space after: 12 pt. (Adding space after the last bullet point helps to create separation between your list and other paragraphs. This design choice is optional.)
- Symbols: Don't use Format > Numbering to insert symbols or numbers for your list, as this creates some design issues (see Sec. 3.7). Rather, insert the bullet (•) symbol for unordered lists or type the number (1, 2, 3… or Roman numerals or letters, for example) directly followed by a space. In Word, use Insert > Symbol, adjust Font at the top to "(normal text)" and adjust "from" at the bottom right to "ASCII (decimal)," then select symbol 149 to insert a bullet. We'll discuss lists again in Sec. 3.7.
- Style for the following paragraph: Choose the paragraph style for non-indented body text. (Whether or not to indent after a list will be addressed in Sec. 3.7.)
- Suggested name: ListPointSpaceAfter.

Recommended settings for **footnotes and endnotes**:

- What it's for: These are the paragraph styles that Word automatically uses for footnotes or endnotes.

- **Note**: The footnote and endnote styles already exist in Word, and these styles are used automatically. However, these styles aren't easy to find and modify. Click the Insert Footnote or Insert Endnote button on the Reference ribbon to insert footnotes or endnotes. Once you've inserted a footnote or endnote, place your cursor within the text in the note, right-click,[30] and click Style. Then you will find a Modify button which will allow you to adjust the settings for that paragraph style. (If you have both footnotes and endnotes, you must do this separately for each.) Keep the note options simple as a simple design is more likely to work well across all devices and apps.

- Font size: 12 pt. Although print books often use a smaller font size for footnotes or endnotes, there really is *no* reason to do this in an eBook. Depending on the device or app, the note may pop-up or the device may take the customer to a new screen, so it is automatically set off from the body text. Unlike a print book, there appears to be no typographical reason in an eBook to make the customer strain his or her eyes to read a footnote or endnote.

- Font style: Use the default font style (Calibri or Times New Roman).

- Font color: Automatic.

- Alignment: Justified (i.e. full).

- Indent: Format > Paragraph > Special > First Line > 0.01". Look closely to make sure it is 0.01", and not 0.1". Anything smaller than 0.01" can lead to big problems. (Both Left and Right, which are different from First Line Indent, should be set exactly to 0.) However, if you have any footnotes or endnotes that will include multiple paragraphs in a single note, you may prefer to adjust First Line to 0.2" (or whatever you use for your other indents, although the default 0.5" would be huge on a cell phone), or you could change Spacing After to 12 pt to create separation between the paragraphs (but *don't* both indent *and* add Spacing After).

- Line spacing: Single. Leave the At field empty.

- Space before: 0 pt.

- Space after: 0 pt.

- Style for the following paragraph: Choose the same style (by default it is called Footnote Text or Endnote Text).

- Suggested name: Leave the default name (Footnote Text or Endnote Text).

---

[30] But don't right-click on a word with green or red underlining (from the spelling or grammar checkers) as that will give you different options.

You may need additional styles, such as variations of the common styles listed previously. Following are a few examples:

- If you need additional subheadings, Kindle can support up to five heading levels, from Heading 1 thru Heading 5, but beware that any heading text may show up in device navigation.

- If you have headings or subheadings that you *don't* want to show up in device navigation, create a separate heading or subheading style for those. Give these a completely different name, like Subhead. (If the names are too similar to Heading 1, Heading 2, etc., they might get picked up in device navigation.) Create a new paragraph style to make these; don't simply change the name of the default heading styles.

- You may want to incorporate a page break into a paragraph style that you want to begin on a new page. Create a separate style for this. Here is how to incorporate the page break into the paragraph style: Click Modify, then Format > Paragraph > choose the Line and Page Breaks tab at the top of the pop-up window > Page Break Before. This is better than inserting a manual page or section break.

- If you have large pictures, you may want to use the paragraph styles recommended in Sec. 4.7 for the image and for the paragraph following the image.

- You will need special styles for the table of contents. There are actually automatic styles for the table of contents, which are hard to find. We'll discuss this in Sec. 3.8.

- Many books use a smaller font for the copyright page, so you may want special paragraph styles for the copyright page with a smaller font size (10 pts in Word, but we'll use a different measure in Chapter 5 that's better than pts).

- Any other kind of paragraph where the paragraph formatting isn't exactly the same as a paragraph style that you already have requires creating a new paragraph style. Sometimes, you need a variation of a paragraph style that adds space after the paragraph, for example.

You can save your style set as a template. Click the Change Styles button near the far right of the Home ribbon, click Style Set, and Save as Quick Style Set.

Sec. 3.5 includes a variety of notes regarding the recommended settings for common paragraph styles. Sec. 3.7 discusses design issues for Kindle eBooks.

This is the styles menu for the book that you are reading.

3.5 Notes on the Recommended Settings

If you will follow the instructions in Chapter 5 for going one step beyond Word, the font sizes that you set in Word's styles won't matter (we'll update them when you reach Chapter 5).

However, if you will be uploading a Word document, then the font sizes **do** matter:

- Use 12 pts for body text. If you upload a Word document (as opposed to following the instructions of Chapter 5), this translates best to Kindle devices, Kindle apps, and the Look Inside feature.

- Adjust the font size by modifying the paragraph (and heading) styles, and by associating the appropriate paragraph style with each paragraph, as described in Sec. 3.6. **Don't** highlight an entire paragraph (or more) and change the font size, and don't adjust font size on the Home ribbon.

- The point values won't mean the same thing on Kindle devices or apps as they mean in your Word file. For example, 12 pts in Word doesn't force 12 pts on a Kindle screen. The user has the option to adjust font size. Font size is a relative indicator. What matters is that your headings have a larger font size than body text, for example.

- Font size choices are limited. A font with 16 pts will appear larger than a font with 12 pts, but a font with 11 pts will probably look the same as either 10 or 12 pts. This means that you want to keep a noticeable difference in font size. For example, use 10 pts for smaller than body text, 12 pts for body text, 16 pts for subheadings, 20 pts for main headings, and 24 pts for the title. This makes the title roughly double the body text, while creating separation between the various levels and sublevels of font size. (We'll learn a better way to achieve this in Chapter 5.)

- Don't make the font size too extreme. Avoid going below 10 pts or above 24 pts. If you make very large text, long words can get broken in strange places on small screens.

Prefer to use Spacing After rather than Spacing Before when you wish to add space between paragraphs. Certain devices or apps (especially older devices) may ignore Spacing Before. That's why, for example, it's recommended to add 12 pts Spacing After to the BodySpaceAfter style instead of adding 12 pts Spacing Before to the NoIndent style. It's also why the subheading style recommends Spacing After, but not Spacing Before. Using Spacing After works more reliably across all devices than using Spacing Before.

Anywhere you wish to add space between paragraphs, think about which kind of paragraph style is likely to precede the space (instead of thinking about which kind of paragraph style is likely to follow that space) and use the Spacing After option in the paragraph style settings. (Most paragraphs should *not* have space between them, as discussed in Sec. 3.7. Usually, Spacing After only appears after headings, subheadings, and special body text paragraphs that happen to appear before images or subheadings, for example.)

Note that the settings in Sec. 3.4 are **recommended**. You can change them to some extent. For example, you may prefer to have your subheadings set in normal or italics rather than bold-face (if so, do this by modifying the subheading style, not by highlighting the subheading text and applying the formatting directly to what's highlighted).

The font color should generally be set to **automatic**. Avoid using white, black, green, or sepia colors for text (or hyperlinks), as these will disappear against one of the four possible reading backgrounds (you have no control over which background a reader selects). Using automatic for the font color, the text will be black unless the reader selects night mode. (Don't set the font color to black because then it will still be black when the reader chooses night mode, and then the text will disappear completely.)

You can use a paragraph style to make headings or subheadings a different color, for example (just don't choose black, white, green, or sepia). If you want to color only *part* of the text of a paragraph, as opposed to the entire paragraph, then you should highlight the text and apply the font color change directly to what's highlighted—and that will override the paragraph style for that selected text. (If it's an entire paragraph—realizing that headings or subheadings are entire paragraphs—then you need a paragraph style with the font color you wish to use; don't highlight an entire paragraph and apply formatting directly to what's highlighted—create a new paragraph style and simply associate that paragraph style with the paragraph.)

When you use a font color (instead of automatic), give some thought to how that color will stand out on a white, black, green, or sepia (a creamy color) background. Kindle customers can change the background to normal (white), sepia, green, or black (night mode), so you must design your book with these possibilities in mind. Also note that the font color will appear in grayscale on a black-and-white display, where it won't stand out like it would on a color display. Your normal body text should be set to **automatic**. Avoid long sections of text in any color other than automatic.

Headings and subheadings should either be centered or left (but follow the steps of Sec. 5.4 to prevent this from automatically becoming justified). Don't use justified (full) for headings or subheadings (as that can lead to large gaps on devices with small screens).

Don't use Exactly in the line spacing options under Paragraph. Either use Single or 1.5, with the At field empty. Most styles in most eBooks should use Single. If you have a special book where similar Kindle eBooks (especially, those by traditional publishers) use extra leading, you can use 1.5 to create a similar effect. Most well-formatted Kindle eBooks use Single line spacing (with no space added between body text paragraphs). Read Sec. 3.7 for further discussion.

The body text paragraph styles should either be indented with no space between paragraphs (recommended), or non-indented with space between (though this is much less common). Sec. 3.7

will discuss this design choice in more detail, along with the choice between left and justified (full) alignment.

Avoid indenting from the right side, as some devices will ignore this and it can exaggerate typographical issues on devices with small screens.

Note the following little idiosyncrasies with Kindle formatting. These options can be found under Format > Paragraph when modifying a paragraph style.

- When you don't want a style to add space after a paragraph (which should be the case for most paragraphs), set the Spacing After field to 0. It's incorrect to set it to 0.01 pt, as that may result in automatic indents on one or more devices or apps.

- When you wish to create a non-indented paragraph style with left alignment or full justification, set First Line Indent to 0.01" (be careful not to use 0.1", which is noticeably larger). It's incorrect to enter 0 or to select "none" for First Line Indent, as that may result in automatically indented paragraphs on certain devices or apps.

- If the alignment is set to center (for an image or heading, for example), then First Line Indent should be set to "none" (and not 0.01"). This works fine for centered paragraphs or headings.

- Make sure that the At field beside Line Spacing is left empty. Don't set it to a number. As mentioned earlier, Line Spacing should either be set to Single or 1.5 Lines (and in both cases, the At field should be empty).

It's better to incorporate a page break into a paragraph style (such as Heading 1 for page breaks at the beginning of a new chapter) than to use a manual page break. One reason is that older Kindle devices may add unexpected spaces. Another is that it avoids a little unnecessary code hidden in the background.

Note that borders and shading may not work across all devices and apps. We'll discuss borders and shading in Sec.'s 3.7, 4.7, and 5.7.

Use only letters and numbers in the paragraph style names. Don't use punctuation or special characters. It's also generally best to avoid spaces, although the default names (like Heading 1 or Footnote Text) that include spaces should work. For example, that's why I have a style named NoIndent (rather than No Indent).

In the dropdown menu for Style Based On, choose "(no style)." Do that *before* you modify the paragraph style (otherwise, your paragraph settings may change on you without you realizing it); this prevents styles from associating with one another. Uncheck the Automatically Update option, but realize that it doesn't prevent paragraph styles from automatically updating (it just prevents any *associated* styles from affecting one another). Also, disable linked styles as described in Sec. 3.3.

If you want to modify a paragraph style and have the change occur throughout your book, just modify the paragraph style and this will ordinarily happen automatically. (Note that the

terminology is confusing: The Automatically Update option only controls whether or not *associated* styles update along with the paragraph style that you modify. The paragraph style you're modifying ordinarily automatically updates throughout your book, even if the Automatically Update option is *unchecked*.) However, if you modify a paragraph style, you should still check paragraphs of that style and verify that the change propagated as expected—especially if you modify the Normal style. If necessary, you can right-click on the style name in the styles menu, and Select All before modifying the style.

Note that when you modify a paragraph style, you are modifying *every* paragraph that applies that paragraph style. If you want certain paragraphs to have one style, and other paragraphs to have a different style, you must create multiple paragraph styles with different names and associate each paragraph with the desired style.

The paragraph style that you choose on the dropdown menu for Style for Following Paragraph doesn't matter if your manuscript is already complete. If you're still writing your book, this option comes in handy when you finish typing a paragraph and press the Enter key: The next paragraph will already have the pre-selected style (if you chose this option wisely).

3.6 Styling Your Book

Once you have your paragraph styles ready (such as those recommended in Sec. 3.4), formatting the paragraphs for your Kindle eBook is easy.

If you're new to Word's paragraph styles, I encourage you to try this out on a simple 'test book,' following the step-by-step instructions in Appendix B, before carrying it out on your actual book. This will give you a confidence boost, too.

Most of your book (if not all of it) is probably already in the Normal style. If so, this makes it very easy to format "normal" body text paragraphs: If they are already in the Normal style, there is nothing[31] to do (assuming you've already modified the Normal style as mentioned in the previous sections). So let's focus on the other kinds of paragraphs in your book.

---

[31] However, you do want to look closely and ensure that the paragraphs with the Normal style have the formatting that you set in the Normal style. This should happen automatically when you modify the Normal style (e.g. following the recommendations in Sec. 3.4). If not, Sec. 3.3 describes a few different ways to go about updating a paragraph style: Try one of those and see if it will update all of the Normal paragraphs to the modified Normal style. For example, try right-clicking on the Normal style in the styles menu (at the right, after opening it as described in Sec. 3.3—not on the Home ribbon), using Select All, then going into Modify (with all those instances still selected), changing something (in the style) and then changing it back to how you want it, and pressing OK. (If you've done any formatting by highlighting paragraphs and applying formatting directly to what's highlighted instead of using the paragraph styles—or if you applied text or paragraph options from the Home ribbon and then proceeded to type one or more complete paragraphs—that can make it harder to propagate the changes through the Normal style. Otherwise, the update to the paragraph style should occur automatically. Remember, the Automatically Update checkbox has nothing to do with this; it only affects associated styles, not the paragraph style you're modifying.)

All you need to do is place your cursor in a paragraph and click on the desired paragraph style from the styles menu. (You could click on a paragraph style from the Home ribbon or a paragraph style from the styles menu: It won't matter. I prefer to do everything from the styles menu that you can open to show at the right, as it includes more options.) Prest-O, Change-O! The formatting of the paragraph will instantly adapt to the new paragraph style.

If you have several consecutive paragraphs that you wish to change to the same style all at once, just highlight them (but don't highlight beyond the last period of the last paragraph, or it will be a step too far: you don't need to highlight an entire paragraph to apply a paragraph style, so the safe practice is to just highlight parts of the first and last paragraphs that you wish to change—along with all of the paragraphs in between) and then click on the desired paragraph style.

You just need to decide which styles to apply to which kinds of paragraphs. Partly, this is a design choice that you must make. We'll discuss the design of Kindle eBooks in Sec. 3.7. Most of the styling doesn't involve too much choice. You apply Heading 1 and Heading 2 to chapter headings and subheadings, use Normal for the bulk of your body text, use a non-indented body text style for the first paragraph of a chapter, use Title and Subtitle for the title and subtitle of your book on the title page, apply a centered style to figures, and so on. Sec. 3.7 will help you with subtler design choices.

There is a handy trick that you can use for a few things like chapter headings. It's almost like magic. Suppose, for example, that your book has 50 chapters, and each chapter heading has the word "chapter" in it (e.g. Chapter 12). Instead of applying Heading 1 to all 50 chapter headings one at a time, you can use the following trick.

Click on the Replace button at the far right of the Home ribbon. Type "Chapter" in the Find What field (without the quotes, of course) and type the same thing in the Replace With field. With your cursor still in the Replace With field, click the Format button. Choose Style, and select the appropriate style (e.g. Heading 1). When you press the Replace All button, this will change every paragraph with the word Chapter in it to the selected paragraph style. (But remember: The next time you proceed to use the Replace tool, you'll need to click the No Formatting button to remove that paragraph style from the Replace With field.)

This trick isn't foolproof, though. In this example, if you used the word 'chapter' anywhere else in your book, those paragraphs will turn into the heading style, also. You could use the Find tool first to see how many instances of "chapter" there are, and compare with the number of chapters in your book, to decide whether or not this trick will work for your book. For example, if your book has 36 chapters and there are 36 instances of the word "chapter" in your book, it's safe to use this trick. As a counterexample, if there are 36 chapters and 42 instances of the word "chapter," the Replace tool would change 6 other kinds of paragraphs to a heading style (but it may be easier to correct those 6 paragraphs than the other 36 headings). Note that you could click the More button on the Replace pop-up window and check the box for Match Case to reduce the number of matches.

Tip: You can add a paragraph style to the Replace With field when using the replace tool. In some cases, such as for chapter headings, this can make it easy to quickly change several paragraph styles at once.

Clearing a paragraph style is easy: Find a Clear All Formatting option at the top of the styles menu, or at the top right corner of the Font group on the Home ribbon. But note that the paragraph will change into another paragraph style: You'll probably need to associate a different paragraph style with the paragraph after clearing the previous paragraph style.

Remember not to highlight an entire paragraph (or multiple paragraphs) and apply formatting directly to what's highlighted. However, you *may* highlight paragraphs and apply a paragraph style to them (but be careful not to highlight all the way to the end of the last paragraph, or it may apply the paragraph style one paragraph too far). If you need to format just *part* of a paragraph, like putting one phrase or sentence in boldface or italics, you should do this by highlighting and applying formatting directly: Don't use character styles to format just *part* of a paragraph.

If you made bullet points or numbered lists before reading this book, you have two choices: restyle them with a list style such as the one called ListPoint from Sec. 3.4 (after first unformatting the original bullets), or leave them as they are (while realizing that there may be a few design issues with them). We'll discuss the design problems with ordered and unordered lists in Sec. 3.7.

Regarding bullet points, you definitely want to undo any fancy list features, like multi-level lists and non-standard symbols. Basic bullets may work okay (but the default bullets include a negative indent, which is problematic on older devices, and produce inefficient instructions hidden in the background—aside from design issues that we'll discuss in Sec. 3.7).

If you have a nonfiction book with lists all over the place, then you must weigh the benefits of restyling them against the hassle of changing them. Fortunately, Word's default bullet tools work better than they used to with Kindle eBooks, provided that you keep them simple (for example, if they aren't multi-level, and if you didn't change the default options).

On the other hand, there are a few tricks available to reformat lists more efficiently. If you have numerous lists already made using Word's default list tools, it may be possible to use the Replace tool to quickly change from the default bullet style to a list style that you create (such as the one called ListPoint from Sec. 3.4). For example, click the More button on the Replace tool, adjust Format > Style to ListParagraph for the Find What field, and adjust Format > Style to your

Word's Default Bullet Tool

the cash register.

- Spellcheck, aisle three. If you can't get the spelling and grammar right in a hundred words or so... Look, it's not an option. You have to get it right.
- Vocabulary. It needs to match your target audience. Words they don't understand can scare them away (but if such words are common in the prose, you also don't want to create false expectations).
- Research. Do your homework. Check out blurbs of successful books similar to yours.
- Feedback. Ask for opinions on your blurb. Before you publish, this can help you generate buzz.

Here is a nonfiction blurb checklist:

- Be concise OR break up a long blurb into paragraphs with bullet points. Still, don't say anything that's unnecessary.
- Inform. Make it clear what information

kindle

Insert > Symbol > 149 + Block Indent

- Spellcheck, aisle three. If you can't get the spelling and grammar right in a hundred words or so... Look, it's not an option. You have to get it right.
- Vocabulary. It needs to match your target audience. Words they don't understand can scare them away (but if such words are common in the prose, you also don't want to create false expectations).
- Research. Do your homework. Check out blurbs of successful books similar to yours.
- Feedback. Ask for opinions on your blurb. Before you publish, this can help you generate buzz.

Here is a nonfiction blurb checklist:

- Be concise OR break up a long blurb into paragraphs with bullet points. Still, don't say anything that's unnecessary.
- Inform. Make it clear what information will be found in your book. If they aren't sure

kindle

own list style for the Replace With field (leaving both fields empty): This will replace Word's default ListParagraph style with your own paragraph style for lists. You will still need to insert the bullet symbol (•) for unordered lists or add the numbers for ordered lists, and if you want to add space after each list, you will need to apply a special style to the last list point (such as the one called ListPointSpaceAfter recommended in Sec. 3.4). For unordered lists, note that you can insert several bullets at once using the Replace tool: Highlight a set of bullets, type ^p in the Find What field, type ^p• (use Alt + 0149, or use Insert Symbol > 149 before opening the Replace tool and copy/paste the bullet symbol into the Replace tool) followed by one space in the Replace With field, and *only* replace for the highlighted selection—*not* the whole document (you may still need to manually adjust the first and last paragraphs of the list).

If you plan to redo several lists, I recommend that you save two copies of your Word file before you begin doing this: That way, if anything doesn't come out right, you have the original to fall back on. The picture on the previous page compares the two options—Word's default list tools vs. manual lists created by adding new paragraph styles—for modern devices. Beware that the issue may be more pronounced than my picture shows with certain devices or apps, especially older Kindle devices. You may wish to read more about bullets and numbered lists in Sec. 3.7 before you decide how to format them.

3.7 Kindle Design

We will discuss a variety of Kindle design choices in this section. When designing your eBook, you should consider:

- How will your eBook look on a variety of screen sizes, from a small cell phone to a huge screen on a tablet, laptop, or monitor? Anything that restricts the margins (like indenting the entire paragraph) greatly impacts the display on a small screen, while anything that can impose large sections of white space (like a page break) can waste a lot of space on a large screen (yet sometimes it's necessary to avoid funny positioning of headings). Images (which we will consider in Chapter 4) need to work well across a variety of devices.

- How will your design be affected if the customer chooses a larger or smaller font, adjusts the line spacing, or increases the margins on the Kindle device or app? Ideally, you want a flexible design.

- What are readers' expectations for books similar to yours? If the design of your Look Inside goes against readers' expectations, it can cost you valuable sales.

- How do different Kindle devices and apps work? Some devices or apps work a little differently than others, and this is especially true of older Kindle devices. Beware that a few features that appear to work fine for modern devices on Amazon's preview don't work well on older devices.

- Will your design work on all Kindle devices and apps, including older devices? To some extent, you can preview your design (Chapter 7) before you publish. When in doubt, simpler designs are more apt to function reliably.

- How do customers use their devices? For example, many hold their devices in portrait mode, but some read in landscape mode, and as a designer you must allow for both. Sometimes customers don't know how to use their devices (e.g. some people don't realize that they can zoom in on an image, such as by double-tapping or pinching on a touch-screen). If possible, don't rely on the customer to know how to use the device to make your book readable.

- What's the worst-case scenario for what you're trying to accomplish? For example, if you want to use a border to set off a paragraph and the worst-case scenario is that the border doesn't display at all, you must weigh the benefits of including the border for the many devices that will support it against how it will look on the few devices where the border is ignored. Do the benefits outweigh the risks? When it's a minor thing, the risk is minimal; when the worst-case scenario is a major design problem, it can lead to a one-star review from a frustrated customer.

One of the big decisions you must make is with regard to the **alignment** of your body text. Almost all varieties of both fiction and nonfiction Kindle eBooks follow one of three schools of thought regarding the alignment of body text:

1. Force justified (full).[32] This forces the text on both the left and right edges of each paragraph to line up neatly, except for the last line of the paragraph, which is shorter.

2. Force left alignment (ragged right). Text lines up on the left side, but the right edge looks ragged. Note that the only reliable way to achieve this result is to go a quick step beyond Word (Sec. 5.4 will show you the most reliable way to do this). If you upload a Word document to KDP, left alignment may automatically become justified in Kindle eBooks (although I will discuss a possible 'trick' later in this section). Beware that Amazon may have a preference for *not* forcing left alignment for body text (other kinds of paragraphs, like bullet points and headings, may be forced left). There are stories of authors whose books have been unpublished because left alignment (ragged right) was forced on the body text.

---

[32] So many people have used the term 'justify' to mean different things, it's important to clarify what you mean. Some people distinguish between justified versus ragged right, but others use the terms 'justified full' and 'justified left' (while a few designers feel strongly that this latter terminology shouldn't be used at all). Henceforth, where I use the term 'justified' I imply full (i.e. not left); I will use 'ragged right' or 'left aligned' to mean that only the left edge is aligned.

3. Don't set any body text alignment at all. Note that this isn't possible to do within Word, but Sec. 5.4 will describe how to do this by going a quick step beyond Word.

The book you're reading now forces justified (full) body text (except on bullet points and numbered lists). I'm a fan of justified text, since the vast majority of traditionally published print books are justified. Readers of most fiction genres and most nonfiction categories are accustomed to seeing justified text (even with eBooks). My personal feeling is that going against this expectation may do more harm than good, though there are designers who feel strongly otherwise.

Some eBook designers who force ragged right (left alignment) do so because they don't like the way that Kindle justifies (typographers know many tricks to improve justification for print books, and their eye for design notices the limitations on Kindle devices and apps), and ragged right is more receptive of using non-breaking spaces (or non-breaking hyphens—but read an important note about this later in this section) to prevent undesirable breaks.

The way I figure it, most of my readers aren't typographers or professional book designers, so they are more apt to think I made a mistake if my book isn't justified like they are used to seeing. But again, this is my personal opinion, and it's not shared by all eBook designers.

It's also worth noting that Kindle justification has improved leaps and bounds with a feature called enhanced typesetting, which applies to many modern devices. Amazon's enhanced typesetting feature automatically hyphenates words and includes typography tricks to improve the reading experience. With this in mind, the issues with justified (full) mainly apply to older devices, which are used more rarely every year. This is another reason that I recommend option 1, justifying the main body text paragraphs (especially, the Normal style) in your Kindle eBook.

There is an interesting idea behind option 3, not setting any body text alignment at all. The idea is to let the customer decide. Well, actually, many devices **don't** let the customer choose between justified and ragged right. The customer has to know a 'trick' to make this 'choice.' My feeling is that most customers won't know this 'trick,' and even if they do, they must be disappointed frequently since most Kindle eBooks force justified body text.

There is also a problem with option 3. If you leave body text alignment unspecified (again, you can't do this in Word—Sec. 5.4 shows how to do this) or if you set the alignment to left, Kindle devices and apps automatically justify the text (except for customers who know a 'trick' to get their device to make it ragged right—not an option when you force alignment one way or the other). However, the body text will be ragged right on the Look Inside.

From a marketing perspective, the Look Inside is quite important. First you have to sell your book before you worry about what it looks like on a Kindle device or app. I want my Look Inside **justified** because I feel that more readers expect it to look that way. That's why I choose option 1.

If you choose option 3 (or 2), the Look Inside will be ragged right. My preference isn't necessarily the 'correct' choice, but it has marketing value. You have to make your own decision.

I recommend browsing Kindle eBooks similar to yours, both traditionally published and popular indie books, and check out their Look Insides on Amazon.com. If you happen to publish in a subgenre or subcategory where ragged right Look Insides are more common, by doing a little research, you won't be caught off guard (but realize that a ragged right Look Inside may be more indicative of option 3 than option 2).

Regardless of the alignment of your main body text paragraphs, you may desire to set a particular type of paragraph (or heading) to be left aligned. For example **bullets** work better *left aligned* (ragged right), and you might have a **subheading** that you want *left aligned*. Note that merely choosing left alignment in Word *won't* work. As mentioned previously, it will automatically become justified unless you follow the instructions in Sec. 5.4 (recommended).

There used to be a 'trick' to preventing Kindle devices and apps from **automatically justifying** paragraphs that are left-aligned in an uploaded *Word document*. The way the 'trick' worked was to select justified (full) in the applied paragraph style, and then highlight the paragraph(s) and click on the left alignment icon on the Paragraph group on the Home ribbon. (Normally, you should refrain from highlighting entire paragraphs and applying formatting directly to them, but this was necessary for the 'trick' to work.) However, this 'trick' doesn't work reliably now (but feel free to test it out in a Word document, upload it to KDP, and see how it comes out in the preview).

If you want to make a bullet point, subheading, or any other paragraph style left aligned (ragged right), the only reliable way to do this is to go a quick step beyond Word. Sec. 5.4 will show you exactly how to do this. Don't attempt the aforementioned 'trick' if you plan to follow the instructions in Chapter 5.

Even if you prefer justified text to ragged right, you shouldn't set your *entire book* justified. **Headings** and **subheadings**, for example, should either be centered or left aligned (if you plan to upload a Word document and not go a quick step beyond Word, there is a clear advantage to choosing centered over left alignment). Justified can be a disaster for headings read on a very small screen (like a cell phone) in a very large font (remember, the customer can change the font size). Since headings usually have a larger font than body text, the gaps in Kindle's justified text would be even more pronounced.

Bullet points and **numbered lists** don't come out as good on Kindle devices and apps as they appear on your computer monitor in Word. Even if you use some other means to make ordered and unordered lists (such as HTML), there are still design issues. There isn't a foolproof method of creating lists for Kindle eBooks. What you need to do is understand the pros and cons of various methods, and then make a design choice.

Word's default bullet and numbered lists tools now work better on Kindle eBooks than they have in the past if you upload a Word document (or if you use Kindle Create). However, they still aren't perfect. For one, these tools automatically include a 0.5" hanging indent, which is quite large for an eBook, especially for a device with a small screen like a cell phone. Unfortunately, if you decrease the size of the indent in Word, bullet points or numbered lists will look worse in other ways: If you use Word's list tools, the *default* settings provide the *best* results for Kindle eBooks (it's one of the quirks of Kindle formatting that messing with these settings in Word adversely affects the way that bullet points display in the eBook). Another issue with Word's list tools is that they include a negative indent in the hidden instructions in the background, which can't be avoided using Word. This negative indent can cause trouble, especially with older devices.

If you plan to follow Chapter 5, I recommend that you *don't* use Word's list tools. Unfortunately, Word's list tools are one of the few features that work better when you upload a Word document than when you go a step beyond Word. Even if you use Word's list tool with the default settings for a simple list, when you go a step beyond Word, the list looks a bit worse compared to uploading a Word document—even if you don't modify the list in any way after going a step beyond Word. (I've tested this out, creating a simple list in Word using the bullet tool in Word, uploading the Word file to KDP, then going a step beyond Word as described in Chapter 5, but without actually modifying anything, and seen firsthand that the bullet points don't look the same.)

Even if you know HTML and make simple ordered and unordered lists and upload your HTML file (or even if you convert to ePub or MOBI), it doesn't come out as well as Word's default list tools. Furthermore, if you take a simple Word file with a simple list created using the bullet tool, convert that list to HTML, and upload the HTML file, the list doesn't look quite as good as it does when you upload the Word file.

I'm **not** saying that uploading a Word file is better than uploading an HTML file, and I'm **not** saying that Word's list tools are the best way to create lists. Later in this section, I will summarize the pros and cons of using Word's default list tools and uploading a Word file compared to the pros and cons of going a step beyond Word (described in Chapter 5) and using your own paragraph style (like ListStyle) to create lists.

What I am saying is that you should *only* use Word's list tools if you plan to upload a *Word* document to KDP: **Don't** use Word's list tools if you plan to follow Chapter 5 and go a quick step beyond Word. Another thing that I'm saying is that Word's list tools now work better than they used to work if you upload a Word document.

Even though results have improved, Word's list tools still aren't perfect. As I already mentioned, you're stuck with a 0.5" hanging indent (since modifying this in Word causes other problems) and negative indents in the hidden instructions. The large indent is a problem for a couple of reasons. For one, it makes issues with Kindle justification more noticeable, as it makes the margin effectively half an inch narrower. This issue is more pronounced if the customer chooses a larger font size, or if the customer reads on a small screen.

Another problem with a 0.5" hanging indent for your lists is that it may be inconsistent with the First Line Indent that you use for your body text paragraphs. Since a large indent like 0.5" increases issues with Kindle justification (especially on smaller screens or when a customer selects a larger font size), I recommend a smaller First Line Indent like 0.2". However, if you indent most of your paragraphs to 0.2" while using the automatic 0.5" for bullet points and numbered lists, this inconsistent indentation may be perceived as a bit of a design mistake. On the other hand, if you consistently indent 0.5" everywhere, the large indent creates its own problems.

In addition to the 0.5" hanging indent, the negative indent value specified in the hidden instructions in Word causes a problem with certain devices (especially older devices). While lists created with Word's list tools may look okay on modern devices, they will look much worse on devices for which that negative indent value causes a problem.

If you choose *not* to use Word's list tools, the best alternative is to create a new paragraph style for bullet points or numbered lists. I recommend the ListPoint paragraph style from Sec. 3.4. If you would like for the last point of your list to add a little vertical space (in order to create a little separation between your list and the following paragraph), apply the ListPointSpaceAfter paragraph style from Sec. 3.4 to the last point on your list.

When using a paragraph style to create bullet points, use Insert > Symbol > 149 to manually insert the bullet symbol (•). When creating numbered lists this way, manually type each number followed by a period and space.

Using a paragraph style (like ListPoint recommended in Sec. 3.4) has its own pros and cons. One benefit is that you can set a much smaller indent size (like 0.2" or 0.3") than Word's automatic 0.5", which helps with justification issues. (Even if you set lists ragged right, they still come out better with the smaller indent than with a larger indent.) One obvious con is that the bullet symbol (or number) won't be set apart to the left of the text, as shown on page 99.

Here is a quick comparison of the two ways to go about formatting lists—using Word's built-in list tools with their default settings and uploading a Word file versus using your own paragraph style (like ListStyle), typing the bullet symbol or number manually, and going a step beyond Word (Chapter 5). I will call the former option A and the latter option B.

- On modern devices, option A may result in a nicer looking bullet symbol that is offset from the text, whereas option B lets you set a narrower indent (which improves justification issues).

- On older devices, option A's negative indent value and hanging indent may cause problems, which can be avoided with option B.
- Your bullet points will be justified with option A (even if you left-align them, they may become justified automatically when uploading a Word file), whereas you can choose to align them left (if you prefer) with option B.

I *didn't* use Word's built-in lists tools for this eBook. As you may have noticed, I created my own list styles, inserting the bullet symbol (•) manually (or typing numbers for numbered lists manually). This allows me to set a narrower indent, and the results work better across all devices and apps (especially older devices).

However, I'm not 100% happy with my list points. Since many of my list points have multiple sentences, my left-aligned bullets (they are justified in the *print* edition, but left-aligned in the eBook) contrast with my justified body text: It's quite noticeable. If most of your list points have little text (like words or phrases), there is a distinct advantage to using left alignment. If your list points have sentences (especially, if they have multiple sentences) like my book, it may be better to justify your list points. With enhanced typesetting, justified list points are better than they used to be. My feeling is that many nonfiction books that use lists have little text in most of the list points (unlike my book), so I went with left-aligned lists as a model for those books. Otherwise, I would have justified my lists for this book (since most of them include sentences).

Whichever method you use, if you decide that you would like to set your lists ragged right, note that setting left alignment in Word won't make your lists ragged right. The only reliable way to do this is to follow the instructions in Sec. 5.4. If you have several bullet points, read Sec. 3.6, which has a suggestion that may help make the transition somewhat less tedious. (Remember, if you follow Chapter 5, I **don't** recommend using Word's built-in lists tools.)

In any case, it's best to keep your bullet points and numbered lists simple. Avoid multi-level lists with multiple indent values, and avoid using special symbols (other than Insert > Symbol > 149 for a bullet). Outline lists with Roman numerals, letters, and numbers are especially problematic: Avoid nested lists, sublevels, and lists that mix letters and numbers, as these features may result in poor and unexpected formatting on some devices or apps (and even worse on older devices). The simpler your lists, the more likely they will come out well across all devices and apps.

Another issue to consider is whether to use **indented paragraphs** with *no* space added between them or non-indented paragraphs separated by vertical space (the latter option is called **block paragraphs**—not to be confused with block indents). The vast majority of both fiction and nonfiction books use indented paragraphs with no space added between them. If you give readers something they are not accustomed to, it's risky, so my advice is to use indented paragraphs and don't add space between them.

There are a few specialized types of books where block paragraphs are relatively common, such as certain kinds of shorter nonfiction books (not like the one you're reading). Those have no indents, but do have space between them. It would be wise to search for traditionally published and popular indie-published books similar to yours to see what your potential readers are accustomed to seeing.

Almost *no* books have *both* indented paragraphs *and* space between them. One exception is the self-published author who doesn't change the factory default settings in Word. So if you format your book this way, that's how it might seem to readers: That you don't know how to change the default settings in Word, or that you aren't familiar with how most books look. Maybe this seems a little harsh, but the reality is that some customers can be harsh (either in terms of not buying a book based on the Look Inside, or by posting harsh comments in a review). What ultimately matters (to many authors) is this: *How should you format your book so that you're more likely to generate sales and positive feedback?*

Here is another issue relating to paragraph indentations: If your body text is indented, you may have a few **special body text paragraphs** that you wish to have *non-indented*. Note that setting First Line Indent to "none" or zero in the paragraph style **doesn't** work for justified or left aligned paragraphs. You must set First Line Indent to 0.01" (look closely: don't use 0.1", which is noticeably larger), as described in Sec. 3.4 (do this to the paragraph style itself). However, don't use 0.01" for centered paragraphs (including centered headings or images): "none" works fine when the alignment is set to center.

For example, most traditionally published books **don't indent the first paragraph of each chapter**. The purpose of the indent is to help find where one paragraph ends and another begins, but it's easy to find the first paragraph, so an indent isn't needed there. Since most traditionally published books don't indent the first chapter, any book that doesn't do the same will seem different, but only to a reader who notices such things (more do than ever before, as very many readers are trying their hand as authors now that self-publishing is very common). As with other body text paragraphs that you wish to be non-indented, create a paragraph style (such as the NoIndent paragraph styles recommended in Sec. 3.4) with First Line Indent set to 0.01" (since "none" won't work from Word).

Similarly, there are other body text paragraphs where an indent may be considered *optional*, as its usual function isn't really needed. For example, you don't really need an indent after a section break, following a picture, after a subheading, following a block indent, or after centered text. This really is a choice. Some books do, while others don't. There are certain kinds of books where one style is more prevalent than the other, so you should research the design of books similar to yours to see which style is common among those. As you can see in this book, I add space after the last bullet point and when the paragraph after the list is body text, I don't indent it. However, not all books follow this same style. To some extent, you're developing your own design and style, but it takes research to help distinguish between a design choice and something that the reader might interpret as a design flaw.

Most eBooks use *single* **line spacing**. (Leave the At field empty for your eBook regardless of your line spacing choice.) Note that most *print* books add a little leading to make the text a little easier to read, such that a line spacing of 1.1 to 1.2 is fairly common among *print* books. However, you should use **single** line spacing for your eBook: <u>**Don't**</u> try setting the line spacing to 1.1 or 1.2 for a Kindle eBook. In comparison, single spacing in Kindle eBooks seems a little tight. However, the alternative is to set the line spacing to 1.5 lines: Whereas single spacing is a little tight, 1.5 is very loose. For this reason, I recommend *single* line spacing.

If you happen to have an eBook in a subgenre or subcategory where a line spacing of 1.5 lines is more common (maybe for kids), you could make an exception. Either choose single or 1.5 lines: <u>**Don't**</u> try other values. Whether you use a line spacing of single or 1.5, leave the At field empty.

Note that single line spacing in Kindle eBooks really *isn't* tight. That's because a customer who prefers a somewhat looser look can achieve that look: *It's possible for the customer to adjust line spacing on most Kindle devices and apps* (provided that the customer knows how to do this). Single spacing works well for Kindle eBooks because most customers are used to that look from reading other eBooks while other customers realize that they can adjust the line spacing right on their device or app. This is another reason that **I recommend *single* line spacing** for Kindle eBooks (even if you feel like single is tight—because the customer can adjust the line spacing).

Drop caps now work better than they have in the past, as Amazon has improved them significantly. However, they aren't foolproof. When the drop cap looks good, it makes a nice impression, which is why you see them used in most traditionally published eBooks. On the other hand, when it looks wrong, it leaves a poor impression. Chapter 7 will show you how to preview your eBook as many ways as possible: If you can get your drop caps to work well in all of the previews, they are probably worth doing. Sec. 5.6 will show you a way to improve upon Word's drop caps.

As with most features of Kindle eBooks, it's best to keep your drop caps as simple as possible. Avoid using a nonstandard font: I recommend leaving the default font even for the drop cap. If you had already formatted your drop cap without a Kindle eBook in mind, consider removing the drop cap and inserting a new, simple drop cap from scratch.

One alternative to the drop cap is to type the first few words of the first paragraph in CAPS (perhaps making the size of the caps slightly smaller). Note that many books use **both**, i.e. they place the very first letter of the chapter in a drop cap and they apply small caps to the first few words. You don't necessarily need to choose just one or the other.

Drop Cap

A bookstore is like a bar where you go to pick up books; internet bookstores are like online dating services. You browse through the books to find one that catches your eye. When you see one you like, you look at it more closely. You scan it up and down, turn it over and examine its rear. The book doesn't mind. In fact, the book yearns for more. It was written for this moment. It is begging, "Pick me! Pick me!"

Satisfied with what you see so far, you look inside. You judge its appearance inside and out. Then you decide to get to know it better. You read the cover blurbs. You check out the contents, browse through the introduction. You're measuring its personality, knowledge, and communication skills; judging its potential.

If the book passes your examination, you take it out on a date. You begin reading the first chapter. The whole time the book is anticipating that first kiss, wondering if you will take it home with you. Meanwhile, you are analyzing the book's every move. Going steady with a book is a big commitment. You don't want to be disappointed.

How do you know if the relationship will work out? Curling up by the fireplace, snuggling in warm covers in bed with a book light, sneaking a quick page or two in the bathroom. You will share these intimate times with your

Caps

A BOOKSTORE IS LIKE a bar where you go to pick up books; internet bookstores are like online dating services. You browse through the books to find one that catches your eye. When you see one you like, you look at it more closely. You scan it up and down, turn it over and examine its rear. The book doesn't mind. In fact, the book yearns for more. It was written for this moment. It is begging, "Pick me! Pick me!"

Satisfied with what you see so far, you look inside. You judge its appearance inside and out. Then you decide to get to know it better. You read the cover blurbs. You check out the contents, browse through the introduction. You're measuring its personality, knowledge, and communication skills; judging its potential.

If the book passes your examination, you take it out on a date. You begin reading the first chapter. The whole time the book is anticipating that first kiss, wondering if you will take it home with you. Meanwhile, you are analyzing the book's every move. Going steady with a book is a big commitment. You don't want to be disappointed.

How do you know if the relationship will work out? Curling up by the fireplace, snuggling in warm covers in bed with a book light, sneaking a quick page or two in the bathroom. You will share these intimate times with your

Both

A BOOKSTORE IS LIKE a bar where you go to pick up books; internet bookstores are like online dating services. You browse through the books to find one that catches your eye. When you see one you like, you look at it more closely. You scan it up and down, turn it over and examine its rear. The book doesn't mind. In fact, the book yearns for more. It was written for this moment. It is begging, "Pick me! Pick me!"

Satisfied with what you see so far, you look inside. You judge its appearance inside and out. Then you decide to get to know it better. You read the cover blurbs. You check out the contents, browse through the introduction. You're measuring its personality, knowledge, and communication skills; judging its potential.

If the book passes your examination, you take it out on a date. You begin reading the first chapter. The whole time the book is anticipating that first kiss, wondering if you will take it home with you. Meanwhile, you are analyzing the book's every move. Going steady with a book is a big commitment. You don't want to be disappointed.

How do you know if the relationship will work out? Curling up by the fireplace, snuggling in warm covers in bed with a book light, sneaking a quick page or two in the bathroom. You will share these intimate times with your

Occasionally, you come across yet another option: Another alternative to the drop cap is to just make the font size of the very first character much larger. This was somewhat more popular when drop caps were a bigger problem. Making the font size of the first character large doesn't look nearly as nice as a properly formatted drop cap, so now that drop caps are a viable option, you rarely see that anymore. Now, you usually see either a drop cap, a drop cap combined with small caps, or just small caps.

Note that if the first paragraph of a chapter is very short, a drop cap could pose a problem. Suppose a customer is reading the eBook on a device with a small font and a large screen, such that the first paragraph of a chapter is only displayed on one or two lines of text. When the drop cap happens to be larger than the height of the paragraph, the drop cap looks out of place. Before you commit to using drop caps, check if any of your chapters open with very short paragraphs.

The first page of a chapter usually stands out in more ways than just a drop cap or small caps. For example, *the chapter heading is often dropped down the equivalent of a few lines in traditionally published books.* Don't use the Enter key to create blank lines in your eBook though, as that will lead to inconsistent formatting (also, some devices or apps may ignore blank lines). Instead, use Spacing Before[33] in the paragraph style (doing so with Heading 1 is recommended in Sec. 3.4) for the first paragraph (or heading) of the chapter. (In general, using Spacing After works more reliably than Spacing Before, but with the first element of a new chapter that includes a page break, only Spacing Before puts the space in the correct place.)

Some eBooks include a small decorative **glyph** above or below the chapter heading. Ordinarily, this is done by inserting a picture (see Chapter 4, and note that you want it *padded* so it doesn't blow up on older devices). If you wish to do this, first spend a few days studying a variety of eBooks that include glyphs to get a feel for the visual design. (Don't copy a design that you see. Rather, try to find inspiration for your own unique design.) A glyph adds value when it looks right, but subtracts value when it looks wrong. The design needs to not only look good, it needs to match the content of your book.

If you use a glyph at the top of the first page of the chapter, then you need a special centered paragraph style for the glyph which incorporates a page break and Spacing Before (if desired), and you don't want a page break or Spacing Before (but if you want space between the glyph and

---

[33] Note that one or more Kindle devices or apps (especially older devices) may ignore the Spacing Before feature in Word when it is applied immediately after a page break. Using the Enter key to drop down a few lines from the beginning of a chapter may also be ignored—in fact, using blank lines is a less reliable and predictable way of adding vertical space. The most reliable way to add space before a heading (or paragraph) following a page break is to create an ePub file (Sec. 5.12). The ePub file format can divide your book up in such a way that Kindle devices and apps will respect the Spacing Before option at the beginning of a chapter. If instead you upload a DOC, DOCX, or HTML file (even a zipped file), it may not work across all devices and apps (especially older devices for which there isn't a proper preview).

heading, add Spacing After to the glyph's paragraph style) included with your Heading 1 style (contrary to the recommendation in Sec. 3.4). If instead the heading text comes first with the glyph below it, then you can incorporate the page break and Spacing Before in the Heading 1 style as recommended in Sec. 3.4 (and just use a centered paragraph style, such as the CenterSpaceAfter style recommended in Sec. 3.4, for the glyph).

Note that the **Look Inside** *doesn't* respect **page breaks**: The Look Inside shows the sample (usually about 10%) of your eBook top down (similar to a scrolling webpage), rather than in pages. The Spacing After feature can help to give separation between headings and text (do this to a paragraph or heading style, not to highlighted text). For example, if you apply the BodySpaceAfter paragraph style recommended in Sec. 3.4 to the last paragraph of each chapter (if the last paragraph has body text), this adds space between the last paragraph of the prior chapter and the heading of the new chapter. (As always, *don't* use the Enter key to create blank lines—the Look Inside may just ignore that.) Another way to create added separation between chapters in your Look Inside is to place your chapter number and heading text on separate lines (which requires applying a different style to the chapter number and heading text, similar to what we just described regarding glyphs).

There are different ways to separate the chapter number and chapter heading text. You might write Chapter 1 or Chapter One on the top line, with the title of the chapter on the next line. Another option is to type something like ~1~ on the top line (without the word 'Chapter'), using a large font size in the paragraph style for this heading. But don't go overboard with fancy symbols around the number and a fancy glyph above. When things look too busy, it can be a visual detractor.

If you effectively have multiple heading lines (like using a **glyph** in addition to heading text, or like separating the **chapter number** and chapter title across two lines), you want to **use Heading 1 for *one* of these lines *only***, and use another style *without* the word "Heading" in the name of the paragraph style for the other line. This is because Heading 1 (and Heading 2, etc.) are automatically used for device navigation: You don't want to double up on the headings by using Heading styles for both lines at the beginning of each chapter. You might want Chapter One, Chapter Two, etc. to show in device navigation, but not the chapter titles,[34] for example. In this case, use the Heading 1 style for Chapter One, and use another paragraph style (without the word "Heading" in the name) for the chapter titles. Similarly, *don't* use a Heading style for a **glyph**.

---

[34] On the other hand, if you do this, you may want both chapter numbers and headings to show up in your table of contents. If so, you may need to doctor your table of contents a bit. When you use Heading styles, these headings automatically show up in an active table of contents created in Word, but they also show up in device navigation. Give some consideration to what you do and what you don't want to show up in your table of contents and device navigation. We'll discuss how to create an active table of contents in Sec. 3.8.

The *most important design principle* may be **consistency**. Whatever design choices you find yourself making, pay attention to them: When you come to the same decision again later in your book, try to make the same choice again. Keep a list handy, if needed.

A relatively common inconsistency occurs with chapter numbers. For example, an eBook may start out with Chapter One, Chapter Two, Chapter Three, and suddenly switch to Chapter 4, Chapter 5, etc. Alternatively, the chapter numbering may suddenly switch to Roman numerals, like Chapter VI. I've also seen it change from Chapter 5, Chapter 6, Chapter 7… to 8, 9, 10… (where the word "Chapter" is no longer used). Authors often do this sort of thing without even realizing it. It's easy to do, especially when you don't see all the chapter headings next to one another, combined with the fact that you may spend a week or more writing one chapter (meaning more time has passed since you typed the previous chapter heading, making it easier to forget what you did last time). Try to be consistent with your chapter headings (and all of your other design choices).

> **Tip**: When you preview your eBook, spend a few minutes checking the chapter headings one at a time for consistency. If you check them all one after another, you are more likely to catch any irregularities.

Another place where I often see inconsistency has to do with indents, alignment, or vertical spacing. Some of these mistakes occur from not applying paragraph styles, or from using the tab key to create indents or the Enter key to create blank lines. Sometimes it's because the author didn't consistently make the same design choice in similar situations.

There are different ways of creating **breaks** between *scenes, points of view,* or *sections.* In non-fiction, it's pretty straightforward: Section breaks are usually introduced with subheadings (like Chapter 3, or Section 2); the section heading or subheading clearly indicates where a new section begins.

* * *

Section headings aren't used in fiction, though: When writing fiction, there are **scene breaks** versus **section breaks**. The difference is that a section break either includes a change in point of view or indicates a complete scene break, whereas a scene break indicates a passage of time or a change of location that continues the same scene. (Section breaks can sometimes involve changes in other things, like mood or tone.)

§

In a print book, scene breaks (in fiction) are traditionally indicated by leaving a blank line between paragraphs, whereas section breaks are traditionally indicated by leaving a line of asterisks (such as * * *) or other symbols (like the section break symbol above). Alternatively, you could use a **glyph** if highly relevant to your book. The most predictable way to format a glyph is when the glyph happens to be one of the supported symbols from Appendix A (as in the example above).

If you use an image as a glyph (see Chapter 4), you want it to be very short (vertically), taking up the equivalent of only one or two lines of text (and the image should include padding, as described in Chapter 4). Note that the impact of a glyph will backfire if it doesn't come out quite right on at least one device or app. The following glyph was formatted as a padded image.

The ideal way to create a **blank line** for a **scene break** in an eBook is to apply a paragraph style that includes Spacing After (such as the BodySpaceAfter style recommended in Sec. 3.4) to the paragraph preceding the scene break. In general, it's best to avoid using the Enter key to create blank lines in eBooks. Adding space to the preceding paragraph achieves the same effect in a more reliable way.

However, something strange can happen when using a **blank line** for a **scene break**, and there is no way to prevent this. If the scene break happens to fall at the very top or very bottom of the screen, readers aren't likely to notice the scene break at all (as shown in the following picture). In print, there are ways to avoid this through typography tricks, but this doesn't work for eBooks, partly because you can't predict when it will happen.

You must make a tough choice: You could use section breaks for *all* of your breaks (including scene breaks), for example, since asterisks will be noticed no matter where the break falls. However, then you run the risk of knowledgeable readers believing that you don't know the difference between **scene breaks** and **section breaks**. If you use different symbols for each kind of break, that might be interpreted as design inconsistency and be viewed as a mistake. The latest trends may also be different from one genre to another. I recommend doing two things. First, read a variety of eBooks in your subgenre that would serve as good models for design. Second, interact with fellow authors in your subgenre and ask them how they handle this challenge (but bear in mind that some authors might not even be aware of this issue).

Another important type of break to consider is the **page break**. Every page break does more than force the text to appear on a new screen: It creates a lot of potential wasted space. Since screen sizes vary and customers can adjust the font, line spacing, and margins, the screen before a forced page break will sometimes have very little text on it—occasionally, it may even be just one little word. The more page breaks you include, the more often readers will come across a page with much wasted space.

That doesn't mean you should avoid page breaks all together. If you don't use page breaks, headings and subheadings can wind up at the very bottom of the screen, separated from the text that follows. It's generally worth including a page break with a heading (such as the Heading 1 style) to prevent it from getting left behind at the bottom of the previous screen. In that case,

At first, this section break seems to be fine.

it needed a cover. He wasn't an artist or a photography. This wasn't going to be easy. As a businessman though, he understood the need to make a good first impression. He wouldn't show up to an interview without a tie, a pressed suit, and a clean shave. So he would get a book cover that could make the right impression. Fortunately, he was able to hire an inexpensive designer to put together a nice cover.

Wait. The writing wasn't complete. The book needed a description. At first, it seemed to be such a small thing. After all, he'd already written 50,000 words. What's a few hundred more?

Yet the more he tried to write a description, the harder this task seemed to be. Why was it so easy to write a story, but so hard to describe it? He knew it shouldn't be a summary: If you already knew what

At a different customer setting, the section break "vanishes" at the top of a screen.

work didn't end there. It was followed with formatting. He learned a great deal about the layout of a novel in his effort to master formatting. He would never look at a book the same way again. It wasn't easy, but he finally made the novel look as beautiful as he reasonably could.

The book was complete, but now it needed a cover. He wasn't an artist or a photography. This wasn't going to be easy. As a businessman though, he understood the need to make a good first impression. He wouldn't show up to an interview without a tie, a pressed suit, and a clean shave. So he would get a book cover that could make the right impression. Fortunately, he was able to hire an inexpensive designer to put together a nice cover.

Wait. The writing wasn't complete. The book needed a description. At first, it seemed to be such a small thing. After all, he'd already written 50,000 words. What's a few hundred more?

Yet the more he tried to write a description, the harder this task seemed to be. Why was it so easy to write a story, but so hard to describe it? He knew it shouldn't be a summary: If you already knew what happened, you wouldn't want to read the story. It needed a few hints regarding what the story was about: enough to know what type of story to expect, but not enough information to spoil it. The description also needed something to entice and interest the reader: a little suspense,

Asterisks would be visible wherever the break occurs.

* * *

Wait. The writing wasn't complete. The book needed a description. At first, it seemed to be such a small thing. After all, he'd already written 50,000 words. What's a few hundred more?

Yet the more he tried to write a description, the harder this task seemed to be. Why was it so easy to write a story, but so hard to describe it? He knew it shouldn't be a summary: If you already knew what happened, you wouldn't want to read the story. It needed a few hints regarding what the story was about: enough to know what type of story to expect, but not enough information to spoil it. The description also needed something to entice and interest the reader: a little suspense, incorporate the page break into the paragraph style for the heading (as shown in the recommendation for the Heading 1 style in Sec. 3.4, but you can also do this with other heading or subheading styles, as desired).

Chapter headings and all major sections of a book should begin on a new page (by incorporating the page break into the paragraph style). Whether or not to also do this for subheadings (more relevant to nonfiction) depends on the situation. If the first subheading appears shortly after the chapter heading, you definitely don't want a new page break with the first subheading (in which case you need a different paragraph style for the first subheading than for the others—though this gets complicated if you wish for all of these subheading styles to be included with device navigation). If many of the sections are very short, so that on a large screen most of the space is liable to be wasted, I wouldn't force each subheading onto a new page; but if the sections are long enough that even on a large screen with a small font most sections span at least a couple of pages, it's probably worth including the page break.

Pay attention to subtle differences between similar paragraph styles. For example, a typical book uses a few different body text styles, such as: a Normal style for indented paragraphs without adding space, a BodySpaceAfter style for indented paragraphs that need space afterward, and a NoIndent style for non-indented paragraphs that don't add space. Most of the body text should apply the Normal style. The first paragraph of a chapter should use NoIndent, as would body text paragraphs following images or section breaks, for example. BodySpaceAfter would be used for the last paragraph of a chapter (if appropriate to indent it), or for indented paragraphs preceding an image or section break, for example.

Similarly, there may be two kinds of centered styles (aside from heading styles), since sometimes you want to add space after the style (such as for images), but sometimes you don't (like when you use asterisks for a section break). For example, compare the Center and CenterSpaceAfter styles recommended in Sec. 3.4.

Some Kindle design issues are *subtle*. For example, sometimes one little character can make a noticeable difference. One character that can come in handy is actually invisible! It's called the **non-breaking space**. In Word, find this with Insert > Symbol > character code 160. You won't be able to 'see' it because it's just a space. However, if you press the Show/Hide button (¶) on the Paragraph group on the Home ribbon, you can tell the difference between a regular space and a non-breaking space. After revealing the codes, a regular space looks like a middle dot (·), while the non-breaking space looks like a degree sign (°). There is an alternative way to insert non-breaking spaces, which is described in Sec. 5.6.

The non-breaking space is different from the space created using a spacebar: It can join two short words together so that they always appear together on the same line. For example, suppose that the short sentence, "I do," comes at the end of a paragraph. Depending on the screen size, font size, and margins (which the customer can adjust), it's possible for the word "do" to appear on the last line all by itself (typographers call this a runt[35]—a short word all by itself on the last line of a paragraph).

However, you can prevent this from happening if you insert a non-breaking space between the "I" and the "do." This way, if the "do" must go onto the next line (because there isn't enough room for it on the previous line), the "I" will move onto the next line with it. The non-breaking space effectively joins two short words so that they always appear together on the same line.

Another place where you might use a non-breaking space instead of a regular space is with numbers and units, such as 6 ft. Here, the non-breaking space prevents the possibility of the "6" ending one line while the "ft." begins the next.

You must be careful with the non-breaking space, or it can do more harm than good, especially in justified text (or left aligned text that will automatically justify later—unless you take the additional steps needed to force it to remain left aligned). In justified text, when two words connected with a non-breaking space are forced onto the next line, it exaggerates the gaps between words that appear in justified text (or in the worst case, it creates a shorter line—Kindle's justification does this when the gaps would be exceedingly long).

Connecting two very short words isn't a problem, even with justified text. However, with justified text, as the length of the combined words grows longer and longer, this increases your chances of very pronounced problems with gaps in justified text. Reserve the non-breaking space for very special cases, such as a number and units that belong together.

You can be somewhat more liberal with left aligned text (but only if you plan to follow the instructions in Sec. 5.4 in order to prevent it from automatically justifying). With left alignment (ragged right), you don't have to worry about gaps between words, but it still has some effect: Instead, it can make one line in the paragraph much shorter than the rest. Try not to overuse the non-breaking space regardless of whether your paragraphs are justified or ragged right.

If a paragraph ends with a short word (4 letters or less), you can use a non-breaking space to prevent a possible **runt** (a short word appearing by itself on the last line of the paragraph), but only do this if the second-to-last word is also short. For example, if a paragraph ends with the words "the day," it may be worth including a non-breaking space between "the" and "day." As a counterexample, if a paragraph ends with the words "breathe air," I wouldn't include a non-breaking space because that would string together 11 characters (plus, "breathe" has no chance of being hyphenated). If you have a possible runt that occurs immediately before a page break (in this case, it's really called a **widow**), you might be a little more liberal with a non-breaking space.

---

[35] Some call it an orphan, though orphan also has another slightly different meaning, similar to a widow, in typography. Widows and orphans refer to one line of a paragraph appearing on a page all by itself. You can prevent that in print books, but there is nothing you can do about them in eBooks (but a non-breaking space can prevent a runt).

As an example of how the non-breaking space may do more harm than good, imagine using a non-breaking space to connect the words "screamed, too." Whereas using a non-breaking space to join "I do" or "6 ft." makes a string of text that consists of 4 characters, using a non-breaking space to join the words "screamed, too" makes a string of text consisting of 13 characters (the comma and space are characters). This can result in excessive gaps in justified text. When the string of text consists of 6 characters (or less), it's fairly manageable. As the string gets longer, the problem becomes more pronounced (and could lead to undesirable hyphenation).

Never Join 3 Words Together with Non-breaking Spaces

An important place to look for possible runts is with **headings** and **subheadings**. If you have a title, subtitle, chapter heading, or subheading that ends with a short word, that word could potentially wind up on the last line of the heading all by itself. Since a customer may read your book on a cell phone, even if the heading seems relatively short, this happens more than you might realize. Since heading styles should either be centered or left aligned (but recall that if you upload a Word file, left alignment may become automatically justified), you don't need to worry about justification issues; use a non-breaking space to prevent a short word at the end of a heading from winding up on a line all by itself.

In print, typographers would also take steps to minimize *widows* and *orphans*, but there really isn't anything you can do about them in Kindle. (Widow and orphan control settings in Word, for example, don't have any effect on Kindle devices and apps.) If you try to prevent widows and orphans from showing up in your Kindle eBook, it will probably do more harm than good. Mainly, this is because you can't predict where widows and orphans will occur in an eBook.

The non-breaking space can also come in handy for creating an **ellipsis**. We already discussed the design challenges associated with the ellipsis (…) back in Sec. 2.7. Beware that non-breaking spaces don't always have the same effect with all punctuation marks as they do with letters and numbers.

There is another special character similar to the non-breaking space called a **non-breaking hyphen**. *Don't* use Word's non-breaking hyphen, optional hyphen, or soft hyphen. (You can use the regular hyphen that you see on your keyboard between the 0 and = sign; it's the special hyphens that pose a problem.)

There is a 'trick' to achieving the effect of a **non-breaking hyphen** using Word, although it may backfire on older Kindle devices (forcing breaks where you don't want them). However, it may be better to prevent broken hyphens connecting short words on new devices and on apps than it is to prevent undesirable breaks on older Kindle devices (unless you use it excessively). Type a regular hyphen, highlight just the hyphen (not the words it joins), and place the hyphen in *italics*. This effectively does what you would want a non-breaking hyphen to do in a way that is compatible with Kindle eBooks. (However, if the hyphen joins italicized words, then highlight the hyphen and ensure that the hyphen *isn't* in italics.)

Like the non-breaking space, you want to be careful not to join long words (or several short words with multiple hyphens) together with non-breaking hyphens (don't use an actual non-breaking hyphen—use the trick described in the previous paragraph instead), else it can cause issues with line breaks. The issue is more pronounced with justified text, where you should only use it to join two very short words.

Another special character similar to these is the **zero-width non-joiner**. In Word, use Insert > Symbol > More Symbols, click the Special Characters tab, and select No-Width Optional Break (be careful not to select No-Width Non-Break). There is alternative way to insert a zero-width non-joiner described in Sec. 5.6.

The zero-width non-joiner (in Word, you get this with the no-width optional break) is used to identify preferred breaks in URL's or very long strings. The problem with URL's and long strings is that they won't be hyphenated (or with the new hyphenation feature that Kindle has recently added, URL's and long strings may hyphenate in undesired locations). The zero-width non-joiner can be inserted in the URL or long string so that if the URL or string doesn't fit on one line, it will break in the desired position instead of some random location.

The zero-width non-joiner isn't foolproof, i.e. it may not work properly on some devices or apps. However, when it works, it aids your design; when it doesn't, there was going to be a problem anyway. One noteworthy problem occurs when the URL appears in justified text, as older devices may add a gap there as part of the justification. However, if you simply put the URL on a centered paragraph all by itself (using a centered style, of course), you won't have to worry about this. Another significant problem occurs when the zero-width non-joiner is inserted at a point where formatting changes: This can cause chaos, so be careful that the text formatting doesn't change (from italics to non-italics) where you intend to insert a zero-width non-joiner.

For those who will follow Chapter 5, the better way to insert non-breaking spaces and zero-width non-joiners is shown in Sec. 5.6 (there is also a better trick shown in Sec. 5.6 that you can substitute in place of a non-breaking hyphen). Beware that most other special characters similar to these three **aren't** supported across all devices and apps. Therefore, I recommend *not* using other special characters that seem similar to the non-breaking space and zero-width non-joiner.

There is another symbol that looks kind of like a hyphen, but is longer: the **dash**. There are two different dashes: the shorter en dash (–) and the longer em dash (—). Compare with the much shorter hyphen (-). Recall that we discussed hyphens and dashes in Sec. 2.7. The best way to insert these symbols is to use Insert > Symbol as described in Chapter 2 (though you should always preview carefully before publishing—see Chapter 7).

Punctuate your book consistently: Don't switch between em and en dashes. Choose one and go with that. Another place to punctuate consistently is with single quotes (' and ') and double quotes (" and "). See how they tend to be used in your subcategory. (Every author should have a handy style guide, but every author should also do a little research to see which conventions are popular among similar books.)

One issue to consider is where a dash will break if the text after the dash is forced onto the next line. With the en dash, you could use a non-breaking space before it to prevent it from beginning a line. The em dash used to have formatting issues with Kindle, but appears to work better across most devices and apps now (however, you should test this when you preview your book). Recall that non-breaking spaces don't always have the same effect with all punctuation marks as they do with letters and numbers.

Which dash is 'best' for your book depends on which kind of book you are publishing. In some genres or subjects, the en dash is much more common, while in others the em dash is more popular. The way to settle the matter is to search for several books very similar to yours, which your intended target audience is likely to be familiar with, and see which kind of dash they will be familiar with. That way your book won't stand out in the wrong way. Whichever dash you opt for, be sure to be consistent throughout your book: Don't mix and match.

Borders and **shading** *don't* work across all devices, so it's generally better to find an alternative. It might be tempting to use a border to set a paragraph off from the main text, kind of a like a sidebar or textbox in print. However, on devices where this doesn't work, the paragraph will just blend into the text, rather than standing apart.

In principle, you could insert a single horizontal line before and after the paragraph, though it doesn't work unless you do it just right (click on the Borders icon on the Paragraph group of the Home ribbon and choose Horizontal Line—don't insert a border) or unless you insert a horizontal line as mentioned in Sec. 5.7 (which is more reliable).

Even if you do it right, using horizontal lines before and after a note still has a problem. For one, one of the lines could wind up on a page just before or just after the note. For another, if you have multiple notes, the reader can't tell whether a line comes before or after a note by simple visual inspection.

One alternative is to use a directional border instead (you can find an example of this in Sec. 4.7). You would need to insert this as two images (see Sec. 4.7): one before and the other after. You also need to design a directional border that looks appealing and fits your content well, and format the image so that it works well. Such an image should be very narrow, taking up very little room vertically (so that it's almost as narrow as a plain horizontal line). It also needs to look good on a narrow device as well as a large screen.

There are few important aspects of Kindle design that we haven't considered in this section: We'll address front and back matter in Sec. 3.9, equations in Sec. 3.11, tables in Sec. 3.12, and designing with pictures in Sec. 4.7.

3.8 Table of Contents

Following are two terms with similar, yet different, meanings:

- An **active table of contents** is an actual section of the eBook, where each entry has a clickable hyperlink. The customer can visit the table of contents as a 'page' in your eBook, and can click any entry of the table of contents to quickly jump to any chapter or section included in the table of contents.
- Device **navigation** doesn't appear as a 'page' in the eBook itself, but is accessed via a menu on the customer's Kindle device or app. Like the table of contents, device navigation includes chapters and sections: A customer can click any entry of device navigation to quickly jump to that chapter or section.

As described in Sec.'s 3.4 and 3.7, use Heading 1 and Heading 2 styles for any chapter heading (or section heading) that you wish to be automatically included with device navigation. (Don't use

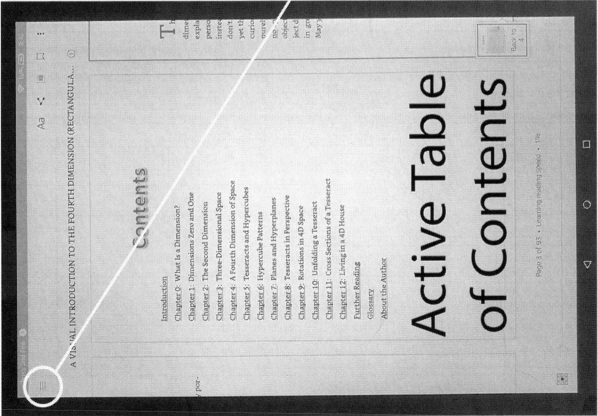

Heading styles for chapters or sections that you don't want included with device navigation. Use a different paragraph style for those, without the word 'Heading' in it—also don't name them h1, h2, etc.)

A table of contents, on the other hand, *isn't* automatically included. You must insert the table of contents into your eBook yourself. (Kindle now *requires* a table of contents in your eBook, so you really 'must.')

If you already have a table of contents that you typed, remove it completely. We will insert a new one. Follow these steps to create your active table of contents:

- Place your cursor in the position where you want your table of contents to appear. Type the heading for your Table of Contents, and place this heading on its own paragraph all by itself (using the Enter key). You might want to call it Table of Contents or just Contents, for example. (Don't use a paragraph style with the word 'Heading' in it for the table of contents heading: You don't want this heading to show up in your active table of contents. However, we will add a bookmark for it later so that it works in device navigation.)

- Use the Enter key to create a blank line below your Table of Contents heading. Place your cursor on this blank line.

- Go to the References ribbon and click on the Table of Contents icon that appears on the far left side. Near the bottom of the list, select Insert Table of Contents. (In newer versions of Word, it's called Custom Table of Contents.)

- Adjust the Show Levels option. For most books, one level is recommended. (The default is three, which is too many.) If you have both headings and subheadings, using Heading 1 and Heading 2 styles, and you want both levels to show in your table of contents, then you would use two levels instead of one (but you'll want to reformat the result using the paragraph styles, as discussed later this in section).

- The other default settings should be fine. The box to use hyperlinks instead of page numbers should already be checked. Formats should be set to "from template." The default Options should be fine.

- Don't make a fancy table of contents. Simpler generally works better.

- Uncheck the box for Show Page Numbers (since you don't want them in an eBook). Do this just before you press the OK button. **Note**: If you click the Modify or Options buttons, after you exit those menus, the Show Page Numbers box automatically gets rechecked. That's why you should wait until just before it's time to press the OK button to uncheck the Show Page Numbers box.

- Press the OK button. This inserts your active table of contents.

- Note that there may be a blank line at the end of your table of contents. We'll discuss this blank line later in this section.

In addition to inserting a table of contents (don't worry; we'll discuss the issue of *formatting* the table of contents shortly), you must also place a bookmark so that Kindle devices and apps can find your table of contents (to include its location in device navigation).

Follow these steps to bookmark the location of your table of contents:

- Highlight your table of contents heading that appears above your table of contents.
- Go to the Insert ribbon and click the Bookmark button.
- Select Bookmark.
- Type "toc" (but without the quotes) in the field for Bookmark name. This is how the Kindle device or app will find your table of contents to include with device navigation.
- Click the Add button.

Now it's time to format your table of contents. Use the styles menu for this. Don't highlight elements of your table of contents and apply formatting directly to what's highlighted; use the paragraph styles instead.

As mentioned earlier, don't use a paragraph style with the word 'Heading' in it for the table of contents heading. You need a similar paragraph style with a different name for this so this heading doesn't become part of your active table of contents. (It will already work in device navigation since we inserted a bookmark for it.) Even though you shouldn't use a paragraph style with the word 'Heading' in it for your table of contents heading, the paragraph style that you use should have similar settings as your other main heading styles so that the formatting appears consistent throughout your book.

The table of contents entries automatically have styles applied to them. There are actually *two* styles applied to each: The first is a paragraph style called TOC 1 (or TOC 2 for the first subheading), and the second is a character style called Hyperlink. You must position your cursor just right in order to see each style in action on the styles menu:

- Place your cursor at the very beginning of the line to see the paragraph style. When you do this, you should see the TOC 1 (or similar) style selected on the styles menu.
- Place your cursor at the end of the line (or within the text, but not at the beginning) to see the character style. When you do this, you should see the Hyperlink style selected on the styles menu.

Place your cursor at the beginning of a line, then modify the corresponding TOC style on the styles menu. Adjust the font settings of the TOC style (i.e. TOC 1 and/or TOC 2) to match the recommendation for the NoIndent paragraph style (but either choose left or centered alignment, noting that left may become automatically justified if you upload a Word document to KDP). Under the paragraph settings of the TOC style, adjust the Spacing After to 0 (Spacing Before should already be 0, and line spacing should already be single with 'at' left empty). If you choose left alignment, remember that you must set First Line Indent to 0.01" in order to achieve a non-indented paragraph (whereas if you choose centered alignment, you should set this to "none").

If you include subheadings in your table of contents, I recommend a non-indenting TOC 1 style and an indented TOC 2 style, using left alignment for both. This way, non-indented lines versus indented lines will make it easy to tell headings from subheadings.

Word's automatic table of contents usually includes a blank line at the end. This blank line can be very stubborn in Word: The line after it may change its paragraph style if you attempt to remove the blank line. Sec. 5.11 shows a way to go beyond Word and easily remove that blank line.

If you revise your book, adding or removing chapters or sections which affect your table of contents, simply place your cursor anywhere within your active table of content and click the Update Table button on the References ribbon (or press the F9 button on your keyboard to update all fields). This will automatically update your table of contents (provided that you used Heading styles for new sections). If you want to keep a section, but remove its heading from the table of contents, simply change the paragraph style for its heading from one with the word 'Heading' in it to one that doesn't (and then click Update Table). Note that you may need to first create a new paragraph style (not named heading) that is similar to the original heading style.

Tip: Consider naming your chapters, like "Chapter 7: Full Moon," instead of just "Chapter 7." For both fiction and nonfiction, this helps to create interest in your book when the table of contents appears in your Look Inside. For nonfiction, it also aids the customer in navigation on the device or app (because some customers like to skip around nonfiction books, rather than read them straight through).

3.9 Front and Back Matter

Books typically include a variety of front and back matter sections. You must decide which sections are appropriate for your book, and then decide which sections to place in the front and which to place in the back of your book.

The first 10% (or so) of an eBook shows up in the Look Inside at Amazon. For a typical full-length book, this ordinarily includes the front matter and first few chapters (longer books tend to have longer Look Insides). Choose your front matter wisely because potential customers will explore your book's Look Inside. Only include sections of front matter that are likely to help sell your book. Ideally, you want your first few chapters to hook the reader, and you want the reader to reach the first chapter as soon as possible. The less front matter you have, the sooner the customer reaches the first chapter.

Tip: Omit front matter (or move it to the back matter) that won't help your book sell. Design the front of your book—from the title thru the first few chapters—so that they will hook the reader.

For example, if you have a dedication or acknowledgments, do you really need to include them at the beginning of the book? These sections don't matter to most of the people who may discover your book and browse through the Look Inside. Therefore, many authors now place these sections in the back of their eBooks.

However, if you place table of contents in the back of your eBook, Amazon may have a problem with this. (Why? For one thing, customers reading older devices who can't access device navigation expect to find an active table of contents at the beginning of the eBook.) I recommend placing your active table of contents in the *front* matter, where Amazon and customers alike expect to find it. (If you're set upon placing your table of contents in your back matter, note that you're *not* allowed to include an internal link to your table of contents anywhere else in your eBook.) Regardless of where you place your active table of contents, note that you're *not* permitted to entice customers to navigate toward the back of your eBook.

If you name your chapters in a way that's informative (e.g. Chapter 9: Book Marketing) or that may create interest (e.g. Chapter 3: The Strange Prince), this may add a little marketing value to your front matter. For nonfiction, informative chapter names help readers see which topics your book covers. For fiction, if you can name your chapters in a way that helps create interest (without giving away the story), it may help to arouse curiosity.

Whatever front matter you decide to include, you want it to help sell your book. Two ways to do this are to generate interest (like my suggestion of informative or interest-arousing chapter names) and to signify professionalism. The first step toward creating a professional brand for your book is to avoid what are often perceived as common rookie mistakes. The second step is to include a couple of subtle, professional design touches.

The following are examples of what some experienced customers may perceive as rookie mistakes: varying indent sizes, ragged right body text,[36] inconsistencies in chapter headings, unsupported characters, unexpected changes in text size, text that appears (by default) much larger or smaller than customers have come to expect, images that don't look right, weird formatting, and strange statements in the front matter that appear out of place or unprofessional.

---

[36] This is not across the board. Many customers don't really care whether the body text is justified or ragged right, so *their* opinion isn't the one you should worry about (they'll buy the book either way). However, I do encounter readers who feel strongly *against* ragged right body text, whereas I seldom find such strong opinions against justified text. It appears that a ragged right Look Inside will deter more sales, which is a risk I don't want to take. (Popular authors can obviously get away with it either way.)

I'm not saying that these are all really 'rookie mistakes.' It's about customer perception. What will some customers think? It also depends on how many issues the customer sees: Just one issue is minor, but multiple issues raises a red flag. Also, this is just formatting that I've mentioned. The customer will hopefully also 'read' a selection of the Look Inside, where the spelling, grammar, punctuation, writing style, and ultimately the storyline and characterization can either help with sales or deter them. It's the whole picture that determines the outcome, but every little part—even the formatting, to some extent—factors into the big picture.

There is more to conveying a professional image for your book than avoiding the common mistakes. Wouldn't you love for the front of your book to provide a bit of a 'wow' factor, so that the customer is in a positive mindset right before starting the first chapter? That's what you want to strive for. You can accomplish this with a few little design touches. Research books similar to yours, especially the top sellers—both traditionally published and self-published. You can get some **good design ideas** this way, in addition to seeing which sections of front matter tend to be included in which order and how they tend to look.

Front matter begins with the title. Print books often include both a half title page and a separate title page. However, the Look Inside doesn't show 'pages,' so these would blend together, and in an eBook having separate half title and full title pages would add one more obstacle on the way to the beginning. If your design of a separate half title page and title page has strong visual appeal, then maybe it's worth having both.

Customers have experience shopping for books and exploring Look Insides, so it *does* matter how your Look Inside compares to what they are accustomed to seeing. Do some research. If a few hours of research today could add a couple of sales per month for the life of your book, would you do it? You don't know if it will, but it does take effort to produce a marketable book— from cover to finish—that will sell itself effectively. Many customers *do* notice when something doesn't seem right, and this *does* deter sales.

The title page is typically followed by the copyright page. A few authors move the copyright page to the back of the book. For one, the copyright notice itself probably isn't going to deter anyone who plans to violate the statements therein. If you have a bland copyright page, or you if don't really know what to put on it, that might be a reason to move it to the back. If you have a long copyright page in a very short book, you might move it to the back matter to increase your Look Inside.

However, the copyright page is also an opportunity. No customer is likely to study your copyright page, but they will see it on the way to Chapter 1 if you include it in the front matter. If, passing through it, the customer senses that it appears professional, it may help put the customer in a better mindset (compared to a customer who sees issues on the way to Chapter 1). The colophon (defined in the next paragraph), in particular, may include an emblem or publisher logo, and some authors are able to add such an image with a nice visual touch. Then the copyright page adds a little value to your book. The picture at the end of this section provides an example of how a colophon might look.

The **colophon** is a brief statement regarding the publication of the book, including the publisher's name, the date of publication, and the location of publication (though location is more relevant to traditional publishing than self-publishing). It may also include a logo. The copyright page may also include the copyright year(s), a copyright statement, edition dates, categories, keywords, and a legal statement for fictional works that the characters, places, and events are all fictitious. Check out the copyright pages of similar Kindle eBooks, both traditionally published and self-published (noting that a few things from traditionally published books may not apply to a self-published book). Don't plagiarize what you see: Instead, use it to as an idea base to help you design a professional looking copyright page.

> **Tip**: Check out the samples of copyright statements, fictional notes, colophons, and other front and back matter sections of similar books before you design yours.

Don't go overboard with front and back matter. Keep the road to the first chapter short: The beginning of your book should be its top selling point. Whatever front matter there is should look professional, maybe even add a little visual appeal (but not too strongly: subtle design elements that look like they belong can make a good impression). Focus on front matter sections that may help you sell your book.

Also, beware of the start reading location. When a customer opens a Kindle eBook, it doesn't begin at the front cover nor the title page: It begins at the start reading location (SRL). The SRL is automatically set by Amazon after you publish, and may not begin where you expect. If the SRL points to the first page of the story, then many customers will automatically skip the front matter. Unfortunately, you don't have control over this.[37]

Nonetheless, the front matter is still very important because Amazon's Look Inside *won't* skip your front matter. Customers who are shopping on Amazon who check out the Look Inside will see your front cover, the front matter, and then the first chapter as they scroll down. These are the customers for whom your front matter can make a difference. The SRL impacts the actual reader who has downloaded your eBook (or at least the free sample), while the Look Inside is a valuable selling tool for the customer who is just checking out your book.

Build interest with Look Inside, but be careful not to give away the story. Arguably, the most important part of the Look Inside is how the book starts in the first chapter. Beware that

---

[37] If you happen to know how to specify the SRL using HTML, note that Amazon may override your preference and set the SRL to a different location.

customers just checking your book out aren't committed to reading the *whole* story. You want to start out with your best stuff, material that will quickly draw the reader into the story and make the reader want more.

Don't include the cover with your front matter. You upload separate files for the cover and the eBook, and Amazon automatically adds your cover to your eBook. So if you include the cover at the beginning of your book, you will wind up with a double cover—a mistake.

Other sections of front matter may include a foreword, dedication, acknowledgments, introduction, prologue, or preface. Only choose what you really need, and if it won't likely help you sell your book, consider moving it to the back of your eBook.

Typical back matter sections may include an epilogue, afterword, about the author section, sample chapter of another book, appendix, glossary, or bibliography (in addition to any front matter sections that may be moved to the back for an eBook). Choose wisely: Most books don't need many sections of back matter.

An about the author section can be a **marketing tool**, helping to direct customers to your blog, email newsletter, or social media feeds. What will the customer find in your newsletter or at your website to make it worthwhile to follow you? Give this some thought (and check out what top selling indie authors do). Customers need a reason to follow you, and you want them to follow you to help build traffic for your next book. Maybe readers can find special features or additional material involving beloved characters from your book. For example, for a fantasy novel, you could offer a map for readers to print out and have handy while reading. There is something you can offer to entice readers to follow you. You just need to give some thought to what that is.

Novelists should include a sample first chapter of another book. Series authors include the first chapter of the next book in the series. Again you can see the importance of writing the first chapter of your book in such a way that it really grabs the reader's interest and hooks the reader. The first chapter can be a valuable sales tool (but it will only work long-term if the rest of the book delivers on the promise that the first chapter makes).

As discussed in Sec. 2.5, an index really isn't needed for an eBook. For one, page numbers are meaningless, so you would use hyperlinks (Sec. 3.10) instead of page numbers. Most eBooks *don't* include an index—even when the print edition has an index—for one simple reason: Kindle devices and apps come with a search tool. Customers can type any word or phrase they wish into the search field and quickly find every instance in your eBook. Therefore, you really don't need to create your own index for the eBook. In addition, after you publish you can add a feature to your Kindle eBook called X-ray (Sec. 8.14), which functions sort of like a handy glossary.

Word to Kindle Formatting Magic

Chris McMullen

Word to Kindle Formatting Magic
Self-Publishing on Amazon with Style

Copyright © 2018 Chris McMullen
chrismcmullen.com

Cover design by Melissa Stevens
www.theillustratedauthor.net

Zishka Publishing
ISBN: 978-1-941691-22-9
Version 3.04.18A

3.10 Hyperlinks

There are three kinds of hyperlinks that you might want to include in your eBook:

- An *external* hyperlink takes the reader out of the eBook when it is clicked on, displaying a webpage URL in a web browser (on devices with this capability, such as Fire tablets, laptops, PC's, Macs, cell phones, or iPads).
- An *internal* hyperlink takes the reader to a different location within the eBook when it is clicked on.
- An email hyperlink opens the reader's default email, initiating a new message with the recipient's email address already filled in.

Create an **external hyperlink** by clicking Hyperlink on the Insert ribbon. On the left column of the pop-up window, select Existing File or Webpage. At the top, in the Text to Display field, type how you want the text to appear (I will provide two examples). (Alternatively, you can first type the text you want to display directly in your Word file and then highlight that text, in which case it will automatically appear in the Text to Display field.) At the bottom, in the Address field, type the URL for the webpage beginning with the http:// part.

Better yet, before you insert the external hyperlink, open your web browser, pull up the webpage, place your cursor in the browser bar, highlight the website URL, and copy it (with Ctrl + c). Although the website URL in the browser bar usually begins with www, when you copy and paste, it will automatically include the http:// part (or https, if applicable). Now paste (with Ctrl + v) the website URL into the Address field when you follow the instructions (in the previous paragraph) for inserting an external hyperlink.

After creating the external hyperlink in Word, hover your cursor over the hyperlink, then hold the Ctrl button and click on the hyperlink. This will open the webpage in your default browser so that you can check that the hyperlink works as expected.

Tip: Visit the actual webpage and copy/paste the URL into the Address field in Word. After inserting the external hyperlink in Word, hold Ctrl and click on the hyperlink to verify that it works.

Here are two examples of external hyperlinks. In my first example, the displayed text is the same as the website URL. When I created the following external hyperlink (for my blog, which includes numerous free self-publishing tips), I pasted the website URL in both the Address field and the Text to Display field—although I deleted the unnecessary slash (/) that automatically appeared after the .com (it had been .com/ instead) from the Text to Display field:

http://chrismcmullen.com

In my second example, the displayed text is different from the website URL. This time, I pasted the website URL in the Address field, but typed "Chris McMullen's blog" (without the quotes) in the Text to Display field.[38] Both examples will take you to my blog (if you're reading the Kindle version of this book), but the displayed text appears different in the two examples.

<u>Chris McMullen's blog</u>

For external hyperlinks, be sure to include the http:// part in the Address field. If you don't include the http:// part, the external hyperlink won't work correctly. You don't necessarily need to include the http:// in the Text to Display field. Compare <u>http://www.amazon.com</u> with <u>www.amazon.com</u>. Both include http:// in the Address field, but only the former includes it in the Text to Display field. A third link to the same website is <u>Amazon</u>, which has "Amazon"—but without the quotes—in the Text to Display field. (All three links work in the Kindle edition.)

Internal hyperlinks require an additional step: Before inserting an internal hyperlink, you must first bookmark the location in your Word file (except for headings created with the heading styles—Heading 1, Heading 2, etc.—which are automatically bookmarked).

Use Insert > Bookmark to create a new bookmark, and Insert > Hyperlink to create an internal hyperlink to an existing bookmark. In the pop-up window, click Place in This Document on the left column, select an existing bookmark, and enter the text that you wish to show in the Text to Display field at the top. (Alternatively, first type the text directly in your Word file and then highlight that text, and it will automatically appear in the Text to Display field.)

When creating a new bookmark, highlight the text that you want to appear at the top of the screen when the reader visits that bookmark, and then click Bookmark on the Insert ribbon. Name the bookmark in a way that will help you remember which bookmark is which. Don't include any space in the name. For example, use Section3 instead of Section 3.

Here is an example of an internal bookmark. When you click on the following bookmark, it will take you to the beginning of this section (if you're reading the Kindle edition of this book). Note that there is space in the displayed text (Visit Section 3.10), which is different from including space in the name of a bookmark. Displayed text can include space and punctuation marks, but the name of a bookmark should only include numbers and letters (with no spaces).

<u>Visit Section 3.10</u>

---

[38] Actually, I cheated to create the curly apostrophe: Examine the apostrophe closely. If I had typed "Chris McMullen's blog" in the Text to Display field, it would look like "Chris McMullen's blog" (with a straight apostrophe) instead because the pop-up window doesn't automatically create curly apostrophes. So what I really did was type the text first in Word, highlight the text, and then when I inserted the hyperlink, the displayed text already had a curly apostrophe in it.

Internal hyperlinks are handy when you want to write things like "see Chapter 4" or "as shown in Figure 8." In each case, you can add an internal hyperlink to the text in order to help the reader visit that point in your eBook directly.

Although hyperlinks come in handy in a variety of ways (for example, they can provide direct links to references, or they can help a reader navigate through a nonfiction book), there are also a couple of potential drawbacks to consider:

- Any time a reader clicks on an external hyperlink, the reader has left your eBook. Would you rather have the reader finish your book or visit an external website? Use external hyperlinks where they are useful, but try not to overdo it.
- When many hyperlinks appear on a screen, it becomes a sort of minefield: One accidental mis-click and the reader is directed off the page. So be careful not to insert too many hyperlinks in a small area.

External hyperlinks aren't an issue at the *end* of your eBook, since the reader must first finish your book to reach that point. Therefore, two good places to include external hyperlinks include an About the Author section and a References section.

The About the Author section might, in addition to briefly describing the author in some way, include links to the author's blog, website, Twitter handle, Facebook author page, Amazon author page, other forms of social media, email address, instructions on how to sign up for an email newsletter,[39] or information about how to follow you directly at Amazon.[40] In addition to listing ways that fans can follow you online, provide a compelling reason to follow you. What will they learn or discover that will make it worth the effort?

While you may include links to external websites and to your own blog or social media pages, don't include hyperlinks that direct readers to advertisements or that direct readers to marketing pages for your affiliates. (The latter won't apply to most authors. What Amazon doesn't want is for authors to publish an eBook that largely serves as an advertisement for something else. Amazon doesn't mind authors providing links for readers to follow them online.)

For email hyperlinks, choose E-mail Address and begin with mailto: in the E-mail address field, as in mailto:chrism@chrismcmullen.com.

---

[39] An email newsletter is a good way to build a list of fans so you can notify them of your next book. MailChimp is popular for this. Note that each email is required to include instructions for how to opt out of receiving future emails.

[40] There is a large yellow Follow button on each author's Amazon author page. Once an author signs up for an Amazon author page via Author Central (see Sec. 8.2 for more info), customers can follow the author at Amazon instead of having to follow the author externally (through social media or the author's personal email newsletter). This way, the customer is only notified if and when the author releases a new book, and the message comes from Amazon. Unfortunately, Amazon currently doesn't tell authors how many followers there are. **Tip**: Follow yourself so you can see what the experience is like from the customer's end.

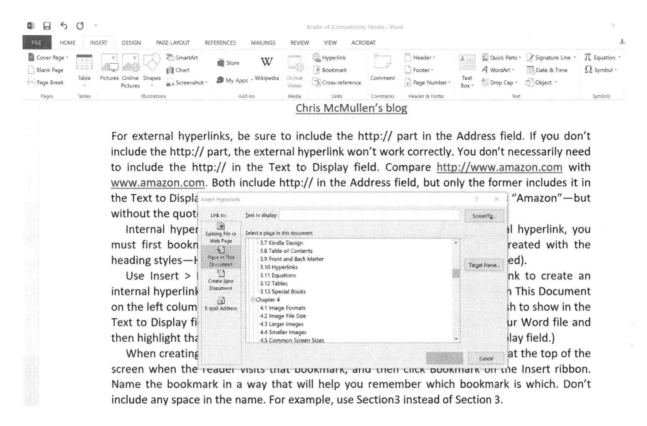

Chris McMullen's blog

For external hyperlinks, be sure to include the http:// part in the Address field. If you don't include the http:// part, the external hyperlink won't work correctly. You don't necessarily need to include the http:// in the Text to Display field. Compare http://www.amazon.com with www.amazon.com. Both include http:// in the Address field, but only the former includes it in the Text to Displa[y] ... "Amazon"—but without the quot[es] ...

Internal hyper[links] ... [interna]l hyperlink, you must first bookm[ark] ... [c]reated with the heading styles—[H] ... [d].

Use Insert > [...] ... [li]nk to create an internal hyperlink [...] [i]n This Document on the left colum[n] ... [wi]sh to show in the Text to Display fi[eld] ... [yo]ur Word file and then highlight tha[t] ... [disp]lay field.)

When creating [...] ... at the top of the screen when the reader visits that bookmark, and then click Bookmark on the Insert ribbon. Name the bookmark in a way that will help you remember which bookmark is which. Don't include any space in the name. For example, use Section3 instead of Section 3.

Test out your hyperlinks when you preview your eBook (Chapter 7) in order to ensure that they work properly.

3.11 Equations

Unfortunately, Microsoft Word's built-in equation tools do **not** convert well to Kindle. There are problems with *both* the new Insert > Equation feature in Word 2007 and up, *and* with the old Insert > Object > Microsoft Equation 3.0 feature that is a carryover from earlier versions of Word. It doesn't matter whether you save the file in the newer DOCX nor the older DOC format: Either way, there are a variety of problems with Word's built-in equation tools:

- The biggest issue is that equations created this way, in general, won't be clearly readable across all devices. For this reason alone, you need an alternative (we'll discuss other options shortly).

- While equations created this way look nice and crisp on your monitor when using Word, they become low-quality images in the conversion to Kindle. The result is that the equations may be blurred beyond recognition on one or more devices. Even though they may look okay when previewed on some devices, they will be unreadable on others.

- Another problem is that the equations don't resize with the text. When the customer changes the font size for the Kindle device or app, it has no effect on equations. Depending on the settings, some customers will see tiny equations compared to the text, while others will see huge equations compared to the text. You can't make them match for every customer.

I've published several math and science books with equations. I've experimented with the old and new equation editors, trying to get them to work reasonably with Kindle, but to no avail. It would be convenient if it worked, but it doesn't work across all devices. However, there are two methods of making equations that do work well:

- Some equations, such as $A^2 + B^2 = C^2$, can be typed as plain text, using only subscripts, superscripts, italics, boldface, and supported symbols (from Appendix A). When it works, this is the **best method**: The equation will automatically display at the same size as the text, which will make it just as readable as ordinary text. Such equations can be typed mid-paragraph without any issues. Unfortunately, many equations *can't* be typed this way.

- When an equation uses potentially unsupported symbols or requires more sophisticated formatting than you can achieve using simple subscripts and superscripts, then you have no choice but to create the equation as a picture. We'll discuss the details involved with this method in Sec. 4.9. You can see an example of this below.

$$C = \sqrt{A^2 + B^2}$$

When typing an equation directly as text, the danger is using potentially unsupported symbols. If you use a symbol that a particular Kindle device or app turns out not to support, it displays as a boxed question mark or as strange characters (see the example below). You don't want to take this risk as it will make your equation completely unreadable on Kindle devices or apps where the symbol is unsupported.

There are very many devices and apps. You can test some of the newer ones with the previewer (Chapter 7), but it's not as easy to test the older devices where the problem is *more* likely to occur. Therefore, I recommend sticking to the supported symbols mentioned in Appendix A (using the method described in Sec. 2.6). When you need a different symbol that might not be supported on every Kindle device or app, use the picture method of creating the equation instead.

Note that it's possible to express the same equation in multiple forms. When one form requires a picture, an alternative form may permit typing the equation as text. For example, consider the equation below. It was formatted as a picture because the squareroot sign can't be properly typed as text.

$$R = \sqrt{x^2 + y^2}$$

However, the above equation can be written in a way that allows typing it directly as text. For example, if you square both sides you can type the equation as $R^2 = x^2 + y^2$. A second alternative is to use an exponent of ½, which means the same thing as a squareroot sign: $R = (x^2 + y^2)^{½}$.

As mentioned in Sec. 2.7, sometimes there are two ways to create a similar supported character, and the decision can make a difference. For example, if you use character codes 178 and 179 to create a square (^{2}) or cube (^{3}), this won't quite match the appearance of higher exponents created with superscript formatting. Compare x^2, x^3, x^4, and x^5 to x^2, x^3, x^4, and x^5. The difference is subtle, but the first set of exponents don't quite match while the latter set of exponents do. The second set used only superscripts, while the first set used character codes 178 and 179 for the first two exponents. It's easier to see that there is a difference when you compare the alternatives together: ^{22} and ^{33}.

Similarly, if you use the character codes for fractions, they won't match other fractions created by typing a slash (/). For example, compare ¾ with 3/4. If you will only use ½, ¼, and ¾, then go ahead and use character codes 188, 189, and 190. However, if you will have other fractions, like 1/3 or 5/8, you won't be able to make them match those typed with character codes. In that case, use the slash (/) for *all* of your fractions so that they match. Compare the pair of fractions 1/2 and 1/3, which looks better than the pair ½ and 1/3.

A non-breaking space (character code 160) may come in handy to help prevent a typed equation from breaking in an unnatural place (but note that the non-breaking space may not have the same effect in a Kindle eBook with all punctuation marks and symbols as it does with letters and numbers). We discussed the non-breaking space in Sec. 3.7 as it relates to text. The same principles apply to equations typed as text. For example, in the equation $y = 3x + 2$, where ordinary spaces have been used around the equal and plus signs, when typed in the middle of a paragraph, there is a chance that the equation will be split across two lines (since every device has a different screen size, and the customer can choose the font style and size). Using non-breaking spaces instead can help force parts of the equation to stay together. However, it's still possible for equations to break at other points (such as punctuation marks or symbols).

Beware of the formatting issues mention in Sec. 3.7: Using a non-breaking space to keep long strings of text together can amplify problems with justified text (and even has issues with left-aligned text). Use the non-breaking space where the potential problem that it may prevent is more important than the potential problem that it may create. (Also, note that some of the symbols used in equations, unlike letters, may themselves break across lines, in which case the non-breaking space doesn't help).

The following are examples of equations that can be typed directly as text.

$$y = mx + b$$
$$y = ax^2 + bx + c$$
$$z = \pm(x^2 + y^2)^{\frac{1}{2}}$$
$$T_F = 9T_C/5 + 32°$$
$$T_C = 5(T_F - 32°)/9$$
$$2H_2 \ (g) + O_2 \ (g) \longrightarrow 2H_2O \ (aq)^{41}$$

Following are equations that couldn't be typed directly. These were formatted as pictures for the Kindle version of this book, following the instructions of Sec. 4.9.

$$y = \frac{1}{x}$$

$$y = x\sqrt{2}$$

$$\sin\theta = \frac{1}{2}$$

$$NH_3(aq) + H_2O(l) \rightleftharpoons NH_4^+(aq) + OH^-\ (aq)$$

3.12 Tables

Kindle supports simple, basic tables with a couple of columns. Formatting for tables is limited. Keep it simple. I would avoid using more than two columns (maybe three columns if every column is very narrow): Just imagine a customer reading your eBook on a cell phone (in portrait mode).

Note that Kindle justification issues with text are much more pronounced with tables. Even left aligned (ragged right) text will be much more ragged than usual. I recommend that you don't justify text in a table: Use left or centered alignment instead.

Note that you can apply paragraph styles to the cells of your table: Thus, as with any other paragraph, you can control the alignment and formatting of table cells through Word's styles.

---

[41] The single-character right arrow is not a symbol that is supported across all Kindle devices and apps: It works on some, but not others. (Using HTML codes, as discussed in Sec. 5.6, *doesn't* completely resolve the problem.) I created this "right arrow" using an em dash (—) and a greater than sign (>): Join the — and > together to make —>.

You can apply different paragraph styles to different cells. If you have multiple paragraphs in a single cell (created by using the Enter key), you can apply different paragraph styles to each paragraph (however, it's *not* a good idea to have "paragraphs" of text in table cells: tables work best when there is little text in each cell).

It may be tempting to create a special paragraph style for the first cell of the table that forces the table onto a new page by incorporating a page break into the style, but note that this doesn't work well on older generation Fire and other Kindle devices. Alternatively, you can add a short line of text before the table and incorporate a page break in its style (like the NoIndentPageBreak style recommended in Sec. 4.7). I did this in the example at the end of this section.

Another way to make a table is to format it as a picture (Sec. 4.8). However, that has its own design challenges. You can make a simple test book: Open a new document, make a few tables with different methods that you're considering, upload the file to KDP, and preview the result (see Chapter 7). As long as you don't publish it, you're the only person who will see the result. **Note**: Tables sometimes display incorrectly in the Kindle previewer and on Kindle for PC. If you have tables, this makes it a priority to test your eBook out on an actual device (Sec. 7.9).

Beware that multiple columns may show up as a single column on older devices. Ideally, you would limit yourself to two columns, and you would organize it in a logical way that a customer could understand it if it shows as a single column on an older device. If one column would be unsatisfactory, the alternative is an image. Since formatting a table as an image has its own design challenges, you must choose between the two options. When a table formats well, it probably looks better on newer devices than an image, and is probably more readable. It's when a table has too many columns or has complex formatting that a well-formatted image may turn out better. If you have a large table with several columns, you really need to split it up into smaller tables.

According to the KDP help pages, if you format your table as an actual table (not a picture), your table should not be cut off at the bottom of the screen when a font size of 3 (the default user setting) is selected. Otherwise, you should split the table into smaller tables.

If a table works well (according to a thorough preview using an actual device—since tables sometimes display incorrectly with the Kindle previewer and with Kindle for PC) as an actual table, that's the best option. It will probably have no more than two columns, and include basic formatting without too much text in a single cell, if the table works well. If it doesn't work well as a table, one alternative is an image (Sec. 4.8). However, text quality can be an issue in a large image or a highly detailed image, so it will still probably be a relatively small table if it works well that way. When a table won't work well as an actual table or as an image, the alternative is to organize the information the same was you would organize information in body text or bullet points (or split a table up into smaller tables, if the information can be understood well that way).

The following table was formatted by applying paragraph styles in Word.

Kindle eBooks Added in Last 30 Days	
Romance	14,076
Fantasy	5,902
Science Fiction	3,695
Thriller	3,512
Mystery	3,172
Suspense	2,841
Literary Fiction	2,591

3.13 Special Books

The majority of Kindle eBooks are either (A) novels or (B) nonfiction books that consist mainly of paragraph text, bullet points, and/or images. However, there are other kinds of eBooks besides these. We will briefly consider a few other types of eBooks in this section.

Poetry eBooks have many inherent limitations compared to print books. The main problem is that a poem consists of lines and stanzas, and poets want all of the text on each line to appear on that line. That is, poets generally don't want line breaks in the middle of what is intended to be a complete line.

However, by the nature of eReader devices and apps, it's impossible to prevent lines from breaking if either the customer makes the font size too large or if the device screen is too small. Depending on the screen size and font size, there is only so much room across the screen, so whenever the text exceeds this width, the line will break. Unfortunately, on a small screen such as a cell phone, or even on a larger screen where a customer selects a very large font size, a single line may consist of just a few words.

You must either accept that on some devices or with some choice of font sizes lines may break where you really don't want them to break, or format the poems as images instead (see Chapter 4). If you have visual poetry, i.e. you want the text to appear on visual backgrounds sort of like an illustrated children's book, then you may be able to format a poetry book as a set of images with the text embedded, or you can format your poetry book as a fixed-format book (review Sec. 1.1 for a brief discussion of the pros and cons of using fixed-format and for a list of Amazon's free tools for creating a simplified fixed-format Kindle eBook, and see Sec. 1.5 for links to free tutorials for how to use these tools). Note that if you decide to format your poems as images (it's probably not appropriate if your book purely consists of text, but may be okay for poetry if every poem is accompanied by a visual element), you want to use a very large font size and not have too much text to read on a single image: You want each poem to be easily read across all devices (without the customer needing to zoom in to read every single poem).

Another issue with poetry is that you can't guarantee that the entire poem will fit onto one 'page.' If the screen size is too small or if the customer chooses a font size too large, a poem intended to fit on one page may run onto the next page. You can't even force all of the lines of one stanza to remain together; it may break across two pages. However, it is possible to force a poem to fit on one page by formatting it as an image, although doing so has its own drawbacks (such as readability on some devices), or by creating a fixed-format book, which also has draw-backs (such as the availability being restricted to certain devices). If you publish your poetry in *print*, you have much more control over the formatting.

The pictures in this section show a couple of examples of how to format poetry. The first picture shows an eBook with the poem formatted as text, and demonstrates how even a relatively short line of text is apt to break across two lines when the customer selects a moderate font size (the left picture used the default font size of 3, while the right picture raised the font size to 5—this *isn't* the font size set in Word: it's the font size that the customer selects on the Kindle device). The last picture shows an eBook with the poem formatted as pictures (with the text embedded in JPEG pictures).

Screenplays and poetry are both affected by yet another issue: Multi-level indents have issues on some devices, especially older Kindles. You can create indented paragraphs and non-indented paragraphs, but if you try to create paragraphs with different indent sizes, first of all this doesn't turn out as expected on one or more devices, and second of all on devices with small screens or if the customer chooses a large font, the second or third indent may be ridiculously large (more than half the screen width).

The best thing is to keep the formatting simple, using just one indent size: This provides the optimum reading experience across all devices. Focus on readability: If the customer really wants multi-level indents or to have the entire poem fit on one page, they can purchase the print edition instead.

A puzzle book is another type of eBook that involves a few formatting challenges. The first challenge is that the book won't be interactive: The customer won't be able to type answers, circle answers, select answers, draw pictures, etc. Most print puzzle books involve writing, selecting, or drawing an answer. Therefore, it's not practical to try to format a crossword puzzle book, a word search puzzle book, a Sudoku book, or a coloring book as an eBook, for example. That's likely to create a frustrating customer experience.

Warning: If you publish a coloring book or certain types of puzzle books in Kindle format that require customers to write or draw answers, if customers complain to Amazon that the Kindle reading experience is frustrating, it's possible that Amazon will block the book and issue a stern warning by email—especially if customers expect the 'book' to function more like an 'app' (like the kinds of interactive games or puzzles that customers might enjoy on a cell Phone). This has happened to some authors. Not all books are a good fit for Kindle.

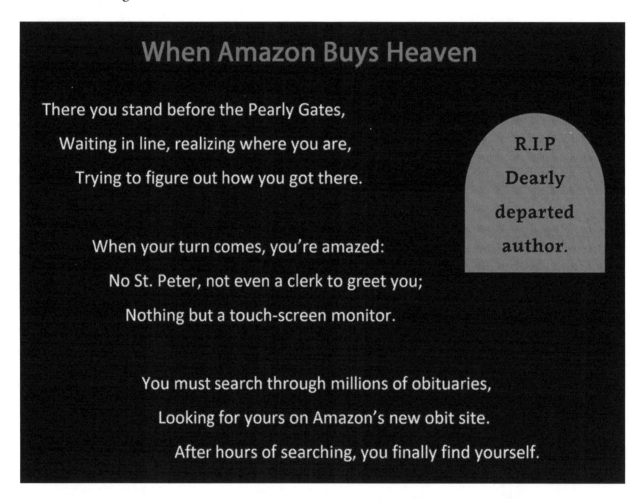

The formatting of a puzzle eBook is different from the formatting of a print book. One way is the location of the answer key: It *isn't* convenient in the eBook to have all the answers collected at the back of the book. It's more convenient to format the answers as endnotes or footnotes so that the customer can check the answer at the click of a button. An alternative is to give a short set of puzzles, then the corresponding answers, then the next set of puzzles, their answers, etc. (with the

Lines of poetry break when a customer selects a larger font size.

When Amazon Buys Heaven

There you stand before the Pearly Gates,

Waiting in line, realizing where you are,

Trying to figure out how you got there.

When your turn comes, you're amazed:

No St. Peter, not even a clerk to greet you;

Nothing but a touch-screen monitor.

You must search through millions of obituaries,

When Amazon Buys Heaven

There you stand before the Pearly Gates,
Waiting in line, realizing where you are,
Trying to figure out how you got there.

When your turn comes, you're amazed:
No St. Peter, not even a clerk to greet you;
Nothing but a touch-screen monitor.

You must search through millions of obituaries,
Looking for yours on Amazon's new obit site.
After hours of searching, you finally find yourself.

Your obit page has a head shot of you,
A blurb about your life, even product info,
Like gender, height, eye color, and age.

A yellow button catches your eye: Apply now.
You click it. It takes you to a form to complete.
Apply to Heaven. Estimated delivery time: two weeks.

The fine print tells you it's based on customer reviews.

Location 2 of 36   5%

answers separated by page breaks). Note that if you intend to have multiple puzzles display on the same 'page,' depending on the screen size and font size, sometimes all of the puzzles won't fit together on the same 'screen.'

One problem with puzzle eBooks is that they are competing against apps, which means that customers can purchase an interactive app instead of your non-interactive eBook. If you have a great puzzle book in mind, you might explore the possibility of creating an app instead of an eBook.

Another type of eBook is a book that contains several pictures. We'll explore how to format images in Chapter 4, including picture books in Sec. 4.12. If your book has numerous pictures, you might want to jump ahead and read Sec. 4.12 now.

3.14 Check Your Styles

There are a couple of simple things that you can (and should) do to help identify common mistakes that are easy to make when creating and assigning paragraph styles for your book.

In Word, go to View and click the Web Layout button. This button shows your book as if it were a very long web page. Scroll down the entire length of your book slowly (when your eyes are fresh) to check the vertical spacing. This will help you see if there are places that are missing vertical space or have too much vertical space. Any issues with vertical spacing are usually easier to spot in the Web Layout view than in the Print Layout view.

For example, is the text at the end of a chapter bunched up against the chapter heading that follows? If so, you want to apply a paragraph style to the last paragraph of the previous chapter that adds space after the paragraph (such as the BodySpaceAfter paragraph style recommended in Sec. 3.4). The Look Inside feature at Amazon (which can have a valuable marketing influence) shows a preview of your eBook that is similar to Word's Web Layout view: The Look Inside feature similarly strips any page breaks out of your eBook and scrolls down like a long webpage. If you don't see vertical space between the last paragraph of each chapter and your chapter headings in Web Layout view in Word, it will likely look the same way in your Look Inside (unless you apply a paragraph style to the last paragraph of each chapter that adds Spacing After.)

When you are finished with the Web Layout view, feel free to return to the View ribbon and click the Print Layout button, if you feel more comfortable with the Print Layout View. I check the Web Layout view just before publishing my eBook, or just before going a step beyond Word to use other software (as described in Chapter 5).

Now open the styles menu: One way to do this is to click on the little arrow-like icon on the bottom right corner of the Styles group on the Home ribbon (you can find a picture showing this menu and how to open it in Sec. 3.3). Click the Options link at the bottom right corner of the styles menu. In the dropdown menu for "Select styles to show," select "In use." Check the boxes for "Paragraph level formatting" and "Bullet and numbering formatting" (but not for "Font formatting").

This will help you find paragraphs that have direct formatting applied to them. Look through the styles that appear in the styles menu. (If the list is full, check to see if there is an option to scroll through it: There may be more styles hidden below. Also, try changing the size of the styles menu window—position your cursor on the bottom edge, until it turns into a vertical double arrow, and then click and drag your cursor to make the styles menu taller.) Look for any style names that seem unfamiliar: That is, are there any styles with names that you didn't choose (other than Word's default styles)?

In particular, see if any style names have a comma (,) or a plus sign (+). For example, if there are style names like "16 pt, Centered" or "NoIndent + Bold," these styles are a **problem** (except for **drop caps**, as noted in the following paragraph). If you find problem styles such as these, hover your cursor over the style name on the styles menu and click on the dropdown arrow that appears at the right of the style name while hovering. This will show you how many instances of that style there are. Click Select All to select all of the instances. If there are multiple instances, you may wish to make some notes on a sheet of paper with a pen or pencil so that you know where each of these problem paragraphs is located (so that you can check each one after correcting the problem).

Drop caps are an exception. When you insert a drop cap, Word creates a variation of that paragraph style for the drop cap. For example, if you apply the NoIndent style that I recommend (in Sec. 3.4) for the first paragraph of a chapter, you will styles with names like NoIndent + 66.5 pt, Lowered by 4.5 pt (but probably with different numbers). For simple drop caps in Word's defaults, these should work fine (though Sec. 5.6 will show you how to optimize drop caps).

What you want to do is assign a proper paragraph style to each of those problem paragraphs (except for drop caps), and to delete the problem paragraph style (simply select Delete from the dropdown menu that appears when you hover your cursor over the style name in the styles menu).

The Style Inspector can help you inspect the styles for a paragraph. The button to open the Style Inspector is the middle button at the bottom of the styles menu. On the Style Inspector window, click the bottom left button to Reveal Formatting: This opens yet another window. The Reveal Formatting window shows all of the Paragraph and Font settings for the paragraph. Near the bottom of the Reveal Formatting Window, check the box beside "Distinguish style source."

If you place your cursor in a paragraph and see the phrase "Direct Formatting" in the Reveal Formatting window, that is a potential problem—especially if it appears in the Paragraph section. If you highlighted an entire paragraph and applied formatting directly to the paragraph, for example, that is one way to get direct paragraph formatting (there are other ways, too). You want to undo direct *paragraph* formatting (whereas direct *font* formatting may be fine). For example, try clicking the Clear All button on the top of the styles menu (there is also a Clear All Formatting button on the Font group on the Home ribbon).

Note that there may be other issues with paragraph styles that don't show up under "Direct Formatting." It's a good idea to check paragraphs one at a time from the beginning of your book, at least until you've sampled one instance of each paragraph style and have confidence that there aren't any issues. Place your cursor in a paragraph, and browse through the information in the Reveal Formatting window, checking for anything that doesn't seem right. If you elect not to do a thorough search of your entire book, try to think of any special paragraphs that may be worth checking. For example, did you copy and paste material into your book? Were you distracted when working on a particular chapter? Which sections of your book were more difficult to format?

When your book is complete and you are either ready to preview your eBook or move onto Chapter 5, the Reveal Formatting window can be helpful. Place your cursor in a paragraph and study the formatting in the Reveal Formatting window. Do this slowly, one paragraph at a time, searching for possible problems.

Another way the Reveal Formatting window can be useful is when you come across a paragraph where the formatting doesn't seem right, but you can't quite figure out why by looking at it. The Reveal Formatting window spells out all of the settings for the paragraph.

If you're trying to correct a problem, but run into an issue where fixing one paragraph seems to mess up other paragraphs, make sure that the Disable Linked Styles box is checked on the styles menu. When this is unchecked, changes that you make to one paragraph style may affect other paragraph styles. (When you right-click a style to modify it, I recommend that you uncheck the box for Automatically Update and adjust Style Based On to "no style"—as recommended in Sec. 3.3. Also, go to File > Options > Proofing > AutoCorrect Options > AutoFormat As You Type and uncheck the box next to "Define styles based on your formatting"—as recommended in Sec. 2.11.)

Web Layout reveals a problem: There is no space before the subheading.

books and pay to have all of them professionally formatted, you could have saved yourself a great deal of money by learning how to do it yourself in the beginning. Another advantage of doing your own formatting is that it's easy to make changes: You won't have to contact the formatter, pay more money, and wait for the changes to be implemented (and what if the formatter has gone out of business?).

https://kdp.amazon.com/en_US/help/topic/G200634410

You really don't need to look for an alternative. Microsoft Word is a great place to start (even if you're willing to go a step beyond Word):

• Microsoft Word is fairly Kindle friendly. Amazon knows that most self-published authors use Word. You do need to learn how to modify your Word file to produce good Kindle formatting, like learning how to use paragraph styles and which features don't convert well to Kindle, but if you do this, then Word is fairly Kindle friendly.

• Word is convenient. Most authors have access to Word. It's fairly affordable and accessible. Most authors already have experience using Word, whereas starting with new software involves a large learning curve.

• You retain the flexibility to go one step beyond Word (for example, if you're willing to use a little HTML). If you style your Word file properly, this makes the transition relatively straightforward. In fact, many formatters who use other software like Sigil actually first prepare their manuscript in Word first. Chapter 5 discusses how to go one step beyond Word to make subtle formatting improvements (though if you submit your polished Word file, that should be pretty good, too).

• For authors who will publish a print book in addition to an eBook, Word can be used to do both (though, as noted in Sec. 1.3, at some point you will need to create two separate Word files for this). This makes Word even more convenient.

1.6 Other Formats, too?

This book is focused on how to format a Kindle eBook. If you also plan to publish your eBook with Nook, Kobo, etc., many of the formatting procedures are the same, but there are a few subtle differences. You'll want to research these differences when preparing your eBook file for other eBook retailers or distributors.

The problem was solved by applying ListStyleSpaceAfter.

books and pay to have all of them professionally formatted, you could have saved yourself a great deal of money by learning how to do it yourself in the beginning. Another advantage of doing your own formatting is that it's easy to make changes: You won't have to contact the formatter, pay more money, and wait for the changes to be implemented (and what if the formatter has gone out of business?).

https://kdp.amazon.com/en_US/help/topic/G200634410

You really don't need to look for an alternative. Microsoft Word is a great place to start (even if you're willing to go a step beyond Word):

• Microsoft Word is fairly Kindle friendly. Amazon knows that most self-published authors use Word. You do need to learn how to modify your Word file to produce good Kindle formatting, like learning how to use paragraph styles and which features don't convert well to Kindle, but if you do this, then Word is fairly Kindle friendly.

• Word is convenient. Most authors have access to Word. It's fairly affordable and accessible. Most authors already have experience using Word, whereas starting with new software involves a large learning curve.

• You retain the flexibility to go one step beyond Word (for example, if you're willing to use a little HTML). If you style your Word file properly, this makes the transition relatively straightforward. In fact, many formatters who use other software like Sigil actually first prepare their manuscript in Word first. Chapter 5 discusses how to go one step beyond Word to make subtle formatting improvements (though if you submit your polished Word file, that should be pretty good, too).

• For authors who will publish a print book in addition to an eBook, Word can be used to do both (though, as noted in Sec. 1.3, at some point you will need to create two separate Word files for this). This makes Word even more convenient.

1.6 Other Formats, too?

This book is focused on how to format a Kindle eBook. If you also plan to publish your eBook with Nook, Kobo, etc., many of the formatting procedures are the same, but there are a few subtle differences. You'll want to research these differences when preparing

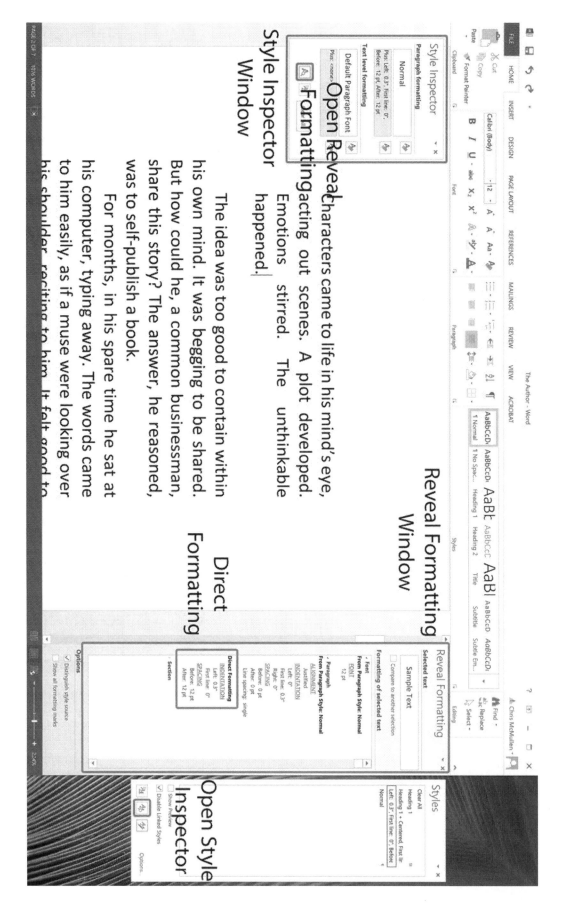

—Chapter 4—

Pictures

4.1 Image Formats

IMAGES SHOULD EITHER be in JPEG or GIF format. (If you know about SVG format and are considering it, you should read Sec. 5.12. The SVG format doesn't work across all devices, and requires going beyond Word.) Other accepted formats, like PNG, are converted to JPEG during the Kindle conversion, so you're better off using JPEG or GIF. (For example, if you have transparency in a PNG file, the transparency will be lost unless you convert it to GIF and use GIF format instead.)

JPEG format is better if:

- The picture is a photograph.
- The picture has a rich color scheme, gradients, or color blends.

GIF format is better if:

- The picture primarily consists of text or line art.
- The picture is a table containing text.
- The picture is a mathematical equation.
- The picture contains transparency that you wish to preserve.

There are reasons behind using JPEG for photos and GIF for line art or text.

- JPEG is better for **photos** because it yields better colors.
- GIF is better for **line art** and **text** because it yields sharper text and lines (provided that your image is sharp to begin with). Text and line art may appear blurry in JPEG format.
- GIF is also a necessity if you wish to preserve **transparency** (but *don't* put black text or line art on a *transparent* background, as it will appear *invisible* in night mode or on older devices). If you convert to JPEG, any transparency becomes white; and if you use PNG (not recommended), it's converted to JPEG in the Kindle conversion with the same result.

Following are a few things to consider when deciding on the image format:

- If an image includes rich color blends (or a photograph) as well as text or line art, a possible compromise is a JPEG image with high enough resolution (and a high enough pixel count) so that the text or line art still appears sufficiently sharp.
- If you format a GIF image with text or line art, be sure that any black text and black line art **isn't** positioned on a **transparent** background: Although GIF supports transparency, black text or line art against a transparent background may appear *invisible* in night mode or on older devices.
- If an image doesn't seem obviously better suited for one format or the other (perhaps it has a color blend that lends itself to JPEG and also has text or line art that lends itself to

GIF, and perhaps neither feature seems more important than the other for the given image), if the image is smaller than 500 × 600, prefer GIF, and if it is larger than 600 × 800, prefer JPEG.

Save **photographs** in JPEG format with high quality (they will be compressed during the Kindle conversion, so you want high quality to begin with). For color photos, use RGB with 24-bit color; neither CMYK nor sRGB are supported. For black-and-white photos, use 8-bit. (If the original photo is in color, I recommend that you keep it in color.)

Photographs should generally be *at least* 600 pixels wide and 800 pixels high (**note**: less than 300 wide or 400 high can cause problems for photographs). I'm *not* recommending 600 × 800; I'm suggesting to think of this as a *minimum* size for photos. We'll discuss image size recommendations for full-screen images in Sec. 4.3 and for smaller images in Sec. 4.4. For design challenges, visit Sec. 4.7.

Line art, black-and-white **drawings**, **equations**, **tables** (that you wish to format as pictures), and images with **text** tend to work better in GIF format.[42]

Any text that appears in images must be readable across all devices. Amazon requires that a lowercase "a" be at least 6 pixels high, though a taller "a" is advisable as a minimum to ensure readability. If you have an image consisting of a single line of text, such as an equation, the text should be at least 45 pixels high.

Since a JPEG works best for the photo, but GIF works best for text, you may be wondering what you should do with a photo that includes text. Treat that as a photo, saving it as a JPEG.

Consider the pictures that follow. I formatted the first picture as a JPEG for its colors and large size, but the second picture as a GIF for its text and line art. In the second picture, note that the text and line art show against a blue background. Note that a white background would be fine behind black text and line art, and that a black background would be fine behind white text and line art. However, if either the text or the line art is black, white, green, or sepia, then you *don't* want *transparency* to lie behind the text or line art on a GIF image—because then it would disappear against one of the four possible reading backgrounds.

---

[42] A few notices regarding pictures that used to be posted on the KDP help pages and in Amazon's publishing guidelines have recently been removed. There used to be a note that if a GIF image exceeds 127 KB in file size, Amazon would automatically convert the GIF image into a JPEG image during the Kindle conversion: This notice has been removed. Amazon also used to advise a maximum pixel count of 500 × 600 for GIF images: This notice has also been removed. Yet another note used to advise authors to compress their pictures before uploading to KDP, but now there is a note advising authors **_not_** to compress their pictures: Rather, Amazon now advises authors to upload high quality pictures. Regarding this last change, Amazon's conversion is now pretty good at compressing pictures for you while preserving picture quality. All of these changes reflect that modern devices now have larger displays and that there is a growing market for eBooks with a significant visual component. As always, it would be wise to test features out with a thorough preview (Chapter 7), since features and recommendations are apt to change with time.

Chris McMullen, Author

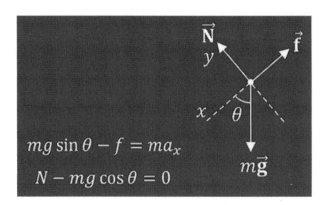

4.2 Image File Size

This section discusses both the file size of individual pictures and the overall file size of a book with pictures. (The size of pictures in *pixels* is discussed in Sec.'s 4.1, 4.3, and 4.4.)

You can check the size of your picture files before you insert them into your eBook. You can do this, for example, by finding the images in a folder under My Computer or My Documents, or on your jump drive or wherever your picture files are saved. You may be able to see the file size by simply hovering your cursor over the file. If not, right-click the picture file and select Properties.

The file size is probably given in kilobytes (KB[43]) or megabytes (MB). Note that one KB equals one thousand (1,000) bytes, while one MB equals one million (1,000,000) bytes.

There is a limit of 5 MB (or 5,000 KB, or 5,000,000 bytes) for a single image file. Note that 5 MB per image is a very generous limit. If you have a single image that exceeds 5 MB, you probably have greater resolution than you need (see Sec.'s 4.3 and 4.5 for a discussion of picture sizes in *pixels* for Kindle).

If you have multiple images, note that each image simply needs to individually be below 5 MB. The total file size of all the pictures combined can far exceed 5 MB.

In fact, the total file size for your Kindle eBook has a very generous limit of 650 MB. The figure that matters isn't the size of the file that you upload, but the converted MOBI file size shown on page three of the publishing process at KDP after you upload your content file (see Sec. 6.13). Most image-heavy Kindle eBooks have converted MOBI file sizes in the 2 to 50 MB range (with 50 MB being very large compared to most eBooks). So 650 MB shouldn't be an issue.[44]

It's possible for the converted MOBI file to be much different (perhaps much lower) than the size of your Word document. The only way to really find out is to upload your file (you could try this with your current draft, just to get a projection) and check page 3 of the publishing process at KDP: Sec. 4.13 will show you a quick way to test this out.

The total file size after conversion to MOBI format is important because it impacts delivery fees and upload times. If you opt for the 70% royalty rate (which requires a list price between $2.99 and $9.99 in the US), you're charged 15 cents per MB based on the converted MOBI file size that you see on page 3 of the publishing process at KDP. (They subtract the delivery fee from the list price *before* applying the 70% to compute your royalty.) The delivery fee doesn't apply to books on the 35% royalty rate. We'll discuss royalties further in Sec. 6.13.

---

[43] In science, we use a lowercase k for the metric prefix kilo, meaning 1000. For example, one kilometer (km) equals 1000 meters and one kilogram (kg) equals 1000 grams. However, computers show kilobytes with an uppercase K, as in KB.

[44] The 650 MB limit is designed to accommodate audio and video clips included with eBooks created with the Kindle Textbook Creator. If you really want to include audio or video with your eBook, check out the Kindle Textbook Creator, but note that these clips will only work with the most recent generations of Kindle Fire devices.

A very large file size also impacts the customer: It requires more memory to store it on their device, and it also takes longer to download a very large file. However, technology keeps improving, so devices can now store more eBooks and download times are faster than they had been in previous years. It's still something to consider, as not all customers have the latest technology.

Amazon now significantly compresses images during the Kindle conversion process. Although each image can be up to 5 MB in the file that you upload to KDP, it will be compressed down to 127 KB (or below) in the Kindle conversion. It's generally best to upload a quality image and let Kindle do the compression.

Tip: If your book is packed with pictures, it's fairly easy to make a test book to see whether or not delivery fees or download times may be significant for your book. It's also fairly easy to test out whether or not you may be able to minimize any such issues. Read Sec. 4.13 to learn more.

One problem with images in Kindle eBooks is that there are occasionally conflicting instructions even from Amazon itself. This is partly because Kindle formatting and conversion have improved over the years. The KDP help pages occasionally have outdated information, whereas the official guidelines are generally more accurate. You can find the official guidelines using the URL below. (However, the official guide is technical, and doesn't go into many details that self-publishers would like to know. I have attempted to provide that pertinent information, along with many other helpful details, in practical terms in my book.)

http://kindlegen.s3.amazonaws.com/AmazonKindlePublishingGuidelines.pdf

For example, the official guidelines advise to save JPEG images with high quality, whereas the KDP help pages advise you to compress images. Compressing images before you publish used to make a significant impact on the file size of the converted MOBI file, but now the Kindle conversion compresses images well and results are better if you begin with a high quality image in the file that you upload to KDP. Thus, I recommend saving high quality images, and not compressing images before uploading (i.e. let Amazon do the compression during the conversion).

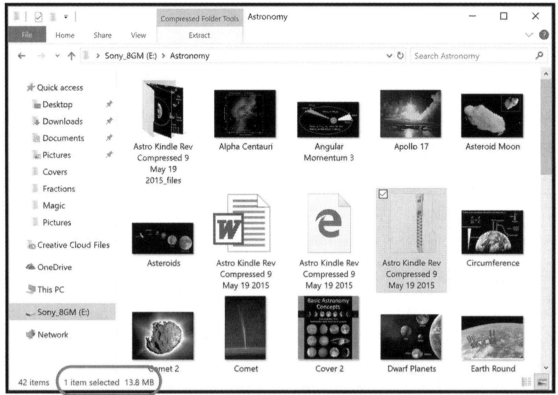

13.8 MB uploaded file size

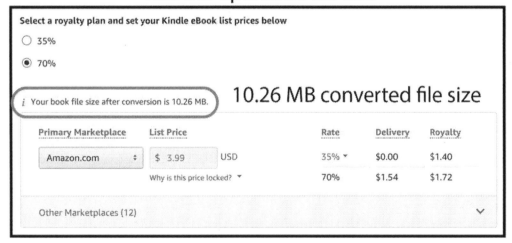

10.26 MB converted file size

4.3 Larger images

Some pictures are intended to fill the width (or height) of the screen, while others are not. This section addresses images that you wish to fill the width or height of the screen. The next section will address images that you want to prevent from filling the width or height (and I do mean *prevent*, as older devices may automatically blow images up to fill the width or height).

Generally, you must choose between full-width and full-height (except as noted in Sec. 4.4 for smaller images, i.e. images you don't want to fill either the width or the height). **Full-screen**, i.e. full-width and full-height simultaneously, images are simply impossible to achieve. That's because different devices have different aspect ratios.

The best you can do is design an image to be full-screen on a particular device. If pictures are a significant component of your eBook, it makes sense to design them with the Kindle Fire aspect ratio (which itself differs slightly across various Kindle Fire devices).[45] However, an image that appears full-screen on a Kindle Fire will look tall and skinny (with wasted space on the left and right sides) on other Kindle eReaders like the Paperwhite. As a counterexample, if you design your picture to appear full-screen on a Paperwhite device, it will look wide and short (with wasted space on the top and bottom sides) on Kindle Fire devices. These inherent problems are illustrated in the pictures that follow.

Note that even if you size the picture perfectly for a specific device, the picture still may not even display full-screen on that device. Why? The customer can adjust the device margins, which forces some white space around your picture. However, if a customer double-taps the picture on most touchscreen devices, it will then display full-width with no margins (if sized with the device's aspect ratio). The third picture that follows illustrates normal device margins for the Kindle Fire (left image), and also shows what happens when a customer zooms in on the picture (right image).

There is yet another important issue with attempts to display large pictures that has to do with what type of eBook file you upload to KDP. Unfortunately, if you upload a Word document to KDP, your pictures may display smaller than their actual size (we'll discuss this further in Sec. 4.11). The only surefire way to prevent pictures from displaying smaller than you intend is to go a step beyond Word, following the steps outlined in Chapter 5. If you want your pictures to display full-screen—or at least full-width—Sec. 5.5 will show you how to achieve this.

Sec. 4.5 provides a list of common eReader screen sizes. If you have images that you wish to fill the screen (at least on your target device), Sec. 4.5 will help you choose an aspect ratio. For example, if you choose to target Kindle Fire devices, you want an aspect ratio of about 1:1.6.

---

[45] In addition, customers can adjust the internal margins on the device, so you can't even guarantee full-screen images on a particular eReader; but you can get very close.

That is, you want the height to be about 1.6 times the width (except for images designed to be viewed in landscape mode, in which case the width should then be about 1.6 times the height).

If you have images that you wish to be full-width (or full-height), but not full-screen, then the aspect ratio isn't relevant. Instead, you should focus on what pixel count to use for the longest side (i.e. between the width and height, whichever side is longer). If you want neither the width nor the height to fill the screen, Sec. 4.4 will show you how to prevent the image from blowing up on older devices.

Note that the Kindle Fire aspect ratio (1:1.6) is somewhat tall and skinny compared to the screen sizes of many other brands of eReaders. For example, the iPad aspect ratio (1:1.33) is short and wide compared to a Kindle Fire. However, before you design your pictures with an iPad (or other non-Kindle brand in mind), you should note that most Kindle customers will read their Kindle eBooks using one of Amazon's free Kindle apps (like the Kindle for iPad, Kindle for Mac, or Kindle for PC). When you read an eBook with a Kindle app, the app mimics the Kindle Fire reading experience to a large degree. For example, if an iPad customer reads a Kindle eBook using the Kindle for iPad app, the visible portion of the displayed eBook may still have the 1:1.6 aspect ratio—wasting portions of the left and right sides of the screen (such that the iPad customer won't enjoy a 'full-screen' experience)—*unless* the customer overrides the defaults. The last picture at the end of this section illustrates this problem for the Kindle for PC app.

Therefore, I recommend designing your eBook with Kindle devices in mind, including Kindle Fire, Paperwhite, and Voyage.[46] The Kindle Fire aspect ratio is 1:1.6 (taller/skinnier), whereas Paperwhite and Voyage have an aspect ratio of 1:1.33 (shorter/wider). However, since Kindle Fire has a color display, the Kindle Fire offers the optimal reading experience for books with color pictures, so I would favor the 1:1.6 aspect ratio (which also suits the default settings for Kindle readings apps for non-Kindle devices).

Whether you want your picture to display full-width,[47] full-height, or full-screen (at least, for your target device), first choose a desired pixel count for the longest side. We will consider a variety of factors that should go into this important decision:

- Will you upload a Word document or follow the steps of Chapter 5 to go a quick step beyond Word?
- What size is your original picture in terms of pixels?

---

[46] Customers don't use an app to read a Kindle eBook on a Kindle device. It's when they read Kindle eBooks on non-Kindle devices that they use a Kindle reading app.

[47] With Kindle, you *don't* have to worry about the picture going off the screen (that is, beyond the edge of the screen). Either the width or height, as needed, will automatically be limited by the device's screen size. Whether an image shows as full-width or full-height depends on the aspect ratio of the image, and also depends on whether the customer holds the device in portrait mode or landscape mode.

- What is the quality of your original picture?
- Does the image involve a high level of detail? If so, how important is that detail for understanding the message that the image conveys?
- Does the picture include text? If so, will customers need to zoom in on certain devices in order to read the text?
- Do you have enough large images for the file size to be a concern?
- How important is regional magnification for your image on large devices?
- Which file format are you using for the image?

In general, I would recommend that the longest side be approximately 2000 pixels if you want the image to be either full-width or full-height, unless one of the exceptions that I describe below applies. Why 2000 pixels? The Kindle Fire HDX 7" and Kindle Fire HD 8.9" have a screen size of 1200 × 1920 pixels, some of the Apple iPads are 1536 × 2048 pixels, and the iPhone 6 Plus has a screen size of 1200 × 1920 pixels. Among reasonably popular eReaders for reading Kindle eBooks, these devices have the most pixels along the longest side. The latest generation of Kindle Fire HD devices are 800 × 1280 pixels. So approximately 2000 pixels across should generally be plenty.

There are a couple of exceptions, like the Kindle Fire HDX 8.9",[48] which measures 1600 × 2560 pixels. It's not yet as popular as the many other Kindle products (it's pricey). There is also a 'trick' for displaying a smaller image full-width (or full-height) on the screen (if you go a step beyond Word), such that you can make a picture that measures 2000 pixels across display full-width (or full-height) on a display that measures 2560 pixels across. There will always be a product with a larger screen size, as technology is constantly improving.

Tip: Making the longest side of your image about 2000 pixels will generally be fine.

Now we will consider possible exceptions.

One possibility is that your original image doesn't measure 2000 pixels across. For example, suppose that you want to use an image that's presently 512 × 1024 pixels. In that case, I *don't* recommend resizing it to 1024 × 2048 pixels because any image software (like Adobe PhotoShop or Gimp) would need to *invent* pixels during the resizing process. That would likely lead to noticeable imperfections in the image.

If you're willing to go a quick step beyond Word (as outlined in Chapter 5), there is a simple way to display any image you want full-width (or full-height) on any device. This is described in

---

[48] Notice the difference between HD and HDX. For example, the Kindle Fire HD 8.9" display is 1200 × 1920 pixels, whereas the Kindle Fire HDX 8.9" display is 1600 × 2560 pixels.

Sec. 5.5. However, you must also look at the quality of your image. Obviously, a quality image that measures approximately 2000 pixels across will look sharp on an iPad or Kindle Fire HDX 7", whereas a quality image that measures 1000 pixels across won't look quite as sharp on those devices. Before you force an image to display full-width (using the technique of Sec. 5.5), ask yourself how it might look when magnified. The smaller the original image, the more important this becomes. For example, most images that are 1000 pixels across look fine when forced full-width on a screen that measures about 2000 pixels across (unless the customer zooms in on the picture to see more detail—we'll consider regional magnification in a few paragraphs), but an image that measures 600 pixels across may look quite blurry if forced full-width on high-resolution devices.

If you will instead upload a Word document for your eBook, then any image that measures less than about 2000 pixels on its longest side simply *won't* be full-width on some devices, like the iPad. However, if it at least measures 1280 pixels across, it will still be full-width (or full-height) on *most* devices—unless the picture gets downsized in the conversion. This can happen if you upload a Word document, though Sec. 4.11 outlines a few measures that you can take to help prevent it. You can safely prevent pictures from downsizing if you go a step beyond Word, following the instructions in Sec. 5.5.

Another possible exception to using images that measure about 2000 pixels along the longest side has to do with file size considerations. If your book is packed with large images, a delivery fee (if you opt for the 70% royalty rate) can cut into your potential royalties, and a very large file size might be a sales deterrent (from the customer's perspective, the eBook takes up more space on their device and requires a longer download time). Before you do anything drastic, like reducing the sizes of all your images, Sec. 4.13 will help you determine whether or not file size may be an issue for your eBook. If you really need to decrease your file size, reducing your images from 2048 pixels across down to 1024 pixels across, for example, may have a significant effect (and you can use the method of Sec. 5.5 to force them to display full-width on all devices). However, Amazon is very good at compressing the pictures in the file that you upload in order to reduce your overall file size: I recommend first using high-quality pictures with the optimal size to see how that turns out. If file size is a significant problem for your converted eBook, then I recommend testing out whether smaller pictures actually makes a significant impact on the converted file size (it might not in some cases) before you do too much work. Sec. 4.13 will help you assess the situation.

There may actually be rare cases where an author wants an image to measure *longer* than 2000 pixels across. One reason might be to 'future proof' your book (though realistically, it could be years before higher resolution screens are more prevalent). Another reason is for rich pictures where **regional magnification** may be desirable on large-screen devices. For example, an image

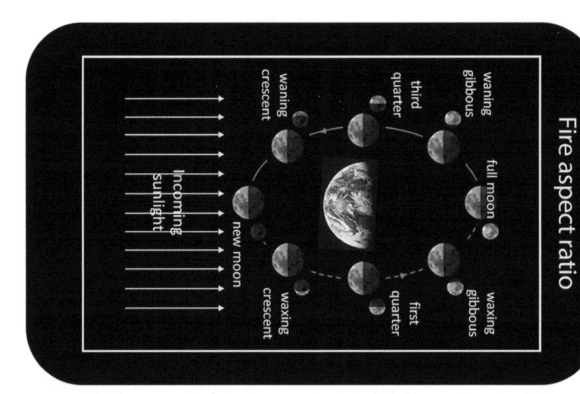

Fire aspect ratio

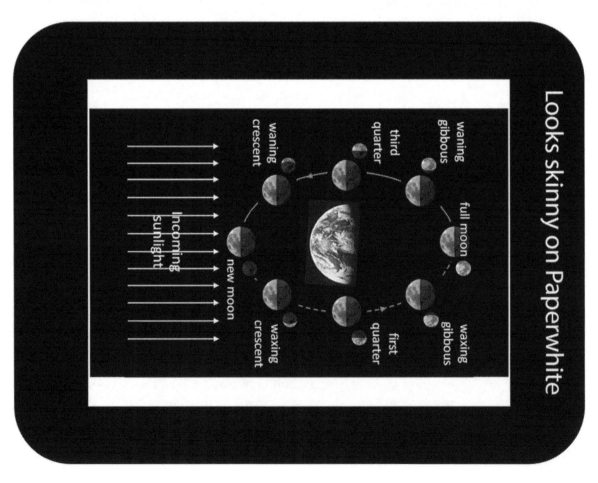

Looks skinny on Paperwhite

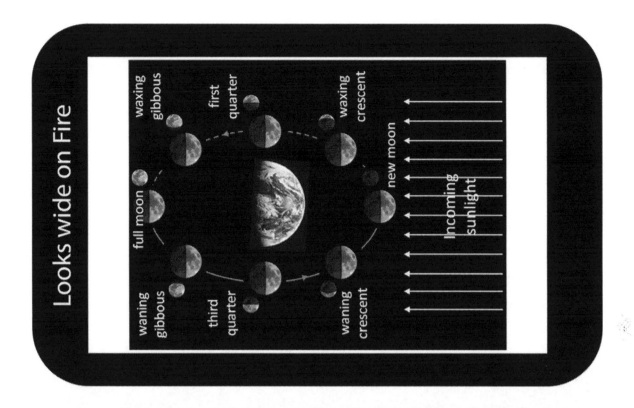

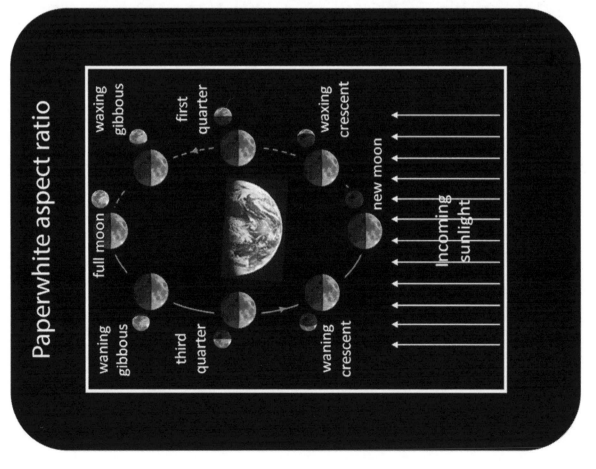

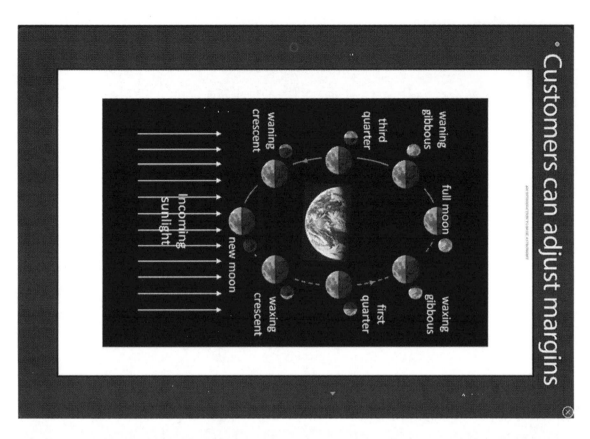

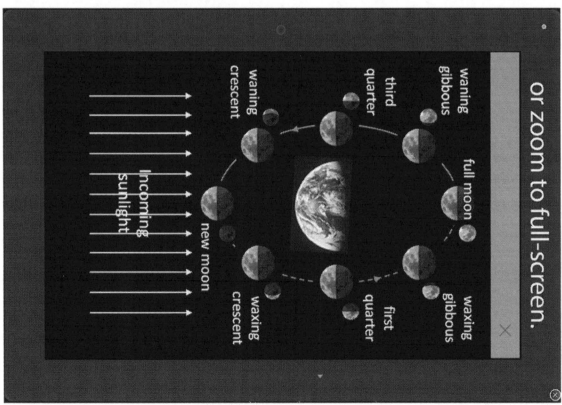

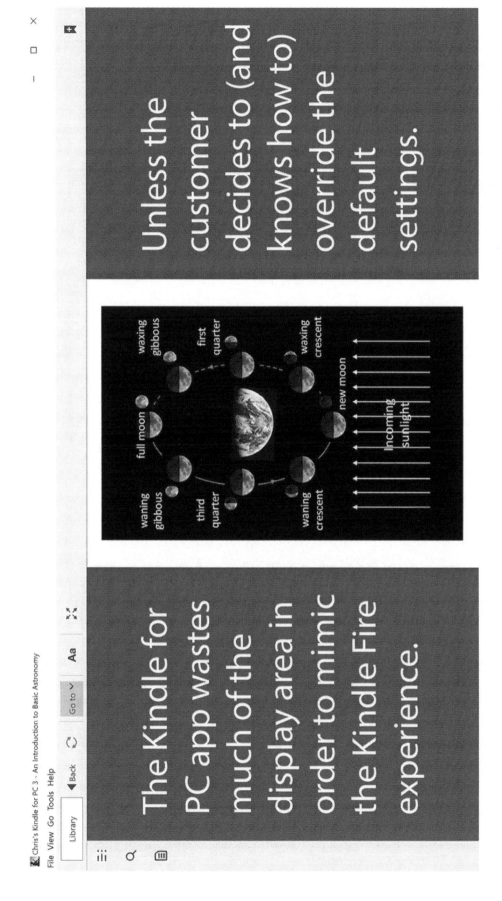

that measures 1920 pixels across will display full-width on most devices (and apps), but if the customer uses regional magnification to zoom in on the picture, the image may appear blurry while it's zoomed in. If your image is about 3820 pixels across, this could help with regional magnification. (This number, 3820, is an Amazon recommendation designed for detailed pictures viewed with maximum zoom on the highest resolution device. Perhaps another reason for this recommendation is to help future-proof your eBook: Someday higher resolution devices may be more common.)

However, in most cases, 3820 pixels is probably *overkill*; 2048 pixels is usually plenty; 1280 pixels is sufficient for most Kindle Fire devices; and 1024 pixels with the full-width trick of Sec. 5.5 is often good enough. Another consideration with very large images (like 3820 pixels across) is that there is a limit of 5 MB for a single picture; make sure you don't exceed this.

Also consider the level of detail involved in the picture. An image with a very high level of detail demands higher resolution, especially when the details of the image are conveying important information (like small text) to the reader. In this case, additional resolution for possible region magnification should merit some consideration.

Ideally, you want to find the right balance point for your eBook. On the one hand, you want to have quality pictures where the details look good even when zoomed in, but on the other hand, if the file size becomes too large, this cuts into your royalties (if you choose the 70% option) and a very large file size can be a problem for the consumer (taking more memory on the device and requiring long download times). If you just have a few pictures, go for the quality. If your book has several pictures, you should test out your options (Sec. 4.13).

Note that neither PPI (pixels per inch) nor DPI (dots per inch) is ultimately relevant for image 'size' in an eBook. All that matters for the picture 'size' are the pixel dimensions of the image and the pixel dimensions of the screen. For example, an image that measures 1024 pixels across will fit on a screen that measures 1024 pixels across, regardless of PPI or DPI. (If you will also be using the same image for a print book, then you do want the image to be 300 DPI for that.[49])

However, the PPI of the picture is important for a different reason, which is why Amazon consistently advises you to ensure that your pictures are 300 PPI in the KDP help pages (and also their technical publishing guidelines). The reason has to do with the quality and sharpness of your pictures. If you create a picture that looks fine at low resolution (like 96 PPI), it might

---

[49] You may need a different version of the same image for your print book and eBook. For example, if you want an image to be 8" × 10" in print, at 300 DPI, it would need to be 2400 × 3000 pixels, whereas you might reduce this to 1638 × 2048 for your eBook. (If the page size is 8" × 10" though, you really need 8.125" × 10.25" for the print book, in order to allow for bleed; or crop the image to 7.5" × 9.5" or smaller to allow for margins. Don't add bleed or margins to your eBook.)

appear blurry or pixilated in your Kindle eBook. There are exceptions, but if you have the opportunity to create 300 PPI images, that is optimal (but see the warning in Sec. 4.11 if you will be uploading a Word document directly to KDP).

Many pictures display fine if they have 192 PPI or even 96 PPI, but if a customer proceeds to zoom in on the image, then the limited PPI becomes much more pronounced. Sometimes, you really don't have an option: If you create a picture using a snipping tool, for example, the PPI will be inherently limited. Most pictures that are 192 PPI will be fine. If a picture is 96 PPI or 72 PPI, you should test out the sharpness in the preview. (Below 72 PPI is strictly not allowed.)

There are certain types of pictures where low PPI are more problematic. One example is when you scan an image with a printer, copier, or phone. Many scans that include text or line drawings don't come out sharp enough to provide a good customer experience in Kindle eBooks (especially, if you try to create an entire eBook with scanned images). If you must use a scan, try to find a way to scan the picture with 300 PPI or higher, if possible, especially if it includes text or line drawings. Be sure to preview your scans before publishing your eBook (Chapter 7 will show you how to conduct a thorough preview).

Finally, you should also consider how large images impact the design of your eBook. For example, a caption may flow onto the next 'page,' or there may be significant white space before or after a large image. We'll consider Kindle design challenges involving pictures in Sec. 4.7.

4.4 Smaller Images

By 'smaller,' I mean images that you *don't* want to display full-width (or full-height). This includes:

- any size picture that you want to prevent from blowing up to full-width on older devices.
- images like logos, which should be small compared to the device width.
- glyphs or borders used to emphasize section breaks (in lieu of the traditional asterisks: * * *).
- pictures with line art or text.
- equations formatted as pictures.
- images used in place of unsupported characters or fancy formatting.
- tiny in-line images, to display math or symbols, that you might intend to blend together with the text.
- small photographs (which have limitations).

There are a few points to consider when designing such images.

The first issue to think about is how the image would look on an older device that automatically blows the image up to full-width (or full-height). If the picture was intended to be smaller, when it blows up to full-width (or full-height) on an older device, the picture may appear *blurry* or *pixilated*. Open the picture with image software and zoom in on the picture: This will help you gauge whether blurriness and pixilation are potential problems.

When a small picture blows up on an older device, this may also impact eBook design. For example, consider a small logo or glyph intended to take up just a small space on the 'page.' If the logo blows up on an older device, this may have an adverse effect on the page layout.

Fortunately, there is an easy way to prevent smaller images from blowing up on older devices. It's called **padding**. This means to make the canvas size larger than the image size. With Adobe Photo-Shop, for example, you can simply change the canvas size, leaving the image size unchanged. If you don't have image software with a canvas size option (separate from the image size), you can create a new image file with a larger image size and insert the original picture into this file.

For example, suppose that you have an image that measures 200 × 300 pixels, and you wish for this image to take up no more than 50% of the width on any device.[50] In this case, you could create a canvas that measures 400 × 300 pixels with the original 200 × 300 pixels picture centered on this canvas.[51] Then if an older device causes the canvas to display full-width, the image itself would only be half-width. You might prefer a particular image to be limited to 25% or 75%, for example, instead of 50%. The choice is yours, but you should preview (Chapter 7) your book carefully on a variety of devices to ensure that the choice works well (though the only way to properly preview an older device is to get your hands on one). You want to ensure that padding your image doesn't create problems with sharpness, affect the readability of text in the image on any device, or prevent adequate zoom magnification where it might be needed.

In general, you would want *transparent* padding (though you don't want a transparent background behind black text or line art). If you use white padding, for example, the padding would stand out to any customer reading in night mode or sepia mode. However, JPEG images don't support transparency, so you can only do this if GIF format is appropriate for the image (as described in Sec. 4.1).

Some smaller images *don't* need padding. For example, a wide and short image, like the picture below, shouldn't require padding. If this particular image blows up on a small screen, it won't influence the page layout noticeably. A square image, like a logo, on the other hand, generally appears better across all devices when it is padded on the sides.

---

[50] The trick from Sec. 5.5 to create full-width images suffers a problem when you attempt to use the same strategy to force a *smaller* percentage. Some older devices ignore a small percentage. The safe option is to pad the image instead.

[51] If you have a compelling reason to want an image to be off-center, you could position it off-center instead.

Another consideration is whether the picture provides enough detail to properly convey its content on any size screen. For example, if the picture contains **text**, ensure that the image is readable across all devices. Sec. 4.13 shows a quick way to test this out, and Chapter 7 discusses at length how to preview your formatting. Also, bear in mind that a customer may zoom in on the image (or use regional magnification).

For **photographs** (as opposed to many other kinds of images), Amazon recommends a minimum size of 600 × 800. Photos less than 300 pixels wide or 400 pixels high are likely to be problematic on some devices.

Positioning is another aspect of smaller pictures that you need to consider. Every image should generally be placed in its own paragraph (with no text or other images beside it in the same paragraph), so basically the picture is on its own line. The text wrap should be set to **In Line With Text**. Pictures format *best* this way. To check this setting, click on the picture and select Wrap Text on the Format ribbon (which only appears when the picture is selected). The picture below (as with almost all of the pictures in this book) was positioned on its own line between paragraphs with the text wrap set to In Line With Text.

If you have a very tiny image—such that the size of the image will be roughly the same height as the characters of text that appear in your eBook's body paragraphs—it is possible to include the image within the paragraph itself, with the text wrap set to In Line With Text. For example, the following symbol was formatted in line as part of the paragraph: ⚒. This might be tempting with equations or special symbols, for example. However, placing an equation—or any type of picture—alongside text in a paragraph introduces some **troublesome design issues** from the customer's perspective. We will consider the issue of in-line pictures (such as for equations or special symbols) in Sec. 4.9.

For tiny images, recall that there are restrictions on minimum sizes for both the image height and text height in pixels: A picture that consists of a single line of text must be at least 45 pixels high, and a lowercase "a" must be at least 6 pixels high. However, you should stay safely above these strict minimums for maximum readability.

I recommend that you *avoid* placing a picture within paragraph text, for the reasons provided in Sec. 4.9. As I mentioned previously, a picture formats *best* when placed on its own line (not alongside text in a paragraph, but with the picture placed between text paragraphs). For example, the picture above comes between two text paragraphs, and the picture that follows was also placed on its own paragraph.

We will discuss the challenge of eBook design as it relates to pictures in Sec. 4.7.

4.5 Common Screen Sizes

The table on the following page shows the screen sizes of eReaders and other devices that customers commonly use to read Kindle eBooks (sizes shown for the latest generation of each model, as of the publication of this book). Read carefully: Whether you see HD or HDX can make a significant difference.

The Kindle Fire HDX 7", Kindle Fire HD 8.9", iPad Air, and iPhone 6 Plus are among the highest-resolution devices that customers commonly use to read Kindle eBooks. These measure about 2000 pixels across. Thus, 2048 pixels along the longest side would cover almost every possibility, except for the Kindle Fire HDX 8.9", which measures 2560 pixels across.

Most of the Kindle Fire HD devices are 800 × 1280. The Kindle Fire HD 8.9", at 1200 × 1920, is a generation older. Kindle Fire (without the HD), including the Kids version, is 600 × 1024. If you are specifically targeting Kindle Fire, then 1280 pixels on the longest side would be sufficient for most, and 1920 pixels would cover all current and older Fire devices except for the Kindle

Fire HDX 8.9" (which measures 2560 pixels across). Applying the trick from Sec. 5.5, 1280 pixels would work satisfactorily for all devices (note that it's exactly one-half of 2560), *unless* your pictures may have issues with fine details, sharpness, or text readability (or if your pictures warrant higher resolution for possible regional magnification).

Common eReader Screen Sizes	
Kindle Fire HDX 8.9"	1600 × 2560
Kindle Fire HDX 7"	1200 × 1920
Kindle Fire HD 8.9"	1200 × 1920
Kindle Fire HD 6", 8", 10"	800 × 1280
Kindle Fire 7"	600 × 1024
Kindle Paperwhite 6"	1080 × 1440
Kindle Oasis 6"	1080 × 1440
Kindle Voyage 6"	1080 × 1440
Kindle 6"	600 × 800
Apple iPad Air	1536 × 2048
iPhone 6/7/8	750 × 1334
iPhone 6/7/8 Plus	1080 × 1920

If you're considering non-Kindle tablets, such as an **iPad** or **Android** tablet, or if you're thinking about a customer who may read your book on a computer monitor (**PC or Mac**), note that customers with non-Kindle devices typically read eBooks using one of the free Kindle apps (such as Kindle for PC, Kindle for Mac, Kindle for Android, or Kindle for iPad). *Kindle apps generally don't display pictures full-screen*, presenting the eBook with the Kindle Fire aspect ratio (and thus wasting some of the screen space)—except for customers who override the defaults. The last picture at the end of Sec. 4.3 illustrates this using the Kindle for PC reading app on a PC monitor.

So, for example, although the Apple iPad 2 has a screen size of 1536 × 2048, when a customer reads an eBook on this device using the Kindle for iPad reading app, the actual display size used by the Kindle eBook may only be a fraction of the total screen size. Also, although the iPad aspect ratio (which is 1:1.33) is relatively square compared to the skinny Kindle Fire aspect ratio (which is 1:1.6), pictures viewed on an iPad using the Kindle for iPad reading app will fill the available display area best (with the default reader settings) if they have the same aspect ratio (1:1.6) as the Kindle Fire. However, there are customers who adjust the default settings.

You are probably wondering, "**Which device do most customers use to read Kindle eBooks?**" If there were one device that were dominant, that would help, wouldn't it?

Unfortunately, customers read Kindle eBooks across a variety of devices, without one really strong favorite. I've conducted surveys to determine these results, and researched other surveys. For example, you can see the results of one of my surveys below. The survey is still open: If you visit the URL that follows the survey, you can take the survey. (You will be able to view the most up-to-date results after you take the survey. I recommend the 5th survey on the page, although the first survey is more elaborate.) Feel free to share the URL: The more people who take the survey, the more helpful the results will be.

Survey Results	
Kindle Fire	15%
Kindle Paperwhite	15%
iPad	14%
Other Kindle device	12%
Android device	13%
Kindle for PC app	9%
Other option not listed	4%
iPhone	3%
Kindle for Mac app	1%

https://chrismcmullen.wordpress.com/2015/02/21/survey-about-reading-habits-how-do-you-read

From my survey (and others like it), it appears that a significant proportion of Kindle customers read via Kindle Fire, Kindle Paperwhite, iPad, other Kindle device, Android device, or the Kindle for PC reading app. Rather than seeing a clear favorite, it was a close race all the way across.

Although the iPad is among the frontrunners, it appears that a significant majority of Kindle customers use a Kindle device. If only 1 out of 6 customers uses iPad, for example, it makes sense to design a Kindle eBook with the Kindle aspect ratio in mind. A possible exception is if you will also publish your eBook with Apple, and have good reason to expect at least half your sales to come through Apple. Most authors who publish with Kindle Direct Publishing find that the vast majority of their sales come through Kindle customers: You would need a compelling reason to expect more sales to come through Apple customers (though there are a few authors who have such a reason).

If your goal is to optimize the display area, or if your goal is to make full-screen images, as mentioned in Sec. 4.3, the problem is that the aspect ratio varies considerably across devices. For example, the Kindle Fire HD aspect ratio is 1:1.6, whereas the Paperwhite and Voyage have aspect ratios of 1:1.33. An image that is 1200 × 1920 matches the aspect ratio of the Kindle Fire HDX 7" or Kindle Fire HD 8.9", whereas an image that is 1080 × 1440 matches the aspect ratio of the Paperwhite and Voyage. For the Kindle Fire HDX 8.9", 1600 × 2560 is optimal (unless you really need fine detail with zooming or regional magnification).

Kindle Fire devices, iPhones, and Android phones are tall and skinny, with heights at least 1.6 times their widths. Kindle Paperwhite and Voyage devices are much more square, with heights 1.33 times their widths.

Here are a few possibilities:

- Target the Kindle Fire aspect ratio. In this case, 1200 × 1920 matches most Fire devices. Some formatters like the number 2048, in which case it would be 1280 × 2048. If you want to match the Kindle Fire HDX 8.9", use 1600 × 2560. In the extreme case of optimizing detail for maximum zoom on a high resolution screen, this translates to 2388 × 3820. In each of these cases, the images will fit very well on Kindle Fires and iPhones, but will appear a bit skinny on Paperwhite and Voyage (leaving gaps on the left and right sides). If my original picture has high enough resolution, my preferred size is 1200 × 1920 or 1280 × 2048.

- If you feel that the Kindle Fire aspect ratio is too skinny for your pictures, you might feel more comfortable with the Paperwhite and Voyage aspect ratio (though of course, these are black-and-white devices), which is a bit more square. (The iPad has the same aspect ratio, though customers who read with the Kindle for iPad reading app get a display that mimics the Fire reading experience—unless they override the default settings.) The Paperwhite and Voyage measure 1080 × 1440, which may be good enough for other devices (especially, if you follow Sec. 5.5). To accommodate the Kindle Fire resolution, this becomes 1440 × 1920 (though of course this will appear a little square on a Kindle Fire or an iPhone, leaving gaps at the top and bottom). For those who like 2048 pixels, this becomes 1536 × 2048 (which matches the iPad screen, but remember that it will appear somewhat smaller with the Kindle for iPad app). With the Kindle Fire HDX 8.9" in mind, this becomes 1920 × 2560 (though it leaves gaps at the top and bottom). If you're aiming for 3820 pixels, this translates to 2865 × 3820. If my original picture has high enough resolution, I would prefer 1440 × 1920 or 1536 × 2048.

- Compromise somewhere in between the Fire and Paperwhite aspect ratios. For example, use 1312 × 1920, 1400 × 2048, 1750 × 2560, or 2610 × 3820. In this case, the images won't fit precisely on *any* device (meaning that there will *always* be a mismatch), but the mismatches will be somewhat smaller. My personal preference for a picture that I would like to show full-screen is to go with the first option (target the Kindle Fire). I don't design *every* picture to show full-screen though: It depends on the picture. Sometimes, the nature of the picture itself suggests a certain aspect ratio. Other times, the picture will look best at a smaller size. There may also be times when you don't want a large picture to disrupt the flow of text too much, and opt to use a smaller picture with the text showing above and below. Don't get so carried away with matching the screen size that you forget to consider how the picture impacts the design and formatting of your eBook.

- A more modest image size is sufficient for many eBooks, and can help keep the overall file size of the eBook down if the book contains numerous pictures. For example, 640 × 1024 targets the Kindle Fire aspect ratio, and if you go a step beyond Word and follow the instructions in Sec. 5.5, the picture will still display full-screen (aside from the customer's choice of margins, of course) on Kindle devices that have a larger display size. The only reason that 640 × 1024 might be insufficient is if the sharpness of the original picture is lacking or if the picture requires better resolution when zoomed in on a higher resolution screen (for example, to see important details or to read text that can't easily be read without zooming).

In general, **I recommend the Kindle Fire HD aspect ratio**. If you have **color** pictures, they will look *best* on Kindle Fire devices, iPads, and iPhones. Most Kindle customers reading with color devices use a Kindle Fire. Thus, it makes sense to target Kindle Fire if your images are in color.

A second reason is that Amazon's recommendations generally fit the Kindle Fire aspect ratio, and hence there are many Kindle picture books using this aspect ratio. Customers who read Kindle picture eBooks with a squarer display (such as the Paperwhite) shouldn't be surprised to see tall, skinny images: It's pretty common.

Customers who buy Kindle Paperwhite or Voyage probably purchased the device more for reading and less for pictures. Customers who really like to enjoy the picture quality are more apt to read eBooks on a Kindle Fire or other brand of tablet. Therefore, I wouldn't base the aspect ratio of my images specifically on Paperwhite or Voyage devices.

Remember, the discussion in this section has specifically been about large pictures that you would like to approximately fill the screen as well as possible. *Not every picture in an eBook necessarily needs to try to fill the screen.* If you consider the many pictures that I have included in this eBook, you should note that a few approximately fill the screen, but many were obviously not intended to fill the screen. It depends on the nature of the picture.

If you will be publishing your eBook with Nook, Kobo, and other e-retailers besides Kindle, you may want to check out which devices those customers typically use. However, *Kindle presently commands the majority of the eBook market*, so it makes sense for Kindle to be the main target. If you do publish with other eBook retailers (Sec. 6.16), you could publish a different version of your eBook using different versions of your pictures for those retailers: When you publish your Kindle eBook, focus on Kindle customers.

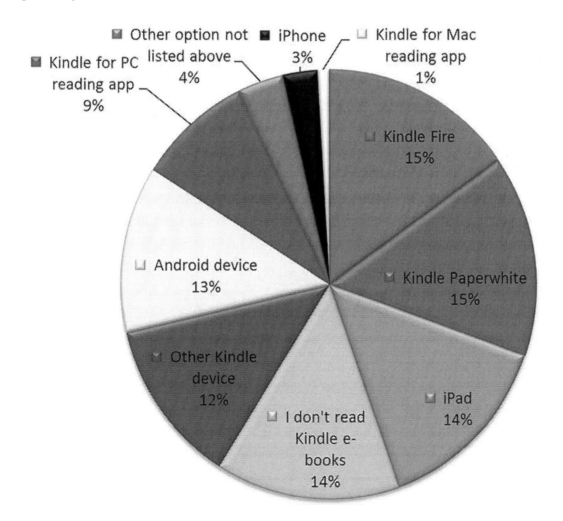

4.6 Perfecting Your Images

The most important aspect of a picture *isn't* the size: It's the *quality*. This means that the original image file must be sharp, clear, free of imperfections, and of sufficient resolution.

You will have better quality images if you avoid common issues:

- Blurriness—the image isn't as sharp as it should be.
- Pixilation—there are stray pixels where they don't belong.
- The text is unreadable. This is very important to preview across all devices. Note that text tends to come out better in GIF format, if the picture suits that format (Sec. 4.1).
- Aspect ratio—the picture appears squeezed or stretched.
- The author rotated the picture sideways, incorrectly assuming that was the proper way to treat landscape images (Sec. 4.7).
- The image doesn't have high enough quality to show the intended level of detail.
- The images were scanned with poor quality. (It's even more challenging to produce a scan of sufficient quality for Kindle eBooks when the scan contains much text.)
- There are photography issues (red-eye, shadows, reflection, etc.). This can include Photo-Shop issues (like inappropriate use of a filter, or reflecting a picture that contains text such that the text appears backwards).
- There are drawing issues (perspective, scale, etc.).
- Text or line art appears in front of a transparent background in GIF format. It will appear *invisible* on some devices or apps when the customer selects night mode.
- Screenshots show Word's spelling or grammar marks. Be sure to successfully turn all editing marks off before taking a screenshot. Note that many websites and programs now feature such editing marks (the problem isn't just in Word).
- Necessary contrast is lost in grayscale. Sometimes, two colors that ordinarily contrast well blend together in grayscale. Even if your pictures are in color, some customers will read your eBook on black-and-white devices (like the Paperwhite or Voyage).
- There is too much text in an image.[52] You should separate the text from the image and include it in a paragraph before or after the picture instead.
- A small image blows up on older devices due to lack of padding (Sec. 4.4).

You can also achieve better quality images by working with professional image software. Adobe PhotoShop and Gimp are used by many professionals; Gimp is available for free. Note that the simpler program called Paint tends to result in pixilated and blurry images.

---

[52] Two notable exceptions include fully illustrated children's books and comic books, although you might instead format those as fixed-format eBooks using the Kindle Kids' Book Creator or the Kindle Comic Creator (mentioned in Sec.'s 1.1, 1.5, and 4.12).

Don't compress images for your Kindle eBook. Images are automatically compressed after uploading the book to KDP, so there is no need for this. A few years back, it was necessary to compress pictures before the upload, but things have improved. Now KDP's automatic compression is pretty good (and quite convenient).

Insert and wrap your images following the method described in Sec. 4.11.

Preview your pictures across all devices before you publish to ensure that your pictures come out well. Sec. 4.13 shows you how to run a quick test, and Chapter 7 discusses how to preview your eBook in detail.

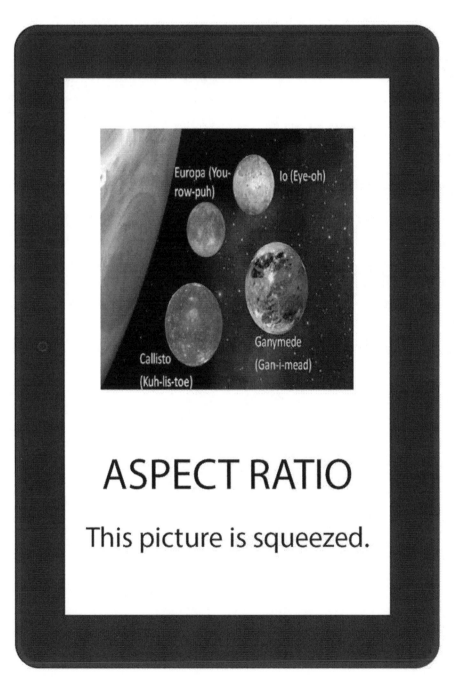

ROTATED

Don't rotate a picture.

It will appear sideways

in both portrait

and landscape.

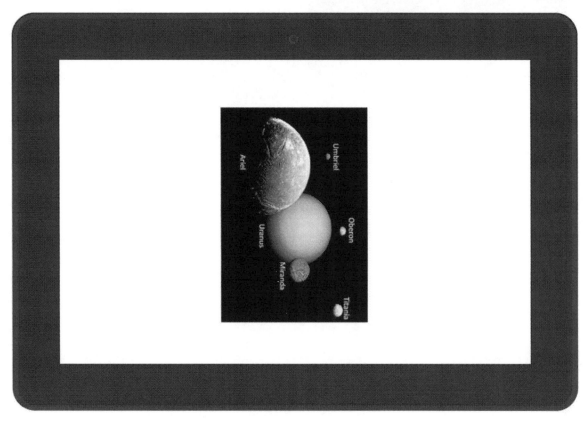

4.7 Kindle Design Considerations with Images

When a Kindle eBook contains pictures and text that are mixed together, the following design issues may arise:

- A large gap of white space may appear at the bottom of a 'page' of text. This happens when the picture doesn't fit into that gap at the bottom of the previous 'page.'

- One or two lines of text may appear above or below a picture. (For a very large picture, there may be one or two lines of text both above *and* below the picture.)

- A short paragraph of text between two pictures may be split across two 'pages,' with the short paragraph beginning below a picture on one 'page' and ending above a picture on the next 'page.'

- There is no guarantee that a figure caption will fit on the same 'page' beneath the figure. We'll consider figure captions in Sec. 4.10.

- It can be difficult to achieve a good flow of both text and images throughout the book.

These issues become more significant when there are numerous images interspersed with text throughout the book, and when many of the images take up at least half of the screen size. The pictures on the following pages illustrate some of these issues. In fact, if you're reading the eBook edition, chances are that you see white space at the bottom of the current 'page.'

In a print book, since each page is well-defined, a typographer would apply a variety of tools to prevent such problems. Unfortunately, (except for fixed-format books) there is no way to predict which text or images will appear on a given screen at any given time (since eReaders come in a variety of screen sizes, and since customers can change the text size and line spacing). The design of an eBook must allow for a variety of scenarios, with customers reading the book on different devices and using different display settings.

Following are a few suggestions for how to minimize the aforementioned problems. You can't eliminate these issues completely, but if you can reduce the occurrence of these problems, the overall design of the eBook will be improved.

- Sometimes you may have a little flexibility in where to place an image. For example, if you have just a few large images, you might be able to collect them together at the end of a chapter (or section). This may improve the readability of the text. When referring to one of these pictures in the text, you can mention that the picture can be found at the end of the chapter. Alternatively, you can number figures (like Fig. 7).

- For a very large picture—one that will take up much of the screen height on most devices—you could apply a paragraph style that incorporates a page break (see the sample paragraph style at the end of this section) to the image.

White Space at the Bottom

2 Understanding the Lunar Phases

2.1 Lunar Motion

As the Earth revolves around the sun, the moon revolves around the Earth. It takes 29 and ½ days for the moon to complete its orbit around the Earth. That's about one month ("moon-th").

One Line of Text Below

Sun

Earth

Moon

The Earth's orbit is only slightly ellip-

Across Two Pages

left to right, appear in order every 29.5 days.

After one-fourth and three-fourths of the lunar cycle, the moon appears as a half-moon. Hence the names first and third quarter.

Bottom Paragraph Split

It takes 29.5 days for the moon to complete its orbit around the Earth.

All of the phases of the lunar cycle, as shown in the following figure from

- When possible, avoid putting a short section (like one short paragraph) of text between two large figures (or between one large figure and one smaller figure). This reduces your chances of a short paragraph of text being split across two 'pages' between the figures.[53]
- If paragraph text follows a large picture, you can incorporate a page break into the paragraph style of the paragraph text to force it onto the next 'page.' There are two recommended paragraph styles at the end of this section: The second paragraph style shows how to incorporate a page break into a paragraph style for paragraph text.
- Crop images to remove any large sections of solid white, transparent, or black space that may appear on the top or bottom of the image.[54] For example, when a very thick white strip appears at the top or bottom, it will look like wasted space before or after the image (except in night or sepia mode, where it will stand out like a sore thumb). A solid black strip has a similar issue (as do green or sepia strips). A *thin* strip (border) at the top or bottom is less of a problem.

Another important consideration has to do with viewing images in **portrait** or **landscape** mode. Most customers prefer to read Kindle eBooks in portrait mode, but a few read in landscape. You should design your eBook with portrait mode in mind, since that's the dominant reading habit, but consider how it may look in landscape mode (you can preview your book both ways—see Chapter 7). Bear in mind that customers are reluctant to turn their device sideways. A few will rotate the device to view a picture in landscape mode, but many customers won't (except for the rare image that is so compelling that it requires a closer look).

You must ask yourself how the picture will look when it's viewed differently than you intended (that is, when a picture designed to be viewed in landscape mode is viewed in portrait mode instead, or vice-versa). One possible problem is that important detail can be lost when the picture is viewed the 'wrong' way. Another possibility is that one orientation may adversely impact the design of your eBook. The best thing is to preview your images both ways to see how it looks.

The biggest issue with landscape mode has to do with a mistake that some authors make, misunderstanding how landscape mode works. **It's a mistake to rotate the image sideways**, since that will make it *impossible* for the customer to view the picture correctly. The 'bottom' of the picture needs to be on the 'bottom.' Don't rotate the 'bottom' to the 'left' (or 'right'). Leave the 'bottom' on the 'bottom.' See the example landscape pictures that follow.

---

[53] A short paragraph of text gets split across two pages all the time in Kindle eBooks. However, when this happens between two pictures, the problem stands out more.

[54] White space on the left or right sides is okay. In fact, in Sec. 4.4, I mentioned how to pad smaller images with a transparent canvas in the background.

The important point is that landscape is *automatic*. There really is *nothing* to do. If you try to do something to accommodate landscape, that's when a mistake may be made. If a picture is longer than it is tall, when a customer rotates the device, the long side will automatically stay on the 'bottom' when the device rotates, so it automatically works in landscape.

> **Tip**: Make sure that every picture has its 'bottom' at the 'bottom.' Don't rotate your pictures sideways. If you have to turn your head to view the picture right while looking at your computer monitor, you have made a big mistake.

The examples on the following pages show both the correct and incorrect methods of inserting a picture that is designed to be viewed in landscape mode. Just to be clear, the second picture, which is labeled 'ROTATED,' is **incorrect**. If you're reading the eBook version of this book, try rotating your device to see how these pictures look in both portrait and landscape mode. Note that when the author does this correctly, the picture displays with the proper orientation regardless of whether the customer reads in landscape or portrait mode (whereas if the author does this incorrectly, the picture has the incorrect orientation in both modes.)

Beware that some large screen devices automatically show two pages side by side with portrait orientation when a customer changes the orientation to landscape, rather than one large page in landscape orientation.

The intended **size** of a picture is another consideration. There are basically three kinds of picture sizes:

- pictures intended to display full-width (or full-height)
- pictures you want to prevent from blowing up to full-width (or full-height)
- pictures where it doesn't really make a difference

For pictures that you want to display **full-width** (or full-height), apply the trick from Sec. 5.5 to force them full-width (or full-height) on all devices, including displays that may be more than 2048 pixels across. (This also helps to make your eBook relatively future-proof.)

To prevent a smaller image from blowing up on an older device, pad the image as described in Sec. 4.4. Before you pad the image (or afterward, while checking the preview), consider whether the **padding** may pose a problem on any devices. For example, padding an image is a *mistake* when doing so prevents a customer with a small screen size (like 600 × 800 pixels) from seeing the intended detail.

You generally don't need to pad an image unless the picture is small (in width), and even then you don't need to pad it unless it wouldn't look good blown up to full-width on older devices. Ideally, you would use GIF format with transparent padding, but recall that GIF is better for pictures with line art and text, whereas JPEG is better for photographs and color blends (Sec. 4.1).

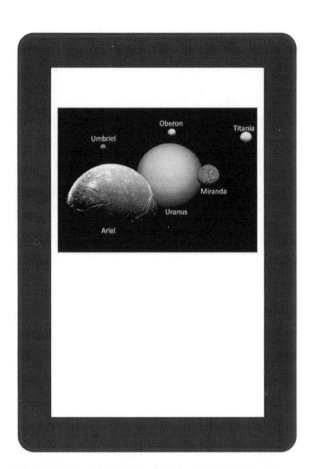

CORRECT

Not rotated.

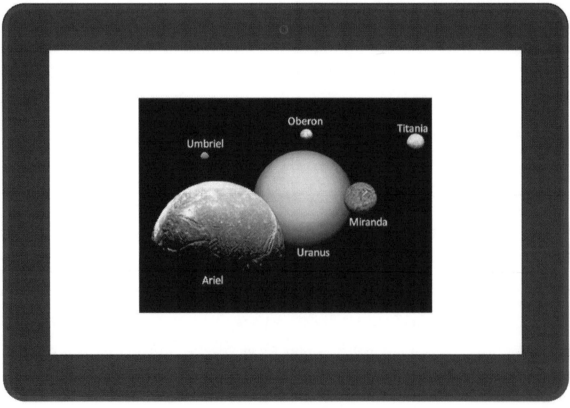

ROTATED

Don't rotate a picture.

It will appear sideways

in both portrait

and landscape.

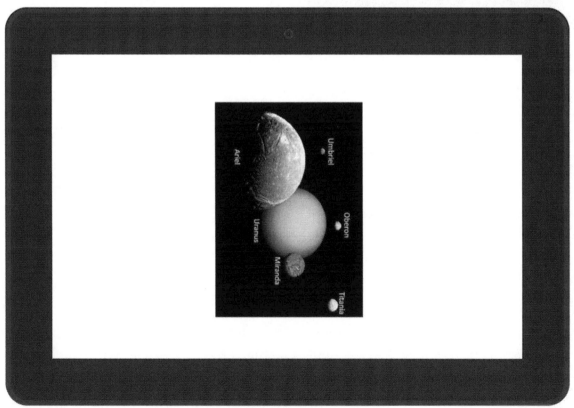

If you pad an image with JPEG format, when you choose the color of your padding, consider how it will look in normal reading mode, in night mode, or on a green or sepia background. When you pad an image with older devices in mind, keep in mind that most of the problematic older devices have limited display sizes (like 600 × 800 pixels), so the canvas size probably doesn't need to be more than about 600 to 1000 pixels wide.

Another issue related to size is **zoom**. On touch-screen Kindle devices, customers can zoom in on images by double-tapping them. Some recent Kindle devices include other options, like pinch-to-zoom or regional magnification. This allows the customer to zoom in for greater detail. However, you can't count on this: Unfortunately, not all customers know how to use their devices (and although some know how to zoom, it doesn't always occur to them to do it). Reading an eBook is also most convenient when the reader doesn't need to do extra work (zooming requires the customer to do some work). In a well-designed eBook, zoom wouldn't be required to see sufficient detail, but would be an option to see improved detail.

Zoom has a second impact on eBook design: A picture may look fine to begin with, but may appear blurry when it is zoomed in. Try zooming in on your pictures when you preview your book to ensure that they look fine when customers enlarge them.

Note that the **background color** of your image can stand out in certain reading modes. In general, you want the *foreground* to stand out, *not* the background. Some notable issues have to do with transparency. Others have to do with customers reading in night mode, sepia mode, or with a green background.

The worst case occurs when part of the image is rendered invisible. This can happen with black line art or black text on a transparent background in GIF format, for example. The problem is that solid black shows through the transparency. A similar effect can occur on older devices even though it may seem like the screen is white. Don't create a GIF image with black line art and text against a transparent background. Putting black line art or text against a white background is fine (though in that case you want to preview how that white space looks in night mode). The problems occur when you have text or line art that is black, white, green, or sepia in color, and when that text or line art appears directly over a transparent background on a GIF image (either change the background to a color that works well against the foreground, or change the color of the text or line art so that it stands out against any reading background).

When designing your images, consider how the background would look in normal, night, sepia, and green reading modes. A solid white background blends into the screen in normal mode, but may stand out in night or sepia mode, for example. While many customers don't read in night or sepia mode, you don't want there to be significant design problems for those customers who do.

In a print book, a small image is sometimes placed beside a paragraph, or a small section of text may be set apart from the rest with a **sidebar** or **textbox**. In an eBook, images are generally best placed *between* paragraphs, *not* beside them. Placing a picture beside a paragraph wouldn't work well on a small screen, and older devices wouldn't support it. Even on a large screen, it would amplify problems with justification (or with ragged right text, it would still create significant problems).

Set the text wrap to In Line With Text and place the picture on its own line (really, it will be on its own *paragraph*) between paragraphs, as described in Sec. 4.11. If you have a tiny figure, like an equation or an unsupported character formatted as a picture, it is possible to place the image within a paragraph besides text, but doing so introduces significant problems (discussed in Sec. 4.9). Pictures used for the purpose of unsupported characters, fancy text, or equations are generally formatted best between paragraphs (not within a paragraph of text, and not beside a text paragraph) with text wrap set to In Line With Text (in GIF format with transparent padding to prevent them from blowing up on older devices). Remember not to put text or line art that is black, white, green, or sepia in color directly over a transparent background on a GIF image.

Now suppose that you have a picture that you wish to place all by itself between two page breaks: That is, suppose that you want the picture's paragraph style to incorporate a page break, and you also want the paragraph of text that follows the picture to include another page break, so that the picture appears all by itself on the same 'page.' (I *don't* recommend doing this will all of your pictures. There may be some cases where this is worth doing: You have to consider how it may impact the eBook design, weighing the pros against the cons—one obvious con is the potential white space that may be left on the previous screen.) If you do this, you might want to **center** the image **vertically** on the screen. Centering the picture *horizontally* is easy, provided that you use a paragraph style with centered alignment. Centering the picture *vertically* can't be pulled off satisfactorily (for all devices, apps, and customer settings) using just Microsoft Word. If you add Space Before immediately following a page break (or by incorporating a page break into the paragraph style, which is the better way to create a page break), some Kindle devices (especially, older devices) or apps may ignore this instruction. Even if you could add Spacing Before the picture following a page break, the problem with doing this in Word is you have no idea how much space to add to center the picture, since every device has a different size screen. (On a very small screen, you might even wind up with a blank page before the image.) You need to work with a special type of file in order to center a picture vertically, and even then it's not 'easy' (Sec. 5.12).

My recommendation is to *not* try to center the picture vertically. You're more likely to do more harm than good (on some device or app, or for certain customer settings), even if you look into advanced techniques that go beyond Word. If you're really intent on vertical centering (remember, we're talking about centering vertically—horizontal centering is easy: just use a paragraph style with centered alignment, like the one recommended at the end of this section), you could pad the picture with a border (so that your original image is centered vertically with the border). If you make the height match the maximum possible display height, and if the overall aspect ratio (after adding your border) matches the Kindle Fire aspect ratio (1:1.6), it will automatically center vertically on every device. Note: If the picture is in JPEG format (or if you use GIF format, but don't use transparent padding), whichever color you use for the border will stand out on some background (though some pictures will look okay with a white or black border—test it to find out).

Sidebar

One way to create a sort of sidebar is to use a pair of directional borders, as I have done here. In an eBook, this sidebar isn't 'beside' the text; it's between paragraphs instead. If you do this, your directional borders should be very wide and very short. Note how these two borders point toward one another. If the note in the sidebar isn't vital to the reader, you might format it as a footnote instead. Some eBook formatters prefer to omit the border, simply using paragraph styles that apply Spacing After to the paragraph preceding the sidebar paragraph and to the last paragraph of the sidebar, and applying paragraph styles to the Sidebar paragraphs that have even left margin (with First Line Indent set to 0.01") to set the paragraph off (see the IndentBlock paragraph style recommended in Sec. 3.4).

If you want to place a **page break** before any picture, do this by using a paragraph style that incorporates a page break (see the recommended paragraph style that follows). A possible consequence is a large gap of white space at the end of the preceding 'page.' Therefore, you probably don't want to format *all* of your pictures this way. For very large images (those that will take much of the screen height on most devices), there is likely to be white space on the preceding 'page' anyway. With smaller images, the page break may introduce white space that wouldn't have been there otherwise. The following paragraph style is better suited for very *large* (or tall) pictures.

Two recommended **paragraph styles** follow. The first paragraph style is for the *picture*. If you want the image to appear by itself (with no text after it), use the second paragraph style below for the *paragraph* of text that follows the picture. These supplement the paragraph styles recommended in Sec. 3.4. I'm not recommending that you apply the first style to every picture, or that you apply the second style to the text that follows any picture. You must decide on this on a case by case basis. Every page break may introduce white space on the previous screen, so any page break must supply a benefit that's worth this risk.

Recommended settings for **centered images** that incorporate a **page break**:

- What it's for: This style is for centered images or text where you wish to incorporate a page break. (You probably don't want a page break before *all* of your pictures, especially if you have smaller pictures in your eBook.) For images where you *don't* want to incorporate a page break, see the CenterSpaceAfter style recommended in Sec. 3.4.
- Font size: 12 pt.
- Font style: Use the default font style (Calibri or Times New Roman).
- Font color: Automatic.
- Alignment: Centered.
- Indent: Format > Paragraph > Special > First Line > "none."
- Line spacing: Single. Leave the At field empty.
- Space before: 0 pt.
- Space after: 12 pt.
- Page break: Format > Paragraph > choose the Line and Page Breaks tab at the top of the pop-up window > Page Break Before. This is the best way to incorporate a page break with a picture.
- Style for the following paragraph: Choose the paragraph style for non-indented body text or for Normal text. (It's not really necessary to indent a paragraph after a centered line, as we noted in Sec. 3.7, but some books do indent such a paragraph anyway.)
- Suggested name: CenterPageBreak. The words 'PageBreak' may help remind you that this centered style incorporates a page break.

Recommended settings for **paragraph text** that incorporates a page break:

- What it's for: If you want the text following a picture to begin on a new page, apply this paragraph style to that paragraph text. Like the first paragraph of a chapter, it's not really necessary to indent a paragraph that follows a page break. This paragraph style is similar to the NoIndent paragraph style recommended in Sec. 3.4, except that it incorporates a page break into the style.
- Font size: 12 pt.
- Font style: Use the default font style (Calibri or Times New Roman).
- Font color: Automatic.
- Alignment: Justified (i.e. full).
- Indent: Format > Paragraph > Special > First Line > 0.01". Look closely to make sure it is 0.01", and not 0.1". Anything smaller than 0.01" can lead to big problems. (Both Left and Right should be set to 0.) As discussed in Sec. 3.7, it is customary to only indent a paragraph of text when another paragraph precedes it.
- Line spacing: Single. Leave the At field empty.
- Space before: 0 pt.
- Space after: 0 pt or 12 pt. **Note**: Use 0 pt if another paragraph of text follows this paragraph, and use 12 pt if an image follows this paragraph, for example. Create two separate paragraph styles like this (one with 0 pt and one with 12 pt Spacing After) if there are occasions in your book where you need both 0 pt and 12 pt Spacing After.
- Page break: Format > Paragraph > choose the Line and Page Breaks tab at the top of the pop-up window > Page Break Before. This is the best way to incorporate a page break with a text paragraph.
- Style for the following paragraph: Choose the paragraph style for normal body text.
- Suggested name: NoIndentPageBreak. The words 'PageBreak' may help remind you that this paragraph style incorporates a page break.

4.8 Formatting Tables as Images

Formatting a table as an image may not be the magic solution to a table that doesn't format well as a table. There are a few cases where it can work, and some where it can't.

The main challenge with formatting a table as an image is with the text. There are two issues. First, you want the text to appear very sharp, even when a customer zooms in on the image with regional magnification. Recall that GIF images are better suited for pictures with text. You need a high-quality image with sharp text with high enough resolution that the text still appears sharp when zoomed in. Secondly, you want the text to be easily readable across all devices. Ideally, the text would be readable without relying on the customer to zoom. This limits the amount of information that can appear on a table on a small screen (just imagine a customer reading with a cell phone).

Most tables would format best as actual tables (Sec. 3.12): Use a table instead of an image when that will work. The larger the table, the smaller the text, or the more text that appears in the table, the more challenging it becomes to format the table well as a picture (that will display well across all devices).

One example of when a smaller table may work well as an image—but wouldn't be feasible as an actual table—is when the table includes unsupported characters, equations, fancy text, or formatting that a table wouldn't support across all devices.

If you're attempting to format a **large** table as a picture (and can't break it up into smaller tables), you want the original picture to be sharp and have a high pixel count, if possible. Some devices can accommodate 2000 to 2560 pixels across the longest side, and this may be worth it to help read the text in the table. (You can go upwards of 3820 pixels for the longest side to optimize the zoom on a high resolution device, but note that this extra resolution won't help with low resolution devices.)

Following are recommendations for formatting either a table or colophon (Sec. 3.9) as an image:

- Prefer GIF format, which tends to render text more clearly. Also, for a GIF image of a table, don't include a transparent background behind text or line art that is black, white, green, or sepia in color, as the text will become *invisible* in one reading mode—or on older devices (Sec. 4.7).
- If instead you use JPEG format, a sharp image with a high pixel count is preferable.
- Fewer columns and smaller tables tend to format better. Try formatting it as an actual table (Sec. 3.12) before testing it as an image.
- Preview the result carefully (Chapter 7) to ensure that the text is readable and sharp across all devices. Note that Kindle's previewers may not display tables properly, so it's best to preview your eBook on actual devices (Sec. 7.9).

- Amazon requires that a lowercase "a" be at least 6 pixels high, but this an extreme lower limit, *not* a recommended size. Larger text is recommended: The larger, the better.

There is a more advanced option (which requires going a step beyond Word) for formatting tables, which involves SVG format and a media query (Sec. 5.12). However, that still requires using GIF format for devices that don't support SVG, so it doesn't completely remove the limitations.

This table was formatted as a picture.

	Kindle Fire 7	Kindle Fire HD 8	Kindle Fire HD 10
Display Size	7"	8"	10"
Aspect Ratio	600 × 1024	800 × 1280	1200 × 1920
Resolution	171 ppi	189 ppi	224 ppi
Weight	10.4 oz	13.0 oz	17.7 oz
Dimensions	4.5" × 7.6" × 0.4"	5.0" × 8.4" × 0.4"	6.0" × 10.3" × 0.4"
Storage	8/16 Gb	16/32 Gb	32/64 Gb

4.9 Equations, Unsupported Symbols, and In-line Images

I will refer to tiny images placed in paragraph text as **in-line images**, in contrast to most images which need to be placed between two paragraphs. The image should have the text wrap set to In Line With Text either way (so what I call an "in-line image" doesn't refer just to the text wrap).

In-line images should be very tiny, so that they are comparable to the height of the characters of text that appear in your eBook's body paragraphs. You definitely don't want to format a large picture in-line with paragraph text. You might be tempted to use in-line images in place of an otherwise unsupported character (like ✘) or to format an equation (like $C = \sqrt{A^2 + B^2}$). However, you should beware that pictures have formatting issues when they are placed in-line with paragraph text.

Since in-line images come with inherent formatting problems, it's generally best to **avoid** them. In most cases, you can insert the picture between two paragraphs, just as you would any other picture, and if needed, simply mention in the paragraph that the picture follows the paragraph (e.g. "as shown below").

If you feel the temptation to format an unsupported character or equation as an in-line image (instead of on its own line between paragraphs), you must weigh the drawbacks against the benefits. Here are some problems with in-line images:

- In-line pictures don't scale with text, so as the customer adjusts the font size, the font may become much smaller or much larger than the picture.[55] (Note that the online previewer doesn't show in-line pictures properly. The downloadable previewer displays them more reliably, although results may still vary on some devices or apps.)

- In-line images are more likely to format poorly on one or more devices.

- The vertical position of in-line pictures may be shifted relative to the text. For example, in-line pictures may appear raised compared to text.

- In-line images may display smaller or larger than you expect (even if your expectation is based on Kindle's previewer). The downloadable previewer is more reliable than the on-line previewer (both are discussed in Chapter 7), but it still isn't a perfect representation of all devices and apps.

- Readability is a greater challenge with in-line images.

When possible, the best way to format an **equation** is by using ordinary text, superscripts, subscripts, and supported symbols, as shown in Sec. 3.11 (with examples at the end of the section). When that's not possible, the next best solution is to format the equation as a picture placed between two paragraphs (with the text wrap set to In Line With Text—but this isn't what I referred to earlier as an in-line equation). In-line images (alongside text in a paragraph) should be a *last resort*, and you should preview (Chapter 7) them carefully for readability across all devices.

Compare these options. The following equation was typed directly with the keyboard using standard supported symbols and the Superscript button on the Font group on the Home ribbon: $(x + y)^2 = x^2 + 2xy + y^2$. When possible, that's the *best* option. When it isn't possible, the second best way to format an equation is to insert it as a picture on its own line between two paragraphs (with the text wrap set to In Line With Text). You can find an example of this after this para-

---

[55] If you know about HTML, beware that setting the image size in em's instead of pixels won't work on Kindle devices and apps. If you know about SVG images, it is possible to make pictures that scale with text, but beware that SVG doesn't work across all devices, so you must use a media query (Sec. 5.12) with an alternative for devices that don't support SVG.

graph. If you want to place a picture for an equation (or unsupported character) in-line with paragraph text (like this: $R = \sqrt{x^2 + y^2}$), first ask yourself if you could instead place the picture between two paragraphs (like the example below), as that will format better.

$$R = \sqrt{x^2 + y^2}$$

Note that equations typed with Word's built-in equation tools will format quite poorly on some devices or apps. I've personally tested out Word's Insert > Equation feature (as well as the older version accessible through Insert > Object > Microsoft Equation 3.0), and encountered severe problems with readability. It looked fine in the Kindle previewer, but when tested out on actual devices, I came across cases where a simple equation was completely illegible. The KDP help pages also advise that Microsoft Word's built-in equation feature doesn't work well with Kindle eBooks.

> **Tip**: If you typed any equations with Word's built-in equation tools, reformat them as GIF pictures instead. Otherwise, the equations may be completely unreadable on certain devices or apps (even if they seem okay in the preview).

Make a GIF image out of the equation and format the equation as a picture to obtain **better results**. One way to utilize Word's built-in equation feature is to copy and paste the equation into photo-editing software (such as PhotoShop or Gimp), or to use a Snipping Tool or take a screenshot (and then crop the equation as desired). It may be desirable to increase the font size of the equation in Word *before* you copy/paste or snip the equation and open it with image-editing software. If you're using the Snipping Tool, it may help to zoom in on the equation first. It's easier to reduce the size of your equation later if you decide that it's too big (whereas trying to enlarge a picture after creating it will likely result in stray pixels or blurriness).

Note that if you use the Snipping Tool to snip an equation or symbol that has black text (or line art) on a white background, if you save the picture in GIF format (or PNG, but PNG isn't recommended for your eBook), it may save the picture as black text on a transparent background, which would appear **invisible** in night mode (or on older devices).

This is a common problem because your equation probably has black text on a white screen in Microsoft Word, and since GIF is the recommended format for pictures of equations or symbols in your eBook. If you use the Snipping Tool to create a GIF image of an equation, the equation will appear invisible in night mode (or when the eBook is read on older devices).

Make sure that the background isn't transparent when the text is black, white, green, or sepia in color. Either change the background from transparency to a suitable color, or change the color of the text.

If you use photo-editing software (like PhotoShop or Gimp), it is possible to edit the picture and set it on a truly white background (rather than a transparent background). With PhotoShop, if you copy and paste the equation or symbol from Word, if you select to create a new file in PhotoShop, you should see the option to select a transparent or other color background when you create the new PhotoShop file. Similarly, if you open a GIF image in PhotoShop that has black text on a transparent background (e.g., created with the Snipping Tool), you can also open a new file with a white background, return to the GIF image, right-click the background (which is the equation), select Duplicate Layer, and adjust the Document under Destination to Untitled (that's the default name of the new file that you created—but if you already saved and named the new file, then select that filename instead).

Whenever you use the Snipping Tool (or take a screenshot), be sure spelling and grammar marks are turned off. Also note that snips and screenshots come with limited resolution, meaning that you may lose sharpness. Many of these provide 72 or 96 PPI (though I have a newer computer with a very large monitor for which the Snipping Tool yields 192 PPI). The reasons that I suggested first increasing the font size and zooming in is to help combat the limited resolution (though in some cases these steps may not be necessary).

If you originally typed equations in Word using the built-in equation tools, save your original equations in a separate Word file before you turn them into pictures. That way, if you need to revise your equations, you will have access to them. (If you decide to make a print edition of your book, for the *print* edition it will be better to use Word's built-in equations than to use pictures, whereas for the *eBook* edition it is much better to use pictures than to use Word's built-in equations. Compare $C = \sqrt{A^2 + B^2}$, which I typed for the print edition, to $C = \sqrt{A^2 + B^2}$, which is the equation that I inserted into the eBook.)

One of the greatest challenges with equations and symbols—regardless of whether they are in-line with paragraph text or if they are placed on their own line—is to make them the right size so that they appear a decent size in every possible reading situation (different display sizes, both portrait and landscape orientations, different font size settings, different reading backgrounds, etc.). Furthermore, if they look great on all devices, they might appear way too large on the Look Inside. You want to ensure readability in all situations, which means it's probably best to make them too large than to make them too small, since a customer may be reading on a cell phone in portrait mode. However, it would be nice for equation text to be approximately the same size as paragraph text in the most common reading situations, but since there are so many display sizes, from cell phones to the Look Inside on a PC, this is a really difficult challenge.

Tip: Make a few sample equations in several different sizes with paragraph text in between in a new document, and preview your "test book" extensively: That will help you decide which size is best for your eBook. Sec. 4.13 provides instructions for testing pic-tures, and Chapter 7 will show you how to preview your test book with the different previewers, actual devices, and free Kindle reading apps.

Following are recommended guidelines for **equations** or **symbols** formatted as pictures:

- Equations formatted as pictures should be saved in GIF format, since text tends to render best in GIF format.
- An equation formatted as a single line should be at least 45 pixels high. This is a **minimum**, *not* a recommended size; most equations will be taller.
- A lowercase "a" needs to be at least 6 pixels high, but again this is a **minimum**, *not* a recommended size. Adhering to a taller minimum will make the equation more readable across all devices.
- Don't use a *transparent* background behind text that is black, white, green, or sepia in color, as it would appear *invisible* in some situations (described in Sec. 4.7). It's okay to have black text against a white, non-transparent background (or white text against a black background), but consider how the background may stand out in night, sepia, or green reading modes.
- If you will be formatting the picture in-line beside paragraph text, **cropping the picture to the very bottom of the equation text** may help to limit problems with the picture appearing raised relative to the text.
- **Don't crop, resize, or otherwise edit the pictures** *after* inserting them into Microsoft Word. Cropping and resizing must be done with image-editing software (like PhotoShop or Gimp) *before* inserting the picture into Word.
- Follow the advice given in the previous tip to help figure out the best size for your equations or symbols.
- If desirable, pad the image to prevent it from blowing up on an older device. The padding may be transparent (if you use GIF format), provided that text or line art doesn't disappear appear against a transparent background (for example, black text may disappear in night mode or white text may disappear in the default reading mode). Note that it's possible to place a white rectangle behind black equation text, but otherwise have transparent pad-ding (so long as the text itself isn't directly over the transparent background): This com-bination allows padding to be less obtrusive on other reading backgrounds, without causing the text to go invisible. The picture below provides an example of this.

$$\text{transparency} \quad \frac{43}{18} = 2\frac{7}{18} \quad \text{transparency}$$

Word's built-in equation tools don't work well with Kindle. It's better to format every equation as a picture.

Word's Equation Tools

Coulomb's Law

Consider the two pointlike charges illustrated below. The left charge, q_1, creates an electric field everywhere in space, including the location of the right charge, q_2. We could use the formula $E_1 = \frac{k|q_1|}{R^2}$ to find the magnitude of q_1's electric field at the location of q_2. We could then find the electric force exerted on q_2 using the equation $F_e = |q_2|E_1$. If we combine these two equations together, we get Coulomb's law, as shown below.

$$F_e = |q_2|E_1 = F_e = |q_2|\left(\frac{k|q_1|}{R^2}\right) = k\frac{|q_1||q_2|}{R^2}$$

Similarly, we could use the formula $E_2 = \frac{k|q_2|}{R^2}$ to find the magnitude of q_2's electric field at the location of q_1, and then

Reformatted as Pictures

Coulomb's Law

Consider the two pointlike charges illustrated below. The left charge, q_1, creates an electric field everywhere in space, including the location of the right charge, q_2. We could use the formula $E_1 = \frac{k|q_1|}{R^2}$ to find the magnitude of q_1's electric field at the location of q_2. We could then find the electric force exerted on q_2 using the equation $F_e = |q_2|E_1$. If we combine these two equations together, we get Coulomb's law, as shown below.

$$F_e = |q_2|E_1 = F_e = |q_2|\left(\frac{k|q_1|}{R^2}\right) = k\frac{|q_1||q_2|}{R^2}$$

Similarly, we could use the formula

As the customer adjusts the font size, in-line pictures don't scale with the font size.

Larger Font Size

Coulomb's Law

Consider the two pointlike charges illustrated below. The left charge, q_1, creates an electric field everywhere in space, including the location of the right charge, q_2. We could use the formula $E_1 = \frac{k|q_1|}{R^2}$ to find the magnitude of q_1's electric field at the location of q_2. We could then find the electric force exerted on q_2 using the equation $F_e = |q_2|E_1$. If we combine these two equations together, we get Coulomb's law, as shown below.

$$F_e = |q_2|E_1 = F_e = |q_2|\left(\frac{k|q_1|}{R^2}\right) = k\frac{|q_1||q_2|}{R^2}$$

Similarly, we could use the

kindle

Smaller Font Size

Coulomb's Law

Consider the two pointlike charges illustrated below. The left charge, q_1, creates an electric field everywhere in space, including the location of the right charge, q_2. We could use the formula $E_1 = \frac{k|q_1|}{R^2}$ to find the magnitude of q_1's electric field at the location of q_2. We could then find the electric force exerted on q_2 using the equation $F_e = |q_2|E_1$. If we combine these two equations together, we get Coulomb's law, as shown below.

$$F_e = |q_2|E_1 = F_e = |q_2|\left(\frac{k|q_1|}{R^2}\right) = k\frac{|q_1||q_2|}{R^2}$$

Similarly, we could use the formula $E_2 = \frac{k|q_2|}{R^2}$ to find the magnitude of q_2's electric field at the location of q_1, and then we could then find the electric force exerted on q_1 using the equation $F_e = |q_1|E_2$. We would obtain the same result, $F_e = k\frac{|q_1||q_2|}{R^2}$. This should come as no surprise, since Newton's third law of motion states that the force that q_1 exerts on q_2 is equal in magnitude and opposite in direction to the force that q_2 exerts on q_1.

kindle

4.10 Formatting Captions

It's very common among print books to include a numbered caption below each figure, such as: "Fig. 23. This figure illustrates a gamma-ray burst emanating from a supernova."

The inclusion of captions in an eBook poses a design challenge. Unlike a print book, you can't guarantee that the caption following a picture will appear on the same 'page' as the picture—unless you embed the caption text in the figure (but that creates a readability challenge).

I prefer to avoid captions in my eBooks. Rather, whatever I want to write in the caption, I convey that idea in a paragraph before or after the picture. In the paragraph that mentions the picture, when I mention the concept conveyed by the image, I write something like, "as shown in the following[56] figure."

If you elect to place a caption below a figure, you must choose between the following two options. I recommend the *first* option.

- Format the caption as paragraph text after the figure, with the risk that part or all of the text may sometimes appear on the following 'page.' If you incorporate a page break into the paragraph style for the picture, and if the picture isn't too tall (and the caption isn't too long), it improves the chances that the caption will fit on the 'page' below the image (but the customer can choose a very large font size, or read the book on a small screen, so there are no guarantees). However, this may create significant white space on the page prior to the picture. (Don't include a page break in the paragraph style for the caption, of course. The goal is to get the caption to display on the *same* page as the figure, if possible.)

- Embed the caption text in the image itself. Using image-editing software such as Photo-Shop or Gimp, you can open the image file and insert a textbox with the caption. The problem with this is that it's challenging to make the text both sharp and large enough such that it will be readable across all devices (without needing to zoom in). If the picture is a photograph or otherwise formats best as a JPEG file, this poses an additional problem, since pictures with text are better-suited to GIF format.

Yet another option is to number each figure by embedding just a little text in the corner (for example), but omit the caption. This way, it's easy to refer to any figure throughout the book, as in, "See Fig. 42," while avoiding design problems associated with captions.

---

[56] Be careful here. If you refer to the "figure below," for example, the picture might instead appear on the following 'page,' not *below*. Referring to the "following figure" is clear whether the image appears below or on the next 'page.' Also, be careful not to write things like "the figure on page 72," since a page number has no meaning in a reflowable eBook.

Fig. 42. The phases of the moon are shown for one lunar cycle. Waxing

There is no guarantee that a caption will fit on the 'page.'

4.11 Inserting Pictures into Your Word File

This is the proper way to insert your images into Microsoft Word:[57]

- Use the Pictures button on the Insert ribbon: Insert > Pictures. Don't copy and paste images into Word.

- Perfect your image (with photo-editing software like PhotoShop or Gimp) *before* inserting it into Word. Don't crop, resize, or otherwise edit your picture in Word.

- If you plan to upload a Word document, it's best to keep your picture at 192 PPI[58] (or less) before inserting it into Word.[59] If instead you plant to follow Chapter 5 to go a quick step beyond Word (highly recommended, especially if your eBook has pictures), then 300 PPI is optimal for the reasons discussed at the end of Sec. 4.3.

- Right-click the picture, select Size and Position, choose the Size tab, and set Width to 100%.[60] Leave the aspect ratio locked: When you change Width to 100%, Height should automatically do the same.

- If your picture appears too large in Word, like it exceeds the page size, *don't worry*. It won't display too large on a Kindle device (though, of course, you should preview your book carefully before you publish, as discussed in Chapter 7).

If your Word file contains pictures, you will get the *best* results by following Chapter 5 to go a quick step beyond Word. On the KDP help pages, **Amazon recommends that you go a step beyond Word if your eBook contains pictures**. Chapter 5 will show you how to implement Amazon's recommendation (and also make a few other subtle improvements to your eBook).

---

[57] For a **print** book, you also want to find a Word to PDF converter and print to PDF using that. Don't use the Save as PDF option, as this reduces the DPI of your images (but don't use PDF for an eBook). Also, check the box under File > Options > Advanced that says, "Do not compress images in file" **before** inserting your first image. You will also want 300 DPI images for your print book, whereas the only strict PPI requirement for your eBook is a minimum of 72 PPI—though 300 PPI is recommended if you follow the instructions in Sec. 5.2. However, if you upload a Word document to KDP, exceeding 192 PPI may actually be a problem: It's funny, since in principle PPI shouldn't matter at all for the 'size' of a picture in an eBook (though as mentioned at the end of Sec. 4.3, the PPI of your original image may impact *sharpness*), but I've seen pictures that were over 192 PPI get reduced in **size** during the Word to Kindle conversion.

[58] If you also make a **print** book, you will want 300 DPI images for that. You will need two separate files, one formatted for your eBook and one formatted for your print book.

[59] For your Kindle eBook, if you upload a Word document to KDP note that pictures exceeding 192 PPI may have problems regardless of whether or not the box to compress pictures is checked. (For a **print** book, you definitely want to check the box to *not* compress images in the file. This option is fine for the Book, too, since Amazon will automatically compress your images during the Kindle conversion.)

[60] This *doesn't* make your image full-width. Rather, it helps to prevent Word from reducing the size of your image.

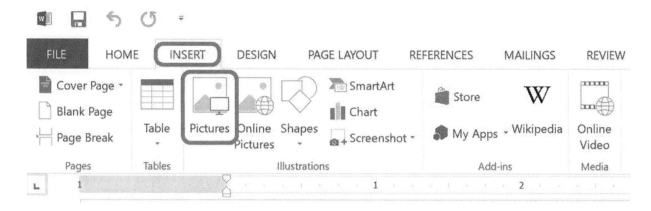

The previous steps help you get the best results out of Word (though you should still follow the above steps even if you go a step beyond Word as outlined in Chapter 5). If you upload a Word document (instead of using the format of Sec. 5.2) to KDP that includes pictures, your Kindle eBook may encounter issues, such as:

- Pictures may be reduced to display at a smaller pixel size. I've seen pictures that measure 2000 pixels across in Word that don't display full-width on a device because they were reduced to 600 pixels across after uploading a Word document.

- One or more pictures may show a drop shadow—a black line along one or more of the edges.

Using the method of Chapter 5 will help to prevent these problems. For example, when you make the compressed zipped folder in Sec. 5.2, you will be able to directly see if Word has reduced the pixel count of any of your pictures (and if so, you can replace the picture file right then and there: simply delete the picture from the image files folder, copy and paste the original picture into the image file folder, and rename the picture to match the name of the file that you deleted—note that these steps will be made clear in Chapter 5).

Another reason to follow Chapter 5 is that you can then make a few improvements to your Kindle eBook that aren't possible when you upload a Word document to KDP. For example, Sec. 5.5 will show you how to display large images full-width across all devices, even when the display size is larger than the picture size.

If you decide to skip Chapter 5 and upload a Word document to KDP, I recommend that you test the pictures out on an actual Kindle device with the largest size screen that you can get your hands on. This will help you see whether or not the size of any pictures have been suffi-ciently reduced during the Kindle conversion.

Uploaded a Word file.

In both cases, the original picture is 300 DPI and sized at 1 280 × 2048.

Uploading a Word file, the pixel size was reduced.

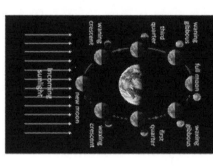

Followed Sec. 5.5.

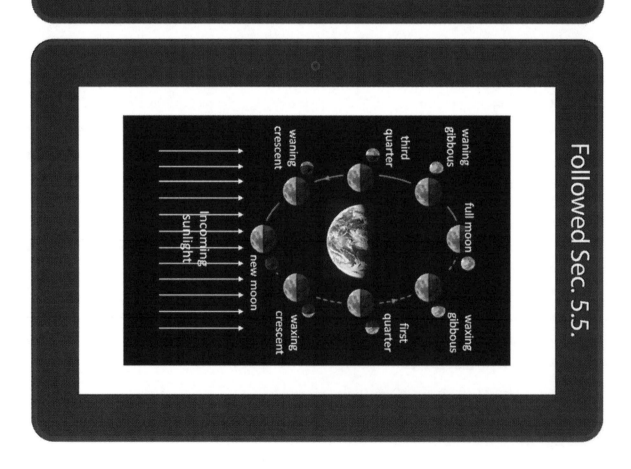

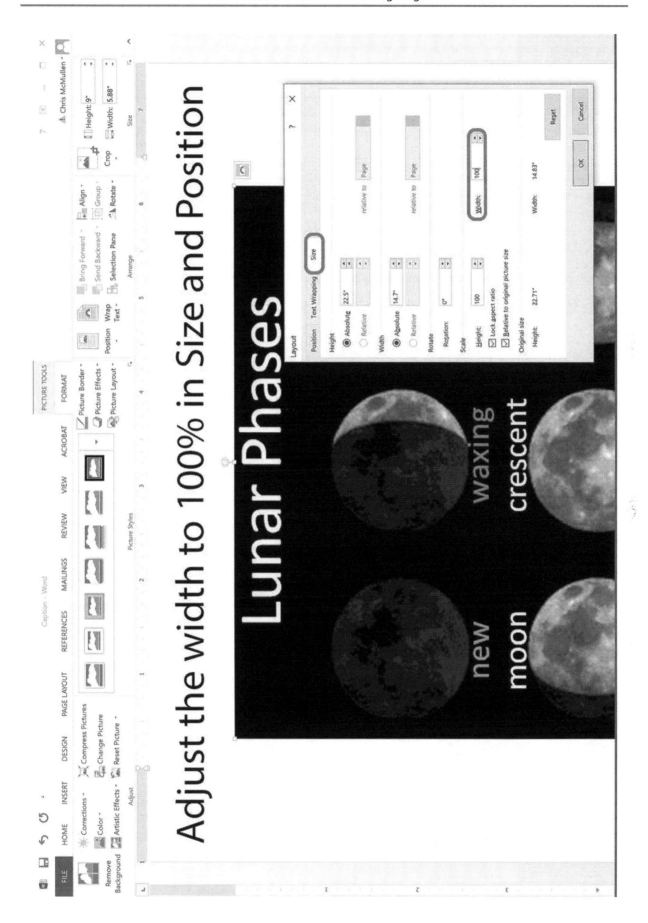

Adjust the width to 100% in Size and Position

If the picture exceeds the margins in Word, that's okay.
It won't exceed the display size in the Kindle eBook.

Warning: According to the Amazon KDP help pages, you should "submit your images separately from your Word manuscript in a ZIP folder" (as this book will show you in Sec. 5.2) "because *Word can decrease the quality of your images*." What Amazon means is that when you finish formatting your Word file, you should go a quick step beyond Word as I outline in Sec. 5.2. (Using Word *isn't* the problem: Uploading the Word file directly to KDP rather than creating the zipped file is the problem.) Sec. 5.5 also shows you how to optimize your images after going a quick step beyond Word.

4.12 Picture Books

We will consider two kinds of picture books in this section:

- books with pictures on virtually every page
- books with frequent pictures that are placed between short paragraphs of text

The pictures at the end of this section show examples of both types of picture books.

If your book has pictures on almost every page, and if there are only one or two lines of text per page, your eBook may be better-suited to fixed-format, using Amazon's free Kindle Kids' Book Creator (Sec.'s 1.1 and 1.5), which allows for pop-up text. A comic book should be formatted using the Kindle Comic Creator (Sec. 1.1).

Otherwise, your eBook will probably format better *without* using those free tools. Text is much easier to read when you format your eBook as I have recommended in this guide. Text is much harder to read when you use the fixed-format tools (like the Kindle Kids' Book Creator). The problem with fixed-format is that the customer can't resize the text to make it larger (and any other method of making the text larger, like pop-up text or region magnification, is an *inconvenient* way of reading a book). If you format your eBook as I have recommended in this guide, the customer will easily be able to make text larger (unless you embed text in a picture).

I have read several illustrated children's Kindle eBooks to my daughter. As a customer, I understand some of the challenges of reading picture books formatted in different ways. Here are a few frustrations that I've experienced trying to read fixed-format picture books on Kindle:

- A few times, pop-up text didn't render quite as intended.
- Even on a large screen, the text often isn't readable without using the pop-up feature (or pinch-and-zoom, depending on how the book was created). It can be tedious reading pop-ups on every page.
- The page can sort of be like a minefield. If you accidentally click the page, pop-up text can open or the picture can zoom in.
- It was difficult to read children's books with two-page spreads, even on my Kindle Fire HD 8.9".

This is a fixed-format eBook created with the Kindle Kids' Book Creator.

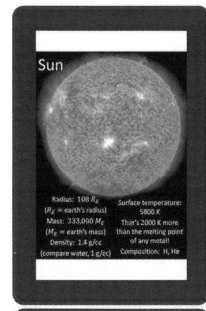

Sun

Radius: 108 R_E
(R_E = earth's radius)
Mass: 333,000 M_E
(M_E = earth's mass)
Density: 1.4 g/cc
(compare water, 1 g/cc)

Surface temperature:
5800 K
That's 2000 K more
than the melting point
of any metal!
Composition: H, He

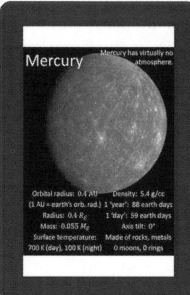

Mercury

Mercury has virtually no atmosphere.

Orbital radius: 0.4 AU
(1 AU = earth's orb. rad.)
Radius: 0.4 R_E
Mass: 0.055 M_E
Surface temperature:
700 K (day), 100 K (night)

Density: 5.4 g/cc
1 'year': 88 earth days
1 'day': 59 earth days
Made of rocks, metals
0 moons, 0 rings

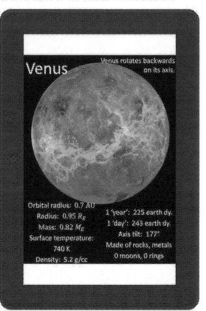

Venus

Venus rotates backwards on its axis.

Orbital radius: 0.7 AU
Radius: 0.95 R_E
Mass: 0.82 M_E
Surface temperature:
740 K
Density: 5.2 g/cc

1 'year': 225 earth dy.
1 'day': 243 earth dy.
Axis tilt: 177°
Made of rocks, metals
0 moons, 0 rings

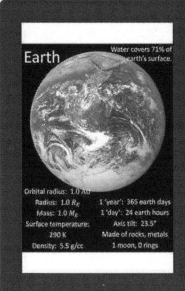

Earth

Water covers 71% of earth's surface.

Orbital radius: 1.0 AU
Radius: 1.0 R_E
Mass: 1.0 M_E
Surface temperature:
290 K
Density: 5.5 g/cc

1 'year': 365 earth days
1 'day': 24 earth hours
Axis tilt: 23.5°
Made of rocks, metals
1 moon, 0 rings

Mars

Mars has the largest volcano (Olympus Mons).

Orbital radius: 1.5 AU
Radius: 0.53 R_E
Mass: 0.11 M_E
Surface temperature:
220 K
Density: 3.9 g/cc

1 'year': 1.9 earth yrs
1 'day': 24.6 earth hrs
Axis tilt: 25.2°
Made of rocks, metals
2 moons, 0 rings

Jupiter

Jupiter is the largest planet.

Orbital radius: 5.2 AU
Radius: 11.2 R_E
Mass: 318 M_E
Surface temperature:
125 K
Density: 1.3 g/cc

1 'year': 11.9 earth yrs
1 'day': 9.9 earth hrs
Axis tilt: 3.1°
Composition: H, He
rings, 63+ moons

This is a reflowable eBook .

Saturn has 95 times as much mass as Earth. Saturn has the lowest density of any planet (0.7 g/cc) – it's even less dense than water at standard temperature and pressure (1 g/cc).

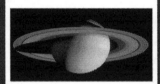

The average surface temperature of Saturn is 95 Kelvin, which is well below freezing. Like the other Jovian planets, Saturn is composed of hydrogen and helium gas. Saturn has an axis tilt of 26.7°, which is a little more than Earth's (23.5°).

One 'year' on Saturn lasts about 29 Earth years. Like Jupiter, one 'day' on Saturn is much shorter than an Earth day – it is just 10.6 hours.

Saturn has (at least) 60 moons. Saturn's largest moon is Titan.

Titan is the second largest moon in the solar system; Jupiter's largest moon, Ganymede, is the largest moon. Titan is the only moon in our solar system that has a thick atmosphere – which, like Earth's atmosphere, is predominantly composed of nitrogen. Saturn's atmosphere also includes two gases – methane and ethane – which have warmed Titan through the greenhouse effect. Although Titan may be too cold for life, its atmosphere does contain numerous organic molecules – the type of molecules that all living creatures on Earth contain. Titan's surface also has several smooth lake-size areas which may be liquid methane.

Saturn has the most prominent rings, which are actually composed of numerous chunks of ice and rocks. There are also gap moons – moons that create gaps between the rings. The rings shown in the following photo appear in false color.

1.9 Uranus

Uranus (Your-uh-nus) is the seventh planet from the sun. Uranus has a radius that is 4 times that of Earth's, while its orbital radius is 19 times that of Earth's. Uranus has 15 times as much mass as Earth. Uranus, like all of the Jovian planets, has a density (1.3 g/cc) that is small compared to the terrestrial planets.

The average surface temperature of Uranus is 60 Kelvin, which is well below freezing. Like the other Jovian planets, Uranus is composed of hydrogen and helium gas.

Uranus has an extreme axis tilt of 97.9°. It rotates about an axis that is nearly perpendicular to its orbit. Its rings and the orbits of its moons are similarly tilted about 90°. This extreme tilt may have been caused by a collision during the early stages of the solar system. Uranus has the most extreme seasons of any planet in our solar system due to its unusual tilt. Because of this tilt, although Uranus has a rotational period of 17 hours (which we would normally call a 'day'), the polar regions are light and then dark for half of a Uranus 'year.' One 'year' on Uranus lasts 84 Earth years, which means it stays dark for 42 years, then light for 42 years, and so on, near the polar regions. This is what creates the extreme seasonal effects.

Uranus has (at least) 27 moons. Uranus has 5 large moons: Titania, Oberon, Umbriel, Ariel, and Miranda. Titania is the largest of Uranus's moons, and is only slightly larger than Oberon. Like Jupiter, but unlike Saturn, Uranus has a faint ring system. The following photo shows Titania.

The following photo shows Uranus with its five largest moons. Titania is actually the largest of Uranus's moons, even though it looks smaller in the following photo. The reason that Titania appears smaller in this photo is simply that it is further away from the camera than a couple of the other moons.

- I occasionally experienced technical problems. For example, a few times every pop-up in the book suddenly opened up and none of the pop-ups would close without exiting and reopening the book.
- A few books that were available for my Kindle Fire were not available for my Paperwhite.

I have also read early children's books with a paragraph or two of text between the pictures, which were formatted as reflowable eBooks (the same format as I have recommended in this guide). These made it easier to read just by turning pages. There was no pop-up text to activate and no need to pinch-and-zoom. When the design worked well (that's the challenge), these reflowable eBooks offered a better reading experience on Kindle, in my opinion as a parent. Keep in mind that opinions vary: Some readers prefer the fixed layout for children's picture books.[61]

What I do recommend is that you browse a variety of illustrated children's books, including some that are reflowable and others that are fixed format. This will help you understand the challenges of each design, and may give you a little inspiration for your own design. If you don't have access to a Kindle device, you can still appreciate the Kindle experience by using Amazon's Kindle reading apps (like Kindle for PC, Kindle for Mac, Kindle for iPad, Kindle for Android, or Kindle for iPhone). It's easy to find inexpensive (or even free) Kindle eBooks, and the Kindle reading apps (like Kindle for PC) are available for free.

Regarding illustrated children's books, another factor may be whether the book is designed for babies (parents read to them) or beginning readers, or whether it is designed as an early chapter book (Disney has a few eBooks of this sort, for example). Those designed for parents to read to babies may work better in fixed-format, whereas early chapter books tend to be a better fit for reflowable format. (Of the Disney early chapter books that I mentioned, some of these are reflowable and came out quite nicely with a paragraph or two of text interspersed between pictures.)

The first picture that follows shows a fixed-format book created with the Kindle Kids' Book Creator, while the second picture that follows shows a reflowable format eBook. Recall that the guide that you're reading right now shows you how to make a reflowable eBook. Note that most Kindle eBooks have a reflowable format.

---

[61] Also, regarding children's books, many readers prefer *print* books over eBooks. Many of the successful children's authors I have net many print sales and personally interact with parents, grandparents, and educators in their marketing (like reading to children at a school, library, church, or hospital).

4.13 Testing Your Images

It can be helpful to create a quick test file (or a series of test files) even if the formatting of your eBook is far from complete. Such tests can help you with design choices, such as seeing how your pictures look before you commit to your method. These tests can also help you assess whether or not the file size and delivery charges may be significant for your eBook.

We'll learn how to perform a very thorough preview of the finished eBook in Chapter 7. For now, we'll focus on quick methods to create a test book and preview your test, even if your eBook is presently just in the initial stages.

Here are a few kinds of test books that you might want to make:

- Insert a variety of pictures into a Word file to test how they turn out.
- Insert different variations of the same picture into a Word file to see which method seems to work best.
- Insert sample pictures into a Word file to gauge the size of the converted MOBI file.[62]
- Test out the method described in Sec.'s 5.2 and 5.5 for going a quick step beyond Word.
- Test out Amazon's free Kindle Create app. If you're determined not to follow Chapter 5 and go a quick step beyond Word, this offers one alternative to simply uploading your Word document. Kindle Create can be quick and easy, especially if you've already formatted your Word file as described in this guide. For Windows, there is even a Word plugin.
- Create a variety of equations to see which option seems to work best.
- Create different sizes of the same equation to determine which size seems to work best across all devices for a variety of reader settings.
- Test other kinds of formatting or design issues to see how they turn out.
- Upload your manuscript in its current form (even if unfinished) to preview how it looks so far.

Decide which file format you want to upload for your test. For ideal results, you would create the same type of file that you intend to upload when your file is eventually complete and ready to publish. If you're undecided, you can test out multiple methods.

---

[62] Neither the file size of the images themselves nor the file size of your Word file is the important number. What really matters, in terms of delivery fees and customer download time and storage space, is the file size of the converted MOBI file that Amazon shows you after you upload your file (and then proceed onto page 3 of the publishing process—don't worry, you will be able to see the file size without completing the publishing process; this is only a test).

- Word document: This is the quickest method. If you plan to upload a Word file as your finished product, you should upload a DOCX or DOC file for your test.[63] I recommend going a step beyond Word as described in Chapter 5. You don't have to read and implement all of Chapter 5 to create a test file (Sec.'s 5.2 and 5.5 would suffice), so I recommend that you choose one of the following two options if you will eventually read and implement Chapter 5.

- Zip file with images: This is recommended for an eBook with pictures. To create your test file, you just need to save your file in the format described in Sec. 5.2. I also recommend applying the trick from Sec. 5.5 to any images that you want to force to display full-width (or full-height). These two steps (saving the file, and applying the trick from Sec. 5.5) are quick and easy, and let you ignore most of Chapter 5 for the time being. However, don't proceed to *edit* your HTML file without first reading Sec. 5.3: So if you elect to apply the trick from Sec. 5.5, **read Sec. 5.3 first**.

- Advanced options: Some authors go yet a step further, creating an ePub or MOBI file. This requires more work for a test file, but if you intend to upload an ePub or MOBI file when you publish (this is optional—also note that Amazon automatically converts whatever file format you upload into MOBI format), you should convert your Word file to the same format for your test (Sec. 5.12 will point you in the right direction).

- Kindle Create: I recommend this if you're planning to upload a Word document. Using Amazon's free Kindle Create tool is free, convenient, and can be quick (especially, if you format your eBook as described in this guide). Simply open your Word document in Kindle Create (or use the Word plugin). You don't need to worry about formatting within Kindle Create if you're making a test file: You can wait until your eBook is completed in Word first. When you export your file from Kindle Create, it will be in KPF format. Upload the KPF file to KDP (as described below).

Note: If you opt to create a zip file (or an ePub or MOBI file) or HTML file for your test, only use that file for your test. Once your test is complete, go back to your Word file and finish preparing that. When your Word file is 100% finished, then read and follow the directions of Chapter 5 to finish your eBook. It's inconvenient to work with those other file formats when there is still work that can be done in Word.

To run your test, you need to upload your test file to Kindle Direct Publishing (KDP). The URL that follows will take you there:

---

[63] Sec. 1.2 discussed the difference between uploading DOCX or DOC to create a Kindle eBook. I recommend DOCX if you decide to upload a Word document. Keep in mind that you can test out both file formats.

http://kdp.amazon.com

If you want, you can sign into KDP with an existing Amazon account.

Follow the steps outlined in Sec. 7.2 to make a quick preview of your test file at KDP. Note that you can skip some of the usual publishing steps (like entering keywords) for the purpose of your test file: Sec. 7.2 will show you how to complete the minimum information needed to upload and preview a test file. The last steps from Sec. 7.2 show you how to determine the converted MOBI file size of your test book and calculate your delivery fee. When you finish creating the quick preview as outlined in Sec. 7.2, return here (you're currently reading Sec. 4.13).

Most of the file size usually comes from the pictures. Consider the pictures that you included in your test book and the converted MOBI file size of your test book to project what your final converted MOBI file size will be.

For example, suppose that you included 5 images in your test book and the converted MOBI file size is 0.6 MB. If all of your images are roughly the same size and your finished eBook will have 80 images, multiply 0.6 MB by 16 to get 6.4 MB as the estimate for your finished MOBI file. (The 16 came from dividing 80 images by 5 images: $80 \div 5 = 16$.)

Books with converted MOBI file sizes ranging from 2 MB to 50 MB are fairly typical of eBooks with many pictures, with 2 to 10 MB more common unless the book is very picture-heavy. The larger the converted MOBI file size, the greater the download fee (with the 70% royalty option), the longer the download time for the customer, and the more space the eBook takes on the customer's device (or cloud).

The delivery fee is 15 cents per MB for US sales. Subtract the delivery fee from the list price, then multiply by 70% to calculate your royalty. The alternative is to multiply the list price by 35% (delivery fees don't apply to the 35% royalty option). For a book with a large enough delivery fee, the 35% option can actually yield a higher royalty, so it's always worth checking.[64]

Let's look at a few examples of the delivery fee:

- Assume a file size of 4 MB. The delivery fee is 60 cents in the US: $4 \times \$0.15 = \$0.60$. For a **$2.99** list price, the royalty equals $(\$2.99 - \$0.60) \times 0.70 = \$2.39 \times 0.70 = $ **$1.67**. If you could reduce the file size down to 3 MB, it would earn 11 cents more per sale. The royalty would then be $(\$2.99 - \$0.45) \times 0.70 = \$2.54 \times 0.70 = $ **$1.78**.

- Assume a file size of 12 MB. The delivery fee is $1.80 cents in the US: $12 \times \$0.15 = \$1.80$. For a **$2.99** list price, the royalty equals $(\$2.99 - \$1.80) \times 0.70 = \$1.19 \times 0.70 = $ **$0.83**. In this case, you would earn a higher royalty with the 35% option: $\$2.99 \times 0.35 = $ **$1.05**. If

---

[64] When you're ready to publish, KDP will show you exactly what your royalties will be in each country based on the list price that you set. You can click the 70% option first and the 35% option second to compare the royalties (Sec. 6.13). This way, there is no guesswork with the finished product.

you could reduce the file size down to 8 MB, it would raise the royalty to ($2.99 – $1.20) × 0.70 = $1.79 × 0.70 = **$1.25**.

- Assume a file size of 40 MB. The delivery fee is $6.00 in the US: 40 × $0.15 = $6.00. Regardless of the list price, the 35% royalty option will pay a higher royalty in this case. You would need to reduce this by several MB before it could make any difference for your royalty.

In many cases, reducing your file size by 25% or so would scarcely make an impact on your royalty. If you can reduce the file size by 50% or more, that could make a huge impact on both the royalty and download time.

If you test out ideas for possibly reducing the file size, and it has an effect of 25% or less, it's often not worth the trouble (but you should do the math, just in case a small change does make a significant impact on your numbers). In this case, it may be better to focus on the *quality* of your images rather than the size of your file. However, if you can reduce the file size by 30% or more, it might be worth doing (but again, do the math first, just to make sure).

Following are some ideas that might help to manage file size. You could try out one or more of these ideas, upload a new test file, and see what impact (if any) it has on your converted MOBI file size.[65] Then you will know whether or not that idea is helpful for your eBook:

- Try reducing the pixel size of your images. For example, if you used 1280 × 2048 images in your original test file, see if reducing the pixel size of the images in your test file to 800 × 1280 or to 640 × 1024 has a significant impact. The trick from Sec. 5.5 will ensure that they still display full-width (or full-height) across all devices (if you want them to). If the resulting images remain sharp and the converted MOBI file size shrinks enough, it's worth considering, but if the pictures don't appear sharp (on the largest displays), it isn't worth it.

- Try uploading your test file in a different file format (DOC, DOCX, zip file, ePub, MOBI) to see if that impacts your converted MOBI file size at all. (What I refer to as the "converted MOBI file size" is the file size shown on page 3 of the publishing process at KDP, as described in Sec. 7.2.)

- You could try compressing your pictures. This used to be helpful in previous years. However, Amazon now automatically compresses your pictures for you, and Amazon's compression is very good. Compressing your pictures before you upload them to KDP

---

[65] You must upload your revised file to KDP the same way that you uploaded your original test file. Just checking the image file size, or just checking the Word document's file size, for example, *isn't* a reliable indicator. You need to find the converted MOBI file size on page 3 of the publishing process for the revised test file. Also, do the math to see how the change might impact your royalty, if at all.

probably won't help with your converted MOBI file size significantly, and even if it does, the quality of the pictures probably won't be worth it. However, it doesn't hurt to run a test, right? For example, you might try reducing your pictures to 75% compression, seeing if that impacts the file size significantly, and examining what the resulting quality is like (on the largest display size). My general advice is to focus on producing *quality* images and let Amazon take care of the compression. However, if your test shows that compression has a significant impact on the converted MOBI file size, and if the quality appears to remain good, this may merit consideration.

- If you have a huge file, even after testing the above suggestions, you may have a couple of extreme options, if you really want to trim the file size down. (For a huge file, the 35% royalty option may pay a higher royalty, and in that case there is no delivery fee. It will be a longer download time for the customer though.) One option is to eliminate some pictures that you really don't need, if plausible. Another is to split the book into smaller volumes. These aren't desirable choices; they are last resorts (I did say that they were 'extreme' options).

4.14 Image Rights and Stock Images

Be sure that you possess the necessary rights to use your images. Most of the pictures that you find on the internet, for example, do **not** grant you permission to use them in your book. (The few that do usually don't have adequate quality.) You generally need written permission from the person (or business) who owns the image rights.

Two common ways that authors use to obtain images are:

- Make the pictures yourself.
- Purchase images from a collection of stock images, such as ShutterStock, Adobe, or iStockPhoto.

If you purchase an image from a company that sells stock images, the watermark won't appear on the image. (Before you buy an image, you can test out the sample that includes a watermark to make sure it will be suitable for your needs.) Check the image rights to verify that you can use the image in your book after purchasing the image. Some companies that sell clipart collections actually restrict commercial use, so you want to find out the details. Other times, a specific image comes with more restrictions than most of the other images available (if so, there is usually a special note at the point of sale).

I have used ShutterStock and Adobe products, so I can personally recommend them. I'm pleased with their images and services. (The pictures of my astronomy books that you see in this chapter include NASA images. The picture below is from ShutterStock.)

Aside from searching for a suitable image and checking on the image rights, you also want to check that the image size is adequate. For your eBook, the picture has to have enough pixels for the intended use (Sec. 4.3 discusses image resolution).[66] Another consideration, if you use stock images, is that other books in your category may use the same (or similar) images.

---

[66] If you will also make a print book, you want the image to be 300 DPI (for the intended physical size on the page). However, if you will be uploading a Word document to KDP (instead of following Chapter 5), see the note in Sec. 4.11 about PPI for your eBook. You will want two different files for a print book and eBook, so if needed you can use different versions of your pictures for the two different book formats.

—Chapter 5—

Touch-Up

5.1 You *Can* Do This (and Why You Should)

IN THIS CHAPTER, we'll learn how to go a quick step beyond Word. I interact with hundreds of authors. It's amazing how many authors I have met who have said something like, "I avoided going a step beyond Word for years because I thought it would be complicated. I thought it would be like learning a new language. Now that I realize how easy it was, I wish I had started doing this sooner."

Here are a couple of secrets:

- You can do just a little. It's your choice. You can keep it very simple.
- You really don't need to learn anything new.

Most authors prefer to go a step beyond Word once they finally take the plunge and learn how to do it, and it usually winds up being *much* easier than they had expected.

If you're feeling intimidated by going beyond Word, you shouldn't. Remember that you can choose to make minimal changes, keeping the process simple. We'll discuss how you can make this stage of the publishing process quick and simple in Sec. 5.3. This chapter is setup so that you can do as little or as much as you'd like.

You don't need to take a course in carpentry to assemble a bookcase: At most, you might need someone to help you interpret the directions. You don't need to know how a car engine works in order to change a flat tire: You just need someone to show you how to do it.

Similarly, I will show you exactly how to go a step beyond Word and exactly what changes to make. This way, you're not learning a new language. Rather, you're just following step-by-step directions.

You can make a variety of improvements to your Kindle eBook by going a step beyond Word. You don't need to make *all* of the improvements: If you prefer, you can take a minimalist approach.

Here is a sample of what you can do by going a step beyond Word:

- Force an image to display full-width (or full-height), even if its size in pixels is smaller than the display size (Sec. 5.5).
- View your pictures in a separate image folder that shows you exactly how large each picture is, and correct any pictures that may have been reduced in size (Sec.'s 5.2 and 5.5).
- Set indents and font sizes in terms of typography units instead of inches in order to create a design that looks better across all devices (Sec. 5.4).
- See the 'hidden' formatting[67] that Word doesn't show you, and resolve any issues therein (Sec.'s 5.4 and 5.7).

---

[67] I'm *not* talking about 'hidden' formatting that can be revealed by Word's Show/Hide button. I'm talking about formatting that's so 'hidden' you have to examine Word's HTML file to see it.

- Remove font specifications to prevent your eBook from specifying a font that the actual Kindle device doesn't support (Sec. 5.6).
- Gain access to a couple of special formatting symbols that aren't supported with Word, which can help with Kindle design (Sec. 5.6).
- Make subtle improvements to the design of your eBook (Sec.'s 5.4 to 5.12).
- Use media queries to create separate formatting instructions for newer devices and older devices (Sec. 5.12 will point you in the right direction).

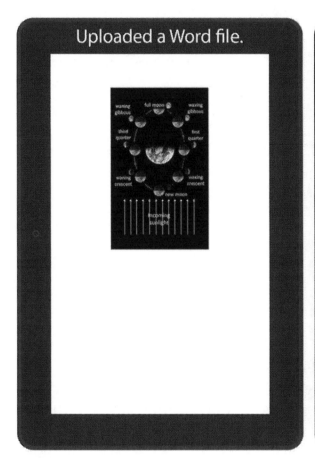

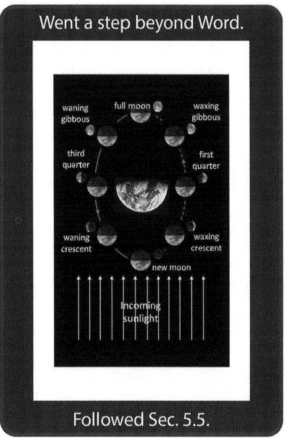

5.2 Going One Step Beyond Word

We're going to make an HTML file, but I want to emphasize that you *don't* need to know any HTML. You're not going to write HTML. You're just going to make minimal revisions to Word's HTML following step-by-step directions.

Don't panic. Here is what we're **not** going to do:
- We're not going to write a program.
- We're not going to write code.
- We're not going to learn a new language.
- We're not going to design a website.

So if you don't have any programming experience, don't know any programming languages, and have never designed a website, *don't worry*. We won't be doing those things.

You don't even need to know HTML. That's because you *don't* need to *write* HTML. We're just going to examine the HTML that Microsoft Word makes and make minimal changes to it. I'll show you exactly what to do.

Let me share a little secret: **It's sometimes better if you *don't* know HTML.** Why? Because many things that you can do with HTML *don't* work with Kindle. The problem for those who are fluent in HTML is that they need to learn which things *not* to do with Kindle.

Here is what we *will* do:

- We'll learn how to automatically generate an HTML file from your existing Word file.
- You'll follow step-by-step directions for how to make small improvements here and there.
- You'll be able to choose which improvements to make. Keep it as simple as you like.

There really is no risk. So why not try it out? If it doesn't work out for you, don't worry: You always have your original Word file to fall back on.

Have you proofread your book carefully yet? You may wish to edit your book to perfection before you go a step beyond Word. If you have *extensive* revisions to make, that may be easier to do in Word now than it would be to do in HTML later. (It's easy to make *small* changes either way.)

Once you start working with your HTML file, you'll want to make any revisions in the HTML file: You won't want to go back to Word, create a new HTML file, and make these improvements a second time.

When you have proofread your book carefully and are ready to create your HTML file, I recommend performing a simple search of your Word document for any possible tabs, double Enters, two consecutive spacebars, or stranded spacebars at the end of a paragraph. You should have already done this when you read Sec.'s 2.1 thru 2.3. However, you probably made some revisions to your Word file since reading those sections, in which case you may have inadvertently reintroduced a few of these into your Word document. It's worth doing a quick search to find out.

Also, before you create your HTML file, double-check that Word isn't tracking changes: Click File > Options > Advanced, look in the Editing Options, and make sure that the box next to "Keep track of formatting" is unchecked. Turn off the spelling and grammar checkers (File > Options > Proofing): Uncheck both boxes to check spelling and grammar as you type, and also check the bottom two boxes to hide spelling and grammar errors for your document. Review the other recommendations from Sec. 2.11 before proceeding.

Finally, I recommend reviewing Sec. 3.14 before creating your HTML file. The suggestions in Sec. 3.14 will help you catch possible issues that would be easier to correct in your Word file.

Looking for unnamed automatically created styles, browsing through the paragraph styles actually used in your book, and checking the Web Layout view often help to catch mistakes before converting from Word to HTML.

Follow these instructions to create an HTML file from your Word file. Note that you don't just want *any* HTML that you can get from Word. You want the specific kind of HTML file that you get by following these steps. These directions are for Word 2010 (and similar versions—basically 2007 and up) for Windows on a PC:

- Click File > Save As and choose "Web Page, Filtered" from the dropdown menu under "save as type." (Be careful: Don't to choose "Web Page" without the filtered, and don't choose "Single File Web Page.") If the name of your Word file currently has any spaces in it (like "My Book.docx"), rename your file without any spaces[68] in the filename (like "MyBook" instead of "My Book"). Also, don't use quotation marks, periods, or anything other than standard letters (A to Z and a to z) and numbers (0 thru 9) in the filename.

- A message will pop open about removing Office-specific tags: Click Yes. (You may also receive a *second* pop-up message, letting you know that your Word document contains features that aren't supported in HTML. For example, if you scaled font size—an advanced feature that you shouldn't use in an eBook—you will receive such a warning. If the feature isn't supported in HTML, it definitely wouldn't be supported in an eBook, so it's okay to remove it.)

- Leave Word. Find the folder on your computer where you just saved your book as a filtered web page (under My Computer, My Documents, or a jump drive, perhaps).[69] Open this folder on your computer so that you can see the files inside.

- You should have two or three files with similar names. For example, if the name of your Word file is Thriller7.docx, you should also have a file called Thriller7.htm (listed as an HTML document under Type when View is set to Details). If you had at least one picture in your Word document, you should also have an image folder called Thriller7_files. **Note**: The image folder ending with _files usually appears at the very top of the list, so you might not see it next to your DOCX and .HTM files.

- If you don't have any pictures and therefore don't have a _files folder (you should check for this folder, just to make sure), then you can skip the remaining bullet points on this list. If you do have pictures in your Word file, look for a _files folder that has the same name as your HTML file (the note in the previous bullet point may help you find it). You will need to be able to find the _files folder for a later step.

---

[68] Not using spaces simplifies the way that image locations are specified. Spaces may also cause problems for some operating systems.

[69] If you don't know where you saved it, return to Word, begin to repeat the previous steps, and in the Save As step, note the file location so that you will be able to find it.

- Find your HTML file on your computer, right-click on the HTML file, hover your cursor over Send To, and select Compressed (Zipped) Folder. This creates a zipped folder named after your HTML file. For example, if your HTML file is named Thriller7.htm, you will see a zipped folder named Thriller7.zip (listed as a Compressed Zipped Folder under Type when View is set to Details).

- Now there are two different **folders** with similar names: One is the image folder ending with _files, and the other is the zipped folder. Select the **image folder** ending with **_files** and drag it into the compressed **zipped folder**. (Alternatively, right-click the image folder ending with _files, click Copy, double-click the compressed zipped folder to open it, right-click in an area inside the folder when it opens, and click Paste.)

- Check to make sure everything worked right. Double-click the compressed zipped folder to open it. You should see a copy of your HTML file and a copy of the image folder ending with _files inside. Double-click the image folder to open that. You should find your images inside, with names like image001.jpg or image002.gif.

- Now open your image folder (the one that *isn't* inside of the compressed zipped folder). Check the pixel size of your pictures, just in case any of them may have been downsized (it happens occasionally, and if it does, it would probably also have happened if you uploaded a Word document directly to KDP). The pixel count of a picture may show if you hover your cursor over the picture for a moment. If not, right-click the picture, choose Properties, and select the Details tab.

- If any pictures were downsized, it's easy to fix. Delete the picture from the files folder. Copy and paste the original picture from its file location into the files folder. Rename the picture file to the exact same name that it had before you deleted it (one way to do this is to right-click on the picture file and select Rename). Now **drag the files folder back into the compressed zipped folder** (just like we did a couple of steps back), and this will update the image folder that's inside the compressed zipped folder (*remember to do this any time you want to update your pictures*).

Note: Don't rename the files folder or the zipped folder. If you do, Kindle won't be able to locate the pictures to display in your eBook.

Why is it helpful to work with HTML?

If you upload a Word document when you publish, Kindle devices and apps (and Amazon's Look Inside) won't see your Word file the way that you do when you view your monitor. Kindle devices and apps see HTML generated from your Word file. There can be important differences between how Kindle devices and apps interpret those HTML instructions compared to how your computer monitor displays your Word document.

In this chapter, we will learn how to examine different parts of your HTML and make minimal improvements to it so that Kindle devices and apps will interpret your HTML for better Kindle design across a variety of devices. You don't need to implement *every* suggestion from this chapter: You can pick and choose.

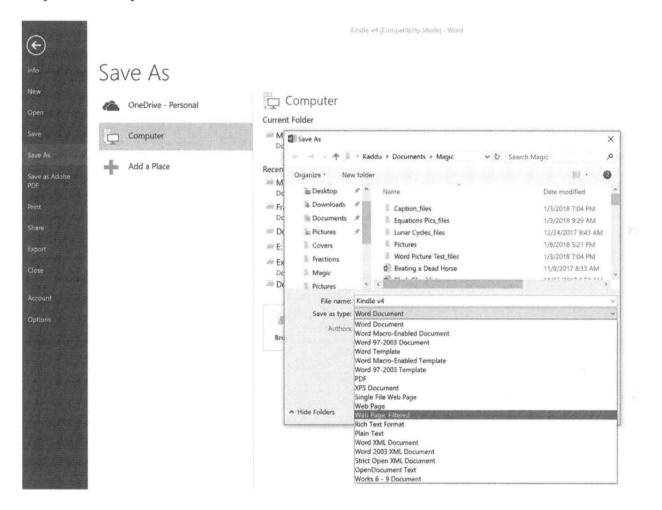

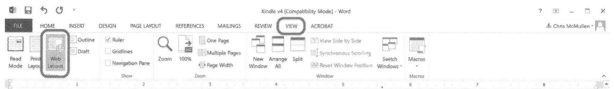

Follow these instructions to create a HTML file from your Word file. Note that you don't just want *any* HTML that you can get from Word. You want the specific kind of HTML file that you get by following these steps. These directions are for Word 2010 (and similar versions—basically 2007 and up) for Windows on a PC:

- Click File > Save As and choose "Web Page, Filtered" from the dropdown menu under "save as type." (Be careful: Don't to choose "Web Page" without the filtered, and don't choose "Single File Web Page.") If the name of your Word file currently has any spaces in it (like "My Book.docx"), rename your file without any spaces[67] in the filename (like "MyBook" instead of "My Book"). Also, don't use quotation marks, periods, or anything other than standard letters (A to Z and a to z) and numbers (0 thru 9) in the filename.
- A message will pop open: Click Yes.
- Leave Word. Find the folder on your computer where you just saved your book as a filtered web page (under My Computer, My Documents, or a jump drive, perhaps).[68] Open this folder on your computer so that you can see the files inside.
- You should have two or three files with similar names. For example, if the name of your Word file is Thriller7.docx, you should also have a file called Thriller7.htm (listed as an HTML document under Type when View is set to Details). If you had at least one picture in your Word document, you should also have an image folder called Thriller7_files. **Note:** The image folder ending with _files usually appears at the very top of the list, so you might not see it next to your .docx and .HTM files.
- If you don't have any pictures and therefore don't have a _files folder (you should check for this folder, just to make sure), then you can skip the remaining bullet points on this list. If you do have pictures in your Word file, you should see a _files folder named after your HTML file.
- When you find your HTML file in its folder on your computer, right-click on the HTML file, hover your cursor over Send To, and select Compressed (Zipped) Folder. This creates a zipped folder named after your HTML file. For example, if your HTML file is named Thriller7.htm, you will see a zipped folder named Thriller7.zip (listed as a Compressed Zipped Folder under Type when View is set to Details).
- Now there are two different folders: One is the image folder ending with _files, and the other is the zipped folder. Select the image folder ending with _files and drag it into the compressed zipped folder. (Alternatively, right-click the image folder

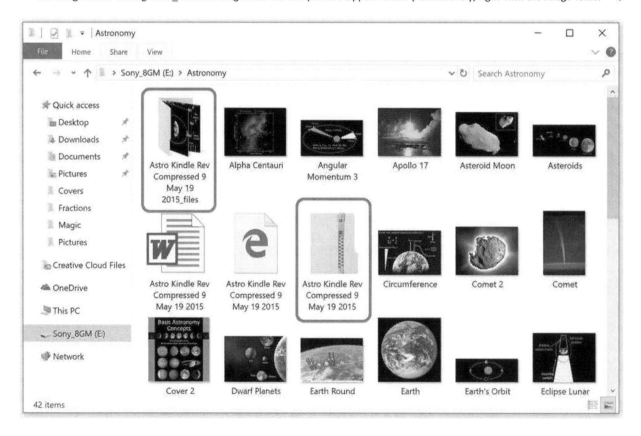

5.3 Making Improvements

Don't open the HTML file with Microsoft Word. Don't open the HTML file with most HTML software either. Most software programs designed for editing HTML (or for editing websites) do **not** result in Kindle-friendly output.

I recommend using either a very simple editor like Notepad[70] (which comes freely available on many computers under Windows Accessories) or Sigil (which is also free) if you prefer to work with something more professional for eBook formatting.

https://sigil-ebook.com

Notepad is handy if you intend to keep the process quick and simple, and intend to upload the HTML file to KDP. Sigil is better if you intend to make extensive revisions to the HTML, or if you intend to create an ePub file (which is handy if you wish to publish across multiple

---

[70] If you want a better editor than Notepad, but don't want to use Sigil, one alternative is Notepad++ (note the second + sign). Some authors find Notepad++ to be somewhat more user-friendly (yet the simplicity of Notepad has its advantages, too). I recommend exploring Notepad first, since it comes free under Windows Accessories on most computers, and if you find that you don't like using it, then search for a suitable alternative. (Don't get Notepad and Wordpad mixed up. Use Notepad, but *don't* use WordPad, to edit HTML.) Personally, I recommend you choose between Notepad and Sigil.

eBook platforms like Nook and Kobo). If you try other software besides Notepad and Sigil, you run the risk of winding up with HTML that isn't Kindle friendly.[71]

I recommend using Notepad. For the advanced author who wishes to create an ePub file, Sigil is the better tool. However, the transition from HTML to ePub is beyond the scope of this book, and carries some pitfalls, so if you decide to make an ePub file, you will want to find a very reliable guide for how to use Sigil to create an ePub file specifically for Kindle (which is a little different from formatting an ePub for other platforms).

In this chapter, I will show you how to make a smooth transition from Word to HTML, with minimal revisions to your HTML. I will also offer some basic guidance for getting started with Notepad. In this section, I will focus on simple tasks like opening your file, how to properly save your file, an important point about find and replace, and simple editing. Later in this chapter, I will include additional details as needed (limited to what you need to know to carry out the instructions in this book).

Right-click your HTML file, choose Open With, and select the appropriate program, such as Notepad. You may need to click Choose Another App if the program you wish to use (like Sigil) doesn't show up on the list, and then browse for the program on your computer. (Alternatively, you can open the program, click Open, and then select your HTML file. If you try this method with Notepad, you will need to adjust Text Documents to All Files in the dropdown menu.)

If your eBook includes images, be sure to edit the HTML file that **isn't** in the compressed zipped folder. When you finish editing your HTML file, click Save (*not* Save As), close the program, and then drag the HTML file into the compressed zipped folder that you created in Sec. 5.2. (First open the folder that contains both the HTML file and the compressed zipped folder, and then you will be able to drag and drop.) This will then overwrite the original HTML file stored in your compressed zipped folder (provided that you haven't changed the filename or extension of your HTML file).[72]

Tip: Don't forget to update the HTML file in your compressed zipped folder by dragging the revised HTML file into the compressed zipped folder.[72]

---

[71] There are a couple of other simple HTML editors that do work, but there are also many HTML editors that don't work very well for Kindle. If you're intent on using something else, at least do your research to ensure that they do result in Kindle-friendly output.

[72] If you haven't changed the file name of your HTML file, this will work. Otherwise, you need the names (and extensions) to match first. (Don't rename your HTML file using Notepad: It will save it as a TXT file instead, and the extension will no longer match. You can use the Save button in Notepad, which will preserve the file as HTML, but don't use Save As with Notepad.)

Don't use Notepad's Save As option, since Notepad only saves TXT files. You can use the Save option, just not Save As. (Well, you can use Save As to back-up the text of your HTML file in a TXT file, but then close the TXT file and continue to work with the HTML file instead. Of course, you should regularly back-up *all* of your files on jump drive, email, etc.—choose at least two methods and you'll likely be covered for the worst-case scenario.)

Note that the Find and Replace tools in Notepad have a couple of peculiarities:

- The Find tool doesn't necessarily search the entire document. It either searches from the position of your cursor to the end of the document (Search Down) or it searches from the position of your cursor to the beginning of the document (Search Up). So if you want to search the whole document, first place the cursor at the beginning of the file and then Search Down (otherwise, you will miss some search results). Note that if you simply scroll up to view the beginning of the file, your cursor may still be positioned elsewhere in your file: Be sure to click at the very beginning of the file so that your cursor is properly positioned before doing a search down.

- The Find and Replace tools won't find matches that are broken across two lines. For example, if the phrase "book publishing" appears in Notepad with "book" at the end of one line and "publishing" at the beginning of the next line, Notepad *won't* find that instance of "book publishing" in a search for the phrase "book publishing."

If you will be relying on the Replace tool to replace text that includes spaces (made using the spacebar), you must take this into consideration (or try using a search engine to find advice for how to work around the problem—with a method that will be compatible with Kindle eBooks).

A few authors prefer to run Word's HTML through a cleaner. This made a bigger impact several years ago. Now, a well-styled DOCX file usually has very clean HTML, such that this step *shouldn't* be necessary (if you used the paragraph styles as described in this book). Personally, I prefer not to run my book through more programs than necessary, so as to reduce the chances of unexpected influences (and my HTML comes out very clean, so there is little to be gained). If you're working with an older version of Word (like 2000), or if you didn't follow some of the formatting advice in this book (perhaps because you had already finished your book before discovering my formatting guide), then you might have more to gain by running your HTML file through a cleaner such as Word2cleanthml.

Word2cleanhtml.com

Every author is unique. Some authors will implement *every* suggestion that they find in Chapter 5, while other authors are looking to take a *minimalist* approach. If you're planning to take a more minimal approach, following are some suggestions for which changes to make or not make:

- If you really want to be an *extreme* HTML **minimalist**, you could follow Sec.'s 5.4 and 5.5 (but read Sec.'s 5.9 and 5.3 before you make any revisions) and skip everything else. In that case, you could even stop reading this list now (though I encourage you to read the next two bullet points).

- Appendix C shows you the sample HTML for a short eBook.

- If you read Sec.'s 5.4 and 5.7, even if you don't implement any of those suggestions, those sections will help you better understand the HTML file and how it relates to your Kindle eBook.

- If your eBook contains any pictures, Sec. 5.5 will help you improve them. It will also show you how to force large images to display full-width or full-height (if you wish to do so).

- If you feel tentative about working with HTML, you can find a list of common mistakes at the end of Sec. 5.9. Compare the mistakes with the corrections and try to learn from them. If those examples make sense to you and if it seems like you could avoid those mistakes (after learning about them), this may lend a needed confidence boost.

- I recommend that you improve your style definitions as discussed in Sec. 5.4. Compare your style definitions to the recommended style definitions that you can find at the end of Sec. 5.4.

- You can be selective in Sec. 5.6. It's relatively easy to remove a few potential font problems from your HTML. You can choose whether or not you feel comfortable editing or removing spans. Don't modify your drop caps and don't apply the media query if you don't want to implement this advanced feature.

- You may choose to skip much (or all) of Sec. 5.7.

- You could skip all of Sec. 5.8, *unless* one of the following situations applies. If you need to add a hyperlink, bookmark, footnote, or endnote after converting from Word to HTML, then you either need to do this in Word, convert to HTML all over, and edit your HTML from scratch—or read Sec. 5.8 to learn how to add these features directly to your HTML. If you discover a problem a hyperlink, bookmark, footnote, or endnote in your preview, you'll need to search for this feature in your HTML file and consult Sec. 5.8 to figure out how to fix the problem.

- If you need to make **revisions** to your content *after* converting from Word to HTML, be sure to *read Sec. 5.9 before you begin*. Also, find the paragraph in Sec. 5.8 that begins "Recall that Sec. 5.3 shows you how to save your HTML file" and follow the instructions for (A) saving your HTML file, (B) dragging your HTML file into your zipped folder, (C) updating your _files folder, and (D) dragging your _files folder into your zipped folder. Note that (C) and (D) only apply if you need to make changes to *pictures*. You may want to consult both Sec.'s 5.3 and 5.9 before making any changes.

- Sec. 5.10 includes a handy checklist of potential problems that I like to search for in my HTML file. There is no harm in using the Find button to see if your file has any of these potential problems. If you find any problems, then you can decide whether or not you feel that they are worth trying to fix. As mentioned in Sec. 5.10, not everything that you find with those searches is actually a problem.

- If you created a table of contents in Word following the method described in Sec. 3.8, you could skip Sec. 5.11, though it may still be worth reading this short section, which has a couple of suggestions for how to improve the table of contents in your HTML file.

- Feel free to skip Sec. 5.12. In fact, some of those advanced features run the risk of doing more harm than good, unless you really know what you're doing.

- If you skim through the handy checklist in Sec. 5.13, you might see something that you feel is worth implementing.

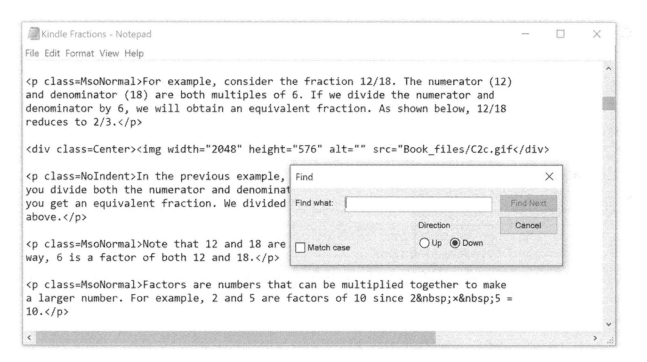

5.4 Improving Paragraph Styles

You can find the paragraph styles in the style definitions. At the top of your HTML file, there is a short <head> section followed by a long <style> section. The <style> section begins with

/* Font Definitions */

and is followed by

/* Style Definitions */

(I recommend deleting the Font Definitions, as described in Sec. 5.6.) Scroll down to the **style definitions**. This is where we will make improvements to your paragraph styles.

(If you see a lot more than just font definitions and style definitions in the beginning of your HTML file, like <xml> info, it's possible that you didn't save your file as "Web Page, Filtered" from Word. Perhaps you accidentally selected "Web Page" or "Single File Web Page" instead. Try deleting the HTML file and saving it as "Web Page, Filtered" again from Word.)

First we'll discuss which improvements to make and how to make them. Then at the end of this section, you can find complete style definitions for all of the recommended paragraph styles from Sec. 3.4. You can also find the HTML for a sample eBook in Appendix C.

Before we begin, note that the syntax is critical. Pay very careful attention to not only the spelling, but also the punctuation, and spacing (from the spacebar). It's very important not to forget (or accidentally delete) the semicolon (;) that appears at the end of a line, or the brace } that appears at the end of a style definition. If deleting the last line of a style definition, be sure to put the closed brace } at the end of the previous line (with the semicolon preceding it). You'll see exactly how everything should look at the end of this section: You can compare with my style definitions, if you wish.

You shouldn't worry: I'll show you exactly what to do. You're not writing HTML: You're just making small changes to it, which is much easier. You mainly need to pay attention to detail, and preview your book carefully (Chapter 7), just in case. The examples of common HTML mistakes and their corrections in Sec. 5.9 will help you focus on important details.

The paragraph styles that you see in the style definitions correspond to paragraph styles that you used in Microsoft Word. Some of your style definitions begin with Mso (which stands for Microsoft Office). For example, MsoNormal is the Normal style. The heading styles are called h1, h2, and so on in the HTML file. Other styles will have the same name from the Word file (except for possibly adding Mso to the beginning).

Note: Some of the style definitions may seem out of order. For example, the style definitions might begin with paragraph styles, then there might be spans, and then later on there may be *more* paragraph styles. *Don't stop looking for style definitions until you reach* </style>. There won't be any style definitions beyond </style>.

Let's begin with one significant improvement that is easy to make: Right now, your indents are specified in inches (like 0.2in), your font size is specified in points (like 12.0pt), and your paragraph margins (not to be confused with page margins) are set in points (like 12.0pt) or inches (like 0.2in). Your book will display better across all devices with a few simple changes.

I recommend making the following changes to indent sizes, font sizes, and paragraph margins.

Change the indent size to 2 em instead of a value in inches. This way, your indent will be based on the size of the letter M. The problem with using 0.2 inches, for example, is that it's the same value regardless of the font size. A value in em's rather than inches makes the paragraph indent match the customer's choice for the font size. I don't recommend using a percentage, as a percentage that looks fine on a small screen blows up to an unsightly amount on the all-important Look Inside. I like to avoid using half an em, so I prefer to work with 2 em or 3 em (larger than 2 em appears very large on a small cell phone screen, and a large indent size becomes a bigger issue if you use two levels of indents—though I recommend using only one indent level: See Sec. 5.12 if you're planning on multi-level indents). If the style definition is *missing* a text-indent line, you should *add* this line to it: Otherwise, a Kindle device or app (or worse, the Look Inside) may *automatically* indent. I recommend changing your paragraph indent to this:

text-indent:2em;

Change the size of non-indented paragraph indents from 0.01 inches to zero inches. Using 0.01 inches is necessary in Word because setting First Linde Indent to "none" or zero in Word doesn't translate to HTML. However, once you're in the HTML, you can correct this. Anywhere you see a paragraph indent of 0.01 inches (or for any paragraphs for which you wish to have zero indent), change this to zero inches. It should look like:

text-indent:0in;

Font size should be set as a percentage. Regular body text (like the Normal style) should have the font size set to 100%. Headings and subheadings should use a somewhat larger percentage, upwards of about 150%: You don't want to overdo it, as the results could prove disastrous on a cell phone screen. Avoid going lower than about 80%, and only go below 100% minimally (use it for special occasions, like small caps, for example). You can find specific recommendations for many standard types of paragraphs at the end of this section. Font size should look like:

font-size:100%;

Edit your paragraph margins (not to be confused with page margins). In each style definition, you should see margin-top, margin-bottom, margin-left, and margin-right. You may also see margin (without a specifier). Occasionally, the same margin (like margin-bottom) may be specified twice in the same style. It's common for one or more of these margin specifications (left, right, top, or bottom) to be missing. I want each of the four margin specifications (left, right, top, or bottom) to be specified exactly once, so there is no ambiguity (and I delete any margin lines that don't mention a specific margin, such as margin:0in;). Note that you may need to add any margin specifications that may be missing (like margin-left). Most of your paragraph margins should be set to 0 inches, like my examples below. We'll discuss exceptions in the next two paragraphs.

```
margin-top:0in;
margin-bottom:0in;
margin-left:0in;
margin-right:0in;
```

The equivalent of Spacing After in Word is margin-bottom in the HTML. Any style definition that adds 12 pt Spacing After in Word should have margin-bottom set to 1 em, as in the following example. The margin-bottom setting creates the effect of a blank line the size of the letter M, and automatically adjusts to match the customer's selection of font size. Note that a single blank line between paragraphs (originally created by pressing Enter in Word, or by inserting a manual line break in Word) may not format as desired across all devices. Therefore, you should apply a style definition (such as the BodySpaceAfter, NoIndentSpaceAfter, or CenterSpaceAfter styles recommended at the end of this section) which sets margin-bottom to 1 em (like the example below) for the paragraph preceding the point where you would like to create the effect of a blank line (this is more reliable than creating a blank line with an effectively empty p-tag).

```
margin-bottom:1em;
```

Note that Amazon's Look Inside feature strips out page breaks (don't worry: they won't be stripped out of the actual eBook, just the preview the customers see when shopping in their web browsers). Because of this, it's a good idea to use a special style definition (such as the BodySpaceAfter, NoIndentSpaceAfter, or CenterSpaceAfter styles recommended at the end of this section) for the last paragraph of each chapter, which sets margin-bottom to 1 em (like the example above). This adds a little space between the last paragraph of a chapter and the heading of the next chapter, creating a little separation in the Look Inside when the page break gets stripped out. You might also add margin-top to the first 'paragraph' (which is likely a chapter heading with an h-tag, not a body text paragraph with a p-tag) of each chapter. (We will discuss p-tags and h-tags in Sec. 5.7, which describes how to apply the style definitions to actual paragraphs and headings in the body of your book. In this section, we will focus on the style definitions themselves.)

Recall that Spacing After is the preferred method for adding space between paragraphs (like between a heading and the first body paragraph of a section)—since some older devices may ignore Spacing Before. The Spacing After field naturally translates to bottom margin. Thus, the top margin should be set to zero for all style definitions, unless you want to add space before the first paragraph following a page break. Beware that on some devices, a top margin may be ignored on the first paragraph following a page break. (You should avoid using a manual page break though: When you want to force a page break, you should call a style definition that applies a page break, such as the h1 and NoIndentPageBreak styles recommended at the end of this section. However, top margin may still be ignored by some devices in that situation.) Don't make the top margin much larger than about 2 em, or it could skip an *entire page* on a cell phone with a large font selected. Following is an example using a top margin.

margin-top:2em;

If you have a style definition that indents *every* line of the paragraph, like ListPoint described in Sec. 3.4, then you will have a margin-left that's nonzero (in that case, text-indent should be set to zero). For such a paragraph, set margin-left in terms of the em, as in my example below. Avoid a large left margin, which can lead to problems on small screens. Also avoid using margin-right, as that may not work on some devices, and if it works on a small screen, the design can become problematic.

margin-left:2em;
text-indent:0in;

The text alignment can be set to justify, left, center, or omitted entirely.[73] Set the alignment to center for each of the following style definitions: images (like the CenterSpaceAfter style from Sec. 3.4), the book title (like Title or Subtitle), centered text (like the Center style from Sec. 3.4), certain heading styles (like h1), or any styles that you wish to have the centered alignment. See the example below. For other alignments (left or justified), see the following paragraphs.

text-align:center;

In Sec. 3.7, we discussed the pros and cons of forcing justified body text, forcing left-aligned (ragged right) body text, or leaving the body text unspecified. Recall that the only way to obtain justified body text in the Look Inside is to force justified body text, as in my example below. Not specifying the alignment of body text (which means to remove this line from the style definition) results in a ragged right Look Inside (but gives customers who know a 'trick' the freedom to choose left alignment, if desired). Since customers are accustomed to justified body text in traditionally published books, it may be a helpful marketing tool to have a justified Look Inside. Note: Don't set text-align to justify (and don't remove the text alignment line[74]) for headings, titles, or other kinds of 'paragraphs' that tend to consist of a short number of words, as these look better centered or left-aligned on small screens.

---

[73] There is rarely a reason to use right alignment. Also, note that if a style definition *omits* the text-align line (or if you delete the text-align line from the style definition), this will result in either left alignment or full justified text, depending on the customer's settings, as noted in the following paragraphs.

[74] The reason being that they would then automatically be justified in many cases.

text-align:justify;

If you prefer to force left alignment,[75] do so by following my example below. Note that when you select left alignment in Word, this doesn't show up in the style definition in the HTML.[76] Instead, you must manually add a text-align set to left in the HTML to force left alignment. Any headings, subheadings (like h2), or other style definitions for short sections of text that you wish to be non-centered should be aligned left instead. Bullet points (see ListPoint and ListPointSpaceAfter from Sec. 3.4) tend to format better with left alignment, as discussed in Sec. 3.7. (For bullet points or numbered lists, I recommend using a style definition like ListPoint and ListPointSpaceAfter, and manually inserting the bullet symbol or number as discussed in Sec. 3.7. I *don't* recommend using <ol> or <ul> to create simple ordered or unordered lists in HTML, as these *don't* come out quite right on Kindle. I also don't recommend using Word's default list tools if you're following Chapter 5.) **To let the customer choose left or full**, remove the text-align line from your HTML.

text-align:left;

Bear in mind that right now, we're discussing the different types of lines that you need to find, modify, remove, or add to your style definitions. At the end of this section, you will see complete style definitions for each paragraph (or heading) style recommended in Sec. 3.4. (Maybe it would help to skip ahead to see how the end of this section looks, and then return here after checking it out. That may help you see how what we're discussing now fits into the bigger picture.)

If you have any style definitions that render the *entire* paragraph boldface or italicized, you should have the font weight or style specified as in my examples below. (Generally, you wouldn't use *both* boldface and italics in the *same* style.) For example, you may wish to put the title, subtitle, heading, or subheading styles in boldface.

font-weight:bold;
font-style:italic;

---

[75] Amazon may prefer for publishers *not* to *force* left alignment for body text (but forcing left alignment for headings, subheadings, or bullet points isn't a problem—if there is an issue, it's regarding the main body text of a standard book format like a novel). Leaving it unspecified gives the customer who knows the 'trick' the option to align left, if desired. My preference is to force justified body text, since a justified Look Inside may be a selling point more often than not. There are stories of authors who have had their books unpublished by Amazon because the body text forced left alignment, whereas justifying body text or at least *not* specifying alignment (which will then automatically justify, except in the Look Inside) should be fine.

[76] Well, it does if you use the 'trick' mentioned in Sec. 3.7. However, you shouldn't be using that trick if you're following the instructions from Chapter 5. You get the best results by not using the 'trick' from Sec. 3.7. Instead, use text-align:left; as described here in the style definitions for paragraphs that you wish to be left-aligned (or ragged right).

A couple of style definitions may incorporate a page break into the style. For example, see the recommendation for h1 or NoIndentPageBreak at the end of this section. If a style definition includes a page break, you should see the following line in the style definition.

page-break-before:always;

If you find any line height settings like the one below, **delete the entire line from the HTML.** Single line spacing formats best across Kindle devices and apps.[77] You might also find a line height specified under MsoPapDefault toward the end of the style section (if so, remove that one, too).

line-height:115%;

Remove all specified fonts. Look for font-family: These appear not only in the paragraph style definitions, but in spans and other places, like under MsoChpDefault. When you remove the font, there will just be a colon followed by a semicolon (:;) at the end of the line, as in my example below. For more information about fonts, like the possible dangers of embedding fonts, read Sec. 5.6. Even worse is calling a font that isn't on the actual Kindle device, without properly embedding it. Removing all mentions of fonts from your HTML is the safest way to go. It also gives each customer the flexibility to choose a font to his or her liking. (For now you may focus on removing specific fonts from your style definitions, by making your font-family specifications look empty just like the examples below. In Sec. 5.6, we'll discuss how to remove fonts from other places in your HTML file.)

font-family:;

If the font-family line is the last line of the style definition, there will also be a closed brace } following the colon and semi-colon, like this:

font-family:;}

Do you see color specified in any of your style definitions? Also look in the span styles in the style definitions (that is, keep looking until you reach </style>). You definitely don't want color set to black, white, green, or sepia anywhere in your HTML file (for example, black will be invisible when a customer selects night mode and white will be invisible in regular reading mode). Your **body text** (like MsoNormal) should have *no* mention of color at all (if it does, remove that line).

---

[77] If you enroll in KDP Select (Sec. 6.12), your KENPC—which impacts royalties for pages read through Kindle Unlimited and Amazon Prime—may be greatly reduced if you include *any* line height specifications. However, the main reason to remove the line-height specification is to ensure better formatting across all devices.

If you set the color to Automatic for each style in Word, you *shouldn't* see color in your style definitions. (Don't change the color:blue and color:purple from your a:visited and a:link spans.)

If you have any style definitions where you want a color (other than black, white, green, or sepia) applied to the *entire* paragraph, then you should have color set for those styles. For example, if you really want a red subheading, it could be done, but it will appear dull gray on black-and-white devices, and may not look good in night and sepia modes on color devices. Generally, designers don't use color in style definitions. You might apply color to a word or phrase using a span within a paragraph (but that's done inside the actual paragraph, not applied to the style definition, as described in Sec. 5.7) for emphasis in a nonfiction book or children's book, for example.

As you modify your style definitions, you will encounter more than just paragraph styles. You may see:

- paragraph styles (like p.MsoNormal, li.MsoNormal, div.MsoNormal)
- heading styles (like h1 or h2)
- span styles (like span.FootnoteTextChar)
- link styles (like a:link or a:visited)

For all of the changes that we've described for style definitions thus far, you want to apply those changes to *all* of the style definitions, *including paragraph, heading, span, and link styles.* As an example, suppose that you find a h1 span style in addition to the h1 heading style. Both will probably mention a specific font. After you strip that font out of the *span* style, it will look like this:

```
span.Heading1Char
    {mso-style-name:"Heading 1 Char";
    mso-style-link:"Heading 1";
    font-family:;
    font-weight:bold;}
```

Later on, when you finally move *past* the style definitions and look at the actual content of your book, you should see that most of the paragraphs have p-tags (with things like <p class=MsoNormal> and </p> surrounding the paragraph text) or h-tags (with <h1> and </h1> surrounding the heading text). The class= part of a p-tag should apply a style definition that you recognize: one that you originally created in Word and which you see in the Style Definitions of your HTML.

Near the end of the style section of your HTML (usually, it's just before @page), you should see MsoChpDefault and MsoPapDefault definitions. These ordinarily specify specific fonts, line heights, and margins. Delete *everything* inside the braces, like this:

.MsoChpDefault

    {}

.MsoPapDefault

    {}

Find the @page part near the very end of the style section of your HTML file. Completely remove the page size and margins using empty braces {} as in my example below. If you have more than one @page WordSection, do this for each.

@page WordSection1

    {}

Following are **recommended style definitions** for each of the paragraph styles listed in Sec.'s 3.4 and 4.7. These style definitions were used in this book (preserved through copy and paste)—though my book has a few additional style definitions (at the end of the list, I describe a few special style definitions that may be relevant for some books).

p.MsoNormal, li.MsoNormal, div.MsoNormal

    {margin-top:0in;

    margin-bottom:0in;

    margin-left:0in;

    margin-right:0in;

    text-align:justify;

    text-indent:2em;

    font-size:100%;

    font-family:;}

p.NoIndent, li.NoIndent, div.NoIndent

    {mso-style-name:NoIndent;

    margin-top:0in;

    margin-bottom:0in;

    margin-left:0in;

    margin-right:0in;

    text-align:justify;

    text-indent:0in;[78]

---

[78] In Word, in order to not indent a paragraph with justified or left alignment, you would need to set First Line Indent to 0.01". However, in HTML, you may set this to 0 inches, which is even better. (Although 0 doesn't work from Word, it *does* work from HTML.) Make sure that there is a text-indent in your style definition (because if a

```
font-size:100%;
font-family:;}
p.BodySpaceAfter, li.BodySpaceAfter, div.BodySpaceAfter
    {mso-style-name:BodySpaceAfter;
    margin-top:0in;
    margin-bottom:1em;
    margin-left:0in;
    margin-right:0in;
    text-align:justify;
    text-indent:2em;
    font-size:100%;
    font-family:;}
p.NoIndentSpaceAfter, li.NoIndentSpaceAfter, div.NoIndentSpaceAfter
    {mso-style-name:NoIndentSpaceAfter;
    margin-top:0in;
    margin-bottom:1em;
    margin-left:0in;
    margin-right:0in;
    text-align:justify;
    text-indent:0in;
    font-size:100%;
    font-family:;}
p.IndentBlock, li.IndentBlock, div.IndentBlock
    {mso-style-name:IndentBlock;
    margin-top:0in;
    margin-bottom:1em;
    margin-left:2em;
    margin-right:0in;[79]
    text-align:justify;
```

---

justified or left-aligned style doesn't specify an indent, Kindle may automatically indent). You have to set text-indent to 0 inches in order to force a non-indented paragraph (unless the alignment is set to center—though as you can see, I prefer to set text-indent to 0 even for centered paragraphs: I generally prefer to tell Kindle what I want it to do rather than leave things up to automation).

[79] It's recommended that you don't set right margins for Kindle eBooks. Block indent with a left margin, with the right margin set to zero. (You *don't* want both margin-left and text-indent to be nonzero. For a block paragraph, create a left margin without adding an additional indent to the first line. For normal paragraphs, we instead added text-indent which indents the first line, but set margin-left to zero.)

```
    text-indent:0in;

    font-size:100%;

    font-family:;}

h1

    {mso-style-link:"Heading 1 Char";

    margin-top:2em;[80]

    margin-bottom:1em;

    margin-left:0in;

    margin-right:0in;

    text-align:center;

    text-indent:0in;

    page-break-before:always;

    font-size:150%;

    font-family:;

    font-weight:bold;}

h2

    {mso-style-link:"Heading 2 Char";

    margin-top:0in;

    margin-bottom:1em;

    margin-left:0in;

    margin-right:0in;

    text-align:left;[81]

    text-indent:0in;

    page-break-before:always;[82]

    font-size:125%;

    font-family:;

    font-weight:bold;}

p.Center, li.Center, div.Center

    {mso-style-name:Center;
```

---

[80] Beware that certain Kindle devices or apps may not respect margin-top following a page break (that would still be the case even if you create a manual page break rather than incorporating the page break into the heading style as I recommend here), unless you create an ePub file that properly separates chapters into different HTML pages (Sec. 5.12).

[81] You may prefer to center your subheadings instead: That's up to you. Either specify text-align:left or text-align: center, but don't omit text-align all together (or your subheading may automatically become justified).

[82] This is optional with the h2 style. My book has lengthy sections (like this section, 5.4), so I incorporated this page break to start each section on a new page (just like h1 starts each chapter on a new page). For a book with short sections, I recommend removing this page break from the h2 style.

```
        margin-top:0in;
        margin-bottom:0in;
        margin-left:0in;
        margin-right:0in;
        text-align:center;
        text-indent:0in;
        font-size:100%;
        font-family:;}
p.CenterSpaceAfter, li.CenterSpaceAfter, div.CenterSpaceAfter
        {mso-style-name:CenterSpaceAfter;
        margin-top:0in;
        margin-bottom:1em;
        margin-left:0in;
        margin-right:0in;
        text-align:center;
        text-indent:0in;
        font-size:100%;
        font-family:;}
p.MsoTitleCxSpFirst, li.MsoTitleCxSpFirst, div.MsoTitleCxSpFirst[83]
        {mso-style-link:"Title Char";
        margin-top:2em;
        margin-bottom:0in;
        margin-left:0in;
        margin-right:0in;
        text-align:center;
        text-indent:0in;
        font-size:200%;
        font-family:;
        font-weight:bold;}
```

---

[83] You don't really need both MsoTitleCxSpFirst and MsoTitleCxSpLast as two separate styles: You could just go with a single title style called MsoTitle. I used two for my book so that *Word to Kindle* appears on the first line and *Formatting Magic* appears on the second line. I applied the MsoTitleCxSpFirst style to the first line and the MsoTitleCxSpLast style to the second line (these Microsoft Office style names automatically showed up in the HTML, but I modified them to suit my needs—I also had to adjust the style= settings in these paragraphs in the body of the HTML to associate each line with the intended title style). Note that the "First" style doesn't include margin-bottom and the "Last" style doesn't include margin-top, such that these two lines won't have space between them.

p.MsoTitleCxSpLast, li.MsoTitleCxSpLast, div.MsoTitleCxSpLast[83]

    {mso-style-link:"Title Char";

    margin-top:0in;

    margin-bottom:1em;

    margin-left:0in;

    margin-right:0in;

    text-align:center;

    text-indent:0in;

    font-size:200%;

    font-family:;

    font-weight:bold;}

p.MsoSubtitle, li.MsoSubtitle, div.MsoSubtitle

    {mso-style-link:"Subtitle Char";

    margin-top:0in;

    margin-bottom:1em;

    margin-left:0in;

    margin-right:0in;

    text-align:center;

    text-indent:0in;

    font-size:150%;

    font-family:;}

p.ListPoint, li.ListPoint, div.ListPoint[84]

    {mso-style-name:ListPoint;

    margin-top:0in;

    margin-bottom:0in;

    margin-left:2em;[85]

    margin-right:0in;

---

[84] As discussed in Sec. 3.7, I use these styles to create my own bulleted and numbered lists (for the eBook, but not for my paperback), and I don't use Microsoft Word's default bullet points. As noted in Sec. 3.7, Word's default list tools *don't* come out well when you upload an HTML file to KDP (or any other format that you might convert to after working with HTML). You might see styles called MsoListParagraph (or variations from it): I delete those from my style definitions (and then search my HTML file to make sure they weren't being used).

[85] Avoid using negative indents or creating multi-level indents. Also avoid combining text-indent with margin-left. If you really want to use negative indents, do it with a media query and a backup plan for devices for which a negative indents causes problems. If you really want multi-level indents, do thorough research on how to do this and be sure that it will come out satisfactorily across all devices: This carries much risk, and usually the possible reward doesn't warrant the risk.

```
        text-align:left;
        text-indent:0in;
        font-size:100%;
        font-family:;}
p.ListPointSpaceAfter, li.ListPointSpaceAfter, div.ListPointSpaceAfter
        {mso-style-name:ListPointSpaceAfter;
        margin-top:0in;
        margin-bottom:1em;[86]
        margin-left:2em;
        margin-right:0in;
        text-align:left;
        text-indent:0in;
        font-size:100%;
        font-family:;}
p.NoIndentPageBreak, li.NoIndentPageBreak, div.NoIndentPageBreak
        {mso-style-name:NoIndentPageBreak;
        margin-top:0in;
        margin-bottom:0in;
        margin-left:0in;
        margin-right:0in;
        text-align:justify;
        text-indent:0in;
        page-break-before:always;[87]
        font-size:100%;
        font-family:;}
p.MsoToc1, li.MsoToc1, div.MsoToc1[88]
        {margin-top:0in;
        margin-bottom:0in;
        margin-left:0in;
```

---

[86] The purpose of ListPointSpaceAfter is to add space after to the last point on the list. Only use this if you want to create space between your list and the paragraph that follows the list. This is a design choice.

[87] The best way to force a page break is to create a style definition specifically for it. I do this with chapter headings, and occasionally find the need to do it with non-indented style definitions or centered style definitions. My advice is to use page breaks for all chapter headings, but to use page breaks sparingly otherwise. If it's overdone, it creates a lot of noticeably wasted white space (on the page before, when the last line of text happens to fall high on the screen). Ask yourself if the benefit of the page break offsets the possible design issues.

[88] By default, Microsoft Word has TOC styles. I use them after modifying them as shown here.

```
        margin-right:0in;

        text-align:left;

        text-indent:0in;

        font-size:100%;

        font-family:;}
```

p.MsoToc2, li.MsoToc2, div.MsoToc2[89]

```
        {margin-top:0in;

        margin-bottom:0in;

        margin-left:2em;

        margin-right:0in;

        text-align:left;

        text-indent:0in;

        font-size:100%;

        font-family:;}
```

p.TocLast, li.TocLast, div.TocLast[90]

```
        {mso-style-name:TocLast;

        margin-top:0in;

        margin-bottom:1em;

        margin-left:0in;

        margin-right:0in;

        text-align:left;

        text-indent:0in;

        font-size:100%;

        font-family:;}
```

---

[89] Most books don't require TOC2. My nonfiction book has both chapter headings and subheadings, and I wanted the titles of both headings and subheadings to show in my table of contents to help shoppers see exactly which topics are covered. As you can see (if you navigate to my table of contents page), I added a left margin to TOC2 to offset it from TOC1. I *don't* recommend using TOC3 (or higher), and I definitely advise against attempting to create multiple levels of indents.

[90] *This* TOC style *isn't* one of Word's default styles: I made it myself. I use this for the last line of the table of contents to create space between the table and the next section (even if the next section begins by applying a style definition that includes a page break—in order to help achieve separation between sections in the Look Inside). If you used References > Table of Contents in Word to create an automatic table of contents before converting to HTML, note that Word adds an effective blank line (that contains basically no other content than nbsp; similar to the examples shown at the end of Sec. 5.10): I remove that blank line (and all other blank lines) from my HTML (when I wish to add vertical space between paragraphs, instead of creating a blank line I use style= in the p-tag or div-tag to apply an appropriate style that includes margin-bottom:1em;).

p.MsoFootnoteText, li.MsoFootnoteText, div.MsoFootnoteText[91]

    {mso-style-link:"Footnote Text Char";

    margin-top:0in;

    margin-bottom:0in;

    margin-left:0in;

    margin-right:0in;

    text-align:justify;

    text-indent:0in;

    font-size:100%;

    font-family:;}

p.MsoEndnoteText, li.MsoEndnoteText, div.MsoEndnoteText[91]

    {mso-style-link:"Endnote Text Char";

    margin-top:0in;

    margin-bottom:0in;

    margin-left:0in;

    margin-right:0in;

    text-align:justify;

    text-indent:0in;

    font-size:100%;

    font-family:;}

You may need additional styles, such as variations of the common styles listed previously. Following are a few examples:

- If you need additional subheadings, Kindle can support up to five heading levels, from h1 thru h5, but beware that any heading text may show up in device navigation.
- If you have headings or subheadings that you *don't* want to show up in device navigation, create a separate style definition for those. Give these a completely different name, like Subhead.
- You may want to incorporate a page break into a specific style definition. Create a separate style definition for this (using page-break-before:always;).
- Any other kind of paragraph where the paragraph formatting isn't exactly the same as a style definition that you already have requires creating a new style definition. Sometimes, you need a variation of a style definition that adds space after the paragraph, for example.

---

[91] These Footnote and Endnote styles appear in HTML generated from Word automatically. I simply modify them as shown here.

5.5 Improving Images

There are two things to consider regarding your images:

- the images themselves (in the image folder inside your compressed zipped folder)
- the line in your HTML file that tells the Kindle device or app how to display your image

We'll discuss the picture files first, and then describe how to improve the image line in your HTML file.

When you created your compressed zipped file, your images may have been reduced in quality or pixel count. I have seen the size in pixels change firsthand, so it's worth checking. Following is one way to check. You may have done this already with a slightly different method (if you followed the directions in Sec. 5.2).

- Open a folder on your computer to view your files. I don't mean to click File > Open in a software program like Word or Notepad. I mean open a folder to view files on your computer: just open a folder on your computer to view the files within it.
- Find the location of your compressed zipped folder.
- Double-click the compressed zipped folder to open it.
- Now double-click the image file folder ending with _files to view its contents. (This is the image files folder that's *inside* of your compressed zipped folder. Sec. 5.2 warns you that there are two copies of your image files folder. You want the one that's inside of the compressed zipped folder. You may recall that in Sec. 5.2 we checked the other copy of your image files folder. That's fine when you first make the HTML file, but afterwards it's a good habit to check the one *inside* the compressed zipped folder because that's the one that ultimately matters.)
- Double-click an image to view the picture.
- Check the picture size in pixels. How you do this depends on which software you use to open the picture. Depending on the image software that you use, you might be able to right-click the picture in the software to find an option for File Info, for example. If you open the picture with PhotoShop (one way is to right-click the picture in the image files folder and select Open With, then choose PhotoShop, provided that you have this program), click Image > Image Size.
- Open the original picture (before you inserted it into your Word file) in a separate folder on your computer. View the pixel count and file size of the original picture for comparison.
- If the picture in your image files folder within the compressed zipped folder has a smaller *pixel size* than the original picture, replace the picture following the instructions in the next set of bullet points.

- Look in the image files folder that's *inside* of the compressed zipped folder *again*. Right-click somewhere in the folder and change View to Details. Now you can check the file size in KB. If the *file size* is smaller than the original picture, that may be okay: Open the picture and also open the original picture and compare the *quality*, which is more important. (Note that the prior bullet point mentioned *pixel* size, like 1024 × 512, whereas this bullet point mentions *file* size, like 378 KB.)

Since Amazon will compress your pictures when you upload your Kindle eBook to KDP, you may not want your images compressed too much beforehand. So even if your pixel counts are unchanged, if the picture file size was reduced and you noticed any reduction in **quality**, you might still consider replacing your images (see the instructions that follow). You should also consider whether file size may be an issue for your book (as discussed in Sec.'s 4.2 and 4.13) and whether or not replacing the images may actually have any impact on how the pictures display on a Kindle device or app. That is, you don't want to waste your time replacing images: You want to know if it will be worth doing.

The good news is that you don't need to guess. Simply upload your compressed zipped folder exactly the way it is right now to create a quick test book and preview both how it looks and the current converted MOBI file size, as described in Sec. 4.13. If you're happy with the outcome, you could just leave it the way it is. If you're not sure about the picture quality, you could try replacing a *few* of the images (as described below), submitting a revised test file, and seeing what impact the replacements have (if any) on picture quality and the converted MOBI file size. This way, you will know whether or not replacing *all* of the images is worth the trouble.

Here is one way to replace one or more images in the image file:

- Find the compressed zipped folder on your computer (not in a software program like Notepad or Word, just in a folder on your computer).
- Double-click the compressed zipped folder to open it.
- Double-click the image file folder ending with _files to view its contents (this is the image files folder that's *inside* of the compressed zipped folder).
- Delete the picture that you wish to replace.[92]
- Find the original picture file (before you inserted the picture into your Word file) on your computer. Right-click the original picture and select Copy.
- Return to the _files folder (the image files folder that's *inside* of the compressed zipped folder). Place your cursor within the _files folder and select Paste.

---

[92] Delete the picture from the _files folder inside of your compressed zipped folder. You might not wish to delete it from the original _files folder outside of your compressed zipped folder. (Remember, you have two _files folders, as explained in Sec. 5.2.) That way, you will have a backup of your compressed image in case you wish to undo the replacement.

- Right-click the picture that you just pasted into the _files folder and select Rename. Type the name of the picture that you just deleted (for example, image001, where those are zeroes, not uppercase O's; don't type a file extension—the extension should be automatic, in most cases).

- Upload your compressed zipped folder as a test book, following the steps outlined in Sec. 4.13, and preview your book to make sure that the images display properly. That way, if you made a mistake while replacing the image, you can catch the problem now.

What if you replace an image, but decide that you want to undo it? You actually have two image folders: one within the compressed zipped folder, and another outside of it. If you replaced an image in the _files folder within the compressed zipped folder, and didn't change the original _files folder outside of the compressed zipped folder, then it's easy to undo the replacement. Find the picture in your original _files folder, copy it, delete it from the _files folder inside the compressed zipped folder, and paste the original compressed picture into this _files folder (the image files folder that's *inside* of the compressed zipped folder).

Now let's examine the image lines in your HTML. They are easy to find: Open your HTML file in Notepad or Sigil and search for "img" (without the quotes). In Notepad, place your cursor at the top of the file, and select Search Down with the Find tool. The results will appear in the body of your HTML file, which follows the styles section. The body section is where the content of your book appears. (The style section ends with </style>, followed by </head>, and then the body section begins. The body section ends with </body> near the end of your HTML file.) The organization of the HTML doesn't really matter right now: The Find tool will find your image lines for you when you search for "img."

When you find an image line, it will look something like this (before you improve it):

<p class=CenterSpaceAfter><img width=1000 height=1600 id="Picture 1" src="Book_files/image001.jpg"></p>

One difference is that your file name will appear in place of "Book" in the source (src) part of the image line. Note that it's simpler if your filename doesn't have any spaces. If your filename does have a space (like My Book.html), you should see 20% in place of the space (like "My20%Book_files/image001.jpg").

Another difference is that your image may be a different size. My example is 1000 × 1600 pixels (which isn't a recommended image size; it's just an example). Also, your class may be different from CenterSpaceAfter (we'll discuss the class= part in a moment).

Note that the image numbers will vary from one picture to another. The picture number in image001.jpg must correspond to the same file in the image folder. I suggest removing the id="Picture 1" label. (Don't worry if the image numbers seem to be out of order, provided that they correspond correctly to the image numbers of the picture filenames contained in the _files folder.)

For your image lines, I recommend changing the paragraph class, which has paragraph tags at the beginning and end, <p class=CenterSpaceAfter> and </p>, to a division class, which has div-tags instead, <div class=CenterSpaceAfter> and </div>. Just change each p to a div at the beginning and end of the image line.[93]

The class= part should call an appropriate paragraph style from your style definitions. The image should ordinarily appear in its own 'paragraph' (the div-tag for the image, like the one shown in the following example, sets the picture in its own 'paragraph'). If you used the paragraph styles correctly in Word, your HTML should already call the correct style definition (such as the CenterSpaceAfter style that I recommended in Sec. 5.4). I prefer to apply a style definition for pictures with alignment set to center and which adds space after the image through margin-bottom. I also apply a style definition to the paragraph *before* the image which adds space after (such as the BodySpaceAfter style from Sec. 5.4, if the previous paragraph has indented body text).

Insert alt="" on your image line (as in the example below). You can optionally place a brief description of the image between the quotes (as in alt="kitten with yarn") for the benefit of any sight-impaired readers who may be using assistive technology. There is a 140-character limit (including spaces) for the alt text. If a picture is meaningful to the content of your book, adding alt text can help to convey that meaning to sight-impaired readers. If a picture is decorative rather than meaningful, it is probably better to leave the alt text null (as in alt="").

If you have an image that you would like to *always* display full-width (or full-height, if the height reaches its limit before the width[94]) on *any* device or app, change your image line to this:

<div class=CenterSpaceAfter><img style="width: 100%; height: auto;" alt=""
src="Book_files/image001.jpg"></div>

You will need to change the source (src) part of the image line: Where my src begins Book_files, you will have the name of your book instead of "Book" (note that if your filename includes a space like My Book.html, you must type 20% instead of the space, as in "My20%Book_files/image001.jpg"). Replace width=1000 height=1600 with style="width: 100%; height: auto;" so that

---

[93] There are designers who prefer to replace every p tag with a div-tag, not just for images. In that case, this change is simple. Use the Replace tool to turn <p into <div and to turn </p> into </div>. Note that the first replacement doesn't include the > symbol. (Leave the heading tags, like h1, alone; don't replace those with div-tags.)

[94] You can't always predict which will happen, since you don't know if the customer will hold the device in portrait or landscape mode, nor do you know what screen size the customer has. It doesn't matter though. If you follow my suggestion, the picture will max out either the width or the height of the screen, whichever it fills first. (You don't need to worry about it overfilling the screen of a Kindle device or app.)

the width of the image will automatically adjust to fill the width of the screen (minus the internal margins of the device, including the customer's choice of margins), except when the height reaches the full height of the screen before the width. If your picture is 1000 × 1600 (for example) and you set width=1000 height=1600 instead of applying 100%, the image would display less than full-width on any screen larger than these dimensions (though for some pictures, that may be fine).

You probably don't want to use style="width: 100%; height: auto;" for *every* picture in your file, unless they are all large pictures designed to show at full width (or height). For example, smaller images may appear with poor quality if displayed full-width on a large screen. Don't use style="width: 100%; height: auto;" for such pictures.

For images that you *don't* want to force to display full-width (or height), your image line should look like this, except for using your filename in place of Book (recall that if your filename includes a space like My Book.html, you must type 20% instead of the space, as in "My20%Book _files/image001.jpg"):

<div class=CenterSpaceAfter><img width="1000" height="1600" alt="" src="Book_files/image001.jpg"></div>

However, you should use the actual width and height of your picture, not the 1000 × 1600 from my example. Open the image folder and check the dimensions of each image (as described earlier in this section) to verify that the dimensions specified in your image line match the pixel size of the actual image.

Note that the size in pixels appears in straight quotes in my example, whereas the size in pixels probably appears without the quotes in your original HTML. I inserted the straight quotes to change from width=1000 to width="1000" in the image line.

I *don't* recommend using a percentage less than 100%. For example, I would avoid using style="width: 50%; height: auto;" in an attempt to display an image half-width across all devices. One reason is that older Kindle devices ignore the percentage, blowing the image up to full-width. The best way to *effectively* display an image at a reduced percentage is to pad the image (Sec. 4.4): Padding prevents the image from appearing full-width on every device.

Combine padding with style="width: 100%; height: auto;" if you want to display the *padded* image full-width across all devices. Instead specify the width and height—as in width="1000" height="1600"—if you want to display the padded image actual width, rather than blowing up the padded image. Use the latter if you're only worried about an image appearing too large on older devices, and prefer how the actual size will display on newer devices. Use the former if you're trying to create a fixed percentage across all devices (like padding the image so it effectively fills half the width of any device).

A few devices have peculiarities. For example, a few older devices may automatically display images at full width unless you specify the dimensions of the image (as in width="1000" height="1600"). On a couple of devices, when forcing full-width (using style="width: 100%; height: auto;"), it may help to display the image quicker by also specifying the width and height in the same image line, like the example below (note that you must replace Book with the name of your file, and recall that if your filename includes a space like My Book.html, you must type 20% instead of the space, as in "My20%Book_files/image001.jpg").

```
<div class=CenterSpaceAfter><img style="width: 100%; height: auto;" width="1000" height="1600" alt="" src="Book_files/image001.jpg"></div>
```

As mentioned earlier, you probably don't want to force *every* picture to display full-width. For example, smaller pictures may look blurry or pixilated if they are forced to display full-width. Other pictures may not have enough quality to look good full-width on a high-resolution display. There are also design issues, where a picture has ample resolution, but the eBook would format better with the picture displaying at a smaller size. In any of these cases (where you don't want to force full width), you want to specify the dimensions of the picture—as in width="400" height="600"—and *not* force full-width. However, note that certain older devices may automatically blow all pictures up to full-width regardless of what you do (but those screens also tend to be smaller in pixel size).

Ask yourself if you really want to set the width to 100%. It may be better to leave it actual size than to force an image full-width. Ask yourself how it may look on a large screen with high resolution if it is forced full width.

If you padded any images, consider the following points:

- In the ideal world, you would prefer transparent padding. However, only GIF format supports transparency; JPEG does not. Recall that images that primarily consist of text and line art format better as GIF images, while photographs or pictures with color blends format better as JPEG images (Sec. 4.1).

- To pad an image that formats best as a JPEG, you must weigh the pros and cons of padding a JPEG image. One of the cons is that the padding will be a border with a solid color, which will stand out against some of the possible reading backgrounds (white, black, sepia, or green).

- You generally don't need to pad an image unless the picture is small (in width), and even then you don't need to pad it unless it wouldn't look good blown up to full-width on older devices. Try to visualize how the picture may look blown up to full-width on an older device (and keep in mind that older devices tend to have screens with smaller pixel counts).

If you wish to include a **caption** that is separate from the picture (as opposed to embedding the text in the image), as discussed in Sec. 4.10 there is no guarantee that the full caption will show on the screen with the corresponding picture. If you do add a caption separate from the picture, place this text in its own paragraph following the paragraph for the image, applying a style definition appropriate for the caption.

If you already typed a caption as a separate paragraph below the picture in Word using an appropriate style definition, it should come out that way automatically in the HTML. If not, you can add it now in the HTML, using appropriate p-tags beginning with <p> and ending with </p> (but calling the appropriate class within the <p> as in my example below, which involves defining a suitable style definition—perhaps with font size set to 80%—called Caption in the style definitions). For example:

<p class=Caption>Fig. 5.9. Describe the picture here.</p>

Centering an image (or text) *vertically* on a screen comes with inherent challenges, whereas centering *horizontally* is easy (just apply a style definition, like the class=CenterSpaceAfter recommended in Sec. 5.4, which sets the alignment to center). Unfortunately, there isn't a magical command that you can add to HTML—which Kindle devices and apps will respect—to center vertically on the screen if you upload an HTML file or Word document. (There is sort of a workaround if you will be uploading an ePub file, mentioned in Sec. 5.12, though even that doesn't quite solve the problem perfectly.[95])

There are several issues with centering an image (or text) **vertically** on the screen. The obvious problem is that you have no idea which information, nor how much content, will show on a customer's screen at any given time, since eReaders come in a wide variety of screen sizes and customers can choose the font size, font style, line spacing, and device margins. So how can you center something on a 'page,' when you have no way of predicting what a 'page' will look like? The short answer is, "You can't." (The long answer is in Sec. 5.12, yet even that isn't optimal.)

Another issue is that you don't know when a new 'page' will begin, unless you use a page break. However, if you incorporate a page break into the style definition for the picture (or line of text) that you're trying to center vertically on the screen, you still run into problems. The first problem has to do with space added before the first paragraph following a page break (unless you

---

[95] However, a picture book formatted as a fixed-format eBook offers more flexibility in positioning: Amazon's free fixed-format tools—the Kindle Kids' Book Creator, Kindle Textbook Creator, and Kindle Comic Creator—make it easy to position images and text anywhere you want on the screen. We discussed fixed-format picture books in Sec. 4.12.

use the ePub method described in Sec. 5.12[96]): When uploading a Word document or HTML file to KDP, Kindle devices and apps may ignore Spacing Before and margin-top on the first paragraph following a page break. Regardless of how you prepare an eBook, Kindle devices may also ignore repeated use of the Enter key or other ways of creating blank lines after a page break. (You *shouldn't* use the Enter key or other ways of creating blank lines to create vertical space in an eBook, as mentioned in Sec. 2.3. You get better formatting using margin-top and margin-bottom settings in the style definitions. Also, while the Enter key has an effect in Word, pressing the Enter key in an HTML file has *no* effect whatsoever on the resulting eBook. HTML uses p-tags, div-tags, and
's to tell the eBook when to end one paragraph and begin another. Pressing Enter in the HTML file just helps you make your HTML file appear more organized when you view it on your computer; Kindle will ignore any Enter that you press while editing your HTML file.)

My advice is *not* to try to center an image vertically (unless you create a fixed-format eBook). Simplicity in design has its advantages when it comes to Kindle formatting.

Formatting pictures, such as equations, **in-line** rather than as separate paragraphs poses a formatting challenge. One problem is that when a customer adjusts the font size, while the text resizes, the pictures don't. Inevitably, for many customers, in-line pictures will either look significantly larger or smaller than the text beside it. Unfortunately, you can't solve the problem by setting the picture size in terms of em's or percentages, as this won't be respected by Kindle devices and apps.

You could solve the problem using SVG format for images, but this is only supported by limited devices, like the latest Kindle Fires. In order to use SVG, you must also use media queries (Sec. 5.12 will point you in the right direction). While it helps display small pictures like equations in-line (that is, alongside the text in a paragraph) properly on a few devices, it doesn't work across all devices and apps, which means that it will still be problematic for many customers. If you're set on formatting an equation in-line, I recommend that you first review Sec. 4.9.

Thus, I recommend that you *avoid* formatting pictures in-line. You get the best formatting of any picture across all devices or apps by placing the picture in its own paragraph, as outlined earlier in this section (search for the img lines). As mentioned in Sec. 4.9, don't leave equations in Word's equation format: Replace them with GIF images instead.

---

[96] Just using ePub itself isn't sufficient. Although this lets you effectively add margin-top to the first paragraph of a new chapter in a way that Kindle devices and apps will respect (provided that you properly split the ePub into separate HTML pages for each chapter), you inherit yet another problem: You have no idea how much space to add because eReader screen sizes vary from tiny cell phones to huge monitors. If you add too much space before, you could introduce a blank page on a cell phone. If you add too little space, it will hardly have any effect on a large screen. If you really want to center vertically, read Sec. 5.12, but also see my warning at the beginning of that section.

Width Set to 100% in HTML

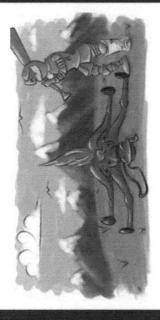

Out of the gate, the detective was bored out of his mind.

Not a single person was even horsing around.

He couldn't hold his horses for a case to work on.

It was a one-horse town, but it wasn't his horse.

Then a damsel in distress strolled into his office.

She was a bombshell; a perfect ten; out of his league.

He was a silly goose to be daydreaming about her.

What chance did a loser like him have with a girl like her?

So he picked his eyeballs off the floor and stuttered like glue.

Turns out her horse had been murdered in the dead of winter.

Picture's Actual Size

Out of the gate, the detective was bored out of his mind.

Not a single person was even horsing around.

He couldn't hold his horses for a case to work on.

It was a one-horse town, but it wasn't his horse.

Then a damsel in distress strolled into his office.

She was a bombshell; a perfect ten; out of his league.

He was a silly goose to be daydreaming about her.

What chance did a loser like him have with a girl like her?

So he picked his eyeballs off the floor and stuttered like glue.

Turns out her horse had been murdered in the dead of winter.

Even worse, she caught someone beating the dead horse.

It was a knight in shining armor beating the poor beast like a drum.

A knight living in 2013? Sounded like an open and shut case.

It would have been a challenge if the knight had had some horse sense.

What kind of fool would linger at the scene of the crime like that?

He told the damsel that he would take care of the matter.

The next morning he went to see the horse with his own eyes.

5.6 Fonts, Characters, and Special Symbols

Near the top of the HTML file, you should see something like the following:

content="text/html; charset=windows-1252"

If you use Mac, you probably see Unicode (UTF-8) instead of Windows-1252. Either Windows-1252 or Unicode (UTF-8) should work for Kindle, provided that your file doesn't specify an unsupported font or unsupported character. The Windows-1252 and Unicode (UTF-8) character sets include the list of supported characters from Appendix A. (We'll discuss special characters later in this section).

I recommend completely removing all mentions of **font** from your HTML. This way, your file won't suffer problems on one or more devices from unsupported font issues. Also, this gives the customer the freedom to choose a font of his or her preference, rather than having a font forced on the customer.

Find the font definitions near the top of your HTML file, shortly below <style>. I recommend that you highlight everything from

/* Font Definitions */

to just before (but not including)

/* Style Definitions */

and press the Delete button on your keyboard. This will remove all of the *font* definitions from your HTML file (but be sure *not* to delete any *style* definitions). That's only *half* the battle.

The other half of the battle involves looking for fonts specified elsewhere in your HTML file. For example, anywhere that you see a font specified after font-family in the style definitions, remove the font as in my example below:

font-family:;

There will also be a } symbol following the colon and semi-colon if this is the last line of the style definition.

Fonts may also appear under spans, .MsoChpDefault, and other sections further down your style definitions than just the main paragraph styles, so be sure to look beyond just the paragraph styles.

Finally, you must search the <body> (it may say something like <body lang=EN-US>) section of your HTML file, which has the content for your book. If you're using Notepad, place your cursor at the beginning of the <body> section, click Edit, select Find, choose Down, and type "font" in the search field (without the quotes). This will help you find all of the places in your file where a specific font may be mentioned. Click the Find Next option on the Edit menu to find the next match. (If you wrote a book that happens to use the word "font" several times in the text, then you might include a hyphen at the end of it to help reduce the search results.)

If this search pulls up any matches, you want to remove the mention of any specific fonts, like Calibri, Times New Roman, or Georgia. These usually show up in spans (as in <span style= 'font-size:12.0pt;font-family:"Calibri",sans-serif'>) within paragraphs (earlier I had mentioned span styles specified in the Style Definitions, but now I'm talking about span instructions that you find in paragraphs in the body of your HTML file). If the problem is widespread, you can use the Replace tool to remove any mention of specific fonts (but always use the Replace tool with care, especially if you're using Notepad—recall the danger described in Sec. 5.3).

We will learn more about spans, including what they are, in Sec. 5.7. For now, we will focus on how to correct possible font problems in your HTML file. (Any such problems are also present in your original Word document, of course. The benefit of the HTML file is that you can find and correct any problems. In your Word file, these problems are hidden. In the HTML file, they can be found.)

Each **span** begins with <span> or something like <span style='color:red'> and ends with </span>. If you remove any spans (see below for when you should or shouldn't), be sure to remove both the opening <span> (or <span style='font-size:150%'> or however it looks) and the closing </span>, but don't remove the *text* that appeared between the opening and closing spans.

Some spans should be left alone, some should be removed, and others should be modified. Examine the span style and ask yourself if it's doing anything useful. Following are common occurrences:

- If a span specifies font-family (like <span style='font-family:"Calibri",sans-serif'>), remove the font-family specification from the style. If all the span does is specify a font family (as does the example I just gave), remove both the opening and closing spans (but don't delete actual text from your book appearing between the spans). See the example below. Be careful with the punctuation marks (< > / ' " : ; = -).

Example: <p class=MsoNormal><span style='font-family:"Calibri",sans-serif'>It was a dark and stormy night.</span></p>

Change to: <p class=MsoNormal>It was a dark and stormy night.</p>

- If a span specifies font-size (like <span style='font-size:12.0pt'>), remove the font-size specification (or remove the opening and closing spans unless the span style also specifies something useful, like a needed font color) unless for some reason you want part of the paragraph to appear in a different size font than the rest of the text in the same paragraph (for example, if you want the first three words to appear in a larger font size). In the latter case, change the font size to a suitable percentage, such as <span style='font-size:120%'>. Recall the recommendations for percentages from Sec. 5.4. See the two examples below. Be careful with the punctuation marks (< > / ' " : ; = - %).

Example: <p class=MsoNormal><span style='font-size:14.0pt;font-family:"Calibri",sans-serif' >IMPORTANT NOTE</span> Don't forget to smile.</p>

Change to: <p class=MsoNormal><span style='font-size:120%'>IMPORTANT NOTE</span> Don't forget to smile.</p>

Note: If the font size is set to the same size called by the p-tag's class (like MsoNormal or h1), remove the font size completely. For example, if the font size is set to 12 pt in a MsoNormal paragraph and that was your default font size in Word, remove it completely (it would be redundant in this case, since MsoNormal sets the font size to 100% in the style definition).

- If a span specifies a property that you wish to apply to the text enclosed between the opening and closing spans, like the color of the text (like <span style='color:red'>), keep this as long as the color isn't set to black or #000000 (or any other HTML color code that is close to black). The color should not be set to white, green, or sepia either. The reason is that the reader can change the background to white, black, green, or sepia on various devices, and the text would appear invisible if it were set the same color as the background (whereas when you don't specify any color at all, the text will automatically appear black on white and white on black). See the example below. Be careful with the punctuation marks (< > / ' " : ; = -).

Example: <p class=MsoNormal>I caught you <span style='font-size:12.0pt;color:red'>red </span>-handed!</p>

Change to: <p class=MsoNormal>I caught you <span style='color:red'>red</span>-handed!</p>

There is another font property that you should search for in your file: Place your cursor at the top of your HTML file and search for all matches of "**color:**" (with the colon, but without the quotes). This will help you discover any possible problems with font color. Most of the matches typically appear in span styles, but you may find a few other matches, too.

Specifying a font color isn't necessarily a problem. When a span applies a font color to just a portion of a paragraph, and you want just that portion of the text to be the specified color (like red or blue), this is fine as long as the color isn't set to white, black, green, or sepia.

Font color should never be set to white, black, green, or sepia because the text would be invisible in some reading modes. White (or any HTML color code close to #ffffff) would be invisible on the default white background. Black (or any HTML color code near #000000) would be invisible when a customer selects night mode. Sepia (or any other creamy color) would be invisible when a customer selects sepia mode. Any greenish color would be invisible against a green reading background.

If you want an *entire* paragraph or a heading to appear in a color other than white, black, green, or sepia, the color should be applied to a style definition rather than to a span (which means creating a new paragraph style definition if you need one in default color and another in a particular color like red or blue). Ideally, a span would be used only to adjust the color of a portion of a paragraph, **like a phrase or sentence**.

If you see numerous spans setting the color to black, it probably means that you set the font color to black in Word, instead of leaving the color set to Automatic. Your HTML comes out much cleaner when you avoid applying font and paragraph settings on the Home ribbon to entire paragraphs—or when you adjust those settings and proceed to type one or more paragraphs. (Applying font or paragraph settings to just *part* of a paragraph in Word is okay, as long as you don't apply a particular font style or one of the taboo colors like black or white. This results in a span that applies to just a portion of a paragraph.)

When you adjust the color of text in your eBook, consider how it will look on a black-and-white eReader, such as the popular Kindle Paperwhite. Some colors which stand out on color displays appear as a dull gray on grayscale displays. For a picture book where the primary audience will use devices with color displays, this is less of a concern.

It is possible to **embed** a font in an eBook, but I personally *recommend against it*. First, if you force the body text to display in a particular font, some customers may be irritated that they can't use a font of their own choosing. More importantly, perhaps, are the horror stories of authors who have embedded fonts (or who attempted to do so), but later discovered some issue on one or more devices. The problem might occur just on one particular device, or it might occur only with certain characters, and when this happens, you probably wouldn't be able to catch the problem *before* you publish. When font embedding goes wrong, it's a *disaster*. My reasoning for not embedding fonts is to avoid the risk and to avoid irritating any customers.

One additional reason is that some fonts which include rights to use them when publishing a print book with a print-on-demand publisher like CreateSpace may not allow for commercial use in eBooks. The legalities of embedding fonts in eBooks appear hairier than for print books, but bear in mind that I'm not an attorney so I'm not qualified to offer any legal advice.

Here is one example of a big problem that some authors run into that relates to font embedding. This example involves the font Times New Roman, which is often recommended for Microsoft Word users (though if you submit an HTML file, you should remove the Times New Roman or any other font specifications, unless you bravely intend to embed one or more fonts in your eBook). When an author applies italics to a paragraph in Times New Roman, Microsoft

Word may (especially for Mac users) treat this as a separate font, Times New Roman Italics. In this case, if the author doesn't save the Word file in HTML format and remove the Times New Roman Italics font specification, the text won't render in italics as the author expects. If you can run into trouble with a common font like Times New Roman, it doesn't bode well for embedding other kinds of fonts.

Despite my warnings, if you research how to properly embed a font in your eBook, in the end you may discover that Amazon strips the font out anyway.

Let's now discuss **specific characters** (like • or ÷) that you can or can't use. Here is the greatest danger: There are characters that work on some Kindle devices and apps, but which don't work on others. These are harder to catch when previewing your eBook, unless you take care to use characters that you *know* are supported.

The characters listed in Appendix A are supported by Kindle devices and apps. The most reliable way to insert these symbols is to use the Insert > Symbol method of Sec. 2.6 in Microsoft Word, before saving your file as a filtered webpage. The one exception is when the symbol appears on your keyboard: For example, to type the dollar sign ($) or tilde (~) symbols, just type them by pressing the corresponding keys on your keyboard.

The symbols from Appendix A could be inserted into the HTML file using XML or HTML entities. However, Amazon KDP recommends using XML or HTML entities *only* for the few symbols mentioned below (and *not* for any others). For all other supported symbols, the most reliable way to insert them is using the Insert > Symbol method of Sec. 2.6 before you save your Word file as a filtered webpage. (If it's too late to go back to Word and do that… there is good news: It isn't too late. Open a blank document in Word, use Insert > Symbol to properly insert a supported character from Appendix A, save this very short Word file as an html file as directed in Sec. 5.2, and open that HTML file in Notepad. Find the equivalent symbol however it turned out in the HTML file, and copy/paste it into the actual HTML file for your eBook.)

There are a few symbols that are automatically converted into XML or HTML codes when you save your Word file as a filtered webpage. These include:

- The less than sign (<) turns into <
- The greater than sign (>) turns into >
- The ampersand (&) turns into &
- The non-breaking space turns into

Let me clarify: Any <, >, or & signs that you may have typed in your Word file turn into their corresponding HTML entities (such as <) in your HTML file. However, you will see <, >, and & signs throughout your HTML file. HTML uses <, >, and & signs to give Kindle devices and apps formatting and design instructions. For this reason, <, >, and & can't appear in the text.

Therefore, once you begin editing your HTML file, if you wish to insert a <, >, or & sign in the text (as opposed to using these symbols to create HTML code, such as p-tags), you must type their HTML equivalents (such as &) instead. Kindle devices and apps will display the actual symbol (<, >, or &) when they read these XML or HTML codes (such as &).

You can't type a <, >, or & sign as plain text in a paragraph because those symbols have other purposes in HTML. Instead, type the HTML codes for these characters. For example, if you want to type the inequality 3x<5, in Word you would just type 3x<5, but in the HTML file you would need to type 3x<5.

Two more instances in which you must use the HTML entity instead of the actual character include the non-breaking space and the zero-width non-joiner. We discussed these special characters in Sec. 3.7 and how they can aid in Kindle design when used sparingly.

When they are needed, I prefer to insert **non-breaking spaces** in the HTML file rather than in the original Word file for the simple reason that they are very easy to see in the HTML file. You can also see them in your Word file if you click the Show/Hide button (¶) on the Home ribbon as non-breaking spaces then appear as ° symbols whereas ordinary spaces created using the spacebar appear as · symbols. In the HTML file, non-breaking spaces look like   which make them stand out better.

As discussed in Sec. 3.7, you want to be very conservative with the non-breaking space, using it only to join two very short strings of text separated by a space. Using a non-breaking space with longer strings of text tends to cause worse formatting problems than what you're trying to prevent. For example, if you have the measurement 30 cm written in a paragraph, you might prefer to write this as 30 cm in your HTML file. This creates a non-breaking space between the "30" and the "cm" in order to ensure that they always appear together on the same line (such that the "30" never winds up at the end of one line with the "cm" appearing by itself at the beginning of the next line). In contrast, you wouldn't want to use a non-breaking space like 367 thousand, since that creates a 12-character string of text, likely leading to problems in the appearance of your body text (in this case, there will be problems regardless of whether it is justified or ragged right).

Note that non-breaking spaces do expand with justified text (they are not fixed width). Don't string non-breaking spaces together in an attempt to create a long space.

Whereas the non-breaking space ( ) is used to join two very short strings of text together, the **zero-width non-joiner** (‌) is used to indicate preferred breaking points in a very long string of text. As described in Sec. 3.7, the zero-width non-joiner comes in handy in lengthy URL's. Again, I prefer to insert zero-width non-joiners in the HTML rather than the original Word file. My example below shows how a URL would look in the HTML. (We'll explore URL's in further detail in Sec. 5.8.)

```
<p class=Center><a href="http://www.chrismcmullen.wordpress.com">www.chrismcmullen.
&zwnj;wordpress.com</a></p>
```

In my example URL above, the ‌ is ignored except when the URL is too long to display on a single line on a screen (for example, with a small screen like a cell phone or when a customer selects a large font size), in which case the ‌ instructs Kindle devices or apps to break the URL with www.chrismcmullen. on one line and wordpress.com on the next line.

Note that what Word calls the no-width optional break becomes the zero-width non-joiner in your HTML file. I prefer to insert the zero-width non-joiner directly in the HTML file (rather than using the no-width optional break in Word before saving it as a filtered webpage).

Don't use any other spaces besides these:

- an ordinary space created using the spacebar
- a non-breaking space using
- the zero-width non-joiner using ‌

There are other types of spaces and non-joiners with different XML or HTML codes that *don't work across all Kindle devices and apps.* That's why you should *only* use the spaces and non-joiners on the list above.

Most of the spaces in your book should be ordinary spaces typed with the spacebar. The non-breaking space ( ) and zero-width non-joiner (‌) should only be used sparingly. For example, if you use a non-breaking space where one of the words isn't short—for example, "10 months"—(or to connect three short words), it will probably introduce formatting problems that are worse than what you're trying to avoid.

You should avoid using XML or HTML codes except when necessary. They are necessary in your HTML file to create the ampersand (&), greater than sign (>), less than sign (<), non-breaking space ( ), and zero-width non-joiner (‌).

The symbols from Appendix A are best typed directly on your keyboard when possible. For example, the hashtag (#) and semicolon (;) can be typed with a standard keyboard. Otherwise, ideally the symbols from Appendix A (except those listed in the previous paragraph) should be inserted using the Insert > Symbol method of Sec. 2.6 in your Word file, before saving it as a filtered webpage. **Only use the equivalent XML or HTML codes when absolutely necessary.**

Avoid using symbols that aren't listed in Appendix A, as they probably won't be supported across *all* devices and apps, such as older Kindle devices or Apple products. There are many XML and HTML codes that don't work across all Kindle devices and apps, so it's best to stick to those that you know work.

For example, avoid using a **non-breaking hyphen**. It really isn't a problem, since there is a more reliable way to create the same effect. In Sec. 3.7, I showed you *how to use italics to create* *the effect of a non-breaking hyphen*: Simply use a regular hyphen (-), by typing it with your keyboard, and italicize the hyphen if you wish to create the non-breaking effect. (If the text before and after the hyphen is italicized, then you want the hyphen to not be italicized.) However, in HTML, you can do this using a **span** that specifies white-space:nowrap rather than using italics, as I will demonstrate in Sec. 5.7.

When I speak of the text being italicized, I don't mean that italics is applied the way that it is done in Word. In HTML, the text won't *look* italicized. The way to apply italics in HTML is to insert <i> before the text that you wish to italicize and insert </i> after the text that you wish to italicize (be sure to put the / symbol in the closing tag, but not the opening tag). For example, if you type <i>italics</i> in HTML, the word "italics" would appear italicized in the eBook.

Following are two examples that effectively create non-breaking hyphens. In the first example, the text is normal while the hyphen is italicized. In the second example, the text is italicized while the hyphen is normal (in the eBook, it would look like this: "my *to-do* list"). However, if you're working with HTML, it's better to do this using and instead of <i> and </i>, as I will show you in Sec. 5.7 (and in either case, you would simply enclose the regular hyphen between the nowrap white-space spans, following my example in Sec. 5.7).

Example: <p class=MsoNormal>I was ecstatic when I finished writing my 500<i>-</i>page book.</p>

Example: <p class=MsoNormal>Writing a bestseller is on my <i>to</i>-<i>do</i> list.</p>

Like the non-breaking space, avoid italicizing a hyphen except when it joins together two short strings of text. Don't use a non-breaking hyphen, and don't use an optional hyphen (or soft hyphen). Beware that an effective non-breaking hyphen may cause issues with some older devices (resulting in breaks in undesirable places).

Finally, let's consider an important font issue that comes at the beginning of each chapter. As we discussed in Sec. 3.7, there are four common methods for beginning the first paragraph of a chapter:

- Use a **drop cap** for the first letter of the first sentence.
- Use a large font size for the first letter of the first sentence (not recommended).
- Type the first few words in all CAPS.
- Type the first few words in **small caps**.

Some books use a **drop cap** in combination with small caps for the first few words.

If you properly inserted a basic drop cap in Word, it should carry over into your HTML file and Kindle eBook fairly well. In the past, there were serious problems with the drop cap showing improperly on some devices. Amazon has improved this significantly, though the drop cap feature may still have subtler issues. However, not every type of drop cap is guaranteed to work: It's best to make it plain and in a default font for your eBook. Some eBook formatters continue to avoid drop caps, perhaps with a "once burned, twice shy" mentality from the original drop cap problems, or perhaps because they are not happy with subtler issues that may still exist for a few devices.

The picture at the end of this section shows a drop cap that was created in Word, and then converted to HTML as described in this chapter. This shows that a drop cap can come out just fine. The optimal way to treat a drop cap is to define a span with a media query. I have an example of how to create a span with a media query (which uses the same values recommended by Amazon in their technical publishing guidelines[97]) at the end of this section (just before the picture of a drop cap). The example also shows how to call the span in the body of your HTML: If you created drop caps in Word and if you wish to follow my HTML example (instead of using the HTML for the drop cap that was automatically generated in the Word to HTML conversion—this is a choice, though my example provides the better alternative), you will want to remove the table that Word creates for the drop cap and make the first paragraph of the chapter look like my example. If you're careful with the syntax, this will optimize your drop caps.

Note that the alternative of setting the first letter in a large font size (without creating a drop cap) comes with undesirable problems, especially the large gap that it creates between the chapter heading and the rest of the first sentence. My current preference is to either use a drop cap or set the first few words in caps (or both). I'm *not* currently a fan of making a large first letter.

No matter which method you choose, be sure to adjust the font size properly in your HTML file, meaning to set the font size as a percentage rather than a value in points. Sec.'s 5.4 and 5.7 both help you make corrections of this nature.

For **small caps**, you want a span (as described in Sec. 5.7) that adjusts the font size of the first few words to about 90%. You might also want to make these words boldface. See the following example.

<p class=MsoNormal><span style='font-size:90%'><b>ONCE UPON A TIME</b></span> a princess saved a knight in distress.</p>

As I mentioned previously, the optimal way to insert a **drop cap** is to define a span with a **media query** and then apply this span to the first paragraph of each chapter. The example that follows will show you exactly how to do this.

First, if you created a drop cap using Word, you will want to *delete the entire table* that Word created in your HTML to do this. You probably see HTML like this for your drop cap:[98]

---

[97] If you would like to read Amazon's technical publishing guidelines, you can find a link to Amazon's PDF for Kindle publishers, called *Amazon's Publishing Guidelines*, in Sec. 5.12.

[98] One problem with the way that Word's drop caps come out in the HTML is that Word creates a table with point values. My example will do this more efficiently with a span, and it will apply percentages and em's rather than point values.

```
<div>
<table cellspacing=0 cellpadding=0 hspace=0 vspace=0 align=left>
<tr>
<td valign=top align=left style='padding-top:0in;padding-right:0in; padding-
bottom:0in;padding-left:0in'>
<p class=MsoNormal style='text-indent:0in;line-height:40.25pt;page-break-after:
avoid;vertical-align:baseline'><span style='font-size:54.5pt'>A</span></p>
</td>
</tr>
</table>
</div>
```

Delete everything from the <div> to the </div> that enclose your table (delete those div tags, too). Note that the first letter of the chapter was included in that table: If you examine the paragraph following that table, you will see that the first letter is missing. You will need to include that letter with a span that calls your drop cap style, like I do in the following example:

```
<p class=NoIndent><span class="DropCaps">O</span>nce upon a time...</p>
```

This won't work until you add a span for the drop cap style to the Style Definitions (which appear above the body of your HTML file). This is best done using a media query. The media query checks which type of device (or app) is being used to read the book, and then displays the drop cap the optimal way for that type of device. (The main idea is that negative margins don't work on certain devices, so the media query lets you use them on newer devices while offering an alternative for devices where negative values would be a problem.) Type the following media queries into your Style Definitions. Pay close attention to the syntax so that everything is typed *exactly* as it appears here:

```
@media amzn-kf8 {
span.DropCaps {font-weight:normal;
font-size:320%;
float:left;
margin-top:-0.3225em;
margin-bottom:-0.3245em;}}
@media amzn-mobi {
span.DropCaps {font-size:3em;
font-weight: bold;}}
```

You only need to type the above span (applied with a media query) *once* in your Style Definitions, whereas you will need to apply the span <span class="DropCaps">O</span> (probably with a different letter than uppercase O) to *each* paragraph that you want to apply a drop cap (most likely, the first paragraph of each chapter). If you originally made your drop caps in Word, you will also need to remove the tables for the drop caps that were generated during the Word to HTML conversion. Be sure to preview your drop caps carefully (Chapter 7).

Tip: After you create one drop cap, upload your file to create a quick preview to test your drop cap (Sec. 7.2 will show you how to make a quick test preview). Wait until you have perfected one drop cap before doing the work to create drop caps throughout your entire eBook.

A BOOKSTORE IS LIKE a bar where you go to pick up books; internet bookstores are like online dating services. You browse through the books to find one that catches your eye. When you see one you like, you look at it more closely. You scan it up and down, turn it over and examine its rear. The book doesn't mind. In fact, the book yearns for more. It was written for this moment. It is begging, "Pick me! Pick me!"

Satisfied with what you see so far, you look inside. You judge its appearance inside and out. Then you decide to get to know it better. You read the cover blurbs. You check out the contents, browse through the introduction. You're measuring its personality, knowledge, and communication skills; judging its potential.

If the book passes your examination, you take it out on a date. You begin reading the first chapter. The whole time the book is anticipating that first kiss, wondering if you will take it home with you. Meanwhile, you are analyzing the book's every move. Going steady with a book is a big commitment. You don't want to be disappointed.

How do you know if the relationship will work out? Curling up by the fireplace, snuggling in warm covers in bed with a book light, sneaking a quick page or two in the bathroom. You will share these intimate times with your book. You want to know that the book is Mr. or Mrs. Right for you.

When you look at the cover, you see the book's handsome or pretty face and stylish suit or dress. As you read, the plot unfolds. The plot is like the book's body. A great plot is like an attractive body. But is that enough to satisfy your needs? Suspense, en-

5.7 Further Formatting Improvements

Recall that we discussed Kindle design in Sec. 3.7, and how pictures impact Kindle design in Sec. 4.7. In this section, we will focus on some Kindle design issues that specifically relate to HTML.

Many formatting problems can be resolved (or even avoided) by knowing specifically what to look for in the HTML. For starters, we'll look at paragraph tags and spans, where some common formatting problems show up.

Note the distinction between paragraph *tags* and paragraph *styles*. Near the beginning of the HTML file (between <style> and </style>), you find paragraph styles defined in the **style definitions**. The paragraph **styles** define the default styles for different types of paragraphs. In the **body** of the HTML file (after the style definitions: after </head>, beginning with <body>), you find paragraph **tags** (or p-tags), heading tags (or h-tags), and division tags (or div-tags). The body text of your actual book is generally contained within the p-tags. The content for every paragraph, heading, picture, or other element (like a table) is contained within opening and closing p-tags, div-tags, or h-tags. In the HTML for this eBook, most of the paragraphs are placed between <p> and </p> tags, headings appear between <h1> and </h1> tags, subheadings appear between <h2> and </h2> tags, and images are placed between <div> and </div> tags.

Paragraph tags begin with <p> and end with </p>, which is why we call them p-tags for short. The opening <p> should include a class, as in <p class=MsoNormal> or <p class=Center>. The class calls one of the paragraph styles defined in the style definitions near the beginning of the HTML file.

A **clean** p-tag for body text just calls the class to specify which style definition to use for the paragraph text. A clean p-tag doesn't include instructions that could have been specified in the style definition. Font style (like italics), font weight (like boldface), font size, font color, text alignment, margins, page breaks, and line height are examples of properties should already be specified in the style definition (Sec. 5.4). These attributes shouldn't be included inside the opening p-tag. The following examples illustrate paragraph tags which are and aren't clean. (For images, these may be div-tags rather than p-tags, as noted in Sec. 5.5.)

<p class=MsoNormal>This sample paragraph has a clean p-tag.</p>

<p class=MsoNormal style='text-align:center'>This sample paragraph includes instructions that could have been included in an appropriate style definition.</p>

The second example above could look like the following example instead, provided that the style definitions include a style definition called Center, with text-align:center instructions (the style definitions recommended at the end of Sec. 5.4 include a paragraph style called Center):

<p class=Center>This sample paragraph calls a centered style definition.</p>

In general, clean p-tags, div-tags, and h-tags result in Kindle eBooks with *more reliable and predictable formatting*. One reason is that the Look Inside—and a few apps or even devices—may not interpret the HTML the way that most programs (like those used for websites) would interpret HTML instructions. Ordinarily, local instructions included in a p-tag should override the paragraph style from the style definitions. However, not all devices and Kindle apps—and especially the Look Inside feature—work quite this way.

Some formatters say that Amazon's **Look Inside** feature interprets HTML more strictly, but you might think of it more like this: The Look Inside doesn't necessarily follow the usual rules for interpreting HTML. Any *contradictions* between instructions included in a p-tag and the corresponding style definition have the potential to be interpreted differently by the Look Inside—or a few devices or apps—than what might be expected from the usual order of operations with HTML. In general, you get more predictable formatting with clean p-tags, h-tags, and div-tags.

It doesn't even need to be an outright contradiction, like the style definition calling for justified alignment and the p-tag calling for centered alignment. It can be more *subtle*. For example, if the style definition doesn't set a text indent, while the paragraph itself says to make zero indent, this may serve as a contradiction. Most Kindle devices and apps automatically indent paragraphs when *no* text-indent is set,[99] so in this example, the style definition is implicitly telling Kindle to indent, while the p-tag says to do otherwise. In general, p-tags should be clean: Any paragraph formatting that could be specified in the style definitions shouldn't be included in the p-tag.

Your p-tags *should* already be clean if you followed my directions in Chapter 3. If your p-tags apply formatting instructions (like text-align, text-indent, or page-break), it's a sign that you applied direct formatting to one or more paragraphs (which I have repeatedly warned not to do because it's a common mistake). In Word, either you highlighted multiple paragraphs and applied formatting directly to what was highlighted, or you adjusted font or paragraph settings and proceeded to type one or more paragraphs with those settings. If instead you used paragraph styles for all paragraph formatting, you will see clean p-tags.

Scan through your book to see how your p-tags (and div-tags and h-tags) look. Are they all clean? If so, pat yourself on the back.

If your p-tags aren't clean, you have a decision to make. The first question is how prevalent the problem is. If only a few p-tags aren't clean, it's relatively painless to clean them up. If the

---

[99] I *don't* recommend this. Each style definition should specify a text-indent. When you want a non-indented paragraph, set the text-indent to 0 in the style definition, as explained in Sec. 5.4. Don't rely on automatic indents, as it could lead to inconsistent formatting, and may even affect spacing between paragraphs. I also recommend clean p-tags, without setting indents or other attributes that should instead be defined in the style definitions.

problem is widespread, it would require a lot of work (even with the Replace tool, which you must use carefully when editing HTML).

If you have numerous p-tags to clean up, upload your file as it is to KDP. Follow the appropriate directions from Sec. 4.13, which describes how to make a test file and preview it at KDP. You may also want to skip to Chapter 7 for now to learn how to preview your file thoroughly. If the results look fine across all devices that you can test, you might settle for the p-tags as they are. However, there is no preview for the Look Inside, which interprets your file differently than most Kindle devices and apps, so there is a significant chance that the Look Inside won't appear as desired if your p-tags are messy. Ideally, you would have clean p-tags, but if cleaning them up appears to be an immense task, you must weigh the pros versus the cons (and since you can't preview the Look Inside, you don't really know if all that work will pay off or not).

To clean up a p-tag, first remove the *direct formatting* instructions from within the p-tag. In my example below, first remove the style= part of the p-tag. Next, change the class= part to call the appropriate style definition. If you don't already have a paragraph style in your style definitions with the desired paragraph formatting, you need to add a new paragraph style to the definitions. You may copy and paste the opening p-tag for an existing clean p-tag and simply revise it (by editing the name of the style definition called by the class= part, if necessary) for the new paragraph style.

<p class=MsoNormal style='text-align:center'>This p-tag includes direct formatting instructions in the style= part.</p>

<p class=Center>This p-tag calls a style definition that already has the desired formatting instructions instead of including direct formatting.</p>

Another place to look for formatting issues is in the **spans**. Sometimes spans are necessary, but other times they are not. We'll discuss both kinds, beginning with the ones you want to correct.

When you see a span, you see both an opening span—like <span style='font-size:12.0pt'>—and a closing span—which is just </span>. The span serves to apply a different style (other than what is defined in the paragraph style) to a *portion* of a paragraph. At least, that's how a span *should* be used for an eBook. The span ordinarily shouldn't apply to the *entire* paragraph (meaning, all of the text enclosed in the p-tag); it should only enclose *part* of the text in a paragraph.

Following are two examples to illustrate the distinction between these two types of spans. The first example shows a span that applies to the *entire* paragraph, while the span in the second example applies only to a *portion* of the text in the paragraph. The first type of span should be **avoided**. The second type of span is sometimes necessary.

<p class=MsoNormal><span style='color:blue'>In this example, the span applies to the entire paragraph. All of the text of this paragraph appears between the opening and closing spans.</span></p>

<p class=MsoNormal>In this example, the span applies only to a portion of the paragraph. <span style='color:blue'>Only this sentence appears within the span.</span></p>

Let's first discuss the type of spans that apply to an *entire* paragraph. Ordinarily, you *shouldn't* have such spans. If you followed my directions in Chapter 3 carefully, you shouldn't have any spans that apply to an entire paragraph. If you do have spans that apply to an entire paragraph, it's a sign that you applied formatting directly to paragraphs in Word, rather than using the paragraph styles to achieve all paragraph formatting.

Ideally, you would remove any spans that apply to an entire paragraph, and apply an appropriate style definition instead. If you have numerous spans that apply to entire paragraphs, you might want to upload your file as it is to KDP to assess whether or not it may be worth the time to clean up all of the spans (though keep in mind that you can't preview the Look Inside, where problems are more apt to show up).

It's okay to have spans that apply to only a *portion* of the text in a paragraph. In some cases, these spans are *necessary*. For example, if you want one phrase or sentence to have a different format than the rest of the paragraph, a span can be used to apply a different formatting style to that portion of the paragraph. Spans are helpful when the formatting *can't* be achieved applying style definitions alone.

Browse through your HTML file to find spans, or use the Find tool to find the word span in your file. Examine several of the spans to see how they look. A necessary span applies formatting instructions needed to make a portion of a paragraph have different formatting than the rest of the paragraph.

If you formatted your book very cleanly in Word, most of your spans should be fine. Following are specific kinds of problems to look for in spans (you can also find a few examples of span issues in Sec. 5.6):

- Do any spans mention **specific fonts**, such as <span style='font-family:"Century", serif'>? If so, you want to remove the font-family from the span. If the span doesn't do anything else besides describe the font family (or if the other things it does are unnecessary), remove both the opening and closing spans from the paragraph. Be sure to also find and remove the corresponding closing </span> whenever you remove an opening span.

Example: <p class=NoIndent><span style='font-family:"Century", serif'>This was totally unnecessary.</span></p>

Change to: <p class=NoIndent>This was totally unnecessary.</p>

- Do any spans set a **font size in points,** like <span style='font-size:10.0pt'>? If so, do you need to change the font size in the middle of the paragraph? If you don't need to adjust the font size, remove the font size specification from the span; of if the span doesn't do anything worthwhile, remove both the opening and closing spans. If instead you do wish to change the font size in the middle of the paragraph, set the value as an appropriate percentage like we did in Sec. 5.4. For example, <span style='font-size:80%'>.

Example: <p class=NoIndent><span style='font-size:10.0pt'>THE MUSE APPEARED</span> in a puff of blue smoke.</p>

Change to: <p class=NoIndent><span style='font-size:90%'>THE MUSE APPEARED</span> in a puff of blue smoke.</p>

- Spans should *only* apply text formatting, like italics, boldface, or font color. Spans should *not* apply paragraph formatting, like paragraph **alignment**, **text indents**, or **line height**. If you find any paragraph formatting in spans (like text-align, text-indent, or line-height), remove the paragraph formatting from the span (and if the span doesn't accomplish anything useful, remove both the opening and closing spans). Such paragraph formatting should instead be specified by applying an appropriate style definition. If the style definition you need doesn't yet exist, add one to the style definitions and call that paragraph style in the p-tag. (Earlier in this section, we described how to call a paragraph style in a p-tag, while Sec. 5.4 discusses paragraph styles and style definitions.)

Spans that only apply a font style (like italics), font weight (like boldface), font color (like red), or similarly just change the text (rather than the paragraph) are necessary if they are only applied to a *portion* of a paragraph (rather than to an *entire* paragraph). These spans should remain in your file.[100] However, in the case of color, you need to check which color is specified. You should not change color to black, white, green, or sepia (or any other colors very similar to these) or the text will be invisible to readers who adjust the background to be the same color as your text.

Note that you may want to **clean** up a span. For example, suppose that a span applies to just part of a paragraph and applies font-color:red, which you wish to keep, but suppose that the span also sets the font size to 12.0 pts, which you don't wish to keep. In this case, you could clean up

---

[100] Well, you really don't need a span to create italics or boldface. It's simpler to enclose text between <i> and </i> to italicize text and between <b> and </b> to make boldface. For example, <p class=MsoNormal>Let me <i>emphasize</i> this.</p> in the HTML would appear like this in the Kindle eBook: Let me *emphasize* this.

the span (to look like <span style='color:red'> and </span>) by eliminating the font size specification from the opening span.

Another type of paragraph to search for in your HTML file is the **empty paragraph**. An empty paragraph is a paragraph that doesn't contain any text. Below is an example of an empty paragraph. You can find a second example (which uses a rather long p-tag to express an effectively empty paragraph—those can fool you because they seem too long to be empty paragraphs) at the end of this section. There are also three more examples of empty paragraphs at the end of Sec. 5.10: It would be instructive to examine those.

<p class=MsoNormal> </p>

The above paragraph consists of nothing more than a non-breaking space. You might see them with h-tags instead of p-tags, and sometimes empty paragraphs appear much longer because they include formatting instructions in the p-tags or include spans.

If you find empty paragraphs in your HTML file, it's usually an indication that you pressed the Enter key two times (or more) in a row to create space between paragraphs. As mentioned in Sec. 2.3, you shouldn't do this. For one, two or more empty paragraphs in a row tend to be ignored on Kindle devices and apps. An empty paragraph that follows a page break also tends to be ignored. The reliable way to create space between paragraphs is to use margin-bottom, as discussed in Sec. 5.4 (but also see Sec. 5.12 if you wish to create space before the first paragraph following a page break).

You might also see **empty spans**, like <span>this</span>. This example does nothing, as it includes no formatting instructions. An empty span should be harmless (whereas you should remove empty paragraphs: if you want to create space between paragraphs, use margin-bottom instead, as described in Sec. 5.4), but it's pretty easy to remove those unnecessary spans.

There is another kind of span that you can add which serves as an effective **non-breaking hyphen** for Kindle. **Don't** use a special non-breaking hyphen symbol or HTML entity.[101] Rather, if you want to make a non-breaking hyphen, *use a regular hyphen and the span style from the following example.* Suppose that you would like for the hyphen in "Read pages 15-22 tonight" to be non-breaking (so that the 15 and 22 never get split across two lines). The following span style could be used to achieve this effect.

Example: <p class=MsoNormal>Read pages <span style="white-space: nowrap">15-22</span> tonight.</p>

---

[101] Only use regular hyphens for Kindle formatting. Don't use an optional hyphen (or soft hyphen), and don't use an actual non-breaking hyphen (using an effective non-breaking hyphen by enclosing a regular hyphen between nowrap white-space spans is fine).

Like the non-breaking space, be careful not to use the non-breaking hyphen in a long string of characters. For example, if you used the nowrap white-space style to achieve a non-breaking hyphen in the hyphenated word "self-publishing," this could lead to very noticeable formatting problems because the string consists of 15 characters. Beware that an effective non-breaking hyphen may cause issues with some older devices (resulting in breaks in undesirable places).

If you want to add a simple horizontal line to separate paragraphs, you can do it using <hr> in your HTML. (This stands for horizontal rule.) That's how I created the horizontal lines that follow this paragraph. After the horizontal lines, you can see the exact HTML code that I used to create them.

This paragraph is set off by horizontal lines.

```
<hr>
<p class=CenterSpaceAfter>This paragraph is set off by horizontal lines.</p>
<hr>
```

Ordinarily, **spellcheck and grammarcheck marks** from your Word file *shouldn't* show up in your Kindle eBook, but I have seen this happen firsthand. It's rare, but you don't want this rare occurrence to show up in *your* eBook, so it's worth double-checking. Fortunately, it's easy to check whether or not such marks have propagated to your HTML file. In Notepad, for example, you can search for "class=SpellE" (but without the quotes) to see if you have things like <span class=SpellE>line spacing</span> (but with different words besides "line spacing" enclosed by the spans). In my example, if you found this match in your HTML file, you would replace <span class=SpellE>line spacing</span> with just the words line spacing. Also search for "class=GramE" (without the quotes) to catch any grammarchecks that may have carried over into your HTML file. Again, ordinarily, you *shouldn't* find any matches, but you want to check just to be sure. In the rare cases where there are such issues, you will also find SpellE and GramE definitions in the style definitions section of your HTML file.

If you study the features described in this section in your actual HTML file, *you can learn how what you do in your original Word document affects the HTML file* that results from saving the Word document as a filtered webpage. The HTML file shows formatting details that are hidden in Word—hidden so much that you can't see them even if you press the Show/Hide button (¶). Your HTML file contains some instructions in p-tags and spans that you *can't* see in Word. The better you prepare your original Word file and the more strictly you use paragraph styles for all paragraph formatting, the cleaner your resulting HTML file will be and the fewer alterations you will need to make to your HTML. If you see p-tags or spans where the HTML isn't clean and efficient, you may be able to learn how to handle Word better in the future to produce cleaner and more efficient HTML.

Following is an example of messy, inefficient HTML generated from Word. The second 'paragraph' is **completely empty** (it would typically result in an unnecessary blank line, but it would also be unpredictable, being ignored by a few devices or apps). On top of that, the font that it specifies, Arial, is especially problematic (it's better not to specify *any* font in the HTML). You may also notice the superfluous non-breaking space (that's what it looks like when you use two spaces after a period instead of one—recall from Sec. 2.2 that it's better to use only a single space after a period). Note that the following example would be problematic whether uploading a Word document or the converted HTML file: **These problems were caused by <u>not</u> styling the paragraphs properly in Word** (as described in Chapter 3).

<p class=MsoNormal style='text-align:justify;text-indent:.01in'><span style='font-family:"Arial","sans-serif"'>Everybody makes mistakes. We are human after all. But we can learn from our mistakes. And we can learn to do a little research to help avoid mistakes in the future.</span></p>

<p class=MsoNormal style='text-align:justify;text-indent:.01in'><span style='font-family:"Arial","sans-serif"'> </span></p>

<p class=MsoNormal style='text-align:justify;text-indent:.01in'><span style='font-family:"Arial","sans-serif"'>Some people seem to be better at learning from their mistakes than others. But one thing is for certain. It's much easier to point out mistakes that others are making than it is to correct our own faults.</span></p>

When the same content is prepared properly in Word, the HTML converted from Word can look clean and efficient (without having to manually edit the HTML):

<p class=NoIndentSpaceAfter>Everybody makes mistakes. We are human after all. But we can learn from our mistakes. And we can learn to do a little research to help avoid mistakes in the future.</p>

<p class=NoIndent>Some people seem to be better at learning from their mistakes than others. But one thing is for certain. It's much easier to point out mistakes that others are making than it is to correct our own faults.</p>

5.8 Hyperlinks, URL's, Bookmarks, Footnotes, and Endnotes

Hyperlinks, bookmarks, footnotes, and endnotes automatically transfer from your Word file into your HTML file and then into your Kindle eBook. However, you may want to know what these are supposed to look like in your HTML file so that you can check that yours came through correctly: I will provide examples showing the syntax in this section.

The main issues to look for in hyperlinks, bookmarks, footnotes, and endnotes are nonstandard **fonts** (though it's best not to specify any font style), a font size specified in **points** (instead of a percentage like those suggested in Sec. 5.4), or a **line height** (even a percentage, like 115% or 108%, is a problem for line height). Such issues may appear in a span within a paragraph in the body of your HTML file, or they may appear in a style definition near the top of your HTML file. Sec. 5.7 describes what to look for in that regard.

Another reason to be familiar with the HTML structure of various types of links is in case you need to move them, modify them, or add new links after you have already created your HTML file. This section will show you by example what your links, bookmarks, and footnotes should look like.

Each hyperlink is enclosed between <a> and </a> tags (called a-tags). The opening a-tag includes the **target** location (or **destination**—where the reader will be directed when the reader clicks on the hyperlink) in the form <a href="target location">. In between the opening and closing a-tags, type the **text to display** (this is the text that the reader will see displayed on the screen). The format is shown below and the examples that follow illustrate how to apply this.

<a href="target location">text to display</a>

An **external hyperlink** includes the URL to a website. In this case, the target location must include the full web address (beginning with the http:// part) in straight quotation marks. For example, if I want to include the URL to my WordPress blog, first I would visit my blog's home page, then I would highlight the URL shown at the top of the page, and next I would copy and paste the URL between the straight quotation marks. When I copy and paste the URL for my blog, here is what I get.

http://www.chrismcmullen.com

The above URL is **inactive**: If you click on it, *nothing will happen*. In order to transform this into an active hyperlink, I will use a-tags, **placing this URL in the target location** (the href part of the opening a-tag). The following example shows what the a-tags look like. What the reader sees is www.chrismcmullen.com, but where the reader goes when the reader clicks on the hyperlink is http://www.chrismcmullen.com.

In each example that follows, the first line shows what the hyperlink looks like in the HTML file, and the second line is the actual clickable hyperlink in action (well, it's clickable if you're reading the Kindle edition of this book).

<a href="http://www.chrismcmullen.com">www.chrismcmullen.com</a>

<u>www.chrismcmullen.com</u>

The href part must include the full URL, but the text to display can be *anything* you want. In the next example, the reader is still directed to the same website when the reader clicks on the hyperlink, but the hyperlink text appears different to the reader than the one above. In the example below, the hyperlink looks like "Chris McMullen's blog" and takes the reader to my blog when it is clicked (if you're reading the Kindle edition).

<a href="http://www.chrismcmullen.com">Chris McMullen's blog</a>

<u>Chris McMullen's blog</u>

I recommend making the appearance text look like a shortened version of the URL, as in my first example. This way, the reader can readily see where the hyperlink leads.

If your appearance text is a lengthy URL, you may want to use the zero-width non-joiner that we discussed in Sec. 5.6. Place the HTML entity ‌ in the positions of desired breaks to reduce the chance of the URL string breaking in an undesired location. The following example includes a zero-width non-joiner as an example. Place this in the appearance text only, **not** in the target location.

<a href="http://www.chrismcmullen.wordpress.com">www.chrismcmullen.‌wordpress. com</a>

<u>www.chrismcmullen.wordpress.com</u>

The a-tag itself will be inside of a p-tag, h-tag, or div-tag. For example, if you want the URL to appear by itself on one line, the format would be as follows. (If you prefer to add space after your hyperlink, you would instead apply a style definition similar to the CenterSpaceAfter style that I recommended in Sec. 5.4. In that case, to create symmetry, you would also apply space after—via margin-bottom—to the paragraph style preceding the hyperlink.)

<p class=Center><a href="http://www.chrismcmullen.wordpress.com">www.chrismcmullen. ‌wordpress.com</a></p>

<u>www.chrismcmullen.wordpress.com</u>

The following example shows you how to include an external hyperlink in a paragraph of text. If you do this, keep the text to display short, include zero-width non-joiners in the text to display, or include spaces in your text to display in order to help prevent justification issues. The first paragraph shows you what the HTML looks like, while the second paragraph shows you the result with the active hyperlink.

<p class=MsoNormal>Alternatively, you can include the URL inside of a paragraph of text, like this: <a href="http://www.chrismcmullen.wordpress.com">www.chrismcmullen.‌ wordpress.com</a>. However, I advise you to avoid doing this with long strings of text, as it increases the risk of serious justification issues.</p>

Alternatively, you can include the URL inside of a paragraph of text, like this: www.chris mcmullen.wordpress.com. However, I advise you to avoid doing this with long strings of text, as it increases the risk of serious justification issues.

Internal hyperlinks work much the same way, except that the **target location** specifies a **bookmark** *within* the eBook rather than the URL of a website. If you created an active table of contents in Word as directed in Sec. 3.8, elements from your table of contents (such as chapter headings) will already have bookmarks. Other locations can be set by manually inserting a bookmark. You can insert a bookmark in your Word file before converting to HTML, as shown in Sec.'s 3.8 and 3.10. Alternatively, you can insert a bookmark directly into your HTML file.

To set a bookmark in your HTML file, use <a> and </a> tags where the opening <a> tag defines the name of the bookmark. Use name= to name the bookmark (inside of the opening a-tag), as in the following example (which names the bookmark RightHere). Don't include spaces in the name of the bookmark. My eBook has a bookmark <a name=RightHere>: This paragraph shows you how to set a bookmark in your HTML file.</a> Later on, I have an internal hyperlink which will return you to this exact location. If you're reading the Kindle edition of this book, you can click that hyperlink to test it out.

The opening a-tag has the format <a name=MakeUpaName>. Place the opening and closing <a> and </a> tags around the text that you would like to bookmark. The complete structure looks like this: <a name=MakeUpaName>Text</a> where "Text" is text that already exists in your HTML file (you're just putting the a-tags around it). In my example in the previous paragraph, I have the sentence following sentence between my a-tags: "This paragraph shows you how to set a bookmark in your HTML file." That text bookmarks the location in my eBook where I want readers to go when they click on a **bookmark hyperlink** created by a *different* set of a-tags (which we'll get to shortly).

Suppose that you want to bookmark an example in your book. Maybe your example looks like this:

Example 3.4. If a monkey throws a banana with an initial speed of 20 m/s at an angle of 30° above the horizontal from a height of 25 m above horizontal ground, how far will the banana travel horizontally before it strikes the ground?

You could bookmark this example so that elsewhere in your document, when you refer to Example 3.4, you can include an internal bookmark to take the reader to this example. In this case, you could add a bookmark using a-tags as follows.

<p class=MsoNormal><a name=Ex3point4>Example 3.4</a>. If a monkey throws a banana with an initial speed of 20 m/s at an angle of 30° above the horizontal from a height of 25 m above horizontal ground, how far will the banana travel horizontally before it strikes the ground?</p>

In my previous example (Example 3.4), the name of the bookmark is Ex3point4. Later in this section, I will show you how to create a bookmark hyperlink that takes the reader to that example.

To create an **internal hyperlink**, use <a> and </a> tags with href in the opening <a> tag, much like we did when we created external hyperlinks. The only difference is that the href specifies the location of a bookmark within your eBook instead of the URL for a website. For internal hyperlinks, the href begins with a # sign (after the first straight quotation mark). Internal hyperlinks have the followings structure:

<a href="#BookmarkName">text to display</a>

The following example shows an internal hyperlink in my eBook. The first line shows you how the internal hyperlink looks in my HTML. The second line is the actual internal hyperlink. If you're reading the Kindle edition and click on this hyperlink, it will take you back a few paragraphs to where it says, "This paragraph shows you how to set a bookmark in your HTML file."

<p class=CenterSpaceAfter><a href="#RightHere">Test out my bookmark.</a></p>

<p style="text-align:center"><u>Test out my bookmark.</u></p>

A few paragraphs back, I showed you how to create a bookmark for a hypothetical Example 3.4. If you want to create an internal hyperlink to Example 3.4, it would look like this: <a href="#Ex3point4">Click here</a> to visit Example 3.4. This hyperlink actually works in my eBook. If you click on it, it will take you back to the paragraph with Example 3.4.

Remember, if your target location is a heading or subheading included in your active table of contents, you *shouldn't* need to create a new bookmark for that location: Bookmarks to headings that are part of your active table of contents *should* have been created *automatically*. You only need to create a bookmark if you want to create an internal hyperlink that takes the reader to a location in your eBook that doesn't already have its own bookmark.

As an example, suppose that you would like to insert a hyperlink to take the reader to Chapter 6. In your HTML file, find the table of contents section and copy the a-tag that links to Chapter 6. When I did this for my book, I found this: <a href="#_Toc506199602">Chapter 6</a>. I pasted this into my HTML right here: <a href="#Chapter6">Chapter 6</a>. This internal hyperlink works in my eBook: If you click on it, the hyperlink will take you to Chapter 6.

Email hyperlinks use the format <a href="mailto:emailaddress">text to display</a>. Put the email address after mailto: as in <a href="mailto:chrism@chrismcmullen.com">text to display</a>.

Footnotes and **endnotes** work much the same way in your HTML, except that these produce a different effect in your eBook. When a reader clicks on a footnote or endnote, the Kindle device or app takes the reader directly to the corresponding footnote or endnote text. When the reader is finished, the reader can then return to the location of the eBook where the footnote or endnote was clicked.

If you create footnotes or endnotes in Microsoft Word, these are automatically included in your HTML file. Such footnotes and endnotes tend to come with spans, which may be relatively harmless. You want to examine your footnotes and endnotes for any spans that set a font size in points, a line height, or a specific font style, as described in Sec. 5.7, since those types of spans cause formatting problems. Otherwise, the footnotes and endnotes should work fine as they are. (Of course, you want to test them out when previewing your eBook before you publish, just to be sure.)

Now we will discuss how footnotes and endnotes should look in your HTML file. This will be helpful, for example, if you need to add any manually to your HTML file after you've already converted your Word document to HTML.

Just like with bookmarks and internal hyperlinks, there is an actual footnote or endnote that contains text for the reader to read, and there is separate link to the footnote or endnote that the reader can click on to visit the footnote or endnote.

First find the actual footnote or endnote text that the reader is meant to read. These should appear between div-tags, as illustrated with the following example.

```
<div id=ftn102>
<p class=MsoFootnoteText><a href="#_ftnref102" name="_ftn102" title="">[102]</a>
This is footnote 102.</p>
</div>
```

Depending on the location of the footnote that you originally set in Microsoft Word, the default class may be called MsoFooter instead of MsoFootnoteText. Whichever class is called, you should find that same class in your Style Definitions.

Endnotes look the same except that ftnref is replaced with ednref and _ftn is replaced with _edn. Look closely: It's edn, not end. The d comes before the n. Also, the default class is MsoEndnoteText instead of MsoFootnoteText.

If you're inserting a manual footnote or endnote, *be very careful to type the syntax correctly*. A single little typo will mess it up in your eBook.

The link to a footnote or endnote looks much like an internal hyperlink. It appears with <a> and </a> tags, like the following example. The opening <a> tag specifies the location of the target footnote or endnote with href. The following example creates an internal hyperlink to footnote 102.

<p class=MsoNormal><a href="#_ftn102" name="_ftnref102">If you click on the following footnote, it will take you to footnote 102.[102]</a></p>

Again, the only difference for an endnote is that _ftnref is replaced with _ednref and _ftn is replaced with _edn.

Both the footnote text and the corresponding link to the footnote include a name and href. Compare the example of a footnote text with the example of a link to a footnote. Note that the _ftn102 and _ftnref102 are swapped between href and name in the two examples. Each one has a different name. One is named _ftn102 and the other is named _ftnref102. Each one links to its counterpart. When you click on the link to footnote 102, it takes you to the footnote. When you click on the link in the footnote itself, it takes you back to the link that called it originally. This is a pair of mutual internal hyperlinks. Whether or not you appreciate the concept, the important thing is to get the syntax correct if you type footnotes or endnotes manually. (**Definitely test out any footnotes or endnotes that you manually create in HTML**. Sec.'s 7.8 and 7.9 will show you how to create previews that allow you to test out footnotes and endnotes.) Also note that href includes a pound (#), but name does not; whereas both include an underscore (_).

If your footnotes or endnotes don't already appear at the end of your HTML file, you may wish to move them there. We discussed where to place footnotes or endnotes back in Sec. 2.5.

Back in your Word document, you could choose to place your footnotes or endnotes at the end of your document. In that case, you wouldn't need to move them later. However, if it's too late for that, and you wish to move them, you can easily move them manually.

Find your footnotes or endnotes in your HTML file. Use cut and paste to remove them from their current location and place them at the end of your HTML file. Well, *not* at the very end. They should appear just *before* the </div> </body> and </html> tags that you find at the end of your HTML file.

(You may move the footnotes or endnotes themselves, which are the notes with the text that you want readers to read when they click on your footnotes or endnotes. Don't move the links that readers will click to visit your footnotes and endnotes. The div-tag <div id=ftn102> labels an actual footnote with text that you want the reader to read after clicking on footnote 102, whereas the link to footnote 102 is part of a p-tag in the content of your book. While you may move the location of the actual footnote or endnote, you don't want to move body text paragraphs.)

---

[102] This is footnote 102.

When you preview your eBook (Chapter 7), be sure to test out all of your hyperlinks, footnotes, and endnotes to make sure that they are working properly. If there are any problems, you have the opportunity to catch them before you publish your book, but only if you test them out in the preview (Sec.'s 7.7 and 7.8 show you how to create previews that will let you test these features out).

The Kindle Previewer (see Chapter 7) lets you quickly navigate through the links in your eBook so that you can test them all out easily. You will be able to do this when you finish with your HTML file.

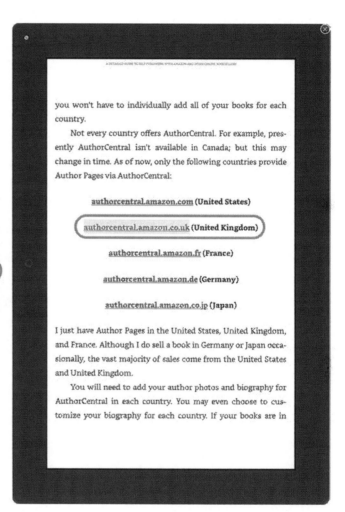

5.9 Making Revisions

Ideally, you would perfect the content of your book as much as possible back in Word, before you save your Word file in HTML format. However, no matter how well you proofread your original Word file, it's almost inevitable that you will discover necessary revisions after saving your file as a filtered webpage.

Once you have put much work into polishing up your HTML file, you really don't want to go back to Word and create a new HTML file: If you go back and make your revisions in Word, you would need to redo all of the improvements to your HTML file. Therefore, once you've made significant improvements to your HTML file, you're better off making revisions directly to your HTML file (especially, if they are minor revisions) instead of going back to Word.

This section will help you make a variety of revisions directly to your HTML file.

The simplest changes to make are minor editing corrections like misspellings and grammatical errors. These are also easy to find. Use the Find tool to quickly pull up all matches of misspelled words, for example (but if you're using Notepad, see the warning about the Find tool in Sec. 5.3). In most cases, what you need to do is simply edit existing HTML, rather than actually write new HTML. Editing HTML is much easier than writing HTML.

In many cases, you can actually avoid writing HTML. If you need to make extensive revisions directly to your HTML file, like adding a brand new chapter, that would require writing HTML. However, there is even a way around this. You could type the new chapter in a brand new Word document, save that Word file as a filtered webpage, and copy paste the HTML of that chapter (not the entire HTML file, just the content from the body of the HTML file) into your original HTML file. It helps if you style the new chapter the same way in the new Word file for the new chapter as you styled the original book. You will still need to make a few changes, like adding this new chapter to your table of contents and adjusting the name of the <a> tag for its bookmark (Sec. 5.8 shows what to look for to make bookmarks and internal hyperlinks work). Be careful to avoid duplicate names. Note that if you have any footnotes or endnotes in the added text, you will need to update their numbers throughout your book.

If you need to type text in boldface or italics, enclose the text that you wish to emphasize between <b> and </b> tags or between <i> and </i> tags. For example, the following HTML paragraph shows how to make a phrase bold or italicized in the HTML, and the repeated paragraph that follows shows how the result would look in the eBook. Don't forget to close your tags: It's easy to type <b>, get distracted, and forget to put the </b> at the end, for example. Also be careful to include the slash (/) in the closing tag (like </b> or </i>), since it's easy to forget. Such "mistakes" are easy to make, but if you make them, they can turn into a formatting disaster. Focus on what you're doing and don't let yourself get distracted. This isn't hard, it just requires focus and a fresh pair of eyes.

<p class=MsoNormal><b>This phrase is bold</b> whereas <i>this phrase is italicized.</i></p>

This phrase is bold whereas *this phrase is italicized.*

Note that using the Enter key in your HTML file doesn't have any impact on your Kindle eBook. If you want to create a line break in your HTML file, pressing the Enter key **won't** achieve this effect. Use p-tags to separate paragraphs. Each paragraph lies between opening <p> and closing

</p> tags. When you want to end a paragraph and start a new one, use </p> to end the current paragraph and use <p> to begin a new one on a new line. The example that follows shows two separate paragraphs in HTML and they are repeated to show you how they appear in the actual eBook.

<p class=MsoNormal>This is the first paragraph in this example. This paragraph ends when you reach the closing p-tag.</p>
<p class=MsoNormal>The opening p-tag creates a new paragraph.</p>

This is the first paragraph in this example. This paragraph ends when you reach the closing p-tag.

The opening p-tag creates a new paragraph.

If you need to write HTML or create style definitions, for example, find HTML examples from this chapter and use these examples as a guide, or try to find similar HTML in your actual HTML file to use as a guide.

When you write any HTML, note that the syntax is critical. Pay very careful attention to not only the spelling, but also the punctuation, and spacing (from the spacebar). The biggest mistakes that you can make are:

- forgetting to end with a semicolon (;) when you type an expression like text-indent:2em; which is supposed to end with a semicolon.
- forgetting to close an HTML tag (like forgetting the </i> after using <i> for italics). Even that little slash (/) makes a big difference. If you accidentally type <b>bold<b> instead of <b>bold</b>, you can wind up with several paragraphs of boldface instead of just one word!

If you preview your eBook carefully (as shown in Chapter 7), that will help you catch any formatting issues that your book might have.

When you need to add images to your HTML, first you need to paste the pictures into the image file folder that's *inside* of your compressed zipped folder. Next you need to add img lines (beginning and ending with div-tags, as in the example below) to your HTML file to display those images. Find existing img lines in your HTML file and use copy/paste, then edit the img line for the new image. Make sure the name matches the name of the image file, and check that the extension matches too (.jpg or .gif). Don't use a space in the name of the image file. For example, name your picture file Fig3.jpg instead of Fig 3.jpg. Sec. 5.5 discusses img lines and how to edit them. As a reminder, following is one of the examples from Sec. 5.5 (note that you must replace Book with the name of your file, and recall that if your filename includes a space like My Book.html, you must type 20% instead of the space, as in "My20%Book_files/image001.jpg"). This example forces full-width (if you don't want to do that, choose a different example from Sec. 5.5):

```
<div class=CenterSpaceAfter><img style="width: 100%; height: auto;" alt=""
src="Book_files/image001.jpg"></div>
```

Recall that Sec. 5.3 shows you how to save your HTML file if you're using Notepad. You can use Save, but don't use Save As when using Notepad because Save As will create a TXT file instead of an HTML file. If you have images in your file and you're using Notepad, you definitely want to reread Sec. 5.3. **Note that clicking Save is not enough**: *You must also drag your HTML file into the compressed zipped folder to overwrite the old HTML file.*[72] (If you run into an error while dragging your HTML file into the compressed zipped folder, save your file in Notepad, close Notepad, and then try dragging it again.)

Following are some examples of HTML that commonly appears in Kindle eBooks.

```
<b>boldface</b>
<i>italics</i>
<p class=MsoNormal>This indicates a paragraph. This paragraph will be styled according to
the MsoNormal style definition.</p>
<p class=NoIndent>This indicates a paragraph. This paragraph will be styled according to
the NoIndent style definition. There must be a corresponding NoIndent style defined in the
Style Definitions at the top of the HTML file.</p>
<h1>Heading</h1>
<h2>Subheading</h2>
<a name=MakeUpaName>This bookmarks the location of the text typed here.</a>
<a href="#NameOfBookmark">This creates an internal hyperlink to the bookmark called
NameOfBookmark.</a>
<a href="http://www.websitename.com">This creates an external hyperlink to
www.websitename.com.</a>
<div class=CenterSpaceAfter><img style="width: 100%; height: auto;" alt=""
src="Book_files/image001.jpg"></div>
```

Following are some examples of common mistakes that are easy to make when typing or editing HTML. These cases show how a slight mistake in the HTML can result in a big formatting problem. When you type or edit HTML, read and type with care, paying special attention to all punctuation marks.

Mistake #1: The b-tag below doesn't actually close (the second b-tag is missing a slash). This will create a **runaway boldface effect**, where the paragraphs that follow will have boldface even when they should be normal.

<p class=MsoNormal>Mass is a measure of inertia, whereas <b>weight<b> is a measure of heaviness.</p>

The HTML should look like this instead:

<p class=MsoNormal>Mass is a measure of inertia, whereas <b>weight</b> is a measure of heaviness.</p>

Mistake #2: The p-tag below doesn't actually close (it opens with a p-tag, but closes with a div-tag instead). This will create a **runaway style problem**, where the paragraphs that follow will be styled incorrectly. Don't mix and match p-tags, div-tags, and h-tags in the same HTML paragraph (or heading).

<p class=CenterSpaceAfter><img width="1024" height="576" alt="" src="Novel32_files/image002.jpg"></div>

The HTML should look like this instead (with the opening and closing tags matching):

<div class=CenterSpaceAfter><img width="1024" height="576" alt="" src="Novel32_files/image002.jpg"></div>

Mistake #3: The following line from a style definition is missing a semicolon. When you edit or type style definitions (for paragraph and heading styles at the top section of your HTML file), make sure that each line ends with a semicolon.

margin-bottom:1em

The HTML should look like this instead:

margin-bottom:1em;

Mistake #4: The following line from a style definition is missing a hyphen.

marginbottom:1em;

The HTML should look like this instead:

margin-bottom:1em;

Mistake #5: The img line below is missing a closing quotation mark. The picture won't display in the eBook.

```
<div class=CenterSpaceAfter><img style="width: 100%; height: auto;" alt=""
src="Mystery_files/image005.jpg></div>
```

The HTML should look like this instead:

```
<div class=CenterSpaceAfter><img style="width: 100%; height: auto;" alt=""
src="Mystery_files/image005.jpg"></div>
```

Mistake #6: The img line below says that the name of the HTML file is Book, but the author actually named the file SweetRomance. The picture won't display in the eBook. (If you copy my suggested img line to make your pictures, replace the word Book with the name of your book.)

```
<div class=CenterSpaceAfter><img style="width: 100%; height: auto;" alt=""
src="Book_files/image006.jpg"></div>
```

The HTML should look like this instead:

```
<div class=CenterSpaceAfter><img style="width: 100%; height: auto;" alt=""
src="SweetRomance_files/image006.jpg"></div>
```

Mistake #7: The img line below uses a space instead of an underscore between the filename and the word "files." The picture won't display in the eBook.

```
<div class=CenterSpaceAfter><img style="width: 100%; height: auto;" alt="" src="SciFi
files/image007.gif"></div>
```

The HTML should look like this instead:

```
<div class=CenterSpaceAfter><img style="width: 100%; height: auto;" alt=""
src="SciFi_files/image007.gif"></div>
```

Mistake #8: The img line below specifies the filename incorrectly. The picture won't display in the eBook. The filename, which is Math Book.HTML, has a space in it. (It would be simpler if the file had been named MathBook.HTML instead.) In the img line, if the filename has a space in it, you must type 20% in place of the space.

```
<div class=CenterSpaceAfter><img width="1024" height="576" alt="" src="Math
Book_files/image008.jpg"></div>
```

The HTML should look like this instead:

> <div class=CenterSpaceAfter><img width="1024" height="576" alt=""
> src="Math20%Book_files/image008.jpg"></div>

Mistake #9: The img line below includes a .jpg extension, but the picture is actually in GIF format. The picture won't display in the eBook.

> <div class=CenterSpaceAfter><img width="1024" height="576" alt=""
> src="BirdsandBees_files/image009.jpg"></div>

The HTML should look like this instead:

> <div class=CenterSpaceAfter><img width="1024" height="576" alt=""
> src="BirdsandBees_files/image009.gif"></div>

Mistake #10: The img line below indicates that the picture size is 1024×448, but the picture size is really 1024×948. The aspect ratio will be distorted, making the picture look much shorter than it should.

> <div class=CenterSpaceAfter><img width="1024" height="448" alt=""
> src="Calculus_files/image010.jpg"></div>

The HTML should look like this instead:

> <div class=CenterSpaceAfter><img width="1024" height="948" alt=""
> src="Calculus_files/image010.jpg"></div>

Mistake #11: The author meant for the following img line to display imgae011, but the author copied and pasted another img line and forgot to change the number of the picture. The wrong picture will be displayed in this position of the eBook.

> <div class=CenterSpaceAfter><img style="width: 100%; height: auto;" alt=""
> src="Mystery_files/image002.jpg></div>

The HTML should look like this instead:

> <div class=CenterSpaceAfter><img style="width: 100%; height: auto;" alt=""
> src="Mystery_files/image011.jpg"></div>

Mistake #12: In the a-tag below, the full web address isn't displayed in quotation marks. It is missing the http:// (or https://) part of the website's full URL. This link won't work in the eBook.

<a href="www.amazon.com">www.amazon.com</a>

The HTML should look like this instead:

<a href="https://www.amazon.com">www.amazon.com</a>

Mistake #13: In the a-tag below, a slash is missing in the web address displayed in quotation marks. There should be two slashes between the https and the w's. This link won't work in the eBook.

<a href="https:/www.amazon.com">www.amazon.com</a>

The HTML should look like this instead:

<a href="https://www.amazon.com">www.amazon.com</a>

Mistake #14: In the a-tag below, back slashes are used instead of forward slashes. This link won't work in the eBook.

<a href="https:\\www.amazon.com">Visit Amazon.</a>

The HTML should look like this instead:

<a href="https://www.amazon.com">Visit Amazon.</a>

Mistake #15: In the a-tag below, the full web address isn't displayed in quotation marks. It is missing the http:// (or https://) part of the website's full URL. (You need the http:// part in quotation marks, whereas between the opening and closing a-tags you can type the text to display however you want, as illustrated in the three corrected examples that follow.) This link won't work in the eBook.

<a href="www.amazon.com">https://www.amazon.com</a>

The HTML should look like one of these instead:

<a href="https://www.amazon.com">https://www.amazon.com</a>

<a href="https://www.amazon.com">www.amazon.com</a>

<a href="https://www.amazon.com">Amazon</a>

5.10 Preventive Measures

This section provides a handy checklist of possible problems that may be worth searching for in your HTML document. If you're using Notepad, each time you conduct a new search, remember to place your cursor at the very beginning of your HTML file before you use the Find tool. Otherwise, it will only search forward (or backward if you adjust the option) from the current point in the document.

(For some of the searches, you might want to search down from \</style\>, where the style definitions end, if you just wish to search the body of your file: If you've already cleaned up your style definitions, this will let you skip matches in that part of your file. Note that if it does pull up any matches, you'll need to return to this point in your file and place the cursor there before searching for a *different* term.)

These are specific things that I search for when I otherwise believe that my HTML file is ready to publish. I sometimes catch a few things that I had previously missed. **<u>Don't</u>** include the quotation marks in your search.

- Search for the word "font" to help find instances where a specific font is specified or where a point value is specified instead of a value in %'s or em's. Some matches will be okay (like font-weight:bold; or font-size:100%;). If you used the word "font" in the text of your book, you might search for "font-" instead.

- Search for the word "text" to help find instances where a text-indent is specified in a point value instead of em's and to help find instances where a p-tag specifies a text-indent or text-align (since text-indent and text-align should instead be controlled by calling an appropriate paragraph style from the style definitions). Again, some matches will be okay. If you used the word "text" in the text of your book, you might search for "text-" instead.

- Search for the closing span tag by entering \</span\> in the search field to quickly check all of the spans in your document. (This cuts down the number of search results by only searching for the closing tags. However, if you typed a span manually and didn't close it properly, this search won't catch that.) Sec. 5.7 describes specific issues that you should look for in your spans, such as specifying a specific font (through font-family) or setting a value in points instead of %'s or em's.

- Search for the word "color" to help find instances where a color may be specified where it shouldn't be. For example, you should never use color:black to create black text, as it would be unreadable when a customer selects night mode. Color should not be set to white, green, or sepia either. Some matches may be okay (such as using style='color:red' within a span in order to emphasize text in the color red). If you used the word "color" in the text of your book, you might search for "color:" instead (this time use a colon, not a hyphen).

- A few more terms that may be worth searching for include "family," "margin-" (with a hyphen), "style=" (with an equal sign), "page-break" (with a hyphen), and "line-height" (with a hyphen). Not all matches will be problems (for example, you should find "style=" in your img lines for full-width pictures), but if there are problems, these searches may help you find them.
- If you want to quickly find all of your img lines in your HTML file, search for "img."
- Searching for "> <" (include everything except for the quotation marks) and for "clear=all" (with an equal sign, *not* a hyphen) can help to find common occurrences of empty paragraphs. These searches typically pull up p-tags or h-tags that effectively include no content. Occasionally, such empty paragraphs can appear really long in your HTML file, setting all sorts of parameters, but not actually enclosing any *text* between the <p> and </p> or <h1> and </h1> tags. If the paragraph truly is empty, delete the entire paragraph from your HTML file. As we have discussed previously, it's better to use margin-bottom in the style definitions to create space between paragraphs: Avoid using empty paragraphs in an attempt to create vertical space.

Following are three examples of **empty paragraphs**. The third example is of the variety that looks so long it doesn't seem like it could be an empty paragraph, but it is. (The third example does include a page break though, so in such a case, you would want to incorporate the desired page break into a style definition suitable for the paragraph that follows the empty paragraph that you are removing.)

<p class=MsoNormal> </p>

<h1> </h1>

<b><span style='font-size:12.0pt;font-family:"Calibri","sans-serif";mso-fareast-font-family:"Times New Roman";mso-bidi-font-family:"Times New Roman";mso-ansi-language:EN-US;mso-fareast-language:EN-US;mso-bidi-language:AR-SA'><br clear=all style='page-break-before:always'></span></b>

When you find and correct issues in your HTML file, keep a list of the kinds of problems that you've encountered. Your list will help you create a customized checklist of issues that you should search for in the future.

5.11 Table of Contents

Recall (from Sec. 3.8) that there are really *two* tables of contents:

- One is an actual list in your eBook file with clickable hyperlinks. I refer to this as an **active table of contents**.
- The other is a list that Kindle adds so that customers can navigate from the device menu. I refer to this as **device navigation**.

These two tables of contents are independent. As we discussed in Chapter 3, any heading tags (like h1 or h2) that you use in your eBook automatically create the second kind of table of contents (the kind that Kindle adds to the menu for device navigation).

In this section, we'll first describe how to modify the active table of contents (which has clickable hyperlinks) in your HTML file. Next we'll discuss how you can optimize device navigation for your eBook.

We discussed how to create an **active table of contents** in Sec. 3.8 that will carry over into your HTML file. In your HTML file, each table of contents entry will look something like this:

<p class=MsoToc1><span class=MsoHyperlink><a href="#_Toc458844695">Chapter 1</a></span></p>

There will probably be a blank line at the end of your table of contents. This blank line is stubborn in Word, but is easy to remove in the HTML. If you see a line similar to the following line in your HTML, remove the entire line. (If you want to create vertical space between the last element of your table of contents and the paragraph or heading that follows, do it by creating a special style definition for the last table of contents entry and including a margin-bottom setting for it as described in Sec. 5.4. Don't use blank lines or empty paragraphs in an attempt to add vertical space.)

<p class=MsoNormal> </p>

The clickable table of contents works using bookmarks and internal hyperlinks, which we discussed in Sec. 5.8. If you need to add new sections to your table of contents (and you don't wish to go back to Word and start over with the HTML), copy and paste one of your table of contents entries and then modify the HTML for the new entry. Review Sec. 5.8 to remember how to make bookmarks and internal hyperlinks, and study the HTML of the other entries of your table of contents and the corresponding bookmarks. The new entry will work the same way. If you add or edit bookmark hyperlinks to your active table of contents, be sure to **test those links out when you preview your book** (Chapter 7).

You can find the style definitions for your table of contents in the style definitions section of your HTML file. They have names like MsoTOC1 and MsoTOC2. You want to revise these style definitions following the instructions from Sec. 5.4. If these style definitions don't already have a text-align specified, you want to add text-align:left; to these styles. Definitely, don't use text-align: justify; for the table of contents, and don't leave the text alignment unspecified for table of contents styles, as that can lead to significant formatting problems. (In some cases, centered alignment may be okay.)

If you want any of your table of contents style definitions to be indented, you may prefer to do this via margin-left and not via text-indent (specify zero text-indent), following the instructions from Sec. 5.4. On a small screen (like a cell phone) with a large font size, even a short line of text may get split across two lines: Decide whether you would prefer for that second line to be indented or not: If so, use margin-left with zero text-indent; if not, use text-indent with zero margin-left.

As noted in Sec. 3.8, if your table of contents includes both heading and subheadings, you may wish to set a margin-left for MsoTOC2, but to set margin-left to zero for MsoTOC1 (as I did in my recommendations in Sec. 5.4).

Regarding the other type of table of contents, which is really built-in **device navigation**, ordinarily Amazon will *automatically* create that for you after you publish your eBook. Amazon uses your heading tags (like h1 and h2) to create the built-in navigation entries and locations (which is why you should *only* use h-tags for headings that you want to have included in device navigation).

However, if you use the downloadable previewer (called Kindle Previewer) to preview your eBook before you publish (Sec. 7.8), or if you download your MOBI preview file to test it out on an actual device (Sec. 7.9), note that *you won't be able to preview the device navigation*. In fact, you will see an incomplete device navigation menu (which will just have Cover, Beginning, and Table of Contents). Although device navigation isn't ready yet when you preview your eBook, Amazon usually adds device navigation to the actual eBook within a few days of publishing the eBook.

It is possible to get device navigation to work in the downloadable previewer and to have it working before you publish your eBook. To do this, you must go beyond the scope of this guide to create an ePub file with a logical TOC or NCX. Progressing from an HTML file to ePub carries its own pitfalls, so you must find a reliable guide if you wish to do that. Amazon's automatic device navigation is simple and convenient, and lets you skip having to learn how to make a successful transition from HTML to ePub.

5.12 Advanced Options

In this section, I will list some of the advanced features that are possible in Kindle. I'm not recommending all of these features. Rather, I'm listing them to make you aware of them.

In Sec.'s 5.1 thru 5.11, I've described what I consider to be *essential* knowledge for how to go a quick step beyond Word. Some of the features described in Sec. 5.12 are not so quick.

The features listed in Sec. 5.12 also carry more risk. It's easy to introduce unexpected formatting mistakes trying to use these advanced features. You really don't want to create a significant formatting problem while trying to improve a subtle design issue. The "keep it simple" philosophy carries many advantages when it comes to Kindle design, and sometimes proves to be most effective.

With this in mind, I'm *not* going to describe how to implement every feature listed in this section. I'll list the features so that you're aware of them. If you decide that one of these advanced features may be worth looking into for your unique book, you can search for more information on them. Or you can look for an advanced book focused solely on the HTML aspect of Kindle formatting (whereas in the book you're reading now, HTML is just one of multiple chapters on Kindle design). Before you implement any of these advanced features, I suggest that you take a look at Amazon's free technical formatting PDF, which lists the HTML possibilities of Kindle formatting:

http://kindlegen.s3.amazonaws.com/AmazonKindlePublishingGuidelines.pdf

If you implement any of these advanced features, you really want to get your hands on an older device with a small screen, a newer Kindle device with a large screen, and a newer Apple product with a large screen—at a minimum—and preview how these features work on each of those actual devices before publishing (Sec. 7.9).

In specific situations, one of these advanced features may provide enough potential to make the risk more worthwhile. You must consider your unique book and your potential HTML abilities to decide which of these features may be a good fit for you.

Let's begin with a media query. This feature helps you combat formatting issues related to different types of devices. The media query lets you create different formatting instructions for different devices.

One common use for a media query is to take advantage of images in SVG format. Some newer devices support SVG images, but many devices don't. Some eBook formatters use media queries so that they can display images, tables, or equations in SVG format on devices which do support the SVG format, and use an alternate set of images in JPEG or GIF format for devices that don't support SVG.

It's possible to use HTML with more flexible design instructions with SVG images. However, since many devices don't support SVG, this can only be done properly using a media query. The media query basically tells the eBook to display the SVG image with one set of formatting instructions for one class of devices, and to display a JPEG or GIF image with a different set of formatting instructions for other devices.

On one hand, the media query lets you optimize the formatting of newer Kindle devices, but on the other hand, it doesn't solve the formatting issues of other devices. So even if you use a media query, you still need to come up with a satisfactory solution for other devices. Note that support for SVG is limited: SVG doesn't work with iOS devices, nor does SVG work with Enhanced Typesetting.

Media queries have other uses besides SVG format. For example, a media query can be used to format a drop cap differently on different types of devices. The example at the end of Sec. 5.6 shows specifically how to use a media query with a drop cap.

In some cases, a media query may be unnecessary. There are a few features that come out okay on an older device even though the older device doesn't support that feature. However, some features result in detrimental formatting issues on older devices. Therefore, before implementing a media query, you should do your homework and also test things out on both older and newer devices to see exactly what happens with or without the media query. If an advanced feature works okay across all devices (including older devices and Apple products) without the media query, I recommend that you avoid using the media query. When an advanced feature leads to poor readability on certain devices, either use a media query to treat all devices sufficiently, or find a simpler alternative to the advanced feature that you're trying to implement.

If you want to add space at the very beginning of a chapter, the most reliable way to do this effectively is to create an ePub file. Some devices or apps may ignore margin-top instructions with the first paragraph (regardless of whether it's a p-tag, h-tag, or div-tag), unless you use an ePub file to get around this problem. (Note that inserting a blank paragraph at the beginning of the chapter won't work: Some devices or apps simply ignore any empty paragraphs at the beginning of the chapter.)

https://sigil-ebook.com

You can use Sigil, for example, to create an ePub file from your HTML file. Your ePub file will separate each chapter in such a way (it's called "splitting pages" as it creates a new HTML page) that Kindle devices and apps will respect margin-top instructions for the first paragraph of the chapter. Sigil allows you to "split pages" wherever you wish (even if it's not really the beginning of a chapter). If you do this, you want to set the margin-top as a percentage (like 20%). Otherwise, the first paragraph will drop down insanely far on any device with a small screen (or if a customer selects a huge font size).

Many formatters prefer to work with ePub format. One reason is that the ePub format is ideal for other kinds of devices like Nook and Kobo. Another reason is that you can take advantage of Sigil's ePub validator. A validated ePub file doesn't mean that your eBook will be perfect, but the process of validating your ePub file can help you catch some obvious problems. Also, Sigil is a friendlier way to edit your HTML than Notepad.

On the other hand, progressing from HTML to ePub carries its own set of pitfalls, so you want to find a very reliable guide to formatting an ePub file specifically for Kindle (which is a little different from formatting an ePub for other platforms) before you attempt this. You would hate for all the work that you've done already to create a beautiful Kindle eBook to backfire on one or more devices because you made some mistake going from HTML to ePub. Ask yourself what you hope to gain from ePub that you can't get from your HTML file: The few subtleties that you might gain may not be worth the effort or the risk. If you learn how to make this transition from a very reliable source, that will help to minimize the risk.

If you really want to center an image or text *vertically* on the screen, you could achieve this approximately using Sigil to split pages before the image or text, and then using margin-top as a percentage. For a picture, you also want to learn how to center it vertically on its own line (which is different from centering it vertically on its own HTML page). For text, you must consider that the text has its own height (which will vary from one customer to the next, as the customer can control the font size). A big problem with trying to center *text* on a 'page' vertically (you must "split pages" with Sigil wherever you want to create a new HTML 'page') is that the text may wrap onto two (or more) lines. Since a customer can read an eBook on a small cell phone with a large font size, you simply can't prevent the possibility of text wrapping onto multiple lines, and then it won't be centered vertically. (For most kinds of eBooks, there should be **no** good reason to try to center text vertically, and in most cases, there **isn't** a good reason to try to do this with images either. Most eBooks should be designed with an optimal reflowable experience in mind, without creating new HTML pages except at the beginning of each chapter.) My recommendation is that you try to *avoid* centering anything vertically.

If you create an ePub file, you should consider using Amazon's free KindleGen tool. This software converts your ePub file to the Kindle MOBI format, and displays informational messages if it encounters any issues.

www.amazon.com/kindleformat/kindlegen

When uploading a MOBI or ePub file to KDP, check your book cover in the preview. You want to make sure that you don't have a double cover (where it shows twice in a row) or a missing cover. If you have a double cover, you simply need to remove the cover from your interior file and try again. If your cover isn't showing at the beginning of your eBook (sometimes you must navigate backward in the preview to find it), consult Amazon's publishing guidelines (follow the URL below) regarding cover image guidelines, which explains how to define the cover in the OPF file. (If you upload a Word document, HTML file, or zipped folder, fixing a double cover or missing cover problem should be easy: Either remove the cover from the beginning of your interior file or add it to the beginning.)

http://kindlegen.s3.amazonaws.com/AmazonKindlePublishingGuidelines.pdf

If you plan[103] to publish your eBook with other eBook retailers like Nook or Kobo, you must consider that formatting instructions that work great for Kindle don't always translate as well to Nook and Kobo. Most of the formatting does, but there are specific things that don't. The guide you are reading presently is specific to Kindle. If you also plan to publish with Nook or Kobo, you want to find an eBook formatting guide that discusses HTML specific to Nook and other eReaders, or a reliable guide that describes how to optimize an ePub file for Nook and other eReaders. Also note that the latest version of ePub has compatibility issues for many Kindle devices and apps.

There are a few advanced formatting tricks that one can learn. You have to be careful because some 'tricks' can backfire, not work as expected, or not work across all devices.

One example of a formatting trick is used to create multi-level indents. If you have a poetry book, for example, and really need multi-level indents, you might look into this trick. One problem is that you need to learn the limitations of older devices and exactly how your eBook will appear on those devices. Another problem is that on a small screen with a large font size, text that is intended to be on a single line may wrap onto two (or more) lines. Multi-level indents introduce formatting and design complications.

If you really want to learn how to use multi-level indents, you need to research the 'trick' to pulling it off. If you simply use multiple indents in your HTML without researching this trick, you will run into big problems, especially on older devices. You will also want to test this out as extensively as possible before publishing. Multi-level indents carry much risk, and usually the possible reward doesn't warrant such risk.

Similarly, if you really want to learn how to create negative indents, research how to do this with a media query and a backup plan for devices for which a negative indent poses a problem.

---

[103] You're probably wondering, "Why wouldn't I publish my eBook with every possible eBook retailer?" That is, why might you publish exclusively with Kindle? That's a good question, and one that every author must wrestle with. In Sec. 6.12, we'll learn that Amazon actually provides an incentive for authors to publish exclusively with Kindle. We'll consider the pros and cons of this decision in Sec. 6.12.

5.13 HTML Formatting Checklist

Following is a quick summary of the improvements that you can make to your HTML file, which we have discussed in this chapter:

- Adjust the text indents of your style definitions (Sec. 5.4). Use text-indent:2em; for indented paragraphs and text-indent:0in; for non-indented paragraphs (if left-aligned or justified).
- Adjust the font size to a percentage in your style definitions (Sec. 5.4). Use font-size:100%; for normal body text and keep within the range 80% to 150% for other types of paragraphs.
- Adjust the paragraph margins in your style definitions (Sec. 5.4). Most of the margins should be set to zero. Use margin-bottom:1em; to add space after to a style definition. If you would like every line of a paragraph indented (to create a block indent), use margin-left instead of text-indent (since text-indent only indents the first line).
- Check the text alignment of your style definitions (Sec. 5.4). If there is no text-align in the style, it may automatically justify. Each style definition should have text-align set to justify, left, or center (I'm *not* talking about the instructions in the paragraphs them-selves: I'm talking about the style definitions at the top of your HTML file).
- Remove any specified font families from your style definitions (Sec. 5.4).
- Remove any line-height specifications from your style definitions (Sec. 5.4).
- Remove any page size or *page* margin settings from the Style Definitions section (Sec. 5.4). I'm not talking about *paragraph* margins like margin-bottom: I mean *page* margins like those found under @page WordSection (review Sec. 5.4).
- Compare the recommended style definitions at the end of Sec. 5.4 to the style definitions for your eBook.
- Search for img in your HTML file to find your images, and then improve the HTML for each image (Sec. 5.5).
- Remove the Font Definitions from your HTML file (Sec. 5.6). Also search for any men-tion of font family, font size, or font color set to black, white, green, or sepia in the body of your HTML file.
- Add non-breaking spaces with   to connect two very short strings of text (Sec. 5.6). Use   sparingly.
- Add zero-width non-joiners with ‌ to very long strings of text like URL's to iden-tify preferred breaking points (Sec. 5.6).
- Check your p-tags and spans for possible formatting issues (Sec. 5.7).
- Search for any empty paragraphs (Sec.'s 5.7 and 5.10). Also check for a possible empty paragraph at the end of your table of contents (Sec. 5.11). If you had any tables in your Word file, you may also find an empty paragraph after the table.

- Examine the sample eBook in Appendix C. Compare the HTML for that eBook to the HTML for your eBook.

- Search for class=spellE and class=GramE in the body of your HTML file and also browse through your style definitions for mentions of them (Sec. 5.7).

- Search for possible problems by searching for the terms font, text, span, color (set to black, white, green, or sepia), family, margin, style, page-break (include the hyphen), line-height (include the hyphen), and > < (for a common form of empty paragraphs).

- Remove the tables that Word creates for drop caps in the Word to HTML conversion and apply a span (via a media query) instead (Sec. 5.6). This step is optional, but it will optimize your drop caps.

- If you will also publish with Nook, Kobo, or other eBook retailers, you want to research possible formatting issues regarding the differences between Kindle formatting and eBook formatting for other eBook retailers. You may need to make a second version of your file with a few minor revisions for other formats.

- If you need to make significant revisions to the content of your eBook after you've already done extensive work to your HTML file, review Sec. 5.9.

- Save your HTML file (Sec. 5.3). If you use Notepad, just click Save, don't use Save As. If your eBook has any images, remember to drag your HTML file into the compressed zipped folder to update the copy of your HTML that's in the compressed zipped folder.[72] If you've updated any images, make sure they have been properly updated in the image files folder that's inside of the compressed zipped folder (Sec.'s 5.3 and 5.5). The compressed zipped folder is what you will upload to KDP when you publish your eBook. If instead you use Sigil, you may prefer to create an ePub, validate your ePub file, and upload the ePub file to KDP.

—Chapter 6—

Publishing

6.1 Before You Publish

CONGRATULATIONS! WRITING YOUR book is quite an achievement. Take a moment to pat yourself on the back. On top of that, since you're reading this guide, it shows that you really care about your readers and the quality of your book. This is a good sign. I wish you a great self-publishing experience. There are a few things that you will need when you go through the publishing process. It would be a good idea to get everything together before you begin.

Here is what you will need in order to publish your eBook:

- An image file for your **front cover**, preferably in JPEG format.
- The **content file** for your eBook in DOCX, DOC, HTML (or a compressed zipped folder containing an HTML file and a corresponding image files folder), ePub, or MOBI format.
- A **description** (but *not* a summary) of your book to appear on your book's product page.
- Your desired Amazon browse **categories**.
- Your desired **keyword searches** relevant to your book.

(If you just want to make a quick "test file" of your book, and you're not yet ready to publish your eBook, all you need are the book files. If that's the case, consult Sec. 7.2.)

This chapter will discuss all of the steps of the publishing process in detail. You can find a quick summary of the steps in Sec. 6.17. It's handy to prepare your **description** (Sec. 6.4), choose your desired **categories** (Sec. 6.7), and make a list of your ideal **keywords** (Sec. 6.6) *before* you begin the publishing process. You might also find it helpful to read the suggestions in Sec. 6.10 regarding cover design before you prepare your cover file.

6.2 Signing in and Exploring KDP

Visit Amazon KDP. (KDP stands for Kindle Direct Publishing. This is Amazon's self-publishing service for indie authors—and also for small publishers.) Once there, you can sign in with an existing Amazon customer account, or you can create a new Amazon KDP account.

https://kdp.amazon.com

Once you sign in, you should see 4 blue links at the top of the webpage:

- **Bookshelf**: Visit your KDP Bookshelf to publish a new Kindle eBook, to republish an existing Kindle eBook, or to edit an eBook (but note that none of the changes will take place until you republish the eBook to overwrite the existing eBook—see Sec. 8.4). If your eBook is also enrolled in KDP Select (see Sec. 6.12), you can check KDP Select info or take advantage of KDP Select features from your Bookshelf. It's also possible to publish a paperback edition through KDP (Sec. 8.11).

- **Reports**: Once you publish a Kindle eBook, you can find royalty data in the Reports section (see Sec. 8.5).

- **Community**: If you can't find the answer to a question regarding your Kindle eBook, you can try searching for it in the KDP community forums (or post a question there). At the end of Sec. 7.11, you can find a few tips for searching the KDP community forums effectively.

- **KDP Select**: Clicking this link merely takes you to a page with information about KDP Select. We will discuss the pros and cons of enrolling a Kindle eBook in KDP Select in Sec. 6.12. If you want to check the KDP Select info for a Kindle eBook that you publish or if you want to take advantage of the KDP Select features, you actually want to visit your **Bookshelf** (Sec. 6.12 discusses KDP Select, and the beginning of Sec. 6.16 explains how to check the KDP Select status for your Kindle eBook from your KDP Bookshelf).

Three of these blue links—Bookshelf, Reports, and Community—help you navigate your way through Amazon KDP. Two other helpful areas include:

- You can find your account info at the top of the page. Look for your name. For example, if your name is Jane Doe, you should see a link called Jane's Account at the top of the page. Click this link to enter or edit your **tax** information or to add **bank** information so that you can receive payments.

- To the right of the link for your account info, you should see a Help link. This link takes you to the **KDP help pages**. If you spend some time exploring the KDP help pages, you can find some helpful information there. It may not be as thorough and organized as you may like—and you should find most of the pertinent information in the book you are reading now—but you can find a few cool and helpful things in the KDP help pages if you spend some time exploring them.

6.3 Getting Started: Book Information

When you're ready to publish your Kindle eBook, visit your KDP Bookshelf (Sec. 6.2) and click the button labeled "+ Kindle eBook." You don't need to complete the process all at one sitting. You can use the Save as Draft button at the bottom of each page to save your progress. If so, when you're ready to return, visit your KDP Bookshelf, find your book, and click the yellow Continue Setup button. Alternatively, you can click the small gray "…" button next to the larger button (which is usually yellow and called Continue Setup when you haven't yet published, but which may have a different message and may also be gray instead of yellow). If you click the small gray "…" button (or just hover the cursor over it), click Edit eBook Details to visit page 1 of the publishing process, click Edit eBook Content to visit page 2, and click Edit eBook Pricing to visit page 3.

The first step is to select the language for the content of your eBook. This step is asking you what language you wrote your book in (it's **not** asking about your native country or native language, which may be different). Note that not every language is supported. If you choose a language that uses nonstandard characters (see Appendix A and Sec. 2.6), you should contact KDP support to make sure that your book (or at least the special characters used) will be readable before you publish.

Your title, subtitle (optional), and series title (for a series) can make a significant impact on the marketability of your book. These are the first words that a prospective customer will read. When a customer is shopping for a book, they see dozens of thumbnails of covers alongside the titles. It's very important for your cover and title to indicate what kind of book you have written at a glance. In addition, the words in your title, subtitle, and series title can help your book show up in relevant searches (along with the keywords that you enter—see Sec. 6.6).

Note that fiction and nonfiction titles are a bit different. With fiction, an effective title is often short and catchy. A nonfiction title usually makes it clear what the book is about. Therefore, a nonfiction book title is more apt to include relevant keywords. One way to get a couple of helpful keywords in a fiction book title is to use a subtitle.

The title and subtitle definitely need to sound good and read well. You don't just want to pack keywords together. A good fiction subtitle often helps to clarify what the title doesn't. If the title doesn't make it clear what type of novel a book is, a subtitle like "A Sci-fi Thriller" or "A Paranormal Romance" can help with this (and it also gives you a couple of keywords in addition to the keyword list that you prepare). **Most bestselling novels have just one to three words in the title.** If they have a subtitle, it's usually also very short.

Nonfiction titles tend to be longer than fiction titles. They usually include a few relevant keywords (sparingly, in a way that reads well) and attempt to make it very clear what the subject matter is. Your title and subtitle together must be fewer than 200 characters. Generally speaking, the title and subtitle are more effective when they are concise, so in most cases you shouldn't come near this 200-character limit (especially in fiction). As a general rule, customers are likely to skim past titles that are over 60 characters long in search results: **Their eyes are more likely to stop and read titles that are *shorter* than 60 characters long.**

Tip: Don't type your title, subtitle, and series title into these fields at KDP. Instead, copy and paste them from the Microsoft Word file for your book. Actually, first copy and paste them into a blank document in Microsoft Word, enable Spellcheck in this new document, check any spelling suggestions (don't rely on Word to be right, just use it to help you identify possible mistakes), and then paste them into the respective fields at KDP. It's very easy to make a typo while trying to type them directly at KDP, which is why I recommend copying and pasting from your book (where you hopefully have checked them very carefully). Recall that we discussed Word's spellcheck feature in Sec. 2.11 (including the reason for disabling this before you publish). Check your character count in Word: Highlight the title and subtitle, and then click on the number of words shown on the bottom left corner of the window (or select the Review ribbon and then click the Word Count button).

The title that you enter should match the title that appears on your cover. (Your subtitle and series title—if you enter these—do not need to appear on your cover.) Note that you can't copyright a title, but that a phrase in a title may be trademarked. This means that you must be careful not to include trademarked names in the title of your book (unless you first obtain written permission from the trademark owner).

If you will be publishing a series of connected books, enter a title for the series (this is separate from, and in addition to, the title of each book in the series). Don't include the volume number as part of the series title. Enter the numerical value of the volume number in the field to the right of the series title. For example, for the third volume of a series, you would just enter the number 3 in the field to the right. Don't include any text with volume number (for example, don't write Book 3 or Volume 3 in this field).

When you enter a series title and volume number for each volume of a series, Amazon will present the customer with information about the series on the product page, including an option for the customer to purchase the entire bundle at once.

If your book has a subtitle or a series title (or both) in addition to the title, following is how your information will appear at Amazon.com:

- Your Book Title: Your Subtitle
- Your Book Title (Your Series Title Book 2)
- Your Book Title: Your Subtitle (Your Series Title Book 2)

The first example above has just a title and subtitle. Amazon automatically inserts the colon and space. The second example above has just a title and series title. Amazon automatically includes the parentheses, the word Book, and the volume number (which will be the actual volume number, which appears as a 2 in my examples above). The third example shows how your book's information will look if you have a title, subtitle, and series title.

Since Amazon automatically separates the title and subtitle with a colon, I would avoid using a colon in the title or subtitle when you have a subtitle (otherwise, it will look funny to see multiple colons). Similarly, since Amazon automatically places series information in parentheses, when publishing a series I would avoid using parentheses (otherwise, it will look funny to see parentheses appearing twice).

Speaking of which, I would avoid punctuation marks and special characters (except for necessary commas) in the title, subtitle, and series title. Some punctuation marks and special characters may not be supported in the title information. If there is a punctuation mark or special character that you strongly feel that you need in your title, subtitle, or series title, contact KDP support to see if it will be supported (well, a question mark shouldn't be an issue).

The field for edition number (not to be confused with volume number) is optional. The main purpose of this field is if you need to republish your book later with significant changes. The first time you republish with significant changes, you would enter a 2 in this field (Sec. 8.4 discusses how to revise your eBook).

There is currently one field for the primary author and a separate place to add additional contributors (which may include coauthors, editors, and more). You want to properly credit all contributors to their satisfaction, though you don't want to clutter your product page with several contributors if it isn't necessary. For example, adding a photographer as a contributor would be necessary for a photobook, but shouldn't be necessary when there are only a few images in the book (though you should work out an agreement with each contributor before you publish). Similarly, most cover designers should be satisfied to have a mention (with perhaps a link to their illustrator website) in the front matter rather than a role as a contributor, whereas an illustrator for a children's picture book should be a main contributor (but again, you should work the details out on an individual basis).

One contributor where it may add a little market value is when you can list an editor. The book obviously needs to *be* well-edited—especially, the Look Inside sample and the description—to reinforce the notion that the book is virtually free from spelling or grammatical errors. If so, listing the editor as a contributor (if the editor is okay with this) might have a little value. Some customers won't notice this. Customers also know that there are a few books on the market that list an editor, which aren't well-edited: That's why it's important that your description and Look Inside appear well-edited (and the whole book needs to back up that impression in order for the book to generate good reviews and recommendations).

Do you wish to use a **pen name** instead of your real name? Amazon lets you do this, provided that you do your research of author names and book titles already in use, so that your choice of pen name doesn't create possible confusion with customers' buying decisions. In general, it's easier to market your book (Sec. 8.7) when you publish with your own name, but there may be occasions where you prefer to write anonymously. If you use a pen name, do some research to see if the name may be trademarked (in which case, don't use it), if the author name is already in use, or if the name may cause possible confusion among customers (perhaps by being too similar to popular author names or popular characters, in which case Amazon will require you to change it).

If you also have a print book (or if you publish a print edition later), be sure that the spelling and punctuation of the book details (such as the title, subtitle, and the author's full name) are entered exactly the same way when you publish both editions. Sec. 8.11 mentions where to get started if you want to self-publish a print edition.

There are two more book details to decide on when you publish, but which you won't fill out until page 2 of the publishing process:

- An ISBN is *optional* for an eBook. There really is *no* advantage to obtaining an ISBN for the Kindle edition of your eBook. Amazon automatically assigns every Kindle eBook an ASIN (Amazon Standard Identification Number). Adding an optional ISBN will not give your Kindle eBook any worthwhile distinction, in my experience and opinion. Note that you're technically not supposed to use the same ISBN from a print edition or from another eBook retailer with your Kindle eBook (for example, you shouldn't use a CreateSpace or Smashwords ISBN for your Kindle eBook). If you publish versions of your eBook with other eBook distributors, then it may be worthwhile to include an ISBN (which typically you can get for free, with Smashwords, for example) with the other distributor (but again, you shouldn't use that same ISBN for the Kindle edition).

- You can choose to enter a "publisher name" even when you self-publish. You are your own publisher, but since you're taking on the task of self-publishing, you can adopt the name of a "publishing company" (an imprint name) to include with the books that you publish (or even multiple imprints if you publish different types of books or if you use pen names and don't want all of your books to feature the same imprint). You may want to look into possible legal issues with setting yourself up as your own publishing "company" (though I recommend **not** investing big money to start a "business" if you can plausibly avoid it—there is no guarantee that you will sell books, so if you minimize your investment, you lessen the risk that you will lose money). Keeping in mind that I'm not an attorney and so I'm not qualified to give legal advice, it is relatively common to include an imprint name with your family name (like an imprint name that includes the name McDougal for an author named Kevin McDougal). You should definitely check that the imprint name is not already in use, and that there are no trademarked names or other publishing companies that are similar to the imprint name that you wish to use.

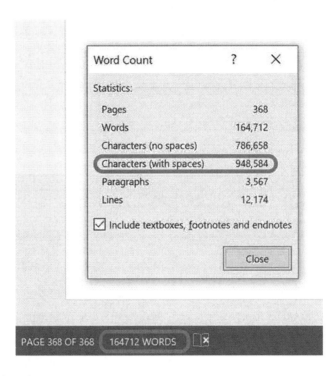

6.4 Book Description

An effective book description is one of the hardest things for an author to learn how to write. It's worth investing the time to develop and then polish your book description because this is the first writing sample that most customers will see of your work. Your description is your opportunity to show indirectly (don't come out and say it) that your book is high quality. It's your chance to generate interest in your book.

A book description *isn't* a summary. It's a **mistake** to summarize the story in the description because then the customer doesn't need to read your book to find out what happens.

There are two important goals that your description must accomplish:

- Your description must **generate interest** in your book.
- It should be clear *what type of book* you have written.

Start out by listing the qualities of your book that make it seem interesting (but which don't give the story away). For fiction, what will hook your reader into your story? For nonfiction, what valuable information or skills will the reader learn from your book?

An occasional question can help draw interest. Don't answer the question: The customer should want to read your book to find the answer.

Make sure that the customer will be able to quickly determine what type of book you have written. For fiction, the genre should be clear. For nonfiction, the subject matter should be clear. Many customers are shopping for a specific type of book and get frustrated (and leave the product page) when it isn't clear from the description what the genre or subject is.

Your KDP book description may include up to 4000 characters (that includes the spaces between the words). However, **most customers will only read the first few sentences of your description**. Note that *Amazon only shows the first few sentences of the description*. Customers have to click a *Read More* link in order to see the rest of the description. Therefore, you want the **beginning** of your description to be **very good at selling your book** (by generating interest and making it clear what type of book you have written).

I recommend that you invest time to browse Amazon for books similar to yours and *read their descriptions*. This will show you what customers are accustomed to seeing in the description. You may read a few descriptions and find yourself interested in the book: If so, that will help you learn how to generate interest. (Don't copy things that you read. Rather, learn from the techniques that appear to be effective.) It may help if you can discover successful indie authors and read the descriptions of the books that made them successful.

Get **feedback** for your book description. You want your description to be polished. *If a customer discovers a single mistake in your description, the customer will wonder how many mistakes are in your book.*

> **Tip**: Asking for feedback regarding your book description is a good **marketing opportunity**. Don't ask for feedback on your draft: Try to perfect your description and then get feedback on that. You want the people giving you feedback to become interested in your book. Sec. 8.7 will point you in the right direction to get started with marketing your book (something that you should start *before* your book is published).

Ideally, a few relevant **keywords** (Sec. 6.6) would naturally fit into the text of your description. Don't include a "list" of keywords (that's actually against the rules, and likely to deter sales). Rather, when you write the text for your book description, you may find that a few of your keywords naturally fit into the wording. You don't just want to throw a keyword in where it seems out of place. You want your description to read well and be effective. If a few keywords naturally fit into your description, this may help your book establish relevance in Amazon keyword searches.

Bullet points can be an effective way to highlight important information for a *nonfiction* book. (Bullet points are less common with fiction book descriptions.) *A few relevant keywords may be more effective towards establishing relevance for Amazon searches if they appear in bullet points.*

Note that you're not supposed to include contact info (such as an email address) or website URL's in your book description. You can include this in the front matter of your book, which will appear in your Look Inside on Amazon.

You may include the following limited, basic **HTML** in your book description. The following features can only be implemented through HTML (or by visiting Author Central after you publish, as discussed in Sec. 8.2). If you try to make italics or bullet points by copying and pasting from Word, for example, it **won't** work. More advanced features of HTML, such as text color or pictures, **don't** work in the Amazon book description. **If you don't know HTML**, don't worry: Skip over to the last tip of this section regarding Author Central.

- Enclose text between <b> and </b> tags to make **boldface**. For example, if you type <b>power</b> in your KDP book description, the word **power** will appear bold in your Amazon description.

- Enclose text between <i> and </i> tags to make *italics*. For example, if you type <i>funny</i> in your KDP book description, the word *funny* will appear italicized in your Amazon description.

- Create **bullet points** by placing <ul> where your bulleted list (the "ul" stands for "unordered list") begins and placing </ul> where your bulleted list ends. Also, place <li> (for "list element") where each bullet point begins and </li> where each bullet point ends. For example, <ul><li>first</li><li>second</li><li>last</li></ul> creates a simple bulleted list.

- Create a **numbered list** by placing <ol> where your numbered list (the "ol" stands for "ordered list") begins and placing </ol> where your numbered list ends. Also, place <li> (for "list element") where each point begins and </li> where each point ends. For example, <ol><li>first</li><li>second</li><li>last</li></ol> creates a simple numbered list (using numbers instead of bullets).

- Typing <br> has the same effect as using the Enter key ("br" stands for "break," as in "line break"). If you want to create a **blank line** between paragraphs, you could type

. However, note that, unlike typical HTML editors, KDP respects the actual Enter key. In ordinary HTML, use of the Enter key has no effect on the text output. So if you're well-versed in HTML, you use the Enter key out of habit to make it easier to read your HTML. However, *every time you use the Enter key in your KDP description, it will create a line break in your Amazon description.* (It's also unnecessary to use the <br> feature in the KDP book description: You could simply press Enter instead.) *Another quirk is that if you edit your book description later from Author Central (Sec. 8.2), that HTML mode will ignore the Enter key* (so there it is necessary to use <br> to create a line break).

Warning: Unlike ordinary HTML, if you press the Enter key in the KDP *book description* field (not to be confused with the HTML for the content file of your eBook that we discussed in Chapter 5), it will actually create a line break. (Author Central, on the other hand, ignores use of the Enter key when using HTML mode.)

The problem with using HTML in the KDP book description is that you __can't__ properly test it out. You could copy and paste your KDP book description into a basic HTML editor and test it out there, but it won't be foolproof, in part because the HTML of the KDP book description is a little quirky (such as the unusual Enter feature mentioned previously). Even worse, I've heard of bizarre cases where an unclosed tag in the description caused a formatting issue with the Look Inside. With this in mind, I recommend that you __don't__ apply HTML at KDP, but read the following tip instead.

> **Tip**: After you publish, edit your book description from **Author Central** (Sec. 8.2). Author Central will let you apply boldface, italics, line breaks, bulleted lists, and numbered lists. *You don't even need to use HTML to do this.* Author Central also shows you a preview of how your book description will look before you make the changes. If you edit your Kindle description at Author Central, copy and paste the HTML from your Author Central description into your KDP description and save the changes at KDP. (Note that you will need to carefully remove the <div> and </div> tags from your Author Central description before you paste it into the KDP description, as div-tags aren't supported in the limited HTML for KDP book descriptions.) This way, if you ever republish your Kindle eBook, the KDP description will already be identical to your Author Central description. (If you forget to do this and later republish your book, KDP will replace your updated Author Central description with your original KDP description.)

Note that if you want to change your book description, simply saving the book description at KDP isn't enough. You must either republish your book through KDP, or edit your book description at Author Central. If you choose to edit your description at Author Central (that's recommended, since Author Central lets you preview the changes), see the note at the end of the tip above about also saving the changes at KDP.

Following is an example of a *nonfiction* book description. It's not a good model for how to write the description for a novel, but it does illustrate how to implement basic HTML. Although it looks like one giant paragraph below, you can see (in the picture that follows) that this description comes out fine with proper line breaks on its Amazon page. As mentioned previously, although almost all HTML editors ignore use of the Enter key, the KDP description field *doesn't* ignore the Enter key (so it's incorrect to type the HTML with Enters the way that HTML often appears): I didn't press the Enter key once in the KDP book description field for the HTML description that follows. The <br /> and </li> tags that you see automatically result in line breaks (so if you also press Enter after each of these, it may add an additional line break). Again, *it's easier to type a plain description in KDP and later reformat it with Author Central* (where you don't even need to use or know HTML).

This eBook provides a highly visual and colorful introduction to a variety of basic astronomy concepts:
<ol><li>Overview of the Solar System</li><li>Understanding the Lunar Phases</li><li>Understanding Solar and Lunar Eclipses</li><li>Understanding the Seasons</li><li>Evidence that the Earth is Round</li><li>Models of Our Solar System</li><li>Laws of Motion in Astronomy</li><li>Beyond Our Solar System</li></ol>This eBook features numerous NASA space photos. (NASA did not participate in the writing or publication of this eBook.) Many diagrams, like the heliocentric and geocentric models or explaining the phases of the moon, were constructed by combining together NASA space photos instead of simply drawing circles.

 The content is suitable for a general interest audience, as well as those who may be learning astronomy and are looking for some supplemental instruction that is highly visual and focused on a variety of fundamental concepts.

Tip: First type your book description in Microsoft Word. Print it out and preview it carefully. Use Word's spellcheck and grammarcheck features to help identify possible mistakes. Get feedback on your description. Once you are happy with your description, copy and paste it into Notepad (to prevent any Word formatting from propagating into your KDP description) and then copy and paste it from Notepad to KDP.

6.5 Copyright and Digital Rights Management

Technically, in the United States your work is **copyrighted** when you first put it in written form. If you are interested in **registering** your work with the US copyright office, visit

https://www.copyright.gov

The copyright registration could come in handy in a rare instance in which Amazon asks an author for proof of copyright (usually, something prompts this, like an author claiming copyright **infringement**). It could also come in handy if you discover someone else trying to use your content without your permission. Keep in mind that I'm not an attorney, so I can't offer legal advice.

Amazon asks you whether you own the copyright and hold the necessary publishing rights to your book, or if you are publishing a public domain work. If you are publishing a **public domain** work, you should click the links at KDP to learn more about publishing public domain content with Amazon KDP, as they outline specific requirements that you must follow. First click the link called, "What is a public domain work?" In that pop-up window, click the link called, "Learn more about publishing public domain content on KDP." You can also type "public domain" (but without the quotes) in the search field at the KDP help pages.

An Introduction to Basic Astronomy Concepts (with Space Photos) Kindle Edition

by Chris McMullen ▾ (Author)

★★★★☆ ▾ 27 customer reviews

▸ See all 4 formats and editions

Kindle	Paperback
$0.00 kindleunlimited	$9.36 ✓prime
This title and over 1 million more available with Kindle Unlimited	11 Used from $8.42
$0.00 to buy	18 New from $9.36

Also available in paperback (full-color ISBN **978-1478169383**, black and white ISBN 978-1478169727).

This eBook provides a highly visual and colorful introduction to a variety of basic astronomy concepts:

1. Overview of the Solar System
2. Understanding the Lunar Phases
3. Understanding Solar and Lunar Eclipses
4. Understanding the Seasons
5. Evidence that the Earth is Round
6. Models of Our Solar System
7. Laws of Motion in Astronomy
8. Beyond Our Solar System

This eBook features numerous **NASA space photos.** (NASA did not participate in the writing or publication of this eBook.) Many diagrams, like the heliocentric and geocentric models or explaining the phases of the moon, were constructed by combining together NASA space photos instead of simply drawing circles.

The content is suitable for a general interest audience, as well as those who may be learning astronomy and are looking for some supplemental instruction that is highly visual and focused on a variety of fundamental concepts.

Look inside ⤴

Basic Astronomy Concepts

Chris McMullen, Ph.D.
Northwestern State University of Louisiana

READ ON
ANY DEVICE
›Get free Kindle app

If you wrote the content yourself (and it's unique—you didn't plagiarize or borrow content from elsewhere) and if you haven't published the content with a publisher, then you should own the copyright and hold the necessary rights to your work. If you've previously published the work with a traditional publisher, you first need to obtain the rights for your work before you can publish it yourself (specifically, for the eBook, you need the digital rights).

Author Central

Edit review   close ☒

Guidelines
If you are copying and pasting text from another text editing program, we recommend you use only a plain text editor like Notepad. Rich text editors like Microsoft Word often cause formatting issues which delay or prevent your request from processing.

What "Product Description" should include:

- An objective summary of the book's subject matter and genre. Think of the content on the back cover of most books.
- Up to 4000 characters (about 600 words)

What "Product Description" should not include:

- Spoilers! please don't reveal crucial plot elements.
- Phone numbers, mail addresses, URLs.

If you want to make a change to the content provided by your publisher, we advise to consult them before making changes. More details on "Product Description" guidelines here ⬀.

`COMPOSE`   `EDIT HTML`

Format: **B** *I* ≣≣

Also available in paperback (full-color ISBN **978-1478169383**, black and white ISBN 978-1478169727).

This eBook provides a highly visual and colorful introduction to a variety of basic astronomy concepts:

1. Overview of the Solar System
2. Understanding the Lunar Phases
3. Understanding Solar and Lunar Eclipses
4. Understanding the Seasons
5. Evidence that the Earth is Round
6. Models of Our Solar System
7. Laws of Motion in Astronomy
8. Beyond Our Solar System

This eBook features numerous **NASA space photos**. (NASA did not participate in the writing or publication of this eBook.) Many diagrams, like the heliocentric and geocentric models or

 Preview ⬇

Separate from the issue of copyright and publishing rights is the issue of **Digital Rights Management** (DRM). When you reach the second page of the publishing process, Amazon asks you whether or not to enable DRM on your Kindle eBook. Consider this carefully because **once you publish, this setting _can't_ be changed.**

The idea behind DRM is to inhibit people from sharing your work. However, if a person wants to share your work and knows how to do it, DRM will not prevent it from happening. There have been some interesting **Author Earnings Reports** (such as the one that you can access via the URL below) that suggest that indie books without DRM actually sell better (but it depends on other factors, like price—in the report referenced below, the effect was most noticeable in the $3.99 to $5.99 range).

http://authorearnings.com/report/july-2014-author-earnings-report

It seems unusual: I would bet that most customers have no idea whether or not DRM is enabled for a book they are thinking about buying. It's possible that the report is establishing a correlation between author habits and sales rather than a correlation between reader habits and sales. (That is, maybe successful indie authors have a tendency not to enable DRM, and maybe that's why the reports favor books without DRM. But that's just a 'maybe.') With this in mind, I usually enable DRM for my books. However, most authors who are aware of the Author Earnings Reports probably disable DRM, as they don't want to take a chance that this setting will inhibit possible sales.

6.6 Keywords

Amazon KDP lets you enter up to 7 keywords (or phrases, or groups of related words) to help improve the discoverability of your book in search results. If you enter multiple words (like "paranormal romance") in the same keyword field, separate them using the _spacebar_. Don't use an underscore (_). Don't use quotation marks.

> **Tip**: Don't waste keywords by repeating words from your title and subtitle. Any words used in your title and subtitle are _automatically_ associated as keywords for your book. Don't use the keyword "book" (since that's also automatic). Note that you're not allowed to use "Kindle" as a keyword or as part of a key phrase.

Keywords tend to be most effective when they are **highly relevant** to your book. Start out by making a list of words that are very relevant for your book. You want to have a long list of words to choose from, and later narrow it down to what to enter into the 7 keywords fields. Many of your words might not get used, but that's okay: You want to build a large pool of ideas and then select the best ones for your keywords. It's better to have too many ideas than too few.

Let me list a few kinds of keywords to help get you thinking. Variety can help you attract customers in different ways.

- **Genre** examples: action thriller, romantic suspense, post apocalyptic,[104] sword and sorcery.
- **Subject** examples: motivational self help,[104] fourth grade math, how to self publish[104]
- **Setting** examples: Victorian London, colonial America, French revolution.
- **Audience** examples: gifted teens, working mothers, college students.
- **Content** examples: funny stories, vegan recipes, science workbook.
- **Character** examples: strong female protagonist, military veterans, shape shifters.
- **Story type** examples: coming of age, who dun it, dystopian.

Visit Amazon.com and try typing a variety of keywords into the search field. Note the search suggestions that you receive. Although it's possible for different customers to see different search results for the same keyword (especially if one customer has mature content turned off while another customer does not), the **search suggestions** can be helpful. For one thing, the suggestions often give me a few good ideas that I hadn't thought of on my own. (Try also using a thesaurus to find similar words to the keywords that you already have in mind.)

Note that the search suggestions depend upon whether you are typing keywords in All Departments, Books, Kindle Books, or specific categories (like Romance). I try typing keywords in all of these fields separately: First I type them in All Departments, then Books, and so on, until I reach the specific categories for my book.

Also type complete keywords and study the search results. This will help you see firsthand which kinds of books are showing up in the search—but remember, it's possible for other customers to see different search results for the same keyword search. Note the distinction between search **suggestions** (the keywords and phrases that Amazon suggests as you type keywords) and search **results** (the list of books that you see on Amazon's product page after you finish entering your keyword or phrase).

Your goal is to help relevant customers find your book among the millions of books on the market. Keywords can help with this if you learn how to use them properly. They can also take time to help boost your book in the searches. If customers happen to find your book in keyword searches, buy your book, and have a **positive customer experience** (Amazon has many ways of trying to track such things—something you learn if you ever try to sell products through Amazon Seller Central), the algorithm associates relevance to your keywords and it is more likely to show higher in relevant searches.

It may help to try considering the customer perspective. The customer wants to find a specific type of book, yet there are millions of books on Amazon, and only a dozen or so showing on

---

[104] I suggest *not* including a hyphen—as in post-apocalyptic, self-help, or self-publish—when entering keywords.

each page of search results. If the customer enters "suspense" in the Books category, there will be several thousand search results. You're wondering how this will help *you*, especially since, as a new author, your book would be buried deep in the results. But don't worry: The search that I just described doesn't help the typical customer either. Several thousand search results doesn't help *anybody*.

It's what most customers do next that not only helps the customer, but can potentially help a lucky author, too. The customer is likely to **filter** the search results one of a few different ways.

- The customer might try a more **specific keyword** search like "legal thrillers" or "Victorian mystery." A specific keyword search can greatly reduce the number of search results. That's why specific keywords that are highly relevant for your book can aid with discoverability.

- The customer might click on one of the category suggestions at the left. For example, clicking on Psychological Thrillers reduces the number of search results from around twenty thousand to about six hundred.

- The customer might click the **Last 30 Days** or **Last 90 Days** link at the left. (The Coming Soon link applies to pre-orders—see Sec. 6.8.) *This gives newly released books a little window of opportunity to get discovered.* This is more helpful with a specific keyword search like "Victorian ghost stories" than it is for a broad keyword like "suspense."

- The customer might use the **dropdown menu**. If the customer chooses one of the review options, that won't help most new books from new authors, but some customers search by *Publication Date* to find new books. With a broad keyword like "romance," a book quickly drops off this list, but with a more specific keyword like "coming of age," a book can stay on this list longer.

Some customers will filter search results in two or more ways. Other customers will use a very specific keyword (or combination of keywords). It doesn't help the customer or most authors when the customer sees thousands of search results, but for the customer who figures out how to reduce the number of search results down to a manageable level, it not only helps the customer, but it also helps authors who are otherwise struggling to get discovered.

Amazon's system tends to help authors who scrupulously help themselves. One way to do this is to write content that customers are looking for and which satisfies most of your audience. Another way is generate sales of your own through effective marketing (Sec. 8.7).

Once you have a list of prospective keywords, you will probably need to narrow it down, but not as much as you might think. There are 7 keyword *fields*, but *you can have more than 7 keywords*. That's because **you're allowed to enter multiple keywords in the same field**. As long as you separate them with spaces and **<u>don't</u>** use quotation marks (or underscores), any of those words will serve as individual keywords. Any combination of individual words from your keyword list and book title will automatically show up in search results. (However, it's best to organize your keywords in a logical order rather than jumble them together in any order.) **You can enter up to 50 characters (including spaces) in a single keyword field.**

> **Tip**: Simple plurals are automatic. For example, if you already have the keyword "ghost," there is no reason to also use the keyword "ghosts." One form may actually work slightly better than the other, but pick *one* form only: Don't use both the singular and the plural. (It's also unnecessary to include variations in punctuation, spacing, and capitalization.)

Note that certain keyword combinations can also get your book listed in **special categories**. For example, if you want to get your book listed in the Sword & Sorcery category, there is a specific combination of keywords that you must enter into one of the keyword fields. It's worth knowing about this for the opposite reason, too: You don't want your book to inadvertently be listed in an irrelevant category. We'll discuss how keyword combinations affect categories in the next section.

You may change your keywords after you publish. However, note that you must republish your book (Sec. 8.4) in order for the changes to take place (simply saving the changes at KDP without republishing won't have any effect). **Beware**: If your book has developed keyword relevance at Amazon (one way is when customers click on your book in search results and then purchase it), if you change that keyword you may lose that relevance. (If your book isn't selling or is hardly selling, it's not really an issue. When a book is selling, be careful what you change.)

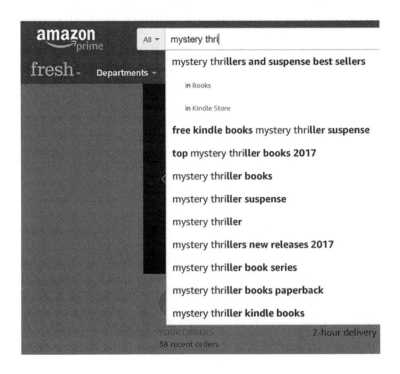

6.7 Browse Categories

You may select up to *two* Amazon browse categories for your book. Unfortunately, *the list of categories that you can choose from isn't exactly the same as Amazon's actual browse categories.* A few categories can't even be found on the list. Some categories can be found, but not where you first expect to find them. Explore the categories thoroughly to discover all of your options so that you can find the two best options.

Here is my strategy for choosing categories:

- First, I visit the Kindle Store at Amazon.com. I search for books similar to mine and write down what their actual Amazon browse categories are. This helps me target my intended categories.

- Next, I spend much time exploring the category choices at KDP. I try to find the two categories at KDP that are the closest match to my targeted Amazon browse categories.

- I also compare my **keyword** list with my targeted Amazon browse categories. We'll discuss how keywords can impact categories later in this section.

- My last recourse has rarely been necessary. After publishing, if your book isn't listed in the desired Amazon browse category, there is a chance that a polite request to KDP support can help get your book into the desired category. There is no guarantee that this will work (and occasionally a subcategory that you discover on Amazon has actually been "closed" for some time, in which case a new book can't get into that subcategory). Also, note that if your book is already listed in two (or more categories) and you request to have it listed in another category, you will likely lose one of your existing categories. (Technically, a book shouldn't be listed in more than two categories, but as noted later in this section, a book can become automatically listed in additional categories.) A few categories are also restricted, such as Kindle Short Reads (even a representative can't help you get into a restricted category).

Very often, there are more than just two categories that seem appropriate for a book, and you must choose which two categories you feel will work best. It's not always an easy decision, and sometimes one choice would be much better than the other.

In which category are customers most likely to be searching for books like yours? That's the question you should be asking. You want the categories that you choose to be highly **relevant** for readers browsing those categories.

Try to do a little research to understand the differences between similar categories. If you can figure out which kinds of customers tend to browse which kinds of categories, and what they are looking for in each category, it can help you choose your categories wisely.

There are **special categories** that you can only get into with the proper list of **keywords** entered in one of the keyword fields. We discussed keywords in Sec. 6.6, but now we will discuss *how keywords relate to categories.*

For example, suppose that you wrote a fantasy book that would be a great fit for the Sword & Sorcery subcategory. The *only* way to get your book listed in this category is by fulfilling the keyword requirements for this subcategory, which are sword, sorcery, magic, dragon, and quest. If you don't have this combination of keywords in a keyword field, your book *can't* get into that category.

Amazon KDP maintains a list of categories with keyword requirements and the keyword combination needed to unlock each category on the KDP help pages. You can access this page through the URL below: When you get there, select **Categories with Keyword Requirements**. However, note that KDP updates their help pages periodically, and sometimes the links to 'important' pages (like the one below) get changed. An alternative way to reach the page (currently this works) is to type "browse categories" (without the quotes) in the search field in the KDP help pages, and click the link called Selecting Browse Categories. Then select **Categories with Keyword Requirements**. (Even the KDP help pages themselves could be easier to find: Look for a Help link near the top right corner of the page after landing at KDP.)

https://kdp.amazon.com/en_US/help/topic/A200PDGPEIQX41

When you select the keywords for your book, it's possible for certain combinations of those keywords to automatically put your book in a category that you *don't* want it to be in. A few categories are enabled by a single keyword. For example, if your book involves vampires and you use vampire as one of your keywords, your book will *automatically* show up in the Paranormal > Romance > Vampires category—even if your vampire book is completely non-romantic. That could create a negative impact if customers buy your book expecting it to be a romance.

This gives you *two* reasons to browse through KDP's tables of keyword combinations and categories. For one, you might discover a suitable category that you hadn't even been aware of. For another, you might realize that a keyword that you had been planning to use will automatically put your book in an irrelevant category.

Are you publishing a **children's** book? If so, it's worth noting the following special keywords:

- The keyword **baby** gets your book listed in the Children's Age Range/Baby-2 category.
- The keyword **preschool** gets your book listed in the Children's Age Range/Ages 3-5 category.
- The keyword **ages 6-8** gets your book listed in the Children's Age Range/Ages 6-8 category.
- The keyword **preteen** gets your book listed in the Children's Age Range/Ages 9-12 category.

In addition to selecting categories, there is an option to select a **grade** and **age** range for your book. This information is relevant for the Children's Kindle Store and Schools and Teaching Store on Amazon. The age designation helps with juvenile categories, while the grade designation helps with both juvenile and education categories. The grade level is based on US grade levels. Narrower age and grade selections better help you target your book to the most relevant customers. Amazon recommends choosing age and grade ranges that span no more than 3-4 years. As an example, selecting ages from 9-12 meets this criteria, whereas selecting ages 6-18 does not.

You may change your categories after you publish. However, note that you must republish your book (Sec. 8.4) in order for the changes to take place (simply saving the changes at KDP without republishing won't have any effect). **Beware**: If your book has developed any browse category visibility at Amazon (one way is when customers click on your book in search results and then purchase it), if you change that category you may lose that improved visibility. (If your book isn't selling or is hardly selling, it's not really an issue. When a book is selling, be careful what you change.)

Product details

File Size: 6598 KB
Print Length: 176 pages
Publisher: Astro Nutz; 3 edition (August 16, 2012)
Publication Date: August 16, 2012
Sold by: Amazon Digital Services LLC
Language: English
ASIN: B0090U01P0
Text-to-Speech: Enabled ⊠
X-Ray: Enabled ⊠
Word Wise: Enabled
Lending: Enabled
Screen Reader: Supported ⊠
Enhanced Typesetting: Enabled ⊠
Amazon Best Sellers Rank: #8,980 Paid in Kindle Store (See Top 100 Paid in Kindle Store)
   #1 in Books > Teens > Education & Reference > Science & Technology > **Chemistry**
   #1 in Kindle Store > Kindle eBooks > Nonfiction > Science > Chemistry > **General & Reference**
   #2 in Kindle Store > Kindle eBooks > Teen & Young Adult > Education & Reference > Science & Technology > **Science & Nature**

6.8 Pre-orders

When I first self-published back in 2008, indie authors didn't have the option to arrange pre-orders for Kindle eBooks. This was reserved strictly for the big publishers. It took several years, but Amazon finally made pre-orders available for anyone who publishes with KDP.

Pre-orders offer potential two ways:

- Your book shows up in the **Coming Soon** filter at Amazon when pre-orders are available. The Last 30 Days and Last 90 Days filters provide valuable exposure for some self-published books, so the Coming Soon filter adds to that exposure for those books that would benefit from it (not all books do).

- The primary benefit of pre-orders is for authors who have already established a significant following either through effective marketing or from previous success (or both). Existing fans may help to generate strong sales before the book is officially released, which can help boost exposure when the book goes live.

Presently, nobody is allowed to review a book during pre-order status. This lets authors generate some sales before reviewers can attempt to sway opinions. If a book generates many pre-orders, those early sales when the book goes live are also likely to generate a few reviews. (Ordinarily, a book might earn about 1 review for every 50 to 200 sales, though this can vary considerably. However, when pre-orders are generated by an authors' top followers, a book is somewhat more likely to be reviewed.)

You should avoid doing a pre-order *unless* you have good *reason* to expect the pre-order period to be somewhat successful. A book generates a pre-order sales rank that indicates how well it is (or isn't selling), so if it doesn't sell during this period, customers will know that it isn't selling. Lack of sales during the pre-order period diminish a book's exposure.

If you're a new author and you haven't already done effective marketing to build strong prospects for early sales, pre-orders probably aren't for you (unless you happen to have several supporters planning to buy your book during the pre-order period).

Pre-orders come with a *responsibility*. I recommend that you **don't** initiate a pre-order **until** your book is 100% ready to go live (meaning that you have already properly previewed it as discussed in Chapter 7). If you use the pre-order option and your book isn't complete, isn't formatted well, or otherwise isn't really ready for customers to read by Amazon's **deadline**, this not only creates a negative customer experience that may lead to negative customer reviews, but you may also lose future pre-order privileges.

Note that Amazon's **deadline** for uploading your **final** book content file is typically about 72 hours (3 days) **prior to** the release date: When you submit your eBook for pre-order, a **timer** will appear on your Bookshelf, announcing the official deadline. Check the timer periodically: Once the timer expires, it will be **too late** to upload corrections (until *after* the book is already published). After that deadline, if you wish to upload a revised file (Sec. 8.4), you must wait until after your book is published, and all of your pre-order customers will receive the original file (with any errors that it may have had). I recommend waiting until your book is as perfect as you can make it **before** setting up your pre-order. This removes the stress associated with trying to revise and perfect your book before the deadline to submit your final file.

If you're publishing an eBook for the first time, even if you have a strong following ready to purchase your book, I recommend that you **don't** use the pre-order option for your *first* Kindle eBook. You would hate to publish your book, sell a large number of pre-orders, and discover after the book is published that there is a significant formatting issue. Although in Chapter 7 we'll discuss how to preview your eBook, there is nothing better than being your own first customer and inspecting the actual published eBook firsthand–especially, when you don't have any Kindle publishing experience. (This way, in the worst-case scenario that you discover an unforeseen problem, you have a chance to quickly correct it and republish—or even unpublish and publish a new book later—before telling everyone that your book is available.) Once you publish a Kindle eBook successfully and see firsthand that there appear to be no problems, then you can use the pre-order option more confidently in the future. You definitely want your first book launch to be as successful as possible (by minimizing any risks): *It's the very first impression that you will make as an author* (and you only get one chance to make a first impression).

6.9 Uploading Your Content File

You should now have reached page 2 of the publishing process at KDP. Recall that we discussed Digital Rights Management (DRM) in Sec. 6.5. You may wish to review Sec. 6.5 before you select your DRM option.

> **Note:** Don't include your front cover at the beginning of your content file. Amazon automatically includes the front cover (that you upload separately—we'll get to that in Sec. 6.10) with your eBook, so if you include the front cover at the beginning of your content file, you will end up with a **double cover**. (However, if you upload a MOBI or ePub file and encounter a double cover or missing cover, check Sec. 5.12.)

Following are my recommendations for which type of file to upload to Amazon KDP for your interior Kindle eBook file.

- If you followed my advice from Chapter 5, and if your interior file includes any **images**, upload a **compressed zipped folder**. (However, if you used a program like Sigil, you should upload a validated ePub file instead.) We discussed how to create a compressed zipped folder in Sec. 5.3. Remember that we also discussed how to replace the original HTML file in that folder after revising your HTML file (Sec.'s 5.3 and 5.5). Make sure that the HTML file in your compressed zipped folder contains the most up-to-date version of your HTML file (by copying and pasting your HTML file into the compressed zipped folder such that it overwrites the previous version of the HTML file in that folder).[72] Similarly, double-check that the image files folder *inside* of your compressed zipped folder contains all of your updated pictures (see Sec. 5.5).

- If you followed my advice from Chapter 5, but your interior file *doesn't* include any images, upload the **HTML file** that you created by saving your Word file as a *filtered webpage*. (However, if you used a program like Sigil, you should upload a validated ePub file instead.)

- If you skipped Chapter 5 of this book, upload your **Word file** in DOCX or DOC format. We discussed the distinction between these two Word formats in Sec. 1.2. (However, if you used Amazon's **Kindle Create** software, upload the KPF file that was generated by Kindle Create.)

- If you went beyond the scope of my book and used a program like Sigil after following my advice from Chapter 5, try uploading an unzipped, validated ePub file. (An ePub file should work fine, if you know what you are doing with a program like Sigil. According to the KDP help pages, only MOBI files created with Amazon tools like KindleGen are supported. A MOBI file created by MobiPocket Creator, for example, is *not* supported.) Validate your ePub file with Amazon's KindleGen or Kindle Previewer, or use the IDPF ePub validator tool at http://validator.idpf.org. (Beware that the latest version of ePub *may not be compatible with Kindle eReaders*, and that there are important differences between how to format an ePub file for Kindle compared to other brands of eReaders.)

- Although Amazon accepts RTF, TXT, and PDF files, I do **not** recommend using any of these formats. These formats—especially PDF—are known to result in many common formatting problems. However, if you have a textbook, illustrated picture book, or comic book, then you should try running your PDF file through the Kindle Textbook Creator, the Kindle Kids' Book Creator, or the Kindle Comic Creator. Although uploading a PDF file to KDP is problematic, the KPF or MOBI files that Amazon's free tools create work fine (but they are only appropriate for certain kinds of books like illustrated books and textbooks—nobody would want to read a novel or a book with mostly text created by one of those programs).

- If you used one of Amazon's free tools—**Kindle Create**, the Kindle Textbook Creator, the Kindle Kids' Book Creator, or the Kindle Comic Creator—to create your Kindle eBook, upload the KPF or MOBI file that was created using Amazon's free tool.

Note: If you encounter any issues, sometimes switching web browsers (Explorer, Fire-Fox, or Chrome, for example) or updating your web browser resolves the issue. (If you uploaded a KPF file, the wait can be several minutes or more. If you receive an error message uploading a KPF file, try again with another web browser, and if it persists, you may need try it again another day. It happens occasionally with KPF files.)

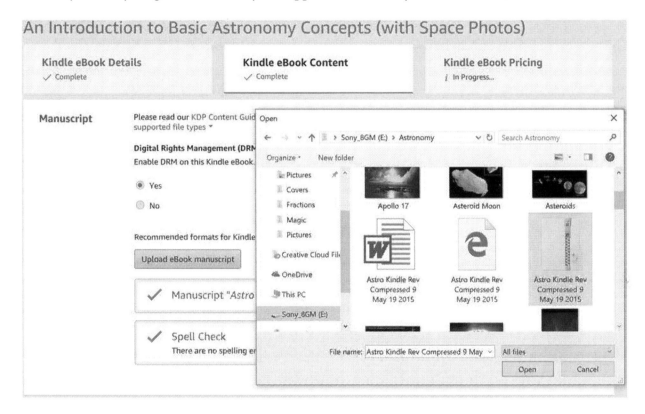

6.10 Uploading Your Cover File

Amazon gives you two options for your cover file:

- Upload a JPEG or TIFF file for your cover.
- Use Amazon's free Cover Creator tool.

I recommend creating your own cover file, or least make your best effort to create a cover and compare with what you can make using the Cover Creator. If you use the Cover Creator, you must either supply your own image or choose from Amazon's stock images. The problem with stock images is that if several authors use the same stock image, your book will look similar to other books on the market.

There is actually a third option: You can invest money on cover design. I don't recommend investing a *large* sum of money on cover design for your *first* book because you have no idea if the book will sell enough copies to recover your investment. There are ways to keep cover design expenses to a minimum. One way is to pay a small fee for a stock image from one of many sites like Shutter Stock. (Be sure to pay the fee to get a licensed image: You definitely **don't** want to use the unlicensed image that has the company's watermark on it.) However, it's possible that other authors will use the same stock image, creating a book cover very similar to yours. Recall that we discussed image rights and stock images in Sec. 4.14.

There are so many cover designers that it *is* possible to find a reasonably priced cover designer who can do very good work. Note that it's not always easy for an author to look at an illustrator's portfolio and determine the prospects that the illustrator (or graphic designer) will produce a highly marketable book cover for his or her unique book. I've seen good covers designed on small budgets, so it *is* possible to keep it affordable and obtain good results.

Regardless of whether you do it yourself or seek hired help, it's good to learn some elements of cover design. One way to help improve your eye for cover design is to *spend time browsing through covers* for books similar to yours. It will also show you what customers are seeing when they browse for books. Following are my **cover design tips**.

- **Three-second rule**: In three seconds, *can complete strangers tell what kind of book you have written without reading the title*? If so, the book sends the proper visual message and has a chance to get noticed when customers are browsing through thumbnails.
- **Three-color rule**: Many of the most effective covers primarily use three colors. The two main colors should go well together (usually by *contrast*), and the third color is used more as an *accent*.
- **Rule of thirds**: The central image in artwork and graphic design sometimes catches attention by being positioned at a fraction of one-third (rather than being centered at a fraction of one-half).
- The title must be large enough to read the text on a tiny thumbnail. Open up Amazon in one window and open your cover in another window side by side on your computer. In the window with Amazon, browse through book covers in search results. Change the view (zoom) for your cover until it is just as small as the thumbnails on Amazon. *If you can't easily read the text of your title, you need to make it larger until you can.* (If you have a long title—even though the most effective book titles have three words or less, especially in fiction—make the most important words larger and the less important words smaller.)
- Use a font that is appropriate for your genre or subject. *Take time to research fonts.* Also study the fonts used on book covers similar to your book. There are many fonts that grant free commercial use, but there are also many fonts that require purchasing a

license, so you need to check the font licensing terms before you use a font that you like. Avoid using Comic Sans (except maybe for young kids) or Book Antiqua (it doesn't tend to kern properly) on your cover. Avoid using Times New Roman for your title font. After you choose your font, make sure that it is *easy to read* when the cover displays at thumbnail size.

- **Three-font rule**: You don't need more than three fonts on your cover. Two fonts may be enough for the Kindle cover.

- Prefer black text on a light background or white text on a dark background. *Avoid using red text on a black background.* (Although red and black can work well together, this particular combination is harder to read than it seems like it should be.)

- Don't go overboard and make a cover that is **too busy**. From a marketing perspective, your cover should attract attention and convey the type of book it is at just a passing glance. A cover with too much clutter or too much going on can't meet this goal as effectively.

- Seek honest **feedback**. You want your cover to have visual appeal, which only honest feedback can establish. You also want feedback to help you determine if your cover is a good fit for your genre or subject.

Tip: A **cover reveal** is a good marketing opportunity. Try to perfect your cover before doing a cover reveal. You want the people giving you feedback to become interested in your book. Sec. 8.7 will point you in the right direction to get started with marketing your book (something that you should start before your book is published).

Note: Save the JPEG file for your cover with a RGB color profile. Note that Amazon doesn't support covers saved with a CMYK color profile.

6.11 Preview Options

It is very important to preview your book thoroughly and carefully. Even when an author takes great pains to learn and try to do everything right, an author is still human. The preview is your opportunity to catch any formatting mistakes before a customer purchases your book. In addition to previewing your book for formatting mistakes, you should also proofread your book carefully for editing mistakes.

We will discuss how to preview your book thoroughly in detail in Chapter 7. For now, I will just briefly mention your preview options.

- The **online previewer** lets you preview your book in your web browser during the second step of the publishing process at KDP. However, while this is convenient, many eBook formatters feel that doing only this is insufficient.

- The **downloadable preview** option lets you download the converted MOBI file for your book. You may then view the converted MOBI file on the downloadable previewer. You may also preview the MOBI file on an actual Kindle **device** or app.

I recommend using *both* the online and downloadable previewers. You also want to explore the variety of devices on both previewers. In addition, you should try to preview your converted MOBI file on at least one actual device. If you don't own an actual Kindle, you might know someone who does and is willing to let you put your Kindle eBook on their device (that's a fair trade: they get to read your book for free, and you get to see how it looks before you publish it). If you have an Android phone, an iPhone, an Android tablet, or an iPad, you can preview your book on those devices, too. At the very least, you can view your book on a PC or a laptop (using one of Amazon's *free* Kindle reading apps, such as Kindle for PC, Kindle for iPad, Kindle for Mac, or Kindle for Android).

It would be wise to read Chapter 7 and preview your Kindle eBook as thoroughly as possible before you continue with the publishing process. I also recommend reading Chapter 8 before you publish your eBook.

Before you advance to page 3 of the publishing process at KDP, you have the option to enter an ISBN and enter a publisher name. Recall that we discussed the ISBN and publisher name options near the end of Sec. 6.3.

Kindle eBook Preview

Online Previewer
The Online Previewer is the easiest way to preview. It lets you preview most books as they would appear on Kindle e-readers, tablets and phones.

> Launch Previewer

Downloadable Preview Options

If you would like to preview your book on Kindle Touch or Kindle DX, you will want to use the downloadable previewer.

▾ Preview on your computer

Use the downloadable previewer if you would like to preview your book on older Kindle models, like Kindle Touch or Kindle DX.

Step 1: Download and install the previewer fo[Mac or Windows]

Step 2: Download and open your converted book file: HTML o[MOBI]

▸ Preview on your Kindle device

Step 1: Download your converted book file: HTML o[MOBI]

Step 2: Send the book file to your Send-to-Kindle e-mail address to view on your Kindle. Learn more about sending files to Kindle via email.

Step 3: Open the file on your Kindle

6.12 KDP Select

You should now have reached page 3 of the publishing process at KDP. The next step (after thoroughly previewing your book file) is to decide whether or not to enroll your eBook in KDP Select.

First note that KDP and KDP Select are two different things:

- You're already using KDP when you publish a Kindle eBook at kdp.amazon.com.
- KDP Select is an *optional* program that you can enroll in. If you enroll your eBook in this program, it comes with a **contract** that automatically *renews*. Therefore, you want to make sure that you understand both the terms and the benefits before you sign up for KDP Select.

We'll discuss the pros and cons of enrolling in KDP Select in order to help you with your decision. There really is just one disadvantage, but it's a big one.

Important note: If you enroll a Kindle eBook in KDP Select, you're **not** permitted to publish your eBook *anywhere* else besides Amazon Kindle. You can't publish your eBook with Nook, Kobo, Smashwords, Draft2Digital, BookBaby, on your own website (although you may post up to 10% of your eBook, starting from the beginning, on your website), or anywhere else unless and until (A) your enrollment period ends and (B) you successfully opt out of KDP Select.

So that's the disadvantage: Your eBook must be **exclusive** to Amazon Kindle if you wish to take advantage of the benefits that KDP Select offers (we'll discuss those next). The question you must ask is whether or not the possible benefits of enrolling in KDP Select outweigh the disadvantage of not being able to publish your Kindle eBook elsewhere.

Following is a list of benefits that KDP Select offers.

- Books that are enrolled in KDP Select are automatically included in Kindle Unlimited and Amazon Prime. I will discuss what **Kindle Unlimited** is and how it works later in this section, and I'll also briefly mention Amazon Prime (the main benefit comes from Kindle Unlimited). Some authors earn good royalties through Kindle Unlimited, but, of course, not every book does well in Kindle Unlimited. A nice side effect of Kindle Unlimited is that when a customer borrows your book, it improves your **sales rank** just like an ordinary paid sale does.
- You may run a single **Countdown Deal** or free book promotion (but not both) every 90-day period for which your eBook is enrolled in KDP Select. We'll discuss Countdown Deals and free book promotions later in this section.

- Another benefit of enrolling in KDP Select is that you won't need to learn how to format your eBook for Nook, Kobo, Smashwords, Draft2Digital, BookBaby, or anywhere else. The formatting is a little different for other eBook retailers than it is for Kindle: A few things that apply to Kindle result in problems with Nook, for example, and there are a few things that you need to learn about other devices that aren't relevant to Kindle. If your eBook is rich in images, your content file may exceed the **file size limit** at one or more other retailers (whereas Amazon KDP has a generous limit that you shouldn't come close to). When you agree to publish your eBook edition exclusively on Kindle, you gain **convenience**: You save yourself the hassle of additional formatting (and previewing) for other platforms.

- There are a few other minor benefits from KDP Select, such as higher royalty rates in select countries (like India and Japan), depending upon your list price.

Now I will describe these potential benefits of KDP Select, and after that I will mention a few other things that you may wish to know about KDP Select (such as how to properly opt out of the program if you change your mind, and how the program impacts boxed sets).

Note: If you enroll in KDP Select, you're still allowed to publish a print edition (for example, through CreateSpace). Your *print* edition (Sec. 8.11) may be sold through other retailers. It's only the *digital* version (the eBook) that requires exclusivity with Amazon Kindle.

We'll begin with **Kindle Unlimited**. Customers who subscribe to Kindle Unlimited may borrow Kindle Unlimited books for free. (It's not really free: Customers pay $9.99 per month in the US—that's the rate as of the publication of this book—to subscribe to Kindle Unlimited.) Customers can keep up to 10 Kindle Unlimited books at a time on their device, and can read as much of as many Kindle Unlimited eBooks as they want each month. (Once they reach 10 books, they simply return one book to check out a new one.)

Amazon pays authors a royalty based on how many pages are read as part of Kindle Unlimited. This payment varies, but has typically been from $0.004 to $0.005 per page. (This is in addition to the royalties that authors receive for *sales*. When a customer purchases a book, as opposed to borrowing a book through Kindle Unlimited, the customer keeps that copy of the book forever. There is no limit to how many books customers can store on their devices—provided that their devices have enough memory—when they *purchase* books. The 10-book limit only applies to *borrowing* books through Kindle Unlimited.)

Note that $0.01 equals one penny. Therefore, a rate of $0.004 to $0.005 is less than half a penny per page. It doesn't sound like much, right? But you can't expect to be paid much when a single customer reads a single page of your book. If a single customer reads 100 pages, you receive up to 50 cents. If your book has the equivalent of 400 pages, you receive up to $2 when a customer reads the entire book. Many authors receive about $2 to $3 for paid *sales* (we'll explore royalties for paid sales in Sec. 6.13) for books priced around $2.99 to $3.99, and many full-length novels have a few hundred pages or more. Therefore, when a Kindle Unlimited customer reads an entire full-length book, it isn't unusual for the royalty earned by the author to be comparable to what the author earns for a paid sale (two exceptions are when an author publishes a short book or when an author sets a high list price).

It's actually *better* than it sounds: What Amazon calls a 'page' for the purpose of this calculation is usually somewhat generous. The official page count for your book is called KENPC, which stands for Kindle Edition Normalized Page Count. If you write a novel or book with mostly text, in most cases you should find that your KENPC is significantly larger than the number of pages that your book would have if it were published as a printed book. So your official page count for the purposes of Kindle Unlimited payments might be larger than you think. Also note that pictures count towards your page count (so that if you publish a children's book with illustrations, for example, those pictures help boost your page count).

Unfortunately, you can't predict what your KENPC will be before you publish your eBook. After you publish your Kindle eBook, if you enroll in KDP Select, then you will be able to check your KENPC (though it might take a couple of days to show): Visit your KDP Bookshelf, hover your cursor over the gray ellipsis (…) button, and click the Promote and Advertise button. You may need to scroll down the page a little to find your KENPC value.

Kindle Unlimited royalties can become significant if your book is borrowed and read by many customers. If 1000 Kindle Unlimited customers read your book in one month, and if each customer reads an average of 400 pages of your book, you would see a total of 400,000 pages read for the month, and would earn upwards of about $2000 for that month (in addition to any royalties you earn from ordinary sales). But that's a big "if." You don't know how many customers will borrow your book or how many pages they will read. (Amazon also awards All-Star bonuses—ranging from about $250 to $25,000—to the top-performing books and authors in Kindle Unlimited.)

What we do know is that Kindle Unlimited draws a significant share of the eBook market. Amazon has been paying upwards of $20,000,000 in monthly royalties for Kindle Unlimited books, and this amount (called the KDP Select Global Fund) has steadily risen for the past few years (it was closer to $10,000,000 shortly after Kindle Unlimited was introduced). That comes to over $200,000,000 in Kindle Unlimited royalties for the year 2017 (and that's on top of royalties that these books earn from ordinary sales). Since a single customer pays about $10 per month, this is a huge customer base (it would take a few million customers per month for Amazon just to break even—Amazon actually pays *more* than $20,000,000 per month for Kindle Unlimited, since this figure is separate from All-Star bonuses and is also separate from what Amazon pays the few traditionally published books that participate in the program).

Since Kindle Unlimited accounts for about $200,000,000 in eBook royalties per year (and this rate is climbing), it accounts for a **significant** share of the overall eBook market. Kindle Unlimited is also a relatively indie friendly market, meaning that many customers in Kindle Unlimited are reading self-published books. There are a few traditionally published books in Kindle Unlimited (like *Harry Potter* and *The Hunger Games*)—which are paid separately from the KDP Select Global Fund—which help to attract readers, but the vast majority of the books (percentage-wise) in Kindle Unlimited come from KDP authors who enroll their eBooks in KDP Select.

This doesn't guarantee that your book would be successful in Kindle Unlimited. It just shows the potential. There are many indie books that are thriving in this program. One thing you might do is browse the Kindle Unlimited books on Amazon to see how well books like yours seem to be doing (by looking at the Amazon.com overall sales rank in the Kindle Store—described in Sec. 8.5).

For what it's worth, my books are available in Kindle Unlimited (through KDP Select), and I also subscribe to Kindle Unlimited as a customer. As an author, I'm content with how my books perform in Kindle Unlimited. As a customer, it's a great value since I'm an avid reader: I would spend way more than $10 per month if I had to buy the books that I read through Kindle Unlimited.

A side benefit of Kindle Unlimited is that it helps with **sales rank** (Sec. 8.5). When a customer borrows your eBook through Kindle Unlimited, it has the same impact on sales rank as an ordinary paid sale. (The moment the book is borrowed is what matters for sales rank, but the reports show when pages are read, which may came days or weeks after the book was actually borrowed.)

Technically, you get paid for pages read when customers borrow your book through Kindle Unlimited or Amazon Prime. The distinction is that **Amazon Prime** only lets customers borrow one book per month, whereas **Kindle Unlimited** subscribers can borrow as many books as they would like. Therefore, the majority of your royalties for pages read through KDP Select come from Kindle Unlimited (Amazon Prime royalties aren't significant in comparison).

Now let's talk about a different type of benefit that KDP Select offers. There are two types of promotional tools available for books enrolled in KDP Select: Countdown Deals and free book promotions. You can only use one or the other in each 90-day enrollment period (we'll discuss enrollment periods later in this section).

If you elect to run a **Countdown Deal**, you can put your eBook on sale for up to 7 days. Although a Countdown Deal can last up to 7 days, you *can't* schedule the days separately. You can only schedule *one* Countdown Deal in a 90-day period (even if the Countdown Deal only runs for a day or less). *To maximize your book's exposure for a Countdown Deal, schedule it to include all 7 days.*

As opposed to simply reducing your price and republishing (the alternative way to put a book on 'sale'), a Countdown Deal shows customers the sale price and the regular price so that the customer can see the savings (whereas republishing with a reduced price just makes the regular price lower—customers have no idea if your list price used to be higher). When you run a Countdown Deal, you don't need to republish your book to adjust the price: Amazon will do this automatically. If you ordinarily earn a 70% royalty rate (see Sec. 6.13), you earn the same rate during the Countdown Deal (but applied to your sale price, of course), although the usual delivery fee (see Sec. 6.13) applies. For a book with a large file size (that's usually only the case if your book has several pictures), the delivery fee could be substantial: In that case, it's worth calculating the royalty you would earn during the Countdown Deal (Sec. 6.13 shows you how to calculate your royalty, accounting for the delivery fee).

Simply scheduling a Countdown Deal often doesn't bring increased sales all by itself. When authors have a successful Countdown Deal, it's usually because they used effective marketing techniques to call attention to their temporary sale prices. Sec. 8.7 will help get you started with marketing. There are a variety of websites (some more effective than others) which can help you advertise a sale price at Amazon. The most popular one among authors is called BookBub, but it's also pricey and difficult to get accepted into. Most of the other sites aren't as effective, but are much more affordable or even free. If you find a few affordable and relevant sites to advertise your Countdown Deal and combine this with other marketing of your own, you have better prospects for a successful Countdown Deal than merely scheduling the sale price.

Amazon does have a **landing page** for Countdown Deals, but many customers don't come across that page, and not all Countdown Deals are lucky enough to be included on that page. Rather than rely on *luck*, it's a good idea to have a *plan* to help promote your Countdown Deal. (If the URL below is no longer working—which may happen if Amazon updates their website—visit Amazon's Kindle Store, click Kindle Book Deals at the top left, and then click Kindle Countdown Deals.)

https://www.amazon.com/Kindle-eBooks/b?ie=UTF8&node=7078878011

To be eligible for a Countdown Deal, your book must have a list price from $2.99 to $24.99 in the US (or £1.99 to £15.99 in the UK), and your book needs to be enrolled in KDP Select for at least 30 days before the promotion. You're not allowed to change the list price of your book for 30 days before and 14 days after a Countdown Deal. You must schedule your Countdown Deal at least 24 hours in advance. I recommend scheduling a Countdown Deal several days in advance, if possible. If you advertise your Countdown Deal, consider starting your Countdown Deal early and finishing later than the promoted period (just in case there are technical issues and it doesn't start or end exactly when you plan—this does happen, though it's rare).

An alternative to a Countdown Deal is a **free book promotion**. Like the Countdown Deal, it's only available for KDP Select books. But unlike the Countdown Deal, you earn *zero* royalty when customers 'buy' your Kindle eBook for free during a free book promotion.

You can use up to 5 free book promotion days in the same 90-day period, and you can schedule them non-consecutively (unlike a Countdown Deal). However, if you run a single free book promotion, you're **not** eligible to run a Countdown Deal during the same 90-day period (and vice-versa).

Why would any author ever give their book away for free? Well, some authors do, and they have a variety of reasons for behind their decision. One possibility is to attempt to gain exposure as a new author. Another reason is to try to build and grow a following. When an author publishes a series (or a set of related books), it's a common tactic to give the first book away for free (or at a lower price, like 99 cents), hoping that the reader will get hooked on the series from the first book and buy the remaining books later.

I'm **not** recommending that you give your book away for free. I'm just stating that it's possible to do so, and noting that some authors have done this. Several years ago, when Amazon first introduced this option, there were a number of authors who used the free book promotion effectively. The general consensus is that it usually isn't as successful these days. However, if you advertise a free book promotion with a book promotion site that has a large, active following, this improves your chances for using this tool successfully. Again, BookBub is thought to be the most effective place to advertise a sale price, but BookBub is also pricey and very hard to get into. There are several other sites (most of which are far more affordable or even free), some more effective than others.

Note that for both Countdown Deals and free book promotions, there are some **bloggers** with popular followings who sometimes mention authors' sale prices. If the blogger is very popular, there might be a very long waiting list. If the blogger is relatively new and rapidly growing, you have good prospects, but this is hard to find. In between, there are many bloggers with mild followings who are looking for authors to help promote (when doing so also helps create interest in their blogs). Note that many bloggers don't promote books at all. You want to find those who do, and you want to visit their sites and follow their directions for submitting a request: If you follow their rules, your chances are greatly improved.

Now we'll discuss some other issues regarding KDP Select. One issue is that a book's enrollment in KDP Select **renews automatically** every 90 days unless you uncheck the box for automatic renewal. To do uncheck the box for automatic renewal, visit your KDP Bookshelf, find your book, hover your cursor over the gray ellipsis (…) button, and click KDP Select Info. Then you will see the checkbox in a pop-up window. **Note that your eBook must remain exclusive to Amazon until the current enrollment period ends**—even if you have unchecked the automatic renewal box (per Amazon's terms and conditions). After the current 90-day enrollment period ends, visit your KDP Bookshelf to confirm that you have, in fact, successfully opted out of KDP Select (if not, contact KDP support).

If you publish your eBook with other eBook distributors and later decide that you would like to enroll that eBook in KDP Select, you must first successfully unpublish your book with all other eBook distributors *before* enrolling in KDP Select. Note that your eBook may not immediately disappear from other sites' catalogs. If Amazon discovers your eBook for sale at other eBook sites (they have a program that does this automatically), **you will receive an email indicating that you are violating the terms and conditions of enrolling in KDP Select**. If you have already unpublished your eBook from the site in question, you will need to contact KDP support to try to straighten it out.

When you publish multiple books, note that enrolling one book in KDP Select doesn't require your other books to also be in KDP Select: You can decide on KDP Select separately for each book. The exception is when one book is also part of another book, such as a *boxed set*. If you enroll one volume of a set in KDP Select, **the boxed set (or omnibus) must also be enrolled in KDP Select**.

If you're struggling with the decision of whether or not to enroll an eBook in KDP Select, you could try it out for 90 days, use the features, and see how it works for your book firsthand. This will also give you time to research how to format your eBook for other devices, and to learn more about other eBook distributors (Sec. 6.16 discusses your main options). If you decide that KDP Select isn't for you, uncheck the automatic renewal box, and once the first 90 days have passed, you can publish your eBook elsewhere in addition to KDP (provided that you successfully opted out after the 90-day period).

6.13 List Price and Royalties

Before you set your list price, you must select the territories for which you hold the distribution rights for your book. If you wrote the content yourself (and it's unique—you didn't plagiarize or borrow content from elsewhere) and if you haven't published the content with a publisher, then you should hold worldwide distribution rights. If you've previously published the work with a traditional publisher, and the publisher released the *digital* distribution rights to you but only for certain territories, then you can only publish in those territories.

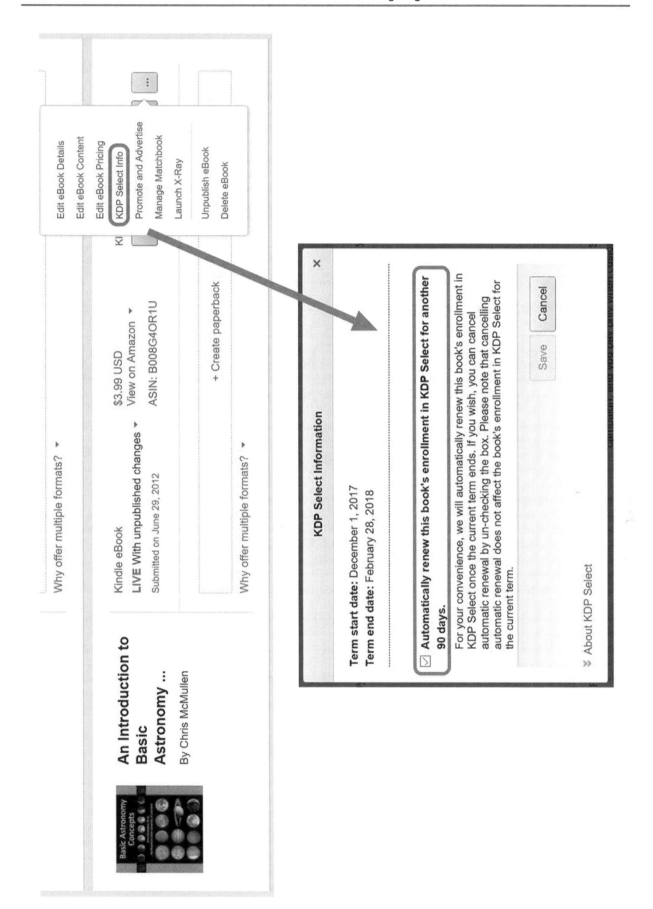

If you are publishing a **public domain** book, note that copyright laws and durations vary in different countries, such that a book that is in the public domain in one country might not be in the public domain in another country. In that case, you need to do some research and select the appropriate countries. Also note that Amazon has specific requirements for public domain books: Type "public domain" (but without the quotes) in the search field at the KDP help pages.

Next you must select either the 35% or 70% **royalty plan**. Ordinarily, you should choose the 70% option unless your book is in the public domain or you wish to set a list price below $2.99 or above $9.99 in the US (the list price requirements vary in other countries). You **must** select the 35% royalty option if your book is in the **public domain**. If you wrote the content yourself (and it's unique—you didn't plagiarize or borrow content from elsewhere[105]), your book is eligible for the 70% option provided that you meet the list price requirements.

If your book has several **pictures**, it could have a large enough file size that you would actually *earn a higher royalty on the 35% option* than the 70% option. That's because the 70% option subtracts a **delivery fee** based on the size of your content book file (after Amazon's automatic conversion to MOBI format) before applying the 70% to determine the royalty. Don't worry: You don't actually have to do the math yourself (although I will show you the formula and provide examples). **You can use Amazon's pricing page to compare your royalty for both plans.**

If your book doesn't have several pictures, the delivery fee should be rather small, and the 70% royalty option should be best for you, unless you wish to set a list price below $2.99 or above $9.99 in the US (for which the 70% royalty wouldn't be applicable).

See what the actual **converted MOBI file size** is for your book: Just above the royalty table (below the place where you choose either the 35% or 70% royalty rate), you should see a sentence that begins, "Your book file size after conversion is…" This tells you your file size in megabytes (MB).

If you select the 70% royalty option, Amazon charges you a **delivery fee** of 15 cents per MB in the US (the delivery fee varies by country) based on the converted MOBI file size. If you select the 35% royalty option, there is **no** delivery fee.

According to Amazon, the average delivery fee is 6 cents, so in most cases, the delivery fee has little impact on an author's royalties. If you publish a novel, for example, your converted MOBI file size should easily be less than 1 MB (it might even be under 0.5 MB, unless it's a very long novel or includes illustrations).

---

[105] If you did copy or paraphrase content from elsewhere that isn't in the public domain, you're **not** allowed to publish your book *at all* unless you obtained written permission or unless you did so in a way that satisfies the *fair use* law in the US—for other countries, copyright laws vary. Keep in mind that I'm not an attorney. If you have legal questions regarding copyright, the public domain, the fair use law, or any other topic, you should consult an attorney for legal advice. If an author publishes a book for which the author doesn't hold the necessary publishing rights, Amazon may unpublish the book, withhold the royalty payments, or even suspend the author's KDP account.

Select a royalty plan and set your Kindle eBook list prices below

○ 35%

◉ 70%

i Your book file size after conversion is 10.26 MB.

10.26 MB converted file size

Primary Marketplace	List Price		Rate	Delivery	Royalty
Amazon.com ⇕	$ 3.99	USD	35% ▾	$0.00	$1.40
	Why is this price locked? ▾		70%	$1.54	$1.72
Other Marketplaces (12)					⌄

If your converted MOBI file size is more than 1 MB, your eBook probably includes pictures. The more pictures an eBook has, and the larger the pixel size of the images, the greater the file size. When an eBook includes dozens of images, the converted MOBI file size can exceed 10 MB. I have seen eBooks with hundreds of images with converted MOBI file sizes of over 50 MB, but that's rare: Picture books with converted MOBI file sizes ranging from 2 MB to 20 MB is more typical.

My point is that the delivery fee can be significant for a book that includes many **pictures**. For example, if the converted MOBI file size is 10 MB, the delivery fee is $1.50 in the US. Note that the delivery fee is subtracted from the list price *before* applying the 70% rate.

First, I will show you the formulas, and then I will work out a couple of examples. Don't sweat the math: *KDP will do the math for you*. My goal is to show you how the royalties work and to help you choose the appropriate royalty option.

To determine the **delivery fee** (which is only relevant for the 70% royalty option) in the US, multiply your converted MOBI file size (in MB) times $0.15.

$$\text{delivery fee} = \text{file size} \times \$0.15$$

Example: If the converted MOBI file size is 0.4 MB, the delivery fee is 0.4 × $0.15 = $0.06.

Example: If the converted MOBI file size is 2 MB, the delivery fee is 2 × $0.15 = $0.30.

Example: If the converted MOBI file size is 10 MB, the delivery fee is 10 × $0.15 = $1.50.

To determine your **royalty** on the 70% plan in the US, first subtract the delivery fee from the list price and then multiply by 0.7.

$$\text{royalty on 70\% plan} = (\text{list price} - \text{delivery fee}) \times 0.7$$

Example: If the list price is $0.99 and the delivery fee is $0.09, the 70% royalty is ($0.99 – $0.09) × 0.7 = $0.90 × 0.7 = $0.63.

Example: If the list price is $2.99 and the delivery fee is $0.30, the 70% royalty is ($2.99 – $0.30) × 0.7 = $2.69 × 0.7 = $1.88.

Example: If the list price is $2.99 and the delivery fee is $1.50, the 70% royalty is ($2.99 – $1.50) × 0.7 = $1.49 × 0.7 = $1.04.

To determine your **royalty** on the 35% plan in the US, multiply the list price by 0.35. There is **no** delivery fee on the 35% royalty plan.

$$\text{royalty on 35\% plan} = \text{list price} \times 0.35$$

Example: If the list price is $0.99, the 35% royalty is $0.99 × 0.35 = $0.34.

Example: If the list price is $2.99, the 35% royalty is $2.99 × 0.35 = $1.05.

KDP will do this calculation for you. Once you enter a list price and select the desired royalty plan, you will see both the delivery fee and the royalty to the right of your list price. If you choose the 70% royalty plan, KDP will actually show you the royalties for both the 35% and 70% plans so that you can compare.

When setting your list price, note that you must meet KDP's **list price requirements**.

- If you choose the 70% royalty option, your list price can't be less than $2.99 or greater than $9.99 in the US.
- If you choose the 70% royalty option, the list price of your Kindle eBook must be at least 20% lower than the print edition (if you have one) of your book.
- You can only set the list price at $0.99 in the US if you choose the 35% royalty option and your converted MOBI file size is under 3 MB.
- If your converted MOBI file size is between 3 MB and 10 MB, the minimum list price is $1.99 in the US and that requires choosing the 35% royalty option.
- If your converted MOBI file size exceeds 10 MB, the minimum list price is $2.99 in the US regardless of whether you choose the 35% or 70% royalty option.
- If you wish to set a list price higher than $9.99, you must choose the 35% royalty option. The maximum possible list price is $200 in the US.

Deciding on your list price isn't easy, so I will offer a variety of suggestions for you to consider. First of all, *try not to undervalue your work*. Did you put a great deal of time, thought, effort, preparation, and revisions into your work? Did you invest any money in cover design or editing, or did you put additional time and effort into these areas? If you invested much time, effort, or money into delivering what you believe is a quality book to the marketplace, you should expect for customers to pay a **fair** price for your book.

Many authors are tempted to underprice their books. One common notion among new authors is, "Who would pay for a new book by a new author?" Another common idea among new authors is that a lower price should result in more sales. But customers don't buy a **price**. They buy a **book**. *Price itself doesn't sell a book.* Good packaging (cover, description, Look Inside) and good content (the story or information) sells books.

Another issue to consider is **perception**. A common perception among customers is that *you get what you pay for.* So if you price your book too low, what message does your price send to potential customers? Think about that.

My suggestion is to try to think about what might be the *appropriate* **value** of your book. There are cases where a very low list price like $0.99 or $1.99 might be appropriate. For example, suppose that you're publishing a series of **short stories** called *Commuter Fiction*, and you're targeting people who wish to read a short story while riding a train, bus, or subway to work. In this case, you might feel like none of the stories includes enough content to be worth more than $0.99 individually, and you might want to keep the price low so that the customer can read your whole collection over the course of a month.

If you wrote a **full-length novel**, a list price of $0.99 doesn't pay much for all of your effort. At this list price, you would earn a mere $0.34 for each sale. With a negligible delivery fee, you would have to sell at least 7 times as many book priced at $0.99 as you would at $2.99 just to earn the *same* royalty: On the 70% royalty plan, with a negligible delivery fee, you would earn about $2 for each sale at $2.99 compared to $0.34 for each sale at $0.99. A customer may also look at the list price of $0.99 and *wonder if there is a 'reason' that the book is so cheap.*

If your book is eligible for the 70% royalty rate (it isn't in the public domain), *I recommend pricing your book high enough to earn that 70% royalty* (assuming you don't have a very large delivery fee). **Avoid pricing under $2.99** unless your book is somehow *lacking in content* compared to a full-length novel or full-length nonfiction book.

There are a few situations where a lower price may have merit for a full-length book. One case is when you have a **series** (or a set of related books). Pricing the first volume of the series lower can sometimes pay dividends later. Another case is when you're just doing a **short-term promotion** to try to generate a spurt of sales (usually, you need effective marketing to accomplish this: just lowering the price often doesn't drive extra sales). A new author might also have a **low introductory price** to try and grow a fan base, and raise the price later.

Now let's consider list prices of $2.99 and up. Suppose that you have written a full-length novel or equivalent nonfiction book that consists mostly of text with a negligible delivery fee. *If a customer is willing to pay $2.99 for your book, the same customer would probably also be willing to* *pay $3.99 for your book.* It's just a dollar more. There is often a degree of **elasticity of price**, where you can raise your price a little without losing many customers.

With a list price of $2.99 and a negligible delivery fee, your royalty would be about $2.09, whereas with a list price of $3.99 and a negligible delivery fee, your royalty would be about $2.79. In this example, you make $0.70 more with a list price of $3.99 compared to $2.99. Let's suppose that 10% of your potential customers who would have purchased your book at $2.99 decide not to buy it at $3.99. If you would have sold 100 copies at $2.99, you would have earned $209 in total. Since 10% of your potential customers walked away in this example, you would sell 90 copies at $3.99. In this case, you earn a total of $251 by pricing your book at $3.99.

Of course, you don't *know* how many customers would walk away from the higher price. If you knew that, it would be easy to price your book perfectly. Here is another consideration: Would you rather have 10 extra customers, or would you rather make $42 more? *Some authors would prefer to have more readers than more royalties.* (Keep in mind that *the more readers you have who enjoy your work now, the more books you might sell later.*) A lower price doesn't always give you more readers though. If a book is priced lower than what customers perceive to be the appropriate value, *a lower price may actually deter sales.*

A list price of $3.99 or $4.99 is a good fit for many self-published, full-length books with good packaging (cover, description, and Look Inside), **good content** (the story or information), and **good editing**. This price range is above the *low point* ($2.99 or less), helping to establish *perceived value*, and is also a *good value* compared to many traditionally published eBooks.

In general, customers who read Kindle eBooks expect to save money compared to buying print books. *As the list price climbs to $5.99, $6.99, $7.99, and beyond, the higher price starts to deter more sales*, in general. There is a point where the higher price deters more sales than the higher royalty can make up for. **For a new author with a new book, in most cases, it will be hard to generate strong sales with a high list price** ($6.99 or higher). *An author with an effective marketing plan may be able to command a higher price point.* Once you make a name for yourself and grow a substantial fan base, you may also be able to command a higher price point.

Another case where a higher list price may be appropriate for a new author is *when the information in the book is quite valuable* to the target audience. This is the case with certain types of **nonfiction** books and **eTextbooks**. If you have relevant *expertise* or *experience* in a field (be sure to show this in your biography—Sec. 8.2—and perhaps briefly mention it early in your description) and write a nonfiction book that *imparts valuable knowledge to the reader*, you can command a higher price point.

However, pricing above $9.99 may backfire. With a list price of $9.99, you can earn a 70% royalty rate (unless you have a public domain book), which means that you can earn a royalty as high as $6.99 (it will be less if your book has several images, such that there is a significant delivery fee). If you price your book above $9.99, you earn a 35% royalty. **There is almost <u>no</u> benefit to pricing your eBook between $10 and $20.** If you price your eBook at $19.99, for example, you earn a $6.99 royalty at the 35% rate, which is the same royalty that you would earn with a list price of $9.99 at the 70% rate (unless your book has a really large delivery fee). *I would avoid setting the list price higher than $9.99* unless your eBook has a large delivery fee or unless you have a very valuable book that can command a very high eBook price of $24.99 or more.

There is one price point that we haven't yet discussed: **free**. Amazon KDP won't let you set a list price below $0.99 in the US. Therefore, you *can't* adjust your price to free. In most cases, you **shouldn't** want to give away your book for free. However, there are series authors who give the first volume away for free, hoping to hook more readers on the series. A few authors have done this by publishing the eBook with other eBook distributors (Sec. 6.16) in addition to Amazon KDP (which you **aren't** allowed to do if you enroll your eBook in KDP Select), and making the eBook price free on eBook distributors that allow this price point. If the author and/or customers contact Amazon to let Amazon know that a competitor has a lower price, Amazon may choose to price-match. This is one way that some authors have made their eBooks free at Amazon (your royalty would be **zero** in this case). If you succeed in doing this and later change your mind, you will need to contact KDP support to undo it (after raising the price at the other eBook distributors), and Amazon will probably warn you that they won't raise your price in the future if it happens again.

Per Amazon's terms and conditions, you're **not** allowed to set a lower price with other eBook distributors than you set for your Kindle eBook. So, for example, if you price your Kindle eBook at $2.99, you can't set a list price lower than $2.99 anywhere else.

Keep in mind that my suggestions regarding how to set the list price for your eBook are based on general considerations. Your unique book may be different. **You should spend some time browsing the Kindle Store for books similar to yours** (including self-published books, especially by relatively new authors who seem to be having early success—you can learn much by studying their product pages, author pages, and social media pages). This will help you see what list prices similar books set. You can also check their overall sales ranks (Sec. 8.5) in the Kindle Store to see how well those books are selling. Customers who frequently shop in your genre or subject will be familiar with typical price ranges for books like yours, so it would be wise for you to be aware of this, too.

If you enrolled your eBook in **KDP Select** (Sec. 6.12), another consideration is **Kindle Unlimited**. When customers borrow your book through Kindle Unlimited, you are paid based on the number of pages read, and the royalty that you earn isn't related to the list price that you set (the list price that you set only determines the royalty for *paid sales*—Kindle Unlimited borrows aren't sales).

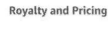

Royalty and Pricing

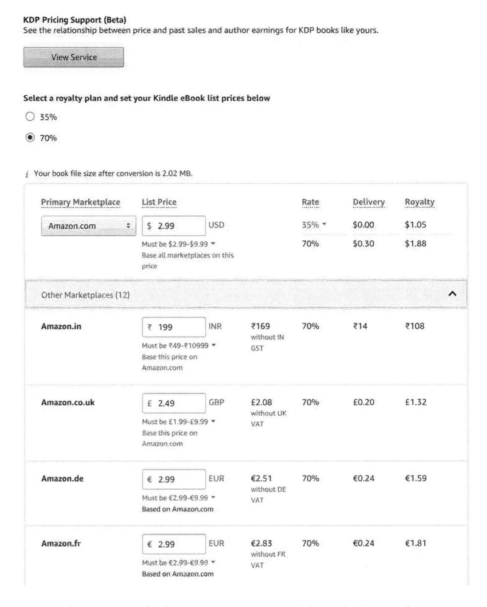

Kindle Unlimited helps you reach customers looking to save money without having to lower your list price. Kindle Unlimited subscribers pay $9.99 per month in the US (that's the rate as of the publication of this book), and can then read as many Kindle Unlimited books per month as they would like. This is a great value for avid readers.

A Kindle Unlimited subscriber would have to read more than 10 books priced at 99 cents each month to justify the expense, whereas a subscriber who reads 4 books priced at $4.99 each month is getting a great value for the money spent. *Kindle Unlimited subscribers who borrow books interpret prices differently than customers who purchase books.* A higher price doesn't deter a Kindle Unlimited borrower. If anything, a higher price may help create a *better perception of value.* However, if you price your book higher and your book doesn't deliver the quality or quantity of content that the customer expects, your book is less likely to receive a valuable review or recommendation—and more likely to receive a critical review. Even with Kindle Unlimited in mind, *you still need a fair price that establishes an appropriate value for your book.*

You may have noticed a yellow button on the pricing page below **KDP Pricing Support** labeled View Service. If you click this button, Amazon's program will attempt to find books similar to yours and show you data that it has on list prices, sales, and royalties. Any information is better than no information, but *you shouldn't interpret this literally as necessarily being the best price for your book.* Depending on what kind of book you have written, the 'similar books *may not be all that similar.* It's worth exploring to see what information it has, but it should just be one piece of information that you consider when setting your list price.

Note that you can change your mind. If you decide to **change your price**, simply visit your Bookshelf, hover your cursor over the gray ellipsis (…) button, and click Edit eBook Pricing. You must **republish** your book in order for your new price to take effect (simply saving without republishing won't change your price in the Kindle Store). *If your book isn't selling, lowering the price probably isn't the solution you're hoping for* (you can always try though). Sec. 8.5 discusses a variety of sales factors.

Until now, I have focused on US prices. List prices and royalties work in a similar fashion in **other countries**, except that the minimum and maximum prices are different, the delivery fees are different, some countries charge a value-added tax (VAT), and a few countries (like Japan and India) only offer a 70% royalty if you enroll your eBook in KDP Select.

When you select a royalty rate and choose a list price, Amazon *automatically* sets your list prices in other countries. You must click the link called **Other Marketplaces** in order to see the list prices and royalties for other countries.

You may adjust the list prices in other countries. *You don't need to use the list price that Amazon automatically sets.* In fact, I recommend that you check the prices that you see in the table and make a few adjustments.

First, you will probably notice that most of your list prices in other countries don't end with 99. **I would adjust all of the prices to end with 99.** For example, if you see a list price of 3.15 in a given currency, consider changing it to 2.99, and if you see a list price of 3.84, consider changing it to 3.99.

Next, check your royalty for each country in the native currency. You might want to Google the current exchange rate to see what the royalty equates to in terms of US dollars. Similarly, check how the list price in that country corresponds to the US list price. If the royalty is less than you feel comfortable with, for example, you might consider raising the price in that country. However, *note that eBook prices tend to be lower in India's market,* so a lower list price and royalty are typical there.

If you look closely, you will also see that most other countries charge a **value-added tax** (VAT) or other tax. (Authors no longer need to calculate the VAT to determine their royalties in other countries.) You set the list price the way that you want it to appear to customers, and Amazon shows you what your royalty will be after subtracting the VAT. Amazon treats the VAT the same way as Amazon treats the delivery charge.

To determine your royalty on the 70% plan, first subtract the delivery fee and the VAT from the list price and then multiply by 0.7. To determine your royalty on the 35% plan, first subtract the VAT from the list price and then multiply by 0.35. There is no delivery fee on the 35% royalty plan. Amazon KDP does this automatically and shows you the results to the right of the table.

$$\text{royalty on 70\% plan} = (\text{list price} - \text{delivery fee} - \text{VAT}) \times 0.7$$
$$\text{royalty on 35\% plan} = (\text{list price} - \text{VAT}) \times 0.7$$

If you run a **Countdown Deal** in the US or the UK (which you can only do if you enroll your eBook in KDP Select—see Sec. 6.12), then you must use my royalty formulas to determine what your royalty will be during the promotion (since KDP doesn't show this when you create your Countdown Deal). If your eBook has a very large delivery fee, *you could actually earn zero royalty during the promotion*, so it's worth doing the math before you run a Countdown Deal.

6.14 MatchBook and Kindle Book Lending

In this section, we will discuss two more Kindle programs:

- MatchBook applies to authors who also publish a **print** edition (Sec. 8.11 describes how to make a paperback edition of your book).
- Kindle Book Lending (which is different from Kindle Unlimited) is required if you choose the 70% royalty rate, but is optional if you choose the 35% royalty rate.

First we'll discuss **MatchBook**. If you publish a print edition to go along with your eBook (or if you've already published the print edition), you may choose to enroll your Kindle eBook in MatchBook. You'll also want to learn how to link the Amazon detail pages for your print and Kindle editions (so that customers who find the page for one version can see that the other version is available, too): Sec. 8.11 discusses how to get the print and Kindle editions linked together (in case the link doesn't occur automatically).

MatchBook offers the customer an *incentive* to purchase *both* the print and Kindle versions of your book. When a customer purchases the print edition **before** purchasing the Kindle edition, if the book is enrolled in MatchBook, the customer will be able to purchase the Kindle edition at a reduced price. You can earn the 70% rate on the reduced price even if your MatchBook price is $0.99 or $1.99 (but the delivery fee will apply as usual). When you set the MatchBook price, Amazon KDP calculates your royalty and displays what your MatchBook royalty will be. (If you make the MatchBook price free, your Kindle royalty will be zero.)

I actually get some MatchBook sales every month, although many authors seldom receive MatchBook sales. Most customers don't discover MatchBook on their own. (It's not as visible on the product page as it could be.) To make the most out of MatchBook, an author needs to do a little marketing to help customers realize the benefits of MatchBook.

Sometimes, it is handy to have both print and eBook editions of the same book. If customers realize this, and if customers know that they can receive a discount on the Kindle edition through MatchBook, more customers would purchase both editions. Here are a couple of examples of **how MatchBook can be helpful for customers**.

- A customer could give the print edition to a family member as a gift, while keeping the Kindle edition for himself or herself. This could come in handy during the holidays.
- If the book is suitable for students, MatchBook lets the student keep the print edition at home, while having access to the Kindle edition at school via a smart phone, tablet, or laptop.

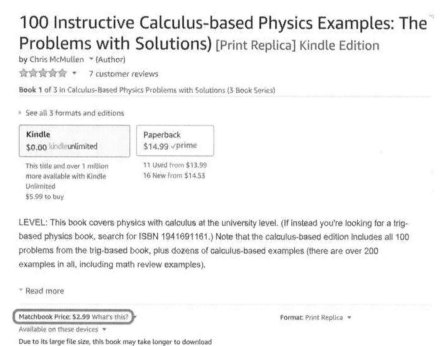

Another program that you must decide on when publishing your Kindle eBook is whether or not to participate in **Kindle Book Lending**. If you opt for the 70% royalty rate, you don't have a choice: In that case, your book is *automatically* enrolled in Kindle Book Lending.

Note that Kindle Book Lending has **nothing** to do with Kindle Unlimited, though authors and customers sometimes confuse the two because of the term "lending."

When Kindle Book Lending is enabled, it allows a customer to loan the Kindle eBook to a **single customer only** (so you don't have to worry about one customer buying your eBook and lending it to multiple people—they *can't* do that). The purpose of Kindle Book Lending is to let a customer lend a Kindle eBook that they have purchased to one friend or family member. The book can only be loaned for up to 14 days, and the original customer won't have access to the book for the duration of the loan.

Few customers use Kindle Book Lending, and since they can only loan the book to one customer one time, *there is very little to worry about.*

6.15 Publishing Your Book

Before you publish your Kindle eBook, read the **KDP terms and conditions**. You will see a link to the KDP terms and conditions below the Book Lending option and below the button to publish your book.

Now you're just one button from making your Kindle eBook available for the whole world to see. Are you ready for this? *You may want to go through the handy checklist in Sec. 6.17.*

- **Have you previewed your eBook thoroughly and carefully?** Are you satisfied that there won't be any formatting, spelling, or grammatical mistakes?
- Have you **proofread** your book details, including the *title*, *subtitle*, *series title*, and *book description*?
- Are you prepared to *market* your book? Have you started marketing already? (Sec. 8.7 will help get you started.)

Once you're ready to publish your Kindle eBook, press the yellow button at the bottom labeled "Publish your Kindle eBook." Your book will probably go live on Amazon.com within 24 hours, and within 72 hours in other countries. Sometimes an eBook goes live on Amazon.com much sooner, but occasionally it may take up to 72 hours. You should receive an email when your eBook goes live. (If your book doesn't go live, you should receive an email with some explanation. For example, you're not supposed to use the word "Kindle" in your keyword list, and if you use the word "Kindle" in your description sometimes they are picky about how you use the word.) Don't contact KDP support unless it has been more than 72 hours since you published your Kindle eBook (and then check your KDP Bookshelf to see what the status is: your KDP Bookshelf may indicate if there was a problem).

Once your Kindle eBook is live, you can view your Amazon product page by clicking a link from your KDP Bookshelf. Hover your cursor over the View on Amazon link, and then click the link for the country where you would like to view your product page. Check your product page carefully, especially your book details: title, subtitle, series title, author name, and book description.

Note that *your product page is built in stages, and that it may take several days to fully develop.* Initially, your product page may only have the essentials. It may take a few days before the Look Inside becomes available. **Once the Look Inside shows up, proofread it carefully for possible formatting issues**: The Look Inside is the most challenging part of your Kindle eBook to format correctly. Also proofread your Look Inside carefully and thoroughly for possible **typos**. Your Look Inside is a highly visible sample of your book, so you want it to be as polished as possible.

I encourage you to read Chapter 8 once your book is published. (It would be wise to read Chapter 8 *before* your book is published.) Chapter 8 will show you how to get a **handy link** that you can share with people you know who might want to read your book, it will help you get started with **marketing**, it will help you setup an Amazon **Author Central** page, it will tell you how to go about making **revisions** (or, if necessary, to unpublish your book), it will show you where to go to publish your book in print or audio formats, and much more.

You should be the first 'customer' to purchase your book. Even if you don't own a Kindle device, you can read your Kindle eBook on one of the many Kindle reading apps (available for PC, Mac, tablet, iPad, iPhone, Android phone, etc.). This way, *if there are any formatting issues with your published eBook, you will be in a position to be the first person to know about it* (and swiftly correct the problem).

The next section discusses how to publish your eBook on **other platforms**, such as Nook and Kobo.

6.16 Other eBook Retailers

Before you publish your eBook with other retailers, like Nook or Kobo, read the following note.

> **Important note**: If you enrolled your Kindle eBook in KDP Select (Sec. 6.12), *you're **not** allowed to publish your eBook anywhere other than with Amazon Kindle.*

Visit your KDP Bookshelf. Hover your cursor over the gray ellipsis (…) button, and choose KDP Select Info. Check the current KDP Select status. If it indicates that your book is enrolled in KDP Select, you *can't* publish your eBook anywhere else unless and until you successfully opt out of KDP Select. **You must do two things in order to properly opt out of KDP Select**: First uncheck the box that says to keep your book enrolled in KDP Select, and also wait until the current 90-day enrollment period has ended. (When the current 90-day enrollment period ends, visit your KDP Bookshelf and check your KDP Select Info just to verify that you have successfully opted out of the program.) Don't publish your eBook anywhere other than with Amazon KDP until your current 90-day enrollment period is over and your eBook is no longer enrolled in KDP Select.

When you proceed to publish your eBook with Nook, Kobo, and other eBook retailers, you face two challenges:

- The **formatting** for Nook, Kobo, and other platforms is a little different from Kindle formatting. You need to research how to format an eBook for other platforms: Specifically, you want to research the little differences between Kindle formatting and other platforms. A few things that we do for Kindle don't work for other eReaders, and there are a few things that you must do for other eReaders that we don't do for Kindle. Note that most other platforms have a much smaller file size limit than Amazon's generous limit (which may be an issue if your eBook has **several images**). The list of **supported characters** may also be different (and a couple of standard characters, like the em dash and ellipsis, may not work as well as they do on Kindle, especially with Amazon's enhanced typesetting in place).
- **There are many brands of eReaders**: Nook, Kobo, Apple, Sony, etc. It's a pain to try and publish with each eReader platform, to research little formatting differences, to upload all of your book details each time, etc. A few platforms don't even let you publish directly with them.

There is a solution which can help you overcome both challenges: Publish your eBook with an **aggregator** such as Smashwords, Draft2Digital, or BookBaby. For example, the free *Smashwords Style Guide* will help ensure that your eBook is properly formatted (your Word document should not be too different from what you already have for Kindle) for Smashwords, and if your book successfully passes through the Smashwords Meatgrinder, you will be able to distribute your eBook with virtually all of the other digital platforms. Smashwords also lets you sell your eBook directly from the Smashwords website, and lets you generate discount codes for your eBook. Draft2Digital and BookBaby are two popular alternatives to Smashwords. I recommend that you choose one of these eBook distributors to help you publish your eBook with other platforms, rather than publishing your eBook with each separate retailer.

www.smashwords.com
www.draft2digital.com
www.bookbaby.com

After you publish your eBook with the aggregator, you will want to try to find out how your eBook looks on Nook, Kobo, Apple, and other devices. If you don't have any of these devices, try to find someone who does. No amount of previewing is better than seeing your actual book on an actual device. (Some of these retailers also have reading apps that you can use on a computer, tablet, or phone.)

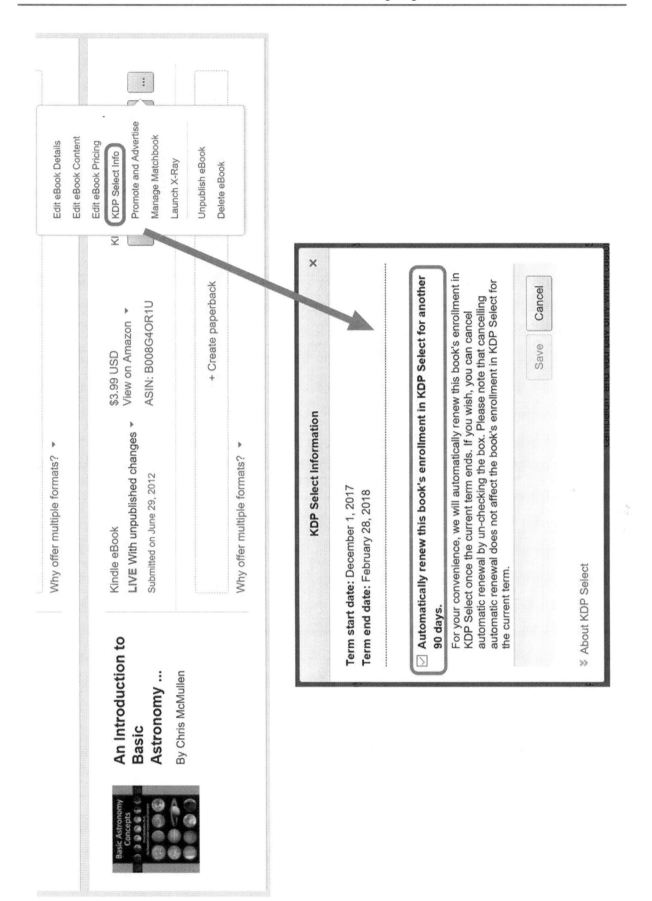

6.17 Publishing Steps Checklist

Following is a quick summary of the steps involved in publishing your Kindle eBook:

- Visit Amazon KDP at https://kdp.amazon.com.

- Log into Amazon KDP. You can login using your Amazon account.

- Visit your KDP Bookshelf. Click the button "+ Kindle eBook" to add a new eBook.

- Select the language for your eBook. (This is the language in which the book was written.)

- Enter the book title. A subtitle is optional. On Amazon, the title and subtitle will show together, separated by a colon.

- If this book is part of a series, enter the title for the series and the volume number. On Amazon, the series title and volume number will show in parentheses after your title and subtitle. Amazon also uses this information to present information about your series to customers, including the option to purchase the entire series at once. (According to the KDP help pages, this may not be available for short stories or novellas.)

- An edition number is optional. If you republish a book with significant changes, you can enter an edition number of 2. If you republish with significant changes again later, you can enter an edition number of 3, and so on.

- Enter the author's name. You may publish with a pen name (provided that your choice of name doesn't create possible confusion with—or otherwise impair—customers' buying decisions).

- Add any other contributors, such as a coauthor or the illustrator of a children's picture book.

- Enter your book description. I recommend that you type this in Word, use Word's spelling and grammar checkers, and proofread this in Word (or print it out on paper first), and then copy and paste your description from Word into the KDP description field. Note that limited HTML is supported (Sec. 6.4), though it may be better to enter plain text now and format your description after you publish (Sec. 8.2).

- Indicate whether you hold the necessary publishing rights or if your book is in the public domain (Sec. 6.5).

- You may enter keywords in up to 7 different keyword fields, as discussed in Sec. 6.6. Each field may contain up to 50 characters. **<u>Don't</u>** use quotation marks or underscores. Separate words with spaces.

- You may choose up to two Amazon browse categories. Note that some categories require a certain combination of keywords (Sec. 6.7).

- For a children's book, you may enter the appropriate age and US grade levels (Sec. 6.7).

- Decide whether you wish to have your Kindle eBook go live when you press the publish button (which appears at the end of page 3 of the publishing process), or if you wish to make your book available for pre-order first (Sec. 6.8).

- Decide whether or not to enable Digital Rights Management (DRM). We discussed this choice in Sec. 6.5.

- Upload the interior book file. Sec. 6.9 recommends which type of file format you should upload depending upon how you made your eBook.

- Upload the cover file in JPEG or TIFF format. Sec. 6.10 lists some cover design tips.

- Preview your book thoroughly and carefully, following Chapter 7.

- An ISBN and publisher name are optional. Note that you're not supposed to use the same ISBN as your print book, and you're not supposed to use an ISBN that you got from an eBook distributor like Smashwords. There really is no advantage to having an ISBN for your Kindle edition, as every Kindle eBook is automatically assigned an ASIN (Amazon Standard Identification Number).

- Decide whether or not to enroll in KDP Select. This was discussed at length in Sec. 6.12.

- Select the territories where you hold the distribution rights for your eBook.

- Select either the 35% or the 70% royalty option (Sec. 6.13). If your book is in the public domain, you must select the 35% option. Otherwise, you should select the 70% option unless your book has such a large file size (usually, from several images) that the royalty would actually be larger with the 35% option. You don't have to guess: Look at the royalties that Amazon KDP displays at the right side of the table.

- Enter the list price for the US.

- Click the link to view the pricing and royalty info in other marketplaces. Check your royalties and list prices. You may adjust any of these list prices if you wish (Sec. 6.13 recommends that you make a few little changes).

- If you have a print edition of your book, you may choose to enroll your book in Kindle MatchBook and set a MatchBook price for your Kindle eBook (Sec. 6.14).

- If you choose the 70% royalty option, your book must be enrolled in Kindle Book Lending (which has nothing to do with Kindle Unlimited). If you choose the 35% royalty option, you must decide whether or not to enable Kindle Book Lending (Sec. 6.14).

- Read the KDP terms and conditions.

- When you have previewed your book and book details carefully and are ready to publish your Kindle eBook, take a deep breath and click the yellow button.

- Usually in less than 24 hours, but sometimes it takes 72 hours, you should receive an email that your Kindle eBook is now live at Amazon.com (or an email explaining that there is a problem). It may take a couple of more days for other countries. You can also check on the status from your KDP Bookshelf.

- Once your Kindle eBook goes live, visit your product page. Check the book details and description carefully. It may take a few days for the Look Inside to show. Once the Look Inside becomes available, check it carefully. If you need to make changes (or unpublish your eBook), see Sec. 8.4.

- Read Chapter 8 to learn more about your book's Amazon product page, how to setup an author page at **Author Central**, several **marketing** tips, how customer **reviews** work, how **sales rank** works, promotional prices, contests and giveaways, gifting your book, how to make a **paperback** edition, how to make an audio book, pirate sites, and how to add **X-Ray** to your Kindle eBook (a cool new feature that you can implement from KDP).

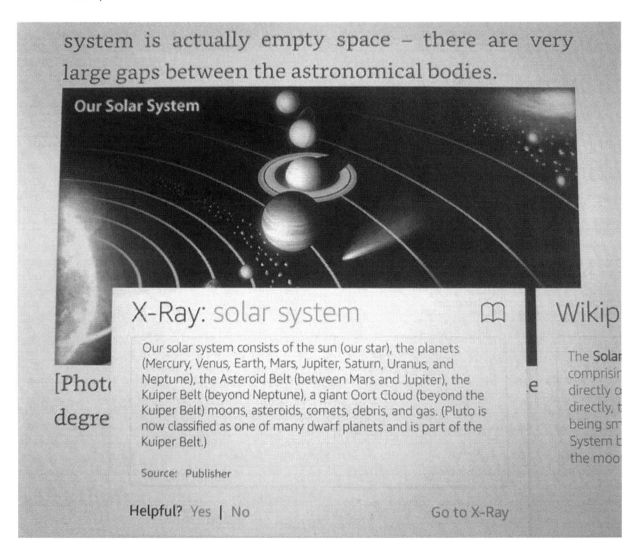

—Chapter 7—

Preview

7.1 What to Look for in a Preview

WHEN YOU PREVIEW your eBook, imagine that you are already your own first customer. As you begin to look through your book, consider what impression it might make. How does it look as you pass the front matter on your way to Chapter 1? Does anything seem odd or out of place? As you read the text, do you notice anything that seems like it might be a typo? Imagine the variety of things that may distract a customer (even subconsciously). Your goal is try to catch as many of those things as possible *before* you publish your book. The different preview options will help you with this. Slow down, take your time, and try to keep your eyes fresh. This stage of the publishing process demands much patience.

> **Note**: If you just need to make a quick test file, and you're not yet ready to do a thorough preview of your eBook, skip ahead to Sec. 7.2.

There are a variety of things that you should look for when you preview you Kindle eBook:

- Are there formatting problems, like indents where you don't want them (or missing indents where you do want them), paragraphs that aren't aligned or justified as you intended, or images that don't display as you expected? Sec. 7.4 lists a variety of **formatting** issues that you should look for when previewing your book.
- Does the formatting look good across *all* devices and apps? Does it look good on both color and black-and-white devices? Does it look good in **night mode**, with a sepia background, and with a green background? Sec.'s 7.7 thru 7.9 will help you test your Kindle eBook out.
- Are there spelling or grammar mistakes? Sec. 7.5 has suggestions for common **proofreading** mistakes to check for.
- Does the writing flow well? Are there any plot holes (for fiction)? Is the information clear and logically ordered (for nonfiction)? Sec. 7.6 offers some ideas for what to look for in the way of **editing** (beyond simple proofreading).

It's virtually impossible to catch all kinds of mistakes at a single sitting. You really need to go through your book multiple times, each time focusing on something different.

I recommend printing out a **hard copy** (or creating a proof for a print edition), and reading the hard copy carefully to help with proofreading and editing (Sec. 7.10): Research shows that our brains don't process digital text that we read on a screen the same way as we process printed text on a page. I always catch several typos in print that I had missed on the screen. Using **text-to-speech** (see Sec. 7.5) can also help you catch some typos: Certain types of mistakes are sometimes more obvious when you *hear* them.

Once you are satisfied with proofreading and other stages of editing, you can focus on scrolling through the various preview options for possible formatting issues.

Note: If you followed Chapter 5 of this book, read Sec. 5.3 before you make any revisions to your HTML file, and read Sec.'s 5.3 and 5.5 if you need to make changes to any pictures.

7.2 Previewing Just to Run a Test

If you haven't finished formatting your eBook and you're not ready to publish yet, but wish to make a quick preview (or if you just want to see what your current converted MOBI file size is), you can skip most of the steps of the publishing process and run a quick test by following these steps:

- Login to Amazon KDP: http://kdp.amazon.com. If you want, you can sign into KDP with an existing Amazon account.
- Click on the Bookshelf link at the top of the page.
- Click on button labeled "+ Kindle eBook."
- Enter something like "Test Book" in the title field (since we're just creating a test, not publishing the actual book). You can just type "test" for the author's last name and for the book description.
- You must choose a publishing option and *some* category in order to move onto the next page. (It won't matter: If you wish, you can delete your 'test' book when you finish. Once you're ready to actually publish a book, you can start over by adding a new Kindle eBook.)
- Leave everything else blank for now. There is no reason to enter keywords, for example, just to make a test run.
- Click the yellow Save and Continue button at the bottom of the page.
- Choose a DRM option. Click the Upload eBook Manuscript button. Find and select your test file.
- If you made a compressed zipped folder following the directions in Sec. 5.2, upload the compressed zipped folder (be sure to read Sec. 5.3 to ensure that you saved it properly, especially if you used Notepad). If your book has pictures, read Sec. 5.5 to make sure that your latest pictures are included with your file. If you made an HTML file, and don't have pictures, upload your HTML file (again, read Sec. 5.3 first), unless you went a step beyond Chapter 5 and created an ePub or MOBI file (for a MOBI file, read the note in Sec. 6.9). If you just worked with Word, upload your DOCX or DOC file (Sec. 1.2 discusses the difference). If you used one of the free Kindle apps (Kindle Create, the Kindle Kids' Book Creator, the Kindle Textbook Creator, or the Kindle Comic Creator), upload the KPF or MOBI file. (Note that PDF, TXT, and RTF are **not** recommended: PDF, especially, tends to be problematic.)

- It may take some time to upload your file. If you encounter any issues, sometimes switching web browsers (Explorer, FireFox, or Chrome, for example) or updating your web browser resolves the issue. (If you uploaded a KPF file, the wait can be several minutes or more. If you receive an error message uploading a KPF file, try again with another web browser, and if it persists, you may need try it again another day. It happens occasionally with KPF files.)

- (If your only goal with the test was to determine the converted MOBI file size, and if you're not interested in previewing your eBook yet, skip down to the bullet point that begins, "If you also want to check your converted MOBI file size.")

- Once your file uploads successfully, there are two ways to preview your book on KDP. One is the Preview Book button (Sec. 7.7). The second option is to click the Download Book Preview File link and also click the link below Download Previewer (Sec. 7.8). I recommend trying *both* preview options. The downloadable previewer includes a few options that aren't available on the online previewer (like the option to change the background color). The downloadable previewer is also considered to be the more reliable previewer (pictures, for example, may not display properly on the online previewer).

- In each preview, check how your book looks on every type of device, including tablet, phone, and eReader. Note that no single mode, such as tablet mode, can properly mimic every possible device of that kind (like Fire, iPad, Samsung, etc. for tablet). Thus, if you do something nonstandard (like using a nonstandard symbol), seeing that it turns out okay in the preview isn't a guarantee that it will work across all devices.

- In addition to previewing how your eBook looks on each device, you may also want to see how your eBook (or specific features therein) look in landscape mode, night mode, with a sepia background, or with a green background. You may also want to explore what happens as you vary the font size, click on links, or zoom in on your images. Note that night mode, a sepia background, a green background, and the option to zoom in on images are only available with the *downloadable* previewer. We'll discuss how to preview your Kindle eBook more thoroughly in the remaining sections of this chapter: If you're just making a quick test, it may be sufficient for your test just to preview quickly for now (depending on the reason for your test).

- *The truest results come from sideloading your eBook onto actual devices.* If you wish to do this with your test book, you can find instructions in Sec. 7.9.

- **If you also want to check your converted MOBI file size**, simply press the yellow Save and Continue button in order to advance to page 3 of the publishing process. (It isn't necessary to upload a cover just to run a test: The only things you need to complete on page 2 right now are selecting your DRM option and uploading the interior book file.)

- On page 3 of the publishing process, scroll down to Royalty and Pricing. Just above the pricing and royalty table, look for the words, "Your book file size after conversion is ___ MB." That's where you will find the converted MOBI file size for your test book in megabytes. If you click the 70% royalty option and enter a price in the range $2.99 to $9.99, KDP will also show you your delivery fee and prospective royalty. Click the Other Marketplaces link to see your delivery fee and prospective royalty in other countries. (Prices and royalties are discussed at length in Sec. 6.13.) Note that the delivery fee only applies to the 70% royalty option.

- Be careful **not** to press the yellow Save and Publish button. As long as you don't click that button, your test book will not go live. If you wish to delete the test book from your Bookshelf, visit your Bookshelf and hover your cursor over the gray ellipsis (…) button, then click Delete. You might prefer to leave the test book there (with the title Test Book) for any future test books that you might wish to upload and preview (if so, anytime you visit your Bookshelf, you should see that it's in Draft mode, and you'll know that it hasn't been published).

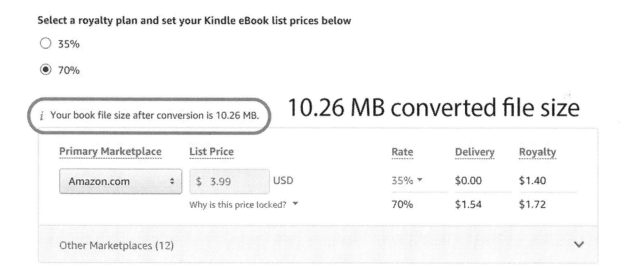

7.3 The Most Important Publishing Step

A thorough and careful preview is your opportunity to catch as many potential mistakes (both formatting and editing) as possible before your book hits the market. You only get one chance to make a good impression as an author, so you want your first book to be as good as you can plausibly make it.

When you've put so much time into writing, formatting, and preparing to publish, and you've finally reached the preview stage, it's common to feel an overwhelming sense to "just finish up and press that publish button." As tempting as it may to be preview quickly and press that golden publish button, it's better if you can overcome that urge, find some patience, preview carefully, and publish with the peace of mind that you did everything that was reasonably in your control to deliver a quality book to the market.

Imagine being a customer for a moment. When you pay money for a product, you expect to receive a quality product. How would you feel if you purchased a product that a manufacturer didn't test out, and you discovered a problem with the functionality of the product? By the same token, when a customer purchases your book, that customer will expect your book to be virtually free of formatting and editing mistakes.

If you're human, there will be an occasional, minor mistake. When you first preview your book, usually there are quite a few mistakes that you can and should catch. You want to fix those until your book just has a very rare and minor mistake that is very difficult for you (or anyone else) to notice.

Iron out your book description and Look Inside to virtual perfection because any mistakes that customers see before they buy your book may result in a lost sale. *If customers see multiple mistakes in these short and highly visible writing samples, they will expect the entire book to be riddled with such mistakes.*

If customers notice more than just a rare typo after buying your book, they may choose to stop reading. Too many mistakes—spelling, grammatical, and formatting—might also determine whether or not they choose to recommend your book to others. Customers may also call attention to mistakes in reviews.

Every mistake that you catch and fix *before* you publish means that your book will have fewer mistakes *after* you publish.

That feeling that you probably have now, like you really want to get your book published… so that you can feel that great sense of accomplishment… Well, that feeling gets replaced by another feeling once you press the publish button: It gets replaced with a feeling of **anxiety**, where *you begin to wonder if people will buy your book and what people will say about your book in customer reviews.*

Remember that. The more time you put into previewing your book, and the more mistakes you catch and fix now, the more **confidence** you should have that your book is virtually free of errors. When that feeling of anxiety comes up after publishing, remind yourself that you did everything you reasonably could. *There should be no reason to feel regret.*

7.4 Formatting Checklist

Read through the following list of common formatting issues before you preview your book. When you have these issues on your mind, it may help make it easier to catch them. A few of these issues are illustrated in pictures at the end of Sec. 7.11.

Keep in mind that this is *not* a comprehensive list of *every* possible problem. These are many of the common problems, but not all of them. You don't want your book to have *any* formatting issues, common or uncommon. Look at each 'page' and ask yourself if anything seems unusual or out of place: This can help you find other potential problems.

Note: The following checklist is specifically for a reflowable eBook made as described in this book. (If you used the Kindle Kids' Book Creator, Kindle Textbook Creator, or Kindle Comic Creator, many of the items on this checklist do not apply to your fixed-format book.)

What should you do if you encounter one or more of the following formatting problems? **Sec. 7.11 will help you troubleshoot the problem.**

- The most common formatting problem found in Kindle eBooks relates to **paragraph indentation**. Are any paragraphs missing indentations? Is the size of the indentation the same in every paragraph? Are there are any paragraphs or lines that weren't supposed to be indented, but which appear to be indented?
- Examine the *vertical* spacing between consecutive lines. Is the **line spacing** consistent? Do you see some paragraphs with tight line spacing, and others with loose line spacing?
- Also check the **space between paragraphs**. Do you see more space between paragraphs than you expected? Did you want space between paragraphs that you're not seeing? (For most types of books, the space between *paragraphs* of text should be no different than the space between *lines* of text—meaning that *no space* should be added between two text paragraphs. The exception is called block paragraphs, which we discussed in Sec. 3.7.)
- Do you see any unexpected **line breaks** in the middle of a paragraph? If so, occasionally this is caused by a long word that didn't quite fit on the previous line, but it could also be a formatting mistake. (Sec. 7.11 will help you tell the difference.)
- Check the text **alignment** of your body text *paragraphs*. Is the alignment consistent among all of the paragraphs of your book? (They should either be justified or ragged right, not some of each—unless, for example, you have bullet points, and you want your bullet points to be ragged right while you want your body text to be justified, as discussed in Sec. 3.7.)

- Also check the text **alignment** of *headings* and subheadings: These should either be centered or left-aligned. You don't want justified headings. One way to look for justified headings (and to see how it can be a problem) during a preview is to (temporarily) make the text size somewhat large (but not drastic) and choose a device with a smaller screen.

- If you used **drop caps** (or any other way of emphasizing the first letter or first words of a chapter), check them all carefully. Try adjusting the text size and line spacing (this can be adjusted on an actual device or app) in the preview to make sure that the drop caps look good across all settings. Also preview drop caps carefully across all devices.

- **Does the body text change font size?** Your body text should have a consistent font size throughout the book. (Headings and special types of paragraphs may appear larger.)

- Do you see any unexpected **page breaks**? If so, first check to see whether they may have been caused by a picture at the top of the next 'page.' Also try switching between portrait and landscape orientation, and adjusting the font size in the preview, to see if the page break persists. If so, there is a forced page break that needs to be removed from your file.

- Is any text **missing**? Do you see any **duplicated** text?

- Check for **boldfaced**, *italicized*, and <u>underlined</u> text. Are there any paragraphs that have boldfaced, italicized, or underlined text, which shouldn't have it? Is there any text that should appear boldfaced, italicized, or underlined, which doesn't?

- Check different parts of the body text of your book to **ensure that the font size changes** when the customer adjusts the font size and that **the typeface of the font changes** when the customer selects a different font style.

- Click on each link in your **table of contents** to ensure that it jumps to the correct location.

- Check all of your **hyperlinks**, including external hyperlinks (to websites) and internal hyperlinks (that is, links that take the reader to a specific location within the eBook). Click on the links to ensure that they work as intended.

- Are there any **blank pages**?

- When you first open the preview, try to back up to any previous pages (in case the preview doesn't open at the location of the book cover). Is the **cover** *missing*? Do you see a **double cover** (where the cover image repeats itself at the beginning of the preview)?

- Do you see any **pictures** that have an unexpected **black or gray line at one or more of the edges**? (These are called *drop shadows*.) If so, this usually results from uploading a Word document instead of following the steps outlined in Sec. 5.2 to create a compressed zipped folder. Note: This issue might show in the actual book even if you don't see it in a preview.

- Look for **missing pictures**. For this, it helps to know the layout of your book well (or have a printed hard copy handy), so that you can see places where there *should* be a picture, but the picture *isn't* there. However, you can also look for little **camera icons** like the one shown below. If you see this icon anywhere in your preview, it's a problem: Anywhere you see a camera icon, a customer will **not** be able to see the picture that was supposed to be there.

- Check the **size** of your **images** on a variety of devices with different sized screens. Check your images in both portrait and landscape orientation. Do the images appear about as large or small as you intended? Note: The downloadable preview may display pictures more reliably than the online previewer.
- Check the **aspect ratio** of your images (this is different from just the size). If the aspect ratio is different than intended, the pictures will appear distorted (either too narrow or too wide for the height).
- Are your **images** *clear, sharp,* and *centered* (if that's how you aligned them)?
- Make sure that any **text** that appears in your images is *legible, sharp,* and *clear.*
- Do your color images look fine on a screen with a black-and-white display?
- How do your *images* look in **night mode**, with a **sepia** background, and a **green** background? Note: You must use the downloadable previewer or sideload to an actual device in order to check this feature.
- How does your *text* look in **night mode**, with a **sepia** background, and a **green** background? If you changed the text color anywhere, you want to ensure that it reads well on any background. With night mode, you want to scan the *entire* file: If any text completely disappears, it's probably a sign that you set the text color to black (instead of leaving it automatic in Word, or instead of removing the text-color designation from the HTML).
- If you used **special symbols** or nonstandard characters, search for these to ensure that they display across all devices. Note: If you used any symbols that aren't listed in Appendix A, beware that there may be some actual devices (including older devices) that may not support them. It's possible that a symbol that isn't on the list will show on all of the devices for which Amazon offers a preview, but won't display correctly on an actual device for which there isn't a proper preview.

- If you applied any **text effects** other than boldface, underlining, italics, strikethrough, superscripts, and subscripts—like highlighting—check these features across all devices to ensure that they work. Note: There are many text effects that Word offers (such as shadows or outlines), which will **<u>not</u>** work on one or more actual devices. Similarly, there are many paragraph effects that Word offers (such as borders and shading), which will **<u>not</u>** work on one or more actual devices.

- Check that your **tables** display in full, and that all of the information in your table is easy to read even on a device with a small screen. According to the KDP help pages, your table should not be cut off at the bottom of the screen when a font size of 3 (the default user setting) is selected. Otherwise, you should split the table into smaller tables. **Note**: Tables sometimes display incorrectly in the Kindle previewer and on Kindle for PC. If you have tables, this makes it a priority to test your eBook out on an actual device (Sec. 7.9).

- If you typed any **equations** in your eBook, you want to ensure that they are displaying properly on every possible device. Note: Many of the common ways of creating equations (like the Insert > Equation option in Word) result in a variety of **problems** on one or more actual devices (and it might be worse on a few devices for which there aren't proper previews). If your eBook includes any math, I recommend that you review Sec.'s 3.11, 4.9, and 5.5 before proceeding. If you made different equations different ways, you want to preview each type of equation.

- Do you see any **page numbers** in your eBook? (You shouldn't. If you do, you need to remove them.)

- Look closely to see if any **spelling or grammar marks** from your Word file have carried over into your Kindle eBook. These are rare, but it has happened (usually, from not converting from Word to HTML properly). If it happens, it is easy to find and remove them from your HTML file (Sec. 5.7).

- Spend some time previewing different features of your eBook on a wide **variety of devices**, using both **portrait** and **landscape** orientation. Try adjusting the reader's settings for the *text size*, *line spacing*, and *margins*. Note that the downloadable previewer includes options that you can't find in the online previewer (such as previewing different font styles, changing the background color, and quickly checking your images and links).

- Also spend some time previewing your eBook where you *select a device with a small screen and choose a very large text size*. This makes certain issues more pronounced to help you catch them, but most of the time you want to preview your eBook with settings that are more typical of what most customers will see. Note: The rare customers who choose a very large font size on a very small screen should be accustomed to some degree of formatting issues.

- Note that there are other formatting issues that aren't on the list. If you see anything that seems unusual or out of place, ask yourself if you could prevent that (without making the problem worse or introducing a new problem).

- There are a few subtle issues that you really can't do anything about, such as Kindle's justification (although Amazon has new typography features for Kindle devices and apps that support them, which does help). We discussed a few of these issues, such as orphans and justification, in Sec. 3.7. If you have an eye for typography (or if you have print formatting experience), you must be careful not to try to 'fix' a subtle issue for which the 'solution' may only make the problem worse.

Tip: If you come across other formatting issues, write down the issue and the solution (after you solve the problem). A list of formatting issues that you've dealt with in the past will be handy when you publish your next book.

Tip: Read Kindle eBooks. (If you don't have a Kindle device, try reading on a PC, laptop, phone, or tablet using a Kindle app.) The more experience you have reading Kindle eBooks on different devices, the more experience you will have with how Kindle eBook formatting should look and what some common problems are.

Tip: Find knowledgeable eBook formatters who share tips and advice regarding Kindle formatting. They might maintain a blog or website with such information, for example. (Of course, you're welcome to follow my blog at https://chrismcmullen.com.)

Tip: There isn't a foolproof way to preview the **Look Inside**. However, previewing your eBook as a webpage can help to catch a few problems that would show up in the Look Inside, but which wouldn't show up on other methods of previewing your eBook. To learn how to do this from a Word file, see Sec. 3.14, and for HTML, see the last paragraph of Sec. 7.10. For example, the Look Inside strips out page breaks and blank lines, displaying your preview similar to how it would show as a webpage. If you view your eBook in Web Layout and don't see space between the last paragraph of a chapter and the chapter heading that follows, try applying a paragraph style to the last paragraph of the previous chapter that adds Spacing After in Word (or margin-bottom in HTML).

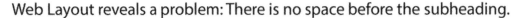

Web Layout reveals a problem: There is no space before the subheading.

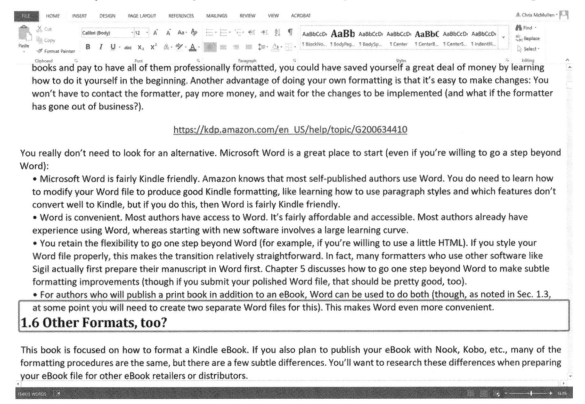

books and pay to have all of them professionally formatted, you could have saved yourself a great deal of money by learning how to do it yourself in the beginning. Another advantage of doing your own formatting is that it's easy to make changes: You won't have to contact the formatter, pay more money, and wait for the changes to be implemented (and what if the formatter has gone out of business?).

https://kdp.amazon.com/en_US/help/topic/G200634410

You really don't need to look for an alternative. Microsoft Word is a great place to start (even if you're willing to go a step beyond Word):
- Microsoft Word is fairly Kindle friendly. Amazon knows that most self-published authors use Word. You do need to learn how to modify your Word file to produce good Kindle formatting, like learning how to use paragraph styles and which features don't convert well to Kindle, but if you do this, then Word is fairly Kindle friendly.
- Word is convenient. Most authors have access to Word. It's fairly affordable and accessible. Most authors already have experience using Word, whereas starting with new software involves a large learning curve.
- You retain the flexibility to go one step beyond Word (for example, if you're willing to use a little HTML). If you style your Word file properly, this makes the transition relatively straightforward. In fact, many formatters who use other software like Sigil actually first prepare their manuscript in Word first. Chapter 5 discusses how to go one step beyond Word to make subtle formatting improvements (though if you submit your polished Word file, that should be pretty good, too).
- For authors who will publish a print book in addition to an eBook, Word can be used to do both (though, as noted in Sec. 1.3, at some point you will need to create two separate Word files for this). This makes Word even more convenient.

1.6 Other Formats, too?

This book is focused on how to format a Kindle eBook. If you also plan to publish your eBook with Nook, Kobo, etc., many of the formatting procedures are the same, but there are a few subtle differences. You'll want to research these differences when preparing your eBook file for other eBook retailers or distributors.

7.5 Proofreading Checklist

It's best to focus on proofreading and formatting issues at *separate sittings*. Proofreading requires much time, as you must carefully read through the entire book, and looking for formatting mistakes can distract you from the focus required to catch little typos. Checking your formatting is quicker, as it just requires studying each 'page' for enough moments to identify any visual problems (though you shouldn't check formatting *quickly*—**taking your time when your eyes are fresh** will help you catch the most mistakes). I prefer to proofread first, since it's possible to introduce a new formatting issue when making the corrections to the proofreading.

Although when I sit down to proofread, I'm focused on finding mistakes in the *writing*, rather than *formatting* issues, when I do happen to notice a formatting issue while proofreading I note it down (so that I don't miss it later). In this section, I'll list common proofreading issues, and in the next section, I will list additional editing issues that go beyond a simple proofreading.

Personally, I prefer to make my first proofread with a **hard copy** printed on paper, and the next proofread with a digital version. There is research to show that how we process information that we read is actually different when reading printed text compared to reading digital text (although they both involve reading text, the brain evidently processes the task a little differently). I always find mistakes in print that I miss when reading digital text, and the printed page is convenient as it lets me write comments in the margins (though it is possible to highlight and take notes with many digital readers), so I prefer to do my first proofread in print. If you're wondering how to go about making a printed copy, read Sec. 7.10.

I also prefer to proofread my book carefully before I reach the HTML stage of the formatting. Especially, if you use Notepad to edit the HTML, revisions to the text are more convenient *before* you convert from Word to HTML. (Recall in Sec. 5.3 that we discussed Notepad and a couple of alternatives for editing HTML. Note that some other HTML editors that we *didn't* discuss are **not** ideal for making a Kindle eBook. I recommend working with Notepad, Notepad++, or Sigil.)

- You want to check the **spelling** and **grammar** carefully. (If these are not your strong suits, you might seek the help of a professional proofreader or editor.) Note that Word's spelling and grammar checker does **not** catch many common typos. For example, if you accidentally miss the first "o" while typing "thorough," you instead type the word "through," which is still a valid word, so a spellchecker might not catch this mistake. There is a program called Grammarly that can help with spelling and grammar, but it also isn't foolproof. **Note:** If you made corrections to the text in your eBook after creating an HTML file, there is a way to check the spelling and grammar of your HTML file: Open your HTML file as a webpage. For example, if you open your HTML file with Word (open Word and choose File > Open), it will open it as a webpage, and Word's spelling and grammar checker can be used to flag possible mistakes. **However, don't make changes to your HTML file in Word, and don't save your HTML file in Word.** Instead, note where the problems are, find the same locations in your HTML file with a program like Notepad or Sigil (as discussed in Sec. 5.3), and save the changes to your HTML file instead. Simply close Word without saving your HTML file.

- Keep a **dictionary** handy and use it to check the spelling of anything you're not sure about. Similarly, it may help to have a grammar book handy, such as *The Chicago Manual of Style*. **Note**: If you use *text-to-speech* software, it *won't* help you catch many simple misspellings.

- When you see the words "its" and "it's," make sure that you didn't accidentally mix them up: "it's" should only be used if it would make sense to say "it is" in place of "it's," whereas "its" indicates a sense of belonging. **Examples**: *It's* a beautiful day. That paint lost *its* shine.

- Check if "there," "their," and "they're" are used correctly: "They're" means the same as "they are," "there" is a place, and "their" refers to something that belongs to "them." **Examples**: I left my book *there*. They left *their* books behind. *They're* far away now.

- Look for other pairs of words that sound alike (called **homophones**). It's easy to accidentally make a homophone mistake while writing, even when you're very knowledgeable about the difference: The trick is to catch and fix your mistake when proofreading. A few more examples include are/our, to/too/two, wear/where, and one/won. **Note**: If you use *text-to-speech* software, it *won't* help you catch problems with homophones.

- **Repeated words** like "the the" and "that that" are often overlooked. It seems like they should be obvious, but the combination of the eye and mind sometimes see what they should be (a single word) instead of what they really are (repeated words). Microsoft Word can identify some of these (it underlined my second "the" above), but not all of them (in fact, it didn't underline my second "that" above because there are actually sentences in English where it can make sense to write "that that"). You can use Word's Find tool to search for "the the," "that that," "and and," (without the quotes) and other common repeated words. Text-to-speech software is also helpful for catching repeated words.

- Search for **capitalization** mistakes, not just with the first letter of a sentence, but also with proper nouns (like Wednesday, Albert Einstein, or California). **Note**: If you use *text-to-speech* software, it *won't* help you catch problems with capitalization.

- Double-check that **contractions** like can't, that's, don't, isn't, and won't are used properly.

- Sometimes, a slight **misspelling** of one word results in the wrong word. For example, suppose that you meant to type the "through," but the 'r' got left out by accident: In that case, you would type "though," which is also a word. A spellcheck may not catch such a mistake, since the result is still a valid word. If you actively think through your proof-reading, slow yourself down, and take breaks to rest your eyes and feel refreshed, it improves your chances for catching these little mistakes.

- Check your **punctuation marks**, especially commas and dashes. Make sure that you were consistent with your dashes: Either use the short dash (–) or the long dash (—), but not both (Sec.'s 2.7 and 3.7). Also, make sure that you didn't accidentally use a hyphen (-) where a dash should be used: A dash serves to separate ideas, whereas a hyphen connects short words together to make a compound word. If you made a print edition first, make sure that you don't have any stray manual hyphens that you may have used to improve paragraph formatting (those will appear out of place in an eBook). Keep a grammar book handy to help with punctuation, such as *The Chicago Manual of Style*. **Note**: If you use *text-to-speech* software, it *won't* help you catch problems with punctuation marks.

- Make sure that present (like "he runs fast") and past **tense** (like "he ran fast") aren't mixed up. Similarly, check singular and **plural** forms (like "that tomato" and "those tomatoes"). Another thing to check is **subject** and **verb agreement** (a simple example of such a mistake is "they was" instead of "it was" or "they were").

- Any time you read (or write) something where you don't feel 100% confident with the rules of English, look it up in a **grammar book**. *The Chicago Manual of Style* is a popular recommendation, but there are viable alternatives. There will surely be readers who know the rules and conventions well. When you do look something up in a grammar book, write it down. This list will be handy when you write and proofread future books.

- Not all proofreading mistakes involve rules of English. For example, if you refer to Chapter 3, figure 7, or table 9, check to make sure that the number is correct. (If not, it will be really frustrating for any reader who proceeds to find the referenced object.) If you referred to a page number, that's a **mistake** for your eBook and must be replaced by a different choice of words (or an internal hyperlink—see Sec.'s 3.10 and 5.8) unless you created a fixed-format eBook (for example, by using the Kindle Kids' Book Creator or the Kindle Textbook Creator).

- This is not a comprehensive list of all kinds of proofreading mistakes. If you would like to see more examples of common proofreading issues to look for, try entering "proof-reading tips" (but without the quotes) or a similar phrase in a search engine.

Tip: A text-to-speech program can help you catch a few kinds of mistakes. Certain mistakes are obvious when you hear them, such as missing words, incorrect tense, repeated words, or mistaking singular and plural. However, text-to-speech is **not** a substitute for proofreading, as there are many common mistakes that it **won't** help with (like homophones, capitalization, punctuation, and many common misspellings).

Tip: Make a list of the different kinds of proofreading mistakes that you find in your book. This customized checklist will be useful when you publish your next book.

Tip: Proofread your corrections carefully: *It's very common to introduce a new mistake when you make revisions.* Your eyes are strained from all of the proofreading, and it's easy to feel impatient. Get a good night's sleep and read through each of your revisions carefully with a fresh pair of eyes.

Note that if you already have separate files for a print edition and an eBook edition, remember to make any proofreading revisions to *both* files.

7.6 Editing Checklist

As I mentioned in the previous section, when it comes to editing (beyond simple proofreading), I prefer to do this with a **printed** copy of my manuscript, and I do this *before* converting my Word file to HTML.

Following are some examples of editing that is more involved than just looking for spelling and grammar mistakes.

- Look for places where you 'tell' information that might have been better to 'show.' As a simple example, instead of writing, "She was visibly angry," you could describe how she looked ("She clenched her jaw") or what she did ("She jostled him in the elbow as she passed by"). A common place where we tell rather than show is when we use an adverb like "quickly" or "wonderfully." However, note that there are occasions when it may be better to tell rather than show: For example, you may not want to disrupt an action scene to 'show' a minor point when 'telling' it quickly in passing would help to keep the action going. In cases where showing serves as an unnecessary distraction, telling may be better—but the more common mistake is to tell when we should show.

- With fiction, you want to make sure that there aren't holes in your plot, that you resolve all subplots, that characters have enough dimension, and so on. You can find handy checklists online to help edit your plot, characters, setting, point of view, and scenes—and even things like conflict and the pace of your story. You can even go beyond *editing*, and think in terms of *marketing*. For example, does the story **create enough interest** in the beginning, does it **hook the reader early** and continue to do so, and will the ending **satisfy** the reader?

- For nonfiction, double-check the *subject matter* and *content*. This is the heart of a non-fiction book, so you want to make sure that the information is **accurate**, **clear**, and **logically ordered**.

- Check your **facts**. This applies to both fiction and nonfiction.

- How well does your writing **flow**? Does the sentence structure vary? Does it read well? Will readers stumble through the words? If such ideas are on your mind when you read your book, it is easier to catch such things. Reader **feedback** can also help with this. (You can potentially obtain valuable input from *beta readers*.)

- Does the **point of view** of your narration inadvertently change anywhere? All it takes is to be distracted in your thoughts why typing, and accidentally write one wrong word.

- Are **names** used consistently throughout the book? If you vary what a person is called, will it be clear to readers? For example, you might call a character by his first name (Mark), last name (Mr. Smith), his profession (the teacher), or a trait (the man with the red beard). There are times when it is appropriate, it's clear, and it works well, but there are books that abuse this in a way that makes it difficult for readers to follow along.

- You also want to make sure that you use the **correct name** every time. If one time you accidentally type Sarah when you really meant Julie, for example, the confusion will distract readers from the story.

- Almost every author has **favorite words** that they *use a little too often*, for which they don't even realize it.[106] When it's pointed out, if the author searches the manuscript for that word, the author usually can't believe how often that word was used. I'm not talking about very common words like "a" or "the," I don't mean conjunctions like "and" or "or," and I'm not referring to pronouns like "it," "that," "he," or "I." Try to find less common words that you may be using too frequently. It could be an adverb like "really" or "slowly," an adjective like "beautiful" or "angry," or some other type of word. If you know people who are familiar with your writing (who may offer honest feedback), ask them if they can think of any words that you might use more frequently than you should. I'm not saying to avoid these words all together: Try using the Find option in your file to see how many occurrences there are, and consider reducing the repetition. Once you know some of your 'pet' words, keep a list near your workstation.

- In addition to favorite words that you might use too frequently, you might have some **favorite phrases** that you *repeat several times* throughout your book. Again, you might not even realize that you do this. A few examples of phrases that get used more commonly than they should include, "not a day went by," "save face," "for all intents and purposes," "pricked up their ears," "tall, dark, and handsome," "not rocket science," and "the point was moot." If you have phrases that you use too often, they probably aren't one of my examples: You want to try to find out what they are, which isn't easy (without feedback) when you don't realize that you may be doing it.

- Sometimes a less common word is **needlessly repeated**[107] a few times in a short span (like a paragraph or two). Sometimes this repetition[108] distracts the reader from the story.

---

[106] I'm no exception to this rule. In nonfiction, especially when you're trying to show or teach something, certain words (like "however") and phrases (like "in addition to") are commonly repeated. Aside from those common words and phrases, there are certain less common words and phrases I could and should use less frequently. Every writer can always improve, including myself. The first step is knowing how.

[107] Note the key word 'needlessly.' Sometimes repetition is useful or necessary. When you write on a specific nonfiction topic, for example, certain vocabulary terms are apt to be repeated several times. You can probably think of several self-publishing terms that I've repeated in this guide.

[108] With a book that aims to teach something, repetition can sometimes be helpful. For one, some students learn and retain information faster than others. It's much easier for the student who grasped the information the first time to ignore the repetition than it would be for the student who still has forgotten pertinent information to fill in the pieces if it is omitted. For another, many readers don't read instructional books straight through like a novel. Many readers jump directly to the section that has the information they need "right now," in which case you can't rely on that reader to be aware of information that you've written earlier. You either need to refer to previous sections that have the relevant prerequisite information (so they can consult those sections as needed), or you need to repeat some information to help readers who don't read the book straight through (keeping in mind that some readers who *should* consult previous sections will choose not to do it). If you've noticed the repetition in my book (yes, I know it's there) and it has upset you, I sincerely apologize (I could repeat the third sentence of this footnote, but...). I hope

This is a separate issue from a possible 'favorite' word. The word might only be used three times in the entire book, but if all three occurrences happen to be in the same paragraph, readers may notice the repetition. When that particular word needs to be used (there is no better alternative to create variety), there is no helping it, but often when you discover repetition, the English language provides a few equally good ways of saying effectively the same thing.

- Another form of repetition is a **cliché**, such as "easy as pie," "scared to death," or "up his sleeve." Even if you only use a common phrase or saying one time in your whole book, the reader recognizes the repetition from having heard a similar expression many times before.

- Are there any **useless words** or expressions that really serve *no purpose*? Does your book seem to have '**fluff**'? (In nonfiction, these may be used to a limited extent. An extremist might argue that words like "however" and "therefore" are unnecessary in nonfiction, yet they are pretty common.)

- Note that certain sections of your book merit **extra scrutiny** for both proofreading and editing (but no section deserves to be under-appreciated). Obviously, it's not good to have frequent mistakes in *any* portion of your book. But since the beginning of your book is used for the **Look Inside** and for the free sample, you want to be even more careful with these sections. The **description** is similarly important. There are a few more sections that are worth extra scrutiny, and require some thinking on your part: Try to remember parts of your book that, when you were writing them, you felt partly uncomfortable with the writing, you were stressed out that day, you were more distracted than normal, or the kind of writing involved isn't one of your strengths. It helps if you can identify your relative strengths and weaknesses as a writer (though beware of being too confident while proofreading your strong suits, as you can miss mistakes with too much confidence), and it also helps if you can remember how you were feeling and what was going on when you were writing different parts of your book. (**Tip**: When you're writing on a day where you're not feeling well, stressed out, or distracted, jot this down in a notebook. As you can see, this information may be handy when you need to edit your book, as these sections are likely to have even more mistakes than usual.)

---

that the repetition that I included is helpful for those readers who need it to be that way, without causing too much frustration for other readers who don't need the repetition. As an example, I bet you can remember me writing "but don't highlight an entire paragraph and apply formatting directly to what's highlighted" too many times: However, if a reader happened to jump straight into a section that mentioned that, then that point was quite necessary for that reader (even though it may have frustrated other readers).

- This is not a comprehensive list of all kinds of editing issues. If you would like to see more examples of common editing issues to look for, try entering "editing tips," "editing a novel," or "editing nonfiction" (but without the quotes) in a search engine.

Tip: Make a list of the different kinds of editing mistakes that you find in your book. This customized checklist will be handy when you publish your next book.

Tip: Proofread your corrections carefully: *It's very common to introduce a new mistake when you make revisions.* Your eyes are strained from all of the editing, and it's easy to feel impatient. Get a good night's sleep and read through each of your revisions carefully with a fresh pair of eyes.

Note that if you already have separate files for a print edition and an eBook edition, remember to make any editing revisions to *both* files.

7.7 The Online Previewer

The online previewer is *convenient* because it opens up in your web browser during the publishing process. (It *should*: If you have any issues with functionality, try switching web browsers—FireFox, Explorer, Chrome, etc.) I recommend that you try using *both* the online and downloadable previewers. *The downloadable previewer offers options that aren't available with the online previewer* (like the option to change the background color or to quickly check your images).

Warning: The *downloadable* previewer (called Kindle Previewer) is *more reliable* than the online previewer. **Pictures**, for example, may display more reliably on the downloadable previewer. See Sec. 7.8.

On page 2 of the publishing process at KDP, simply click the Launch Previewer button in order to open the online previewer.

The options are fairly limited with the online previewer:

- You can adjust the **font size** from a scale of 1 to 9 for a tablet, 1 to 14 for a phone, or 1 to 8 for a Kindle eReader (these are not pt sizes), designed to mimic the customer's font size selection on actual devices or apps. The higher end of the scale is pretty extreme.
- Don't worry if the **table of contents** option shows nothing more than your cover and the beginning. If you used heading tags as discussed in Chapter 3 or 5 (to create a proper table of contents as discussed in Sec. 3.8 or 5.11), the customer will find your chapter headings in device navigation (although it's possible that device navigation won't appear

in your eBook immediately after publishing). The only way to the make **device navigation** function for all of your chapters in the preview (and immediately after publishing) is to create an ePub file (Sec. 5.12 will point you in the right direction). If you didn't make an ePub, don't worry: *Amazon typically adds this feature to your published eBook* (although it may not appear immediately). On the other hand, the **active table of contents** that you created in Sec. 3.8 or 5.11 *should* function in the preview: View this 'page' in your eBook and click on the links therein. (The previewer contains a Table of contents button, which mimics *device navigation*, not to be confused with your *active table of contents*, which is a 'page' inside the eBook.)

- You can change the orientation from **portrait** to **landscape**.
- The **location** is just a helpful way to navigate through an eBook. These locations are **<u>not</u>** 'pages.' If you knew that you wanted to open an eBook to about the halfway point, and if you knew that there were 280 locations in the book (this number varies depending on the length of the book), then you could go straight to location 140, for example.
- **Hyperlinks** work if you click on them. For example, if you click on a link to a website, the webpage opens up in a new window (provided that your link is properly setup). You should click on the links in your table of contents, external hyperlinks (to websites), and internal hyperlinks (that take the reader directly to a location within the book). Check that all of your links work as expected. **Note**: The *downloadable* previewer (Sec. 7.8) provides a convenient means of checking all of your links one after another.
- There are so many different brands of tablets (like Fire, iPad, Samsung, etc.), which come in a wide array of aspect ratios and screen sizes, that you can't expect the single option for "tablet" to provide a completely accurate representation for how *every* tablet will function. The same goes for the phone and eReader settings. So, for example, if a non-standard symbol appears to work in the preview, there may be actual devices that **<u>don't</u>** display it properly. However, if you see any problems with the formatting in the previewer, it will *definitely* be a problem on multiple devices: In this way, the previewer does help you identify important problems.

Note: The online previewer may not display **picture size** correctly, and may make it seem like in-line images will scale with font size (although in-line images **<u>don't</u>** actually scale with font size in Kindle eBooks).

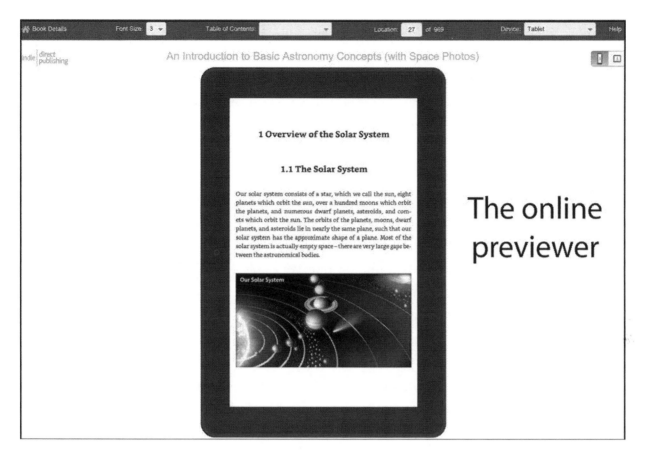

7.8 The Downloadable Previewer

The downloadable previewer (called the **Kindle Previewer**) is fairly easy to install and use. Look below the Launch Previewer button for the link called "*Preview on your computer.*" Click this link, and then click *Mac* or *Windows* to **download and install the downloadable previewer**. With Windows, ordinarily a window should prompt you to click Run, Save, or Cancel. The Save option can be adjusted to Save As (an easy way to know exactly where it is saved on your computer). Eventually, you want to '*run*' the installation. If a window doesn't pop up, find the list of *recent downloads* on your browser (some browsers even have a button for this). If it doesn't seem to be working for you, try switching **web browsers** (FireFox, Chrome, Internet Explorer, etc.).

The installation file is called KindlePreviewInstaller, but once the software is installed, it is called **Kindle Previewer** (followed by a number, like 3, to indicate which version it is). It may automatically show up in Windows Shortcuts. In the future, if you have trouble finding it, or if the shortcut isn't working, you might need to search your computer for Kindle Previewer (or try reinstalling it).

If the Kindle Previewer is the *only* software that you've downloaded that opens MOBI files, when you proceed to open a MOBI file, the Kindle Previewer should automatically be the software that attempts to open it. Once you have additional software that opens MOBI files, the Kindle Previewer may no longer be the default software for MOBI files. In that case, you must open the Kindle Previewer manually (either from a Windows shortcut or by remembering the file location so that you can find it). For example, if you download the **Kindle for PC** software (an app for reading Kindle eBooks on your PC), it may become the default software for MOBI files from that point on.

Once you successfully download and install the Kindle Previewer, you must *also* download your **converted MOBI file** from Amazon KDP. This option is immediately below the link that you clicked to download the Kindle Previewer. Click the **MOBI** link. If you're prompted with options to Open, Save, or Cancel, I recommend adjusting Save to Save As so that you can monitor where the file saves. (The default location is usually a Downloads folder, but I recommend instead saving it on your computer in My Documents or wherever you normally store files on your computer—or saving it to an external drive if you don't want the file stored on your computer.) This way, if you want to find the file on your computer, you should know where it is.

Note: The downloadable preview option (and downloadable MOBI file) doesn't always show right away. *You may need to wait a few minutes* (or longer) for your uploaded interior book file to finish its Kindle conversion before this option becomes available. Just be patient.

(Note that if you used Amazon's Kindle Textbook Creator, Kindle Create, or Kindle Comic Creator and if that resulted in a KPF file, you *won't* be able to use the downloadable previewer. However, in that case, there was a previewer in Amazon's app that you can use instead.)

Open your converted MOBI file with the Kindle Previewer. The Kindle Previewer will check if **enhanced typesetting** is supported for your eBook. If so, you will see a green checkmark next to Enhanced Typesetting on the left (in previous versions, it was called the Inspector window).

The downloadable previewer has a few options that the online previewer doesn't have:

- You can see how a variety of Kindle **fonts** look, such as Bookerly or Caecilia.
- It's convenient for checking your **pictures**, as you can choose to navigate by image instead of by 'page.' Simply adjust the dropdown menu beside View All from Pages to Images (in previous versions, this was instead under Navigate By in the Inspector Window). Then either use the left/right arrows on your keyboard or the left/right arrows in the preview window to advance from one picture to another (previous versions also had left/right arrows in the Inspector Window).
- You can similarly check your **hyperlinks**, **drop caps**, or **lists** quickly by adjusting View All (it used to say Navigate By) to Links, Drop Caps, or Lists.

Note: Although the downloadable previewer offers the option to change the background color to black, sepia, or green, transparency in GIF images may be lost in the preview. To properly see how transparency displays against various backgrounds for GIF images, sideload your MOBI file onto an actual device (Sec. 7.9).

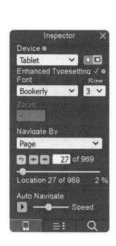

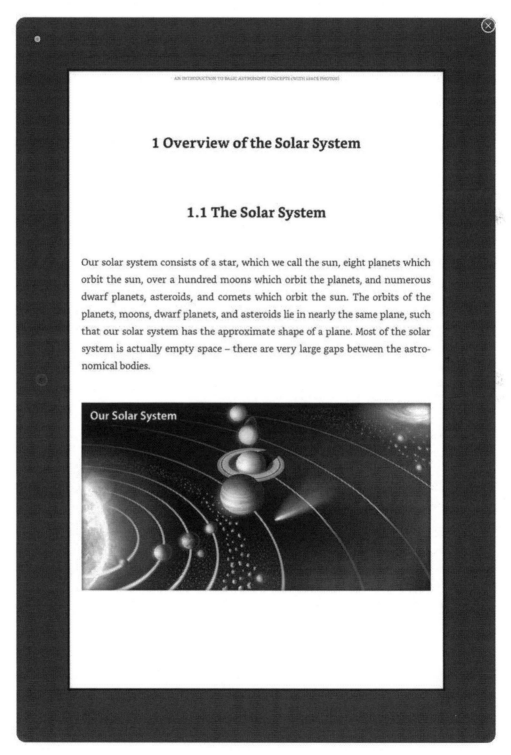

- You can preview your eBook with different **backgrounds**, including *night* (black), *sepia*, and *green*. To adjust the background, choose View and select **Color Mode**.

- You can use the new **Auto-Advance** feature (with adjustable speed) instead of clicking.

- **Tables** sometimes display *incorrectly* in the Kindle previewer and on Kindle for PC. If you have tables, it's best to also test your eBook out on an actual device (Sec. 7.9).

- Choose View and select Conversion log (in older versions, click the little white circle at the top left of the preview window). You will probably see a few **warnings**. Don't panic if one mentions the start reading location (since Amazon will set that automatically) or if there is a corresponding hyperlink warning ending with #start. If you didn't bookmark the table of contents location as described in Sec. 3.8, there will also be a hyperlink warning that ends with #toc. If you can't figure out what a warning is from the description, you can try searching online (or see Sec. 7.11 for suggestions about where to seek help).

Note: The device navigation menu will be *incomplete* (and what little there is will have limited functionality), unless you created an ePub file with a logical TOC or NCX. That should be okay though, since Amazon usually adds device navigation *automatically* within a few days of publishing your eBook using your heading styles.

For older versions of the Kindle Previewer, note that if you close the **Inspector** window and decide that you would like to reopen it, you need to click on the second white circle (with an "i" inside of it) that appears at the top left of the preview window.

7.9 Previewing on Devices or Apps

Nothing beats seeing your Kindle eBook on an *actual* Kindle device or Kindle reading app. The limitation is that you *can't* possibly preview your Kindle eBook on *every* possible device or app that a customer can use because there are hundreds of different devices (with new kinds coming to the market year-round).

Preview your eBook on as many devices as you can get your hands on, which may be more than you think. **Even if you don't own a Kindle device**, you probably have family, friends, acquaintances, or coworkers (that's a huge pool to choose from) who do. Somebody would probably not mind having you put your Kindle eBook on their device for free in exchange for helping you preview your eBook.

You surely have access to a PC, Mac, laptop, tablet, iPad, or smart phone. (Otherwise, how are you even publishing your Kindle eBook? Whatever computer or device you're using to publish your eBook, *you can use the same device to preview your eBook on Amazon's Kindle reading app.*) Amazon has several free apps (like Kindle for PC) for reading Kindle eBooks. Therefore, you must have a means to preview your Kindle eBook on at least one device (probably more).

(The least expensive Kindle devices are quite affordable, so you might consider investing in one device. Any time that you spend reading Kindle eBooks would help you develop your eye for Kindle formatting and offer some firsthand experience with formatting issues from the customer perspective. Since I publish Kindle eBooks regularly, I own several devices, including a Fire HD 8.9", Fire HD 7", Fire HD 8, Fire HD 7, Paperwhite, Fire for Kids, an older Kindle, an iPad, and an iPhone—in addition to PC's, laptops, and Android tablets for which I can use the free Kindle reading apps, including the Kindle Cloud Reader. That's probably overkill: *One Kindle device would be a great place to start*, and you probably have a PC, Mac, laptop, tablet, or phone that will work with a free Kindle reading app.)

If your eBook includes any large **pictures**, I highly recommend finding a way to preview your MOBI file on a Kindle Fire with the largest display that you can get your hands on. This is one way to determine if your pictures are displaying significantly smaller than you expect.

You can use the same MOBI file that you downloaded in Sec. 7.8 to preview your eBook on most devices. (If you skipped Sec. 7.8, go back and read about how to download the MOBI file.) I recommend that you download the MOBI file to your computer or to a jump drive connected to your computer.

To preview your Kindle eBook on a Kindle device, you need to **sideload** your MOBI file onto the Kindle device (*this is better than emailing it*). This means to connect the Kindle device to your computer via the USB cable that the device came with, find the converted MOBI file for your eBook on your computer (or jump drive connected to your computer—the jump drive and Kindle device should be connected to your computer simultaneously in this case), copy the MOBI file, and paste it into the appropriate folder for the Kindle device (which you must also find and open on your computer).

After you copy and paste the MOBI file onto the Kindle device, search for your eBook on the device. **Note**: You might need to browse **Documents** on your device *instead of Books* (that's the case with Kindle Fire devices, for example).

Important note: Don't email the MOBI file. When you email a MOBI file, it may be possible for some features to be altered. Instead, use a jump drive or USB cable to transfer the MOBI file from one device to another.

If you have trouble with this, you can find articles or videos online if you search for "**sideload** MOBI file onto Kindle _____" (where you replace the blank with your specific device, like Fire or Paperwhite, and where you omit the quotes) or a similar phrase.

You can also preview your eBook on your PC, laptop, Android tablet, Android phone, or Mac using one of the *free* **Kindle reading apps** from Amazon, such as Kindle for PC. For a PC, laptop, or Mac, connect a jump drive that has your MOBI file on it, download the appropriate app (such as Kindle for PC, Kindle for Mac, or Kindle for Windows 8), and open the MOBI file with the app. For an Android tablet or phone, you can connect the device to your PC or laptop, also connect the jump drive to your PC or laptop, download the Kindle for Android Tablet (or Phone) app to your Android device (but for a Samsung device, there is a Kindle for Samsung app—and if you have a Windows or Blackberry phone, there is Kindle for Windows Phone, Kindle for Blackberry 10, and Kindle for Blackberry), and then open your MOBI file with the Android device.

If you have trouble with this, try searching for help online (for example, "sideload MOBI file onto Android phone" or "open MOBI file with Kindle for Mac").

Previewing your eBook on an **iPad** or **iPhone** is different. The best way to preview your Kindle eBook on an iPad or iPhone is to use an AZK file instead of a MOBI file. The AZK extension stands for "AmaZon Kindle," and allows you to download an eBook to an iPad or iPhone using iTunes (in which case it will probably show up in Books instead of Documents, unlike Kindle devices).

You can get an AZK file for your book from the Kindle Previewer (Sec. 7.8). First, open your MOBI file in Kindle Previewer. Click the white dot in the top left corner of the preview window, choose File, and select Export. Change MOBI to AZK in the dropdown menu next to "Save as type," and then save the AZK file for your book.

Follow these steps to open the AZK file with an iPad or iPhone.

1. Install the Kindle reading app on your iOS device.
2. Close the Kindle reading app. Then connect your iPad or iPhone to your computer using the USB charging cable for the device.
3. Open iTunes on your computer. Don't click on the device name that appears in the left column. Instead, click on the icon for your device to the right of Music.
4. Click on File Sharing and select Kindle. Drag the AZK file into Kindle Documents.
5. Open the Kindle for iPad (or iPhone) app on the iPad (or iPhone). You should find your eBook in Books (not Documents). You may need to wait a short while.

Again, if you have trouble with this, try searching for help online (for example, "sideload AZK file onto iPad" or "sideload AZK file onto iPhone").

Note: When you preview your AZK file on an iPad or iPhone, the formatting may be considerably different from when you preview your MOBI file on a Kindle device. This is typical of the AZK preview experience.

Following is the current list of **Kindle reading apps**. It's worth checking this list, since Amazon adds to it periodically. If the URL that follows isn't working (which may happen, since Amazon updates their help pages periodically), try visiting Amazon, hovering your cursor over

Departments, hovering your cursor over Kindle E-Readers and Books, and clicking Free Kindle Reading Apps near the top right column (unfortunately, Amazon updates this periodically, too—if neither is working, you'll have to look for the Kindle reading apps: they should be in place where you would look for Kindle eBooks on Amazon).

Note: Just as I finished writing this book, Amazon released a **new Kindle reading app**. Amazon is streamlining the Kindle app so that there is one app for each *platform*—iOS, Android, Mac, PC, and Google Play—whereas in the past there was one app for each *device*. Eventually, the first URL below that lists a dozen separate reading apps may be replaced by the second URL below for the new Kindle reading app. Don't worry: You should still be able to use the app—just pick the appropriate app for your *platform* (instead of looking for the name of your device). If the first link isn't working, or if you can't find all the separate reading apps that I've listed, it may be because the new reading app has taken precedent. (I recommend trying the *new* app rather than one of the old apps.)

https://www.amazon.com/gp/help/customer/display.html?nodeId=200783640

https://www.amazon.com/kindle-dbs/fd/kcp

- Kindle for PC
- Kindle for Windows 8
- Kindle for Mac
- Kindle for iPhone, iPad, and iPod Touch (also called Kindle for iOS)
- Kindle Cloud Reader
- Kindle for Samsung
- Kindle for Android Tablet
- Kindle for Android Phone
- Kindle for Windows Phone
- Kindle for Blackberry 10
- Kindle for Blackberry

As I noted, Amazon's new Kindle reading app is streamlined by platform rather than by device. The *new* choices are:
- PC
- iOS
- Mac
- Android
- Google Play

Important note about the Kindle reading apps: If you make revisions to your eBook, when you create the new MOBI file, <u>**change the file name**</u>. If you don't change the name of the MOBI file, the Kindle reading app will automatically open the previous version of your eBook (it will pull it from your Kindle library), unless you delete the eBook from your library first.

You may be wondering, "**How do customers read Kindle eBooks?**" If there were one device (like Kindle Fire) that most Kindle customers used for reading eBooks, it would make sense to try to get that device and place emphasis on the formatting for that specific device. Unfortunately, there *isn't* one primary device that Kindle customers use to read eBooks.

I have conducted multiple **surveys** with hundreds of participants, and my research shows that *customers read Kindle eBooks on a wide array of devices* (as shown in Sec. 4.5). I found that about 10% of those surveyed read on a Kindle **Fire** (with about a third of Fire customers using the largest size screen), about 8% read on a Kindle **Paperwhite**, about 10% read on some other Kindle device (or didn't even know which type of Kindle they had), about 10% read on **iPad** (with the Kindle for iPad app), about 10% read on a computer (with the Kindle for PC or Kindle for Windows app), about 8% read on an **Android phone** (with the Kindle for Android Phone app), about 5% read on an **iPhone** (with the Kindle for iPhone app), about 3% read on a **Mac** (with the Kindle for Mac app), about 5% read on some other tablet or phone, and there are still a host of other options for eBooks (like Nook, Sony, and Kobo). The highest percentage, coming in at 12%, selected that they didn't read eBooks at all: They only read **print books**.

While the percentages may be somewhat different if the survey were done again, or if the survey had a wider audience, the variety would probably still be there. *There isn't one main device that you can focus on for formatting.* It doesn't make sense to target the Kindle Fire, for example, if upwards of 90% of customers may read something else. (The percentage is lower, even for my survey. You're not going to sell eBooks to the 12% who only read print books. If you don't publish with Nook or Kobo, you won't sell eBooks to those customers. If you publish a fully illustrated color eBook, you'll probably sell to more Kindle Fire customers than if you publish a novel. So, it's possible that 70% of your eBook customers will read something other than Kindle Fire. But the percentage doesn't matter that much: With 70% or 90% of your customers reading on some other device, it doesn't make sense to target a single device.)

What is significant is that many customers do read eBooks (though there are also many customers who read both print books and eBooks). Another thing that is significant is **that the majority of eBook customers read Kindle eBooks** (keep in mind that a few customers actually read Kindle eBooks and also read other kinds of eBooks).

After you publish your Kindle eBook, you should be your own first customer. If you don't own a Kindle device, use one of the many free Kindle reading apps to read your book on a PC,

Mac, tablet, iPad, iPhone, Android phone, or other device. *You want to be the first person to see how your book looks after publishing* (just in case).

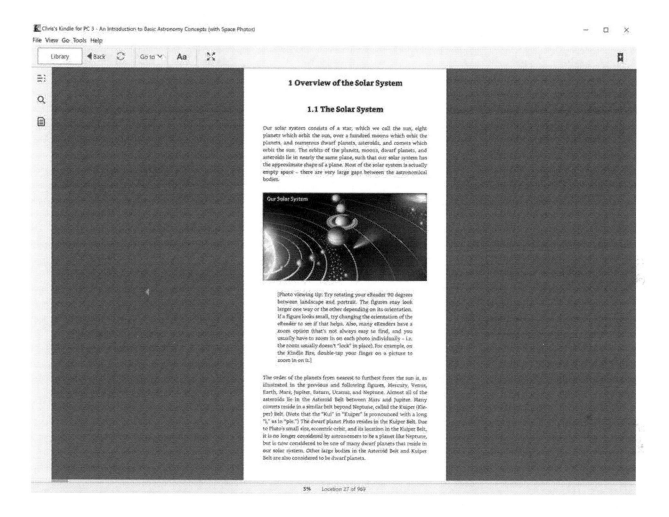

7.10 Printing a Hard Copy

As I mentioned in Sec.'s 7.5-7.6, it can be handy to print out a hard copy of your manuscript for **proofreading** and **editing** (but don't use the hard copy to check eBook *formatting*).

One way to do this is to print out your manuscript directly from your Word file. Ideally, you would do this *before* converting your Word file to HTML, since it's easier to make revisions (especially, extensive revisions) in Word.

Another way to get a hard copy is if you also publish a print edition. Amazon KDP will let you publish a paperback edition of your book, and CreateSpace is Amazon's original print-on-demand self-publishing service. Sec. 8.11 will help you choose a print-on-demand service and format your book as a paperback.

KDP and CreateSpace each allow you to order a printed proof of your paperback before you publish (KDP recently added this feature). The proof copy of your paperback can be used for proofreading and editing.

What if you've already converted your eBook to HTML, and you've already done extensive work to your HTML file? That is, you would like to print out your book using your HTML file instead of your Word file. One way is to open your HTML file as you would open a webpage (if you simply proceed to open your HTML, it should open with your default web browser), and then print that—but if you do this, **don't** save the HTML file. Just open, print, and exit without saving. You can even open your HTML file in Word, where it will appear as a very long web page, and you can print it—but again, **don't** save the HTML file after you open it in Word. If you want to edit and save your HTML, use Notepad, Notepad++, or Sigil (as explained in Sec. 5.3). Printing your HTML file as a webpage may not seem ideal, but it's *better than nothing*.

7.11 Troubleshooting

If you encounter a formatting problem when previewing your Kindle eBook, the first thing you should do is try to find the exact same location in your Word file (if you didn't go beyond Word), your HTML file (if you followed Chapter 5), or Amazon's app (if you used Kindle Create). Write down the chapter number (or section number), write down a unique phrase near the problem, and then try using the Find tool to search for that phrase in your file. Examine your file closely to try determine what may be causing the problem. If you are working with a Word file, inspect the paragraphs, and also open the paragraph dialog box (place your cursor in a paragraph and click on the little arrow-like icon in the bottom right corner of the Paragraph group on the Home ribbon). It may also be useful to use the Style Inspector (Sec. 3.14). If you are working with an HTML file, inspect the HTML instructions in the paragraphs near where the problem occurred, and also inspect the style definitions (Sec. 5.4) that those paragraphs call.

If that doesn't help, see if you can find your issue on the following list of common problems. If not, *after the list ends* I will offer a couple of more suggestions regarding how to get help with formatting problems.

Note: Most of the bullet points contain two sets of possible solutions—the first set applies to a Word file, while the second set applies to an HTML file. Look for **IF YOU DIDN'T USE HTML** for possible solutions for Word, and look for **IF YOU USED HTML** for possible solutions for HTML. However, beware that a few bullet points don't have these phrases in caps because the troubleshooting for those issues is organized differently.

Note: The following list is specifically for a *reflowable* eBook made as described in this book. (If you used the Kindle Kids' Book Creator, Kindle Textbook Creator, or Kindle Comic Creator, many of the formatting issues and solutions are different for your fixed-format book.)

Note: If you used HTML and if your eBook has pictures, when you make any alterations to your HTML file (which should be done in Notepad, Notepad++, or Sigil—see Sec. 5.3), after clicking Save, copy and paste your HTML file into your compressed zipped folder to overwrite the previous version of the HTML file in your compressed zipped folder.[72] Also review Sec.'s 5.3 and 5.5 regarding how to properly update the pictures in the folders file that's *inside* of your compressed zipped folder.

- If you have inconsistent **indentations**, missing indentations, or indented paragraphs that weren't supposed to be indented, first make sure that you removed every instance of pressing the tab key as instructed in Sec. 2.1 (which should be done in Word before converting to HTML). **Note**: If your indentation issue relates to bullet points or a *numbered list*, we will address formatting issues with lists a few paragraphs down. **IF YOU DIDN'T USE HTML**, check that you properly styled every paragraph as discussed in Sec.'s 3.3, 3.4, and 3.7: Indentations should be controlled through the *paragraph styles* (Chapter 3). If necessary, try highlighting the entire paragraph, clicking the Clear All Formatting button on the Font group of the Home ribbon, and then associating the desired *paragraph style* with the paragraph (this might remove a hidden problem). Next, right-click on the *paragraph style* for that paragraph (click Modify > Format > Paragraph) and check the indentation settings (Special > First Line controls the indent, while Left controls the left margin) for that *paragraph style*. Recall that you must set the First Line indent to 0.01" in Word if you want a non-indented paragraph because setting the First Line indent to zero or "none" will **not** work (the paragraphs may indent on Kindle even though you set the indent to zero or "none" in Word) if the paragraph is justified or ragged right ("none" only works for centered paragraphs). **IF YOU USED HTML**: It's easier to see your indent settings in the HTML (Sec. 5.4), though remember that ideally the *style definition* would set the indent (rather than specifying a text-indent size directly in the p-tag). Check that the p-tag (or h-tag, div-tag, or span) doesn't specify a text-indent, and also check that the *style definition* that the p-tag calls properly specifies the text-indent. Also check that your indent sizes are consistent values (ideally, values in em's). Also check the margin-left settings for the style definition (and also look for margin-left in the paragraph's HTML instructions, and check for possible spans—remove margin-left from the paragraph, and control this from the called style definition instead). Remember that setting *multi-level indents* is an advanced option (properly done in HTML), which carries many pitfalls (it's easy to create a *disaster* if you attempt this, especially on certain devices). I recommend sticking with one uniform indent size, if at all possible. (Keeping it simple is effective formatting advice for Kindle.)

- If there is inconsistent vertical **line spacing**, or if you're not happy with the line spacing, check your line spacing values. **IF YOU DIDN'T USE HTML**, check that you properly styled every paragraph as discussed in Sec.'s 3.3, 3.4, and 3.7: Line spacing should be controlled through the *paragraph styles* (Chapter 3). If necessary, try highlighting the entire paragraph, clicking the Clear All Formatting button on the Font group of the Home ribbon, and then associating the desired *paragraph style* with the paragraph (as it might remove a hidden problem). Next, right-click on the *paragraph style* for that paragraph (click Modify > Format > Paragraph) and check the line spacing. Recall from Sec. 3.5 that single spacing formats best for Kindle. If you really need greater spacing, the alternative is to change the Line Spacing from Single to 1.5 in Word (which isn't suitable for most eBooks). Don't use any other Line Spacing values. Also see the next bullet point. **IF YOU USED HTML**, search for any occurrences of line-height in your HTML file. If you find any line-height settings—such as line-height:115%;—remove them (check in the offending paragraphs, check for possible spans that include this, and check the style definitions). Also see the next bullet point.

- If you see extra **space between paragraphs** that you would like to remove, or if there is a place where you would like to add space after (or before) a paragraph, check your spacing before/after or your top/bottom paragraph margins. **Note**: If you're trying to add space before the first paragraph (or heading, or image) following a page break, see the next bullet point. **Note**: For most types of books, the space between paragraphs of text should be no different than the space between lines of text—meaning that no space should be added between two text paragraphs. The exception is called block paragraphs, which we discussed in Sec. 3.7. **IF YOU DIDN'T USE HTML**, check that you properly styled every paragraph as discussed in Sec.'s 3.3, 3.4, and 3.7: Space between paragraphs should be controlled through the *paragraph styles* (Chapter 3). If necessary, try high-lighting the entire paragraph, clicking the Clear All Formatting button on the Font group of the Home ribbon, and then associating the desired *paragraph style* with the paragraph (as it might remove a hidden problem). Next, right-click on the *paragraph style* for that paragraph (click Modify > Format > Paragraph) and check the Spacing Before and Spacing After settings: Spacing Before and Spacing After should both be set to 0 for most paragraphs of *normal body text* (except for a few specific kinds of books where block paragraphs are common), but one of these should be adjusted when you need to add space before or after paragraphs (in Sec. 3.4, I recommended using Spacing After to control this, and setting Spacing Before to zero—that's because some older devices may ignore Spacing Before). Make sure that they are set to 0, and **not** set to Auto, in places where you want them to be zero. **IF YOU USED HTML**, the equivalent settings are controlled through margin-top and margin-bottom (in Sec. 5.4, I recommended using margin-bottom when you want to add space after a paragraph, and setting margin-top to zero—that's because some older devices may ignore instructions to add space before a paragraph). This should be controlled through the *style definitions*: Remove any margin controls that you find in p-tags (or h-tags, div-tags, or spans).

- *If there is no space before the first element* (whether it be a heading, paragraph, or image) *following a page break* (or at the beginning of a new chapter), and you wish to add vertical space at this position, note that the most reliable and predictable way to achieve this is via ePub (see Sec. 5.12). Some Kindle devices or apps may ignore[109] the Spacing Before or margin:top setting for the first element (heading, paragraph, or image) following a page break when you upload a Word document, HTML file, or compressed zipped folder. If you try inserting blank lines at the beginning of a chapter following a page break, Kindle may ignore those, too. If you create a validated ePub file properly, then Kindle will respect the instructions to add space to the first element following a page break (provided that the ePub properly splits the HTML file into HTML pages). Do thorough research before you attempt the ePub option, as there are some potential pitfalls to navigate through. Beware that if you use ePub and add "too much" space (do this properly via the margin-top setting in the style definition), the text for the first paragraph may drop down "too far": This can happen very easily when the customer reads your book on a cell phone, for example (the vertical space could even cause a blank page—with the phone held in landscape orientation and a moderate text size). **IF YOU DIDN'T USE HTML**, apply a paragraph style with Spacing Before in an attempt to add space before the first element following a page break. Ideally, the paragraph style will incorporate the page break (Sec. 3.4). **IF YOU USED HTML**, apply a style definition with margin-top in an attempt to add space before the first element following a page break. Ideally, the style definition will incorporate the page break (Sec. 5.4).

- For **bullet points** or **numbered lists**, recall that there are a number of inherent challenges. I recommend that you reread about bullet points (which is also relevant for numbered lists) in Sec. 2.9 and also in Sec. 3.7. The safest and most effective way to format ordered or unordered lists is to keep it very simple. In my eBook, I just insert a bullet point (•) via Insert Symbol (Sec. 2.6) or type the number (like "5.") followed by a space: I didn't use Word's built-in list options for the Kindle edition of this book, and I didn't do anything fancy. I did create special paragraph styles (Sec. 3.4) for my lists: I use ListPoint

---

[109] The very beginning of the file, which is usually the title, can successfully drop down a few lines using the Spacing Before option. Elsewhere, some Kindle devices or apps may ignore Spacing Before and may also ignore blank lines following a page break.

and ListPointSpaceAfter (the latter adds vertical space after the last point on each list, which is a personal style preference). My list paragraphs don't "hang" in my eBook: The left margin is even (which was initially 0.2″ in Word, but which I later adjusted to margin-left:2em; in the style definitions—for ListPoint and ListPointSpaceAfter—in my HTML file). Special is set to "none" in my Word file for my list paragraphs. I chose to set my list paragraphs ragged right, even though my main body text paragraphs are justified: My reason for this is that the left margin for my list paragraphs makes my list paragraphs more susceptible to Kindle's justification issues. (If you have an issue regarding paragraph alignment, such as ragged right or justified text, we'll discuss that in another bullet point later in this section.) If you try to get fancy with your bullet points or numbered lists (especially, using HTML), it can backfire, or it can seem to work in the preview while causing problems on select devices. When it comes to list paragraphs (and Kindle formatting in general), simple can be quite effective. (However, in my experience the simple <ul> and <ol> tags *don't* work well for HTML, which is why I prefer the list styles recommended in Sec. 5.4.)

- If you have **alignment** problems—ragged right, justified, or centered—with paragraphs, headings, or images, check that you controlled this through paragraph styles. **IF YOU DIDN'T USE HTML**, check that you properly styled every paragraph as discussed in Sec.'s 3.3, 3.4, and 3.7: The alignment of paragraphs, headings, and images should be controlled through the *paragraph styles* (Chapter 3). If necessary, try highlighting the entire paragraph, clicking the Clear All Formatting button on the Font group of the Home ribbon, and then associating the desired *paragraph style* with the paragraph (as it might remove a hidden problem). Next, right-click on the *paragraph style* for that paragraph (click Modify > Format > Paragraph) and check the alignment (the options in Word are Left, Centered, and Justified). **Note:** If you attempted to make your text ragged right (left aligned), but it instead appears to be justified (full), recall that we first discussed this in Sec. 3.7, and that Sec. 5.4 shows you the only reliable way to achieve this: In your HTML, include text-align:left; in the *style definition*. **IF YOU USED HTML**, paragraph alignment is controlled through text-align (set to center, left, or justify). Check that the p-tag (or h-tag, div-tag, or span) doesn't specify a text-align, and also check that the *style definition* that it calls properly specifies the text-align. Also check that your indent sizes are consistent values (ideally, values in em's).

- If you see a problem with a **drop cap**, try keeping the drop cap *simple*. Also try deleting the drop cap and reinserting it. If you revise a drop cap and it appears to work in a preview, remember to try adjusting the font size, orientation, background color, and device to ensure that it works as desired on every device and setting (on an actual device or Kindle reading app, try adjusting the line spacing, too). If have a persistent problem, see my suggestions towards the end of this section regarding how to seek further help (for example, through the KDP community help forum). If you can't get a drop cap to come out to your satisfaction, one alternative is to put the first few words in caps (or small caps). **IF YOU DIDN'T USE HTML**, review Sec. 3.7. **IF YOU USED HTML**, review Sec. 5.6.

- If your body **text changes font size**, examine the font size settings in your file. **IF YOU DIDN'T USE HTML**, check that you properly styled every paragraph as discussed in Sec.'s 3.3, 3.4, and 3.7: Font size should be controlled through the *paragraph styles* (Chapter 3). If necessary, try highlighting the entire paragraph, clicking the Clear All Formatting button on the Font group of the Home ribbon, and then associating the desired *paragraph style* with the paragraph (as it might remove a hidden problem). Next, right-click on the *paragraph style* for that paragraph (click Modify > Format > Font) and check the font settings. Place your cursor in a paragraph and look at the font size on the Font group on the Home ribbon to double-check the size (but remember, the font size should be set through *paragraph styles*, not by adjusting this value on the Font group on the Home ribbon). Review the recommended font sizes for Word in Sec.'s 3.4-3.5. **IF YOU USED HTML**, remember that ideally the *style definition* would set the font size (rather than specifying the font size directly in the paragraph): Check that the p-tag (or h-tag, div-tag, or span) doesn't specify a font size, and also check that the *style definition* that it calls properly specifies the font size. Review the recommended font sizes for HTML in Sec. 5.4: The font sizes should be set as percentages, using 100% for body text.

- If there is an **unexpected page break** (which wasn't caused by a picture at the top of the next 'page'), look for a forced page break in your file and remove it. **IF YOU DIDN'T USE HTML**, press the Show/Hide Codes button (¶) on the Paragraph group of the Home ribbon in Word and see if it reveals a manual page break (or next page section break). Next, check the paragraph style: Click Modify > Format > Paragraph > Line and Page Breaks, and see if the Page Break Before box is checked. **IF YOU USED HTML**, look for page-break in the p-tag (or h-tag, div-tag, or span), and also check for a page-break in the corresponding style definition.

- If there is **duplicated text**, you simply need to remove the repeated text.

- If there is **missing text**, see if the text is in your file (Word or HTML—whichever you uploaded). If you find the text in your file, but it's missing from the preview, look closely to determine the cause. For example, if your text color is set to white, it will appear invisible on the default white background. In that case, if you used **WORD**, change the text color to Automatic, or if you used **HTML**, remove the font color specification. **IF**

YOU DIDN'T USE HTML, find the location of the missing text in your file and examine the font color and any other properties carefully. **IF YOU USED HTML**, make sure that the text appears between <p> and </p> tags, or between h-tags (like <h1> and </h1>). Examine the p-tags (or h-tags) closely, including the punctuation marks. Also look for comment tags, which are /* and */ for Kindle (but are <!-- and --> in ordinary HTML), since any text appearing between /* and */ comment tags won't show in your eBook.

- If you have problems with **boldface**, *italics*, or <u>underline</u> (either you see it where you shouldn't, or you don't see it where you should), find a unique phrase in or near that text and search for it in your file with the Find tool. Examine that text closely. **IF YOU DIDN'T USE HTML**, place your cursor in the text in Word, and check that the bold, italics, and underline buttons on the Font group on the Home ribbon are set as desired. If necessary, try highlighting the entire paragraph, clicking the Clear All Formatting button on the Font group of the Home ribbon, and then reformatting the text in the paragraph. (If you want an *entire* paragraph set in bold, italics, or underline—as opposed to just a section of a paragraph—you should do this with an appropriate paragraph style, as described in Sec.'s 3.3, 3.4, and 3.7, instead of applying the formatting directly to the paragraph.) Also read the note at the end of this bullet point. **IF YOU USED HTML**, if just a section of a paragraph is (or needs to be) in bold or italics, this should be done via <b> and </b> tags or <i> and </i> tags (Sec. 5.4). Look closely at the offending paragraph—and also study the preceding paragraphs—for any possible unclosed tags (or improperly closed tags). These tags should come in pairs: For example, if you find a <b> tag to begin boldface, you need to have a </b> tag to close boldface. If you typed <b> to begin boldface and accidentally typed <b> (instead of </b>) to end the boldface, for example, it won't end where you wanted it to end. Many formatting problems relating to boldface, italics, and underline involve missing closed tags or incorrect syntax—it can sometimes lead to a runaway boldface or italics problem. Note that the root of the problem may actually lie in a p-tag, h-tag, or div-tag for a *prior* paragraph. It's also possible that boldface or italics is controlled through <span> and </span> tags instead, so look for these, too. If you want an *entire* paragraph set in bold or italics—as opposed to just a section of a paragraph—you should ordinarily do this with an appropriate style definition (using font-weight:bold; or font-style:italic;), as described in Sec. 5.4, instead of applying the formatting directly to the paragraph. Underlining isn't used as much in eBooks as boldface and italics (partly because underlined text could be confused with hyperlinks). There are different ways of underlining in HTML. It could be done via text-decoration:underline, for example. Amazon includes <u> and </u> in their list of supported tags (though the use of the <u> tag has changed with recent versions of

HTML). Also, see the examples of common HTML mistakes at the end of this chapter. **NOTE FOR BOTH WORD AND HTML**: If you used the paragraph style (in Word) or the style definition (in HTML) to apply boldface or italics to an entire paragraph, *but still encountered problems* doing this on at least one device, experiment with what you ordinarily shouldn't do: In Word, try highlighting the entire paragraph, and applying boldface or italics to what you highlighted, or in HTML, try using font-weight or font-style within the p-tag for the paragraph itself. (In general, you should apply formatting for an entire paragraph to the paragraph style or style definition, not to the paragraph or p-tag itself. I'm only suggesting this as a last recourse when the 'right' way isn't working as intended on at least one device. If this happens to resolve your issue, don't make this a new formatting habit; treat it as the exception. If you used HTML, I suspect that your problem has to do with an unclosed tag or improper syntax—perhaps similar to one of my examples at the end of this chapter.)

- If you have a problem with an **external hyperlink** (to a website), the most common reason is that the website URL is incorrect, incomplete, or outdated. For example, make sure that the target URL includes the http:// part. Visit the actual webpage in your web browser, and then copy and paste that web URL into the target address field. For example, when I visited Amazon's webpage and did this, I got https://www.amazon.com/ to display in my target address field to create the following hyperlink: www.amazon.com. (Here, I removed the https:// part from the text to display field, but kept it in the target address field.) For an email hyperlink, remember to begin the email address with mailto: (including the colon), as in mailto:chrism@chrismcmullen.com. **IF YOU DIDN'T USE HTML**, review Sec. 3.10. Test the external hyperlink out in your Word file: Hold the Ctrl button while clicking on the external hyperlink to open the webpage. For a troublesome hyperlink, highlight the paragraph and the adjacent paragraphs in Word, cut them from the document, and then use Paste > Special > Unformatted Text to reinsert the paragraphs back into your document without any formatting (one way to do this is to click the little arrow below the word Paste at the left end of the Home Ribbon and choose Keep Text Only)—or cut/paste the paragraphs into Notepad and then copy/paste them back into Word. You'll need to restyle these paragraphs and then make the external hyperlinks from scratch. (Occasionally, hyperlinks in Word get confused or messed up, and sometimes there are even hidden hyperlinks. Replacing all of the text, even the paragraph before and after, with plain text gives you a chance at a fresh start.) An email hyperlink should begin with mailto: (including the colon) in the E-mail Address field, as in mailto:chrism@chrismcmullen.com. **IF YOU USED HTML**, review Sec. 5.8. Following is an example using HTML: I typed <a href="http://www.amazon.com/author/chrismcmullen">

Chris McMullen's author page</a> in my HTML to create the following external hyperlink: Chris McMullen's author page (this link works in the eBook edition). An email hyperlink should have the format <a href="mailto:chrism@chrismcmullen.com">text to display</a>. Also, see the examples of common HTML mistakes at the end of this chapter.

- If you have a problem with an **internal hyperlink** (that is, a link that takes the reader to a specific location within the eBook) or a hyperlink that is part of your table of contents, check that the internal hyperlink uses the correct bookmark (for example, does the internal hyperlink point to Chapter 3 when it it's supposed to point to Chapter 4?), and also check that the bookmark points to the right place in your eBook. **IF YOU DIDN'T USE HTML**, review Sec. 3.10. Test the internal hyperlink out in your Word file: Hold the Ctrl button while clicking on the internal hyperlink to make sure that it takes you to the right location. For a troublesome hyperlink, highlight the paragraph and the adjacent paragraphs in Word, cut them from the document, and then use Paste > Special > Unformatted Text to reinsert the paragraphs back into your document without any formatting (one way to do this is to click the little arrow below the word Paste at the left end of the Home Ribbon and choose Keep Text Only)—or cut/paste the paragraphs into Notepad and then copy/paste them back into Word. You'll need to restyle these paragraphs and then make the internal hyperlinks from scratch. (Occasionally, hyperlinks in Word get confused or messed up, and sometimes there are even hidden hyperlinks. Replacing all of the text, even the paragraph before and after, with plain text gives you a chance at a fresh start.) **IF YOU USED HTML**, the bookmarked location will have the form <a name=MakeUpaName>Text</a> and the internal hyperlink to that bookmark will have the form <a href="#BookmarkName">text to display</a>. Review Sec. 5.8. Also, see the examples of common HTML mistakes at the end of this chapter.

- If you see an **unexpected line break** in the middle of a paragraph, you want to determine whether or not this may be a formatting issue. Occasionally, when a long word is a little too long to fit at the end of one line of a paragraph, when it moves down to begin the next line of the paragraph, it leaves a large gap of space at the end of the previous line—even if the paragraph style is justified. Kindle justification isn't perfect (though it has improved considerably, especially for devices and apps that support Kindle's enhanced typesetting). However, it's also possible that a formatting mistake is creating the line break, so you want to explore this possibility. Try changing the orientation between portrait and landscape, and try adjusting the font size. If there had been a long word at the beginning of the line following the line break, and if adjusting the orientation and font size resolves the issue, it may be a Kindle justification issue. If the problem persists, it's *definitely* a formatting issue. Examine the paragraph closely in your book file. **IF YOU**

DIDN'T USE HTML, in Word press the Show/Hide Codes button (¶) on the Paragraph group on the Home ribbon: There may be a soft return (←⏎) or hard return (¶) in your paragraph. There should be one hard return (¶) at the very end of the paragraph. Remove any soft returns (←⏎). Also, remove any hard returns (¶) that come *before* the end of the paragraph. **IF YOU USED HTML**, make sure that the text that makes up the 'paragraph' appears between a single pair of <p> and </p> tags (or <div> and </div> tags), instead of being split across multiple paragraphs. Also check for any <br> tags in your HTML, since these tags force line breaks.

- If you find a **blank page** in your Kindle eBook, find the same location in your file, and see if you can identify a possible cause. For example, the blank page might consist of a blank line followed by a page break (or followed by a paragraph style that forces a page break): In that case, try removing the blank line. Another way to get a blank page is when a paragraph adds "too much" space before or after: For example, if you hold a cell phone in landscape mode and select a moderate font size, it's possible for space before or after to shift the text clear off the screen. Yet another way to see a blank screen is when the eBook sets the font color to the reader's choice of background color—black, white, sepia, or green. A GIF image that has black, white, sepia, or green text or line art over transparency can similarly be rendered invisible. If the problem involved a GIF image with transparency, review Chapter 4. **IF YOU DIDN'T USE HTML**, look for possible blank lines or page breaks. Check the paragraph settings for both the *paragraph style* (click Modify > Format > Paragraph) and the paragraph itself (click the little arrow-like icon at the bottom right corner of the Paragraph group on the Home ribbon) to see if a large value of Spacing After was added (perhaps to the previous paragraph). Also check the Line and Page Breaks tab on the paragraph dialog box that pops up. Press the show/Hide Codes button (¶) on the Paragraph group on the Home ribbon to look for possible line breaks or page breaks. If the problem was caused by applying a text color, you need to clear the formatting of the text and set the font color to *automatic* instead (through a *paragraph style* if it applies to an *entire* paragraph or more). **IF YOU USED HTML**, a p-tag or h-tag that effectively renders a blank line might not seem like a blank line: Any effectively empty paragraph will create a blank line. For example, <p class=MsoNormal> </p> and <h1> </h1> are two ways of creating a blank line. However, sometimes you can find a very long string of characters that boil down to a blank line: This can happen when the opening p-tag or a span within the p-tag includes a very long assortment of instructions. Check the margin-top and margin-bottom settings for a value that may be very large in the p-tag, h-tag, span, or style definition for the problem paragraphs and the adjacent paragraphs. If the problem was caused by applying a text color, search for text-color:black or text-color:white (for example) in the p-tag, h-tag, or span, and also check the corresponding style definition. Most text should have no color declared; never set the text color to black, white, green, or sepia.

- If you see any pictures that have an unexpected *black or gray line at one or more of the edges* (these are called **drop shadows**), this usually results from uploading a Word document instead of following the steps outlined in Sec. 5.2 to create a compressed zipped folder.

- If you see a **camera icon** (like the one below), or if there is a picture that is missing, **IF YOU DIDN'T USE HTML**, ensure that the image was inserted in Word using Insert > Pictures, that the picture is in JPEG or GIF format (as discussed in Sec. 4.1), and that the picture is placed on its own line between paragraphs. Also, right-click on the picture in your Word file, select Wrap Text, and check that it is set to In Line With Text. **IF YOU USED HTML**, check that you uploaded the compressed zipped folder (and not the HTML file—the compressed zipped folder contains both your HTML file and your images) that you made in Sec. 5.2. Also check that your current HTML file is in the compressed zipped folder (by copying and pasting your HTML file into the compressed zipped folder in order to overwrite the previous HTML file).[72] View the contents of your compressed zipped folder to verify that the 'missing' image is, in fact, in the folder, and write down its exact name and the file type (JPEG or GIF—don't use any other file formats for pictures). If the picture isn't in your compressed zipped folder, find it and paste it in there. Now open your HTML file and find the place where it calls your image (one way to find pictures is to use the Find option and type "img" without the quotes). Check that the name of the picture exactly matches the name of the picture from your compressed zipped folder, and check that the extension is correct for the image type (.jpg or .gif). The name and extension should appear in quotation marks after src= (in the example below, the name of the picture is image042.jpg where that is a zero, **not** an uppercase O). These are straight quotes (not curly quotes). The location (in this case, Book_files/ indicates that image042.jpg is located in a folder called Book_files) should automatically be correct if you followed the instructions from Sec. 5.2. (However, if you're merging content from different eBooks together, for example to create a boxed set, you may need to adjust the locations.) **Note**: If the name of your book file or if the name of any of your pictures has a space (created by pressing the spacebar) in it— I recommend **not** doing that—this introduces an unnecessary complication, as the HTML uses 20% in place of the space in the name of the file. It's simpler to remove any spaces from file names and picture names (otherwise, if your filename includes a space like My Book.html, you must type 20% instead of the space, as in "My20%Book_files/image001.jpg").

If you renamed your files folder after creating it, this could be the source of your problem. Also, see the examples of common HTML mistakes at the end of this chapter.

<div class=CenterSpaceAfter><img style="width: 100%; height: auto;" alt="" src="Book_files/image042.jpg"></div>

- If you have a picture that appears *too small*, **IF YOU DIDN'T USE HTML**, select the picture in your Word file, right-click, choose Size and Position, and check that the width and height are both set to 100%. (If you adjust these to 100% and the picture becomes much wider than the page width in Word, **don't worry**—it won't be too wide in your Kindle eBook.) Also open your picture file with image software (like PhotoShop or Gimp) and check that the PPI is 192 or less (this step only applies if you *didn't* create an HTML file):[110] If the PPI exceeds 192, decrease it down to 192 (but *don't* decrease the *pixel count*—if the pixel count reduces when you alter the PPI, see if your software will then let you raise the pixel count back up without changing the PPI). If those suggestions don't solve your problem and if you uploaded a Word document, in order for your picture to appear larger, you may need the picture to have a larger pixel count. One way is to create a new picture with equipment or software that gives you a larger pixel count. If that's not practical (you just can't make a new picture like the old one), you could use image software (like PhotoShop or Gimp) to increase the pixel count, but that comes at a cost: The picture may not look as sharp, and if you look closely, you will probably see imperfections (like stray marks or pixilation) on your images. *Amazon recommends that you don't upload a Word document if your book has pictures* because pictures display more reliably when you convert the Word file to a compressed zipped folder that includes an HTML file and an image files folder as outlined in Sec. 5.2 (in which case you should also read Sec.'s 5.3 and 5.5—and Sec. 5.4 is recommended, too). **IF YOU USED HTML**, if your picture is neither displaying full-width nor full-height (and your picture isn't padded—it doesn't have a border), find the img line for the picture in your HTML

---

[110] In principle PPI shouldn't matter at all for an eBook, but I've seen pictures that were over 192 PPI get reduced in size during the Word to Kindle conversion when a Word document was uploaded to KDP. We discussed this in Sec. 4.11. When you upload an html file, 300 PPI is fine.

file and check that it includes style="width: 100%; height: auto;" (check the syntax carefully) like my example above. If it does include the 100% width instructions, and still doesn't display full-width (or full-height), if it specifies the picture size (as in width="2048" height="1024"), double-check the pixel size specifications or try removing them. Finally, check the actual pixel size of your picture in the image files folder (the one that's inside of your compressed zipped folder), as described in Sec. 5.5.

- Do you have a picture that appears *too large* on at least one device? This might be the case with a glyph or logo, which is intended to appear small, or it might be the case with a picture that isn't sharp (since it looks even less sharp when it's larger) or a picture with a small pixel count (which will look less sharp if it displays full-width, for example). The only surefire way to achieve this is by adding padding (a transparent border) with the picture in GIF format (which supports transparency), as discussed in Sec. 4.4. Beware that older Kindle devices may automatically blow a small picture up to full-width: Padding your image helps to prevent this.

- If you discover a problem with the **aspect ratio** of a picture, first find your original picture and verify that the aspect ratio looks fine there. **IF YOU DIDN'T USE HTML**, find your picture in your Word file, and examine how it looks in Word. Right-click the image, choose Size and Position, check that the aspect ratio is locked, and check that the width and height are both set to 100%. If necessary, try deleting the picture and using Insert > Picture to reinsert it. **IF YOU USED HTML**, open the picture in your compressed zipped folder (in the _files folder contained therein) and verify that the aspect ratio looks fine there. Next, select the picture in your _files folder (*within* the compressed zipped folder), right-click, choose Properties, and select Details: Check the size in pixels against your original picture. If necessary, delete the picture from the _files folder that is *inside* of the compressed zipped folder (note that there is another _files folder *outside* of your compressed zipped folder—be sure to do this to the one *inside* the compressed zipped folder), and replace it. After you replace it, if the name is different from the name it had in the _files folder *within* the compressed zipped folder, right-click on the picture to change the name (for example, the original picture might be named Dragon.jpg, and that may have become image005.jpg in your _files folder when you created the compressed zipped folder, in which case you would delete image005.jpg from the _files folder, copy and paste Dragon.jpg into the _files folder, and change the name of Dragon.jpg to image005.jpg in your _files folder). If the picture looks fine in the _files folder *inside* of your compressed zipped folder, most likely there is a mistake in the size specified in the img line in the HTML file. It should have the form img style="width: 100%; height: auto;" width="1000" height="1600" alt="" src="Book_files/image042.jpg" (except that it should have your filename instead of Book—and recall that if your filename includes a space like My Book.html, you must type 20% instead of the space, as in "My20%Book_files/image001.jpg"). If it specifies the pixel count (as in width="1000" height="1600"), verify that this matches the actual size in pixels of the picture from the _files folder that's *inside* of your compressed zipped folder (if not, adjust these values in your HTML file). Drag the HTML file into the compressed zipped folder to make sure that it contains the latest version of your HTML file.

- If you have an image that isn't as clear or **sharp** as you would like, check the pixel count and quality of your original picture. If you can create a new picture with a larger pixel count or better quality, that may help. One way that a picture may appear less sharp or clear than intended is when the picture displays larger than its actual size in pixels. For example, if the picture measures 512 pixels across and displays full-width on a screen that measures 1024 pixels across, the picture won't appear as sharp as it would on a display that measures 600 pixels across. This can happen when an older Kindle device automatically displays the image full-width, it can happen when you use HTML to force an image to display full-width (using style="width: 100%; height: auto;"), and it can also happen to any image when a customer zooms in on the image on a device with a large screen size. If your image measures about 2000 pixels across (or high), it shouldn't have this problem when displayed normally, but it may lose sharpness when zoomed in on a large screen. In most cases, 2000 pixels should be plenty, but if you have a highly detailed picture or a picture with small text—such that customers will want to zoom in to see that detail or read that text—then sharpness could be an issue when the image is fully zoomed in (but may not be). Recall that we discussed picture size at length in Chapter 4 (along with the related issue of file size and its impact on delivery fees).

- If an image isn't *aligned* properly (for example, if you want the image to be centered, but it appears to be aligned with the left edge of the screen instead), first check the original image to make sure that it looks fine in picture software. If you *padded* the image (Sec. 4.4), check that the padding isn't uneven on the left and right sides. **IF YOU DIDN'T USE HTML**, ensure that the picture is placed on its own line between paragraphs. Also, right-click on the picture in your Word file, select Wrap Text, and check that it is set to In Line With Text. Next, check that the paragraph is properly aligned to center using an appropriate paragraph style (find the bullet point earlier in this section that discusses how to troubleshoot problems with *paragraph alignment*). **IF YOU USED HTML**, look for any instructions in the img line, p-tag or div-tag, or a span that may cause the alignment to be different from your intent. Next, check that the alignment is done properly through a style definition, the same way as any paragraph or heading should be aligned (find the bullet point earlier in this section that discusses how to troubleshoot problems with *paragraph alignment*). The image should appear in its own paragraph, like my example a few paragraphs back with the div tag.

- If you're not happy with the way that a color picture looks on a *black-and-white* display, the solution is to change the colors of your picture. This either means to create a new picture, or to use photo-editing software like PhotoShop or Gimp to recolor the picture. You can find tutorials and YouTube videos to help learn specific skills with software like PhotoShop. Examine your result carefully to ensure that the quality of the full-color picture isn't sacrificed for the sake of looking better on a black-and-white display.

- If you're not happy with the way that a picture looks in **night mode**, with a **sepia** background, or a **green** background, you need to revise your picture. If you have a black and while illustration in GIF format that appears invisible in night mode, consider removing the transparency from the GIF image or recoloring the picture. An alternative is to save the image in JPEG format instead of GIF format (since it will lose transparency with the JPEG format—but review Sec. 4.1, which discusses when JPEG and GIF images should be used). **Note**: Transparency may not show in the downloadable previewer. To properly check how transparency shows against various backgrounds, sideload to an actual device.

- If there is *text that you can't see in night mode*, it's probably because you set the font color to black. Similarly, if you can't see text against a *sepia* or *green* reading background, it's probably due to the text color. Find this text in your file. **IF YOU DIDN'T USE HTML**, find the text in your Word file and change the font color from black (or green or sepia) to Automatic. For an *entire* paragraph, ideally this should be controlled through a *paragraph style*. **IF YOU USED HTML**, search for text-color, color:black (or #000000 or any other HTML color code that is close to black), or any other instructions that would set the color of the text to black (or green or sepia), and remove them from your HTML.

- If a character doesn't display properly, see if the character is on the list of standard **supported symbols** from Appendix A. If so, check that you inserted the symbol properly. **IF YOU DIDN'T USE HTML**, use Insert > Symbol in your Word file (before converting to HTML), as described in Sec. 2.6. Also check the notes at the end of this bullet point. **IF YOU USED HTML**, ideally you would use Insert > Symbol in your Word file *before* converting to HTML, as described in Sec. 2.6. It is possible to use the corresponding HTML entity *after* converting to HTML, but Amazon recommends only using the HTML entity for the following symbols: < (less than sign), > (greater than sign), & (ampersand), and   (non-breaking space). If you type these symbols in your HTML, pay close attention to the syntax, especially the semicolon at the end. If you use any other HTML or XML entities, you run the risk that the symbol won't display properly on one more devices (even if they seem to work fine in the available previews). There is an alternative, even *if you've already converted from Word to HTML*: Open a blank document in Word, use Insert > Symbol to properly insert a supported character from Appendix A, save this very short Word file as an HTML file as directed in Sec. 5.2, and open the HTML file in Notepad. Find the equivalent symbol (however it turned out) in the HTML file, and copy/paste it into the actual HTML file for your eBook. Also, search the top of your HTML file to see that it specifies content="text/html; charset=windows-1252" for Windows or Unicode (UTF-8) for Mac. These two character sets should work fine for the supported characters from Appendix A. **NOTE FOR BOTH WORD AND HTML**: If you inserted a supported character from Appendix A using Insert > Symbol in Word and it still doesn't display properly, check the font for that symbol. In Word, highlight the symbol and it should show you which font is associated with it: It should be Times New Roman, Calibri, or Georgia (I don't recommend trying anything else). In HTML, check to see if a font-family is specified (check the paragraph tag, check for a span, and also check the style definitions): I recommend **not** specifying any font-family anywhere in your HTML file (place your cursor at the beginning of your HTML file and search for font-family). **NOTE FOR BOTH WORD AND HTML**: If you can't use a supported symbol from Appendix A, one alternative is to create a small glyph, though that may be problematic, especially if you wish to place it alongside text in paragraphs. We discussed using glyphs for special symbols in Sec. 4.9, and smaller images such as glyphs in Sec. 4.4.

- If any **fancy formatting** or **text effects** are missing or came out wrong on at least one device (note that you're taking a big risk with nonstandard effects, in that there might be a problem on at least one device even if it seems to work in the available previews), the simple and effective solution is to stick with standard formatting (keep it simple). If you really need an unsupported effect, perhaps you could pull off something similar with a picture (padded, if necessary to limit the size).

- If a **table** doesn't display fully or if there is information in the table that is hard to read, you can try splitting the table up into smaller tables, you can try making the table into a picture (if all of the text will be sharp, clear, and easy to read), or you can try turning the table into a long list. We discussed tables in Sec.'s 2.9, 3.12, and 4.8. **Note**: Tables sometimes display incorrectly in the Kindle previewer and on Kindle for PC. If you have tables, make it a priority to test your eBook out on an actual device (Sec. 7.9).

- If you're not satisfied with how an **equation** is displayed, you should review Sec.'s 3.11, 4.9, and 5.5. **Don't** use the Insert > Equation option in Word. When an equation can be typed with supported symbols (Appendix A), the best way is just to type it. For example,

I simply typed the equation $3x^3 - 2x^2 = 9(x - 4)$ using my keyboard, the superscript feature on the Font group of the Home ribbon in Word, and Insert > Symbol > More Symbols (using character code 150 for the minus signs with Font set to "normal text" and the "from" field set to "ASCII decimal") using the same font (the default font) as the rest of the paragraph. When you can't type an equation with supported symbols, the next best thing is to format the equation as a picture in line with the text, on its own line between paragraphs (Sec. 4.9).

- **Page numbers** don't show up in an eBook if they were inserted via Word's Insert > Page Number feature or if they were otherwise created in a page header or page footer. If you see page numbers, they were probably inserted some other way (like typing them in manually). Search for the page numbers in your file and remove them.

- If you happen to see **spelling** or **grammar marks** in your Kindle eBook like the similar review marks that you find in Microsoft Word, there is a simple and effective way to find these in your book file if you convert your Word file to an HTML file as described in Sec. 5.2. In Notepad (or Notepad++ or Sigil), type "spellE" in the search field (but without the quotation marks). If you find something like <span class=SpellE>keep this text</span>, replace the whole thing with just the text between the spans (which is "keep this text" in my example, but without the quotes). Also, search for "gramE" and make similar replacements.

- Recall that there are a few subtle issues that you really can't do anything about, such as Kindle's **justification** (although Amazon has new typography features for Kindle devices and apps that support them, which does help). We discussed a few of these issues, such as orphans and justification, in Sec. 3.7. If you have an eye for typography (or if you have print formatting experience), you must be careful not to try to 'fix' a subtle issue for which the 'solution' may only make the problem worse.

- After you publish your eBook, once your Look Inside goes live, if you discover a problem with your **Look Inside**, examine the formatting of the beginning of your book closely. Unfortunately, there is no reliable preview for the Look Inside, and the Look Inside is the most challenging part of the Kindle eBook to format correctly. If you followed this guide, you should be in good shape. If you notice problems with indentations or space between paragraphs in your Look Inside that you haven't seen on any preview or even on an actual device, it could be that you have a subtle formatting mistake, for which the preview, actual devices, and Kindle apps are more forgiving than the Look Inside: It's especially important for the Look Inside to use *paragraph* styles in Word (or *style definitions* in HTML) to control paragraph formatting. However, there is one visual property of the Look Inside, which authors sometimes believe is a mistake, but is really a difference with how the Look Inside works: The Look Inside displays more like a scrollable, reflowable webpage, whereas an actual Kindle eBook or app shows the eBook in 'pages.' Due to this difference, the Look Inside does not respect *page breaks*. The Look Inside also sometimes strips out vertical space (especially, that which is created by blank lines) that a Kindle eReader or app doesn't strip out (though even Kindle eReaders and apps may strip out extra consecutive blank lines). If you want to create vertical space between two paragraphs, it's best to do this with a *paragraph style* in Word (or a *style definition* in HTML) that adds space after a paragraph (but note that most books do **not** add space between two body paragraphs of text, except for a few kinds of books that use block paragraphs) using Spacing After (in Word) or margin-bottom (in HTML). *If the Look Inside is missing space between the last paragraph of a chapter and the chapter heading that follows*, try associating a paragraph style (or style definition) with the last paragraph of the chapter that applies Spacing After (or margin-bottom), such as the BodySpaceAfter style recommended in Sec.'s 3.4 and 5.4. **Note**: If you would like to increase or decrease the length of your Look Inside, place a polite request through the contact us option at KDP support. However, note that if you republish your book later, the length of the Look Inside may change again.

If you worked with HTML, read the examples of **common HTML mistakes** at the end of this chapter (just before the last set of figures: you can find them after the paragraphs of text below).

If you didn't find your problem in this troubleshooting section, or if the solution didn't work, I'm sorry: I couldn't list every possible problem and every possible solution (or this book would have turned into an encyclopedia—I included several common problems and solutions, though). The next step is to search online.

At the **KDP community help forum**, it is possible to find several formatting issues, with helpful discussions outlining a variety of possible solutions from helpful experts: I know this because I have seen many of them (and have even participated in some of them) over the years. However, it's not always 'easy' to find what you're looking for, not every discussion on formatting is equally informative, and occasionally what could have been a great discussion ran into a trolling problem (a challenge we all face when interacting with others on the internet—if you're just browsing and just reading, and not participating, note that you really aren't directly impacted by the occasional troll, and sometimes the community succeeds in getting inappropriate comments or spam removed from the discussion).

I have some tips for searching through past discussions on the **KDP community forum** to try to find more of what you're looking for and less of what you aren't. (I search the forum periodically myself, and have learned this through experience.)

- Try to think of the keywords that relate to your issue, such as drop caps, inconsistent indents, missing pictures, left alignment, night mode, or font embedding. Enter the most relevant words into the search field, as this will more likely pull up relevant results.

- After your search, click the Discussions button or View More link to see more than just a handful of search results.

- Click the dropdown arrow next to Top Questions for an alternative way to sort through the search results.

- If necessary, try typing a different set of keywords and conducting a new search. There are usually a variety of ways to discuss a similar issue. For example, if you have a problem with transparency showing in a padded picture, you might search for transparency, but you could also search for padding or search for transparent image (or picture). Your first few tries may not pull up a helpful discussion, but eventually it might work out.

- Click the Home link and select a forum. If you're trying to solve a formatting issue, click on the Formatting forum. If you browse through the first several pages, it's possible that another author will have asked a similar question recently.

If you can't find the answer you're looking for, post a polite question in the appropriate forum (use the **Formatting** forum for formatting questions). First visit your profile and decide whether you wish to post publicly or anonymously. The advantage of anonymity is that if for whatever reason someone gets upset with you or jealous of you, they won't be able to find your book after you publish it. If you post publicly, as with all public activity both online and offline, strive to appear professional, and avoid responding to posts emotionally (if something gets you upset, walk away, calm down, and think it through before responding—*sometimes, the best things we say are the words we don't say at all*).

If you don't find the information you're looking for at the KDP community forum, try searching with your favorite search engine. You might find the information you seek in a formatting guru's blog, or you might find it at another popular spot for authors to discuss eBook formatting. Another community forum where authors discuss Kindle eBooks is Kindle Boards.

https://www.kdpcommunity.com/s/?language=en

http://www.kboards.com

Following are some examples of common mistakes that are easy to make when typing or editing HTML. These cases show how a slight mistake in the HTML can result in a big formatting problem. When you type or edit HTML, read and type with care, paying special attention to all punctuation marks.

Mistake #1: The b-tag below doesn't actually close (the second b-tag is missing a slash). This will create a **runaway boldface effect**, where the paragraphs that follow will have boldface even when they should be normal.

<p class=MsoNormal>Mass is a measure of inertia, whereas <b>weight<b> is a measure of heaviness.</p>

The HTML should look like this instead:

<p class=MsoNormal>Mass is a measure of inertia, whereas <b>weight</b> is a measure of heaviness.</p>

Mistake #2: The p-tag below doesn't actually close (it opens with a p-tag, but closes with a div-tag instead). This will create a **runaway style problem**, where the paragraphs that follow will be styled incorrectly. Don't mix and match p-tags, div-tags, and h-tags in the same HTML paragraph (or heading).

<p class=CenterSpaceAfter><img width="1024" height="576" alt="" src="Novel32_files/image002.jpg"></div>

The HTML should look like this instead (with the opening and closing tags matching):

<div class=CenterSpaceAfter><img width="1024" height="576" alt="" src="Novel32_files/image002.jpg"></div>

Mistake #3: The following line from a style definition is missing a semicolon. When you edit or type style definitions (for paragraph and heading styles at the top section of your HTML file), make sure that each line ends with a semicolon.

margin-bottom:1em

The HTML should look like this instead:

margin-bottom:1em;

Mistake #4: The following line from a style definition is missing a hyphen.

marginbottom:1em;

The HTML should look like this instead:

margin-bottom:1em;

Mistake #5: The img line below is missing a closing quotation mark. The picture won't display in the eBook.

```
<div class=CenterSpaceAfter><img style="width: 100%; height: auto;" alt=""
src="Mystery_files/image005.jpg></div>
```

The HTML should look like this instead:

```
<div class=CenterSpaceAfter><img style="width: 100%; height: auto;" alt=""
src="Mystery_files/image005.jpg"></div>
```

Mistake #6: The img line below says that the name of the HTML file is Book, but the author actually named the file SweetRomance. The picture won't display in the eBook. (If you copy my suggested img line to make your pictures, replace the word Book with the name of your book.)

```
<div class=CenterSpaceAfter><img style="width: 100%; height: auto;" alt=""
src="Book_files/image006.jpg"></div>
```

The HTML should look like this instead:

```
<div class=CenterSpaceAfter><img style="width: 100%; height: auto;" alt=""
src="SweetRomance_files/image006.jpg"></div>
```

Mistake #7: The img line below uses a space instead of an underscore between the filename and the word "files." The picture won't display in the eBook.

```
<div class=CenterSpaceAfter><img style="width: 100%; height: auto;" alt="" src="SciFi
files/image007.gif"></div>
```

The HTML should look like this instead:

```
<div class=CenterSpaceAfter><img style="width: 100%; height: auto;" alt=""
src="SciFi_files/image007.gif"></div>
```

Mistake #8: The img line below specifies the filename incorrectly. The picture won't display in the eBook. The filename, which is Math Book.HTML, has a space in it. (It would be simpler if the file had been named MathBook.HTML instead.) In the img line, if the filename has a space in it, you must type 20% in place of the space.

```
<div class=CenterSpaceAfter><img width="1024" height="576" alt="" src="Math
Book_files/image008.jpg"></div>
```

The HTML should look like this instead:

> <div class=CenterSpaceAfter><img width="1024" height="576" alt=""
> src="Math20%Book_files/image008.jpg"></div>

Mistake #9: The img line below includes a .jpg extension, but the picture is actually in GIF format. The picture won't display in the eBook.

> <div class=CenterSpaceAfter><img width="1024" height="576" alt=""
> src="BirdsandBees_files/image009.jpg"></div>

The HTML should look like this instead:

> <div class=CenterSpaceAfter><img width="1024" height="576" alt=""
> src="BirdsandBees_files/image009.gif"></div>

Mistake #10: The img line below indicates that the picture size is 1024 × 448, but the picture size is really 1024 × 948. The aspect ratio will be distorted, making the picture look much shorter than it should.

> <div class=CenterSpaceAfter><img width="1024" height="448" alt=""
> src="Calculus_files/image010.jpg"></div>

The HTML should look like this instead:

> <div class=CenterSpaceAfter><img width="1024" height="948" alt=""
> src="Calculus_files/image010.jpg"></div>

Mistake #11: The author meant for the following img line to display imgae011, but the author copied and pasted another img line and forgot to change the number of the picture. The wrong picture will be displayed in this position of the eBook.

> <div class=CenterSpaceAfter><img style="width: 100%; height: auto;" alt=""
> src="Mystery_files/image002.jpg></div>

The HTML should look like this instead:

> <div class=CenterSpaceAfter><img style="width: 100%; height: auto;" alt=""
> src="Mystery_files/image011.jpg"></div>

Mistake #12: In the a-tag below, the full web address isn't displayed in quotation marks. It is missing the http:// (or https://) part of the website's full URL. This link won't work in the eBook.

<a href="www.amazon.com">www.amazon.com</a>

The HTML should look like this instead:

<a href="https://www.amazon.com">www.amazon.com</a>

Mistake #13: In the a-tag below, a slash is missing in the web address displayed in quotation marks. There should be two slashes between the https and the w's. This link won't work in the eBook.

<a href="https:/www.amazon.com">www.amazon.com</a>

The HTML should look like this instead:

<a href="https://www.amazon.com">www.amazon.com</a>

Mistake #14: In the a-tag below, back slashes are used instead of forward slashes. This link won't work in the eBook.

<a href="https:\\www.amazon.com">Visit Amazon.</a>

The HTML should look like this instead:

<a href="https://www.amazon.com">Visit Amazon.</a>

Mistake #15: In the a-tag below, the full web address isn't displayed in quotation marks. It is missing the http:// (or https://) part of the website's full URL. (You need the http:// part in quotation marks, whereas between the opening and closing a-tags you can type the text to display however you want, as illustrated in the three corrected examples that follow.) This link won't work in the eBook.

<a href="www.amazon.com">https://www.amazon.com</a>

The HTML should look like one of these instead:

<a href="https://www.amazon.com">https://www.amazon.com</a>

<a href="https://www.amazon.com">www.amazon.com</a>

<a href="https://www.amazon.com">Amazon</a>

Consistency

getting every one of several lights red in two different cities. Oh, but that day I had been in a hurry.

I did manage to reach my destination and jot down some notes on a napkin. Then I went into the restaurant, only to think of yet another idea, with my napkin and pen back in the car.

Very funny, muse. We all know that muses have a great sense of humor. They really put the muse in amusement.

Of course, this isn't the only evidence. We have storage rooms full of it.

Your muse and Murphy's law: They're definitely in on it together.

What has your muse done to you lately?

One Problem with Tabs

in two different cities. Oh, but that day I had been in a hurry.

I did manage to reach my destination and jot down some notes on a napkin. Then I went into the restaurant, only to think of yet another idea, with my napkin and pen back in the car.

Very funny, muse. We all know that muses have a great sense of humor. They really put the muse in amusement.

Of course, this isn't the only evidence. We have storage rooms full of it.

Your muse and Murphy's law: They're definitely in on it together.

What has your muse done to you lately?

Inconsistent Indents

light when you want one? I once drove 70 miles, getting every one of several lights red in two different cities. Oh, but that day I had been in a hurry.

I did manage to reach my destination and jot down some notes on a napkin. Then I went into the restaurant, only to think of yet another idea, with my napkin and pen back in the car.

Very funny, muse. We all know that muses have a great sense of humor. They really put the muse in amusement.

Of course, this isn't the only evidence. We have storage rooms full of it.

Your muse and Murphy's law: They're definitely in on it together.

What has your muse done to you lately?

Uploaded a Word file.

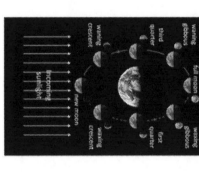

In both cases, the original picture is 300 DPI and sized at 1 280 × 2048.

Uploading a Word file, the pixel size was reduced.

Followed Sec. 5.5.

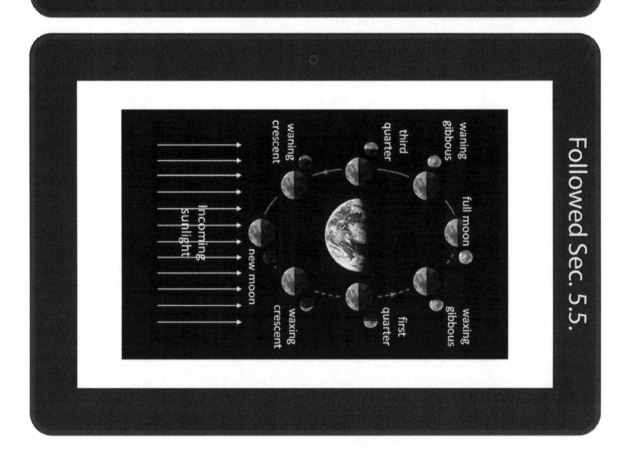

Width Set to 100% in HTML

Out of the gate, the detective was bored out of his mind.

Not a single person was even horsing around.

He couldn't hold his horses for a case to work on.

It was a one-horse town, but it wasn't his horse.

Then a damsel in distress strolled into his office.

She was a bombshell; a perfect ten; out of his league.

He was a silly goose to be daydreaming about her.

What chance did a loser like him have with a girl like her?

So he picked his eyeballs off the floor and stuttered like glue.

Turns out her horse had been murdered in the dead of winter.

Picture's Actual Size

Out of the gate, the detective was bored out of his mind.

Not a single person was even horsing around.

He couldn't hold his horses for a case to work on.

It was a one-horse town, but it wasn't his horse.

Then a damsel in distress strolled into his office.

She was a bombshell; a perfect ten; out of his league.

He was a silly goose to be daydreaming about her.

What chance did a loser like him have with a girl like her?

So he picked his eyeballs off the floor and stuttered like glue.

Turns out her horse had been murdered in the dead of winter.

Even worse, she caught someone beating the dead horse.

It was a knight in shining armor beating the poor beast like a drum.

A knight living in 2013? Sounded like an open and shut case.

It would have been a challenge if the knight had had some horse sense.

What kind of fool would linger at the scene of the crime like that?

He told the damsel that he would take care of the matter.

The next morning he went to see the horse with his own eyes.

ROTATED

Don't rotate a picture.

It will appear sideways

in both portrait

and landscape.

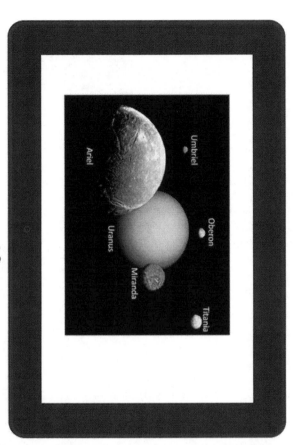

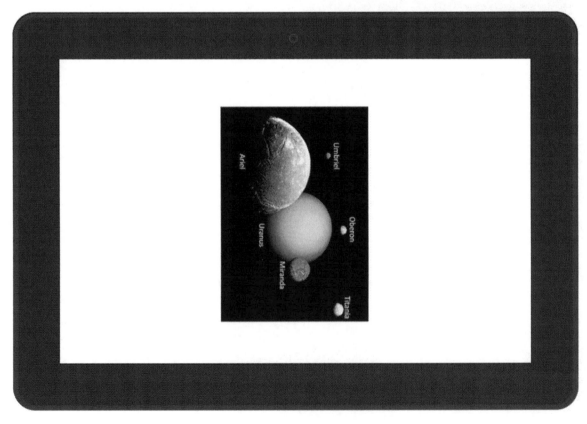

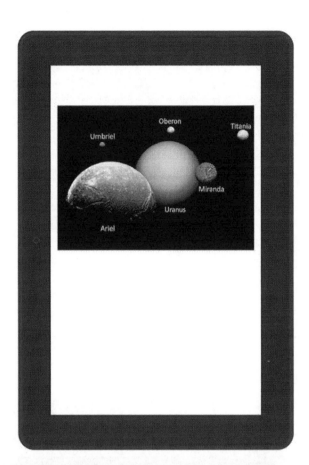

CORRECT

Not rotated.

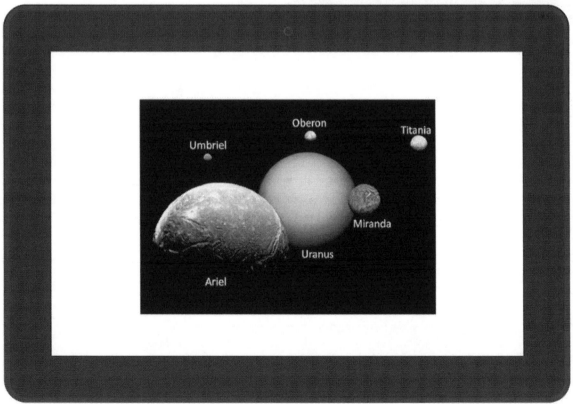

Word's built-in equation tools don't work well with Kindle.
It's better to format every equation as a picture.

Word's Equation Tools

Coulomb's Law

Consider the two pointlike charges illustrated below. The left charge, q_1, creates an electric field everywhere in space, including the location of the right charge, q_2. We could use the formula $E_1 = \frac{k|q_1|}{R^2}$ to find the magnitude of q_1's electric field at the location of q_2. We could then find the electric force exerted on q_2 using the equation $F_e = |q_2|E_1$. If we combine these two equations together, we get Coulomb's law, as shown below.

$$F_e = |q_2|E_1 = F_e = |q_2|\left(\frac{k|q_1|}{R^2}\right) = k\frac{|q_1||q_2|}{R^2}$$

Similarly, we could use the formula $E_2 = \frac{k|q_2|}{R^2}$ to find the magnitude of q_2's electric field at the location of q_1, and then

Reformatted as Pictures

Coulomb's Law

Consider the two pointlike charges illustrated below. The left charge, q_1, creates an electric field everywhere in space, including the location of the right charge, q_2. We could use the formula $E_1 = \frac{k|q_1|}{R^2}$ to find the magnitude of q_1's electric field at the location of q_2. We could then find the electric force exerted on q_2 using the equation $F_e = |q_2|E_1$. If we combine these two equations together, we get Coulomb's law, as shown below.

$$F_e = |q_2|E_1 = F_e = |q_2|\left(\frac{k|q_1|}{R^2}\right) = k\frac{|q_1||q_2|}{R^2}$$

Similarly, we could use the formula

—Chapter 8—

After Publishing

8.1 Your Amazon Product Page

YOUR BOOK'S PRODUCT page at Amazon is built in stages: Not every feature will show up immediately, and the time it takes for a feature to become available varies. Your Look Inside may not be available for a few days, but sometimes it shows up quickly, and occasionally it takes longer. One of the last things to develop on a product page is the customers-also-viewed or customers-also-bought lists: The more sales your book gets, the faster these lists show. If you succeed with a great marketing plan to drive hundreds of sales, these lists can develop quickly and help to bring additional sales. However, for the many books that sell slowly, these lists can take weeks or months to develop.

Inspect your book's Amazon product page closely: This is what customers will see when they are considering your book. There are some things (like the description) that you can revise, if you find ways to improve them.

First double-check the book details: the title, subtitle, series info, author name, other contributors, etc. Make sure there are no mistakes.

Next, read the **description** carefully. Unless your description is very short, you probably see a Read More link. Click the Read More link, and note where it was. (It's possible that the exact position of the Read More link will a little vary depending on the device that you use to visit Amazon's website.) If there is pertinent info after the Read More link, you might consider whether it could be moved closer to the beginning of the description.

You should already have checked your description for spelling and grammar, and you should have already considered whether your description is effective at creating interest (Sec. 6.4), yet it's a good idea to check it carefully again and reconsider how effective it may be. It's very challenging to craft a highly effective description. Most good descriptions go through multiple revisions before they become 'good.'

Buy one copy of your Kindle eBook. If you don't own a Kindle device, you can use one of Amazon's free apps (Kindle for PC, Kindle for Mac, Kindle for Android, Kindle for iPad, Kindle for iPhone, etc.). You should be your own first customer: Be the first person to see how the actual book looks after publishing, and ensure that there are no formatting problems. This will also give your book a sales rank (though it may take up to 48 hours before your product page reflects the sale).

The **Look Inside** plays an important role in customers' buying decisions. It serves as a preview of what to expect. Any formatting issues are red flags. Mistakes with spelling or grammar are also red flags. If customers like the way that the writing flows, and if the beginning of the book grabs their interest and runs away with it, the Look Inside can help sell your book.

Therefore, you need to visit your product page once a day until your Look Inside becomes available. Once your Look Inside is present, check it over carefully. If you find any mistakes, you need to correct them and republish your book (Sec. 8.4): Look for spelling, grammar, writing, and formatting issues. If you find formatting problems in your Look Inside, visit Sec. 7.11.

Does the writing in your Look Inside generate interest? For fiction, does it create suspense? For nonfiction, does it provide valuable content?

If your Look Inside is shorter or longer than you would like, you can place a request with KDP support to alter this. However, note that if you later republish your book, the Look Inside length may change again.

Consider the **marketing** potential of your book's product page, realizing that there is an abundant supply of alternative books on the market, some of which have highly effective product pages.

- Is there **visual appeal**? This includes the front cover, author photo (Sec. 8.2), any images in the Look Inside, and the formatting of the Look Inside. Some customers may not read a single word on your product page if it lacks visual appeal.

- Is there **enticement**? What will draw the reader's interest in the content of your book? Does the description arouse curiosity, create suspense, or describe valuable content?

- Does it send clear signals? It should be clear from the cover (visually), the title (or subtitle), description, and the first chapter exactly what kind of book you have written. All four should send a consistent message about the **genre** or **subject** of your book. For example, if readers look at your cover and expect a mystery, but your description makes it sound like your book is primarily a romance, this creates *buyer confusion*, which doesn't sell books. Customers are wondering if they're in the right place, and it takes consistent messages to reinforce this. Customers who have *doubts* walk away and search for a different book.

- Does it appear **authoritative** and **professional**? Partly, you can demonstrate this by having a professional looking product page: Every element (cover, description, author photo, biography, Look Inside, and the writing itself) needs to appear well done and free of mistakes. In nonfiction, your description can briefly mention any relevant *expertise*, and you can expand upon this in your biography (Sec. 8.2). It's often possible to do this even in fiction, if you have relevant *life experience* (for example, have you lived in or visited any of the cities in your book?) or a qualified background (for example, twenty years of being a Renaissance Fair enthusiast or a hobby relevant to your story). The first chapter(s) reinforce this: For nonfiction, does the writing sound authoritative, and for fiction, does the writing flow well and seem well written?

- Are there any **deterrents**? Unfortunately, it just takes one deterrent to spoil a significant percentage of possible sales. With so many ingredients on your product page (cover, title, description, author photo, biography, Look Inside, etc.), it's easy to have one or more deterrents. Work hard (and perhaps recruit help) to remove deterrents and to give your product page as much customer appeal as you can. Customers can walk away for a variety of reasons: one too many typos, the way the cover looks, bored by the description, author's photo didn't seem professional, formatting mistakes in the Look Inside, bored by the story's beginning, didn't like the writing style, etc. The fewer possible deterrents you have, the better.

- Does the book merit **recommendations** and **referrals**? Everything else is important to get people to try your book, but once people try your book, this is what it takes to make your book successful. Fantastic content with customer appeal can do this. For fiction, a story that is truly amazing or which moves readers greatly, and for nonfiction, content that is very helpful, informative, or filled with tips, can generate valuable recommendations or referrals. Unless there are problems, like too many typos, plot holes, or other kinds of mistakes: It's hard to recommend a book with mistakes (unless they are relatively minor and very rare).

For every sale that you get from a complete stranger, there were several customers who viewed your product page at Amazon, but who chose not to buy your book at that time. A highly marketable product page for a marketable book can sell the book to 10% or more of the customers who happen to discover the book for the first time while shopping at Amazon, but that's relatively rare—most books aren't that marketable. If there is a significant audience for the book and the product page does its job well, 5% is a more reasonable expectation. There are many books for which the rate is 1% or less. If 99 out of 100, or 299 out of 300, or 999 out of 1000 of strangers walk away from the product page without buying the book—the reality is, many books fall into this category—many potential sales are being squandered by some deterrent on the product page (cover, description, Look Inside, author photo, biography, reviews, etc.).

Unfortunately, Amazon doesn't give you these statistics. If you knew that 500 people viewed your product page this week, but you only sold 5 copies (and 3 of those you had been expecting because they were friends or family), the knowledge that 495 people were looking at your book but chose not to buy it would motivate you to try to improve the effectiveness of your product page. **The traffic potential is actually there**, even when a lack of sales makes it seem otherwise: The trick is to make your product page and book as compelling as possible.

If Amazon doesn't provide these statistics, then where did I get the numbers of 10%, 5%, and less than 1% (two paragraphs back)? That's a good question. I know this from ample experience advertising a variety of books on Amazon in multiple pen names, and also from many discussions with fellow authors (some highly successful, some struggling, and most somewhere in between) who have advertised their books. When you advertise on Amazon (Sec. 8.10), Amazon provides data that lets you determine what percentage of people who click on your advertisement actually proceed to purchase the book.

You can expand your Amazon product page by using Amazon **Author Central**. There you can add formatting (like boldface or bullet points) to your description, post an author photo, add an author biography, and gain access to a few other cool features. We'll discuss Author Central in Sec. 8.2. Every author should use Amazon Author Central.

Another important section of your Amazon product page depends on customers: the **customer review** section. The best way to influence this section is to deliver a high quality book with content that readers will feel strongly enough about to post a review. Another way to help with reviews is through effective marketing, as it can take hundreds of sales to generate a few reviews from complete strangers. Sec. 8.6 discusses customer reviews.

If you have a paperback edition of your book, you can get it linked with your Kindle eBook so that customers who discover one edition can easily find the alternative. Visit Sec. 8.11 to learn more.

If you need to make changes to your book, note that you must republish your book through KDP (Sec. 8.4). If you simply click the button to save changes at KDP, these changes do **not** take effect at Amazon unless you reach page 3 of the publishing process and press the button to publish your book (again). However, if you just need to update your description, you can do that through Author Central (Sec. 8.2).

8.2 Author Central

Amazon Author Central lets you add formatting to your Amazon book description (such as boldface or bullet points), add an author picture and biography that will show on your book's product page, and access other helpful features. Visit Author Central via the URL below. Note that your usual Amazon login information will work at Author Central.

https://authorcentral.amazon.com

When you setup your account with Author Central, you will need to **claim your book**. One way to find your book is to type your title and name. Another way is to use your ASIN, which you can copy and paste from your KDP Bookshelf.

Once your Author Central account is setup, login and click on the Author Page tab. You should add at least one **author photo** that is a quality picture (check the lighting and shadows, look for red-eye, make sure that your facial expression is appropriate, check the background, etc.). If you browse the author photos of a variety of a popular authors, it may inspire an idea of your own. You may include up to eight author photos. If you have any book events, like an author signing, include a photo from the author event. When you have two or more author photos, click the Manage link to reorder the images: Position your primary author photo at the top left (using drag and drop).

Next, add your **biography**. Like your description, your biography needs to read well and be free of mistakes. It should be *relevant*: For nonfiction, identify your *expertise* early, but even for fiction, you may have relevant expertise (life experience, travels to cities in your book, several years spent with a relevant hobby, etc.). Ideally, you don't want your biography to come across as just a boring, dry summary, yet you do want your biography to be appropriate and professional. If you browse the biographies of a variety of popular authors, it may help you think of the kinds of things to write about in your own biography.

Create your author page URL. Your default author page URL includes a bunch of numbers. When you create a custom author page URL, you can make this more concise and professional. For example, my default author page URL is:

https://www.amazon.com/Chris-McMullen/e/B002XH39DS

Compare that to the custom author page URL that I made at Author Central:

http://amazon.com/author/chrismcmullen

When you include the link to your author page on all of your *printed* **marketing** tools, such as business cards and bookmarks, you can see how the custom author page URL is convenient: If a customer had to type the URL for my default author page, there is a good chance that the customer would type B002XH39DS incorrectly and not find the page. The custom author page URL is easier for a customer to *type* and find.

Author Central lets you post **videos** on your Amazon *author* page. Authors **can't** post videos on their *product* pages (that's by invitation only, which means you need to be extremely popular for Amazon to 'invite' you to post a video on your product page). However, you can post a video on your Amazon *author* page, and your author page is accessible from your book's Amazon product page, so this is the next best thing. If you have an iPhone or a smart Android phone, you can make a fairly high quality video. Use a search engine to try to find tips for making a video: You may find good suggestions for lighting, sound, etc.

Feed your author **blog** into your author page, and your recent posts will show on your author page. Every author should maintain an author blog. If you create a WordPress blog (as I recommend in Sec. 8.7), visit the main page for your blog, put your cursor in the address bar in your web browser, copy/paste the URL for your blog (it will include the http:// part), and add /feed/ to the end of it. For example, my WordPress author blog is:

https://chrismcmullen.wordpress.com

When I add /feed/ to the end of it, I get this:

https://chrismcmullen.wordpress.com/feed/

When I added this blog feed to my author page, my blog posts started showing up on my Amazon author page. If you don't use WordPress for your author blog or website, the structure of your blog feed may be somewhat different. For example, instead of adding /feed/, you may need to add something like /rss.xml, /atom.xml, or /index.rdf. If you used Google's Blogger (or BlogSpot), add /feeds/posts/default?alt=rss instead of /feed/. To find the RSS feed for your blog, try logging into your blog and looking for help or support info (or try using a search engine).

If you do a *book signing*, attend a *writing conference*, give a *workshop*, or anything else that is author-related, you can add the **event** to your author page (I recommend also adding a photo from the event to your author page).

The Books tab at Author Central allows you to add a few features to your Amazon product page. Visit the Books tab and click on your book. This gives you access to Editorial Reviews, Product Description, From the Author, From the Inside Flap, From the Back Cover, and About the Author.

The Reviews area is for **editorial reviews** (whereas *customer reviews* appear in a separate area on your product page). For example, if a small local newspaper or online magazine reviews your book, you could ask for permission to include a snippet of their review in your editorial reviews section on your product page, quoting a line from their review and indicating the source of your review. Editorial reviews give you the chance to include a review quote from someone with *authority*.

Click the edit button next to Product Description in order to edit your **book description** or add formatting to your description. This allows you to add *boldface, italics, bullet points*, or a *numbered list*. You *don't* need to know any HTML. Author Central lets you preview your description before making the changes. When you preview it, make sure that there aren't any line breaks in the middle of a paragraph (it happens occasionally, as if the Enter key were pressed in the middle of a paragraph—even when you feel 'sure' that you hadn't).

When you're happy with your description, click the Edit HTML tab, copy the HTML for your description, and paste that into the description field at your KDP Bookshelf. (Note that you will need to remove the div-tags from your Author Central description before you paste it into the KDP description, as div-tags aren't supported in the limited HTML for KDP book descriptions.) **Why do this?** Because if you ever republish your book at KDP (if you just want to change your price, keywords, or categories, you must republish, so there is a good chance that you will), **your KDP description will overwrite your Author Central description**. By copying and pasting the HTML for your description into KDP, both descriptions will be identical.

> **Tip**: Copy and paste your description into Word to check for possible spelling and grammar flags. However, **don't** copy and paste from Word into Author Central, as that usually introduces serious formatting issues into your Author Central description. If you type a description in Word and wish to paste it into Author Central, first copy/paste it into Notepad and then copy/paste it into Author Central (this removes the problematic formatting instructions that arise from pasting from Word).

After you update your book description, check it out at Amazon after it goes live. It's not uncommon to discover a strange line break in the middle of a paragraph, for example, in which case you'll want to return to Author Central to correct the problem.

Another section that may be useful is the From the Author section. When this section is used, it appears further down the product page. If there is something you want to add to your product page that isn't a good fit for your description or biography, the From the Author section provides another option.

The About the Author section, on the other hand, probably isn't useful. You already have a biography, so you probably don't also need an About the Author section.

Once you have sales and reviews, you can monitor customer reviews and sales rank at Author Central. We will discuss sales rank and author rank in Sec. 8.5. The Nielsen BookScan data is specifically for *printed* books. If you publish a *paperback* edition (Sec. 8.11) and have significant paperback sales, the Nielsen BookScan section lets you see your sales by geography, which is pretty cool (but note that Nielsen doesn't include 100% of your print sales, and sometimes there are reporting delays at KDP or CreateSpace, so the numbers may not quite match up). Unfortunately, Amazon *doesn't* provide geographic data for *Kindle* sales.

When you publish your next book, visit the Books tab to add your new book. You will need to claim your book, just like you did when you first signed up.

If you publish in two or more author names (using a **pen name**), note that you may use the same Author Central account for up three author names (after that, you need to create a separate account). When you proceed to claim a book written in your pen name, Author Central will ask if that's your pen name, and you will be able to claim your pen name.

Author Central is available in the United States, United Kingdom, France, Germany, Japan, and India. You must login to Author Central in each country where you would like to enable the service (except for India, which is automatically the same as your author page in the United States). Your same account information should work in each country's Author Central. It should eventually pull up your books. You may need to add your author photo or biography again, and there may be a few features from the United States that aren't supported at other countries (like your blog feed).

- United States: http://authorcentral.amazon.com
- United Kingdom: http://authorcentral.amazon.co.uk
- France: http://authorcentral.amazon.fr
- Germany: http://authorcentral.amazon.de
- Japan: http://authorcentral.amazon.co.jp
- India: same as the United States

Product details

File Size: 6598 KB
Print Length: 176 pages
Publisher: Astro Nutz; 3 edition (August 16, 2012)
Publication Date: August 16, 2012
Sold by: Amazon Digital Services LLC
Language: English
ASIN: B0090U01P0
Text-to-Speech: Enabled
X-Ray: Enabled
Word Wise: Enabled
Lending: Enabled
Screen Reader: Supported
Enhanced Typesetting: Enabled
Amazon Best Sellers Rank: #61,938 Paid in Kindle Store (See Top 100 Paid in Kindle Store)
   #2 in Books > Teens > Education & Reference > Science & Technology > **Chemistry**
   #5 in Kindle Store > Kindle eBooks > Teen & Young Adult > Education & Reference > Science & Technology > **Science & Nature**
   #6 in Kindle Store > Kindle eBooks > Nonfiction > Science > Chemistry > **General & Reference**

Would you like to **tell us about a lower price?**

More about the author

› Visit Amazon's Chris McMullen Page

Biography

Dr. Chris McMullen has over 20 years of experience teaching university physics in California, Oklahoma, Pennsylvania, and Louisiana. Dr. McMullen is also an author of math and science books. Whether in the classroom or as a writer, Dr. McMullen loves sharing knowledge and the art of motivating and engaging students.

Chris McMullen earned his Ph.D. in phenomenological high-energy physics (particle physics) from Oklahoma State University in 2002. Originally from California, Dr. McMullen earned his Master's degree from California State University, Northridge, where his thesis was in the field of electron spin resonance.

✓ Following   Show More

Chris McMullen

$8.99 Paperback $8.42 Paperback $9.98 Paperback $9.99 Paperback $3.99 Kindle Edition $3.99 Paperback $7.97 Paperback $7.04 Paperback $19.99 Paperback

✓ Following

Dr. Chris McMullen has over 20 years of experience teaching university physics in California, Oklahoma, Pennsylvania, and Louisiana. Dr. McMullen is also an author of math and science books. Whether in the classroom or as a writer, Dr. McMullen loves sharing knowledge and the art of motivating and engaging students.

Chris McMullen earned his Ph.D. in phenomenological high-energy physics (particle physics) from Oklahoma State University in 2002. Originally from California, Dr. McMullen earned his Master's degree from California State University, Northridge, where his thesis was in the field of electron spin resonance.

Dr. McMullen is well-known for:
• engaging students in challenging ideas through creativity
• breaking difficult problems down into manageable steps
• providing clear and convincing explanations to subtle issues
• his mastery of physics and strong

Author Updates

Blog post
Tips For the New Goodreads Giveaways
GOODREADS GIVEAWAYS As you may have heard, Goodreads Giveaways have changed.
One change is that KDP authors can now give eBooks away. Anoth...
1 week ago   Read more

Blog post
How Kindle Unlimited Clears Half a Penny per Page (December, 2017)
KINDLE UNLIMITED UPDATE FOR DECEMBER, 2017 The Kindle Unlimited per-page rate finished 2017 with a bang, paying over $0.005 per page read ($0.00506394 to be preci...
1 week ago   Read more

Blog post
How to Add X-Ray to Your Kindle eBook
X-ray picture licensed from ShutterStock.
X-RAY FOR KINDLE Authors can add X-ray to their Kindle eBooks via KDP. Here is how to do it:
1 week ago   Read more

Books by Chris McMullen

Showing 1 - 12 of all Results Books : Advanced Search   Sort by Featured

All Formats Kindle Edition Paperback Large Print Audible Audio Edition

Algebra Essentials Practice Workbook with Answers: Linear & Quadratic Equations, Cross Multiplying, and Systems of Equations (Improve Your Math Fluency Series 12) Sep 11, 2015
by Chris McMullen
Kindle Edition
$0.00 In Unlimited   ★★★★☆ ▾ 123
Subscribers read for free.

amazon Author Central   **Author Page**   Books   Sales Info ▾   Customer Reviews   Help | Chris McMullen ▾

Author Page

Content you provide will appear on Amazon's Chris McMullen Page after a short delay.
› Visit Amazon's Chris McMullen Page ⬈

Biography   edit biography | delete

Dr. Chris McMullen has over 20 years of experience teaching university physics in California, Oklahoma, Pennsylvania, and Louisiana. Dr. McMullen is also an author of math and science books. Whether in the classroom or as a writer, Dr. McMullen loves sharing knowledge and the art of motivating and engaging students.

Chris McMullen earned his Ph.D. in phenomenological high-energy physics (particle physics) from Oklahoma State University in 2002. Originally from California, Dr. McMullen earned his Master's degree from California State University, Northridge, where his thesis was in the field of electron spin resonance.

Dr. McMullen is well-known for:
• engaging students in challenging ideas through creativity
• breaking difficult problems down into manageable steps
• providing clear and convincing explanations to subtle issues
• his mastery of physics and strong background in mathematics
• helping students become more fluent in practical math skills

As a physics... › Read More

Blogs   add blog

Blog Feed	Status
http://chrismcmullen.wordpress.com/feed/	✓ New posts will appear on the Author Page within 24 hours of posting. Learn More 🗑
http://improveyourmathfluency.com/feed/	✓ New posts will appear on the Author Page within 24 hours of posting. Learn More 🗑
http://readtuesday.com/feed/	✓ New posts will appear on the Author Page within 24 hours of posting. Learn More 🗑
https://monkeyphysicsblog.wordpress.com/feed/	✓ New posts will appear on the Author Page within 24 hours of posting. Learn More 🗑

Events   add event

Share your upcoming speaking engagements, bookstore appearances, and other events.

Author Page URL   learn more

Cut and paste the text below to share your Author Page:

amazon.com/author/chrismcmullen

Share this URL: 🔵 🔷 ✏

Photos   add photo | manage

Videos   add video | manage

8.3 Sharing Your Book

Share your book to help people find it. You can link to your book from your author blog, from social media, or through an email newsletter, for example (Sec. 8.7).

There are a variety of ways to share a link to your book's Amazon product page. You can get a **short link** to your product page by visiting your product page, looking for the Share link (is usually beneath the pricing and other info at the top right of the page), and clicking the Share link. For example, when I did this for one of my books, I got the link http://a.co/ebN3J7m, which is much shorter than the URL displayed in the address bar of the web browser.

Tip: Test out your link to make sure that it works *before* you share it.

Another way to obtain a fairly short link is from your KDP Bookshelf: Hover your cursor over the View on Amazon link and click the desired country. When I did this for the same book as my previous example, I got the link https://www.amazon.com/dp/B00AA5CJ7C. One thing that's convenient about this is that you can quickly get a short link to your book for **any country**. I like this link because it clearly says "Amazon," so that customers can see that the link will take them to a site that they **trust**. My previous example was shorter, but doesn't make this as clear. (If a customer hovers over the link and looks at the bottom left of their browser, it will show where the link would take them, but many customers don't think to do this, and many customers also prefer to view web pages via mobile devices, where they don't have a mouse to "hover.")

Amazon also provides a cool, visual, and engaging way to share your Kindle eBook. It's called the **Kindle Instant Book Preview**. You can get a link for this (or the HTML code to embed it so that it works right on your own webpage) by clicking the <**Embed**> link next to the Share link (which we discussed earlier in this section). Anyone can read a *free preview* of your book with a single click of the mouse, *without needing to login and without having to first get a Kindle app*. The Kindle Instant Book Preview serves two useful purposes: First, people can see a preview of your book, but secondly, **people can see how easy it is to read your Kindle eBook even if they don't own a Kindle device**. From the preview, customers can then click a link that takes them directly to the Amazon store to purchase your book, and if needed, they can also click a link to get a **free Kindle reading app** to let them read your book on a PC, laptop, tablet, phone, iPad, Mac, etc.

Amazon Associates is a program that *pays you* to share your book (or anything else on Amazon that you might like to share). If you sign up for Amazon Associates, you can earn a *commission* on *referrals*. If someone clicks on an Amazon Associates link to your book and winds up purchasing a Kindle Fire, for example, you can earn a commission on the sale. Visit Amazon's home page, scroll down to the bottom, look for Make Money With Us, and click the link Become an Affiliate.

https://affiliate-program.amazon.com/home

Once you've published multiple books, it's convenient to provide a link to your Amazon **author page**, where customers can see all of your books at once. Sec. 8.2 describes how to make a link to your author page.

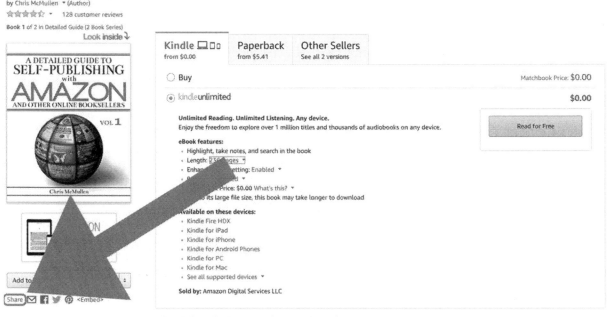

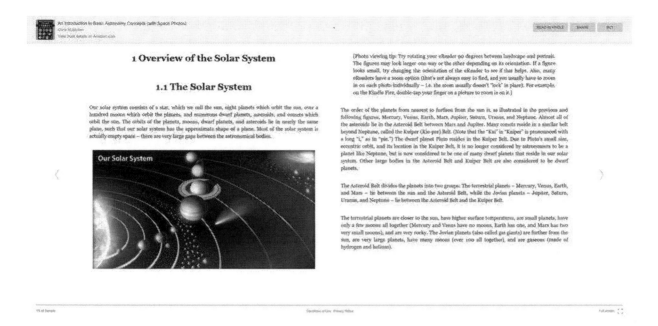

8.4 Revising or Unpublishing

Republishing is very common for Kindle eBooks. If you just want to do something simple like change your price, change your keywords, or change your browse categories, **you must republish your book**: If you simply click the save button, your revision will **not** take effect at Amazon (until you reach page 3 of the publishing process and click the publish button).

There is one thing that you can change without having to republish: *You can edit your description through Author Central* (Sec. 8.2).

Beware of changing your keywords or categories. If your book has already developed **keyword associations** or improved **visibility** in a browse category, *you risk losing this when you change your keywords or categories*, respectively. If a book is getting sales, I don't change anything (if I can avoid it). When sales are stagnant, then a change may be worth the risk.

Certain revisions you want to make swiftly. For example, if you discover mistakes in your book description or **Look Inside**, you want to fix those and republish as soon as possible—but take time to preview any changes to the content of your eBook as described in Chapter 7.

Tip: If you revise your interior book file, make a small change to your **copyright page** so that you will know *which version* of your book you are looking at. For example, if you examine the copyright page of my book, you will see something similar to "Version 3.19.18A." When I see this, I know that I'm looking at a version that I published on March 19, 2018 (you could change the letter from A to B if you happen to publish a second version on the same date). Since it may take a few days (or more) for your Look Inside to reflect the new version, such a note helps you determine which version is showing. If you're trying to download the latest copy of your eBook (which is tricky, as we'll discuss next), adding a version or edition number will tell you whether you're looking at the latest edition or not.

If you've already purchased your Kindle eBook, then you republish with revisions, and then proceed to purchase your Kindle eBook *again*, you will discover that you still have the *original* version. Once you own a Kindle eBook, it becomes part of your Kindle library. The version that you purchased is the version that you will *always* have—*unless* you contact KDP support and ask them to "push" the new version to your device. That's the language that you want to use.

The same is true for your customers. Once a customer buys your book, the customer is stuck with the version that the customer bought. If you republish your book, the customer will still have the previous version. The customer would similarly need to contact Amazon and request for the latest version to be "pushed" to the customer's device.

There is a reason behind this, and occasionally there is a way around it. The reason that a republished version doesn't automatically override the customer's previous version is that *the customer would lose any annotation or highlighting*. Imagine this from the perspective of a customer who purchased a book and had highlighting and numerous notes written (yes, it's possible to do this in a Kindle eBook) in the book, and then suddenly all of those valuable notes are gone. That's why Amazon doesn't automatically "push" new versions onto customers' devices.

However, if you make **significant changes** to a book, Amazon KDP will consider a request to notify customers and "push" a new version onto their devices. Place a polite request through KDP support. Be clear and specific about what you changed and how extensive the revisions are.

Generally speaking, Amazon is hesitant to automatically deliver an update to customers, since any customers who lose notes or highlighting will become frustrated: Amazon must determine that the benefits of a forced update outweigh such possible frustration. This generally means that Amazon will only automatically "push" your book onto customers' devices if they feel that the previous version was very difficult to read (perhaps there were significant formatting mistakes, which have now been corrected).

If Amazon feels that your revisions are **major corrections** (destructive or critical), Amazon will notify all customers about your update via email, and each customer will have the option to download the new version through their Manage Your Content and Devices page at Amazon. Every customer will know that your book was updated, so before you place your request with KDP support, you should consider if it is worth spreading this knowledge (that there may have been a significant problem with your book).

If Amazon feels that your revisions are **minor** (distractions, but not destructive or critical), Amazon *won't* notify customers about the update. This is the most common outcome. However,

Amazon will arrange it so that any customers who visit their Manage Your Content and Devices page can download the new version. Most customers won't know that there is an updated version, so they won't go looking for it. However, if a customer who has the old version contacts you, then you can let that customer know that an updated version is available.

It's also possible that Amazon will look at the book and deem that major corrections still need to be made. This could be the case if a significant formatting mistake impairs the reading experience. In this case, Amazon will make the book temporarily unavailable for sale, notify you of the issue, give a chance to correct the issue, and once it's resolved Amazon will notify customers that an update is available.

Until now, I've been talking about revisions that *you* want to make. There is another possibility to be aware of: Customers who discover mistakes may report them to Amazon.

Occasionally, Amazon sends an author or publisher a **Kindle Quality Notice**. Some of these simply point out a minor issue, like a few spelling mistakes. However, occasionally a quality notice indicates that there are critical errors, and Amazon has already removed your book from sale or will do so soon. In this case, you must correct the error swiftly and republish your book. (There is yet another possibility: If a book violates the KDP terms and conditions, a title may be suspended indefinitely, or an author's publishing privileges may be revoked. Such action is usually taken against someone who does something unscrupulous, like plagiarizing from another author's work.)

If you publish a *paperback* edition through KDP or CreateSpace, for example, note that you can also upload revisions to the paperback edition (through the respective company, of course).

Let's discuss an alternative to republishing: In the worst-case scenario, you may want to **unpublish** your book. I don't recommend unpublishing unless the circumstances seem dire: Save the option to unpublish as a **last resort**. If you have a nightmarish situation, like accidentally publishing a draft that had numerous mistakes and a missing chapter, unpublishing will remove the book from sale (though the effect isn't immediate). You can unpublish your book from your KDP Bookshelf.

If you're on the fence about whether to republish or unpublish, or perhaps temporarily unpublish, consider the following. If you unpublish and republish later, your **sales rank** and **searchability** on Amazon may be affected just as if you had left the book available for sale and had zero views, activity, and sales in the meantime: If you go weeks or months without a single sale, your sales rank climbs into the high millions. When a sale finally does come through, sales rank will climb very fast due to the recent inactivity. If instead you simply republish by uploading new files, advancing to page 3 of the publishing process, and pressing the publish button, your book remains available for sale and any sales will help your sales rank.

If you unpublish and then publish the revision later by adding a new title (as opposed to republishing the original title) to your KDP Bookshelf, you lose your **sales rank** history and you also lose your **reviews**. (However, if your book has the same title and author info, sometimes the reviews do come back. If this happens and you don't want the old reviews, if you've made significant corrections to the original book, try emailing KDP support to explain the situation politely, emphasizing the corrections that you've made. There is no guarantee though. Of course, a customer who reviewed your original book can choose to write a new review for your new book.) **If you had semi-regular sales or positive reviews, it may be better to upload revised files to your original book** (and press the publish button to republish).

Note that if you unpublish a *print* edition, the book listing remains on Amazon forever, whereas when you unpublish a Kindle eBook, the book should become unavailable for sale and unsearchable at Amazon in about a day or so. The reason that Amazon keeps unpublished print editions available is that it allows customers or booksellers to resell any used copies that they may have (authors earn royalties when a new copy of a print book is first sold, but don't earn royalties when it is resold).

8.5 Sales

You can view sales figures at KDP. After you login, click Reports to see your Sales Dashboard. Note that the report shows units "ordered," which isn't the same as units "sold." Click the Month-to-Date tab to see units "sold." While often a sale appears at about the same time as an order, occasionally there is a delay of one day to a few days, and rarely the delay can be a week or more. Don't freak out if your units ordered report seems slightly different from your month-to-date report. In addition to a possible delay, the month-to-date report also shows returns.

Also note that the Sales Dashboard shows sales from *all* marketplaces. Below your Sales Dashboard charts you can find a table of royalties earned for sales in each country. Note that the Royalties Earned table *doesn't* include royalties for pages read through Kindle Unlimited or Amazon Prime.

If you enrolled your book in KDP Select (which means that you're not allowed to publish your eBook anywhere other than Amazon Kindle unless you successfully opt out of KDP Select and then wait for your enrollment period to end—see Sec. 6.12), you will see Kindle Edition

Normalized Pages (KENP) read in addition to sales. The KENP read shows how many pages of your book have been read by Kindle Unlimited and Amazon Prime customers who borrow your book. **You won't know how much you are earning for KENP read until the 15th day of the following month**: 15 days after the month ends, you can click the Prior Months' Royalties tab and generate a report for the previous month, which will finally show your earnings for KENP read. (It typically varies from about $0.004 to $0.005 per KENP read.)

If your book is available for pre-order, note that there is a separate tab for pre-orders. There are also tabs for Payments, Promotions (Countdown Deals and free book promotions for books enrolled in KDP Select), and Ad Campaigns (Sec. 8.10 discusses advertising).

If you complete the tax information and sign up for direct deposit, you should be paid two months after a month ends. So, for example, if you sell books in January, you would be paid royalties for January near the end of March. (Keep in mind that you will need to pay **taxes** on your author earnings, unless for some reason you're legally exempt from doing so. You can learn more about taxes at irs.gov, and when April approaches, there are usually some discussions about taxes on the KDP community forum.)

Another indication of how well your book is selling is your Amazon.com **sales rank**. The main idea is this: The more a book sells, the lower the sales rank number. For example, a book that has a sales rank of 15,000 is selling much better than a book that has a sales rank of 340,000.

Sales rank combines **recent sales** frequency together with **sales history** (and also reflects other factors which are more difficult to determine—plus, Amazon occasionally changes the method for computing sales rank). When a book doesn't sell, its sales rank climbs. If a book has a history of steady sales and suddenly stops selling, its sales rank climbs slowly. If a book hasn't sold much and suddenly sells, after the sale its sales rank climbs rapidly (unless it gets another sale). Books that sell multiple copies per day have better sales ranks (the numbers are lower). The books that sell the most frequently in each category are ranked #1 in that category: That's what it takes to be an Amazon bestseller (at least temporarily: if you have such amazing fortune, take a picture, and consider mentioning it in your description).

There are **overall ranks** and **category ranks**.

- The **Kindle Store sales rank** is the overall rank compared to all other Kindle eBooks. If you sell about one book a day, you would have a sales rank in the low hundred thousands (200,000 to 300,000 or so, depending on how many eBooks have sold one copy in the last 24 hours—this number consistently grows, so that soon there may be 1,000,000 eBooks that have sold in the last 24 hours, and it also depends on the season). A book with an overall Kindle sales rank consistently below 100,000 is selling multiple copies per day. When a book hasn't sold for a while, its overall Kindle sales rank eventually climbs into the millions.

- A sales rank in **Books** (as opposed to a sales rank in the Kindle Store) includes both print books and eBooks.

- A sales rank in a **category** is more difficult to interpret, as it depends on how many books are in that category and how well the other books in the category are selling. For example, a book with a sales rank of 1800 in Sword & Sorcery might have an overall Kindle Store sales rank of 150,000. It's also easier to rank well in a subcategory than a category: For example, Sword & Sorcery is a subcategory of Fantasy.

- Note that there are separate **free** and **paid** Kindle sales ranks. If you run a free book promotion through KDP Select to temporarily make your eBook free (Sec. 8.8), your paid sales rank will be replaced by a separate free sales rank during the promotion. If you check your sales rank while your book is free, don't get too excited: The free sales rank that you see is temporary. Once your free promotion ends, the free sales rank will be replaced by a paid sales rank. Note that the paid sales rank will likely be worse than it was before the promotion, since you won't have any paid sales during the promotion. (I'm **not** recommending that you give your book away for free. Presently, I'm just providing information about sales ranks. We'll discuss promotions in Sec. 8.8.)

- There is also an **author rank**, separate from sales rank. You can find your author rank at Author Central (Sec. 8.2). The author rank tallies sales for all of your books, and ranks you relative to other authors. If, on average, you can get your author rank to improve (become a lower number) with time, this is a good sign. Usually, it takes continued writing and publishing along with some effective marketing (Sec. 8.7).

Don't try to interpret your sales rank too literally, as there are *multiple factors* involved. If you enrolled your book in KDP Select, note that *every time your book is borrowed, that boosts your sales rank the same as a sale.* (It's when your book is borrowed that matters, not when the pages get read, as far as sales rank is concerned.) So if you see a big improvement in your overall sales rank in the Kindle Store (a huge drop in value), it may be a sign that your book was **borrowed** rather than *sold*. Note that there are sometimes **significant delays** in reporting at Amazon, for sales rank as well as for orders and sales, and the sales rank is complicated by the fact that it depends on a *variety of factors*.

If you enrolled your eBook in KDP Select, note that this significantly complicates the interpretation of sales rank. Each time a Kindle Unlimited customer borrows your eBook, this helps your sales rank. The problem is that you have *no idea* when a customer borrows your eBook through Kindle Unlimited: Your reports *don't* show this at all. Your sales report does show how many pages are read, but that's *not* the same thing. If you see that 100 pages are read, you have *no idea* whether 1 customer read 100 pages or 10 customers each read 10 pages, and you also have *no idea* whether those customers borrowed your book today or sometime in the past. Some customers borrow a book and wait weeks or months before they start reading it. The bottom line is that if your eBook is enrolled in KDP Select, you really *can't* interpret your sales rank reliably (and even if you don't enroll in KDP Select, there are other complicating factors). However, Kindle Unlimited borrows do help with sales rank, which is a *good* thing.

Realize that sales rank *changes*. It **fluctuates** with sales and dry spells. *It's very common for sales rank to drop off after 30 or 90 days.* Many books receive initial sales from fans, and get initial exposure from the Last 30 Days and Last 90 Days search filters, but see sales drop off after a few months. Thus, although a book might have a sales rank of 2,000,000 right now because it hasn't sold for a while, it may actually have sold fairly well when it was first released. It sometimes works the other way, too: When an author publishes a new book, interest in the new book sometimes helps to generate sales in the old book, such that a book with a sales rank over a million occasionally sees new life in the low hundred thousands. It usually takes continued writing and publishing combined with effective marketing (Sec. 8.7) to keep books selling well long-term. Another way is to write such a compelling book that it continues to receive word-of-mouth recommendations and referrals for years to come, but that's much more challenging to do (it has been done though).

It's tempting to watch your sales reports like a hawk. After all, you're hoping to see more sales. However, it's more productive if you **focus on writing the next book**, and spend a little time **marketing** (Sec. 8.7). These activities may *help* your sales.

Product details

File Size: 6598 KB
Print Length: 176 pages
Publisher: Astro Nutz; 3 edition (August 16, 2012)
Publication Date: August 16, 2012
Sold by: Amazon Digital Services LLC
Language: English
ASIN: B0090U01P0
Text-to-Speech: Enabled
X-Ray: Enabled
Word Wise: Enabled
Lending: Enabled
Screen Reader: Supported
Enhanced Typesetting: Enabled
Amazon Best Sellers Rank: #8,980 Paid in Kindle Store (See Top 100 Paid in Kindle Store)
> #1 in Books > Teens > Education & Reference > Science & Technology > **Chemistry**
> #1 in Kindle Store > Kindle eBooks > Nonfiction > Science > Chemistry > **General & Reference**
> #2 in Kindle Store > Kindle eBooks > Teen & Young Adult > Education & Reference > Science & Technology > **Science & Nature**

Would you like to **tell us about a lower price?**

8.6 Reviews

Once you get some sales, you will probably be hoping to get some customer reviews of your book. It's not uncommon to only get one review for every 50 to 200 sales, on average. The sales-to-reviews ratio can vary considerably, depending on a number of factors, such as the type of book. I once sold several hundred copies of a book before I finally got the first review, but a few times one of the first customers reviewed my book. Those extremes are rare: Usually, it's somewhere in between.

Note that Amazon is highly effective at *blocking* and *removing* reviews suspected of being left by **friends and family members**. Nobody except Amazon knows exactly how it works, but judging from the number of authors who have started discussions about reviews not showing up, Amazon is pretty effective at knowing. (Think about this: How does the author 'know' that a review was 'supposed' to show up? When a complete stranger reviews your book, you generally have *no idea* that this was going to happen. Evidently, when the author 'knows' that a review is 'missing,' Amazon 'knows' that the author 'knows.')

There is a reason that Amazon blocks and removes friend and family reviews. Back in the early days of self-publishing, unfortunately, some authors abused the review policy. It had reached the point where there were high profile articles in the *Wall Street Journal* and *New York Times*. Amazon needed to do something to restore customer faith in the review system, and that's when Amazon began implementing the new system. It's now common knowledge that Amazon blocks and removes friend and family reviews.

There was a nice **side benefit** to this: Most customers approach reviews—both good reviews and bad reviews—with a degree of **suspicion**. Many customers examine the Look Inside to see if the reviews that they read seem to have merit. So if you're unfortunate enough to receive a bad review, fortunately, some customers will give the book the benefit of the doubt, or at least see if they can corroborate the information provided in the review before being swayed.

The *best* reviews that you can receive are **organic reviews**—the reviews that are left by complete strangers without your knowledge. Reviews that show the **Verified Purchase** label also tend to hold more sway and receive more visibility (all other things being equal). When a customer purchases a book directly from Amazon, the review will show up as a Verified Purchase (except when, for whatever reason, a few customers exercise the option to **not** have this label displayed).

Reviews are helpful to customers because they offer an assortment of opinions about different aspects of the book. The three important words here are "customers," "opinions," and "books."

- Reviews are primarily there to serve the *customers*, not to serve the author. Note that some customers feel very strongly that this space is "for customers only." Consider this before you comment on a review as an author.

- Reviews generally contain *opinions*, **not** facts. Everyone is entitled to his or her opinion.
- Customers are reviewing the *book*. They generally aren't criticizing the author. Try not to take criticism personally.

When your book receives reviews with praise and encouragement, reviews will seem like the most wonderful thing in the world. But when your book receives a review with criticism or spite, it may seem like an awful, gut-wrenching experience.

It's challenging for many authors, but it's best if you can develop a *thick skin*, and let reviews easily roll off your back. If you struggle with this, avoid reading your reviews, or at least check on them less frequently.

Don't comment on a review emotionally. It's generally good advice *not* to comment on *any* reviews: It looks more professional to *not* comment, and you avoid the many **pitfalls** involved in doing otherwise. If you can't stop yourself from commenting, at least try to force yourself to *walk away from the computer for a few days* before you post your comment (this gives you time to cool down, and for reason to settle in), avoid responding *emotionally*, and try to keep your comment professional, polite, and concise. Many experienced authors would advise you **not** to comment on reviews at all. (Some of the wisest things that we write are the words that we don't write at all.)

If you do comment on a review, beware that **it's easy to get trapped**. You might think that you're just going to leave one quick comment and be done with it, but it's not always so simple. Once you comment, you might open a *can of worms*. The reviewer might reply to your comment. What if the reviewer asks you a question? Now you feel obligated to reply again, and **before you know it, what you intended to be one quick comment turns into a lengthy discussion**, where you've left several comments. It doesn't look good to potential customers. It was better when it was just a critical review with no comments at all.

Instead of commenting on the review, see if you can find another way to turn the negative experience into something **positive**. Examine the review to see if any of the criticism may actually have merit. Is it worth making a revision? If so, the criticism may help your book improve. Does the review create a false perception about your book? If so, *perhaps you can revise your book description to make that point more clear*.

Note that bad reviews don't always hurt sales, and good reviews don't always help sales. *Reviews don't always have the impact that authors expect.*

It's better to focus on **sales** than reviews. **Marketing** (Sec. 8.7) can help you create more sales, and the more sales you get, the more organic reviews will come. There are two kinds of sales: One type of sale is when a complete stranger discovers your book on Amazon, and another kind of sale is when someone first discovers the book through marketing. If a critical review appears to have stifled the first type of sale, focus more on the second type of sale. When you interact with potential customers in person through marketing, the impression that you make is more likely to result in sales and new reviews.

You're **not** permitted to offer anything in exchange for a review. You may offer one free copy of your book in exchange for an honest review, with no strings attached. We'll discuss options for gifting your book in Sec. 8.13.

Note that Amazon isn't the only place where a customer can post a review. Many avid readers post reviews at **Goodreads**, for example. There are some bloggers with a large following who regularly post reviews. If your book receives such a review, some customers may learn about your book through reviews before they ever visit Amazon. We'll consider Goodreads and blogging in the next section, along with several other marketing suggestions.

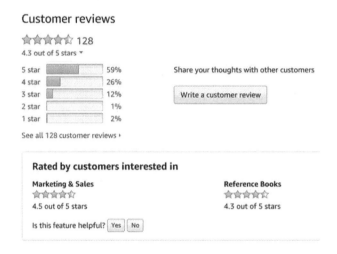

8.7 Marketing

There are millions of Kindle eBooks on Amazon, plus tens of millions of print books, with tens of thousands of new books added each day. With so many books to choose from, how will customers ever discover your book? The answer is marketing.

There are two important factors that help to sell books:

- *Marketability* is about customer *appeal*. Does the cover offer instant visual appeal, and clearly convey the genre or subject? Does the description create interest? Is the Look Inside appealing? Does the beginning of the story grab the customer's interest? Do customers want to read a book like yours?

- *Marketing* is about *helping* to make your *target audience* aware of your book.

Marketability and marketing go hand in hand. If you do a lot of marketing, but your book lacks marketability, results can be dismal. If your book has strong marketability, but you're ineffective with marketing, customers won't find your book. Strive to get your marketability as strong as you can, and then learn and try out various forms of marketing.

In this section, I will list several tips and suggestions to help get you started with marketing. If you feel overwhelmed, realize that you don't need to do it all at once. Try out one thing at a time, do a little here and there, and your *marketing net* will grow. Even if it starts out small and slow, it can become significant over time. The main thing is to keep at it, and try your best.

Marketing should actually start **before** you publish your book: It's called **premarketing**. If you haven't published yet, you still have a chance to do this. If it's too late to do premarketing for this book, there is always the next book. Following is a list of premarketing suggestions.

- Start a free WordPress **blog** and post regular, short articles with nonfiction content (or poetry) that relates to your book.

- Create social media accounts at Twitter and Facebook (at a minimum), set up your profile, and begin to grow a following.

- Start an **email newsletter** with MailChimp. Send out a short email with engaging content relevant to your book once a month or so (but try to make it regular).

- Print business cards and **bookmarks** to give potential customers when you interact with them personally.

- Find people who carry influence among your target audience and get them involved when your book is developing. Try to *earn* their recommendations and referrals.

- Get feedback regarding your book as you write it. Try to involve people who might help you create **buzz** for your coming book and share it with people they know (who aren't likely to spoil the story).

- Do a **cover reveal** before you release your book. You can also do a blurb reveal, where you reveal your description (and you might receive valuable suggestions for revising it). The idea is to get people interested in your book before the release date.

- Arrange for a special activity when your book is released. For example, for a horror book, you could arrange for a zombie run. If you prefer to keep things simple and normal, you could have a **book signing** (if you have a print version available—see Sec. 8.11).

- Offer free **review copies** (Sec. 8.13 describes various options for sending copies of your book). This can help to create buzz. If the recipients are strangers,[111] it may help to get a few customer reviews shortly after you book launches. If you find bloggers who sometimes review books similar to yours (follow their submission guidelines) or if you can get media attention (through a small local paper or a small online journal, for example), it may help also with publicity.

---

[111] As mentioned in Sec. 8.6, Amazon is highly effective at blocking and removing reviews where the reader may have a personal connection with the author (such as a friend or family member).

- Be prepared to spread the word about your book when it comes out. You want to build a following before release day, hoping that a few of your followers will be interested in your book. Try to recruit a few people who may help announce your book's release.

- Follow fellow authors. Interact with them periodically, support their work, and help them share their books. Hopefully, a few will help you spread the word when you release your book.

- Don't *overhype* your book: It's hard to live up to lofty expectations. You do want to create a little buzz (people talking about your book) and awareness for your book, but refrain from making it sound like the best book ever (even if it is).

Now we'll discuss **marketing** (though some of the premarketing ideas work for regular marketing, too). When most authors think of marketing, they usually associate this with strategies for trying to create an avalanche of short-term sales. While there are strategies for trying to achieve a burst of sales, the success of such strategies can vary. When you hear authors say, "Don't buy a book on marketing that's over three months old," they usually have this kind of marketing in mind.

However, there is another kind of marketing: When I think of marketing, I think about trying to generate **long-term** success. *Long-term marketing is more likely to pay dividends.* There are some forms of marketing that you can do which, after putting in the work now, can become almost self-reliant in the future. Long-term marketing strategies are less susceptible to changes in the market, such that if you read a book on long-term marketing that is a few years old, many of the strategies may still be useful for creating long-term success.

Keep in mind that some long-term marketing strategies start out very slowly, and may not yield significant results for some time, but have the potential to eventually grow strong and almost self-reliant if done right. For example, if you start a blog, you will only have a few views at first, and it may take months of posting weekly articles to really gain traction. But if those weekly articles (which can be short and still be effective) contain the kind of information that people might search for on the internet, your content can eventually accelerate traffic to your blog, so that after a year or two, you might have hundreds of daily visitors. (I've done this, so I know it can work: My blog was very slow for several months, but after a year it started to grow, and now hundreds of visitors discover my articles through search engines every day).

When I do marketing that brings short-term results, I do it thinking more about the potential for long-term dividends. A fan who reads one book now may come back to read more books later. A customer who finds my book valuable is more likely to recommend my book to others. That's the *best* kind of marketing you can get, but the *hardest* kind to earn: **word-of-mouth recommendations** and referrals. You need for a customer to find a nonfiction book to be very helpful or a fiction book to be highly compelling, moving, or amazing. Consider this as you write and publish new books: What can you do to take your books to the next level, making them even more compelling?

Remember that marketing usually starts out slow and small. Keep it up and your marketing net can grow. Useful content that you post now is more likely to pay dividends down the road. Keep your eye on continued improvement and possible future success: Sell more books next year than this year, publish more books, get your average author rank to improve each year, grow your following, and get more traffic to your blog each year. These are all positive indicators that things may eventually take off.

Following are several **marketing suggestions**. What are you waiting for? Get started!

- Create a free **blog** with WordPress.com. I've created multiple blogs and websites—both free and paid—with WordPress, GoDaddy, and Blogger, and I've had by far the greatest success with my free WordPress blog (over 700,000 views and 8000 followers as of the publication of this book, with hundreds of daily visitors finding my articles through search engines).

- Post regular (weekly is good enough) articles (they can be short) that have nonfiction content relating to your book (and your background) in some way. If your articles answer questions that people search for on the internet, and if most of your articles fall in the same general category (in my case, the broad category is self-publishing), several months down the road they might start to gain significant visibility through search engines. Valuable content can bring long-term success (and you can find relevant nonfiction topics to write about even if your books are *fiction*). This is called **content marketing**, and valuable content *attracts readers*. It starts out very slow, but can be highly effective long-term.

- Create **social media** accounts. Do this at Twitter and Facebook at a minimum. LinkedIn is a networking platform for professionals (useful for nonfiction). Instagram and Pinterest are visually oriented social media platforms. Note that you can sometimes feed posts from one platform to another: For example, my WordPress posts automatically feed into Twitter and Facebook so that people who prefer Twitter of Facebook can follow me from their preferred platforms (but don't double feed: if you accept Twitter's offer to feed to Facebook and vice-versa, you can get double or triple posts).

- Start an **email newsletter** using MailChimp. One advantage of an email newsletter is that the followers are more likely to be interested in your content, whereas social media followers are sometimes just hoping for a follow-back. When you publish your new book, an announcement through your email newsletter thus has the potential to be more effective. (On the other hand, customers may be more reluctant to subscribe to yet another email. You may need compelling content, or a free gift—maybe a PDF booklet with valuable information—to entice the subscription.) **Don't** add email contacts without their consent. You **must** include an unsubscribe option in each email.

- Most of your social media posts should include **valuable content**. Only an occasional post should mention your book. Blog posts and email newsletters should primarily include valuable content (briefly at the end, you may mention your book and ways to follow you on Twitter or Facebook).

- Post a short, **free sample** for your next book in the back of your current book. Put it in the back so that it doesn't hamper the reading experience. Keep it short (like one chapter), just enough to draw interest (definitely, not longer than the Look Inside sample). Make sure that the sample is similar to the actual book so that it's likely to be relevant to the readers.

- At the end of each book, include a short thank-you note and encourage the reader to follow you. If they follow you on Amazon, when you publish your next book, Amazon will email them. Include a link to your author blog and information so they can follow you on Twitter and Facebook. Consider including your email address in your book so that fans can contact you. If you have an email newsletter, include instructions so that they can follow your newsletter.

- Put your book on sale and spread the news of your **book promotion** (Sec. 8.8).

- Run an Amazon or Goodreads **giveaway** for your book (Sec. 8.9).

- Find **bloggers** with significant followings among your target audience who are willing to review books. Read and follow their submission guidelines.

- Print **bookmarks** and business cards. Bookmarks are nice because readers may actually use them, especially if they look nice and don't seem primarily like an advertisement. Business cards are handy because they can fit in a wallet or pocket.

- Consider **advertising** your book (Sec. 8.10).

- Write an **article** that relates to your book and try to get it published in an appropriate newspaper, magazine, or website. If, at the end your article, you get to write Your Name, author of Your Book, you will gain some publicity with your target audience. There are so many websites that post articles, you have good prospects of getting your article accepted somewhere.

- Enter your book in a **contest** for writing or cover art.

- Create a sell sheet and a **press release kit**. These will help you appear more professional, and contain handy information, if you interact with the media or bookstore managers, for example. Do a little research for what these should include.

- Contact **local newspapers**, radio stations, and t.v. stations. They might have column inches or minutes available, and may be willing to use them to help support a new local author.

- If you have a book that may be relevant for a K-12 school, contact **teachers** in appropriate subjects and grade levels. If a teacher finds your book useful, it might be recommended to parents, for example. I've seen a few schools really help local authors out, even sending home letters about the authors' books. Results will vary, but if you don't try, it can't happen to you.

- A **paperback** edition (Sec. 8.11) gives you additional marketing opportunities. For example, if people are seen reading your book on a train, airplane, bus, or subway, it may help create interest and recommendations. It also lets you do a book signing. Always have a few copies on hand, since you never know when someone might ask about your book.

- If you have a paperback edition, visit local libraries, **bookstores**, and other stores that carry books but which don't specialize in books (some of these stores may be more receptive). See if they may be willing to keep a few copies in stock.

- Try to arrange for **workshops**, seminars, or presentations if you can provide valuable skills or information. This is common in nonfiction, where an author has expertise, but I've also seen fiction authors do it. For example, a few fiction authors have done seminars to share their self-publishing knowledge and experience, teaching new authors the art of formatting, for example. Some authors sell several paperback copies after the event. Authors who are really good at these events sometimes even receive invitations (in some cases, with pay) to host more events.

- Create an **audio book** (Sec. 8.12).

- Post a **video** on YouTube, start your own YouTube channel, setup a vlog (like a blog, but using video), or start your own radio or video show online.

- Offer free **review copies**[111] (Sec. 8.13 describes various options for sending copies of your book) in exchange for an honest review (no strings attached). Note that you're not allowed to pay for reviews, or offer any incentive other than one free copy of your book. If the recipient has a blog relevant to your audience, this can bring helpful exposure. Some authors go to extremes looking for reviews (for example, finding top reviewers on Amazon in their genre or subject who reveal their email address, contacting them with a polite email, asking if they might like to read a free copy of their book). Generally speaking, **the best reviews are organic reviews that naturally come from sales**, such that if you focus on marketing and succeed in generating hundreds of sales, a good assortment of reviews is likely to come naturally.

- If a reader contacts you to say that he or she enjoyed your book, consider politely asking the reader to post a review on Amazon. (Don't put any pressure on the person.)

- *Avoid blatant self-promotion*, like, "Check out my latest book." Get people interested in you, and through you they may learn about your book. For example, if you walk into a room full of people and say, "I'm an author: I bet you'll love my new book," you come across as a salesman, but if you start up a conversion and someone asks what you have done recently, it's a perfect opening to let them discover that you're a (humble) author. It makes a difference.

- Once people discover that you're an author and show interest, let them indirectly see your **passion** for your book.

- Always be **professional** and **courteous**. *You are your own public relations department.*

- **Personal interactions** can be especially valuable for a struggling new author. When potential readers experience positive interactions—in person or online (though in person has the chance to make a stronger impact)—with authors, they are more likely to purchase the book and review or recommend it.

- Think long and hard about the nature and habits of your **target audience**. Where are you likely to meet them, both online and in person?

- What makes your book special? Have you done anything that goes above and beyond? Whatever the answers are, when they happen to get mentioned in conservation, they might help to create interest in your book.

- Make valuable **contacts** and **connections**. Sometimes, just knowing the right person can make a huge difference. I've seen a few authors receive major publicity via theaters, radio, television, etc. just by knowing the right person.

- Many **children's books** sell better in print than they do as eBooks, so it may be worth creating a paperback edition (Sec. 8.11). Many successful children's authors set up readings, are involved with teachers or parent-teacher associations, and take advantage of a variety of in-person marketing opportunities.

Much of marketing revolves around the concept of **branding**. When a customer visits a store to purchase a particular type of product (such as a television or a pair of shoes), the customer usually purchases a product by a brand that the customer recognizes. Marketing a book is similar in this regard: Each time a customer comes across your book, the customer is being branded.

Books involve multiple forms of branding:

- The cover of your book establishes a visual brand when a customer sees it on multiple occasions. If you publish multiple books, if the covers have a distinguishing feature or if the covers share a similar style, this expands your visual brand.

- The title of your book brands the book with one or more words each time a customer reads or hears it.

- The author name is also an important brand. Your goal is to become a household name among your specific target audience. As you write and publish more books, as people discover your blog, as people follow you on social media, etc., you expand your author brand.

- Even a character can become branded. One example is Sherlock Holmes.

A customer rarely purchases a book the first time that the customer discovers it. A typical customer might need to see the book on four or five separate occasions, spread over a period of weeks or months, before the customer becomes truly interested in the book. (Over-branding can have the opposite effect: When a customer sees the same book repeatedly over a very short period, the customer may associate the book with frustration. That brands a negative perception.)

Effective marketing often involves a **long-term** approach. If you expect instant results, you're likely to be disappointed. Most marketing strategies start out very slowly. As your marketing net widens (as you try out new techniques, and as you gain more experience with one technique), with time branding starts to have a greater impact. After several months, marketing can finally start to take hold.

Tip: Browse through Appendix D. It is packed with links to several essential author resources.

8.8 Promotional Pricing

It's possible for a short-term promotional price to create interest in a book, though for it to be effective it usually needs to be done in conjunction with some effective marketing. In many cases, just lowering the price of the book has little to no effect. *Price alone doesn't sell books.* What you want to do is create the **perception** that the sale price is a **good value** through marketing.

When a customer sees a book selling for 99 cents or $1.99, for example, it's just one of several thousands of low-priced books. However, if a customer discovers the book through your marketing, and if the marketing shows that the book is regularly $3.99 and is on sale for $1.99 for one week only, for example, now the $1.99 seems like a better value. **The limited-time offer** also creates a **sense of urgency**.

The challenge of promotional pricing is spreading the message. Look through my marketing suggestions in Sec. 8.7 and try to find some that can help you tell customers that your book is on sale. Follow successful indie authors and see how they promote their sale prices.

There are several online websites and newsletters that specifically **advertise** eBooks that are *temporarily on sale*. The most well-known place to advertise your eBook's sale price is called BookBub. However, BookBub is also among the most expensive and is also highly selective (most of their submissions get turned down). Many other online websites and newsletters that advertise sale prices are much more affordable and less selective. There are dozens of such services, some more effective than others (it also depends on the type of book, and the marketability of your book). Some authors have used Ereader News Today, Kindle Books & Tips, Book Gorilla, Book Blast, and Pixel of Ink, for example (there are several others).

There are a few ways that you might be able to put a book on sale. If your book is enrolled in KDP Select (which requires publishing exclusively with Amazon—Sec. 6.12) and if your book has a list price from $2.99 to $24.99 in the US (or £1.99 to £15.99 in the UK), you can run a Kindle **Countdown Deal**. A Countdown Deal shows both the regular price and sale price of your book, along with a timer that shows customers when the sale will end. Note that there are a few restrictions for when you can run a Countdown Deal (see Sec. 6.12): For example, you can't run a Countdown Deal until your book has been enrolled in KDP Select for at least 30 days. A cool thing about a Countdown Deal is that if you normally earn 70% royalties, you still earn 70% royalties during the discounted price (but your delivery fee still applies—Sec. 6.13: If your book has pictures, you should do the math to see what your royalty would be, especially if your delivery fee is significant). When you run a Countdown Deal, note the time zone (which by default is Pacific time for a Countdown Deal in the US, but is GMT for a Countdown Deal in the UK). Also note that you must run separate deals for the US and for the UK. Note that occasionally the start or end dates may be delayed a bit (the times do not come with guaranteed precision—consider starting the sale early, just in case).

If your book isn't in KDP Select, and if your book isn't already at the minimum possible price, you can run a **short-term price reduction** manually: Republish the book with a reduced price before your sale starts, and republish the book with the original price when your sale ends. There are a couple of disadvantages of this method compared to a Countdown Deal. For one, if your sale price is below $2.99, you must select the 35% royalty option (but there won't be a delivery fee on the 35% plan). Another problem is timing: You need to republish at the reduced price about 24 hours in advance of the start date (even longer outside of the US), whereas with a Countdown Deal you can schedule the start and end dates. Although updates to the list price ordinarily occur within 24 hours, it's not always 100% consistent. Also, unlike a Countdown Deal, customers won't be able to see the regular price: The only way for customers to know that your book is on sale is through your marketing.

When you're manually dropping a price (by republishing), make sure that your book isn't already at the minimum possible list price. If your regular list price is $0.99, you can't go lower than that (without doing a KDP Select free promo). If your regular list price is $1.99, you can only lower your price if the converted MOBI file size of your book is below 3 MB. If your regular list price is $2.99, you can only lower your price if the converted MOBI file size of your book is below 10 MB. You'd hate to put effort into marketing a short-term sale price, only to realize later that you can't put your book on sale. (The 3 MB and 10 MB restrictions don't apply to Countdown Deals.)

For books enrolled in KDP Select, an alternative to the Countdown Deal is a **free book promotion**. With a free book promotion, customers can read your book for free, and you earn no royalties. Furthermore, customers who would normally have borrowed your book through Kindle Unlimited will 'purchase' your book for free, and you won't earn royalties for those pages read. (This doesn't impact pages read by customers who borrowed your book through Kindle Unlimited *before* your promotion began.) Note that Amazon separates free sales ranks from paid sales ranks: Your paid sales rank will slide during the free promotion because you aren't earning sales. If you check on your sales rank during the free promotion, the number will probably 'seem' good, but it will be a free sales rank, not a paid sales rank. When the free promotion ends, the paid sales rank will replace the free sales rank, probably a much higher number (where higher is worse) than it was before the free promotion started. However, if your free promotion succeeds in drawing interest in your book and earning new customers, in the long run your paid sales rank may recover and improve.

The idea behind the free book promotion is to generate exposure for your book and you as an author: You can gain some readers. If the readers love your book, there is potential for valuable word-of-mouth **recommendations** and referrals. However, there are no guarantees. When this feature originally rolled out, there were authors who greatly benefited from it, drawing in thousands of readers during the promotion. Since the early days, the effectiveness of the free book promotion has dropped off tremendously in most cases. To get the most out of it, you usually need to find online websites or newsletters to help promote your freebie (and also supply your own marketing). You might intuitively expect customers to be grateful for the opportunity to read your book free, and thus be more inclined to leave a favorable review, but it doesn't quite work that way: Customers generally have the same high expectations for the time that they invest in a book. Plus, customers know that there are hundreds (or thousands) of free books out there. I'm *not* recommending that you give your book away for free: I'm just mentioning that this is one option available, and that a few authors use this tool (some use it more effectively than others).

Are you wondering about **discount codes** or **coupons**? Unfortunately, at this time, these are *not* available for Kindle eBooks. You must either put your book on sale (as discussed previously), or give your book as a gift (although then you are giving your book for free) as described in Sec. 8.13.

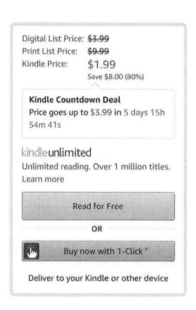

8.9 Contests and Giveaways

One way to generate a little interest in your book and to gain a few readers or followers is to host a contest or giveaway for your book. If you run a giveaway through Amazon or Goodreads, be sure to follow their rules. (If you opt to host your own contest instead—that is, not running your giveaway through a company like Amazon—you should first research the laws governing giveaways and contests.)

To run an Amazon giveaway for your book, visit your product page on Amazon.com (in the United States), and scroll down the page looking for the Setup a Giveaway button.

- Select the number of prizes that you wish to offer. Note that you pay for the prizes now, but unclaimed eBook prizes are **not** refunded (but you can run a new giveaway for the unclaimed prizes at no additional cost). If your book happens to be on sale during the giveaway, it will cost less to run the giveaway. (You should also earn a royalty, though it might not be until after the prize is claimed.)

- If you're running a giveaway for your own book, you should enter your **author name**. Note that you can run a giveaway for *any* product on Amazon (such as a $5 Amazon gift card, which sometimes creates much interest).

- Add an image in JPEG, PNG, or GIF format. You may use your cover file or author photo, for example. Note that the maximum file size is 1 MB: If your cover file exceeds this (or even if it comes close, sometimes it won't upload), try reducing the pixel size of your picture.

- Choose which type of giveaway to run. I prefer **Random Instant Win** with a minimum of two prizes (with only one prize, there is a chance of a very short giveaway with minimal exposure, for this option): The winner knows right away that he or she has won, and since it's random, everyone has an equal chance regardless of when they enter. The **Lucky Number Instant Win** guarantees a certain amount of exposure: For example, if you set the value to 199, the 199th entrant will win. The **Sweepstakes** option randomly selects the winner(s) after the giveaway wins. Unlike the Instant Win giveaways, the Sweepstakes option doesn't limit the number of entrants, but then there is a delay in notifying the winner: All other types of giveaways (besides Sweepstakes) immediately notify the winner. I **don't** recommend First-come, First-served, as it gives virtually no exposure.

- For an Instant Win giveaway, you must set the odds of winning. If you set it too low, you limit your exposure, but if you set it too high, you don't have a winner and sometimes the odds discourage participation. It takes a little trial and error, since participation can vary significantly from one book to another. (My best giveaways have received nearly 3000 entrants, but that is rare: 200-500 is much more common for me, and I know some authors who have struggled to get 100.) If you don't have a winner, you will have the option to use the unclaimed prize(s) in a new giveaway. (The Sweepstakes giveaway doesn't require setting the odds, so it *maximizes participation*. The only drawback is that the winners aren't immediately notified.)

- You may select one requirement for entrants. Having tried various options, I prefer to have entrants follow me on Amazon. When you publish your next eBook, Amazon will send an email to your Amazon followers, announcing your new book. You need to sign up for Author Central and claim your book first, if you haven't already done so (Sec. 8.2). If you choose "No additional requirements," you will get somewhat better participation.

- Set the duration of the giveaway.

- Check the box to make the giveaway **public** to gain **additional exposure** for your giveaway.

- Note: The Instant Win giveaways will ask if you wish to offer a discount to entrants. However, you *can't* offer a discount to entrants for your eBook giveaway. (That option is for Amazon.com sellers who sell products via Seller Central.)
- If you are given the option to limit sharing, I **don't** recommend it, as it would reduce your exposure.
- Note that you **can't** edit your giveaway once you press the button to create your giveaway. Check your details carefully.
- You will receive an email when your giveaway goes live. I recommend that you share your giveaway in a tweet: This gives you extra exposure (even if you have few or no Twitter followers), as there is a special landing page for Amazon giveaways at Twitter. A few people who discover your giveaway through Twitter may even help to share it. You can also share your giveaway on your blog, Facebook, and other forms of social media.
- After your giveaway has begun, one way to find it is to visit Amazon.com, log in, click the Orders button near the top right of the page, and select Digital Orders.

https://www.amazon.com/ga/giveaways

Goodreads (now owned by Amazon) is a website used by millions of avid readers to explore and review books. Goodreads is another option for hosting a giveaway for your book. If you're already familiar with Goodreads giveaways, note that they made some changes at the beginning of 2018: You can now run an eBook for a Goodreads giveaway, but there is now a setup cost to host a giveaway.

A good percentage of winners will post a review at Goodreads (but a much smaller percentage will also post the review at Amazon). Your book will automatically be added to readers' To-Read lists, which helps to show some activity on your book's Goodreads page (though realize that, in general, people mark books as To-Read that they never actually get around to reading). If you run a print giveaway at Goodreads, note that you must pay for shipping and packaging (plus you're re responsible for ordering copies in advance and sending them to the winners). A print giveaway offers you the option to include a brief note, bookmark, or business card. Your note can politely request an honest review, but you're **not** permitted to use persuasion and the winner is **not** required to review your book: You should emphasize that reviewing is optional. Be sure to read the rules and conditions carefully.

https://www.goodreads.com/giveaway

https://chrismcmullen.com/2018/01/17/tips-for-the-new-goodreads-giveaways

Set up an Amazon Giveaway

Amazon Giveaway allows you to run promotional giveaways in order to create buzz, reward your audience, and attract new followers and customers. Learn more about Amazon Giveaway

This item: An Introduction to Basic Astronomy Concepts (with Space Photos)

Set up a giveaway

8.10 Advertising

There are a variety of ways to advertise your book, including the option to advertise directly on Amazon.com itself. If you're starting out as a new author, my advice is to keep your initial advertising expenses to a minimum ($100 or less). Advertising carries risk, so the less you invest, the less you risk losing. With pay-per-click advertising (this is available through Amazon Marketing Services via KDP), you can advertise on a small scale to test it out, and the results will help you decide whether or not advertising may be helpful for you. In the future, if you begin to earn steady royalties, you can afford to invest a percentage of your royalties in advertising (and in that case, you'll be playing with the house's money, so to speak).

Note that advertising is probably **<u>not</u>** the solution for a book that isn't selling. If a book isn't selling, I would instead focus on improving the book's marketability (cover, description, Look Inside, formatting, writing, story, maybe even reconsider the book idea), look for free and low-cost marketing ideas (Sec. 8.7), and put time into writing and publishing a new book (consider doing more research to find an idea that's likely to be more marketable, while still being a good fit for you to write).

What advertising can do is bring additional exposure to your book. Sometimes, the exposure doesn't bring enough immediate sales to cover the advertising expenses. When you advertise an expensive product, like a car or television, each sale brings significant profits: When you advertise a book, one sale only brings you a royalty of a couple of dollars. When you see a commercial for toilet paper, that's a product that people need, whereas a book is a luxury that people want. Also, when you shop for toilet paper, there are only a dozen or so brands to choose from, whereas when customers shop for books, there are millions of choices. All of these factors make it more challenging for advertising to yield short-term profits for books compared to many other products.

Sometimes, taking a small loss on an advertisement may still be worth doing. There are possible long-term benefits to advertising. For example, if the content of your book is quite compelling, any readers you gain now may purchase more books in the future, and may recommend your book to others. If you have a series, a customer who reads the first book may wind up purchasing the entire series over time.

It is possible for an advertisement for a book to yield short-term profits, or at least to keep losses to a minimum. It largely depends on how marketable the cover, product page, and content of your book are. A highly marketable book can sell to 10% or more of the customers who click on the advertisement, but the vast majority of books aren't this marketable. A more modest rate like 3% to 6% is more realistic, yet there are many books that fall short of this. Less marketable books (which is all too common) see a rate of 1% or less (for the percentage of customers who purchase a book after clicking on an advertisement). This figure (the conversion rate) is very important for the success of an advertisement, especially for pay-per-click advertising (this is the type of advertising available through Amazon Marketing Services via KDP).

If you knew your conversion rate (the number of sales divided by the number of clicks), you could calculate how much you can afford to bid when you use pay-per-click advertising. Although you don't know what your conversion rate will be, you can estimate this with a little data. Run an ad on a small budget with a modest bid for a short period, until you get a significant number of clicks. Then figure out how many sales you had (you may need to wait a few days or more for possible reporting delays). Divide the number of sales by the number of clicks to estimate your conversion rate in decimal form. The fewer clicks you have, the less reliable the estimate, but the more clicks you have, the more it costs you to get this data.

Example: Suppose that you bid $0.25 per click for a book with a list price of $2.99 and a royalty of $2.00, and after a few days the ad report shows 100 clicks and $14.95 in sales (this data is available when you advertise through Amazon Marketing Services via KDP). Divide the sales amount ($14.95) by the list price ($2.99) to determine that you sold 5 books ($14.95 ÷ $2.99 = 5). The ad in my example would cost you $25 to run (multiply the number of clicks by your bid: 100 × $0.25 = $25), and it resulted in a short-term loss: The royalties from the sales amount to $10 (multiply the number of sales by the royalty: 5 × $2.00 = $10), so the loss is $15 (subtract the royalties from the cost of the ad to determine the loss: $25 – $10 = $15).

In my example, the bid is higher than you can afford (unless you don't mind taking a short-term loss). Now I will show you how to estimate your bid based on this data. First calculate the **conversion rate**: Divide the number of sales (5) by the number of clicks (100): 5 ÷ 100 = 0.05. (In this example, the conversion rate is 5%, which is fairly good. I multiplied by 100 to turn 0.05 into a percentage, but I will use the decimal form, 0.05, and *not* the percentage, in the math that follows.)

Multiply your conversion rate (in decimal form) by your royalty to figure out the **estimated break-even bid**: In my example, that's 0.05 × $2.00 = $0.10. If the bid had been

$0.10 instead of $0.25, the little data that we have estimates that the ad would break even.

Realize that this is an *estimate*. The conversion rate tends to fluctuate, so you could still take a loss if you set your bid according to this estimate. The next 100 clicks may result in only 3 sales, or they might result in 7 sales, but they could result in 0 sales. There are **no** guarantees. However, an estimate is an *educated* guess: It's better than a *blind* guess.

Remember, also, that there may be long-term benefits (which I mentioned earlier), which may offset any short-term loss. If you keep your advertising losses minimal, advertising may pay off in the long run. If you're fortunate to earn a short-term profit (the royalties from your ad exceed the cost of the ad—but be sure to figure out your royalties, **not** the sales, following my previous example) or at least break even, you can afford to continue advertising over a long period. If your advertising results in a significant loss, my advice is to terminate your campaign at some point, hoping that the possible long-term benefits eventually help you recover from your short-term loss. In the future, you might try varying some parameters of your ad, trying to make your next ad more effective.

Amazon lets you advertise your Kindle eBook through **Amazon Marketing Services** (AMS)— although you must check the conditions, as advertisements are not allowed for a few types of eBooks (there are restrictions on category and on the nature of the cover, for example). You actually place your ad from KDP (don't visit AMS directly to try setting this up over there).

Follow these steps to **advertise** a Kindle eBook with AMS via KDP.

- Visit your KDP Bookshelf, click the gray ellipsis (…) button, and choose Promote and Advertise. Click the yellow button labeled Create an Ad Campaign. This will take you to a special AMS page that is specifically dedicated to Kindle eBooks published through KDP.
- Choose which type of ad campaign to run. A **Sponsored Products** ad lets you enter a list of keywords and phrases. Your ad displays in search results and on product pages based on your keyword targeting. A **Product Display** ad lets you compile a list of specific books (or other products). In this case, your ad displays on product pages and Kindle eReaders based on your targeting list, but note the following. The ad *doesn't* target the *product pages* of the books on your list: Rather, it targets product pages of customers based on their *search history*. So, for example, if you target romance books, your ad will sometimes show on the product page of a sci-fi book when a customer who happens to be browsing for a science fiction book has searched for a romance book at least one time in the past. **Sponsored Products ads seem to have more effective targeting for most types of nonfiction books.**

- Enter a name for your campaign. Nobody will see the campaign name except for you. If, like me, you have several ad campaigns in your AMS report, you want to type something that will help you tell your campaigns apart. If you tried something different with your targeting, for example, you might include a word or phrase that will help remind you what you tried with your ad. If you publish multiple books, you might include language to help you remember which book was advertised.

Note: The order of the steps is different for Sponsored Products ads and Product Display ads. I have ordered these bullet points for Sponsored Products ads. I have included information for both types of ads, but if you're following these instructions as you place a Product Display ad, the steps will be in a different order.

- Set the budget for your campaign. For a Sponsored Products ad, enter a maximum daily budget. What is the most that you are willing to spend per day? For a Product Display ad, you must set a minimum budget of $100, but you are **not** required to spend the entire budget: At any time, you may pause or terminate your campaign (but note that due to reporting delays, you may continue to see clicks for a few days after stopping your ad). You're **not** charged up front: You are billed periodically for the clicks that your ad generates. You may edit your ad and increase your budget in the future (if your ad is successful, you might want to do this before your ad reaches the budget and ends).

- Set the duration for your campaign. For a Sponsored Products ad, you can let your ad run indefinitely, or you can select start and end dates for your ad. If you choose to let it run indefinitely, you can always pause or terminate your campaign later. For a Product Display ad, select the start and end dates for your ad. If you want your ad to run longer than the end date that you initially set, as the original end date approaches, you can edit your ad to revise the end date. For a Product Display ad, choose whether you want the campaign to run as quickly as possible or to spread the campaign evenly over its duration. In most cases, I would run the campaign as quickly as possible.

- Select the targeting for your campaign. For a Sponsored Products ad, select either automatic or manual targeting. I prefer **manual targeting**: When you choose manual targeting, Amazon shows you suggested keywords, and you can add to this list. First, look over the suggested keywords and click the Add button next to all of the keywords that you would like to approve (or click the Add All button to add all of them). There are usually a few **irrelevant keywords** on the list that I choose not to add. When you finish adding suggested keywords, click on the link to add your own keywords. You should see the suggested keywords that you added already listed below. Place one word or phrase on its own line and use the Enter key to go onto the next line. For a Product Display ad, choose Product targeting or Interest targeting. Interest targeting lets you choose specific categories: This is handy when one of the subcategories happens to be a perfect fit for your book. For example, if you have a paranormal romance, the paranormal romance category provides ideal targeting. As a counterexample, the category Science & Math (find it in Other) would be way too broad for a chemistry book. Product targeting lets you target specific products, and there is also a new option to target related categories. If Interest targeting didn't have a category that was an ideal fit, see if the Target Related Categories option under Product targeting has better options. The Target Specific Products option in Product targeting lets you compile a list of books to target (it can be a very long list with hundreds of books). You can search for popular authors of books that are very similar to yours, for example. Note that you generally need a long list with some popular authors to get significant results (but you should also add highly relevant books that are less popular, too). Realize that you're not actually targeting the *books* on your list: The ad targets the *search history* of the customer, *not* the book itself. So, for example, if you target a popular fantasy book, it could show up when a customer is shopping for a cookbook (simply because that customer has shopped for a fantasy book at some point in the past).

- Set a bid for your campaign. For a Sponsored Products ad, you can place a different bid for each keyword (or you can place the same bid for every keyword). Note that if you adjust the bid from the default value, when you click on the link to add your own keywords, *the bid value will have returned to its default value*, so you must adjust the bid again. For a Product Display ad, there is just one bid to set. **Note**: Earlier in this section, I showed you how to estimate what bid you can afford once you have some data. Before you have data, I recommend bidding low (you can bid a dime or less—the minimum bid is $0.02). If after a few days you're not getting many views and clicks, you can edit your campaign and try raising your bid a little. This strategy helps you get views and clicks with the **minimal possible expense**. If you find yourself raising your bid high, like $0.50, *it probably isn't the bid that's the problem*: Try adjusting the *targeting* (either it was too narrow and you need to widen it a lot, or it was too wide and you need to make the targeting more relevant). **Successful ads** (those that get better click-through rates and conversion rates—sales compared to clicks) **tend to generate more views and clicks**. Ads that aren't as successful in the early going are more apt to remain slow, *even if you raise your bid* (sometimes it's better to terminate the ad and *create a new one with revised targeting*). Ads that the program determines to be more **relevant** also tend to be more successful.

- Type customized text for your ad (up to 150 characters). You want your customized text to generate interest in your book: You need a 'hook.' For fiction, sometimes a question can help arouse curiosity. With nonfiction, the value of the information in the book can lure customers. Along with the title and cover, your customized text should also help make it clear what type of book you have written. A Product Display ad lets you type a headline (up to 50 characters) in addition to customized text. Copy and paste your customized text into Microsoft Word. Check the spelling and grammar carefully, and double-check any spelling or grammar flags. Read your customized text aloud (sometimes, you catch a mistake when you 'hear'" it): Read slowly word for word what your eye sees (try not to read what you 'meant' to write instead of what you actually wrote). Be sure to capitalize the first letter of your text. **Tip**: Spend some time browsing search results and product pages at Amazon. The ads that you see will help you get ideas for different ways that this customized text can be used.
- Check your preview carefully. When you are happy with your preview, click the Launch Campaign button.

After you place your ad, monitor the performance a few times per day. If your ad accumulates clicks rapidly, but isn't yielding sales, you'll want to pause or terminate the ad before you blow your entire budget. If you bid low (closer to a dime), there is less risk that this will happen. If you bid high (half a dollar or more), it's possible (depending on your targeting and other factors) to zip through a budget quickly. The only way you can know how quickly or slowly your expenses are accumulating is to monitor the progress regularly.

Click the Reports tab at KDP, choose Ad Campaigns, and then click on the link to view your ads dashboard page. This takes you to your ad report page at AMS. It sometimes takes a while to load the page when you first get there (though if it takes very long, try switching web browsers).

Important note: It is common for there to be reporting delays. It can take a few days (even more) for all of the views, clicks, and sales to show up (in the worst case, it can take up to 14 days for all of the data to come through, though a few days is more typical). If you see numbers right away, it doesn't mean there aren't delays: It might be that some of the data is reporting quickly while some of it is delayed. If you pause or terminate your ad, you may continue to see clicks for a few days afterward. **Always wait a few days before you raise your bid**, just in case your ad is doing better than you realize (due to possible reporting delays).

As of now, I have placed over 100 ads since January, 2015, on dozens of books (some of which were written in pen names). I've had 30 different ads result in over 1,000,000 views each, and 70 different ads result in at least 100,000 views. My most popular ad brought over 12,000,000 views and over 10,000 clicks over a period of 2 years. However, I've also placed some ads that really struggled to get views: I actually have an ad that has been running for 2 years and only has 19,000 views (I continue to let it run since the bid is merely $0.04, it has brought me two sales, and the ad has only cost me $1.77—although the results are extremely slow, the ad has made a profit). Results can vary considerably from one ad to another, and especially from one book to another. So **how do you know how well your ad is working?** That's a good question.

The **impressions** column shows you how many times your ad has shown on a screen that a customer was viewing. Although most customers don't click on your ad, these impressions still have value. When the same customer sees your book cover multiple times, it helps a little with **branding**. (Sure, it would help more if some of the ads were larger. On the other hand, smaller ads make advertising less intrusive, which helps keep online advertising more effective in the long run.) Impressions are **free**: You only pay for *clicks*.

The clicks column shows you how many different customers have clicked on your ad. Typical **click-through rates** (ctr's) are on the order of 0.001, meaning that 1 out of 1000 customers tend to click on an ad (this is fairly typical of online advertising in general). With Amazon's pay-per-click advertising, the ctr isn't nearly as important as it is with many other forms of online advertising (where you instead pay for impressions). However, the ctr does make a difference. If your ctr is too low (like 0.0005, or 1 out of 2000), Amazon may *terminate* your ad due to *low relevance*. (They may also look at other factors besides the ctr, but the ctr is one important factor.) If this happens, you can create a new ad with different targeting.

Another way that the ctr matters is that **ads that perform better tend to land more impressions**. All else being equal, an ad with a higher ctr (like 0.002, or 1 out of 500 customers) is performing better than an ad with a lower ctr. However, the ctr is just one of the performance metrics. Your ad must also perform well other ways, such as the conversion rate (see below)— and the value of your bid is also factored in. From my experience with Amazon Seller Central, I know that Amazon places a premium on customer satisfaction metrics, and this surely factors into their ad performance metrics, too.

The clicks column is important to you because you pay for every click. Sometimes, you pay less than your bid: Your bid represents the highest value that you will pay for one click. The spend column shows you how much you have paid for your ad thus far (but keep in mind that due to possible reporting delays, your actual expenses may be higher than the spend column currently shows).

The sales column ultimately determines whether your ad is running at a *profit* or *loss*. However, you really want to know the royalties, **not** the sales. First, divide the sales column by the list price of your book. For example, if the sales column shows $128.57 and your list price is

$2.99, you have had approximately 43 sales: $128.57 ÷ $2.99 = 43. Note that if you change the list price of your book during the ad campaign (for example, with a Countdown Deal), this gets more complicated, and this estimate will be significantly off if many of your sales occurred at a lower price.

Look at page 3 of the publishing process—click the gray ellipsis (…) button from your KDP Bookshelf and select Edit Pricing Info—to see what your actual royalty is in the United States. Multiply the number of sales by your royalty for one sale to determine the total royalties earned by the ad. For example, if you have 43 sales and your royalty is $2.00 for each book, your total royalties are $86. Once again, if your price changed during the ad campaign, this estimate may be significantly off.

Compare your total royalties earned through the ad (by performing a calculation similar to my previous example) to the total cost of the ad. If the total royalties earned exceed the total cost of the ad, your ad is turning a *profit* (congratulations!). If the total royalties earned are less than the total cost of the ad (the spend column), your ad is running at a short-term *loss*. If your ad is suffering a significant loss, I recommend that you revise or terminate your ad. You might consider revising the targeting method or list, changing your customized text, reducing your bid, or improving your book's marketability (cover, description, Look Inside, etc.). Many authors bid higher than they can afford, and sometimes it takes trial and error to create an effective targeting list. So it's possible that adjusting your bid and targeting will improve your ad performance (if your current ad had a slow impression rate, I would terminate the current ad and create a new ad, rather than edit the current ad—but if it had a good impression rate, it may be better to edit the current ad).

Is your book enrolled in KDP Select (Sec. 6.12)? If so, your ad may actually be doing better than you realize. Unfortunately, at this time the ad doesn't show **Kindle Unlimited** data. If a Kindle Unlimited subscriber clicks on your ad and reads your book, you earn royalties for the pages read, but this data doesn't appear in your ad report.

There may also be long-term benefits to advertising, which you don't see in your ad report. For example, if the ad nets you new readers who really enjoy your book, they might recommend your book to others, and they might purchase more of your books. If an ad runs at a small loss for a short period of time, such possible long-term benefits may make the ad worthwhile.

One important aspect of advertising is **branding**. This works best when you also apply other marketing strategies (Sec. 8.7) other than just advertising. Each time a customer sees your book, it helps with branding.

When a customer sees a commercial on t.v. or hears an advertisement on the radio, the customer usually doesn't drive straight to the store and purchase the product. Months later, when the customer is in the store, the customer will prefer a brand that the customer recognizes from branding. Book advertising is no different. The impressions and clicks that your ad creates now might result in a few purchases weeks or months from now through branding.

Even if your ad campaign suffers a significant loss (in which case, hopefully you were able to terminate the ad before losing too much), you still get some **valuable data** from the AMS ad report: You would have no information about impressions and clicks in relation to sales without that report. Following are a few *things that you can learn from your AMS ad report data.*

- If your ad struggled to make **impressions**, even with wider targeting and a higher bid, this suggests that your book is struggling to find an audience at Amazon.

- If your ad had a low **ctr** (divide the number of clicks by the number of impressions)— less than 0.001, meaning 1 customer out of 1000 who saw your ad clicked on it—this suggests that you could improve your cover, your title, your customized text, or your approach towards targeting the audience for your book. The book cover is one of the most marketable features of a book: If the relevant audience is seeing your book, but isn't clicking on it, it's probably a sign that your cover isn't effective at generating interest in your book. If you believe in your cover, the alternative is your approach to targeting: If your book isn't relevant to many of the customers who saw your ad, that would explain a low ctr. Spend more time thinking about who your target audience really is, what their habits are, which categories they are likely to browse, what keywords they search for, and which similar books they purchase.

- If your **conversion rate** (divide the number of sales by the number of clicks, then multiply by 100 to make it a percentage) is low—3% or less—this suggests that you have room to improve the marketability of your product page. It's probably the description or the Look Inside, but another possibility is that the cover or title suggest that your book is one type, while your description makes it seem like your book is a different type. Try to improve your description and Look Inside (formatting, editing, writing style, writing flow, and how well the beginning of the book grabs and holds interest), and check to ensure that every component of your book (cover, title, description, and beginning of the book) sends a consistent message about what type of book you have written.

- Your ad data is probably reflected in your typical product page data. If your ad generated many impressions, but few clicks, even when you don't advertise, your book is probably seen in category and keyword searches on Amazon, but gets frequently overlooked. If you had 100,000 views, 100 clicks, and 3 sales, for example, you're losing 99,997 customers out of every 100,000. In this example, **even when you're not advertising, if you normally sell 3 books per week, your ad data suggests that there are usually 100,000 customers who see your book and 100 customers who view your product page every week**. *In this case, the traffic is there, but your book is lacking the marketability needed to* *fully take advantage of that traffic.* This is actually quite common: Many books get much better visibility and traffic on Amazon than authors realize from their sales reports. The trick is creating a highly marketable book and learning how to maximize the marketability of the product page.

- If you revise your cover, description, Look Inside, or the beginning of your book, try running a new ad so that you can compare the new ad data to the old ad data. This valuable information will help you see whether or not your revisions are improvements.

The option to advertise directly on Amazon—where customers are already shopping for books (rather than someplace else, where you are interrupting what the customer is doing, asking them to check out your book instead)—through AMS via KDP is nice, but it's not the only place to advertise. Another place where you can advertise directly to a large gathering of readers is Goodreads (Sec. 8.9): The self-service option provides inexpensive cost-per-click advertising that is fairly similar to AMS in many ways (except that you can choose to target specific authors)—whereas the book launch packages can be quite expensive and carry much more risk. A few other options that have a wide reach include Google, Facebook, and Twitter. Websites with a smaller audience, but where the audience is highly relevant for your book, may also be a good fit. When you have promotional pricing, there are a number of websites that can help you advertise the reduced price (Sec. 8.8).

If you advertise externally (that is, not through AMS), keep an eye on your sales ranks and sales reports. If you're not seeing improved sales, consider tweaking or terminating the ad.

When your advertisement (or even your regular marketing) drives traffic to your Amazon product page, note that Amazon's program may be measuring your new traffic pattern and analyzing this data. For example, **if you drive thousands of customers to your product page, and this results in very few sales, the program sees that your product page isn't very effective at closing sales.** The program looks at a variety of factors, including established category or keyword relevance (when a customer finds your book in a search and clicks on it, this helps to establish relevance with that search method—but if many customers click on your book and don't purchase it, this may suggest a lack of relevance), the percentage of customers who are likely to click on your book (the click-through rate), the percentage of customers who are likely to purchase your book once visiting the product page (the conversion rate), appropriate pricing for the customer, and customer satisfaction metrics (you can learn more about how this is determined through Amazon Seller Central, but it includes return rates and customer reviews, for example). Amazon's program is measuring and analyzing these sorts of things all the time. **When you drive increased traffic to your product page through marketing or paid advertising, this additional traffic may have a significant impact**—which may be good or bad, depending on the average tendencies of those new customers. Your sales ranks and sales reports can help you determine whether this additional traffic seems to be helping or hurting. Another thing that additional sales may do over time is improve your book's reach through **customers-also-bought lists**.

8.11 Paperbacks

Some books actually sell better in print than they do as eBooks. This is common among many types of informative nonfiction books, textbooks, guides, young children's books, and travel books, for example. A print book can be handy, is more convenient for highlighting and notes, and makes a better gift. Some parents prefer for their children to read print books. There are also a few types of books that shouldn't be published in eBook format, such as coloring books, certain types of puzzle books, or any other books where the customer is intended to draw or write in the book (in a way that the customer may expect the 'book' to function more like an interactive app rather than a non-interactive eBook).

There are other types of books that sell much better as eBooks. Novels and short stories tend to sell better in eBook format, for example.

Even if the book sells better in eBook format than in print, there may still be value in creating a print edition:

- You can **autograph** or personalize a print book for a customer.
- Print books make for better **gifts**.
- If any customers read your print book on a train, bus, airplane, or subway, this can be good **marketing** for you. People see that the book is worth reading, so they might ask which book it is.
- If a customer leaves your book lying on a coffee table or counter and has a guest over, your book might become a **conversation piece**.
- Your print book is a constant reminder of your book. A customer who set your book down a week ago might be reminded of your book when passing by and resume reading it: When a customer closes your eBook, the customer might not get such a reminder.
- Print books create additional marketing opportunities. You might get it stocked in a local library or **bookstore**. Some reviewers may prefer print format.
- Some authors feel a sense of satisfaction when they see their book in print.
- Family members or friends may be impressed by the print edition. That might be the moment when they finally realize that you're a 'real' author.
- Always keep extra copies of your print book on hand. (Do the same with bookmarks and business cards.) You never know when you might get into a conversation with someone that you meet. If you happen to have a copy of your book in the trunk of your car, for example, you can pull it out and show it to a potential customer (you might even sell it right there in person).

I recommend publishing a paperback edition with KDP or CreateSpace. Since CreateSpace is Amazon's original print-on-demand publishing company, these are the two natural feeds for print sales on Amazon. The main alternative is Ingram Spark, which includes higher setup fees. If you have a special reason to expect many more print sales than normal in other countries (perhaps due to the nature of your marketing, your biography, or the setting of your book), or if you have a book that is more likely to sell in hardcover (such an illustrated children's book), then it may be worth comparing Ingram Spark to KDP and CreateSpace. If, like most self-published authors, you expect to derive most of your print sales online through Amazon, I recommend KDP or CreateSpace.

As of the publication of this book, KDP had only recently begun offering a paperback option, whereas CreateSpace has offered this for several years. Initially, CreateSpace was the better option, as it offered printed proofs, author copies, and better expanded distribution. However, KDP is catching up: KDP now offers printed proofs and author copies. In fact, for authors in the UK or continental Europe, KDP has an advantage over CreateSpace: If you use KDP, you can get your printed proofs and author copies printed and shipped from within Europe (whereas if you use CreateSpace, they will be printed and shipped from the United States).

As KDP's paperback service continues to grow, CreateSpace has removed a couple of features. CreateSpace's eStore now redirects customers to Amazon, and CreateSpace no longer offers paid services. (KDP doesn't offer an eStore, and also doesn't offer paid services.) It seems likely that KDP and CreateSpace will eventually be comparable (or that the two companies will merge into KDP).

As of the publication of this book, **CreateSpace still had a slight advantage over KDP**: CreateSpace offers better Expanded Distribution. All books enrolled in the Amazon.com channel at CreateSpace automatically become available in Canada, and CreateSpace pays the standard Amazon.com royalty for Canada sales. CreateSpace also offers distribution to Mexico. Another benefit is that CreateSpace's Expanded Distribution makes your book available to bookstores and websites not owned by Amazon. (KDP has one advantage in distribution, and that's the Japanese market.)

Most self-published authors sell the vast majority of their books through Amazon.com, and derive few sales through the Expanded Distribution channel. In that case, KDP's print service is comparable to CreateSpace. If you've done thorough research on how to effectively utilize the Expanded Distribution channel or if you have a strong international market, you may be better off publishing with CreateSpace. Otherwise, I recommend using KDP print.

Using KDP for both eBooks and paperbacks is convenient. You setup a single account, you use a single website, and can you see all of your sales collected in the same report.

KDP also appears to be the way of the future, as it is quickly catching up to CreateSpace. *You should check to see if KDP's paperback option has already widened its distribution to match CreateSpace*: If so, then I would definitely recommend KDP's paperback option over Create-

Space. If it hasn't yet, it probably will soon, and there is a possibility that all of the books published through CreateSpace will eventually be migrated to KDP. (I love CreateSpace and KDP both. I've published several paperbacks with CreateSpace and my experience with them has been great. I have nothing against CreateSpace.)

www.createspace.com

Note that your Amazon account information **won't** work at CreateSpace. You'll need to setup a new account with CreateSpace, whereas you can use your Amazon login with KDP.

Before you publish your paperback, you'll need to modify your Kindle eBook file. You need to have two separate Word files: You want to keep your original Kindle eBook file, and you also want to save a copy of your eBook file with a new name and modify it for your paperback edition.

Following are some of the features of your eBook that you should consider changing for your paperback. Be sure to only make these changes to the Word file for the paperback version of your book. Don't change these features for the Word file for the Kindle edition of your book. (You may recall that we discussed creating separate files for your print and Kindle editions back in Sec. 1.3.) If you make any proofreading, editing, or other revisions to the text of your book, be sure to do this to both files (print and eBook). **Note**: CreateSpace offers interior design templates, but I **don't** recommend using them, especially if you've already completed your eBook. For one, they include settings that you will want to override (such as the advanced paragraph options: One of the following bullet points, which discusses lining up the bottom of your pages, shows you how to uncheck the appropriate boxes in the advanced paragraph settings). The templates are fairly simple, so they don't offer much advantage. Some authors also have trouble adjusting the settings: It's easier to modify a file that you made yourself than one that somebody else made, since you understand what you did to make your own file.

- Adjust the **page size**. Browse through the available trim sizes, making sure that your book will have the proper number of pages for the trim size that you select (note also that the available trim sizes are different for color and black-and-white books). Be sure to adjust the Apply To setting to Whole Document when you change the page size. The 6" × 9" trim size is popular among *trade* paperbacks. If you think that's too large, you're probably used to reading *mass market* paperbacks. It's almost impossible for a paperback self-published novel to compete with low-priced *mass market* paperbacks (but your Kindle edition *can* compete with those): However, a self-published paperback *can* compete with the higher-priced, somewhat larger *trade* paperback. You can choose a smaller print size, if you wish, though it will probably still be a little larger than mass market size. Workbooks and children's picture books are often larger, 8" × 10" or 8.5" × 11". Browse through a local bookstore to see what trim size is popular for books similar to yours.

Note: If you have any images that need to extend to the very edge of the page, you must select the option with **bleed** when you upload your interior file, and you must add 0.125" to the width and 0.25" to the height of your pages (for example, a book with a trim size of 6" × 9" would have a page size of 6.125" × 9.25"). This is common for children's picture books and photography books, for example. If this applies to you, read the instructions relating to bleed at CreateSpace or KDP.

https://www.createspace.com/Products/Book/#content4

- Decide whether you want to have a **full-color** or **black-and-white** interior. Note that you must select full-color even if you only want a single page to be in color. Color books cost more to print, require setting a higher list price, and result in a lower royalty (unless you raise the price higher to compensate for the higher printing cost). You can use the royalty calculator at CreateSpace to determine how a color interior and how the page count would impact your list price (the **minimum** list price gives you **zero royalty**— I encourage you to set a *higher* list price so that you can earn a respectable royalty). If your book would be fine in black and white, that's what I recommend. If color is necessary for your book, then you should choose color instead.

https://www.createspace.com/Products/Book/#content6:royaltyCalculator

- Adjust the page **margins**. If you have a long book (hundreds of pages), narrower margins can save you money: For a black-and-white book over 100 pages (or a color book over 40 pages), each additional page cuts into your royalty. Avoid making your margins narrower than 0.5" (as that will accentuate any trimming errors), unless you really need to reduce your page count. Check CreateSpace or KDP to find the **minimum inside margin**, which depends on the length of your book. You'd hate to set your inside margin to 0.5", only to discover later that for your page count the minimum inside margin is 0.75". If page count isn't a pressing matter, *you should be more concerned with the visual layout of your book*, in which case larger margins (up to 1") might be better. For a textbook or other book where annotation is likely, readers may appreciate generous margins. Visit a local bookstore with a ruler and notepad and see what size margins are common for books similar to yours. **Note**: If you have any images that need to extend to the very edge of the page, you must select the option with **bleed** when you upload your interior file, and you must allow for the extra 0.125" that will be trimmed off the top, bottom, and outside margins (that's why you had to make your page size larger than your trim size in the first step). You must also be careful not to put any text within 0.25" of the actual page edges after trimming (which means they must be at least 0.375" from the top, bottom, and outside edges in your print book file). If this applies to you, read the instructions relating to bleed at CreateSpace or KDP.

https://www.createspace.com/Products/Book/InteriorPDF.jsp

Important note: Print books make a distinction between pages and leafs. Each piece of paper is called a **leaf**: There are two **pages** on each leaf (a front side and a back side). For example, you would count 80 sheets of paper (leafs) on a book that consists of 160 pages. The front side of a leaf is odd-numbered, while the back side of a leaf is even-numbered.

- Insert **page numbers** and add **page headers**. Most traditionally published print books don't number the early front matter pages, use lowercase Roman numerals (like vii) from the introduction onward, and switch to Arabic numbers (0-9) starting with the first chapter. The first chapter doesn't ordinarily begin with page 1, but uses the actual position from the very beginning of the book (for example, the first chapter might begin on page 9 if there are 8 pages of front matter). It's also common to have no header in the front matter, an odd-page header with the book title, an even-page header with the chapter number and name, and no header on the first page of each chapter. Another common feature is for the chapter heading to drop down a bit from the top of the page (add Spacing Before to the first paragraph—use a paragraph style to automatically do this to every chapter heading). **Browse through a variety of print books that are similar to your book. Use these books to help you decide on your page layout and book design** (without copying everything that one book does exactly). **Note**: In order to have different types of page numbering or page headers in Microsoft Word, you must insert **section breaks** between chapters, and use the Header & Footer Design ribbon (not to be confused with another Design ribbon that may also appear at the top of the screen) to allow for different odd and even pages, make a different first page, and to link or unlink the current header or footer from the previous header or footer. Press the **Link to Previous** button to make the **Same as Previous** flag appear or disappear: This helps you control the linking between the previous section's header or footer (note that it's possible to have the footer linked, but the header unlinked, for example) and the current section's header or footer. If you use Microsoft Word, click on the URL below, which will take you to a tutorial on my blog to help you setup your headers and footers. You can also search Microsoft Word's help pages for tutorials on this. An alternative program that some book formatters use for print books is Adobe's InDesign: That software is in some ways better suited for controlling typography and page layout. However, a book can be formatted quite well with Microsoft Word, if you know what you're doing. If you're already fairly proficient with Word, it may be easier (and cheaper and more convenient) to learn a few new things (like how to use section breaks) in Word than it would be to learn everything from scratch for InDesign (but if you may wind up publishing several books in the future, time spent learning InDesign now may pay dividends in the future). If you get Adobe Acrobat DC (not to be confused with the Acrobat Reader), which is also handy for PDF conversions (you will need some type of PDF converter), click the footnote at the end of this sentence for an alternative method.[112]

https://chrismcmullen.com/2014/07/04/page-numbers-in-microsoft-word-2010

https://chrismcmullen.com/2013/06/13/different-headers-in-each-chapter-microsoft-word-2010

Tip: Backup your file and save a new copy of your file with a new name before you start messing with headers and footers. This way, if your file becomes corrupt (which sometimes happens if you work with one huge file that has headers and footers), you will have a backup available without headers and footers.

Important note: The two-page view in Microsoft Word doesn't show your document the same way that it will appear in a book. The two-page view in Microsoft Word incorrectly makes it look like odd pages are on the left and even pages are on the right: *When you actually open your book, you will see even pages on the left and odd pages on the right.* Once you finally create a PDF file, if you open it with Acrobat Reader (which is free), if you select Two Page View and also select Show Cover Page in Two Page View, then you will see a proper book view with the odd pages on the right and the even pages on the left.

- Choose a **font face**. I **don't** recommend using Times New Roman (the most recognizable word processing font), Book Antiqua (which is difficult to kern properly), or Comic Sans (though for an illustrated children's book, this one may be okay). Popular book fonts for self-published authors include Garamond (especially for novels, though it is a little light) and Georgia (a darker alternative, though it's a little similar to Times New Roman).

---

[112] Adobe Acrobat DC will let you combine multiple Word files into a single PDF. Thus, you can save each chapter (and even your front matter) individually. This makes it easy to have different headers and footers in each chapter. It also reduces the chances of your file becoming corrupt, since you will have several small files instead of one huge file. However, you need to take care that the page numbering is continuous from one file to the next, and that you have consistent page layout and design (like margin settings) across all of your files.

Personally, I'm fond of Minion (for a serif font—although each letter of Minion also resembles Times New Roman closely, it displays better than Times New Roman) and Myriad (for a sans serif font). Century may be a good fit for K-12 texts, study guides, and workbooks. If your book includes math typed with Word's equation editor (which you may use for a print book, but shouldn't use for a Kindle eBook, unless you reformat the equations as pictures for your eBook), Cambria will match the font of your equations (with recent versions of Word for Windows). Note that it is common to use a **serif** font (which adds short lines to the edges of the letters—see my example below) for the *body text* and **sans serif** for *headings* (though there are exceptions). I recommend that you browse through a variety of traditionally published books, studying fonts and other features (this will also help to develop your own eye for book design). Although you're trying to find font styles that are suitable for your genre or subject, the main goal of the font that you choose for your body text should be **readability**. *Some of the fonts that most clearly signify your genre or subject work best on the cover, but aren't suitable for body text*—because they aren't as readable as more standard fonts. If you search for fonts online, check the font licensing to see if it permits commercial use: This is necessary since customers will be purchasing your book. Adobe TypeKit offers a good selection of fonts that don't come preinstalled on your computer (but you should check whether or not you have the right to use them for your self-published book). If you check the font properties on your computer, it will tell you whether or not the font is embeddable (if so, you should be able to use it to print to PDF). Now whether or not you have the legal rights to include a font that is embeddable and have CreateSpace or KDP print your book for you is a separate matter: I'm not an attorney, so I can't offer legal advice (if you would like legal advice, consult an attorney). You can find good discussions about this on the CreateSpace community forum, and you can search online for more information. Some popular embeddable fonts are frequently used by self-publishers (whether it's right or wrong—of course, that doesn't necessarily mean that it's 'right'). Beware that some font kits that you can purchase in a store specifically state that they are *not* for commercial use (just because you pay for it doesn't mean that you can publish a book with it).

This is a serif font.

This is a sans-serif font.

- You may wish to resize your **indents** for your print book. If you controlled indents through paragraph styles in your eBook, it should be very easy to resize them for your print book: Simply adjust the paragraph settings in the affected paragraph styles. If you used a word processor in school, you might have developed the habit of using 0.5" indents, which are *much larger than most traditionally published books use* (especially for trade paperbacks, which are smaller than a sheet of school paper). One problem with a 0.5" indent is that it accentuates any justification problems for the first line of each paragraph. An indent size of 0.2" to 0.3" is more modest.

- Adjust the **line spacing** for your print book. You should have used single spacing for your eBook with zero space between paragraphs (except for certain kinds of books where block paragraphs are common). You should preserve this, except for one thing: Change the line spacing to include a little 'leading.' Set the line spacing to Multiple and enter a value around 1.15 to 1.2 for most books that format like a novel. For certain types of fonts (you can research this online), a little extra leading may be appropriate; there are also a few fonts where the leading should be a little tighter. For children's books, more generous leading (1.5 to double) may be appropriate (the younger the reader, the greater the leading).

Tip: Format a full page of text and print it out at home. Compare it to a variety of traditionally published books that are similar to yours. This will help you adjust things like line spacing, space between paragraphs (usually no added space between two text paragraphs), the size of the indent, the position of the header, the location of the page number, the style of the font, etc.

- Update the **table of contents** for your print edition to include page numbers. If you inserted an automatic table of contents with Word as described in Sec. 3.8, you just need to uncheck the box that says to use hyperlinks instead of page numbers, and the page numbers should automatically appear (unless you saved each chapter as its own file).[113]
- You probably need to replace (or at least delete and reinsert) all of your **pictures**. Ideally, the images for your print book should be at least 300 DPI. Otherwise, the pictures may appear blurry or pixilated. Unfortunately, **Word automatically compresses your pictures unless you follow each of these steps to prevent it from doing so**: (1) Click File > Options > Advanced and check the box that says, "Do not compress images in file." This must be done *before* inserting your images. If you have an older version of Word (before 2010), or if you work on a Mac, search online for the instructions, which are a little different. Try right-clicking on a picture with Word 2007 or earlier. (2) Use Insert >

---

[113] I **don't** recommend using Word's optional Master documents feature to try to tie separate files together. The extra memory required greatly increases the chances that your file will become corrupt or that the processing may become very slow.

Pictures. Don't copy/paste images into your file. Check the DPI of your images to ensure that they are 300 DPI to begin with. If they aren't 300 DPI and you don't replace them with higher resolution images, they may appear blurry or pixilated in print. However, in many cases, 200 DPI may be satisfactory. (3) Don't crop, resize, or otherwise modify your pictures in Word. Use image software to perfect your image, then insert it as-is, without any adjustments in Word. (Make sure that the picture isn't wider or taller than your margins allow.) (4) Find a Word to PDF converter and print to PDF. **Don't** use Word's Save as PDF option. Adobe Acrobat DC offers excellent PDF conversion, if you can afford it. Otherwise, browse the CreateSpace or KDP community forums for recommended PDF conversion software that is free or low-cost (and then research that software online to learn more about it before you download it). **Note**: It's very common to learn, after submitting your files for review, that you have one or more images with less than 300 DPI. If you follow all of these steps to the letter, it reduces the likelihood that this will happen. (Rarely, though, the 'picture' they are referring to may be some other feature of your Word file, such as a border.) Once you order a printed proof, you can see whether or not you are satisfied with the appearance of your pictures.

- You may wish to apply certain types of formatting to your print book which is lacking in your Kindle eBook. For example, you can replace simple, basic tables in your eBook with larger, more complex **tables** with rich formatting in your print book. You can use the full array of **special symbols** that Word offers[114] for your print book, instead of just the supported Kindle eBook symbols from Appendix A. Your print book will support the full assortment of **bullet** and **numbered list** options, and you can use **multi-level indents**: If you chose to have justified body text paragraphs, but ragged right bullet points (Sec. 3.7) for your eBook, you might prefer to have bullet points justified in your print book. You can use highlighting, double underlining, text outlines, fancy drop caps, borders, shadows, multiple columns, and a host of other features that you should have avoided in your eBook.

- If your book is a novel or other kind of book that mostly consists of text, if a customer thumbs through the book, it will seem strange if any of your pages has a different number of lines (such that the bottom line of text on that page doesn't line up with the bottom line of text in adjacent pages). In a traditionally published book, every page would typically have **the same number of lines** (except, of course, the last page of the

---

[114] For your print book, the only limitation is ensuring that the font needed is properly embedded. You should order a printed proof and check that your special symbols printed fine. In very rare instances, even a common font with regular symbols can run into embedding or printing issues, so it's important that you order a printed proof and check it carefully.

chapter, which may be shorter), and **every page will line up at the bottom**. With self-published books, it's a common mistake not to do this. Check the paragraph settings (hopefully, you're in the habit of doing this in a paragraph style, and not for a specific paragraph: Look at the Normal style, and then check your other styles next): Go to the Line and Page Breaks tab, and **uncheck the top three boxes**. That should help solve *this* problem (though perhaps not perfectly), but it will probably introduce a *different* type of problem: widows and orphans (described in one of the following bullet points).

- Does the last page of any chapter appear to be centered *vertically*? If so, click the little arrow-like icon in the bottom right corner of the Page Setup group on the Page Layout ribbon, choose the Layout tab, and adjust the Vertical Alignment from Center to Top. This will **align the text at the top of each page**, instead of centering it vertically.

- To give the print layout maximum visual appeal, print book formatters look for possible issues like widows, orphans, runts, and rivers. A **widow** occurs when the very last line of a paragraph appears at the top of the next page. The word **orphan** has multiple meanings: It can refer to a short line appearing at the very bottom of a page, the first line of a new paragraph appearing at the very bottom of a page, or a single word at the end of a paragraph appearing on a line all by itself (this is also called a **runt**). A **river** occurs when the gaps in consecutive lines of text happen to line up to create a vertical column of white space. Formatters try to remove all widows from the book, as well as short runts (about three letters or worse), but often don't remove all of the orphans (it's not as common to find a river with computer word processors). To deal with unwanted widows, orphans, or runts, first read your paragraph text carefully: If the writing may have room for improvement, try to revise the writing and see if that helps. The alternative is to apply subtle formatting tricks to the paragraph, like tracking, kerning, or scaling (see the next bullet point). **Note**: Don't try to remove these features from your book **until** your text is completely written and proofread. If you revise your text to correct a typo or rewrite a sentence, you will likely need to undo the formatting that you had previously applied to deal with widows, orphans, or runts—and you may find new widows, orphans, or runts that you didn't have before. Formatting is easier once the text has already been perfected.

- You may be able to improve the visual design and layout of your book by adjusting things like hyphenation (see the next bullet point), tracking, kerning, scaling, the size of the spaces between words, the font size of a selection, leading, or the spacing between paragraphs. **Kerning** is usually a correction applied to a font for which the spacing between the letters of a word appears non-uniform: Some fonts have more notable kerning problems than others (like Book Antiqua). **Tracking** is when you add (or remove) the same amount of space between each letter of a word. **Scaling** makes the text smaller or larger. **Leading** refers to the vertical space between consecutive lines of text. In Word, click on the little arrow-like icon at the bottom right corner of the Font menu to open the Font dialog box, and then click the Advanced tab. Check the box labeled "Kerning for fonts." To apply scaling in Word, first highlight one or more lines of a paragraph, and adjust the percentage: A value like 98% will be difficult for a reader to notice, whereas a value like 90% will be quite noticeable. If you adjust the scaling in Word, note that it may impact the leading a little, too: Watch closely. To apply tracking in Word, first highlight one or more words, change Spacing from Normal to Condensed or Expanded, and specify a point value: You want to apply a small change that will be difficult for the reader to notice. **Note**: Don't apply kerning, tracking, scaling, etc. <u>until</u> your text is completely written and proofread. Otherwise, when you correct a typo or rewrite the text, you will likely need to undo some of this formatting (and reapply it elsewhere). For example, suppose that you want to make one line of text of a paragraph slightly shorter, so that a short word at the beginning of the next line comes up to the end of the previous line: You might select that line and the short word, and apply either tracking or scaling. Typography is an art form, and you must be careful not to make the page design worse while attempting to correct one minor issue. To learn more about widows, runts, tracking, and scaling, for example, search online or consult a book dedicated to the art of typography. **Tip**: If you apply kerning, tracking, scaling, etc. to a small section of your book, select that formatting, and apply highlighting to it (in Word, you can find the highlighting tool on the Font section of the Home ribbon). This highlighting will help you remember which sections of your book have special formatting. That way, if you discover a typo that you need to fix, it will be easier to find previous formatting that you may need to undo. Obviously, you don't want to publish your book with highlighting in it: So when your book is 100% complete, save your book with a revised file name, and then remove that highlighting. You want to have two files, one with and one without the highlighting: Publish the version **without** the highlighting (the purpose of the highlighting is just to help you remember where you have tracking, kerning, scaling, etc.—use different colors for different features). **Tip**: If you decide to use automatic hyphenation (see the next bullet point), do that **before** you adjust things like tracking or scaling.

Note: I recommend that you first try *tracking*. I recommend that you avoid *scaling*.

• If you see large gaps between words in your print book, you can fix it. One adjustment you can make is to add a **hyphen** at the proper position in a long word (consult a dictionary to determine the proper breaking points). If you only need to insert an occasional hyphen, you can do this manually. However, if you would need to insert multiple hyphens on every page of your book, it's more convenient to do this automatically. In

Word, go to File > Options > Advanced and check the box labeled, "*Do full justification the way WordPerfect 6.x for Windows does*" (if you have Word 2010, you will first need to click Layout at the bottom of the list, and if you have an older version of Word, search online for how to do this). Next find the Hyphenation button on the Page Layout ribbon. Adjust the options before you turn on automatic hyphenation. I recommend that you **increase the hyphenation zone** from the default value to something closer to 0.4" (or you may get excessive hyphenation) and limit the number of consecutive hyphens (you probably don't want to see more than two in a row). After enabling automatic hyphenation, you may still feel the need to add a few manual hyphens. Suppose that you wish to avoid an automatic hyphen: In Word, place your cursor just before the word that was automatically hyphenated, and press Shift + Enter to move the entire word onto the next line (but beware that if you later revise the paragraph—for example, to correct a typo—this may cause a big problem later unless you then remove the Shift + Enter by deleting it: Click the show/hide button (¶) in the Paragraph group on the Home ribbon, and if you look closely you can see a special mark that shows where your Shift + Enter is). **Note**: At the end of a paragraph, simply press Enter (**not** Shift + Enter). The combination (holding shift while pressing Enter) is useful in the middle of a paragraph (not at the end of the paragraph) to force a word that appears at the end of one line down onto the next line of text. This is sometimes also helpful when dealing with widows and runts.

- **Upload a PDF file** to CreateSpace or KDP for your paperback book interior. Although CreateSpace accepts DOC and DOCX formats, these are **not** recommended: It's fairly common for the layout of one or more pages to change significantly, or to experience other unexpected changes to your file, when you upload a Word file instead of a PDF file. To convert from Word to PDF, **don't** use Word's built-in Save as PDF option: It's better to find a PDF converter and print to PDF instead, especially if your book has any images. Adobe Acrobat DC offers excellent PDF conversion, if you can afford it. Otherwise, browse the CreateSpace or KDP community forum for recommended PDF conversion software that is free or low-cost (and then research that software online to learn more about it before you download it). For optimal results, if your PDF converter has these options, you would flatten your images and embed the fonts.

If you would like a more thorough introduction to publishing a paperback version with CreateSpace or KDP, and if you would like to format your print book using Word, you may be interested in my other book, *A Detailed Guide to Self-Publishing with Amazon*. If you would like to learn how to use InDesign (or other software) to format your print book, search online for tutorials or look for a book on formatting using your desired software.

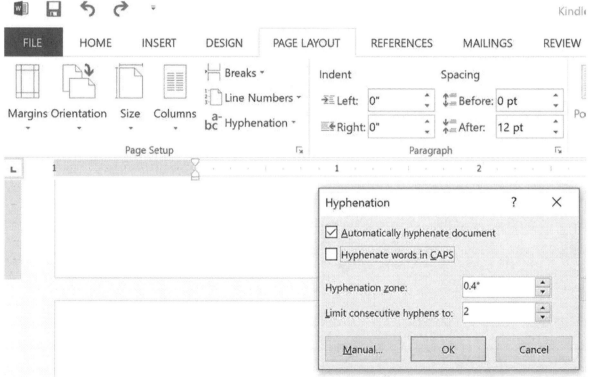

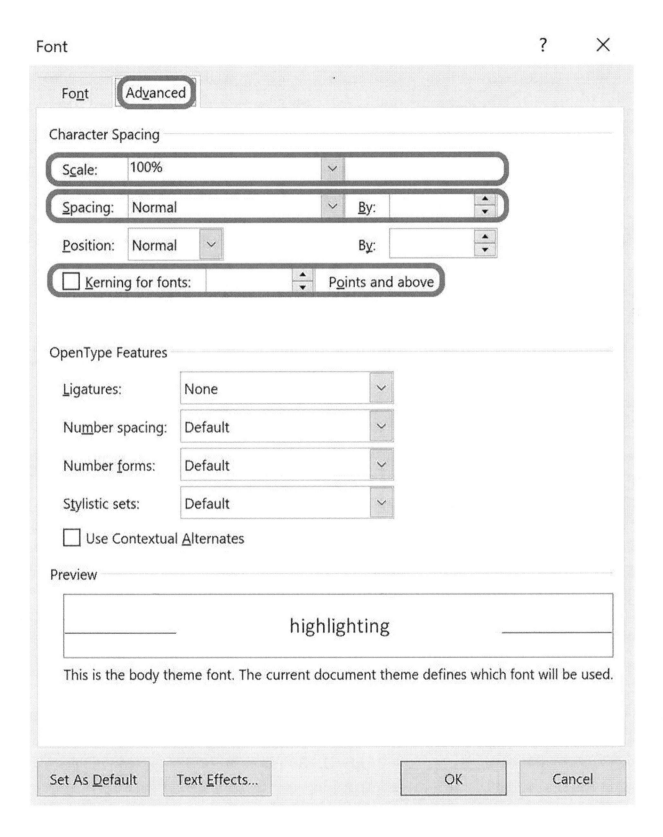

https://www.amazon.com/dp/B00AA5CJ7C

https://www.amazon.com/dp/B00CSDUP66

You will also need to create a single PDF file for your book cover that accommodates the front cover (on the right), the back cover (on the left), the spine width (in between), and trim (add 0.25" to the width and height, since 0.125" will be trimmed from each side to create your cover). The spine width depends on your page count, whether your interior is black-and-white or color, and whether the pages are white or cream: For a black-and-white interior on white pages, multiply the page count by 0.002252; for a black-and-white interior on cream pages, multiply the page count by 0.0025; for a color interior (which requires white pages), multiply the page count by 0.002347. You can also download a cover template for your book. Any images should be at least 300 DPI. If you used the Cover Creator at KDP for your eBook, you might consider also using the Cover Creator at KDP or CreateSpace for your paperback book.

https://www.createspace.com/Products/Book/CoverPDF.jsp

https://www.createspace.com/Help/Book/Artwork.do

Note that colors tend to show darker in print than they do on a computer screen. Thus, if you use the same picture on the front cover of your paperback as you use for your Kindle eBook cover, the paperback cover will probably look noticeably darker.

An ISBN is another thing that your paperback book needs, which your Kindle eBook doesn't need (since Amazon automatically assigns an ASIN to every Kindle eBook). CreateSpace and KDP both have an option where you can receive a free ISBN for your paperback (note that you're not supposed to use an ISBN for a print book for your Kindle eBook—and as I already mentioned, there is no reason to do that). The only reason to pay for an ISBN is if you want to list a 'publishing company' in the publishing field, instead of having the 'publisher' appear as Create-Space Independent Publishing Platform or Kindle Direct Publishing (technically, neither Create-Space nor KDP is your *publisher*—you are: CreateSpace or KDP serves more of a role as a *printer*, which aids with distribution). **My advice is to use the free ISBN** *unless* you have thoroughly researched what it takes to get a self-published book stocked in small local bookstores and libraries, you have put together an amazing press release kit, and you have solid marketing reasons to expect to sell several print copies in bookstores and libraries. Most self-published authors sell print books primarily on Amazon, and struggle to get their books stocked in stores or libraries: In that case, the free ISBN would be better. *The free CreateSpace or KDP ISBN might even net you a few sales.* Suppose that you like to read books, and wish to support fellow self-published authors: How can you find self-published books on Amazon to read? One way is to type

CreateSpace or Kindle Direct Publishing as one of the words in the search field. (I myself have discovered, purchased, and read self-published books by searching for CreateSpace books—even when I was searching for an eBook to read: First I searched for the print edition, and then purchased the eBook.)

Once you've published both print and Kindle editions of your book, you will want both editions of your book to get **linked** together at Amazon. What I mean by 'linking' the two editions together is this: Once they are linked, a customer who discovers your Kindle edition will be able to see that your book is also available in print, and vice-versa.

If all of your book details (title, subtitle, author name, etc.) have the *exact* same spelling and punctuation for both the paperback and Kindle editions, the Kindle and print versions usually link together automatically within two days. If this doesn't happen within two days, visit KDP, click the Help link at the top right of the page, click the Contact Us button (usually in a corner near the bottom of the page), and look specifically for the option regarding linking print and Kindle editions together (it's currently under Amazon Product Page > Linking Print and Kindle Editions). If you do this right, you will get a form to fill out. In the subject, type something like, "Please link my print and Kindle editions together." Fill out the form, including the ISBN of your print edition and the ASIN of your Kindle edition, and submit your request.

Don't accept CreateSpace's free offer to transfer your files to Kindle. If you've already published a Kindle eBook following my guide, simply ignore CreateSpace's offer. (If you accept it, you will have two Kindle eBooks, and you don't want that.) *CreateSpace's free offer to transfer your PDF files to Kindle almost always result in formatting problems*, so even if you haven't already published a Kindle eBook, you wouldn't want to make your Kindle version by accepting that offer.

8.12 Audio Books

One way to make an audio book is through the Audiobook Creation Exchange (ACX), which is an Amazon platform. Your audio book will be available on Amazon and Audible. Certain types of books sell fairly well as audio books. For example, there are truck drivers who avidly read audio books, and there are parents who buy audio versions of children's stories.

http://www.acx.com
https://www.audible.com

Take the **mystery** out of Kindle formatting. Find detailed, step-by-step help using Word to format your e-book for Kindle:

- Achieve predictable, consistent formatting from Word by mastering Word's styles.
- Format images that display well on a variety of devices.
- Understand the semi-reflowable nature of Kindle e-books and how this impacts design choices.
- Discover which features to revise or remove for Kindle compared to print books.
- Treat special characters, punctuation, glyphs, and equations properly.
- Control Microsoft Word's hidden formatting.
- Learn how to sideload your Kindle preview .mobi file onto actual devices.
- And much, much more.

Put some **magic** into your Kindle e-book. Learn how to go a quick step beyond Word to make subtle improvements:

- Display pictures full-width, even when the display size exceeds the image size.
- Create indents that vary either with font size or display size for customized formatting.
- Find recommendations for a variety of HTML style definitions designed specifically for formatting a Kindle eBook.
- Clean up hidden formatting in your Word file.
- Learn how to use media queries to deal with drop caps.

The author, Chris McMullen, has self-published several books with Kindle. He is experienced with the techniques and details, and is sharing his knowledge with you through this guide. This handy reference helps you self-publish a well-formatted Kindle e-book with Amazon.

WORD TO KINDLE FORMATTING MAGIC   MCMULLEN

WORD TO KINDLE FORMATTING MAGIC

Chris McMullen

The biggest challenge with producing an audio book is narration. If you feel like you could do your own narration, first read as much information as you can find at ACX's website. For example, in Video Lessons and Resources, you can find tips for setting up a home studio (it's really important to remove all background noises). If you need to work with a narrator, you either need to pay for the narration service up front (at a price that you negotiate through ACX), or you need to split your royalties. I've gone through this process, worked with a narrator, and had a great experience producing an audio book.

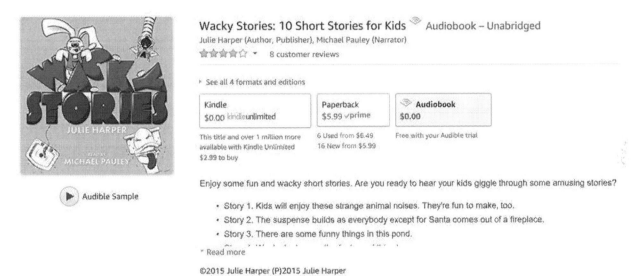

8.13 Sending or Gifting Your Book

There are a number of reasons why an author might want to send a copy of their book to someone else, such as:

- to send one copy in exchange for a possible *honest* review (you're allowed to do this if it's done with *no strings attached, without any payment or compensation* other than one free copy of your book, and *without any persuasion* regarding the number of stars or the nature of the review—the recipient may choose not to review your book, and if the recipient does review your book, they could leave a one-star review or include criticism; that's the chance that you take)
- to send a copy to an editor for proofreading
- to send a copy to an acquaintance who has a specific device that you want to check the formatting on
- to gift a copy to a family member or friend

There are different ways that you can go about sending or gifting a copy of your book:

- Once the book is published at KDP, you can send the book as a gift from the Amazon product page. However, note that the customer *isn't* required to purchase your book:

The customer can use that money towards *anything*. (If the customer uses your gift to redeem your book within 24 hours, it will help with sales rank.) **Note**: Amazon is setup to gift a Kindle eBook who lives *in the same country* as you: If you're trying to gift a Kindle eBook to someone who lives in a different country, you should search online for more information about this.

- If you've already purchased your own book (you should be your own first customer, to be the first person to inspect the actual formatting after publishing), you may be able to loan one copy of your Kindle eBook to a family member for a period of up to 14 days (Sec. 6.14). Note that you can only loan your book one time this way, and that you won't have access to your book while it is loaned.

- If you downloaded your converted MOBI file following the instructions in Sec. 7.8, you could email the MOBI file to the customer. It's possible for certain advanced features to be altered when you email a MOBI file, though if your eBook consists mainly of text, like a novel, it may be okay (as a test, first try emailing it to yourself at a second email address, or emailing it to a friend or family member, and see how it appears on the other end). You must also trust that the recipient won't then give (or sell) your eBook to anybody else.

- You could create a PDF version of your Word file and email that. You must trust that the recipient won't then give (or sell) your PDF to anybody else.

- If you created a paperback edition of your book (Sec. 8.11), you could send an author copy. Unlike sending a MOBI or PDF file, if the person decides to give (or sell) the printed book, they can only do that one time (since they only have one physical copy of the book—and anything else they might do with the book, they could just as well purchase one copy from Amazon and then do it anyway). It costs more to send a printed book than it does to send a digital copy, yet this is my preferred option. I see marketing value in having printed copies of my book out there (Sec. 8.11).

- If you don't have a print edition, you could print out your Word file and make copies with a local office supply company, for example.

- If the recipient happens to be a Kindle Unlimited subscriber and your book happens to be enrolled in KDP Select, there is no reason to gift the eBook: **The subscriber can already read your book for free.**

- If your book isn't enrolled in KDP Select, and if the recipient reads books through Smashwords, for example, you could publish your book with Smashwords and offer the recipient a discount code that allows the recipient to redeem a free copy of your book from Smashwords.

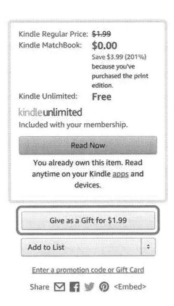

8.14 Add X-Ray to Your Kindle eBook

X-Ray is a cool feature that Amazon recently made available to KDP authors. X-Ray offers a way to pass more information onto readers in the background. There are two ways that readers might access X-Ray in your Kindle eBook (once you activate this feature). One is to visit the X-Ray section directly. For example, on a Kindle Fire one of the icons on the ribbon that appears at the top has an X on it: If a customer presses this icon, it opens the X-Ray section, allowing the customer to review Notable Clips, People, and Terms. Another way happens when a customer happens to highlight a term or name that has an X-Ray note associated with it.

X-Ray can be useful for both nonfiction and fiction. An obvious use of X-Ray for nonfiction is to define relevant terminology or offer explanations. With fiction, X-Ray could be helpful to keep track of names or places in a book that has a complex plot or is part of a long series. There is also an option for an author to share commentary: Some readers enjoy it when an author shares the inspiration behind a character's name or an event that occurs in the book, or when an author offers personal background that relates to a specific part of the book, for example.

Remember, X-Ray doesn't detract the reader from the story. The reader doesn't see X-Ray while reading the book. If the customer wants to see a list of characters and terms, the customer will choose to visit the X-Ray feature. Alternatively, if the customer wants to know more about a term or place, the customer can highlight a word in the book, and if that word happens to be included in X-Ray, then a window will pop up with the relevant information.

The Amazon product page for a book shows whether or not X-Ray is enabled for the Kindle eBook (scroll down to the product details section). Some customers who enjoy the X-Ray feature look for this, and when they read the book, they think of X-Ray as valuable bonus content (and thus have expectations for how it will work).

Here is how to enable X-Ray for your Kindle eBook:

- Visit your KDP Bookshelf.

- Position your cursor over the gray (…) button to the right of your book title, and hover it there for a moment. Once the X-Ray feature becomes available for your book, one of the options will say, "Launch X-Ray."

- The first time you visit the X-Ray setup page, *you won't be able to do or explore anything*. All you can do right now is click the yellow button labeled Request X-Ray. When you click this button, a timer will countdown from 20 (unless KDP changes how it works, of course) and then it will automatically return you to your KDP Bookshelf.

- If your account is set up to receive emails from KDP, you should receive an email within a few hours (sometimes it just takes a few minutes), letting you know that X-Ray is ready for you to set up (if not, check your spam filter or junk mail, or just check the X-Ray option from your KDP Bookshelf a while later).

- Once X-Ray is enabled for your KDP eBook, you need to click the Launch X-Ray option again. This time you will be able to explore it and set it up for your book. **Tip**: Click the Begin Tutorial button—it's quick and effective.

- The items that you see on the left are suggested names or terms. If you don't want to include an option, you will be able to select Exclude for it. If something is set to *character* and you wish to call it a *term*, or vice-versa, there is an option to switch it. (A character is usually a person or creature, while a term is usually a word or phrase. The choice is up to you, though it would be wise to try to do what readers who enjoy X-Ray may expect.)

- **Tip**: Click on the number which shows how many occurrences of the term there are. The link will show you actual terms in context to help you see how it was used and to decide whether you think it's worth displaying to readers.

- You can either write a custom description or search for a relevant Wikipedia article. Sometimes a Wikipedia article already appears, but you can search for a different article and change it, or you can write a custom description instead. Any article that already appears was automatically selected, and might not be relevant.

- **Tip**: Make sure that it says Item Reviewed at the bottom if you wish to display the term to readers. Otherwise, your changes won't be published. You may need to click this little button to change it. Occasionally, you may need to click No to the top question to temporarily exclude it, and then click Yes to change it back before it will let you change it to Item Reviewed.

- **Tip**: Think of other terms that you might have typed that you might want to include together with the same description. For example, if you may have used both the singular or plural form of a word, or if you used an adjective and noun version of basically the same term, you might want them linked together (there is an option to add variations). As another example, imagine that you wrote a description of the difference between acids and bases: If so, you might want *acids and bases* (and *acid*, and *base*) all linked together with the same description.

- **Tip**: The option called Remove only applies when you have two or more terms linked together. When you click on Remove for an automatically generated term, the term will move somewhere else on the list at the left (sometimes far away). When you click on Remove for a term that you added yourself, it gets deleted (so if you wanted to keep that term, but have it separate it from the other term, you need to re-add it).

- You can probably think of helpful terms or characters that didn't automatically appear on the list. It may help to browse through your book. Click the option to Add new terms. Unfortunately, it won't show you how many occurrences there are like it does for automatically generated terms. Well, not right away. **Tip**: If you add a new term, after you publish the changes and after the changes take effect, return to the X-Ray setup page and check the number of occurrences.

- **Tip**: When you're ready to publish the changes, first browse through all of the items. Check that the first question is marked Yes or No as you intended. If it's marked Yes, check that it shows Item Reviewed at the bottom. Then sort by X-Ray status (like Modified, Pending Publication, or Excluded) to make sure that everything is marked correctly. It's also helpful to filter by Type or Character to quickly catch anything that is out of place. Click the Remove All Filters option at the bottom when you're ready to see every item.

- **Tip**: Be sure to click the yellow button labeled Review and Publish X-Ray at the top right corner, otherwise **nothing will happen** (and you will have wasted your time). You should receive an email when your X-Ray changes are published. Sometimes it just takes a matter of minutes, but it can be a few hours.

- Check the KDP help page for X-Ray (one way is to type X-Ray in the search field) to see what is or isn't allowed.

- **Tip**: After the changes have been published and have taken effect, visit your X-Ray page once again. Filter by X-Ray status. Sometimes, a few items appear to have the incorrect status even though you're 'sure' that you had marked it correctly before, so it's worth checking.

The following picture below shows X-Ray in action on my Kindle Fire HD 8.9" for my astronomy book.

8.15 Write More

Very few authors who write and publish a single book become successful. I've met and interacted with dozens of fairly successful authors (and hundreds who are mildly to moderately successful), and every one of them has an Amazon author page with dozens of books (and a few of them have at least one more author page under a pen name).

Although publishing multiple books doesn't guarantee success (you need to produce quality books with marketable content), there are many benefits to writing and publishing more books:

- Each book that you publish gains renewed visibility with the Last 30 Days and Last 90 Days search filters. It's not uncommon for the sales of your first book to taper off when you reach the 30-day or 90-day marks: If that happens with your book, it's an indication that your book benefited from such early exposure. Publishing a new book gives you a chance to gain from it again.

- When customers click on your author page (or simply search for your name, or when they look at the customers-also-bought lists), when they see that you've published multiple books, each book has multiple reviews, and some of your books are selling fairly well (as indicated by the overall sales rank), this adds to your credibility as an author.

- Each book that you publish creates new marketing opportunities: cover reveals, creating buzz, pre-orders, book signings, book launch announcements (via social media and your blog), Goodreads giveaways, Amazon giveaways, advance review copies, etc.

- Fans who enjoyed your previous book may be interested in your new book.

- Instead of selling one copy of your book to one customer, a single customer may purchase multiple books all at once.

- Your following grows over time, so when you publish your tenth book, for example, you may have many more readers who are ready to help support your book launch.

- If you publish a series, customers who enjoy your books may wind up purchasing every book in your series.

- You can put a few books together and package them as a boxed set at a reduced price.

I recommend that you **don't** publish more than one book every 90 days (at the very least, try to stagger the release dates 30 days apart). This maximizes your exposure with the Last 30 Days and Last 90 Days filters. I've seen too many authors publish several books at the same time and see little to no sales. When customers see a flood of matching books appear all at once, for whatever reason, it's a common reaction to shudder and then to try to navigate past it. Plus, you lose several of the benefits that I just mentioned in the previous list (for example, your fan base hasn't grown before you published the next book, and you waste so much new release exposure).

Before you get too excited about publishing more books (which may wear off a bit when you start writing and remember just how much work is involved and how much motivation it takes), remember that, for this to be effective, **quality** is even more important than quantity. Focus on producing quality books with highly marketable content (if selling books is a strong goal).

Chris McMullen

8.16 Pirate Sites

Inevitably, you will come across multiple websites that appear to be selling *unauthorized* copies of your book, or worse, will appear to be giving your book away for free. Most of these websites do **not** actually have the books that they claim to have. It may be a trap to lure unsuspecting customers or inexperienced self-published authors to click on the link—which may give your computer a virus, spyware, or malware (or perhaps they have some other ulterior motive—for example, they may pretend to offer free books to get businesses to pay them money to advertise on their website).

The following situations are rather common. A new author's book was selling, and then after 90 days sales stopped (it's probably because the book no longer shows in the Last 90 Days filter, and the author hasn't learned any marketing strategies). The author happens to search for his or her own name on the internet, and discovers that some unknown site is giving away (or just claims to be doing this) the book for free. The author incorrectly concludes that the reason for the 'missing' sales is that customers are going to this unheard-of website instead (after all, the book is 'free').

Here is another situation: Someone sends you an email, letting you know that some website is selling (or giving away) unauthorized copies of your book. (Maybe the person who emailed you has good intentions. Maybe it's a fellow author who discovered this website, and is contacting all the other authors whose books were affected.)

When this happens to you, keep the following things in mind:

- The website probably *doesn't* actually have your book.
- If you click on the link, you may wind up with a virus, spyware, or malware on your computer.
- Even if the website does have your book (and isn't authorized to do so), almost **no** customers are going to download your book from an unheard-of website (because they

don't want to risk getting a virus, spyware, or malware). Most customers shop for books at Amazon, Nook, Kobo, Smashwords, or a popular website that they have heard of before: Customers tend to get their books from places they **trust**. Amazon has put billions of dollars into marketing and growing in order to attract customers to their site. Some unknown site isn't going to quickly gain traction in the eBook market (not even by giving away free books).

- **What you can do** is report the pirate website's unauthorized distribution (or claim to distribute) of copyrighted material, perhaps with a DMCA takedown notice. Personally, I don't want a web browser on one of my electronic devices opening such a website, but if you do visit the website, look in the fine print at the bottom to see where the site is hosted (if it happens to be hosted by a big company with a trusted brand name, contacting that big company will likely help you put a quick end to any piracy that occurs on their territory).

- If you discover another author or publisher selling your book (or any book that plagiarizes content from your book) in the Kindle Store, contact KDP support. (It helps if you have registered your copyright—it's the easiest way to prove to Amazon that you're the copyright owner. However, if you didn't register it, don't let that stop you from contacting KDP support.)

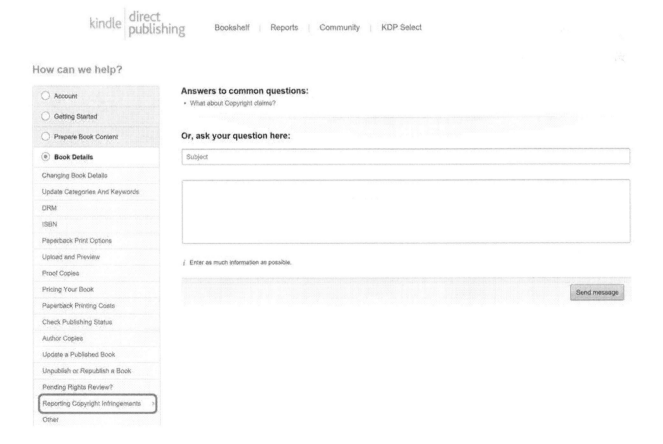

8.17 Common Questions

Following are the answers to some questions that authors commonly ask after publishing a Kindle eBook.

- *Why isn't a sale showing in my reports?* First of all, note that your Sales Dashboard shows books ordered, whereas other reports (such as the Month-to-Date report) show books sold. Orders and sales aren't quite the same thing: An order may be canceled, or an order may be delayed due to credit card processing issues before it turns into a sale. Also, there can be a wild variation in the time it takes for sales to show in reports: Although sales often appear very quickly, but there are occasions where it takes several days for a sale to show. However, Amazon's reporting is far more transparent and swift than the reporting you get with most other major storefronts and publishers (where sales reports may be monthly or quarterly).

- *Why didn't a sale show up in my reports after my sales rank improved?* Amazon KDP actually states in their help pages that sales rank is not a reliable indicator of whether or not a sale has occurred. The sales rank algorithm is complicated (Sec. 8.5 discusses how it works), and provides an idea of how well a book has sold over time, but doesn't tell you reliably whether a sale occurred recently. When the **overall** sales rank (**not** category ranks) makes a huge jump (like from a million down to a hundred thousand), this usually signifies a sale, but **not** always. To complicate matters, Kindle Unlimited borrows also impact sales rank. So if your book is enrolled in KDP Select, sales rank may have improved because the book was borrowed, not because it sold. (If a Kindle Unlimited subscriber borrows your book, sales rank is improved when the book is borrowed, **not** as pages are read.) Note also that there are common delays both with sales rank and sales reports.

- *Why isn't my review showing?* If you 'know' that a friend or family member left a review for you, chances are that Amazon also 'knows' that the review was left by a friend or family member. Amazon may have blocked or removed the review. Amazon will only discuss reviews with the customer who posted the review: Amazon won't disclose review information with the author. (Sometimes, also, a customer says that he or she will leave a review, but doesn't actually get around to it. A customer occasionally even claims to have posted a review, when the customer didn't do it. This happens.) For more information about customer reviews, read Sec. 8.6.

- *What can I do about a bad review?* The best thing is to focus on marketing your current book and writing new books. If you can succeed in generating new sales, this gives you a chance to get new reviews. Personal interactions can be quite valuable when you have a discouraging review on your product page: Potential customers who interacted directly with you (offline or online) and who had a pleasant experience are more likely to ignore bad reviews and are more likely to write a review of their own. Avoid commenting on the review: Perhaps the **biggest mistake** an author can make regarding reviews is to post an emotional response to the review (partly because your comment will be public and seem unprofessional, and partly because that opens the door for the many ways that the reviewer can then drag you into a lengthy discussion—even if you feel 'sure' that won't happen). Try not to take the review personally: The customer reviewed the book, **not** the author. No book will please everyone. After a few days, when you've calmed down, re-read the review, and try to think as objectively as possible whether any comments in the review may have merit. For example, if a review called attention to possible typos, if there may be truth to this, consider having your book edited. If the review pointed out something that the customer didn't know or didn't expect, try making this point more clear early in the product description.

- *Why isn't my book selling?* Either the book lacks marketability, the book idea doesn't have a significant audience, or you need to learn how to market your book effectively. Sec. 8.7 offers several marketing suggestions, while parts of Sec.'s 8.5 and 8.10 discuss factors that relate to a book's marketability.

- *How do I edit my book description?* The best way to do this is through Author Central. However, you should also copy/paste the HTML version of your book description from Author Central to your KDP Bookshelf for the reason described in Sec. 8.2.

- *How do I change my list price, keywords, or browse categories?* To change just about anything other than the book description, you must republish your book (Sec. 8.4). One thing that you can change easily without republishing is your book description (see the previous bullet point).

- *Can I create a discount code for my Kindle eBook?* Unfortunately, as of the time this book was published, Amazon does not offer discount codes. If your eBook is enrolled in KDP Select, you can create a temporary sale price by running a Countdown Deal (Sec. 6.12) unless it's already priced below $2.99 (or above $24.99) in the US. Whether or not your eBook is enrolled in KDP Select, you can change your list price by republishing (Sec. 8.4), provided that your book isn't already at the minimum possible list price based on its file size. Promotional prices are discussed in Sec. 8.8.

- *How can I give away free copies of my book?* You can run a giveaway on Amazon or Goodreads (Sec. 8.9), or you can gift a copy of your book (Sec. 8.13).

- *What can I do about a website that is giving my book away for free?* Read Sec. 8.16.

- *Can I unpublish my book?* You can unpublish a Kindle eBook, as described in Sec. 8.4. While you can also unpublish a print edition (if you used CreateSpace, you can make the book unavailable for sale), a print edition won't completely disappear from Amazon's website (the reason Amazon does this is so that any customers who may happen to have a used copy and resell it on Amazon).

- *How do I link the Kindle and print editions of my book together at Amazon?* Normally, this occurs automatically in 1-2 days, provided that the spelling and punctuation of the title, subtitle, and author name(s) match exactly. If the Kindle and print editions don't automatically link together at Amazon within 48 hours, use the Contact Us option at KDP. You will need the ASIN of your Kindle edition (available from your KDP Bookshelf) and the ISBN of your print edition.

- *Why don't page breaks show up in the Look Inside?* Amazon's Look Inside feature shows your Kindle eBook differently compared to how it looks on an eReader or Kindle app: The Look Inside scrolls down like a reflowable webpage. There aren't any 'pages' in the Look Inside, so it can't respect page break instructions. The Spacing After and Spacing Before options (or margin:bottom and margin:top if you followed Chapter 5) provide the most reliable to add vertical space between paragraphs in the Look Inside—provided that you implement this properly through paragraph styles (Chapters 3 and 5). Note that Spacing After (or margin:bottom) is more reliable than Spacing Before (or margin:top). Try applying a special paragraph style to the last paragraph of each chapter that adds space after to help create separation between chapters in your Look Inside (or at least try including space before to the chapter heading that begins each chapter).

- *Why does the formatting look wrong?* For common formatting issues and solutions, review Sec. 7.11.

If you didn't find the answer to a question that you have about your Kindle eBook, try searching the KDP community forum. You can find some tips for how to search the forum more effectively towards the end of Sec. 7.11. Alternatively, you can post a question on the KDP community forum or use the Contact Us feature at KDP to ask an Amazon KDP representative.

8.18 Stay Up-to-date

The publishing industry is constantly evolving. Amazon itself introduces new or altered features periodically. New eReader devices are released each year with improved technology. There can be trends among what readers are looking for, styles for formatting books, and short-term marketing strategies.

For these reasons and others, it can be an advantage to keep current with the self-publishing world. If Amazon brings a new feature to KDP, for example, you could be among the first authors to take advantage of it.

How can you stay up-to-date? There are a few ways. One way is to follow blogs or sign up for email newsletters of reliable self-publishing sources. Another way is to visit the KDP and CreateSpace websites (and help forums) periodically. Interacting with other authors via social media will also help keep you in the loop.

Following are a variety of ways to keep current:

- Check out the KDP help pages. Amazon updates these help pages periodically to reflect changes. Whenever I publish a new Kindle eBook, I spend some time browsing through the KDP help pages to see if anything has changed (and on multiple occasions I was glad that I checked).

- Subscribe to the email newsletters of self-publishing services, like KDP, CreateSpace, Goodreads, and Smashwords. Most publishing websites offer to let you subscribe to their email newsletter when you sign up. Amazon has a special page with access to several email subscriptions: Visit the URL below to access that page. Once there, I recommend that you subscribe to KDP and Success Stories.

  https://www.amazon.com/gp/gss/home

- My self-publishing blog draws hundreds of visitors per day via search engines. People come for the free self-publishing articles (and often browse the pages on my website to find valuable tips). If you click on the option to follow my blog via email (no strings attached), you'll be among the first to know when I write about recent changes to KDP or CreateSpace.

  https://chrismcmullen.com

- There are dozens of excellent self-publishing blogs. Following are a few suggestions to help you get started.

  https://www.thebookdesigner.com
  http://www.aaronshep.com
  http://www.hughhowey.com/blog
  https://the-digital-reader.com
  http://nicholasrossis.me
  https://notjohnkdp.blogspot.com
  https://kimwrtr.wordpress.com
  https://thestoryreadingapeblog.com

- Follow KDP and CreateSpace at Twitter and Facebook. They regularly share self-publishing tips. Their Twitter handles are @AmazonKDP and @CreateSpace.

  https://www.facebook.com/KindleDirectPublishing
  https://www.facebook.com/CreateSpace

- Interact with your fellow authors in person and via social media. As writers, you will have something in common to talk about. This is a great way to exchange information and stay current with the writing and publishing industry.

- Periodically check out self-publishing community forums, like the KDP and CreateSpace community forums, or like Kindle Boards. You don't need to participate: There are numerous authors who just read discussions from the background without ever posting. (If you do post, strive to maintain professionalism. Also, consider trying to preserve your anonymity. Beware that, like all online forums, there may be occasional trolling.)

  https://kdp.amazon.com/community/index.jspa
  https://forums.createspace.com/en/community/index.jspa
  http://www.kboards.com

- Find helpful self-publishing hashtags like #pubtips and search for them on Twitter periodically. This will show you recent tweets about self-publishing.

- Follow myself and other authors on Amazon. Visit any author's Amazon author page and click the yellow Follow button. You can similarly show your readers how they can follow you.

  https://amazon.com/author/chrismcmullen

—Publish a Paperback, Too—

There are many benefits to publishing a paperback edition, including:

- Expand your audience: Some readers only buy printed books.
- Increase your exposure: Every time somebody sees your book being read on a bus, train, subway, airplane, park bench, or at a restaurant, for example, the person might inquire, "Which book are you reading?"
- Widen your distribution: A paperback book gives you the opportunity to sell copies to local bookstores, libraries, and other stories that occasionally stock a few books.
- Gain marketing value: Print books are great for advance review copies, local newspaper exposure, bookstore signings, local readings, review copies, book giveaways, and more.
- Improve your reputation: When people see your printed book, especially when they see it on a local bookstore shelf, they are more likely to see you as a 'real' author. Of course, you are already a 'real' author, but sometimes it's nice to hear that from friends and family, and it can be a nice confidence boost to see your own printed book on a shelf.

If you found this book helpful, you might be interested in my books that show you how to format and publish a paperback book: *A Detailed Guide to Self-Publishing with Amazon*, volumes 1-2. Someday, I will publish a *Paperback Formatting Magic* companion to the *Word to Kindle Formatting Magic* book that you're reading now. Until then, *A Detailed Guide to Self-Publishing* is the next best thing. Volume 1 covers the basics of formatting and publishing a paperback edition, while volume 2 includes a few important formatting subtleties and a thorough introduction to how to get started with effective long-term book marketing strategies.

—Was This Book Helpful?—

Thank you for reading my book, *Word to Kindle Formatting Magic*. I hope that this book has proven helpful in various ways.

Three years of effort and thought were put into this book:

- It went through two major overhauls where it was completely rewritten and reorganized.
- You can only imagine the time it took to compile all of the information for this book.
- It took much more time to test everything out. I made hundreds of test books and previews to experiment with problems and solutions to everything from unsupported characters to displaying pictures to line spacing issues.
- With over 500 pages on 8.5" × 11" paper and a word count exceeding 150,000 words, this book is packed with information. I proofread print and digital copies of this book for what seemed like an eternity in my quest to perfect this book.
- If you read Chapter 7, you should have a good idea of how much time and effort I put into previewing this eBook on various previewers, devices, and apps.
- I interact with hundreds of aspiring authors. I receive a few emails every week from a writer who is interested in self-publishing (many discover me from my blog). I also spent much time from 2010 thru 2015 actively participating on the KDP and CreateSpace community forums. This experience helped me to understand the types of problems that self-published authors face. I have done my best to incorporate valuable advice in my book.

If you appreciate the effort that went into making this book possible, there is a simple way that you could show it:

Please take a moment to post an honest review. Thank you.

Even a short review can be helpful and will be much appreciated. Which parts of this book did you find most helpful? I would appreciate the answer to this question, as it will help me when I write future publishing guides. (You could make a similar request for reviews at the end of your book.)

—Support Fellow Authors—

Most authors are readers, too. You have the chance to support fellow authors.

- Interact with indie authors on social media.
- Offer words of encouragement and support.
- Try to be a positive influence. If negativity starts to spread, if it isn't put out quickly, try not to add to it. Complaining is easy. Staying positive can be a challenge. But it's worth trying.
- Discover and read indie books. Write helpful reviews.
- Reviews aren't the only way to support an author. If you like a book, you can thank the author, tell your friends, review the book on your blog, or give the book as a gift.
- Maybe there is a little truth to karma: When you do good deeds for others, you believe that you deserve for good things to happen to you, you might feel more motivated toward your own goals, and you're more likely to interpret events in a positive light.
- Similar books can help one another or sink together. A foolish author slams the competition: When books on the customers-also-bought lists sell well and provide good customer experiences, all of those books thrive together (few customers read just one book). If one of those books begins to discourage customers, all of those similar books are adversely affected.
- If you see an author who is looking for guidance, lend a hand. (Note that unsolicited advice isn't always welcome, though in certain cases it may still be needed.)
- Help brand a good name for indie authorship. Help the companies (like Amazon) which make indie authorship possible maintain a positive image—authors and readers both benefit from this. (If there is a change that you would like to see, send the company a polite suggestion privately.)
- Pay it forward. Help make the future bright.

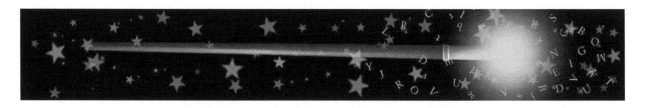

—The Author—

CHRIS McMULLEN HAS self-published several books in both print and eBook format since 2008. His first book, *A Visual Guide to Extra Dimensions*, provided a geometric tour of the fourth dimension of space. He has since published numerous math workbooks (algebra, fractions, and trigonometry), a few science books (astronomy, chemistry, and physics), and a few self-publishing guides.

With over 20 years of experience as a passionate university physics instructor, Dr. McMullen has become skilled in the art of teaching. Whether in the classroom or as a writer, Dr. McMullen loves sharing knowledge and the art of motivating and engaging students. He maintains a few blogs to help share his knowledge. His self-publishing blog, which is packed with informative articles, draws hundreds of visitors per day through search engines.

Chris McMullen earned his Ph.D. in phenomenological high-energy physics (particle physics) from Oklahoma State University in 2002. Originally from California, Dr. McMullen earned his Master's degree from California State University, Northridge, where his thesis was in the field of electron spin resonance.

https://chrismcmullen.com
https://improveyourmathfluency.com
https://monkeyphysicsblog.wordpress.com

—Appendix A—

Supported Characters

THE FOLLOWING SYMBOLS are supported across Kindle devices and apps. Find the character code next to each symbol. Using the Insert > Symbol method—selecting "normal text" and ASCII (decimal) in the pop-up window, with a default font (Calibri or Times New Roman) in the paragraph—**as described in Sec. 2.6** is the most reliable way to insert these symbols into your Kindle eBook (except, of course, for those supported symbols that can be typed directly using a standard keyboard,[115] like % or &). Each symbol that follows was created using the Insert > Symbol method.

> 32 spacebar
> 33 ! exclamation mark
> 34 " straight quote

See the note in Sec. 2.7 regarding quotes.

> 35 # number sign
> 36 $ dollar sign
> 37 % percent sign
> 38 & ampersand
> 39 ' straight apostrophe

See the note in Sec. 2.7 regarding apostrophes.

---

[115] Not every symbol that can be typed with a standard keyboard is a supported symbol. However, if a symbol is supported and if it can be typed with a standard keyboard, then that is the best way to type the symbol (but be sure *not* to adjust the font from the default style, which is usually Calibri or Times New Roman). When you can't use a standard keyboard to type a supported symbol directly (without using keyboard shortcuts), then you should use the Insert > Symbol method.

40 (open parenthesis

41) close parenthesis

42 * asterisk

43 + plus sign

44 , comma

45 - hyphen

46 . period

47 / slash

48-57 digits 0-9

58 : colon

59 ; semicolon

60 < less-than sign

61 = equal sign

62 > greater-than sign

63 ? question mark

64 @ commercial at

65-90 uppercase A-Z

91 [open bracket

92 \ backslash

93] close bracket

94 ^ circumflex accent

95 _ underscore

96 ` grave accent

97-122 lowercase a-z

123 { open brace

124 | vertical line

125 } close brace

126 ~ tilde

Note: Regarding character codes 127-159, see the note following character code 255 below.

160 non-breaking space

161 ¡ inverted exclamation mark

162 ¢ cent sign

163 £ pound sign

164 ¤ currency sign

165 ¥ yen sign

166 ¦ broken bar

167 § section sign

168 ¨ diaeresis

169 © copyright symbol

170 ª feminine ordinal indicator

171 « left double angle

172 ¬ not sign

173 - soft hyphen

Note: The soft hyphen may result in formatting issues with some Kindle devices. Sec.'s 3.7 and 5.6 discuss hyphenation with regard to Kindle design.

174 ® registered symbol

175 ¯ macron

176 ° degree sign

177 ± plus or minus

178 ² square

179 ³ cube

See the note in Sec. 2.7 regarding superscripts.

180 ´ acute accent

181 µ micro prefix

182 ¶ pilcrow sign

183 · middle dot

184 ¸ cedilla

185 ¹ superscript one

186 º masculine ordinal indicator

187 » right double angle

188 ¼ one-fourth

189 ½ one-half

190 ¾ three-fourths

See the note in Sec. 2.7 regarding fractions.

191 ¿ inverted question mark

192 À grave A

193 Á acute A

194 Â circumflex A

195 Ã tilde A

196 Ä diaeresis A

197 Å ring A

198 Æ uppercase AE

199 Ç cedilla C

200 È grave E

201 É acute E

202 Ê circumflex E

203 Ë diaeresis E

204 Ì grave I

205 Í acute I

206 Î circumflex I

207 Ï diaeresis I

208 Đ uppercase Eth

209 Ñ tilde N

210 Ò grave O

211 Ó acute O

212 Ô circumflex O

213 Õ tilde O

214 Ö diaeresis O

215 × multiplication sign

216 Ø stroke O

217 Ù grave U

218 Ú acute U

219 Û circumflex U

220 Ü diaeresis U

221 Ý acute Y

222 Þ uppercase thorn

223 ß sharp S

224 à grave a

225 á acute a

226 â circumflex a

227 ã tilde a

228 ä diaeresis a

229 å ring a

230 æ lowercase ae

231 ç cedilla c

232 è grave e

233 é acute e

234 ê circumflex e

235 ë diaeresis e

236 ì grave i

237 í acute i

238 î circumflex i

239 ï diaeresis i

240 ð lowercase eth

241 ñ tilde n

242 ò grave o

243 ó acute o

244 ô circumflex o

245 õ tilde o

246 ö diaeresis o

247 ÷ division sign

248 ø stroke o

249 ù grave u

250 ú acute u

251 û circumflex u

252 ü diaeresis u

253 ý acute y

254 þ lowercase thorn

255 ÿ diaeresis y

There *are* additional supported symbols (see below). The characters listed above are the supported characters listed on the KDP help pages, which are character codes 32-126 and 160-255 of the 'Latin-1' (ISO-8859-1) format. However, there are certainly other symbols that are supported, which aren't listed in the table from the KDP help pages.

For example, the following characters are frequently used in Kindle eBooks (see the notes in Sec. 2.7 regarding quotes, apostrophes, dashes, and ellipsis):

133 … horizontal ellipsis
145 ' begin single quote
146 ' end single quote
147 " begin curly quote
148 " end curly quote
149 • bullet
150 – en dash
151 — em dash
153 ™ trademark symbol

The above symbols are part of Windows-1252 (mentioned in Sec. 5.6). The Windows-1252 character set contains a few more symbols than the 'Latin-1' (ISO-8859-1) character set.

For any symbols that aren't listed above, rather than taking a chance, it would be prudent to insert them as images (see Chapter 4), except for the few symbols mentioned in Sec. 5.6. You want to use symbols that are supported across *all* devices. Note that there are symbols other than those mentioned here that work on a few devices, but not all Kindle devices and apps: In fact, a few unsupported symbols may appear to work fine in the preview, but experience problems on older devices. The safest bet is to use symbols that are *definitely* supported—and even then, preview your eBook thoroughly and carefully (see Chapter 7).

When you use a symbol that isn't supported on at least one device (or app), customers will have no idea what the symbol was supposed to be. It may look like some other random symbol instead, like one of these:

—Appendix B—

Styles Tutorial

THIS TUTORIAL SHOWS you how to use Word's styles with a hands-on approach. You will be able to see how it works firsthand before you begin applying styles to your book. In addition to applying styles, you will learn how to modify a paragraph style, how to create a new paragraph style, how to change your mind after applying a paragraph style, and we will explore some of the options and features associated with styles.

First, we will make a quick test file. Open a blank document in Microsoft Word.

Don't adjust the font style, font size, line height, or any other formatting at this point. Just type the text first, and then we'll learn how to format the text using the paragraph styles. Leave everything in Word's default settings for now.

We will type a few words in your file so that you have simple text to practice formatting on. Don't worry: There really is very little to type. The typing won't take long.

Type the words Chapter One and press Enter.

Type the sentence, "This is the first paragraph." Copy this sentence and paste it several times to make a quick paragraph. Press Enter at the end of it.

Make three more paragraphs just like that one, but change the word "first" to "second," "third," or "fourth." (I copy and paste the previous paragraph, highlight the new paragraph, and use the Replace tool to change "first" to "second" in the selection only, for example.)

Type the words Chapter Two and press Enter.

Type the sentence, "This paragraph has block indent." Copy this sentence and paste it several times. Press Enter at the end of it.

Type the words Centered Text on its own line and press Enter.

Type the words Last Line with a period. (Don't press Enter.)

Your document should now look like the following picture.

Chapter One

This is the first paragraph. This is the first paragraph. This is the first paragraph. This is the first paragraph. This is the first paragraph. This is the first paragraph. This is the first paragraph.

This is the second paragraph. This is the second paragraph. This is the second paragraph. This is the second paragraph. This is the second paragraph. This is the second paragraph.

This is the third paragraph. This is the third paragraph. This is the third paragraph. This is the third paragraph. This is the third paragraph. This is the third paragraph.

This is the fourth paragraph. This is the fourth paragraph. This is the fourth paragraph. This is the fourth paragraph. This is the fourth paragraph. This is the fourth paragraph. This is the fourth paragraph.

Chapter Two

This paragraph has block indent. This paragraph has block indent. This paragraph has block indent. This paragraph has block indent. This paragraph has block indent. This paragraph has block indent. This paragraph has block indent. This

Centered Text

Last line.

Now we will modify and apply paragraph styles to format the text.

Place your cursor in the very first line, where the words **Chapter One** appear. Click on the little funny-looking arrow-like icon at the bottom right corner of the Styles group on the Home ribbon (this icon appears at the far right, just left of the word Editing for recent versions of Word for Windows). This opens the styles menu at the right of the screen.

Click the bottom-right corner to open the Styles menu.

Check the box beside **Disable Linked Styles** at the bottom of the styles menu.

Right-click on the style called **Heading 1** and click Modify. Make the following changes to the Heading 1 style in the Modify Style pop-up menu (don't apply any of this formatting directly to the heading text: apply it to the Heading 1 style instead):

- Adjust the font style to the default font style (Calibri or Times New Roman), size 20 pt, and set the font color to Automatic.
- Set the alignment to **centered**.
- Click the **Format** button in the bottom left corner of the Modify Style pop-up menu and select **Paragraph**. Under Special, set First Line to "**none.**" Both Left and Right indents should be set to zero. **Set Spacing Before to 24 pt and Spacing After to 12 pt.** Adjust Line Spacing to Single with the At field empty.
- Click the Format button in the bottom left corner of the Modify Style pop-up menu and select Paragraph. Click on the Line and Page Breaks tab, and check the box beside **Page Break Before**. (The best way to create a page break is to incorporate a page break into the desired paragraph style. The first chapter heading won't do this because nothing comes before it in this simple example, but the second chapter heading will.)
- At the top of the Modify Style pop-up menu, adjust Style Based On to "no style" and leave the box beside Automatically Update *unchecked*.

Apply the **Heading 1** style to the first chapter heading (called **Chapter One**). Just place your cursor anywhere in the chapter heading (no need to highlight it) and click on the Heading 1 style. You should see the entire chapter heading change formatting from the original plain text to the Heading 1 style.

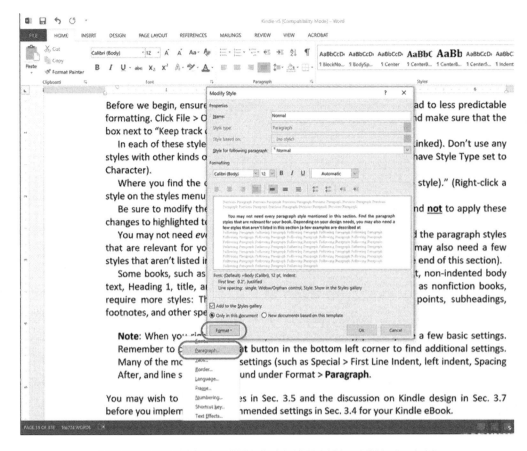

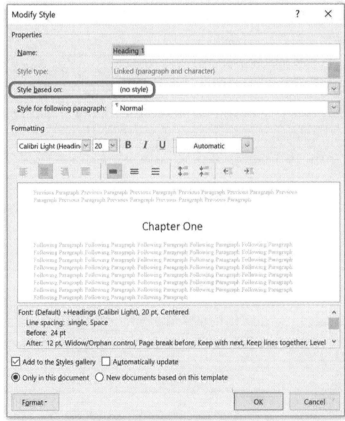

Now apply the **Heading 1** (note that this is a 1, not a 2) style to the second chapter heading (called **Chapter Two**). Although it took some work to modify the Heading 1 style for the first chapter heading, you should appreciate how easy it is to format all of the subsequent chapter headings.

Place your cursor in the first paragraph of Chapter One (the one that says, "**This is the first paragraph**"). On the styles menu that appears at the right of the screen (open the styles menu by clicking on the little funny-looking arrow-like icon at the bottom right corner of the Styles group on the Home ribbon), click the bottom left button to create a new paragraph style. Change the name of the paragraph style to **NoIndent**. Right-click on the paragraph style called NoIndent and click Modify. Make the following changes to the NoIndent style:

- Adjust the font style to the default font style (Calibri or Times New Roman), size 12 pt, and set the font color to Automatic.
- Set the alignment to **justified** (i.e. full).
- Click the Format button in the bottom left corner of the Modify Style pop-up menu and select Paragraph. Under Special, **set First Line to 0.01"**. Look closely to make sure it is 0.01", and not 0.1". Both Left and Right indents should be set to zero. Set Spacing Before and Spacing After both to 0 pt. Adjust Line Spacing to Single with the At field empty.
- At the top of the Modify Style pop-up menu, adjust Style Based On to "no style" and leave the box beside Automatically Update *unchecked*.

Apply the **NoIndent** style to the first paragraph of Chapter One (the one that says, "**This is the first paragraph**").

Place your cursor within the second paragraph of Chapter One (the one that says, "**This is the second paragraph**"). Right-click on the paragraph style called **Normal** and click Modify. Make the following changes to the Normal style:

- Adjust the font style to the default font style (Calibri or Times New Roman), size 12 pt, and set the font color to Automatic.
- Set the alignment to **justified** (i.e. full).
- Click the Format button in the bottom left corner of the Modify Style pop-up menu and select Paragraph. Under Special, **set First Line to 0.2"**. Both Left and Right indents should be set to zero. Set Spacing Before and Spacing After both to 0 pt. Adjust Line Spacing to Single with the At field empty.
- At the top of the Modify Style pop-up menu, adjust Style Based On to "no style" and leave the box beside Automatically Update *unchecked*. (Actually, the Normal style wouldn't let you change this anyway.)

Apply the **Normal** style to the second and third paragraphs of Chapter One (the ones that call themselves the **second** and **third** paragraphs). Since these paragraphs were "normal" to begin with, they may update automatically. The last paragraph of Chapter One may also update, but we're going to modify it slightly in the next step.

Place your cursor in the last paragraph of Chapter One (the one that says, "**This is the fourth paragraph**"). On the styles menu that appears at the right of the screen (open the styles menu by clicking on the little funny-looking arrow-like icon at the bottom right corner of the Styles group on the Home ribbon), click the bottom left button to create a new paragraph style. Change the name of the paragraph style to **BodySpaceAfter**. Right-click on the paragraph style called BodySpaceAfter and click Modify. Make the following changes to the BodySpaceAfter style:

- Adjust the font style to the default font style (Calibri or Times New Roman), size 12 pt, and set the font color to Automatic.
- Set the alignment to **justified** (i.e. full).
- Click the Format button in the bottom left corner of the Modify Style pop-up menu and select Paragraph. Under Special, **set First Line to 0.2"**. Both Left and Right indents should be set to zero. Set Spacing Before to 0 pt and **Spacing After to 12 pt**. Adjust Line Spacing to Single with the At field empty. (It may seem unnecessary to add 12 pt to the Spacing After field of the last paragraph of the chapter, but it can matter: This can help to create vertical spacing between chapters in the Look Inside, which displays a sample of your eBook more like a webpage than like a book. Although the Heading 1 style adds Spacing Before to the Chapter Two heading, note that Spacing After is more reliable for the Word to Kindle conversion.)
- At the top of the Modify Style pop-up menu, adjust Style Based On to "no style" and leave the box beside Automatically Update *unchecked*.

Apply the **BodySpaceAfter** style to the last paragraph of Chapter One (the one that says, "**This is the fourth paragraph**").

Right now, you may be thinking that each time you have to modify a paragraph style, it seems like a lot of work, but this will be a real time-saver later. Once you have all the paragraph styles in place, you can format your paragraphs like a *magician*, simply placing your cursor in a paragraph and applying the paragraph style to it. After you master the paragraph styles, you can write your next book using paragraph styles from the beginning, and anytime you change your mind about a paragraph style, it can automatically change every paragraph of that same style (instead of having to manually change the paragraphs one by one).

However, the main reason to use the paragraph styles for your Kindle eBook *isn't* to save time: It's to achieve more predictable and consistent formatting across all devices and apps (as well as the Look Inside feature).

Place your cursor within the first paragraph of Chapter Two (the one that says, "**This para-graph has block indent**"). On the styles menu that appears at the right of the screen (open the styles menu by clicking on the little funny-looking arrow-like icon at the bottom right corner of the Styles group on the Home ribbon), click the bottom left button to create a new paragraph style. Change the name of the paragraph style to **BlockIndent**. Right-click on the paragraph style called BlockIndent and click Modify. Make the following changes to the BlockIndent style:

- Adjust the font style to the default font style (Calibri or Times New Roman), size 12 pt, and set the font color to Automatic.
- Set the alignment to **justified** (i.e. full).
- Click the Format button in the bottom left corner of the Modify Style pop-up menu and select Paragraph. Set a block indent of Left = 0.2" with Special > First Line = 0.01" (in order to indent the entire left margin rather than just the first line). Set Spacing Before to 0 pt and **Spacing After to 12 pt**. Adjust Line Spacing to Single with the At field empty.
- At the top of the Modify Style pop-up menu, adjust Style Based On to "no style" and leave the box beside Automatically Update *unchecked*.

Apply the **BlockIndent** style to the first paragraph of Chapter Two (the one that says, "**This paragraph has block indent**").

Place your cursor within the paragraph that just has the words, "**Centered text**." On the styles menu that appears at the right of the screen (open the styles menu by clicking on the little funny-looking arrow-like icon at the bottom right corner of the Styles group on the Home ribbon), click the bottom left button to create a new paragraph style. Change the name of the paragraph style to **CenterSpaceAfter**. Right-click on the paragraph style called CenterSpaceAfter and click Modify. Make the following changes to the CenterSpaceAfter style:

- Adjust the font style to the default font style (Calibri or Times New Roman), size 12 pt, and set the font color to Automatic.
- Set the alignment to **centered**.
- Click the Format button in the bottom left corner of the Modify Style pop-up menu and select Paragraph. Under Special, set First Line to "**none**." Both Left and Right indents should be set to zero. Set Spacing Before to 0 pt and **Spacing After to 12 pt**. Adjust Line Spacing to Single with the At field empty.
- At the top of the Modify Style pop-up menu, adjust Style Based On to "no style" and leave the box beside Automatically Update *unchecked*.

Apply the **CenterSpaceAfter** style to the paragraph that just has the words, "**Centered text**."

Simply apply the NoIndent style to the paragraph called Last Line.

Your document should now look like the following picture.

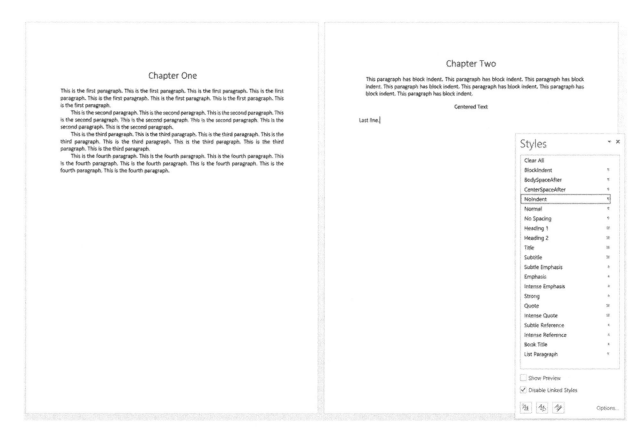

Experiment with your file a little to better understand the paragraph styles. Following are a few suggestions:

- Type a few new short paragraphs, and associate the NoIndent or CenterSpaceAfter paragraph styles with them until you have a few paragraphs of each of these styles. Highlight an entire paragraph with a NoIndent or CenterSpaceAfter paragraph style, and modify the corresponding paragraph style: Try adjusting the alignment, the indent size, the font size, the Spacing After, or apply boldface, for example. Does it automatically change any other paragraphs? If so, note which paragraph style(s) those other paragraphs have. Press Undo until all of these changes are removed. Now try highlighting a Normal paragraph and modifying the Normal style to see what happens (if anything) to other paragraphs.

- Type a few new short paragraphs, and associate the CenterSpaceAfter style with them. Right-click on the CenterSpaceAfter style and choose Select All. Right-click on the Center-SpaceAfter style again, and this time select Modify (while all instances are still selected). Adjust the settings. Check if all of the highlighted instances changed automatically.

- Highlight a word or phrase (but not an entire paragraph), and apply boldface or italics directly to what is highlighted. Then try switching the paragraph style (i.e. apply a different style to that paragraph) to see what happens. Does the boldface or italics change? First try this to a NoIndent paragraph, and then try it with a Normal paragraph.

—Appendix C—

Sample eBook Formatting

I WROTE AND formatted a little story called "The Muse" to show you a sample eBook that has a structure similar to a novel. This formatting sample is organized into three parts as follows:

- It begins with pictures of my Word file for the story. The pictures are labeled to show you which paragraph styles (or heading styles) were applied to which paragraphs.
- This is followed by the HTML that I used. This will be helpful if you followed Chapter 5.
- At the end you will find pictures showing how it looks on the online previewer.

For this story, I applied the following styles. Most of these styles are recommended in Sec. 3.4, but I did create a couple of special styles (such as LeftSpaceAfter) for this story.

- Title: This has the same settings that are recommended in Sec. 3.4.
- Subtitle: This has the same settings that are recommended in Sec. 3.4.
- LeftSpaceAfter: This is like the NoIndentSpaceAfter style from Sec. 3.4, except that it is aligned left instead of justified. I applied this to short lines that wouldn't look good if they justified on a small screen with a large font (as discussed in Sec. 3.7, I followed Chapter 5).
- NoIndentSpaceAfter: This has the same settings that are recommended in Sec. 3.4.
- CenterBold20: This is like the Heading 1 style, except that it doesn't incorporate a page break into the style and it doesn't add space before.
- Toc1 is Word's automatic table of contents style (Sec. 3.8), while TocLast adds space after.
- Heading 1: This has the same settings that are recommended in Sec. 3.4.
- NoIndent: This has the same settings that are recommended in Sec. 3.4.
- Normal: This has the same settings that are recommended in Sec. 3.4.
- BodySpaceAfter: This has the same settings that are recommended in Sec. 3.4.
- CenterBold20PageBreak: This is identical to the Heading 1 style. The reason that I didn't use Heading 1 was so that this 'heading' wouldn't show in device navigation.
- CenterSpaceAfter: This has the same settings that are recommended in Sec. 3.4.
- LeftIndentSpaceAfter: This is like LeftSpaceAfter (see above), but this is indented.

Title `The Muse`

`Chris McMullen`

Subtitle `LeftSpaceAfter`

CenterBold20 `Contents`

TOC 1

Acknowledgments `CenterBold20`

I would like to thank my muse for the inspiration for this story. I couldn't have done it without her. `NoIndentSpaceAfter`

Heading 1

-1- The Gift `NoIndent`

I was content doing the 9 to 5. Really, I was. My life was simple. I had a routine: Wake up to the alarm, shower, shave, get dressed, grab a bite, take the subway, work, eat lunch, work some more, commute home, eat dinner, relax, unwind, sleep, and repeat.

But one day, she showed up. She fed me irresistible ideas. That's how she hooks you. The ideas seem too good not to write about. `Normal`

You find yourself slaving over your keyboard night and day. Your job can't finish soon enough so that you can get to the work that you really want to do.

It doesn't seem like work. You enjoy it. You live for it. You dream about it. The book is everything.

Writing the book isn't enough. You must publish it, too. Share it with the world.

So you do. And it feels wonderful to be the author of such a masterpiece. `BodySpaceAfter`

CenterBold20PageBreak

–Thank you–

NoIndentSpaceAfter

Thank you for reading my story, *The Muse*. I hope that you enjoyed it.

LeftIndentSpaceAfter

–Chris McMullen   www.chrismcmullen.com

NoIndent

CenterSpaceAfter

CenterSpaceAfter

Heading 1

–2– The Cost

NoIndent

Nothing is free, of course. Not even ideas. There is always a price to pay. Your muse will surely put the 'muse' in amusement. She will have fun with you. Toy with you. It's all just a big game to her.

Just as you begin your shower, she will whisper a most amazing idea in your ear. There is just one problem: How will you write this idea down so that you don't forget it before you finish your shower? If you turn off the shower, dry off, and grab your writing supplies, guess what: She'll whisper another idea in your ear when you return to the shower.

Once you solve that problem, she'll change it up on you. Maybe you'll be stopped at a red light, struggling to pay attention during a meeting at work, or wake up in the middle of the night. She's ready for it. *Whisper.*

Normal

Soon enough you're armed with two writing utensils (because one time the ink or lead ran out) and a notebook 24 hours a day.

That's just lesson one. Then she brings out her A game.

While you're seething over a scathing review, she fuels your fire. She gives you what seem like magical words that you could write in response to the review. Oh, but you know you're not supposed to respond to reviews emotionally. Yet the words are so good.

Torment. She thrives on your anguish.

But in the end, it was all worth it. I wouldn't change it for the world.

Yes, I had been content before. But now I am alive.

My muse and I. Till death do us part.

BodySpaceAfter

```
<html>
<head>
<meta http-equiv=Content-Type content="text/html;
charset=windows-1252">
<meta name=Generator content="Microsoft Word
15 (filtered)">
<style>
<!--
/* Style Definitions */
p.MsoNormal, li.MsoNormal, div.MsoNormal
     {margin-top:0in;
     margin-bottom:0in;
     margin-left:0in;
     margin-right:0in;
     text-align:justify;
     text-indent:2em;
     font-size:100%;
     font-family:;}
p.NoIndent, li.NoIndent, div.NoIndent
     {mso-style-name:NoIndent;
     margin-top:0in;
     margin-bottom:0in;
     margin-left:0in;
     margin-right:0in;
     text-align:justify;
     text-indent:0in;
     font-size:100%;
     font-family:;}
p.BodySpaceAfter, li.BodySpaceAfter,
div.BodySpaceAfter
     {mso-style-name:BodySpaceAfter;
     margin-top:0in;
     margin-bottom:1em;
     margin-left:0in;
     margin-right:0in;
     text-align:justify;
     text-indent:2em;
     font-size:100%;
     font-family:;}
p.NoIndentSpaceAfter, li.NoIndentSpaceAfter,
div.NoIndentSpaceAfter
     {mso-style-name:NoIndentSpaceAfter;
     margin-top:0in;
     margin-bottom:1em;
     margin-left:0in;
     margin-right:0in;
     text-align:justify;
     text-indent:0in;
     font-size:100%;
     font-family:;}
p.LeftSpaceAfter, li.LeftSpaceAfter,
div.LeftSpaceAfter
     {mso-style-name:LeftSpaceAfter;
     margin-top:0in;
     margin-bottom:1em;
     margin-left:0in;
     margin-right:0in;
     text-align:left;
     text-indent:0in;
     font-size:100%;
     font-family:;}
p.LeftIndentSpaceAfter, li.LeftIndentSpaceAfter,
div.LeftIndentSpaceAfter
     {mso-style-name:LeftIndentSpaceAfter;
     margin-top:0in;
     margin-bottom:1em;
     margin-left:0in;
     margin-right:0in;
     text-align:left;
     text-indent:2em;
     font-size:100%;
     font-family:;}
h1
     {mso-style-link:"Heading 1 Char";
     margin-top:2em;
     margin-bottom:1em;
     margin-left:0in;
     margin-right:0in;
     text-align:center;
     text-indent:0in;
     page-break-before:always;
     font-size:150%;
     font-family:;
     font-weight:bold;}
p.MsoTitle, li.MsoTitle, div.MsoTitle
     {mso-style-link:"Title Char";
     margin-top:2em;
     margin-bottom:1em;
     margin-left:0in;
     margin-right:0in;
     text-align:center;
     text-indent:0in;
     font-size:200%;
     font-family:;
     font-weight:bold;}
p.MsoSubtitle, li.MsoSubtitle, div.MsoSubtitle
     {mso-style-link:"Subtitle Char";
     margin-top:0in;
     margin-bottom:1em;
     margin-left:0in;
     margin-right:0in;
     text-align:center;
     text-indent:0in;
     font-size:150%;
     font-family:;}
```

```
p.CenterSpaceAfter, li.CenterSpaceAfter,
div.CenterSpaceAfter
      {mso-style-name:CenterSpaceAfter;
      margin-top:0in;
      margin-bottom:1em;
      margin-right:0in;
      margin-left:0in;
      text-align:center;
      text-indent:0in;
      font-size:100%;
      font-family:;}
p.CenterBold20, li.CenterBold20, div.CenterBold20
      {mso-style-name:CenterBold20;
      margin-top:0in;
      margin-bottom:1em;
      margin-left:0in;
      margin-right:0in;
      text-align:center;
      text-indent:0in;
      font-size:150%;
      font-family:;
      font-weight:bold;}
p.CenterBold20PageBreak,
li.CenterBold20PageBreak,
div.CenterBold20PageBreak
      {mso-style-name:CenterBold20PageBreak;
      margin-top:2em;
      margin-bottom:1em;
      margin-left:0in;
      margin-right:0in;
      text-align:center;
      text-indent:0in;
      page-break-before:always;
      font-size:150%;
      font-family:;
      font-weight:bold;}
p.MsoToc1, li.MsoToc1, div.MsoToc1
      {margin-top:0in;
      margin-bottom:0in;
      margin-left:0in;
      margin-right:0in;
      text-align:left;
      text-indent:0in;
      font-size:100%;
      font-family:;}
p.TocLast, li.TocLast, div.TocLast
      {mso-style-name:TocLast;
      margin-top:0in;
      margin-bottom:1em;
      margin-left:0in;
      margin-right:0in;
      text-align:left;

      text-indent:0in;
      font-size:100%;
      font-family:;}
@media amzn-kf8 {
span.DropCaps {font-weight:normal;
      font-size:320%;
      float:left;
      margin-top:-0.3225em;
      margin-bottom:-0.3245em;}}
@media amzn-mobi {
span.DropCaps {font-size:3em;
      font-weight: bold;}}
a:link, span.MsoHyperlink
      {color:blue;
      text-decoration:underline;}
a:visited, span.MsoHyperlinkFollowed
      {color:purple;
      text-decoration:underline;}
span.MsoPlaceholderText
      {color:gray;}
span.Heading1Char
      {mso-style-name:"Heading 1 Char";
      mso-style-link:"Heading 1";
      font-family:;
      font-weight:bold;}
span.TitleChar
      {mso-style-name:"Title Char";
      mso-style-link:Title;
      font-family:;
      font-weight:bold;}
span.SubtitleChar
      {mso-style-name:"Subtitle Char";
      mso-style-link:Subtitle;
      font-family:}
.MsoChpDefault
      {font-family:;}
.MsoPapDefault
      {}
/* Page Definitions */
@page WordSection1
      {}
div.WordSection1
      {page:WordSection1;}
-->
</style>
</head>
<body lang=EN-US link=blue vlink=purple>
<div class=WordSection1>
<p class=MsoTitle>The Muse</p>
<p class=MsoSubtitle>Chris McMullen</p>
<p class=LeftSpaceAfter>Copyright © 2018</p>
<p class=LeftSpaceAfter>All rights reserved by the
author.</p>
```

<p class=NoIndentSpaceAfter>The characters and places of this work are purely fictional. Any resemblance that they may have to real people or locations is pure coincidence.</p>
<p class=CenterBold20><a name=toc>Contents</p>
<p class=MsoToc1><a href="#_Toc507332472">1 The Gift</a></p>
<p class=TocLast><a href="#_Toc507332473">2 The Cost</a></p>
<p class=CenterBold20>Acknowledgments</p>
<p class=NoIndentSpaceAfter>I would like to thank my muse for the inspiration for this story. I couldn't have done it without her.</p>
<h1><a name="_Toc507332472">–1– The Gift</a></h1>
<p class=NoIndent><span class="DropCaps">I</span>was content doing the 9 to 5. Really, I was. My life was simple. I had a routine: Wake up to the alarm, shower, shave, get dressed, grab a bite, take the subway, work, eat lunch, work some more, commute home, eat dinner, relax, unwind, sleep, and repeat.</p>
<p class=MsoNormal>But one day, <i>she</i> showed up. She fed me irresistible ideas. That's how she hooks you. The ideas seem too good not to write about.</p>
<p class=MsoNormal>You find yourself slaving over your keyboard night and day. Your job can't finish soon enough so that you can get to the work that you really want to do.</p>
<p class=MsoNormal>It doesn't seem like work. You enjoy it. You live for it. You dream about it. The book is everything.</p>
<p class=MsoNormal>Writing the book isn't enough. You must publish it, too. Share it with the world.</p>
<p class=BodySpaceAfter>So you do. And it feels wonderful to be the author of such a masterpiece.</p>
<h1><a name="_Toc507332473">–2– The Cost</a></h1>
<p class=NoIndent><span class="DropCaps">N</span>othing is free, of course. Not even ideas. There is always a price to pay. Your muse will surely put the 'muse' in amusement. She will have fun with you. Toy with you. It's all just a big game to her.</p>
<p class=MsoNormal>Just as you begin your shower, she will whisper a most amazing idea in your ear. There is just one problem: How will you write this idea down so that you don't forget it before you finish your shower? If you turn off the shower, dry off, and grab your writing supplies, guess what: She'll whisper another idea in your ear when you return to the shower.</p>
<p class=MsoNormal>Once you solve that problem, she'll change it up on you. Maybe you'll be stopped at a red light, struggling to pay attention during a meeting at work, or wake up in the middle of the night. She's ready for it. <i>Whisper</i>.</p>
<p class=MsoNormal>Soon enough you're armed with two writing utensils (because one time the ink or lead ran out) and a notebook 24 hours a day.</p>
<p class=MsoNormal>That's just lesson one. Then she brings out her A game.</p>
<p class=MsoNormal>While you're seething over a scathing review, she fuels your fire. She gives you what seem like magical words that you could write in response to the review. Oh, but you know you're not supposed to respond to reviews emotionally. Yet the words are so good.</p>
<p class=MsoNormal>Torment. She thrives on your anguish.</p>
<p class=MsoNormal>But in the end, it was all worth it. I wouldn't change it for the world.</p>
<p class=MsoNormal>Yes, I had been content before. But now I am alive.</p>
<p class=BodySpaceAfter>My muse and I. Till death do us part.</p>
<p class=CenterBold20PageBreak>–Thank you–</p>
<p class=NoIndentSpaceAfter>Thank you for reading my story, <i>The Muse</i>. I hope that you enjoyed it.</p>
<p class=LeftIndentSpaceAfter>–Chris McMullen</p>
<p class=CenterSpaceAfter><a href="http://www.chrismcmullen.com">www.chrismcmullen.com</a></p>
<div class=CenterSpaceAfter><img style="width: 100%; height: auto;" width="1448" height="1150" alt="" src="TheMuse_files/image001.jpg"></div>
</div>
</body>
</html>

The Muse

Chris McMullen

Copyright © 2018

Contents

Acknowledgments

I would like to thank my muse for the inspiration for this story. I couldn't have done it without her.

–1– The Gift

I was content doing the 9 to 5. Really, I was. My life was simple. I had a routine: Wake up to the alarm, shower, shave, get dressed, grab a bite, take the subway, work, eat lunch, work some more, commute home, eat dinner, relax, unwind, sleep, and repeat.

But one day, *she* showed up. She fed me irresistible ideas. That's how she hooks you. The ideas seem too good not to write about.

You find yourself slaving over your keyboard night and day. Your job can't finish soon enough so that you can get to the work that you really want to do.

It doesn't seem like work. You enjoy it. You live for it. You dream about it. The book is everything.

Writing the book isn't enough. You must publish it, too. Share it with the world.

So you do. And it feels wonderful to be the author of such a masterpiece.

–2– The Cost

Nothing is free, of course. Not even ideas. There is always a price to pay. Your muse will surely put the 'muse' in amusement. She will have fun with you. Toy with you. It's all just a big game to her.

Just as you begin your shower, she will whisper a most amazing idea in your ear. There is just one problem: How will you write this idea down in your shower? If you turn off the shower, dry off, and grab your writing supplies, guess what: She'll whisper another idea in your ear when you return to the shower.

Once you solve that problem, she'll change it up on you. Maybe you'll be stopped at a red light, struggling to pay attention during a meeting at work, or wake up in the middle of the night. She's ready for it. *Whisper.*

Soon enough you're armed with two writing utensils (because one time the ink or lead ran out) and a notebook 24 hours a day.

That's just lesson one. Then she brings out her A game.

While you're seething over a scathing review, she fuels your fire. She gives you what seem like magical words that you could write in response to the review. Oh, but you know you're not supposed to respond to reviews emotionally. Yet the words are so good.

Torment. She thrives on your anguish.

But in the end, it was all worth it. I wouldn't change it for the world.

Yes, I had been content before. But now I am alive.

My muse and I. Till death do us part.

–Thank you–

Thank you for reading my story, *The Muse.* I hope that you enjoyed it.

–Chris McMullen

www.chrismcmullen.com

—Appendix D—

Author Resources

THIS HANDY APPENDIX is packed with links to several essential author resources.

Book promotion websites:

https://www.bookbub.com/welcome

http://ereadernewstoday.com

http://www.pixelofink.com

http://fkbt.com

http://www.bookgorilla.com

Email newsletter tools:

https://mailchimp.com

Informative self-publishing articles:

https://selfpublishingadvice.org/amazon-sales-rank-taming-the-algorithm

https://chrismcmullen.com/2013/07/06/cover-design-checklist

http://www.fulltimefba.com/5-little-known-facts-about-keywords-amazon-product-listings

Free helpful book marketing guides:

https://www.smashwords.com/books/view/305

https://www.smashwords.com/books/view/145431

Blogs with self-publishing tips:

https://chrismcmullen.com

https://www.thebookdesigner.com

http://www.aaronshep.com

http://www.hughhowey.com/blog

https://the-digital-reader.com

http://nicholasrossis.me

https://notjohnkdp.blogspot.com

https://thestoryreadingapeblog.com

Author Central:[116]

https://authorcentral.amazon.com

https://authorcentral.amazon.co.uk

https://authorcentral.amazon.fr

https://authorcentral.amazon.de

https://authorcentral.amazon.co.jp

---

[116] Once you setup Author Central in the United States, this automatically sets up the same author page in India.

Community help forums:

> https://kdp.amazon.com/community/index.jspa?ref_=FOOT_cm
> https://forums.createspace.com/en/community/index.jspa
> http://kboards.com

Basic formatting guides:[117]

> https://kdp.amazon.com/en_US/help/topic/G200910130
> https://kdp.amazon.com/en_US/help/topic/G202187740
> https://www.smashwords.com/books/view/52

Amazon's technical formatting guide:

> http://kindlegen.s3.amazonaws.com/AmazonKindlePublishingGuidelines.pdf

Social media:

https://www.goodreads.com	https://www.linkedin.com
https://wordpress.com	https://www.pinterest.com
https://www.facebook.com	https://plus.google.com/discover
https://twitter.com	https://www.instagram.com/?hl=en

Places to publish an eBook:

https://kdp.amazon.com	https://www.smashwords.com
https://press.barnesandnoble.com	https://www.draft2digital.com
https://kobowritinglife.com	https://www.bookbaby.com

Places that sell eBooks:

https://www.amazon.com	
https://www.barnesandnoble.com	https://www.apple.com/ibooks
https://www.kobo.com	https://www.smashwords.com

Places to publish print books:

https://www.createspace.com	
https://kdp.amazon.com	https://www.bookbaby.com
http://www.ingramspark.com	https://www.lulu.com

Free Amazon publishing tools:[118]

> Kindle Create: https://kdp.amazon.com/en_US/help/topic/GHU4YEWXQGNLU94T
> Kindle Textbook Creator: https://www.amazon.com/gp/feature.html?docId=1002998671
> Kindle Kids' Book Creator: https://www.amazon.com/gp/feature.html?docId=1002979921
> Kindle Comic Creator: https://www.amazon.com/gp/feature.html?docId=1001103761
> KindleGen: https://www.amazon.com/gp/feature.html?docId=1000765211

Copyright information:

> https://www.copyright.gov

Self-publishing software:

https://sigil-ebook.com	https://www.adobe.com

When you have a little time to relax, you may enjoy a couple of my poems:

> https://chrismcmullen.com/2013/08/21/once-upon-a-time
> https://chrismcmullen.com/2013/09/13/which-part-of-the-book-is-best

---

[117] Amazon updates the KDP help pages periodically, and occasionally this causes URL's to change. If the links to the Kindle formatting guides aren't working, you can find these guides in the KDP help pages. *Building Your Book for Kindle* is also available as a free Kindle eBook (which you can read on a Mac or PC).

[118] If Amazon updates these pages so that the URL's no longer work, try searching for these tools in the KDP help pages or with a search engine like Google.

—X-Ray Sample—

The Kindle edition of this book includes Amazon's X-Ray feature, as described in Sec. 8.14. The print edition includes a sample of the terms from the X-Ray feature of this eBook, whereas in the Kindle edition X-Ray can be accessed directly from a device or app.

active table of contents: a table of contents with clickable hyperlinks that will take the reader directly to each chapter or section.

aggregator: an eBook publishing platform that distributes your eBook to a variety of retailers, such as Nook, Kobo, and Apple. A few of the major aggregators include Smashwords, BookBaby, and Draft2Digital.

block indent: when every line of a paragraph is effectively indented by adding a left margin to the entire paragraph.

block paragraphs: non-indented paragraphs with space between them. (Most eBooks don't use block paragraphs for body text. Instead, for body text most eBooks indent the first line of each paragraph and don't include any space between the paragraphs.)

Book Lending: when enabled, Kindle Book Lending allows a customer to loan a Kindle eBook to one family member for a period of up to 14 days. The original customer won't have access to the eBook while it is loaned. A customer can only lend a Kindle eBook once. (This has nothing to do with Kindle Unlimited borrows.)

Digital Rights Management (DRM): access control technologies that are designed to help protect copyrighted works such as eBooks.

enhanced typesetting: Amazon's new feature for Kindle eBooks which is designed to improve the Kindle reading experience with typographical features. This includes automatic hyphenation and the exclusive Bookerly font.

fixed format: a special type of eBook with a fixed page layout, appropriate for books that consist primarily of pictures.

justified (full): paragraph text that is aligned at both the left and right sides.

KDP Select: an optional program available to eBooks published through Kindle Direct Publishing. KDP Select requires that the digital version of the book be published exclusively with Amazon Kindle. Benefits of KDP Select include participation in Kindle Unlimited and book promotion tools (Countdown Deals or free book promos).

KENP read: the Kindle Edition Normalized Pages read refers to the number of pages that a KDP Select eBook has been read by customers who borrowed the eBook through Kindle Unlimited or Amazon Prime.

KENPC: the Kindle Edition Normalized Page Count establishes the official number of pages for a KDP Select eBook. The KENPC is utilized to determine the number of pages read for KDP Select eBooks borrowed through Kindle Unlimited and Amazon Prime. The KENPC is often somewhat generous compared to the actual page count of the print edition.

Kindle Unlimited: a subscription-based reading service where customers pay a fixed monthly fee to read as many Kindle Unlimited eBooks as they would like each month.

night mode: a reading mode with a black background available on Kindle devices and apps.

non-breaking space: a space used to join two short strings of text like "6 ft." in order to prevent the short strings from becoming separated across two consecutive lines of a paragraph (with the "6" at the end of one line and the "ft." at the beginning of the next line).

padding: a border (often transparent) added to the left and right sides of a small picture to prevent it from blowing up on older devices.

ragged right: paragraph text that is aligned (only) at the left side.

reflowable: an eBook where the page layout varies depending on the device's display size and the customer's choice of font style, font size, line spacing, and internal margins.

sepia: a cream-colored background that is available on many Kindle devices.

zero-width non-joiner: an invisible character used to identify desired breaking points in long strings of text such as website URL's.

—Index—

–E–

–F–

–G–

–H–

–O–

–P–

–Q–

–R–

–S–

─Science Books─

Dr. McMullen has published a variety of science books, including:

- Basic astronomy concepts
- Basic chemistry concepts
- Balancing chemical reactions
- Calculus-based physics textbook
- Calculus-based physics workbooks
- Trig-based physics workbooks
- Creative physics problems

https://monkeyphysicsblog.wordpress.com

—Math Books—

This series of math workbooks is geared toward practicing essential math skills:

- Algebra and trigonometry
- Fractions, decimals, and percentages
- Long division
- Multiplication and division
- Addition and subtraction

https://improveyourmathfluency.com

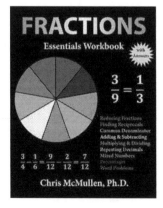

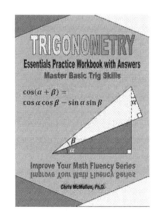

—Puzzle Books—

The author of this book, Chris McMullen, enjoys solving puzzles. His favorite puzzle is Kakuro (kind of like a cross between crossword puzzles and Sudoku). He once taught a three-week summer course on puzzles. If you enjoy mathematical pattern puzzles, you might appreciate:

http://amzn.com/1512044288

Number Pattern Recognition & Reasoning
- pattern recognition
- visual discrimination
- analytical skills
- logic and reasoning
- analogies
- mathematics

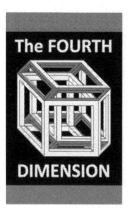

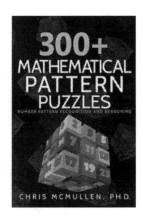

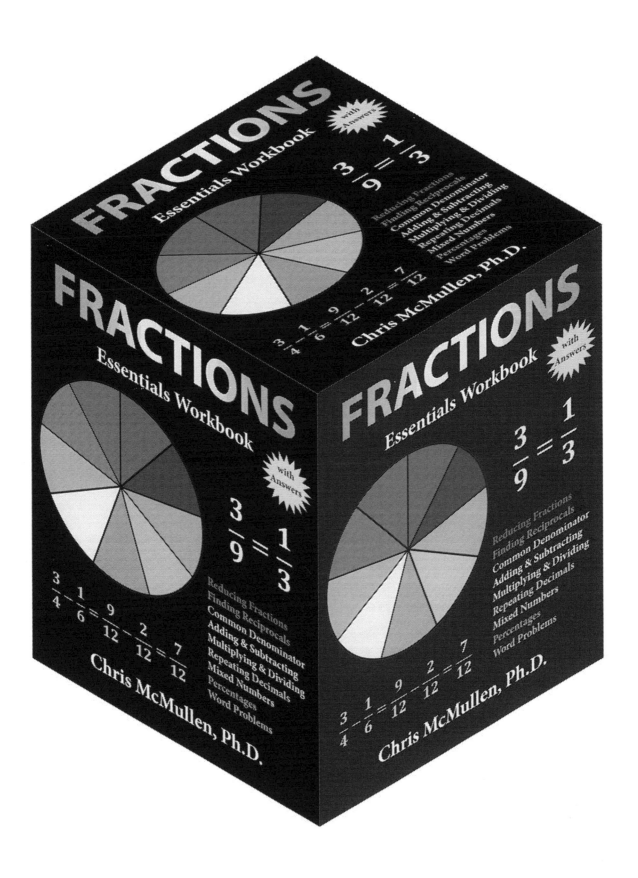

Made in the USA
Lexington, KY
20 July 2019